CAMBRIDGESHIRE RECORDS SOCIETY

(formerly Cambridge Antiquarian Records Society)

VOLUME 10

JOSEPH ROMILLY

ROMILLY'S CAMBRIDGE DIARY 1842 – 1847

SELECTED PASSAGES FROM
THE DIARY OF THE REV. JOSEPH ROMILLY
FELLOW OF TRINITY COLLEGE AND REGISTRARY OF
THE UNIVERSITY OF CAMBRIDGE

EDITED BY

M.E. BURY & J.D. PICKLES

CAMBRIDGE

1994

Published by the Cambridgeshire Records Society
County Record Office, Shire Hall, Cambridge CB3 0AP

British Library Cataloguing in Publication Data

A catalogue record for this book
is available from the British Library

ISBN 0 904 323 10 2

*Printed and bound in Great Britain by
E. & E. Plumridge Ltd., Linton, Cambridge.*

CONTENTS

List of illustrations   vi

Preface   vii

INTRODUCTION   xi

Abbreviations of book titles in the footnotes   xvii

THE DIARY   1

Appendix: Romilly's Family   242

Index of Persons   245

Index of Subjects and Places   267

Plan of Cambridge by R.G. Baker from
  The Cambridge Guide 1845   *Inside back cover*

ILLUSTRATIONS

Joseph Romilly from the water-colour by Miss Hervé   *frontispiece*

A page from the Diary of 1843   facing p.x

Cambridge from Castle Hill   xviii
    From J. Le Keux, *Memorials of Cambridge*

The Meeting of the Cambridge Boat Club   37
    An engraving by Rock & Co., *c.*1850

The Reception of Victoria and Albert   38
    From *The Illustrated London News*, 10 July 1847

Examination of the Register Book   90
    By R.W. Buss. From V.A. Huber, *The English Universities*, 1843

Margaret Romilly   facing p.112
    From a painting in the possession of Mr Peter Romilly

G.T. Romilly   facing p.112
    From a painting by Denning in the possession of Mrs Mary Bain

G.B. Allen   facing p.113
    From a painting in the possession of Mrs Anne David

L. Baugh Allen   facing p.113
    From a painting in the possession of Mrs Anne David

The Railway Bridge   120
    From *Ely Cathedral as it is and as it was*, 1846

William Carus preaching   121
    From a silhouette in the Cambridge and County Folk Museum

The Great Court of Trinity College   121
    From a water-colour by R.B. Harraden in Trinity College

The Reception for The British Association   122
    From *The Illustrated London News*, 21 June 1845

John Lodge   facing p.116
    By F. Walmisley. From a mezzotint

Adam Sedgwick   facing p.116
    From a painting by Thomas Phillips 1832

William Whewell   facing p.117
    From an engraving in the possession of Trinity College

William Carus   facing p.117
    From a crayon by George Richmond

Interior of Holy Trinity   153
    From Le Keux's *Memorials*

A page of the *Graduati Cantabrigienses*   154

Christ Church   187
    From Le Keux's *Memorials*

Electing a Chancellor at Cambridge   188
    From *Punch*, March 1847

PREFACE

Joseph Romilly's Diaries fill forty-one notebooks in a small but legible hand and extend from 1818 to 1864. Apart from three volumes devoted to holiday tours with his brother Cuthbert the entries in the earlier books are both intermittent and scrappy. From February 1829, however, he began to write regularly and from then until his death hardly a day is missed and the entries, at first brief and factual, generally become ampler and more full of human interest. They are an important primary source for life in the Cambridge of those years. The Diaries were given to Cambridge University Library (Additional MSS. 6804-42) in the 1930s by Romilly's great-niece, Miss Rachel M. Allen, a descendant of his sister Caroline and Lancelot Baugh Allen. They were not unknown, having been drawn on by J.W. Clark and T.M. Hughes, the biographers of Romilly's friend Adam Sedgwick, although it was misleading to describe them, as they did, as 'personal rather than public' when they are a vast repository of general facts. Recording events came naturally to Romilly; it was the secret of his professional success. D.A. Winstanley made a careful study of the Diaries for his books on Victorian Cambridge in the 'forties, and they have often been used since for the light they bring to special subjects such as the history of Cambridge University Library, or of Dulwich (see A.T. Milne, *Dulwich Villager,* February and April 1980). His official accounts of the royal visits of 1843 and 1847 were published with annotations by Professor R.S. Walker and Dr E.S. Leedham-Green as *Victoria and Albert in Cambridge* (Cambridge University Library, 1977). Canon Geoffrey Morris of Lampeter Velfrey has for some years been preparing a volume entitled *Romilly's Visits to Wales 1827-1854* with extracts from the Diary, and he hopes it will be published in 1994. Little else of what Romilly wrote seems to have survived apart from official business and a few unimportant letters out of the many thousands which he undoubtedly sent. After the death of his father there is an intriguing reference to a 'private journal', but we find no other mention of it, and assume that it was written to help Romilly come to terms with his grief.

While collecting material for a history of Corpus Christi College, of which he was a Fellow, Dr Patrick Bury concluded that the Diaries deserved to be published in extenso for a wider audience, and his annotated selections were published in 1967 by Cambridge University Press as *Romilly's Cambridge Diary 1832-42.* He had begun to think of a second volume shortly before his death in November 1987, and his preliminary choice of passages for it, somewhat altered, forms the basis of the present book which continues Romilly's chronicle from March 1842 to December 1847. In addition to limiting this volume to those years we have, like Dr Bury, confined the extracts to Romilly's life in Cambridge both for pressing reasons of space and because there is a particular interest in concentrating upon the Cambridge life of a prominent official of the unreformed University. Yet we have done so with regret, for Romilly indulged in long summer holiday tours and in frequent briefer visits to London and elsewhere, and on such occasions often recorded his doings much more fully and no less vividly than when he was at home. We have, however, in passages of connecting narrative, given usually brief indications of his movements and some of his activities when he was away from Cambridge. The publication of extracts from the rest of the Diary has been left for a later occasion, should it arise. We believe that a single volume would do justice to Romilly's last seventeen years, for while the entries grow in length they increasingly become a record of official business as well as of his own doings.

The editors are responsible for the notes and apparatus, and also for a different treatment of the text from Dr Bury's. Romilly habitually used many contractions which, while they add to the immediacy of what he wrote, may hinder the general reader. We have therefore commonly expanded most of them silently. A few have been deliberately retained throughout (e.g. 'wch' for 'which' and the ampersand &), and his characteristic spelling (except for the use of long 's') and sometimes careless punctuation have been followed. The form of dates at the beginning of each entry is standardised. Omissions within entries are signalled by the customary three points '. . .'. In annotating the text we have tried to be helpful to those who may be interested in the customs and procedures of the diarist's times and to social and local historians; such notes are, of course, illustrative and explanatory, not exhaustive, but the sources indicate the wide range of available primary and secondary material. We have attempted to identify as many as possible of the people mentioned in the text, and put them in an index of names at the end of the book with details which would have been out of place among the footnotes. The general index covers places and subjects and is intended to draw together recurrent themes and events, and to guide the reader to information in the footnotes.

It is with pleasure that we acknowledge our gratitude to those who have read the book in draft, and helped in its preparation with advice and information or proof-reading, especially Dr E.S. Leedham-Green, Assistant Keeper of the University Archives, Professor J.P.C. Roach, and Dr Robert Robson of Trinity. In the University Library Mr G. Waller and the staff of the Manuscript Room, and Mr R.H. Fairclough of the Map Room, and in the Cambridgeshire Collection of the city library Mr M.J. Petty and his staff, have supplied our needs with their usual efficient courtesy. We are indebted to Mrs Anne David and Mr Thomas Lloyd for copies of the portraits of L. B. Allen and his son G. B. Allen, to Mrs Mary Bain for Denning's portrait of G. T. Romilly, to Mr Peter Romilly for the portrait of

Margaret Romilly, and to the Registrary for Miss Hervé's water colour portrait of the diarist used as our frontispiece. By permission of the Syndics of Cambridge University Library are reproduced a page of Romilly's manuscript and portraits of William Carus and Adam Sedgwick, and by permission of the Cambridge library (Cambridgeshire Collection) illustrations from *The Illustrated London News.* We have also benefitted from comments by Dr Peter Searby and Mr P.J. Barnwell. Our best thanks are also due to the Governing Bodies of Corpus Christi and Emmanuel Colleges who paid for the typing of successive drafts of the book, and to the Council of Trinity College which contributed most generously towards other costs of publication.

...reputable painstaking woman, & M. puts one of the other
children to school. — Edw. read Churzlewit to us. —
Whist club at Birketts : all the members prest & also Bunch

Wednesday the 1st of Nov. — Nasty wet day : women
not out. — Breakfast to C. J. Bayley (come up for his M.A. deg.)
, Hon. Mansfield, & Edw. Allen. — Cong. day. — 1 DD, 6 AM, 1 MB, 1 AB
— Great batch of Graces for the diff. Ex⁵. — It was thought
indecorous to bring in a Grace for paying the expenses of the
Prince's degree out of the Chest, as it would not look well
to see the announcem̄t of such a Grace in the Papers : — the
payment is to be made quietly by the Univ⁵. — Lodge passed
a very bad night & was dreadfully dejected. — I walked with him &
cheered him a good deal. — Edw. read Churzlewit loud. — H 191

Thursday the 2nd of Nov. — Lucy having taken strong measures &
written letters threatening a summons ag⁵ her son, the poor unhappy
woman contrived to borrow the money & today restored the 10/- stolen
by her son. — Weather fine again : — good walk with M...
L. had caught a cold & did not stir out. — Dined with Sedgwick
& met Mary Shine, to Marchesa, Miss Doria, Prof. & M⁵ Challis & Miss
Copsey, Miss Elizabeth & Miss Agnes Smith M⁵ & M⁵ Hopkins,
Martin (our Bursar) & Ellis (the S. Wr⁵). — Poor M⁵ Challis found
the room too hot & fainted away. She staid in another room
for a couple of hours. The 2 Miss Smiths sang a great deal, epc⁵ —
I outstaid all the comp.y & handed the ladies into their carriages —
& then sat an hour with Sedgwick & smoked a Cigar. — D 115

Friday the 3rd of Nov. — Lovely day. — Long College meet.g
: Hudson (Vic. of Kendall) just dead. — Took M. & L & 3 little
proteges of the latter (viz. Esther Bailey, Eliza Gillmour, &
Eliza Clark, — all 3 uncle⁵ly in mourning, so they looked like
one family) to Trinity Lodge. M⁵ Whewell was very kind
to us & showed us the State Rooms, the Queens Bed, &c, &
also the Bracelet given her by the Queen. — Dined at
the Family at Powers : 3 members absent, viz. Whewell,
Packe & Morblock. — one stranger there, a dull Dr. Williams —
played Whist unsuccessfully, losing every rubber but one.

Saturday the 4th of Nov. — Another fine day. — I sh.d have
said yest. y that Whewell went out of office : both he & the Procts
praised the young men very much in their speeches. — Today
Dr. Hodgson was elected F.C. : — he made a dull speech.
I sent off 3 Doz. Ale to Denning. — Yesterday declined going
with Sedgwick for 3 days to the B. — shd ly to meet Mr Y & H. Yorke
— M. & I paid a visit to Miss Anthony. — H 192
Did not go to the V.C.'s ... went faster. — ... to Town ... 3 doz.

INTRODUCTION

In the Diaries of Joseph Romilly (1791–1864) we meet a clergyman of a very different kind from Parson Woodforde or Francis Kilvert. He was a townsman rather than a countryman, and an academic who was fortunate enough to spend the whole of his active life in Cambridge as a Fellow of Trinity College during a period when 'the life of undergraduates and dons was never more vigorous or more varied'.[1] Essential changes in the late eighteenth century had contributed to the election of a remarkable group of Fellows distinguished in mathematical, classical, philosophical, philological, and historical studies. Yet, unlike many of his colleagues, Joseph wrote no books and would not have claimed to be an inspiring teacher or an original thinker. He was for a few years the non-resident rector of Porthkerry in Glamorgan, but he never had a parish and seldom took duty or preached. Indeed by the time of his energetic canvassing of electors to the important office of University Registrary in 1832 he was probably conscious that his abilities were under-employed. But after his election, apart from being reprimanded in 1835 for too frequent absences from Cambridge, he performed his duties with thoroughness, constant good-humour, and increasing industry. That he also enjoyed the work is confirmed by his diary entry for Easter Sunday 1856, when he wrote 'This very day of March 24 years ago I was elected Registrary & I heartily bless God for having vouchsafed me health & strength to carry on for so great a length of time an employment of which I am very fond and which affords me competence and happiness.' He was in fact to continue as Registrary for another five years.

Romilly was, in Adam Sedgwick's phrase, 'a merry genial man', and a devout and conscientious Christian who shared with many contemporaries a dislike of extremes of observance and belief. He was a cultured and travelled man of moderate means, who, by virtue of his position and his many family connections, was in touch with or had the opportunity to meet many of the ablest men of his day.[2] He gave liberally to the poor and to numerous good causes, and was a devoted brother and uncle and a generous master to those in his employ. Urbane and courteous, well-read in continental as well as in English literature, he had a wide circle of friends and was sought after as a guest in great houses such as Audley End and Madingley Hall as well as in Masters' Lodges and College Halls where

[1] G.M. Trevelyan, *Trinity College* (revised ed. 1972), p. 99.
[2] See Robert Robson (ed.), *Ideas and Institutions of Victorian Britain* (1967), pp. 312-35, 'Trinity College in the Age of Peel', and also R.O. Preyer who writes 'It is beginning to be clear that the intellectual center of early Victorian thought in a variety of fields of learning was located geographically in Cambridge and specifically among a band of friends and colleagues loosely or closely connected with Trinity College', J.G. Paradis and T. Postlewait (eds), *Victorian Science and Victorian Values* (Rutgers University Press, 1985), p. 39.

his reputation as a coiner of puns survived him.[3] He loved a game of whist and the society of children and of pretty, preferably lively, intelligent women. He visited picture galleries, churches, and the theatre at every opportunity, and was an intrepid traveller who enjoyed fine country and sea bathing even when the water was cold and rough. He saw no reason why, as a clergyman, he should not play an occasional game of billiards and attend a race meeting when on holiday.

His sociability did not, however, prevent Romilly from being a man of strong principles and decided views, a firm Whig and 'stout reformer', and one of that group of 'liberal-minded clergymen, ardent educationalists, solid in character and learning, versed in mathematics and in classical scholarship'[4] who helped to guide Trinity and the University into a new age. His courtesy did not hinder him from being an outspoken critic of abuses, nor was he afraid of advocating causes that were unpopular with many in an academic society still predominantly conservative in outlook. He nevertheless disliked political argument, and in the Diaries, which are never introspective until the death of his sister Lucy in 1854 leaves him alone, rarely attempts political analysis. If there are few references to national affairs and the great issues of the 'Hungry Forties' and 'The Bleak Age', as the period has not unjustly been called, there is always a practical concern for the poor, for chimney sweeps, for schools, for the starving Irish, for orphans and widows and for the welfare of servants in College or in Hills Road.

The Diaries show him too to have been a shrewd and humorous — in youth sometimes too critical—observer of his fellow men and women. When entreated, for example, by an anxious father to dissuade his daughter from going into a convent, Romilly writes, 'Miss Bowtell says she is prepared to sacrifice everything for religion, *the very hair of her head* wch I presume therefore is fine'. Of a young poet's account of what is seen by spirits on a flight through the world he remarks he 'has some power of versification, a good deal of imagination & much knowledge of geography'. And again, he notes of a memorial sermon 'Mrs Wheelwright seems to have been as near perfection as a dismal person can be'. They also contain plenty of caustic comment on folly and bad taste and on tediousness and obscurantism, whether in the pulpit, in social intercourse, or in the conduct of University or College business. In July 1843 Romilly had to endure 'an awful sermon from Mr Minor Canon Clay. . . for aught that appeared the Preacher might have been a Jew'. Later in the same month he gave a wine party largely for undergraduates, among whom was Rowe 'who don't go out on Fridays,—& who is so shy & dull & stupid that it would be a comfort to one if he went out on nodays'. And at a great dinner at Wisbech Romilly reported that the host, in proposing Lord and Lady Hardwicke

---

[3]   C. Wordsworth, *Scholae Academicae* (1877), p. 63.
[4]   Trevelyan, *op.cit.*, p. 88.

'made rather too warm a eulogy of their virtues (as they were present); however Ld Hardwicke paid him in coin & made him not only the beau ideal of a vicar but the composer of the best sermon ever writ by mortal pen:— it could not have been that one wch we heard this morning'.

Joseph Romilly, born on 9 October 1791 in Frith Street, Soho, and christened at the nearby church of St Anne's, was one of the nine children of Thomas Peter Romilly (1753-1828) and his cousin Jane Anne, daughter of Isaac Romilly, F.R.S. The family, whose best known member was Joseph's uncle, Sir Samuel Romilly, the great philanthropist and law-reformer, was of Huguenot origin and had settled in England at the beginning of the eighteenth century. Like many other displaced French families they had prospered and been absorbed into the upper classes and the Anglican church (see Appendix, p. 242). Not unnaturally they identified with the Whig oligarchy: among Joseph's cousins John Romilly was Solicitor-General in 1848, Charles was married to a sister of Lord John Russell, the architect of the Reform Bill, and Frederick married a sister of Russell's second wife in 1848. At the same time they had long memories, and their aversion from Tractarianism and Roman Catholicism, their keen sense of religious obligation, self-discipline, and warm family feeling, come as no surprise. Of his youth we know little. It seems probable that his early home was in London, although the family owned a house in Margate. He was educated privately as were his cousins, Sir Samuel's sons, and there are several references in the Diary to his old master, the famous pedagogue James Boyer, formerly of Christ's Hosptial. In 1810 the Romillys moved into a comparatively small house, The Willows, on Dulwich Common, and it was here that he often rejoined his family until it was given up in 1837. In 1834 he describes the hunt galloping 'over the Common by our house', and his walking 'in the Grove field to hear the nightingales'.

In 1808 Romilly was admitted as a pensioner of Trinity, the Cambridge college with which he was to be associated for the rest of his days. He matriculated at Michaelmas 1809, was elected a Scholar in 1810, took his Bachelor's degree as fourth Wrangler in 1813, and became a Fellow of Trinity in 1815. He held the offices of Junior Dean (1822-3) and Senior Dean (1829-31), and in 1840 he was admitted to the 'Seniority', thus becoming one of the eight Senior Fellows who, together with the Master, in those days ruled the College. The greatest event of his career, however, was his election in 1832 as Registry of the University, an office which he held until his resignation at the end of 1861. This imposed upon him a number of regular duties, which are constantly referred to in his Diary, and which included his playing a prominent part in all the chief University ceremonies, some of which he described minutely and evidently enjoyed. He took great interest in the University records of which he had charge, and his most notable service as Registry was their much-needed arrangement, indexing, and annotation. Indeed it has been said that 'he rescued the archives from the neglect and indifference of nearly two centuries. . . His work was. . . invaluable and can hardly be too highly praised'.[5] He also edited the volume of alphabetical lists of graduates of the University together with particulars of their degrees, entitled *Graduati Cantabrigienses,* which covers the years 1760-1846, and later continued it to the year 1856. Much of his time too was spent in providing others with information either personally or by letter; Henry Gunning in his *Reminiscences* (1854) wrote that 'to receive assistance from him seems to be conferring on him an obligation'.

In 1837 Romilly resigned the family living of Porthkerry to which he had been presented in 1830, and accepted the far from onerous post of chaplain to his friend and former Trinity colleague, Thomas Musgrave, Bishop of Hereford and subsequently Archbishop of York. 1837 was also the year in which Romilly's two unmarried sisters, Margaret and Lucy, moved with their maid Betsy from Dulwich after the death of their brother Cuthbert, and came to live with him in Cambridge. Romilly therefore ceased to be a bachelor resident in college and adjusted without difficulty to life as a householder at 50 Hills Road, then on the outskirts of the town. Thereafter he began to chronicle 'the women's' doings almost as fully as his own. The household, moreover, was periodically enlarged and enlivened by the presence of a much loved nephew, George Romilly 'our little man', who had been orphaned as a child and was virtually an adopted son, and by George and Edward Allen, the children of Romilly's deceased sister. They came to stay as schoolboys and reappeared as undergraduates of Trinity College.

'The women' seldom entertained or shared in Joseph's social round, but they provided this confirmed bachelor with agreeable domesticity, and he in turn was their protector and the anchor of their home. At Dulwich he had spent many hours teaching 'M' and 'L' French and German; he also read widely with them, and it is clear from the frequency with which he asks their opinion that he regarded them as intelligent and educated women. Margaret was seven years older than her brother and her portrait shows her to have been a handsome, elegant woman. She worked as indefatigably as Lucy for good causes, but temperamentally seems to have been much closer to Romilly, both in efficiency and attention to detail, than to her sister. The course of her final illness, probably caused by abdominal cancer, and the false hopes raised by Cambridge's best known doctors, cast a long shadow over the pages of the Diary for 1847. Lucy, thirteen years younger than Margaret, was as shy with her social equals as the birds she rescued from rough boys. When, however, she witnessed cruelty to animals or thought her human protégées in danger from immoral influences, she became formidable and quite indifferent to other

---

[5] H.E.Peek and C.P. Hall, *The Archives of the University of Cambridge* (1962), p. 22. Cf. J. and J.A. Venn, *The Book of Matriculations and Degrees* (1913), p. xx where he is described as 'that most careful and conscientious officer' whose 'hand and eye are in evidence everywhere, and it is plain that his paramount interest lay in the records in his custody'.

peoples' opinion. She could even, if she disapproved of a sermon by William Carus, the handsome Evangelical incumbent of Holy Trinity whom she greatly admired, give him 'a withering look' as she left the church. Joseph was frequently irritated by Lucy's untidiness and unpunctuality and what he calls her 'quixoticisms', but his admiration for her selflessness was unbounded. In one morning she 'passed ½ an hour in flapping away with her boa the flies that pestered a horse' and 'did an infinitude of work visiting sick paupers, slanging draymen, patronising asses' and ordering fresh wheels for a donkey cart. He remembered her devotion to man and beast alike when he came to write her epitaph.

After Margaret's death Joseph and Lucy moved to 3 Scroope Terrace where she also died in 1854. Thereafter he lived alone, except for devoted servants, his only surviving brother being in Paris. The last of his generation, he died suddenly of heart failure at Great Yarmouth on 7 August 1864 and was buried beside his sisters in the family grave beneath one of the few monuments now remaining in the churchyard of Christ Church, Barnwell, on the east side of Cambridge. The water-colour portrait of him painted by Miss Hervé in 1836 hangs in the University Registry, and an undated photograph of him taken late in life is preserved in one of the albums in Trinity College Library.

Cambridge in 1842 when this volume begins was a country town of almost 25,000 inhabitants, and the 1841 census shows that the number of inhabited houses had increased from 1691 in 1801 to 4797. Much of this expansion was to the east along the Newmarket Road and in Barnwell, a densely populated development of working class housing which stood in sharp contrast with the fine public buildings of Colleges and University. Charles Bristed, a young American who arrived in 1840, was at once struck by the 'narrow ugly and dirty streets' and the 'low and antique houses' of the old town that often projected over them. *The Cambridge Guide* of 1845, whilst admitting that the general appearance was 'somewhat below what might be expected', nevertheless noted a new 'spirit of improvement' and 'better more genteel housing'. To some of the notable new buildings in the town, such as the County Courts, Christ Church, St Paul's, and to the re-building of St Andrew the Great and the restoration of the Round Church, the Diary makes interesting allusions. But Mr Ranger, Superintending Inspector of the new Board of Health, did not share the complacency of *The Cambridge Guide.* Reporting on the town in 1849 he gave a horrifying picture of overcrowding and filth in some 140 alleys, courts and yards. 'The conditions are so wretched as to be a disgrace to civilisation; it is next to impossible for the inhabitants to be healthy, cleanly, moral, decent or modest'.

Manufactures hardly existed, but the town lay at the centre of an agricultural area whose economy was based on grain and dairy farming. It had busy markets and good communications by road and river. Barges brought up necessities like butter, coal, wood, and stone. A good deal of

Cambridge business depended on provisioning the seventeen colleges and providing for them such services as banking, printing, tailoring, and law. The coming of the railways in 1845 had a calamitous effect on the old coaching routes and water-borne traffic, and when, towards the end of Romilly's life, fresh industries were established it was to the rails that they looked.

The University, on which the town so much depended, had increased considerably in size since Romilly had first arrived in the middle of the Napoleonic wars. By 1842 the resident population during term time numbered 1,787 of whom 1,192 lived in college and 595 in lodgings. It was still an unreformed University whose continued claims to exercise a medieval jurisdiction in the town (over such matters as licensing, the conduct of fairs, and the control of prostitution) caused friction with the civic authorities, and whose inefficiency and narrowness of outlook were coming under criticism from within and without its walls. Fellows of Colleges were mostly debarred from matrimony and required to take holy orders; religious tests were imposed which prevented Jews and Dissenters from taking degrees, and the Heads of the seventeen Colleges formed an exclusive oligarchy. Although a Classical Tripos had been instituted in 1822, mathematics was still the main road to honours; but honours men depended largely upon private coaches to help them through their studies, and more than half the undergraduates then and for long afterwards did not read for honours at all but took the ordinary or 'poll' degree, the standard of which was extremely low. After the reform of Parliament, however, it was not to be expected that the ancient universities would be left undisturbed. The governing body of Trinity College succeeded in ridding itself of some of its more anachronistic statutes in 1844, but it is clear, at least with hindsight, that cautious palliatives would not soothe criticism of the whole university, and the next decade brought a Royal Commission which left little unexamined and unrevised. Of these rumblings of reform there are echoes in this volume, and it is not surprising to find that Joseph Romilly, staunch Whig and supporter of national reform, was also a friend to liberal causes in his own college and University.

In 1842 Romilly had held the office of Registrary for ten years and we continue to see him busy at the tasks which were to occupy him until his retirement, working at his books with his one clerk in the Pitt Building — in other words recording the administrative business of the University, and much more of general interest, in 'Grace books' and other registers — keeping registers of degrees and receiving the appropriate fees from newly made Bachelors and Masters of Arts, attesting the admission of newly elected professors, attending the Vice-Chancellor's court of discipline and the annual proclamation of Sturbridge and Midsummer fairs, and taking part in royal and other ceremonial occasions. These and other duties of his office together with College business, examining, answering requests for information, the alternation of term and vacation, Sunday churchgoing, week-day entertainment, daily walks, and evening reading maintain the basic rhythm of the Diaries .The flavour of a Diary such as this can only be properly tasted if the reader is gradually able to enter into the quiet daily round of the Diarist, to share his interests, and to learn to know his circle of friends. There must be a sufficient continuity of entries. Although the choice of December 1847 as a terminal date for this volume may seem arbitrary, it is not inappropriate. The death of Margaret in that year (foreshadowing the deaths of many of the Diarist's older friends), and the removal of Joseph and Lucy from Hills Road soon afterwards, mark the end of ten happy years there. And the election of Prince Albert as Chancellor with a secure liberal government in place heralds a period in which both University and Colleges as Romilly had known them were to be radically altered.

LIST OF ABBREVIATIONS OF BOOK TITLES USED IN THE FOOTNOTES

Al. Cant.	J.A. Venn, *Alumni Cantabrigienses,* Part II from 1752 to 1900 (Cambridge, 1940-54).
Bristed	C.A. Bristed, *Five Years in An English University* Second edition in one volume (New York, 1852).
Chadwick	Owen Chadwick, *The Victorian Church* 2 vols. (London, 1966–70).
Clark & Hughes	J.W. Clark and T.M. Hughes, *The Life and Letters of Adam Sedgwick* 2 vols. (Cambridge, 1890).
Cooper	C.H. Cooper, *Annals of Cambridge,* vol. IV, 1688–1849 (Cambridge, 1852).
D.N.B.	*Dictionary of National Biography.*
McKitterick	David McKitterick, *Cambridge University Library* (Cambridge, 1986).
R.C.D. 1832–42	*J.P.T. Bury, Romilly's Cambridge Diary 1832–42* (Cambridge, 1967).
UP	University Papers (in the University Archives at Cambridge University Library).
V.C.H.	Victoria County History, *A History of the County of Cambridge,* vols. III and IV (Oxford, 1959, 1953).
Winstanley	D.A. Winstanley, *Early Victorian Cambridge* (Cambridge, 1946).

Cambridge from Castle Hill

1842

From March 17 to 21 Joseph Romilly, who had now been Registrary for ten years, was in London and Dulwich. As Registrary he played an important part in all the chief University ceremonies and the entry in his diary for March 18th describes the presentation of the University's address of congratulation to the Queen on the birth of the Prince of Wales.

Fri. 18 March. Breakfast at the Burlington with Vice Chancellor, Drs Ainslie, French & Graham. — Letter to V.C. from Sir J. Graham,[1] saying that only 2 of the Cambridge Deputation were to kiss hands. — the same instructions sent to the Oxford Deputation. — This arrangement was very distasteful to all the Deputation. Yesterday intimation was sent that the Address would be received at 1¼ instead of 2½, — wch will just throw out Whewell (who leaves Cambr. this morning at 8 and has never kissed hands upon his appointment).[2] — The Cambridge Deputation consisted of V.C. (Archdall), Neville Grenville, Webb, French, Ainslie, Graham & Tatham[3] Dr. Geldart, Dr. Fisher,[4] Birkett & J. Smith (Caput),[5] Crick (Orator)[6] Proctors (Gaskin & Thompson),[7] Gunning & Hopkins[8] & my self. We were joined by Lord High Steward (Chancellor Lyndhurst) etc etc — Two of our young Noblemen (Ld Nelson & Ld Fielding) appeared in their under-graduate Gowns: they wore Court Dresses with swords & added much to the effect. — They unfortunately did not join us in the Presence Chamber & were therefore not presented to the Queen: — they were afterwards presented to Prince Albert & Duchess of Kent by the V.Ch. — The Duke of Northumberland[9] was not in Town: — the V.C. therefore read the

[1]   The Home Secretary.
[2]   Whewell had been installed as Master of Trinity on 16 November, 1841.
[3]   All Heads of Houses (i.e. Colleges).
[4]   Regius Professor of Civil Law and the Downing Professor of Medicine.
[5]   The Caput was a powerful body consisting 'of the Vice-Chancellor, sitting ex-officio, a doctor from each of the three faculties of divinity, law and medicine, a Regent Master of Arts and a non-Regent Master'. It was elected annually by the Heads of Houses, doctors and two Scrutators (Winstanley, p.238). All Graces (formal proposals or decrees put before the Senate) had to be approved by it before being submitted to the Senate and any member of the Caput could veto a Grace.
[6]   The Orator 'is the voice of the Senate upon all public occasions . . . and presents to all honorary degrees with an appropriate speech' (*Cambridge University Calendar* for 1842).
[7]   'Two Proctors, who are peace-officers elected annually. It is their especial duty to attend to the discipline and behaviour of all persons *in statu pupillari,* to search houses of ill fame, and to take into custody women of loose and abandoned character, and even those *de malo suspectae.* Another part of their duty is to be present at all Congregations of the Senate . . . to read the Graces in the Regent-House, to take secretly the assent or dissent, and openly to pronounce the same.' (*ibid*).
[8]   Two of the three Esquire Bedells whose chief duty was to attend the Vice-Chancellor on all public occasions. The Esquire Bedells throughout these years of the Diary were Gunning, Leapingwell and Hopkins. For a history of the office and its holders see H.P. Stokes, *The Esquire Bedells* (1911).
[9]   The Duke was Chancellor of the University.

1

Addresses, wch he did very fairly; but I was obliged to prompt him about giving the Address to the Queen, & also about receiving her Majesty's Reply. — The V.C. & Master of Magdalene alone kissed hands: — the rest of us made our bows. — The V.C. ought to have presented Lords N. & F. & me, but not seeing them he was flurried & forgot me altogether. — The Q. was looking pale and ill: the Prince stood by her and looked well: — Sir R. Peel & most of the Cabinet surrounded the Queen. — We were then shown into the Picture Gallery (where are some recumbent female statues by Canova, covered with gauze, & some excellent pictures by Rubens, Vandyk, Cuyp etc). After remaining here about 20' we were ushered into the Presence of P. Albert: — here I presented the Deputation as usual, & then the V.C. presented Earl Nelson, Viscount Fielding & myself. — Poor Travis (conduct of Trinity,[10] who has recently had an operation on his eyes to cure squinting, — wch has failed & seems to have injured his general health) is said to have behaved very wildly here, to have jumped up & down & spread out his hands to attract the Prince's notice: — in the Presence Chamber too he turned his back on the Queen, & I was obliged to pull him round. — I hear that some of our men clambered on the chairs etc. & that one glass door was broken: this is unfortunate & discreditable to us: — The V.C. exhorted the men to go up the Great Stair-Case in an orderly manner: —they did so & seemed to think that their good behaviour was to cease at the Head of the Stairs. — We then proceeded to Clarence House (the part of St James' Palace where W.IV lived when Duke of Clarence). Here the Deputation alone & the 2 young Lords (to the great discontent of the rest) were allowed to come into the Duchess of Kent's drawing-room. — As before I presented the Deputation, & the V.C. presented the 2 young Lords & me. — Whewell arrived at Buckingham Palace just as the guard was marching off. — About 200 persons accompanied our address from the Thatched House:[11] — the change of hour however threw out a great number who reached the place of rendezvous an hour after we were gone & were loud in their complaints. — The Papers gave Lord Lyndhurst (who as H. Steward was present)[12] credit for giving dinner to the Deputation. The Deputation however got dinner where they could, the V.C. alone dining with Lord Lyndhurst who entertained the Cabinet Ministers this day: — Lord Lyndhurst (as Lord Chancellor) very recently gave a Norwich Stall to Archdall wch accounts for the invitation to him: — Dr. French is said also to have been asked, but to have been engaged . . .

---

[10] I.e. the salaried chaplain.
[11] A well-known tavern in St. James's Street.
[12] The High Steward had 'special power to take the trial of scholars impeached of felony within the limits of the University' (*Cambridge University Calendar* for 1842).

Fri. 25   Good Friday . . . Lucy & I in the Evening to Trinity Church[13] — In spite of the late fracas[14] we found Mrs Bull & son & daughter in our Pew: the old lady gave way & went into the next pew . . .

On 26 March Romilly went off in the Bury coach for an Easter visit to Henslow[15] at Hitcham in Suffolk. On the way a trace broke, one of the horses fell, and the coach was almost overturned. One of the three lawyers who were his fellow-passengers 'was terrified in a ludicrous manner; . . . he became as pale as a ghost and vociferated in the utmost alarm to have the door opened — after all we did not go over & he was rather jeered by his companions for his needless fright.' At Bury Romilly bought presents for the younger Henslow children and admired a newly built church — 'it is of white brick, is an imitation of Early English, has a spire and is very handsome indeed'. The following day, Easter Sunday, he had thought, mistakenly, that he was to preach at the morning service at Hitcham Church and was putting on his gown 'to mount the pulpit when Henslow came into the vestry & stopped me'. One afternoon Mrs Henslow 'took a drive in her garden-chair, Henslow & I accompanying on foot', and on 29 March there was a dinner-party with 'so much pleasant chat that the aid of music was not called in'. On March 30 Romilly returned to Cambridge for the College scholarship examinations.

Sun. 3 April   . . . Today's post brought me a sermon of Henslows about the transportation of 3 of his parishioners for sheepstealing: — read it & thought it very good. — wrote to thank him . . .

13   I.e. Holy Trinity.
14   'It appears that Mrs Bull last Thursday begged to be admitted *into Mr. Romilly's* pew when it was filled by Mr Twiss's brother's wife & family, who very properly said 'it is our Pew':— So to show his right Mr. T. took possession:— it was rather amusing to see that our own cushion had been removed & Mr T's old brown one substituted' . . . (Entry for Sunday 27 February). Mr Twiss, a Cambridge attorney, did indeed own the pew but allowed the Romillys to use it.
15   Henslow, one of the most admirable figures among the early and mid-nineteenth century clergy, had decided in 1839 that he must live in his Suffolk parish and only return to Cambridge to deliver his lectures as Professor of Botany. When Henslow was appointed to his Chair no lectures on botany had been delivered in the University for thirty years.He was able, however, to tell the Royal Commissioners in 1850 that he had given twenty lectures every Easter Term for the last 25 years, and J.W. Clark in *Memories and Customs 1820-60* (reprinted from *The Cambridge Review* Lent Term 1909) says that in his house and Sedgwick's rooms 'the lamp of science was kept burning at a time when good people thought it dangerous'. In his parish he was equally conscientious. He fought a gallant battle to civilise Hitcham, built a school and paid for a teacher, introduced allotments despite fierce opposition from the farmers, started a wives' society, coal and clothing clubs, a Loan and Blanket Fund and a Medical Club. Henslow and his wife would also have been expected to give medical advice and help and, where necessary, to dispense simple medicines (see G.S.R. Kitson Clark, *Churchmen and the Condition of England 1832-85,* 1973).

Tu. 5. Looking over papers all the morning.[16] Walk with M:[17] — we called on Miss Webster; I made the tirade against Brown (the ejected Architect of St. Andrew):[18] she took it in such a way that she must either be a relation or in love with him . . .

Wed. 6. Walk with M. — Dined in Hall — To Trinity Lodge to Tea to settle the scholarships. — Passed ½ hr very agreeably in the Drawing room with Mrs Whewell. — We had a discussion concerning the Election of Young: — a very clever man in his 3rd year who was accused of swearing in hall last Sunday (his accuser was an undergraduate, not produced by the Dean); this charge brought up a reminiscence of the Proctor having once complained of him: — we decided to elect the man, & the Master undertook to lecture him seriously.

On the eighth Romilly and Sedgwick went to pay a brief visit to Mr Gale Townley at Beaupré Hall, Outwell, in the Isle of Ely. On the way he saw for the first time the process of 'claying'[19] the fenland and had his first view 'of the 'Hundred Foot',[20] wch we crossed by a handsome suspension Bridge built at G. Townley's expense'. The Townley's house had been large 'but it has never been restored since part of it was burnt down:— its present appearance is dingy & comfortless: the entrance is thro a handsome tower, wch is the only striking part of the building'. However, the guests, for there was a large house party, seem to have been very well entertained. On the day after their arrival Romilly and Sedgwick set off in their host's pony chaise to see the neighbouring churches. They visited Wisbech, Walsoken, (West) Walton with

---

[16] Examining for Trinity College scholarships was one of Romilly's annual duties. The number of scholarships varied from year to year. In 1839 there were 12 scholarships, in 1840 23 and in 1844 17 and some 70 or 80 Trinity men competing for them. The examinations lasted about 4 days. 'About nine, A.M., the new Scholars are announced from the Chapel gates . . . it is not etiquette for the candidates themselves to be in waiting . . . but their personal friends are sure to be on hand, together with an humbler set concerned —the gyps, coal-men, boot-blacks, and other College servants — who take great interest in the success of their masters, and bet on them to the amount of five shillings and less'. (Bristed p.193). Bristed was a graduate of Yale who was admitted as a Fellow-Commoner to Trinity in 1840 and himself became a scholar. His book is commended for its accuracy by G.M. Trevelyan and F.H. Bowring who became a Fellow of Trinity in 1844.

[17] I.e. Margaret, born in 1784 and the diarist's elder sister.

[18] In 1841 Brown had brought an action at Norwich Assizes against the Vicar of the parish of Great St Andrews for the recovery of £300 for preparing designs for the projected new church. Brown's designs had been approved, but he had agreed that the Vicar's committee should not be obliged to pay anything if they could not be built for a maximum of £4,000. No one could be found to build within this limit and a verdict was found for the Vicar.

[19] 'Claying' had been introduced about 1830 with excellent results. As the drainage of the fens became more efficient the thick peat layer above the clay had shrunk and the clay become accessible. It was then dug up and spread over the surface of the fens in order to make them more fertile. 'The new husbandry quickly extended itself: farmers may be cautious of new improvements, but this was too obvious for dispute, too near at hand for refusal' according to J.A. Clarke* *Fen Sketches* (1852).

[20] The New Bedford or Hundred Foot River was cut in 1651 and ran parallel to the Old Bedford River from Earith to Denver. It was the main channel for the upland waters of the Ouse. The north side of the Old Bedford River and the south side of the New Bedford River had been embanked and a long narrow wash left between them to provide a reservoir for flood water.

its 'lovely detached tower', the 'noble perpendicular church of Walpole St. Andrew', and lastly Walpole St. Peter — 'handsome but vastly inferior to its brother'. They were entertained to lunch by Mr Hankinson, the rector of the last-named parish, who, Romilly noted, had some good pictures including a Hogarth. When they returned from their long drive the Bishop of Norwich and other guests had joined the party. 'Sedgwick did not feel well & never came into the drawing room, tho' (as he left the dining room the 1st) he was supposed generally to have gone to flirt with the pretty Miss Blencowe',[21] sister of the Rector of Walton 'an enthusiastic young man, justly proud of his Church (wch he is exerting himself to restore)'. The next day, Sunday 10 April, the Bishop confirmed 208 children at Upwell, laying his hands on five children at a time and then pronouncing the words of administration. The church, Romilly noted, was in excellent order both inside and out, as Townley had laid out £6000 on it. On 11 April the party broke up and Romilly and Sedgwick returned to Cambridge.

Th.14. To a meeting of the Committee for rebuilding St. Peter's:[22] Salvins Estimate is £14500 !! — Good walk with M. to County Courts etc[23] —Finished 'the Fairy Bower':[24] it is dreadfully too long . . .

Fri.15. Revising Statutes for 2 hours.[25] — observing Carus in a greatcoat he astonished me by telling me that it had been the covering of the Pulpit at Trinity Church. — Tea & whist at Skrines.

Tu.19. Revising Statutes as usual. — The outside of our house painting . . . Evening party at Cummings to hear Miss Brasse (Daughter of our late Fellow) sing: she sang 'those Easter chimes', etc: much pleased with her voice & with her extreme good nature:— she is as round as a dumpling &

---

[21] In 1813 Sedgwick was very seriously ill with what was thought to be inflammation of the lungs. He felt the effects of this illness throughout his life and thereafter was much given to talking about his health. He told Dr. Hooker that he had become 'unfit for sedentary labour after 1813' and this 'conviction more than any other consideration determined him to become candidate for the Professor of Geology in 1818'. (See Clark and Hughes I, 130-1).

[22] Part of St. Peter's had been pulled down in 1781 and it was proposed to rebuild it with a tower and spire. This came to nothing and it was only restored, not rebuilt (see 31 December 1842).

[23] In 1747 a Shire Hall was built in Cambridge market place. It gradually became too small for the conduct of the assizes, and in 1842 a new Shire Hall was completed within the precincts of the castle to designs by T.H. Wyatt and D. Brandon. See Royal Commission on Historical Monuments, *City of Cambridge, Part 2*, plate 298 (77).

[24] A children's book by Harriet Mozley (1841). The author was the wife of a prominent Tractarian and the sister of J.H. Newman.

[25] Soon after becoming Master Whewell had told the Seniors, to which group of 8 senior Fellows Romilly had been elected in 1840, that revision of the statutes must no longer be delayed. Romilly's diary entry for 15 February 1842 reads 'College meeting to revise the Statutes. The Master expounded his views very clearly & well, that we were not to make new Statutes, but to bring our old into accordance with present practice, that we were a Privy Council & ought not to communicate to others our proceedings, etc —'. Between that date and 23 April the Board of Seniority met nearly 30 times and on 20 May Whewell was able to communicate a first draft of the revised statutes to the Home Secretary. 'The revised code was returned to Trinity, with the Great Seal attached in February 1844; and it may be fairly taken as an example of what the colleges then understood by statutory reform . . . A few motes had been removed, but most of the beams had been left; and in the light of subsequent events is it easy enough to see that a great opportunity had been missed'. (Winstanley, p.196).

has a face rather too red for the appearance of gentility.

Wed.20. Revising Statutes . . . I walked with Lodge to Chesterton[26] to see the restoration of the Chancel wch Trinity Coll. is making:— we also went over the County Courts & into the jail to see the very pretty model of them: we also went to St Sepulchres [the Round Church] & saw there a beautiful ancient Font (belonging to St. Edwards) wch has just been restored. — In the Evening I read loud 'the Favorite of Nature'.[27]

Th.21. Sacrament in the College Chapel; I assisted — The Master preached from Proverbs XV. 3 'The eyes of The Lord are in every place, beholding the evil & the good'. —:— for the benefit of the Freshmen there was a long passage about the Oedip. Colon.,[28] & the inability of ancient philosophy to show how an offending creature could be reconciled to God: . . . There was an eloquent passage where Whewell descanted on the majesty with wch Law invested itself, & that its highest force was derived from its reference to Religion (— by Oathes). — But the sermon was in parts hard and too metaphysical . . .

Sat.23. G.B. Allen[29] came of age. Revising Statutes — Epistolam anonymam recepi moerens intimantem viduam Fuscam clam peperisse.[30] — Lovely summer weather; almost too hot. — Walk with M. to the top of Castle Hill (her 1st visit there). — Dined in Hall.

Sun.24. Very hot day, with thunder. — Read prayers at Downing at 8 AM & 6 PM: the Congregation consisted of Dr Fisher, Frere, Sykes & 7 undergraduates. — M, L,[31] Esther Baily & I to Trinity Church where Carus preached from the 2nd Lesson (Acts XX1.13 'What mean ye to weep & break my heart etc:' he recommended imitating the tenderness and firmness of St Paul. — I then went to St Mary's to hear Alford (The Hulsean Lecturer):— the weather was very hot, the sun shone in my face (for in consequence of the suit between the University & Parish there are no blinds),[32] & Alford's matter was dry & his manner monotonous, so that I had all the trouble in the world in keeping my eyes open. — Mem: keep away when Alford preaches . . .

26 According to the *Cambridge Guide for 1845*, Chesterton was 'a large and pleasant village, a mile north of Cambridge'. The Vicar, however, appealing in 1843 for subscriptions for a National School, describes it as a place where 'many idle, disorderly and disreputable persons from Barnwell and Cambridge are continually setting a bad example — where nearly twenty beer shops keep open their doors to the great moral injury of the people'.
27 Mary Ann Kelty was the daughter of an Irish surgeon resident in Cambridge. *The Favorite of Nature* published in 1821, was the first of her many books.
28 *The Oedipus at Colonus* of Sophocles.
29 The diarist's nephew George Baugh Allen who had been admitted to Trinity in 1838. His mother, the Diarist's oldest sister, had died in 1831.
30 Why Romilly should have received an anonymous letter telling him that the widow Gray had died remains a mystery, as does his recording of it in Latin.
31 I.e. the diarist's younger sister Lucy, born in 1797.
32 A faculty was obtained on 15 March 1842, for confirming certain alterations and additions to seating for members of the university. 'The application for this faculty occasioned protracted and costly litigation'. (Cooper III p.306 note (e)).

Wed.27. Margaret all the morning at Mrs Marlows (from 10 to 3) to hear Thurtell & Swinney [sic] examine the children[33] . . . Great Prize fight near Mildenhall between J. Broome & Bungaree (the latter beaten):— the Heads sent out a decree yesterday against attending it:[34] — shoals went over, but only 4 were caught by those zealous men Archdeacon Thorp, Pro-proctor Cooper, & Smith of Caius.[35] — Declined Headly's whist.

Th.28. College meeting about Bursarial business. — Trial before V.C. & Heads from 1 to 4:— the 4 persons caught yesterday were had up viz, Sinclair (a F.C.)[36] & Houstoun, Shelford and Ogier 3 Pensioners, all of Trinity — The 1st 3 were suspended from their deg. for 1 Term, Ogier for 2, because he staid after being warned off, whereas the others went away:—he is a Pupil of G. Allen's . . .

Fri.29. Shortly after breakfast poor M. was seized with bad pain in her side:— I went to Dr Haviland, who did not apprehend anything very serious as she had no cough. — Carus paid Lucy a visit of 1½ hour! . . .

Sat.30. Margaret had not got rid of the spasms in her side: so Dr Haviland prescribed some Pills & Draught:— by a most unfortunate blunder Deck's boy left the Pills at the bottom of his basket & only delivered the draught. — G.E. Childe convened before V.M. & Seniors for Contumacy in riding towards Newmarket after being forbidden by his Tutor Blakesley. — We rusticated him till next October. — Dined at V.Ch's & slept in College, so I knew nothing about the unhappy mistake of the

[33] In 1815 the Governors of the Old Schools Trust replaced their scattered dame schools for girls by a National School in King Street. The school was free until 1820 when fees were charged at 1s. a quarter. The girls were taught scripture, reading, writing, accounts, needle-work and knitting. Cambridge children were comparatively fortunate. In Cambridge in 1835 the ratio of children at day schools was 1 in 8 as a whole. The corresponding ratio in England as a whole was 1 in 10 · 7.

[34] This stated that any person *in statu pupillari* should be liable to suspension, rustication or expulsion if he resorted to or had 'any communication whatever, with any professed teacher of the art of boxing, or be found attending any prize-fight' . . .

[35] 'It was laughable to see the contention between the University authorities and the students under their care . . . Many of the Fellows of colleges were sworn in as special Proctors and were to be seen parading the courts of their various colleges, at three o'clock in the morning. Two of these gentlemen were stationed at the Paper Mills gate' . . . [the gate of the toll-house in the Paper Mills area beyond Stourbridge Chapel was an obvious place at which to check traffic to Newmarket]. 'In addition to these precautions, the horse-dealers were had into the august presence of the Vice-Chancellor, who threatened to stop the licence of any one of them who let a horse to go to the fight: . . . A vast number of the swell mob' [pickpockets who dressed and behaved like respectable people] and London pickpockets were present' *(The Cambridge Independent Press* for 30 April). Romilly noted that some undergraduates 'were disguised in smockfrocks' (See *UP* 14 no. 648).

[36] The Fellow Commoners were wealthy young men and younger sons of noblemen and accorded many privileges. 'But many of them did not trouble to take degrees, wasted their time and money, and set a bad example to the other undergraduates.' (Winstanley, p.415) C.A. Bristed comments that the expenses *necessarily* incurred by Fellow Commoners meant that even the eldest sons of peers sometimes came up as Pensioners, and 'younger sons continually do'.

Pills, wch I should have detected had I been at home as I had read the Prescription. . .

Sun. 1 May Poor M. felt worse, having had a very bad night:— I went for Dr. Haviland before breakfast. — He was much annoyed at the Pills not having been sent, wch he expected would set her up:— Now he found it necessary to order 12 leeches . . .

Mon.2. Delightful day for the May Lords & Ladies.[37] — Margaret happily passed a good night & is (thank God) a great deal better. — Dr. H's 4th visit . . .

Tu.3. . . . Dined at the Woodward Audit[38] at the V.C's, and met there Sedgwick, the 2 Auditors . . . the 3 Esq. Bedells & 6 heads (besides the V.C.). —Archdall gave Sedgw's health with a good deal of heartiness, & S. made an admirable speech, speaking of the recently bought Plesiosaurus & the general prosperity of his museum. — Went home with him & smoked a cigar. — Back to the Hills Road[39] before 10 to read prayers.

Tu.10. . . . Tea with Mrs Lindsay to meet Archbishop of Dublin & Miss Whately: he said that one golden link of Scripture was worth all the Catena Patrum[40] & that he should think much worse of the Fathers than he was prepared to do if many of them would not feel much shocked at finding their writings put almost on an equality with Scripture. He said that he (Whately) examined only in 2 Books, the Bible (as Christians), and Prayer Book (as Ch. of England men) . . . He talked unceasingly & most cleverly, put himself in all manner of ungainly attitudes, & was perpetually taking something off the table. — He wanted Miss Wh. to sing 'The Crabstock' & declared that her declining proceeded entirely from her disliking the wholesome doctrine of Judge Buller inculcated in it[41] — Miss Whately played nicely on the Piano: she is a fat good humoured young Lady of much affability. — Mrs Mill sang 'What tho I trace'.

Th.12. . . . Trial at ViceChancellor's:[42] the Culprit was Forbes of Queens who (on 27th Apr.) at the Prize Fight near Mildenhall denied being a member of university — Rusticated for 2 years. — Also a trial before the V. Master of Ford, Locke & Shakspeare for breaking a lamp in a

37 In 1833 Romilly records giving halfpence to children who were dressed up or had dressed dolls or other figures as Lords and Ladies of the May.
38 Dr Woodward in his will of 1727 had left the University his cabinets of English fossils and the University then bought the cabinets of foreign fossils which he had described in printed catalogues. These formed the nucleus of the Geological Museum.
39 An 1847 directory states that the Romillys' house was No. 50.
40 I.e. biblical commentaries dating from the 5th century onwards in which successive verses of the scriptural text were elucidated by 'chains' of passages derived from previous commentators.
41 Dr. Robson suggests that Judge Buller is Sir Francis Buller and that Whately may have been making a jocular reference to Buller's ruling that a husband may beat his wife so long as the stick he uses is no thicker than his thumb. We have been unable to trace the song, but Dr. Robson thinks that the slender crab apple sapling used for grafting (the crabstock) might conform to the dimensions of the Judge's permissible weapon.
42 It fell to the Registrary to attend the Vice-Chancellor's Court of Discipline, to attest the proceedings as a Notary Public and to enter the proceedings in the *Acta Curiae*.

drunken fit: the 1st gated: the other 2 rusticated. — I escaped this 2d trial as it was at the same time as the V.C's. — Yesterday we decided the long expected Theological-Examination Grace:[43] the Senate House was extremely full: 58 to 25 in Black House; 52 to 19 in White House;[44] the Nonplaceters[45] were J.J. Smith & Williamson of Clare. — The Ornamental Wall N. of Fitzwilliam (for £2000) was thrown out;[46] 31 to 38 in B.H; 32 to 32 in W.H: The Non-Placeters were Birkett (Emmanuel) & Williamson (Clare) . . .

Fri.13. Auditing V.C's Dr. Graham's Accounts till 5 o'clock. (N.B. — The Proctors were very tiresome (Maturin & Dalton) & kept us from 10 to 12. — Dr G's accounts in admirable order . . . M. went to Mrs Marlows School & returned indignant at Perry's having ordered that the rules against plaited hair, necklaces & ear-rings, & bare shoulders are to be superseded![47] Read loud Ch. O'Malley.[48]

Sat.14. . . . In the Evening M. & I went to the Procession of Boats:[49] the weather was charming & the sight very pretty:— both of the G's

---

[43] A syndicate had been appointed 'to consider whether any and what steps should be taken to provide a more efficient system of Theological instruction in the University'. In his *Observations on the Statutes of the University* (1841) George Peacock had stated that 'at least half the students in the University are designed for the Church and no provision (the lectures of the Norrisian Professor alone excepted) is made for their professional education'. As a result of this vote and of Whewell's subsequent circular letter to the Bishops, the Voluntary Theological Examination came into operation in 1843 and soon ceased to be voluntary except in name. The candidates for orders had to have testimonials from their colleges. C.A. Bristed was dismayed by the profligacy of many of them. 'Many of the men whose undergraduate course has been the most marked by drunkeness and debauchery, appear, after the 'Poll' examination, at Divinity lectures'. The colleges were inclined to be too lenient when the Proctors reported undergraduates suspected of sexual offences. They often only imposed 'the same penalty as would be inflicted on one who neglected to attend lectures regularly . . .' (Winstanley pp.375-82).

[44] The Senate was divided into two Houses, the Regent or White House of Masters of Arts and others of a certain standing, who wore their hoods in such a way as to show the white silk lining, and the Non-Regent or Black House of the other members of the Senate who wore their black silk hoods so that the white did not show.

[45] I.e. they signified opposition to the Grace. Non placet means 'not approved'.

[46] The Grace or formal proposal was 'to authorise Mr. Basevi to contract with Mr. Baker for enclosing the north and west sides of the Fitzwilliam Museum; the former with a Portland stone architectural wall, the latter with an iron palisade'.

[47] The National Schools' rules for 1841 said that 'The children must be sent to School clean and neat, with their hair well cut and combed. No necklaces or ear-rings shall be allowed in any of the Schools. If any Child offend against this rule it shall be sent back'. Perry had presumably acted in his capacity as a governor. The governors and subscribers nominated children for the school — an annual subscription of one guinea entitled the subscriber to nominate four.

[48] By Charles James Lever, published in 1841.

[49] The annual procession of racing eights took place between the bridges of Clare and King's. 'The eights row past in order, adorned with flags and flowers, then return and lie side by side across the river; when the line is formed all except those in the first boat stand up, lift their oars in the air and cheer, while the band plays 'For he's a jolly good fellow'. (Charles Dickens, *Dictionary of Cambridge*, 1884). It was possible to stand up in these boats because they were heavy, unrigged, and clinker built.

pulled.[50] Today declined Blakesley's Luncheon. — Began reading Kara Kaplan (a Persian Novel) by Savill of Queens:— Some merit.

Sun.22. Trin: Sund: Read prayers at Downing — M & I to Trinity Church and heard Dr. Ting: he preached from Rev. 19.12 'wore many crowns':— he was in the energetic or ranting stile:— he had 2 merits: his sermon was only 25 minutes & he certainly kept one awake . . . his action was inelegant & particularly offensive from his wearing a pudding sleeved gown.[51]

Fri. 27. Long walk with M. in the round-about &c[52] — Trinity College examination ended today at 2.[53] The 2 G's dined with us at 5: it was a farewell dinner to G. Allen who goes away for good tomorrow. Declined dining with Blakesley.

Sat. 28. . . . Lucy poorly with a sort of influenza. — Called on John Pennethorne (brother of A.P.) Architect who flatters himself that he has made a great discovery about Grecian Architecture, viz. that it is all purely Geometrical. . .

Mon. 30. Gave breakfast to Mr Pennethorne, Geo. Romilly and his friend Graham:— The Master of Trinity & Willis were asked, but one was out of Cambr. & the other was engaged with guests at his Lodge. — At 10 however the Master came to my rooms and gave an hour to Mr. Pennethorne and his plans.[54] — He threw much cold water upon Mr. P's project, who took it greatly to heart & lamented much to me after the Master's departure. — Today a young scoundrel (named Francis) attempted to shoot the Queen on Constitution Hill (— the same place as

50 I.e. Romilly's nephews George Allen, who had become a scholar of Trinity in 1839 and was now about to leave Cambridge, and George Romilly, who had been admitted to Trinity in April 1841.
51 A large bulging sleeve drawn in at the wrist or above, as on a Doctor of Divinity gown.
52 I.e. Trinity Fellows' Garden.
53 Trinity had done great service to the cause of reform by holding entrance examinations, and in 1790 by testing the industry of undergraduates by establishing annual college examinations. By 1818 these examinations were extended to third as well as to first and second year undergraduates. L. Wainewright in *Literary and Scientific Pursuits in the University of Cambridge* (1815) was surprised to find that so few of the smaller colleges had followed Trinity's example. The candidates in 'The May' examinations wrote from 9 to 1 and again from 4 to 8 in the evening. For a detailed and amusing account see Bristed, pp.61–76.
54 Dr. Robson knows of no plans for Trinity which involved Pennethorne. John Pennethorne may well have thought that Whewell, as a mathematician and keen amateur architect, would be interested in the theory to the demonstration of which he devoted most of his life. Pennethorne attempted to show that Greek architects, having designed a rectilinear building, then corrected its dimensions in accordance with the optical conditions of correct perspective. In Nikolaus Pevsner's chapter on Whewell in *Some Architectural Writers of the Nineteenth Century*, (1972) he writes with admiration of Whewell's *Architectural Notes on German Gothic Churches* (1830) which he says was unmatched at that date in England. Dr Searby points out that Whewell designed 4 and 6 Trinity Street, Cambridge, to exemplify his ideas on the Gothic.

Oxford chose).[55] — Dined with Lodge & met the Master of Trinity (— who today was thrown by his horse starting and then backing into a ditch)[56] . . .

Tu. 31.   Walk with M. — Gave dinner to Master of Trinity & Mrs Whewell, Master of Pemb, & Mrs Ainslie, Dr & Mrs Clark, Mr & Mrs & Miss Hughes & Mrs Foster, G.A. Browne, Thorp & Carus. — By the way Carus walked half way up to the house (flattering himself he was going to dine with the Ladies) before he suspected his error. — G.A. Browne was kind enough to lend me his rooms for a drawing room. — The party went off very well — When the rest of the company were gone G.A.B. told me he was in great grief from intelligence that he had just received, that his friend Charles Beales was a defaulter at the Races (just run) for £18,000 & has bolted:— it seems there is a suspicion of his having (with Gully) tampered with a boy to drug one of the horses![57] , . .

Wed. 1 June   Poor Miss B. has got a cancer & is gone to Town for the Operation. — Wrote to her. — Trinity Classes: George, alas! only in the 5th: there were 9 classes (containing 113 names) & 5 posted dunces,[58] among whom was Head (son of Sir. F.). — A meeting of Master & Seniors: we had up 2 Posted men (3rd year) Macleod & Mr Elliott & the Master gave them a stout reprimand upon the disgrace they had incurred, — from wilfulness & perverseness not from stupidity, for they are both expected to take Honors:— they wished to be in the last class, but fell short of their hopes.

Th. 2.   To a grand luncheon at Wauds: we met in the Pepysian Library & looked over books &c: we feasted in the Hall; & a very good feast it was with Ice & Champagne . . . The choristers were engaged:— they sang Grace, & then various catches & glees till the women left us. — We soon joined them & paraded about the walks till coffee time; then more walking till tea-time; we had then more glee-singing. — I attached myself to Miss Hind (who was so near dying of a fever) during the walking time. — Away at 8½ — Found it very pleasant . . .

Mon.6.   Congregation to read an Address of Congratulation to the Q.

---

55 Nineteen year-old Francis shot at the Queen as she and Prince Albert were returning to Buckingham Palace in a barouche and four. He was transported for life, having originally been sentenced to be hanged, beheaded and quartered. Oxford, a maniac, had fired at the Queen and Prince on June 15, 1840.

56 Whewell was both a bold and a careless rider. He died after a fall from his horse.

57 In a report headed 'Tattersalls' — Monday' *The Cambridge Chronicle* (4.6.42) comments that 'it rarely happens that a good settling follows a Derby won by a great public favourite . . . Up to Saturday morning nothing had transpired to induce a suspicion that there would be any serious defecations . . . On Sunday, however, it was announced that Mr. Beales had been hit for £18,000 and could not pay! The news came like a thunderbolt, for independent of the amount of the deficit, it must necessarily place many other parties who lost on the race in a very embarrassing position'. It seems clear from subsequent small reports in the *Cambridge Chronicle* and the *Independent* that the rumours of Beales conspiring with Gully and decamping were without foundation.

58 I.e. they had failed in the college examinations. Their names were 'posted' separately as not worthy to be classed.

on her escape from attempted assassination (by J. Francis). Heard an anecdote of Archbishop Whateley that amused me: he asked a Lady 'What is the feminine of Jack Pudding?' to which she answered 'A Charlotte de Pommes' . . .

Wed. 8. The same glorious weather. — Paget & I over to Shelford to dine with Sir Ch. & Lady Wale . . . Some mouse in a cheese singing from Miss James. — Lady Wale kept a bazaar for the Shelford School:— bought some trifles of her. — When I got home at past 12 was without my key:— fortunately the Porter among a store of keys found one that let me in.

Sun. 12. Lucy rather poorly. — She did not stir beyond the garden all day. — Carus gave us an awful stick (of Peterhouse) to preach on the Queen's Letter for the distressed manufacturers: the insufferable preacher took for his Text 2 Cor. VIII. 9.[59] but did not say above 2 or 3 sentences for the poor . . .

On 14 June Romilly went to London for the presentation of the address to the Queen on her escape from assassination. The ceremonial was much the same as before. The Queen, he thought, looked remarkably well, and the Presence Chamber was 'still adorned with some of the emblazonry of the great Pageant in wch the Q. represented Q Philippa & P. Albert Edw 3rd'. The Duke of Northumberland invited the official party to dine with him at Sion House the following day, and Romilly was much annoyed at the Vice-Chancellor's refusal of the invitation 'because the V.C. did not like the trouble of going to Sion House . . . a bad precedent . . . not respectful to the Chancellor & very distasteful to all the Deputation'. (Note by Romilly on the Order of Precedence for the 15th June in *UP* 1840-43). He stayed in London until the 20th. of the month and passed his time very much as usual. He was much pleased with 'the Dissolving Views' at the Polytechnic and with the mountain scenery depicted in 'the Panorama of Caboul'. He went several times to the theatre, seeing Dobler, 'the Great German conjurer', at the St. James's who 'was very skilful: and the 200 candles on the stage were brilliant: but the heat was insufferable & after an hour I came back again to the Athenaeum'. He also found Rachel in Corneille's *Ariadne* admirable 'but the part is not nearly so effective a one as Camille, the only other character that I have seen her sustain'. He went too to several picture galleries, including an exhibition of Wilkie's work and the Royal Academy. This he thought rather poor. 'The E. Landseers were in general unpleasing subjects (a deer that had escaped thro the water, a hideous badger-dog, an ugly greyhound of P. Alberts etc:) except 2 monkeys (sitting on a melon) frightened at a wasp . . . The Turners are in general detestable, more especially 2 (a misty elongated Bonaparte & the burying Wilkie at Sea)'. On Sunday, 19 June, he and his friend Lodge attended what he calls a 'Puseyite' service where they 'sat in the Free-seats in spite of the Pew openers entreaties'. There were 4 or 5 (I am not sure which) clergymen in their surplices at the communion table, . . . 12 surpliced singing boys (6 on each side of the organ) . . . and different parts of the service read

[59]   I.e. 'For ye know the grace of our Lord Jesus Christ, that, though he was rich, yet for your sakes he became poor, that ye through his poverty might be rich.'

or chaunted by different persons.' They must have had 'Puseyism' much in their minds that day for after church they went to the Athenaeum where Lodge read to Romilly the Bishop of Oxford's charge on the *Tracts for the Times*.[60]

On 20 June Romilly returned to Cambridge by the Star, two days before 'George began with his new Tutor (W. Walton) whose half pupil he is to be for the long vacation'.

Fri. 24 Visit in the Evening from Macfarlan: he seems not entirely to have thrown off his old bad habit of swearing from an anecdote he told me of his little boy (aged 4) saying to another child 'does your papa say 'devil'? mine does when he is in a passion' . . .

One of Romilly's chief duties was preparing for the annual commencement or conferring of M.A. and other higher degrees which was ordained by statute to take place on the first Tuesday in July. In 1842 his duties were made particularly onerous by the festival to celebrate the Installation of the Duke of Northumberland as Chancellor of the University. The Duke had been elected Chancellor and installed at Northumberland House, London, in October 1840. But the Cambridge festival had been postponed because of the political excitement in 1841 which ultimately resulted in a general election.

Mon. 27. Wrote to F. — £10.[61] From 10 till 2 at my office distributing tickets:[62] that was my announced time:— I did in fact stay till 3½. I was assisted by Bunch, Cartmell, Birkett & Mills. — Gave to about 210 people . . .

Fri. 1. July From 10 to 3 tickets with same helps. — In the Evening at my rooms from 8 to 11½ distributing tickets & receiving fees:[63] — helped by Bunch, Birkett, Cartmell & Cookson: Cookson was kind enough to be cash-taker, & made an admirably good one:— coffee etc & afterwards sandwiches:— a great crowd constantly endeavouring to rush into the rooms, & could scarcely be kept back by 2 men whom I had to guard the passage: two or 3 times I had to go & address the unruly mob. — Sedgwick & Peacock came & had a sandwich & discussed the proceedings of the British Association at Manchester from wch they are just come.

Sat. 2. Cartmell most kindly came at 9 to help me in College: so too did Bunch & Lodge: Birkett was (as last night) working for the V.C. —Great influx of people from 7½ to 11:— no time for breakfast. — A grand number of MAs viz 114: the other degrees were few, viz 5 DD, 1 BD, 1 LLB, 2 AB. —

---

[60] Between 1833 and 1841 a total of 90 *Tracts for the Times* had been published by Newman, Pusey, Keble, Froude and other leaders of the High Church movement in Oxford. They exerted great influence particularly on the younger clergy and provoked bitter controversy. For a full account of Bishop Bagot's charge which was delivered on 23 May 1842, in St Mary's Church at Oxford see Chadwick, pp.174-5.

[61] Frank (or Francis) Romilly, the Diarist's younger brother (1793-1863), who lived in Paris with his French wife and three children.

[62] I.e. for the forthcoming ceremonies in the Senate House.

[63] In 1842 B.A.s or A.B.'s (Artium Baccalaurei) paid the Registrary £3.3.0., £3 of which was paid to Government in stamp duty and M.A.s or A.M.s (Artium Magistri) paid £6.6.0. of which six pounds was paid in stamp duty.

Today a Grace for suppressing the Proctorial feasts at the 2 fairs.[64] — This morning Lucy went to St Mary's to hear the Bp of Winchester preach for Addenbrooke's Hospital:[65] his Text was Luk. X1X.23: a prodigious crowd:—a grand collection, £154! — In the Evening I again distributed tickets assisted by Cartmell, Lodge, & Bunch — such a constant rush of clamorous candidates for tickets (most of them undergraduates) that coffee never could be brought in & it was very difficult to take the fees of the subscribers. — Happily however the last of them was gone by 11. —Then sandwiches — very much tired.

Sun. 3. [Commencement Sunday][66] I was so tired & knocked up that I did not go to Trinity Church . . . Lucy went by herself . . . She fell in with Mrs Pryme who took her home to lunch & gave her a ticket for St. Marys side aisle. The Church was tremendously full, the heat very oppressive, the music very loud (being for a Musical degree), & she found the Sermon of the B. of London uninteresting (— it was a good deal about our recently instituted Theological Examinations) . . . I was obliged tho it was Sunday, to sign a large number of cards (all the original issue having been exhausted) & answer an infinitude of letters of application, etc etc. — Declined dining in hall to meet the D. of Cambridge[67] etc — Declined Mrs Whewell's soirée tonight as I had been obliged to do last night also. — M. & I joined the Promenade on Clare Hall piece[68] after Trinity Chapel (wch was made an hour later today, the dinner having also been made an hour later for the sake of our royal guest attending Kings.)

64 The Grace was 'To dispense, in future, with the entertainments given by the Proctors at Midsummer and Sturbridge fairs'. At Stourbridge 'after listening to the proclamation, the Vice-Chancellor and the other representatives of the University adjourned to the Tiled Booth where at the expense of the Proctors they feasted on oysters.' (Winstanley, p.129). The fairs were declining in importance and Romilly remarked in 1853 that they were going, like all other fairs, 'to the dogs'.

65 At the bottom of the leaflet giving particulars of the sermon and preceding anthem 'Ladies and Gentlemen who may chose to visit the Hospital immediately after the service' are told that they will 'find it well worth the inspection of all lovers of order and regularity'.

66 The annual Commencement or conferring of M.A. and other higher degrees was by statute ordained to take place on the first Tuesday in July. Adam Sedgwick writing to his niece about Commencement at this period remembers that 'At this season . . . all was bright and gay as the young M.A's often brought their wives and sisters and we had a week of festivities and dances and concerts, and every third year there was a Grand Commencement, when we had during the week three oratorios and one or two concerts'. See Clark and Hughes, II, 447–8.

67 The Duke, who was the seventh son of George III and Queen Charlotte, had arrived in Cambridge on the evening of 2 July. After his return from Hanover he had become very popular in this country and was active in supporting many learned and benevolent societies.

68 Clare Hall Piece, on the western side of the river, was a favourite promenade of the University and town especially at the July Commencement. 'On Commencement Sunday the whole academic world used to walk up and down there for half an hour after the University Sermon, and a very pretty sight it was, Mr. Vice-Chancellor and all the Heads and Doctors in scarlet and the ladies in their best frocks' (J.W. Clark, *Memories and Customs 1820-60*, reprinted from *The Cambridge Review*, Lent Term 1909).

Mon. 4. That good fellow Cartmell came to help me at 8: Lodge also & Bunch — 68 AM, 8 LLD (Hon), 4 AM (Hon), 1 BD, 1 LLB, 1 Mus D & 1 Mus B. — I remained on the Platform all day.[69] — There was a brilliant assemblage of persons there; the D. of Nd had on his right the D. of Camb, & the A. of Canterbury, on his left the D. of Wellington & Lord Chancellor Lyndhurst:— this was the front row: behind were The A. of Armagh, Bps of London, Winchester & Carlisle, Bunsen (Prussian Minister), Everett (American Minister),[70] Count Kielmannsegge (Hanoverian Minister), Baron Gersdorff (the Saxon Minister) & a great tribe of Lords & Ladies. —

The undergraduates gave 3 cheers for the Belle of the Senate House:— upon wch Lady Jersey said to her daughter (Lady Clementina), 'Clem: that's you'.[71] The Orator's speech was read:— it was dreadfully too long, but (allowing for its idolatry of toryism) it seemed well written. —

The Chancellor conferred the Hon: Degrees only & then left the S.H. about 4, —having come about 12½. — The V.C. then conferred all the ordinary degrees. — The D. of Wellington was ushered into Cambridge this morning by a great concourse & was received most enthusiastically:[72] — he staid a short time in the Senate House: he showed himself at the Promenade at the Master of Magdalene's & also on the grass plot at Emmanuel just before dinner,[73] but at 7 he left C. for London.[74] — By the way M. & L. very amiably sent the maids to Mrs Derry (the Hosier's) to see the entry of the D. of Wellington. — M. L. & I were asked to the Promenade at Magdalene from 4 to 6, but we declined going. — Dined at the V.C's grand dinner in Emm: Hall. We were asked at 6, but (a spit laden with venison having given way) we had to walk up & down the grass for an hour before dinner was announced. — It was in grand stile, turtle, venison & champagne. — Ladies in the Gallery to hear the speeches. — The moment the cloth was removed I went away (to my great regret) to distribute tickets

[69] On 4 July 'the Chancellor held a levee at St. John's Lodge, and proceeded thence to the Senate House, where H.R.H. the Duke of Cambridge was created LL.D., and other honorary degrees were conferred. (Cooper, IV,653).

[70] For a reproduction of R.W. Buss's plate illustrating the installation see Bruce Dickins's article on 'Cambridge in 1842', *Transactions of the Cambridge Bibliographical Society* V,3 (1971). He points out that Edward Everett was in black because 'he was a Unitarian minister, and in any case the U.S. disapproved of diplomatic uniform'.

[71] *The Cambridge Chronicle* records that the fame of Lady Clementina Villiers' beauty 'had long preceded her appearance in our academic groves'.

[72] The Duke had been staying at Bourn Hall, the seat of Earl de la Warr, and several hundred horsemen and innumerable pedestrians left Cambridge early in order to meet him. The road from the Observatory to Cambridge was 'strewed with branches of laurel' (*The Cambridge Chronicle* 9 July).

[73] 'where he walked up and down in delightful converse with the Archbishop of Canterbury; the appearance of those two venerable and venerated men was hailed with great pleasure by every one within the College walks!' (*ibid*).

[74] "I *must* go", said he; 'my carriage is at the gate, and I am very sorry for it. God bless you all —God bless you all!' . . . To Cambridge it is most likely that the Duke of Wellington has now bid a final adieu: one can scarcely hope to see him here again . . .' (*ibid*).

& so missed Mr Everetts speech[75] which was (according to general report) admirable. Cartmell most benevolently came & helped me:— at 10 the demand was supplied & Cartmell & I took a walk — not going to the Dance at Jes. College . . .

Tu. 5.   Tickets for the Senate House & for Creation of M.A's from 7 to 10. — Then assisted the Editor of the Advertiser for 2 hours — Did not go to the Senate House today:— I should like to have heard the 'God save the Q.' with wch the Music concluded.[76] — I took M. & L. into the Fitzwilliam Museum to see the Preparations for the Ball of tomorrow: we were much pleased with the flowers (sent by Widnall). — George and I to the Grand Fête at St. Johns:[77] the day was charming and the banquet delicious; the promenading & dancing very attractive. — Poor Mr Beard begged hard of Crick, the Orator, for a ticket for the Fête today, & when he urged that he was actually lodging in the Cloisters in his son's rooms the Orator conducted him to the Gate & gave orders to the Porter not to admit him again till 10 o'clock at night! — A grand scene took place in the dancing tent:— a brother of the Orator was Curate to a Mr. Potchett & had won the heart of the daughter but not that of the Father: he used to drop love epistles in her pew as he went up the Pulpit stairs, — but the inexorable Papa forbad all correspondence. — In the aforesaid dancing booth however he spied M. le Curé handing his daughter:— he rushed forward, elbowing the crowd right & left, tore away the damsel & bitterly reproached the lover as an unworthy clergyman & a dishonorable man for practising on the weakness of his daughter:— Crick junior whined & said 'it was very hard, for even his brother took part against him'. — In the Evening viz at 9½ I took G. & M. to see the Fitzwilliam lighted up as a Rehearsal of tomorrow:— it was very imperfectly done while we were there, & we were told it would be completed at 10. — I went to the Fireworks at Jesus: they went off very well. —The Entrance was not well managed: most injudiciously the gates were shut: so the crowd (or as the D. of Cambridge called it 'the scrimmage') was very great:— by the way the D. of C. lost his star in this scrimmage:— it was afterwards recovered.[78] I went up into Gaskin's room where the D. of C. &c were assembled:— I was amused by listening to his questions to Gaskin about his office, his rooms &c .

Wed. 6.   Breakf. to G.T.R, P.T. Ouvry & an Oxonian friend of his Roberts. — M. & L. sent the maids to see the Trinity dinner-tables & to hear the band on Clare Hall piece. . . Took M. to see the Trinity Tables; also

[75]   Everett's speech is reported on p.753 of *UP* 14.

[76]   After the creation of Doctors and the recitation of the prize poems, three of them by a scholar of Pembroke, the installation ode was sung. There were no less than twelve long verses set to music by T.A. Walmisley.

[77]   There were more than 1400 people there. (Cooper, IV,657).

[78]   The star was said to be worth 500 guineas. 'The announcement of the loss created a great sensation, it being generally supposed that an expert Thief had stolen it'. The star was found during the night in 'the gardens of the college by Serjeant Langley'. (*The Annual Register,* 6 July 1842).

16

took her to the Anthem at Kings, & then to the Promenade on Clare Hall piece to hear the Band: she was much pleased with all 3. — Procured a ticket from Thorp for Mr Roberts to dine at the Trin: dinner. — Today was the Grand Trinity Dinner — I was very well placed for hearing all the speeches. Our dinner was very tolerably punctual:— we sat down at 5¼:— the gallery was filled with Ladies. — The dinner was all of common things: no turtle, no venison, no champagne:— the best part of it was a dessert of very fine fruit. —The speaking of the Master was very good & had the merit of brevity & terseness. His speech of thanks after the D. of Cambridge gave his health was admirable: he said that he felt the deep responsibility of his position, but that *reponsibility was man's highest dignity.* — When he had concluded the D. of Cambridge turned to him & said 'Very true: the longer I live the more I feel it: — *a confounded thing that responsiblity'!*

The V.M. made a very elegant concise speech in drinking prosperity to Oxford:—Buckland made a flashy mouthy speech in reply:— He spoke by the direction of the Master, but it was a mistake as Ld Devon (the H. Steward) was present, & returned thanks immediately afterwards. — The great speech of the day was the B. of London's: it was of a high order of eloquence; the part concerning his own Academic career ('how kindly he had been assisted with instruction when he could not afford to have a private tutor':[79] — how much humbled he felt at not having made a nobler use of the opportunities afforded him, and yet how deeply grateful to God for having enabled him to gain the — he could find no other word, the *distinctions* he had obtained &c'. — The applause was enthusiastic. — Sedgwick (who was not well) gave prosperity to Dublin University:— his speech was too long & fell heavy & flat wch greatly vexed me as I was sitting between 2 Oxonians whom I wished to admire him. — The D. of Cambr. said quite loud 'Gratias ago' when Sedgwick said 'I will not trouble you longer'. — The A. of Armagh (as perpetual V.Ch. of Dublin) returned thanks[80] — The D. of Northumberland was now so much tired that he begged the Master to break up, whereby we missed his *5th Act* (as he afterwards called it), viz. the speeches of Everett & Bunsen (the American & Prussian ministers). — I was very sorry for this as I missed Mr Everett's speech at the V.C's. — About 9½ we left the Hall. — At 10¼ I went to the Ball wch was most brilliant:— The D. of Northumberland did not go to it. —but the Duchess of Northumberland, the D. of Camb. &c &c all went: —

[79] James Hildyard told the Royal Commissioners that his 'expenses . . . as an undergraduate from 1829 to 1833 for a private tutor in mathematics alone . . . were £72 per annum, inclusive of the Long Vacation, for which I three times over paid £30.' (*University Commission Report* 1852).

[80] *The Cambridge Chronicle* reports that 'Professor Sedgwick in a speech of considerable length which we could not distinctly hear, proposed prosperity to the university of Dublin'. The Archbishop of Armagh replied, 'but in so low a tone of voice that we unfortunately were not able to catch a single sentence.'

out of the 1627 tickets sold, 1602 persons were present.[81] — By the way only 500 tickets were sold up to Tuesday night, so that the prospect was but gloomy early this morning as the expenses were £1200:— now however there is £400 clear for the Hospital.[82] The Committee mean indeed to offer to repay the D. of Northumberland the £300 wch he so handsomely paid for the fittings up of the Fitzwilliam Museum last year for the expected public Commencement, but it is quite certain that he will not accept it. — All today Widnall sold elegant little bouquets (1d each) for the ball: he sold 1000 & gave the £50 to the hospital:— Mr Hope also gave £50 and the D. of Cambridge £10. — A propos of bouquets Miss Spilling sent Lucy a very large no of nosegays wch she had made up from her own garden at the Hospital:— Lucy sent several of them to the Prymes. — The ball was very magnificent, and the ices &c excellent:— no champagne, no sit down supper:— there was but one thing ill managed:— the waxlights had no shades to them, & the draught occasioned the wax to fall abundantly:— the white spots on the Ladies' shoulders looked like leprosy & their hair became powdered. — I went away at 12½. — The rooms were profusely lighted: & the entrance looked very beautiful with all the boat-flags.

Th. 7. Breakfast to G.T.R, P.T. Ouvry, Mr Roberts, & Wray (the Receiver of the London Police). — I then went to a grand breakfast at Dr. Mills to meet 2 picturesque shawled Hindoos (whom the Papers call Indian princes):[83] they are very wealthy & are intelligent men: they speak English well. — Today was rainy. — The Fitzwilliam Museum was thrown open today to all bearers of 2/6 tickets:— there was a band:— M. & L. sent the maids . . .

Sun. 10. . . . G. dined with us because he is the only undergrad. who is not a Scholar & they don't like setting out dinner for 1 . . .

Mon. 11. To a meeting of the Heads:— On Monday last Dr Ainslie said in the S.H. to Leapingwell that he was conducting himself very ill to the Proctors (— the Proctors however took no offence at his somewhat hasty manner & lodged no complaint whatever):— Leapingwell wrote a waspish letter to Dr Ainslie, demanding an investigation of his conduct before the Heads if he had misbehaved:— Ainslie instantly assented. —

---

[81] *The Cambridge Advertiser* reported that 'the distinguished persons under whose auspices the festivities will be conducted' hoped 'that no individuals of respectability among the yeomanry & tradespeople', would 'consider themselves as excluded from sharing in this splendid fete.'

[82] John Addenbrooke, M.D., Fellow of St. Catharine's had left about £4,200 for the erection and maintenance of a small hospital for poor people which opened in 1766. By 1842 expenses were running at about £2,600 per annum. About £900 came from permanent funds and the rest from donations, subscriptions, fund-raising events and the annual sermon.

[83] 'Every room in the college [Trinity] will be tenanted, and the distinguished Indian Prince, Dwarkanauth Tagore, with his nephew, Chunder Mohur Chatturzie, will honour the society with his company'. (*The Cambridge Chronicle* 2 July). In R.W. Buss's plate of the installation of the Duke of Northumberland Dwarkanauth Tagore stands behind the Proctors. See note 70 above.

The Heads however kept us (viz. the 2 Proctors, 3 Bedells & myself) waiting 2 hours in the study: & then happily they called in Leapingwell by himself, an amicable arrangement was made & we were all dismissed . . .

Dined with Eb. Foster Jun. to meet Ch: Ingle:— I met there Eb. Foster Senior, Mr Baldrey (of the Observatory) who was bold enough to defend W. India slavery, Leapingwell, & Dr. Bond. — Ingle was very amusing: he told a story of a patient at a Lunatic Asylum who jumped furiously upon the Doctors toes, declaring that the Dr. had put such a series of wild incoherent questions to him that he must be mad, that madness proceeded from determination of blood to the head, that he had therefore tried to counteract it by making a determination to the feet. Leapingwell gave a long account of 2 ladies & their father who are not in their right mind who came to the Fitwilliam Museum Ball: they are in constant dread of poisoning: the 2 ladies were conspicuous, one by a $\perp$ feather, the other by a horizontal one: Leapingwell danced with both[84] . . .

Tu. 12. Exhibited my office & the Mesman Museum[85] (with its newly acquired treasures of the bronze Cast of the shield of Ach. given by Rundell & Bridge,[86] & the ivory model of the sepulchral monument at Agra (called Taj. Mahal) wch cost Mr. R. Burney of Chr. the donor £7000). From 11 to 3 dedicated myself at my office to a New Englander Mr Savage brought by Prof: Smyth:— he wished to see the signatures of the Puritans educated at Cambridge (particularly at Emmanuel) who went over as the first settlers in 1630:— he was highly delighted as each turned up (particularly Harvard the founder of the College) & said 'Aye, that's the boy; he's the Chap; &c' He is an intelligent enthusiastic man about the history of his own Country;— he amused Smyth (whom he always called Mr. Smith) by asking about *a catalogue* immediately after the Professor had been reciting with greater earnestness to him Gray's Progress of Poesy!

---

[84] Presumably Sophia and Mary Ann Bones. See 4 July 1843. Their father, a solicitor, had died in 1813.

[85] In 1836 Romilly had moved from a cold damp room in the Divinity Schools to a ground-floor room at the south-east end of the Pitt Press Building in Trumpington Street. The William Pitt the younger Memorial Committee, having surplus funds after paying for a statue of Pitt in Hanover Square, London, had offered the University a large sum 'for the erection of a handsome building connected with the University Press'. The Press buidings were completed in 1833 and since 1834 had housed the 248 paintings and 33 drawings and prints bequeathed to the University by David Mesman. These were moved, together with subsequent additions to the collection, to the Fitzwilliam Museum in 1848. Romilly's diary for 8 November 1848 records that after considerable lobbying, he was at last suitably housed — 'this day to my great delight the Grace for giving me the Mesman room with the fine bay window passed unopposed'.

[86] Rundell, Bridge and Co. were the London goldsmiths who had cast Flaxman's shield of Achilles.

Wed. 13. . . . This Evening Edward Allen arrived on a weeks visit to us:—he is much grown during his 10 months' residence at Geneva. — Poor Mr Sismondi is just dead of a cancer in the stomach:[87]— in his 69th year.

Sat. 16. Letter from George Romilly saying that thro' a hole in his pocket he had lost his purse containing £3..10.. — & could not for lack of funds keep his engagement of coming down to Cambridge today:— wrote to him to come on Monday & sent him by the Telegraph my Letter containing a cheque for £1.15. Edward read loud at night.

Sun. 17. Carus being gone for a fortnight Lucy went (for the 1st time) to Perry's Church (St. Pauls):[88] Perry preached from the Text 'Thinkest thou those 18 on whom the Tower of Siloam fell etc:' — a good part about the late dreadful calamity on the Versailles Railroad.[89] . . .

Mon. 18. . . . At 8 o'clock I (as V. Master) & Edleston (as representative of the Seniors) received the Judges (Alderson & Williams).[90]

Tu. 19. Breakfast to Edw. Allen & G. Druce — Dined with the Judges at Trinity Lodge at 7: capital dinner with Turtle and Venison. — The party 31: viz. V.C. & 3 other Heads, 2 Proctors, myself, Gunning & the Bar. — No dessert; no tea: dismissed at 9:— as usual we all had to give 2s to the 2 servants — G.T.R. returned home this Evening from his Dulwich Visit.

Wed. 20. Dinner to the Judges at 6½ in Hall: — Baron Alderson was engaged in an interminable road case & sent word he could not come. . . I presided, having Judge Williams on my right & the mayor on my left:— I asked Worlledge (our late Fellow) to preside at the 2d table. I made no speeches & gave but one Toast 'The Queen'. — Judge Williams seemed to enjoy himself very much & staid till ½ past 10:— I ordered card tables to be set out upstairs & invited the few people who now remained (about 12):— I was extremely annoyed by old Humfrey grossly insulting the Mayor & declaring he would not go up into the same room with him: I was not near when he behaved in this unprovoked brutal manner:— what a misfortune for a man to have such an ungovernable temper. — The Mayor consulted me about what he must do:— I advised him to treat it with silent contempt.

Sat. 23. Walks with M. morning & evening. — M. went to the School yesterday.[91] Late in the Evening came in Humfrey & showed me

---

[87] J.C.L. Sismondi, the Swiss historian had married a sister of Lancelot Baugh Allen and so, like Romilly, was uncle to George and Grim.

[88] On 18 May 1842 Perry had explained in a letter to the *Cambridge Chronicle* why St. Pauls had only 'been licensed for Divine Service and not consecrated . . . I hoped that the rents of the pews would have been regarded as a sufficient income for the Minister; but the Bishop . . . has decided, that an endowment of £1000 must be obtained.'

[89] On Sunday 8 May the passengers in three crowded locked carriages were burnt to death on the Versailles-Meudon railway and many people injured.

[90] Winstanley in *Later Victorian Cambridge* (pp. 20–35) thinks that the custom of the Judges of the spring and summer Assizes being allocated rooms in Trinity Lodge probably goes back to the reign of James I.

[91] Presumably the National School for Girls in King Street.

correspondence between himself & the Mayor, which ended in H. apologising. — Sealing Barton School.[92]

Romilly went to London on 25 July, 'cool pleasant day:— 32 miles (Hockerill to London) in 85'. On the 26th he and Lodge travelled by train to Leeds via Rugby, Derby and Swinton — 'paid £2.12 for 1st class: distance 205 miles'. Before leaving Leeds they went to inspect 'Dr. Hook's new church: it has a noble tower & the exterior altogether is very striking; but the inside greatly surpassed in magnificence anything I had expected:— beautiful painted glass, exquisite wood work, a grand flight of steps up to the Altar (as the Puseyites call it);- it produces the effect of a cathedral'.[93] They attended Evensong, sung by a large surpliced choir and three clergy, with good organ music, and Romilly noted that 'one of the mechanics of the place in dirty rough attire was standing by us ; he joined in the singing.' Romilly thought it 'a very imposing and seductive pageant' but they had to leave early in order to get their coach to Harrogate. They covered the whole stage, 15 miles, without changing horses, 'and were amused with the broad dialect & jocund good humour of our Coachman.' They stayed at Harrogate until 6 August, and each day followed a uniform pattern. Early in the morning they took the waters from 'Betty the veteran nymph of the well'. Then during the day they went walking. They inspected all the Harrogate wells; they made an expedition to Knaresborough, where they saw the castle and Eugene Aram's cave; they admired the scenery round the spa itself — thus one day they went 'along the brook & thro the woods of the pretty valley going up to Pott Bridge: this scenery is very picturesque from the overhanging rocks'. In the evening they generally went to the concert in the Promenade Rooms and then played whist, but one evening they saw a performance of several scenes from Othello. The Othello 'was a woolly haired African of the name of Aldrich: he is a close imitator of Macready & is possessed of considerable theatrical talent & is not undeserving of his travelling designation 'the African Roscius': — his Father is said to be a clergyman at New York:— his accent is perfect:—he must have spoken English from his infancy'. On Sunday, 31 July, they went into Leeds [Romilly wrote Harrogate by mistake] to attend morning service at Dr. Hook's church. The congregation was over 2000, the singing and chanting were admirable, and Dr. Hook's sermon, which he preached in surplice and hood, pleased Romilly very much, as did the beauty of the church which he was able to study with more care than on his previous visit. As usual in the diaries there are a good many vignettes of the people he met. Among those at the Crown Hotel, Harrogate, was 'a Mr Maude (brought up at Hawkshead with Wordsworth our late Master); he is a conversible man: he is just come from Russia and Denmark: he is trying all manner of different mineral waters to get rid of a dryness of the mouth.' A less pleasant acquaintance made at the whist table was 'a disagreeable little man (called Captain Stewart) . . . I took an instinctive antipathy to him: I find that he has killed a man in a duel.' Nor should the curious history of Mrs Simpson, the Vicar of Pannal's wife be omitted. 'She was daughter of a tradesman in Leeds & became governess in a neighbouring family:— here she was greatly admired by a

92 The University owned 271 acres in Barton. Romilly's entry in The Sealing Book 1742-1847 (Misc. Collect. 1) reads 'Seal was affixt to Donation of site of Land for Barton School House. Me present. 23d July 1842'.

93 The chancels of parish churches had been used as storehouses or even schools until the Camdenians decreed that they should be cleansed and a choir sing in them. Hook was Vicar of Leeds and the 'first to put his choir into a chancel; and the example was sporadically initiated in other parishes, though rarely with the choir instantly in surplices lest the congregation be vexed at the unfamiliarity'. (Chadwick, I, 213.) See also 29 October 1842. St. Peter's, Leeds Parish Church, was rebuilt between 1838 and 1841.

Gentleman on a visit at the house: he proposed, was accepted, & married her. They lived very happily together & had 2 children: but at the end of 2 years came a smart Lady, claimed the gentleman as her husband & carried him off triumphantly. — This story reached the ears of young Mr. Simpson who began by pitying & ended by loving:—they have lived a very happy couple ever since'.

From Harrogate they went by coach to Scarborough, stopping at York to visit the Minster. They put themselves 'under the guidance of an obstinate verger who opposed most pertinaciously Lodge's Views about removing the Skreen & would not allow that the 2d fire at the Cathedral brought any discredit on the vigilance of the Dean & Chapter:[94] it is curious to see how well the old painted glass stood the conflagration: — it is scarcely at all injured'. At Scarborough Romilly found much to admire:— 'Scarboro is a very striking place from its natural position: a fine Norman castle (much shattered by Ol: Cromwell's Cannon) on the top of the eminence wch gives name to the place makes a grand landmark to all the country round. — As soon as we had arranged about our lodging we set out for a walk:— all the new part of the Town is very clean & neat & the houses & public buildings in very good taste:— the inequality of the ground afforded excellent opportunities for picturesque effects & they have been taken advantage of. — The grand promenade is over a Viaduct (resting on 4 iron arches almost 100 feet high from the sand: these are supported by 3 stone piers, the middle one of wch stands in a tank for horses):— This Viaduct leads to walks very prettily laid out in wch are reading rooms (in the shape of a Castle), summer houses, a pump area (for it has no roof over it, &c &c):— The flowers & shrubs flourish very well here in spite of the sea breeze.' Each day Romilly bathed before breakfast. The machines, he noted, were very cheap, 'only 6d', though on 7 August, which was a Sunday, he found that machines were not available. 'I was resolved however to bathe, so I walked a very long way out upon the shore to a secluded little bay & there had a swim'. The party at their hotel was, in general, pleasant and companionable, though Romilly disapproved of dining so late (6 o'clock) and of the fact that ladies did not dine in public at the table d'hôte. On 9 August they went out to Hackness Hall, Sir John Johnstone's estate. In the church they admired a beautiful statue by Chantrey to the baronet's sister, and after lunch walked in the grounds and were invited to eat peaches gathered in the kitchen-garden. 'Since we passed so much time in this agreeable promenade. . .(in spite of the extreme sultriness of the weather) we had to walk back at the rate of 4 miles an hour. Our walk from Ayton to Scarboro was a good 12 miles'.

They left Scarborough on 10 August and passed that night at Hull. 'After dinner . . . we went round all the docks, paid our respects to the Wilberforce column', and visited Holy Trinity church, the condition of which, like that of St. Mary's at Scarborough, shocked Romilly's architectural taste. 'It is a very fine building awfully brutified: *part only* of the nave is used for divine service & this is dreadfully bepewed & begalleried: the Chancel is entirely cut off. — Lately indeed the exterior of the W. end has been well restored & I am glad to hear that Archd. Wilberforce[95] is exerting himself to set the whole in order'. He was also anxious to inspect a handsome new Wesleyan chapel, 'but Lodge indignantly refused going to look at it!' The next day they went by steamer to Grimsby, and then made a long journey of 100 miles by coach to Huntingdon, where they arrived at 11.30 p.m. On the way Romilly was able to admire the many fine Lincolnshire churches, including the beautiful tower and spire of Louth and Boston Stump. Lodge, who was a Lincolnshire incumbent, made 'an admirable cicerone for he knew the name of

---

94 In 1829 the woodwork of the choir was set on fire by a madman and in 1840 fire reduced the S.W. tower to a mere shell.
95 He was the second son of William Wilberforce and Archdeacon of the East Riding.

every church & the history of every incumbent.' At Spilsby they picked up Lodge's curate, O'Connor — 'this gay Irishman was married this very morning:— he & his bride got into the Mail Coach & are to be set down at Peterboro: they are going honeymooning to Brussels.' And on the morning of 12 August. the no doubt weary travellers at last arrived in Cambridge.

Sun. 14. M. L. & Hester Baily & I to Trinity Church where the heat was so overpowering that Lucy was much overcome by it, — she did not however leave the Church:— Carus preached from Heb.XIII.11.12.13. a sermon wch Lucy had heard before & did not consider to be one of his best efforts. — The effects of the heat were perceptible:— Hose was languid & gaped awfully; Carus was obliged to mop himself frequently; Hester in our pew, Mrs Pryme in hers, & unknown People in pews & free seats fell into deep sleep . . . Geo. went to Morning & Evening Chapel & heard Kingdon at St Mary's at 2:— This being long Vacation time he dines & drinks tea with us daily.

Mon. 15. All the morning till 4 working in my office — Lucy recovered from her fatigue, but wisely abstained from going to the Hospital as the heat continues very sultry. She sent off a parcel to her former protégée M.A. Walkerley (by Mrs Cockle). Today Margaret lost her scholar Kitty Marlow who went off by Coach to Bourn (in Lincolnshire) to a person who requires every accomplishment & excellence & gives the great salary of £25!! — M. has begun with a new Scholar (viz. Miss Caulfield (Mrs Clark's Governess) in the absence of Mrs Cl. &c on the continent. —Read loud in the Evening.

Sat. 20. Yesterday & today Lucy resumed her hospital practice. — All 3 surgeons (old Lestourgeon, Okes & Abbott)[96] have resigned at Addenbrookes: we have written to Dr. Paget putting our votes in his hands . . . Paget recommends (of the present Candidates) young Lestourgeon (in whose favor Okes resigns), Hammond (in whose favor Abbott resigns) & a clever Londoner of the name of Humphry (brother to our fellow). — The other candidates now are Knowles, Adams, Sudbury, Thurnall & Taylor. We are inundated with the letters of the candidates[97] . . .

Mon. 22. . . . This evening Lucy (accompanied by M. & me) took to Carus's room a great jug of Walkden's Ink, he having declared to us last Saturday that L's last gift was exhausted:— by the way he sent the old jug that morning to our great amusement.

Mon. 29. Great thunderstorm this morning tremendous crash just over our heads:— fire ball struck the sails of the mill close to us.[98] — M. & I to the Havilands to eat mulberries. — Jane returned this Evening, her

---

[96] See W.D. Bushell, *The two Charles Lestourgeons, Surgeons of Cambridge, their Huguenot ancestors and their descendants* (Cambridge, 1936, p.22). Okes had also been surgeon to the Spinning House, the house of correction for women in St. Andrews Street.

[97] Presumably to solicit their votes as subscribers to the hospital.

[98] According to a sale plan of July 1827, the windmill stood on a pasture about 300 yards from the Romilly's house (ms. Plans. Y.I. (Plate 8) in the University Library).

mother being out of danger . . . Today took M. to see the Fitzwilliam Pictures in their new place (in the E. wing of the Library):[99]— they look very well, being more judiciously hung than before:— Yesterday took her to see the new Cattle Market (by Bandy Leg Walk).[1]

Mon. 5 September . . . Emma Shedd came (dressed all in her best) to repeat a hymn, but was so much overcome at having been left in Cambridge by her Mother (who this morning went on a visit in the Country) that when she tried to begin she burst out a crying:— it cost Margaret 7 little books & a good deal of coaxing to bring the spoiled child to a state of calm. — M. & I walk in the Evening.

Wed. 7. Today the cricket-match between the scholars of Mr Jones & Mr Barker stopped by Mr Jones on account of some of the lads being caught smoking:— he had better have let them finish their match & then scold them . . .

Th. 8 Yesterday Emma Shedd drank tea with us & M. & I walked home with her:— we found her a dull spoiled child good for nothing but eating cakes. — :— music & prints & conversation seemed to produce no impression on her. — A rainy day: but in spite of that Lucy contrived to get to the Hospital:— M. never stirred out:— The annual School feast of the Barnwell children today notwithstanding the rain:— two new bonnets of Lucy's making (for 2 of the Grays) out in it. — G.T.R. to the Theatre to see Ducrow's horses[2] — George has within these last 2 days produced some capital drawings of Dick Swiveller[3] &c.

Sun. 11. Carus preached in behalf of his Sunday School: it was also a thanksgiving sermon for the abundant harvest:[4]— Text, Levit. 2. 14.15.16. --about 'the green ears':— a very happy application of the artificial mode of ripening them to education . . . considering the wetness of the day & the deadness of this holiday time I thought the collection of more than £18 not bad . . .

---

[99] The Fitzwilliam pictures and books remained in the east wing until 1848.

[1] On the 7th of June, the Council ordered 'that the Cattle Market formerly held on St. Andrew's Hill, otherwise Hog Hill, should on Saturday the 18th of June, and on every succeeding Saturday, be held at Pound Hill, in the parish of St. Giles'. (Cooper IV,651). St. Andrew's Hill, formerly the Hog Market, lay between Corn Exchange Street and St. Andrew's Street.

[2] Andrew Ducrow (1793-1842), son of the 'Flemish Hercules' had appeared on horseback, aged 7, before George III. He became chief director of Astley's Royal Amphitheatre and the principal attraction of immensely successful equestrian performances such as 'The Sailor Returned', 'Cupid and Zephyr' and 'Death of the Moor'. The theatre had been destroyed by fire in 1841.

[3] The shabby and disreputable young man of Dickens' *Old Curiosity Shop* (1840).

[4] In the starving year of 1842 the abundant harvest saved lives, and public authority issued a form of thanksgiving (Chadwick I, 517). Lord Melbourne had refused to sanction a harvest festival in 1838 and so the new service was not celebrated until 1842.

Tu. 13. M. & L. adorned one of the wards of the Hospital with Vases etc:— they took Miss Corfield to see the establishment:— she was like Gallio,[5] who cared for none of these things. — M. & Miss Corfield to a flower-show:—Miss Corfield is not floral in her tastes. . . .

Sat. 17. We had a visit this Evening from Lady Cotton & Mrs Fisher (without her little girl): Lady C. brought us a present of a brace of hen birds. — Today the Proclamation of Sturbridge Fair: — this was the 1st time of the new oyster-less dispensation. — Read loud Mathew's Memoirs[6] — George dined with his friend Wood.

Wed. 21. Seniority about Coll. Business — First day of Fellowsh:[7]— Greek-day. Examiners Archdeacon Thorp & Martin. — Tea & a Rubber at Mr. Wilson's to meet his Son-in-law Mr Watson . . . Master Watson (not yet 5 yrs old) astonished me by repeating the 1st 6 lines of Homer, especially by his forcible utterance of oulomene[8] — gave the little fellow 6d to encourage him in his precocious scholarship. — Geo. drank wine with his Private Tutor (Walton).[9]

Fri. 23. 3rd day of F. — Examiners the Master & Martin. Mathematics & Metaphysics — Gosset & I looked over papers all the morning at G.A.B's. — Gave wine & tea to G.A.B, Gossett & Martin (who never came):— Gosset with very little help from Browne & of course none from me drank 2 bottles of Port before we parted wch was 12½;— we looked over a good quantity of papers.

5   Gallio was proconsul of Achaea. In 53 he dismissed the charges brought by the Jews against Paul. 'But Gallio cared for none of these things.' (*Acts* 18 v.5).
6   Presumably by the famous comic actor Charles Mathews (1776-1835). The memoirs were edited by his widow.
7   The chief business of a Trinity Bachelor Scholar in residence was studying for a Fellowship. This year there were 22 candidates for 7 Fellowships. Scholars could take the examinations in each of the three years that must elapse between taking their B.A. and M.A. degrees. C.A. Bristed commented that a Fellowship was 'just the thing for a Barrister as it supports him whilst starting in his profession'. Fellowships were only tenable for 7 years by those who were not ordained.
8   Romilly uses the Greek alphabet. The word means destructive or deadly.
9   The Tutors were the most important officers in the colleges. They taught and lectured and acted *in loco parentis* to their pupils for whom they also had financial responsibilities. But there were almost always too few Tutors and Assistant Tutors for the teaching needs of the colleges, and the vast majority of undergraduates therefore engaged private tutors. These varied from distinguished scholars for whose teaching there was keen competition from men seeking high honours, to hacks who crammed the idle in the last few weeks for the ordinary degree examination. See Bristed, pp.150–4, for a spirited description of a private tutorial which Herman Bowring thought 'uncommonly well told and to the life'. George Peacock describes the 'rapid growth of private tuition in late years' as 'an evil of the most alarming magnitude . . . as threatening to supersede the system of public instruction both in the colleges and the university'. . . 'If we assume the average number of students . . . to be 1300' their expenditure on private tuition 'will amount to £52,000 per annum or more than three times the sum paid to the whole body of public tutors and professors in the university'. (*Observations on the Statutes of the University of Cambridge* (1841) pp.153–4 note 1.) However, in order to provide more teaching the larger colleges and some of the smaller were gradually appointing college lecturers. In 1842 Trinity had 12 tutors and 9 lecturers of whom 4 were also tutors. St. Catharine's was not alone amongst the smaller colleges in having only 2 tutors and no lecturers.

Sun. 25.   M's birthday. Very well, thank God:— George gave her a very pretty penknife, & I some Edging. — Carus preached an excellent funeral sermon upon poor Mrs Watson (the Chemist): he told us that her daughter (Mrs Wilkinson) (who was just going to be confined) was lying in her mother's house without any human chance of recovering . . . Prof Scholefield also preached a funeral sermon on Mrs John Deighton who died of premature confinement (as Mr John D's 1st wife had.) . . .

Mon. 26.   . . . Dined with Dr & Mrs Bond . . . In the middle of dinner arrived Mrs B's brother (I think his name is Carpenter) (a very great invalid) from Leamington; 1st out went Mrs Bond, & staid a ¼ hr; then out went Dr Bond & staid another quarter of an hour; all wch made the dinner very comfortable!! — last of all out went the lamp & made a horrid stench. —I made my escape at 9 without going into the drawing room. — Walk with M in the Evening.

Th. 29.   V.C's Court again: Police v. Low & Richardson for keeping bad hours in their booth:— they behaved with great humility & escaped with a reprimand. — Looking over papers the rest of the day.

Fri. 30.   V.C's Court again:— Alger (who keeps the Abomination called the London Booth)[10] did not appear to the summons of the V.C. (for selling wine without licence):— convicted of contempt; fine of £5 sentence:— the University Marshall sent to distrain on his goods if any can be found. — Tea at the Masters Lodge to settle the Fellowships:— we drank tea in Mrs Whewells Boudoir & then adjourned to her bedroom wch (in consequence of the grand alterations making at Hopes expense)[11] is fitted up as a sitting-room . . . If Denman had gone into the Mathematical Tripos & not availed himself of his Privilege[12] we should have elected him, as he far surpassed everybody else (the 2 University Scholars Cope & Munro included) in his Class. — Then to the Master of Catharine's (where I had been asked to dine): met there Dr. French, Mr Pemberton, the

[10]   The Booth was at Stourbridge ('Sturbridge') Fair.
[11]   Dr. Whewell was appointed Master in October 1841 and Mr. A.J. Beresford Hope in writing to congratulate him, asked if he might give £300 towards 'restoring to the Lodge the Oriel and Mullioned windows, exactly as they stood before Bentley's alteration . . .' Work began in 1842 under Salvin's direction and Hope eventually gave £1000. Whewell put up an inscription in which he claimed to have restored the Lodge himself with Hope's assistance. This was much resented by the College which had in fact put up two-thirds of the total of £3765.
[12]   In a very strong letter to the Editor of *The Advertiser,* an anonymous writer, believed by Romilly to be James Hildyard, writes: . . . 'a new case has now arisen which the framers of these several regulations' (i.e. that noblemen could take the classical tripos one year earlier than ordinary students and might sit for the classical tripos without having obtained an honour in the Maths Tripos) 'seem never to have contemplated, that of noblemen coming up as pensioners and contending not only for honorary prizes, but also for scholarships and ultimately for fellowships'. In the opinion of the writer of the letter Denman was guilty of laying aside his nobility in competing for a Fellowship and of resuming it in order to wrest one of the substantial rewards of our university 'from the sons of the poorer Clergy . . . I might add much more and even then only give you a faint idea of the indignation that pervades a large portion of the University'. (*UP* 14 No.587. See also 2 November 1842).

Revising Barristers (Evans & Gurdon), Philpott, Maddison &c: staid playing whist till midnight:—drank some villainous green tea wch kept me awake almost all night. — G. to the Theatre to see the Undergraduates bespeak 'Sch. for Scandal'.

Wed. 5 October. Over to Ely by Lynn Coach:— Before dinner walked with my Host (the Dean) & the Cummings to Cherry Hill & 'The Elysian Fields'[13]. . .

Th. 6. Walked for an hour before breakfast (reading with great Pleasure Jane Austens Sense & Sensibility). — At the Morning Service in the Cathedral we had the Dettingen Te Deum, & an Anthem of Greenes to show off the singing of 2 boys. — The Dean then took me & the 4 Cummings to Mr James [sic] & we saw his mode of teaching his choristers, — making them read the music — making them sol-fa — making them shake — & then perform solos, duetts, & chorusses. We were all highly pleased with the performances. — He exhibited some little probationaries, whose ear was imperfect: it seemed rather hard to make them stand up & hear themselves condemned for singing false. — I then went to the Justice-room & heard the Dean administer justice for 2 hours. Prof. Cumming & I called at the Palace & saw Mrs Allen & her younger son. At the 3 o'cl. service we had an Anthem of Handel's from the 45th Ps. 'My heart is inditing &c: —' very beautiful. — We now mounted to the top of the Cathedral Tower, all except Mrs Cumming who stopped halfway. — At dinner we had the 4 Cummings, Mr. & Mrs Guillemard, & two others —. The Curate of Soham (Mrs Airy's brother) came in after dinner:— Mr Guillemard was very entertaining during dinner, & rather alarming after tea, for he fell asleep & snorted & groaned in the most piteous manner.

Sat. 8. M. & I sallied out to make a call of ceremony on the new Mist. of Downing; — met her & her Lord on horseback near their own gate — We then called on Mrs Bond & Mrs Skinner:— we also left cards at Mrs Hind's: she has broken a blood vessel, but is much better. -- We waited tea till 9 o'clock for Edw. Allen:— he however (as the coach was late) did not come up, but went immediately to the rooms which I have been fortunate

---

[13] 'Nothing survives of Ely Castle, save the conspicuous mound (Cherry Hill) on the south-west side of the cathedral park'. (V.C.H. IV, 28). The Park in which Cherry Hill stands and which slopes downhill towards Broad Street was presumably the Elysian Fields. We are grateful to Mrs Blakeman, historian of Ely, for this information. The note explaining walking 'thro Elysium' at Audley End on 16 November 1832 says that 'such gardens were regarded as especially suited to study and meditation'. (*R.C.D. 1832–42*, p. 22).

enough to obtain for him. — Geo. R. went to the play to hear 'No song no supper'.[14]

Th. 13. Received a barrel of oysters from Mr Beard:— gave them to George; he accordingly had them scalloped & had Grim & some of his friends to eat them. . .

Fri. 14. M. & I called on the Headly's at Jesus Lodge & on the Marchesa:— I took away a chair intended for the Marchesa & down she came all her length on the ground:— fortunately not hurt. — Grim today underwent the Freshman Matriculation Examination.[15]

Sat. 15. Declined the Soirée of Mrs Lindsay. — G. to an Evening party at Trin: Lodge where the Master was very kind to him & spoke of his drawings which he had seen at Mrs Hayles's. — G. enjoyed the party.

Sat. 22. Mrs Clark returned yesterday: so Margaret has lost her zealous scholar Miss Corfield, after having given her 62 lessons (in French & music) of 3 hours each or more, by which she has profited immensely. — Besides presents of Fr. Testament, Fr. Grammar, Hind's Arithmetic, &c, M & I made a M.S. Hamiltonian collection of Fables from Lafontaine & Florian for her.[16] — Pouring day. — Proclamation of Market.[17]

Mon. 24. Carus paid a long visit, & in spite of the rain Lucy took him to see her poor protégée Sarah Folkes (who is lately out of the hospital & seems on her deathbed). — Whist Club at the Marquis's.

Wed. 26. M. & I called on Mrs Clark (just returned from the Continent). — Wrote to Bath about Lucy's rent. In the Evening Grim began reading loud to us Dickens' new Book 'American notes for circulation'.[18] —I thought it tedious & dull & a complete piece of bookmaking:— he gives long accounts of sea voyage, & then is very minute

---

[14] In 1814 William Wilkins built the new Theatre Royal on the (modern) Newmarket Road opposite the present *Cambridge Evening News* building. There was only a three week season during the time of the Stourbridge Fair as in the interest of undergraduates the University forbade professional theatrical performances for the rest of the year within 9 miles of Cambridge. In 1843 the Vice-Chancellor's veto was extended to a radius of 14 miles. *No Song no Supper* was an opera by Prince Hoare (1790) and to hear it George would have sat in a horseshoe auditorium with three tiers above the pit which could hold at least 700 people. (See H.C. Porter, 'The Professional Theatre in Victorian Cambridge', *The Cambridge Review* 28 January 1983).

[15] 'Before you are fairly in your college, you must pass an examination. At many of the Colleges this is little more than nominal . . . but at Trinity there is a regular test, though it must be owned the standard is not very high' (Bristed, p.11). See 27 May 1842.

[16] James Hamilton (1769-1829) was the author of a system of teaching languages which began by word for word translation. He published many books with literal and interlinear translations.

[17] This was an annual ceremony which maintained the University's right to supervise trade. The Vice-Chancellor, Heads of Houses, and various University officials regaled themselves with cakes and wine in the Senate House and then went 'to the two Markets (first Peas Hill) where the Proclamation is read by the Registrary, and repeated by the Yeoman Bedell.' (Gunning, *Ceremonies*, p.41). The second market consisted of stalls on the east side of Market Hill as the centre of the present market was occupied by houses with shops on their ground floors. These were so badly damaged in the great fire of 1849 that the whole site was redesigned.

[18] *American Notes for General Circulation* (October 1842).

in the description of each prison, madhouse & deaf & dumb asylum:— little or nothing that would not do for any other part of the world.

Th. 27. Lady Wale's Bazaar for the Shelford Schools: cleared more than £200. — Lovely day. — Expected Dr Roget, Miss Kate & her Governess by the Lynn Coach today at 12:— they did not come by it: I had asked Ansted to come at 1 to show them Sedgwick's Museum:— they arrived in a Post chaise at 2 (coming from Mr Hewlett's at Hilgay & having stayed an hour at the deanery at Ely). — Gave them an early dinner at 2¼. M, G. & E. & Ansted were of the party. — It was Kate's birthday & we drank her health. — Lucy did not come to the party, having gone to the Bazaar to buy some useful & pretty present for our Minister:— found nothing. — The Rogets went to Town by the Rocket at 3½.

Sat. 29. Good walk with M. Visit from Apthorps. — The witticism of the day is that Perry wished to build a water closet adjoining the vestry: the Camdenites[19] were furious till it occurred to them that it might be consecrated as a chapel of ease. — Qu. Why is a blue striped shirt dangerous in rowing? Ans. Because it is a check to perspiration . . . In the Evening Grim read loud 'American Notes':— an interest [sic] account of the teaching of a child that was blind as well as deaf and dumb.

Sun. 30. M. & I to Trinity Church where we heard W.W. Pym preach a Jew Sermon:[20]— I did not at all like it Text Ps. 102. 13 . . . 16:— he thinks the millennium is to begin in 3 or 4 years. — Lucy went to the Wesleian Chapel (in Green St) to hear a Mr Farrar:[21]— She was highly pleased with his zeal & his rude eloquence in spite of his general vulgarity & his particular omission of the hs — His Text was 'He delighteth in mercy': Lucy gave all the money she had. — Took a walk with M. & then one with Lodge. —

Mon. 31. Election of 3 Surgeons to Addenbrookes: viz Lestourgeon, Hammond & Humphrey:— the other 3 Candidates (who received votes) were Sudbury, Thurnall & Knowles. — Today I stole an umbrella out of Hatt's shop.[22] I discovered my theft but could not recollect Hatts shop: I called at many places where I had been, & nobody owned the umbrella:—

---

[19] The Cambridge Camden Society was formed by J.M. Neale and a group of fellow-undergraduates to study the way in which, in an age of extensive restoration, church architecture could influence worship. They agreed with Pugin that architects should copy medieval Gothic churches and they rapidly attracted a very influential membership. (See 26 July 1842 — link passage.)

[20] The London Society for Promoting Christianity amongst the Jews was founded in 1809 and increased in influence until in 1841 the Archbishop of Canterbury became its Patron and Lord Ashley its President. W.W. Pym, the Vicar of Willian, Herts., was a prominent member of the Society. 'He was called 'the Jews' Man'. 'I would I could work more for them' was ever on his lips.' (See W.T. Gidney, *The History of the London Society for Promoting Christianity amongst the Jews.* (London 1908)).

[21] John Farrar (1802-84), distinguished Wesleyan, was twice president of the Wesleyan Methodist Conference and wrote five theological books. The new Wesleyan chapel, opened in 1819, was approached by a passage almost opposite Gifford Place. (See A.B. Gray, *Cambridge Revisited* (1921) pp.94, 99-101).

[22] John Hatt was a well-known bookseller on Peas Hill who also ran a circulating library.

so I went & hid it in a corner of the Election Room at the Eagle.[23] — This was however all wrong; for a clerk of Mr. Fetch's came up to my house to ask if I had taken an umbrella out of Hatt's shop:— I posted back with the messenger & to my great joy found the umbrella in the corner where I had put it. . .

Tu. 1 November Declined dining at Pembroke Lodge & at Magdalene Lodge — Seniority: in wch we voted £20 additional to Carus (our Dean). — Poor M. passed a very bad night & was suffering this morning from a severe pain in her side. Haviland[24] does not think it likely to be a dangerous illness, but he ordered her 8 leeches:— to whose suction she submitted most cheerfully . . .

Wed. 2. Margaret passed a good night, & the pain in her side is nearly gone:— Dr. H. says that there are no symptoms of Fever, & and that we need not be alarmed. — Congregation:— Great excitement — That firebrand Ja. Hildyard got up an opposition to Bateson as a Classical Tripos Examiner on the ground of his having private Pupils who will be competitors:— this is met by a flat denial on the part of Bateson, he having had none such since May:— people cannot also forget that Hildyard was at feud in Lent with Bateson,[25] Bunbury & Warter about Denman[26] being a Candidate for the Class. Tripos. — The Division was:

B.H. — Pl. 38 : 12 N.P. — Hildyard gave the 1st
W.H. — Pl. 43 : 3 N.P. — Bates ———————— [27]

Th. 3. M. passed a good night but Haviland thought a blister[28] advisable as a matter of security . . .

Fri. 4. Breakfasted with the Senior Proctor (Cookson) during the interregnum:— met the other Proctor & the 3 Bedells & nobody else:— a capital breakf. with 4 hot dishes, — would have done for dinner — At 9 Whewell was elected V.C:[29]— he did not know that he had to make a speech; & therefore when we came to fetch him from the Library (having been just apprised) he was in the act of writing a few sentences in Latin. These he wrote in such desperate haste that he made awful work of reading them in the S.H:— it was a complete breakdown:— I was heartily sorry for

---

[23] The Eagle Hotel was the headquarters of the Cambridge Tory Party and was made full use of during elections. Before 1832, when Cambridge ceased to be a Rutland pocket borough, it was known as the Rutland Club and *'The Ratland Feast'* published in the *Independent Press* in 1820 attacked the freemen and the apostates who
'For a glass of wine
Cringed at the Eagle once a month to dine'.
[24] There is no means of knowing whether Haviland responded equally promptly to the needs of his other patients, but Sir Humphrey Rolleston (*The Cambridge Medical School* (1932)) describes him as a courageous pioneer who by determination and great labour succeeded in revolutionising a course in which virtually no interest had been taken hitherto.
[25] W.H. Bateson of St. John's was an examiner in the Classical Tripos of 1842 as were J. Hildyard and 2 others. Hildyard was clearly a contentious man.
[26] See 30 September 1842.
[27] See 12 May 1842.
[28] I.e. a sharp irritating ointment or plaster applied to raise a blister.
[29] I.e. for the academic year 1842-3. He succeeded George Archdall, Master of Emmanuel.

it, especially as Mrs Wh. & several other ladies were present. — By the way the effect was the more painful from Cookson having just read a very good speech in allusion to the events of the past year. — Wine at the new V.C's:— I & the other Officers were quartered in the bedroom; the heads in the drawing room, & the tail in the dining room:— N.B. — The Henry VIII Drawing Room is still open to the weather in consequence of the new Bay window being unfinished![30] Read loud Mathew's Memoirs in the Evening.

Sat. 5. M. passed a good night & Dr. Haviland took his leave, having prescribed a sope plaster[31] by way of a legacy . . .

Sun. 6. M. slept ill:— probably from eating fat mutton at dinner:— condemned herself to abstention from animal food today . . .

Mon. 7. Whist Club at my rooms: a large party of 13 . . . we elected 2 new members, Eyres & Birkett:— Bateson was elected at the last meeting:—we are now 9. — A ludicrous event:— Skrine and Capt. Doria both came in white hats:— Skrine marched off 1st in Capt. Dorias & left his own which was so beggarly that Capt. D. rather than wear it walked home bareheaded. —

Wed. 9. . . . Cold raw day: neither of the women out. — Election of Mayor (Stevenson):— swore him in at 1 o'clock.[32] . . . Worked at 'Graduati'.[33]

Sun. 13. Complete deluge of a day: M & I staid at home:— Lucy however took the Prophet's direction & did not let the rain detain her. — She had Edward Allen for her companion (he having been too late for morning chapel). Carus preached from Joh. XXI. 17. 'lovest thou me'. — Lucy received a petition from Carus (for a former parishioner of his, now at Biggleswade):— Lucy made from the letters of William Carus all the various names she could contrive, — above 50 — & sent him subscriptions for all. —The 2 youngsters drank tea with us.

Th. 17. Sacrament in Trin. Coll: Mrs Whewell there — a prodigiously large no. of communicants . . . Learned the particulars of the midnight robbery at Sir Ch. Wales a few nights ago:— yesterday some young men were racing in 2 Tandems in Shelford:— both were upset & Nelson of C.C.

---

[30] See Friday, 30 September 1842. The 'two bow windows or oriels, one on each side of the Lodge, two storeys high' gave 'much needed light to the depths of the dining-room and the Elizabethan drawing-room above it.' (G.M. Trevelyan, *Trinity College. An Historical Sketch*). Dr Robson tells us that the portrait of Henry VIII which is now in the Hall used to hang in the Green Drawing Room of the Lodge.

[31] A healing plaster chiefly composed of soap.

[32] The Mayor and Bailiffs on election were required to swear to 'observe the liberties and customs of this university' according to a charter granted to the University by Edward II. There was no justification for this but, as Winstanley points out (p.122) 'the University was never reluctant to cause annoyance to the Town and the Town was always on the outlook for an opportunity to humiliate the University'.

[33] Romilly edited over many years the alphabetical lists of graduates of the University together with particulars of their degrees. His first volume *Graduati Cantabrigienses* for 1760 to 1846 was published in 1846 (see below, p. 159 and references in the Index). He later brought the work down to 1856.

is lying in a hopeless state in a public house there![34] — Subscribed 5s for a copy of Whewell's Translation of Knight of Toggenburg[35] published by Miss Wale for benefit of Shelford Schools. — Heard of an ingenious translation made by a Dunce at the Examination for Degree last Tuesday:—

'Hoc dicunt vetulae pueris repentibus assae'
The old asses tell this to their repentant colts. —

Fri. 18. Vicechancellors Court:— Police v. 4 Publicans for allowing drinking during Divine Service:— 3 reprimanded; 1 Licence suspended for fortnight. — M. & I called on Mrs Hopkins. — This Evening John Mortlock got into his uncle Edmund's room & fired 2ce at him:— slightly grazed him:—the miscreant dropped down into the garden & escaped:— he is said to have also been armed with a dagger.[36]

Sat. 19. Joh. Mortlock taken at Ditton — he fired twice at the men who took him, but did not hurt them — Meeting of Master & Seniors about the Revision of the Statutes — Both the youngsters drank tea with us. — Edw. read loud Dickens' American Notes.

Sun. 20. We all 3 went to Trinity Church: Carus played us a slippery trick: he gave us no warning that he was not going to preach the Charity Sermon (for the Old Schools),[37] & left that dismal hideous Mr Moore to drawl us to death . . .

Wed. 23. To Jones[38] to have my teeth cleaned:— M. also went on the same errand.

Th. 24. Walk with M. — Dined at the V.C's to meet my brother Officers. — In the Evening a grand Soirée. — I got away very early & missed thereby a grand scene:— the floor of the drawing room was found to be on fire:— there was abundant help & a plentiful supply of water so the Lodge was soon in safety, but the party broke up in 'admired confusion'. — The V.C. is said to have dismissed rather uncourteously a large no. of undergraduates who came with their slop pails.

---

[34] George Nelson of Corpus survived his accident and took his M.A. in 1847. On 2 December 1841 a decree had been published stating that 'if any person . . . *in statu pupillari* should be found offending against the good order and discipline of the University, by driving tandems and four-in-hand carriages such person . . . should be liable to . . . suspension, rustication or expulsion, as the case should appear to the Vicechancellor and Heads of Colleges to require.'

[35] By Schiller. Between 1839 and 1851 Whewell made four published translations from the German.

[36] John Mortlock, grandson of John Mortlock the banker and M.P. who ruled Cambridge during his adult lifetime, was the black sheep of the family. He had become obsessively convinced that his uncles Edmund, Fellow of Christ's and Thomas, the banker, were trying to defraud him of his inheritance. See A.E. Clark-Kennedy, *Cambridge to Botany Bay* (1983).

[37] I.e. for the many Church of England and National schools for poor children in Cambridge which were supported by the Old Schools trust.

[38] 'Mr Jones, Surgeon-Dentist', practised at 4 Jesus Lane. See also 9 June 1843.

From December 1 to 6 Romilly stayed with the Edward Romillys at Stratton Street. He was amused to hear that a friend of theirs, a Mr Hallam, 'was quite contradictory enough to justify S. Smith's story of his putting his head out of the window at 28′ past one & railing at the watchman for crying half past'. One reason for Romilly's visit was to take his books to Somerset House for inspection, and he adds ruefully 'also had my Umbrella inspected there: like my books it was approved, for I saw no more of it!'. The rest of his time was spent seeing friends and enjoying himself. He visited 'the great Chinese Exhibition' as a result of which 'the Chinese have risen much in my estimation'; he saw Congreve's *Love for Love* which he did not like, and heard Purcell's music to *King Arthur* which delighted him. On Sunday, 4 December he went to the Temple Church, then newly restored in magnificent fashion — 'the alterations have cost £40000 & do not seem to me dear at that immense sum'. In the afternoon he heard Milman preach at the Abbey. The sermon he thought brilliant and poetic, 'it tickled the ears but it never came near the heart'.

Wed. 7.   Called on Mrs Airy (who is staying at Trinity Lodge) & was very glad to find her in excellent spirits: she gave a very interesting account of her Tour last summer & of the total eclipse of the sun at Turin: she & the Astronomer Royal saw it from the Supurga.[39] The common people were highly excited & kept shouting Vivan gli astronomi: gli astronomi hanno vinto — To an Evening party at the Mills: plenty of music.

Fri. 9.   Nasty wet day: M. not out — Dinner to the Family . . . Ten Members present, (viz. V.C.(Whewell), Dr Graham, Dr Haviland, Dr Paget, Mortlock, Lodge, J.J. Smith, Power, Cartmell, & I the host:—) 4 Strangers, viz. Sir C. Wale, Mr Prest, Col. Pemberton & Mr R.G. Townley. —Prest gave so much offence to V.C. by observing on our smoking & by interrupting his conversation by loud talking across the Table, & such severe & angry reprimand was administered by Whewell that I shall never ask the Master of Trinity & the Owner of Stapleford Lodge to meet again.[40] — We made up 2 whist tables & played into Saturday morning:— Lodge played & very well.

Sat. 10.   Trial in V.C's Court:— Police v. Harrod (Publican) for allowing Gambling:— Licence suspended for a fortnight:— also Police v. Tarrant (Publican, Poacher, Pigeonshooter, Dogstealer, & Rogue in general) for allowing gambling, resisting Police, & having his house open during Divine Service:— The cases against him were far from strong: the resistance (wch was very slight) was against intruding upon a private room (where there was no disturbance) of the Odd Fellows:[41] & the Sunday company was his own relations:— however his bad character ruined his cause, & his Licence was taken away (one fortnight being allowed for selling his stock). — Walk with M. — Passed all the Evening copying out the trial. — Edw. & Geo. drank tea with us: Edw. read loud N. Nickleby.

[39]   The Hill of Saperga is 2,300 ft above sea-level.
[40]   Despite Whewell's disapproval of Mr. Prest's bad manners he did in fact object to smoking as an ungentlemanly habit and in December 1846 addressed a lengthy letter to the Seniors on the subject.
[41]   One of the largest of Victorian friendly societies, founded in 1810.

Sun. 11. M. L. & I to Trinity Church where Carus preached from the Gospel of the day (Matt.X1.4.5.6). He had several smart attacks upon the Puseyites in his sermon. — Lucy to see Sarah Foulks:— M. & I. walked together. — I then walked with Lodge. — Both youngsters drank tea with us.

Mon. 12. Dies Computi[42] — Sixteen Original Dividends —

Modulus	Master 75
	8 Seniors — 200
	2 Labourers — 40 [the 9th and 10th Fellows]
	6 sixt[een] — 102 [the next 6 Fellows in order
£896.7	of seniority]
	33¼ Maj — 415.12 [M.A.s]
	12¾ Min. 63.15 [B.A.s]

Tu. 13. Walk with M. — Declined Arlett's whist. — E.G. Allen had the excitement of driving a friend over to Bishop's Stortford & coming back alone at midnight — G.T.R. drank tea with us — Read loud Redgauntlet.[43]

Wed. 14. . . . Nomination of Wootton & Shackle for 3d Under Library Keeper — There were 13 other candidates . . . Evening party where . . . a young effeminate looking Pembrochian (Anderson) (Called 'the Fair Maid of Pembroke') sang moderately . . .

Th. 15. Congregation:— Grace to dissent from the N. & E. Railway running thro our new Botanical Garden.[44] Wootton elected: he had 44 votes, Shackle only 4 . . .

Fri. 16. Dismissal of term. — Dined with Shaw (being his 58th birthday) & had a magnificent dinner (with real turtle soup). . . Played whist unsuccesfully. — I had better have gone either to the Skrines or Hughes.

Sun. 18. Lovely day: we all 3 went to Trin: Church, — M. in her new Gown & Mantilla. — Carus preached from Phil. IV. 6.7. 'Be careful for nothing &c.' — Lucy afterwards to Sarah Fordham &c. M. & I walked. I also took a walk with Lodge — George was clumsy enough to meet the V.C.

[42] I.e. the annual audit at Trinity at which the amounts of Fellowship dividends were declared. (See Winstanley, Appendix A) Mr. Kucia and Dr. Robert Robson of Trinity College tell us that the Labourers were the ninth and tenth Fellows by Seniority and therefore liable to be called on to do duty when any of the eight Seniors were absent. For this they received a dividend at a higher rate than their juniors. See J.H. Monk *The Life of Richard Bentley D.D.* (1830), I,234.

[43] Sir Walter Scott's *Redgauntlet* (1824).

[44] Between 1763 and 1846 when the Garden on its present site was opened the Botanical Garden lay to the east of Free School Lane and was entered from Free School Lane and Pembroke Street. The site had, however, become too small, the soil was impoverished and it was closely surrounded by houses. In 1831 the University had therefore bought a field for 'the purpose of forming a new Botanical Garden'.

at 11 going in State to St Mary's — he was sent to hear Kingdon to his great disgust . . .

Tu. 20. Miss Watson called on Margaret: — she had got from Margaret 10s towards a subscription for procuring clothes for a very ragged impoverished clergyman of the name of Pulling:— she bought some new shirts & gloves & got a suit of Clothes of Perrys (almost as good as new) & sent them all in 2 Parcels with a Text of Scripture, but without any name of the sender. — The Text was one probably often in her mouth, or her handwriting was recognised, for Mr P. sent every thing back with an indignant letter 'he had never had his feelings so insulted:— he was not a beggar:— what must the people of the house think at his receiving 2 parcels? & such things indeed! the black gloves were worked in white silk at the back! & the waistcoat had been torn at the pocket & attempted to be finedrawn!' — So Miss Watson was in tears & must (like the Goodnatured Man)[45] make up her mind never to do a good turn again. — She may have been a little indiscrete in her mode of serving this poor Clergyman, but he has behaved without the least regard to her feelings, & has shown that tho he had poverty in his purse he had none in his spirit. — Walk with M. — Redgauntlet at night.

Sun. 25. I preached in Chapel from Joh. I.4 'The Word was made flesh'. — I preached from the Deans Seat. — I assisted at the Sacrament:— Mrs Whewell & Mr Goulburn there — M. & L. to Trinity Church where Carus preached from Matt. 2.10.11. 'When they saw the star they rejoiced with exceeding great joy; &c.'. — They staid the Sacrament. — George staid at Trin: Chapel. — Lucy called upon Sarah Foulkes in her new lodgings, which are really comfortable, but which (from a natural love of change) the poor invalid thinks 'earthly paradise'. — Lucy had also an interview with the mad Mrs Murcutt (whom S.F. has just left, — to the old lady's no small annoyance), who however spoke very calmly & expressed good wishes for her late lodger — M. & I paid a visit to Mrs Heaviside. — In the Evening read Mill's sermon on 'the gainsaying of Core':[46]— tried also to read his 'Vindication of the Genealogies'. — When nearly asleep gave it up. — George did not come to tea tonight having a friend at his rooms.

Mon. 26. A wet day: M. & L. not out — Miss Vincent & G.T.R. ate their Xmas dinner with us at 5. — I declined going to the dinner either at Trinity Hall or Peterhouse. — Miss Vincent went away at 8½ (having come at ¼ to 4): her fly did not drive in, & she went off in the rain without an umbrella! (—all this learned afterwards from Betsy:) — wrote to her to express my horror. —Highly amused this Evening by Lucy sitting up till our pet cat chose to return. —

---

[45] A reference to Oliver Goldsmith's comedy *The Good-natured Man* (1768).

[46] Core or Korah and his followers rebelled against Moses and 'the earth opened her mouth and swallowed them up'. (*Numbers* 16 v. 1-34).

Th. 29. Dined at the V.C's to meet all the Trinity Hall members of the Senate (who are not visible except in Xmas Vacation):[47]— Goulburn & Law &c[48] were present: also one Lady (Mrs Webb) besides our hostess . . .

N.B. Last Friday (23d) began a double delivery of Letters in Cambridge:— the Telegraph (starting at 11½) serves for the day-mail.[49] — Asked to St Johns by Bateson.

Fri. 30. Dined in Trinity Hall Hall: the largest party I ever met there, — 42. — Vicechancellor Knight Bruce & his son the smasher (who has made himself known by breaking the windows of the blasphemous-publication shop in Holywell St) [Strand] were there:[50]— a superb dinner:— nearly suffocated by the heat & stunned by the babel-talking in the Combination room. Played whist with Vicechancellor K.B, Dr. Proctor &c.

Sat. 31. Trial at the V.C's of 2 Publicans, reprimanded one; fined the other. . . Breakfast to G.T.R, his Tutor Walton, & 2 friends Brown & Wood — meeting of Committee for rebuilding St. Peters at Swinnys:[51]— we accepted Salvin's Plan — (seats for 450): (cost £2000:— E. English:— Tower & Spire).[52] — All of us, thank God, well at the close of the Year.

[47] As practising lawyers they normally lived and worked in London (see 14 February 1843).

[48] As Members of Parliament for the University.

[49] The *Chronicle* records that 'a second [i.e. evening] delivery of letters took place for the first time yesterday'.

[50] The placard removed from behind the broken panes read as follows:- 'That revolting odious Jew production, called the Bible has been for ages the idol of all sorts of blockheads, the glory of knaves and the disgust of wise men. It is a history of lust, sodomies, wholesale slaughterings, and horrible depravities, that the vilest part of all other histories collected into one monstrous book could scarcely parallel. Priests tell us that these abominations were written by a God: all the World believe it the outpourings of some devil'. The magistrate strongly approved of Mr Bruce's action and asked him to help in following up the prosecution. *The Times* of 23 December deplores the fact that despite the case Patterson's shop was allowed to continue as before. In November 1843, however, Patterson, 'late of Holywell Street' was found guilty in the High Court of Justiciary, Edinburgh, of selling blasphemous publications and was later sentenced to 15 months imprisonment. Patterson spoke for about 4 hours in his own defence.

[51] Henry Hutchinson Swinny was Vicar of St Giles and St Peter's from 1840-4. Before the building in 1908 of the vicarage, the vicars lived in a house adjoining Magdalene College in Chesterton Lane or in the College itself. (H.M. Larke. *Cambs Local History Council.* Bulletin No. 23).

[52] See 14 April 1842.

Meeting of Cambridge Boat Club *c.* 1850

Reception of Victoria and Albert

1843

Tu. 3 January. Another gentle frost — 125 fees.[1] M & I walked as usual. — Dined in hall. — Whist Club at the Marquisse's: — no music: — the only incident was the pet cat jumping upon the table & making off with a chicken — asked to John's Combination by Crick.

Th. 5. . . . Dined in Hall — Began reading Marryatts new novel 'Percival Keene';[2] it is very amusing:— bad taste to make his hero a Bastard.

Fri. 6. Avoided the great twelfth day party at Trinity. — Carus paid the women a visit today: it was one of his short ones, only ½ hour; — he was in a hurry to get away to his grand dinner. . .

Sat. 7. . . . A few days ago I wrote to the V.C. to prepare him for a stormy B.A. Commencement:[3]— he is unfortunately very unpopular[4] . . .

Th. 12. As I was returning from my walk with M received a note from Lodge to say that he was prevented by violent sickness last Monday from going into Lincolnshire & that he was very ill. — I went to him directly after dinner: found him in a very nervous uncomfortable state: his bile is completely out of order, he can keep nothing on his stomach:— he has also received very bad news from Calcutta:— Edmund's[5] health is broken up & he talks of taking a passage home.

Fri. 13. Went to see Lodge directly after breakfast:— very glad to find him rather better: — stormy day, women not out. — Went to see Lodge after dinner:— found him so restless & so depressed that I immediately went to Haviland & described to him Lodge's state. Haviland found him free from

---

[1] See 1 July 1842.
[2] Published in 1842.
[3] The Bachelors' Commencement or conferring of B.A. degrees. All Tripos examinations were taken in the Michaelmas or early Lent Term.
[4] Whewell's dictatorial temperament and his enforcement of petty and long neglected regulations had indeed made him unpopular with undergraduates. In 1843 the Milton Press published *A Letter to the Rev. W. Whewell. B.D., by an Under-Graduate* (copy in University Library). It was written in the hope 'that you may yet conciliate the University, and put an end to the heart-burning which exists' and it reveals 'what aspect the Master of Trinity presents to the Undergraduates of Cambridge . . . He appears, Sir, to speak plainly, for I must do so, a rude, coarse, overbearing man, elevated out of all sense of propriety by a dignity, which to his birth and youthful fortunes appeared inaccesible; an unnecessarily strict and vexatious disciplinarian, scorning to temper discipline (needed or not) with kindness and conciliation' . . . who 'in the undergraduate sees not the future man . . . but a being without a soul, insensible to kindness, between whom and Masters of Colleges nature has set an irreconcileable antipathy, whose principal characteristic is a propensity to walk about without cap and gown and to trespass upon grass-plots . . . The spirit of the age demands that intellect such as yours should be set on high for the worship of the young; believe me, Sir, it is no irresponsible thing to change that worship into irreverence and infidelity'.
[5] Lodge's much younger cousin, who in December 1841 had travelled overland from Alexandria to India where he was to be an inspector of schools.

Fever, but in a most disordered state of stomach, that will require time to rectify:— poor Lodge passes dreadful nights . . .

Sat. 14. . . . Today received from Mr. Ja. Savage of Boston (U.S.) a very kind note and a present of the triennial catalogue of his University (Harvard) — also from Mr Warwick his new publication 'Cambridge University Register'[6] . . .

Sun. 15. . . . After dinner went to see Lodge; happily found him better:— we went to St Giles & heard the whole service performed by Codd the Puseyite:[7] his Text was 1 Sam. XIV.6 'No restraint to the Lord to save by many or by few'. — it was a complete Puseyite sermon, in praise of the daily service at St Giles. — It was very difficult to hear Codd from the Chancel:— the organ & singing pleasing.

Mon. 16. Lodge and his servant set off at 8½ for Brighton via London: he proposes staying out a month visiting Brighton, St Leonards, etc: — I heartily hope he will come back quite set up . . .

Tu. 17. George sent off a parcel of drawings of M's and his own as a present to Miss Smith of Dulwich. — Letter from a Miss Law asking me to subscribe to her Poems: I agreed: — she must be mad, for she calls herself in her title page niece of so & so, granddaughter of etc etc. — Wrote to Mr Denning to ask him if he would take George as a Pupil in painting, to lodge & board him[8] . . . The meeting of the Caput at Trinity Lodge from 10 to 12:— at 12 the Caput broke up & adjourned to 2. — At noon The Electors to the Professorship of Divinity met in the Lecture Room under the Library.[9] The Electors were all present, viz. the V.C (Master of Trinity) Drs Thackeray, Graham, Tatham & King & G.A. Browne & J. Brown. — Upon Graham mentioning himself as a Candidate the Provost of Kings tendered a Protest against the Eligibility of the Master of Christ's;[10] The President of Queens then offered a counter protest *with reasons* (— the Provost had *none* —): it was refused; — Dr Graham then presented a protest *with reasons* in favor of his eligibility :— the part preceding the reasons was ordered to be recorded. — Dr Graham then to the surprise of all & the regret of many handed in a paper stating his now withdrawing to prevent litigation &

---

6 W.A. Warwick's *Register and Almanack for 1843* was 'designed as a Companion to the Cambridge University Calendar . . .' Romilly is thanked particularly by the editor for his 'kind suggestions and assistance'.

7 Pusey had become the leader of the Oxford movement after Newman's gradual withdrawal from it. Newman's disciples were 'delighted to find provision for daily service, private confession, weekly celebration of the sacrament and splendid ornaments if the ornaments rubric . . . were correctly understood', in the prayer book. (See Chadwick, chapter III).

8 Romilly had known Mr Denning for many years both as a resident of Dulwich and curator of the Dulwich Gallery. Denning exhibited at the Royal Academy between 1814 and 1852 and the National Portrait Gallery has several of his portraits. It appears that George only lived with the Dennings until 4 May 1843 as the diary records that thereafter he was to sleep at Mrs Bonham's. 'She asked £20 a year for G's bedroom, offered her £16 wch she agreed to'.

9 Dr Turton had vacated the Chair upon his preferment to the Deanery of Westminster.

10 I.e. as a candidate whilst an elector (see note for 7 February).

controversy. — He would certainly have been elected:— Tatham, King &
G.A. Browne would doubtless have voted for him:— the validity of the
election would as certainly have been disputed. — Upon this the 3
remaining Candidates Mill, Ollivant & Wordsworth were examined by the
V.C.: he asked each of them their opinion concerning a particular Text, &
then to explain the error of a particular Heresy. (N.B. Dr Lee did not
present himself) — The 31st Jan. was fixt for reading the Praelections & 1st
Feb. for the Election.

Fri. 20. Heard from Lodge; not a good account. Meeting at 11 of the
Caput to mark off the Honors:— Adams of St John's is the Senior
Wrangler.[11] — Goodeve of St J would have been 2d (it was expected) but
after 3 days he was seized with a panic terror & bolted:— in spite of this he
is 9th Wrangler. — Our highest man is 3d (Gray) — At 8 in the Evening we
were to meet again; but the Examiners (thro the slowness of one of them,
Dalton), did not send me the List [of the Polloi] till past 10. — I found the
Caput at Trinity Lodge playing a rubber. — After the breaking up of the
Caput I sat up till near 1 sorting the Supplicats.[12] Wrote to Lodge & Miss
Cotton.

Sat. 21. Senate House from 10 till 1½:— there was a peculiarly large
No. of B.A's viz. 264, but we managed the preliminary business with very
great speed that we might allow as little time as possible to the turbulent.[13]
— The V.C. had printed a very judicious circular to all the College Tutors,
upon the strength of which they all this morning exhorted their pupils:—In
spite however of this the V.C. was abundantly made conscious that he is
most unpopular:— a long sustained groan was kept up all the time he
walked up the Senate House:— from time to time the youngsters called out
'3 groans for Whistle' wch were given very effectively: at other times they
kept up whistling for half an hour together, & then some blackguard called
out 'have you had enough? or shall we give you some more?' . . .

---

[11] Between 1753 and 1910 Mathematical Tripos candidates were divided into three classes,
Wranglers, Senior Optimes and Junior Optimes but they were listed strictly in order of
merit. By the early nineteenth century the examination was becoming an increasingly
exhausting high-speed marathon which became even more strenuous as the century
progressed. The examinees often suffered too from cold in the unheated Senate House
where the examinations were held in January. So it was indeed a great achievement to
become Senior Wrangler. Usually *The Times* wrote about the occasion and the Senior
Wrangler became a well-known personality overnight. (Bela Bollobas. 'Some Trinity
Mathematicians'. *The Cambridge Review* 30.1.1984). Between 1843 and 1850 seven of the
eight Senior Wranglers were from St John's. John Couch Adams was the son of a tenant
farmer in Cornwall.

[12] I.e. a formal petition for a degree.

[13] Undergraduates' 'disorderly conduct in the Senate House was a recurrent and distressing
feature of University ceremonies'. (Winstanley p.417).

Th. 26. Mr Drummond[14] (Private Secretary to Sir Robert Peel) died of a pistol shot from an Assassin (Macnaughten)! Dr. Le Blanc[15] died almost [as] suddenly of inflammation by cutting his toenail. Thought M. so ill with her cold that I called upon Haviland (he could not come to her however being laid up with the Gout): he wrote me a prescription against my indigestion & would not take a fee — He begged that Lestourgeon would call on him after seeing M. — Trial in the V.C's Court: Fitzpatrick of Peterhouse for bringing a whistle into the Senate House last Saturday — suspended for 1 Term. — Declined Mrs Haviland's soirée.

Tu. 31. Much refreshed this morning by a good night's sleep: pain of indigestion much abated. — At 10 to the Law Schools to hear Mill's Thesis.[16] — I was a few minutes after the time & just met Johnson who was coming to look after me as the V.C. would not allow proceedings to begin without me. — The 7 Electors were in the Gallery (accommodated with 7 chairs); a few heads and other Doctors & Masters were down below: Mill was dressed in scarlet robe & Cope but did not wear his cap: he recited from the Prof's seat: he began with 'Actiones nostras etc' & 'Pater noster': he ended with a Prayer. — His subject was 6th Hebrews. — Upon descending from the Prof's seat he was attended by Gunning: he transferred his Scarlet Gown etc. to Ollivant, who began with 'Digniss. Dom. Proc.'[17] & ended with a prayer: his subject was Rom. III v. 21 to end. — Dr Wordsworth Jun. concluded the Theses: he wore *the* scarlet gown (for there was but one for all the Candidates): he also began 'Digniss. Domine etc'. He ended with a prayer. — His subject was Luk. I 1 ... 4 : a very oratorical declamation on the stile of St Luke: it was too noisily recited & had too much of 'Judices' & 'Electores doctiss'[18] etc., and it ended (I thought absurdly) with DIXI[19] after his concluding prayer: — Amen would have been more appropriate . . . Of the 3 theses that of Dr Mill was incomparably the most learned, that of Dr W. the most elegant & oratorical, and that of Dr Ollivant the — least striking . . .

Wed. 1 February. . . . At 12 to the Law Schools to be present at the Election of the Pr. of Divinity: it was with closed doors:— I read the Act of

14 Edward Drummond had also been private secretary to the Duke of Wellington. Drummond was walking from Downing Street towards Charing Cross when he was shot from behind. His assailant Daniel M'Naghten, seemed to have had no connection with him although it was suggested that M'Naghten might have mistaken Drummond for Sir Robert Peel. The jury found M'Naghten not guilty on grounds of insanity 'a decision which has occasioned a general burst of indignation and alarm in which the public papers are nearly unanimous'. *The Gentlemans Magazine* 3 March 1843. Prince Albert and a great many other distinguished people were present at the trial.
15 Thomas Le Blanc had become a fellow of Trinity Hall in 1800 and was Master from 1815 to 1843. He was 'a devotee of port and a martyr to gout'. (C.W. Crawley, *Trinity Hall* (1976, p.121).
16 I.e. as one of the candidates for the Regius Professorship of Divinity.
17 I.e. 'Dignissime Domine Procancellarie' or 'Most Worshipful Mr Vice-Chancellor'.
18 I.e. 'Judges' and 'Electores doctissimi' or 'most learned electors'.
19 I.e. I have spoken.

Parl (31 Eliz. Ch.6) against 'abuses at Elections etc';[20] the V.C. read part of the Foundation, & the Electors then proceeded to voting (after a very just tribute of praise from the V.C. to one of the Candidates who in the most considerate manner had retired, to wch Dr Graham briefly and excellently replied).

J. Brown	voted for	Dr Ollivant
G.A. Browne		Dr Wordsworth
Dr King		Dr Wordsworth
Dr Tatham		Dr Ollivant
Dr Graham		Dr Ollivant
Dr Thackeray		Dr Ollivant
Vice-Chancellor		Dr Mill[21]
(Whewell)		

The Registrary was then directed to desire a Bedell to summon Dr Ollivant who could not at first be found. Dr. O. drily and woodenly returned thanks & hoped he should not be deficient in industry. He was directed to attend in Trin. Chapel this day at 1½. — When he there arrived he did not feel prepared to take the oath (about lecturing twice a week, or else paying 10/- forfeit etc.) without time to consider:— he was therefore allowed till tomorrow[22] . . .

Th. 2. . . . At 10½ to Chapel to swear in Ollivant who had now overcome all his scruples . . .

Fri. 3. Edw. Allen's birthday: he is now 19 complete. This morning G.T.R. went on a pictorial visit to Denning. — Heavy fall of snow: women not out. — Read loud Madame d'Arblay[23] — Edward read loud to us Martin Chuzzlewit. — thought his character & Pecksniffs most unnatural.

Mon. 6. Seniority where we refused . . . to sign the testimonials of C. Penrose who has been conducting himself admirably at Oakham (where he is 2d Master) but whom we rusticated (for the battlement-breaking

---

[20] In 1588 an Act of Parliament was passed against abuses in the election of scholars and presentation to benefices. The clauses relating to university elections deal particularly with simony.

[21] Mill was undoubtedly the best scholar of the three and his defeat which was probably due to his Tractarian opinions was regretted by many people who did not share his views. The *Morning Post* commented that 'some impudent or ill-designing persons . . . have endeavoured to get up the stale and stupid bugbear cry of 'Puseyism' ' against Mill. On 11 February 1839 Romilly had called 'also on Dr Mill (at 19 Adelphi) whom I had not seen since his arrival in England'. He is 'in hopes of being today elected into the Athenaeum . . . they cannot help chusing to elect a man so distinguished. I grieve to hear however from Blunt that he is grown wildly high-church & rushes into Puseyism, & fasts weekly'.

[22] 'Lectures on the early Fathers are given by the Professor, in the Lent Term, in the Divinity School'. (*The University Calendar* for 1843).

[23] Madame D'Arblay (1752-1840) was Fanny Burney the novelist. Five volumes of her *Letters* and *Diaries* were published in 1842.

fracas where he was tipsy): C. Penrose was 2d Classical Tripos 1841[24]
. . .

Tu. 7. The nastiest sleety snowy drizzling day imaginable. Dean of Bristol Waud & I over to Ely in a Fly to visit the Bishop . . . I learned from the Bishop that he had received most urgent letters from Dr Wordsworth Senior begging him (the Bp) to use all his influence with the Electors to the Divinity Professorship in behalf of his son!!![25] I learned also a curious story about Mr Neale (who married Miss Webster): he was married by Mr Boodle & begged to receive the Sacrament after the ceremony: Mr Boodle refused:— Mr Neale complained to the Bishop, who thoroughly approved of Mr Boodle's conduct[26] . . .

Wed. 8. Prayers in the Bishops Chapel:— the Litany only — To the Cathedral at 10 . . . Lunch with the Dean of Ely (Peacock) . . . We went to the Cathedral at 3 & heard a dull anthem of Purcell's (95th Ps); we then lionised the place:— the Dean has been making prodigious improvements, — opening 16 windows in the Cathedral,[27] beginning a restoration of the Chapel (in Mr Jenyn's house)[28] — building a wall before the stables — pulling down all the fences etc — & laying out the grounds like a park, etc etc — At his Deanery he has (under Prof. Willis's directions) laid out some very pretty French gardens. — At dinner we had the Dean & Sedgwick &

---

[24] 1839 according to *Admissions to Trinity College, 1801-1850.* Charles Penrose became headmaster of Grosvenor College, Bath in 1844 and of Sherborne School in 1845, so perhaps he was already applying for a headmastership, although testimonials were normally asked for from Trinity before ordination rather than to support an application for a post in a school. Penrose had been ordained deacon in 1842. On 11 February 1834 Romilly records that 'we confined to Gates & Walls Lord Cl. Hamilton, Ld J. Beresford, 2 Ponsonbys & 8 more for a riot in the Court at 2 o'clock on Sunday Morning after a supper at Ld Claud Hamiltons: 2 lamps & part of the balustrade in Nevile's Court were pulled down, but by whom of the party unknown' . . . It is probable that Penrose was one of the '8' as there is no other record of a similar fracas during Penrose's time at Trinity. Venn says that he was admitted pensioner on 30 October 1834 but this may be inaccurate as are the dates given for his headmastership of Sherborne.

[25] Dr Wordsworth had canvassed energetically on behalf of his son, writing also to Whewell even before the vacancy was announced. He had himself stood for the same chair in 1827 whilst an elector. The lawyers then consulted had differed. Pemberton and Roundell Palmer found that electors were not eligible as candidates, but Warren and Lushington in 1816 had been of the opinion that they were. Dr Wordsworth realised that the Master of Christ's would be a formidable rival and now asked, with others, for a fresh legal opinion. Winstanley thinks it 'not improbable that Wordsworth suffered by his father's zeal' (p. 298 note 2).

[26] Mr Boodle presumably refused the Sacrament because of Mr Neale's well-known high church views and support of Puseyism. In 1841 Bishop Sumner of Winchester had refused to license him in his diocese.

[27] 'Restorations, upon a very extensive scale, have been in progress, during several years, in Ely cathedral. More than forty windows, which were wholly or partially closed up with brick or masonry, have been opened' (From an 1847 leaflet appealing for further subscriptions). About 1860 Sir George Gilbert Scott restored the octagon and lantern as a memorial to Dean Peacock 'to whose initative the extensive works of repair of the church during the previous 20 years were largely due' . . . (V.C.H., IV, 65).

[28] Presumably George Jenyns, Prebendary of Ely and Vicar of Swaffham Prior near Newmarket.

Tasker. —The visitors went early & we had prayers in the Chapel:— by the way the Chapel is not warmed & is most damp & comfortless.

Tu. 14.   Election of a Master at Tr. Hall: they chose Sir Herbert Jenner Fust:— we resident Cantabs hoped for Power who would have been chosen if a layman[29] . . .

Th. 16.   Thermometer at 23 at 9 o'clock this morning. — Seniority at 11 to try a ruffian called Peacocke for assaulting Craufurd the Scholar with a life-preserver. — The story is this:— Yesterday Craufurd walked about all day with a horsewhip to insult or chastise Peacocke who had boasted that he had the previous night struck him (Craufurd) & that he (C) had tamely put up with it. The fact was that at a public Lecture on Shorthand[30] in the Union (Archdeacon Thorp presiding) some of the Audience made game of the Lecturer, Archdeacon Thorp rebuked them with dignity & firmness, & said that if such conduct were repeated either he or they must leave the room:— this produced temporary good conduct, but towards the end Peacocke & others repeated their bad behaviour & Craufurd spoke loudly about 'the blackguardly conduct' & insisted on the offender being turned out:— on going out Peacocke struck or pushed Craufurd, but Craufurd declared he was not conscious of it. Peacocke (who had been dining in Magd. Hall) on hearing that Craufurd had been seeking for him all day to horsewhip him & had declared his belief that he (P) avoided Trinity Hall to shirk him, became half-furious, *went* & *bought* a life-preserver & accompanied by 2 friends (Childe & Hughes of Magd) went to Craufurd's rooms at 9 in the Evening. — Craufurd asked Peacocke if he had spread a report of having struck him: Peacocke answered that he knew nothing about the report, but that he had struck him. Upon this Craufurd said 'then consider yourself horsewhipped' & waved a whip over his head:— Peacocke said 'but you have not struck me':— the reply was 'O if that is what you want I will' & Craufurd laid the whip gently on his shoulder — Whereupon Peacocke muttered 'shall I knock him down?' & instantly struck Craufurd on the head with his life-preserver:— before Craufurd's two friends (for he had 2) could rescue him he received 4 or 5 blows:— the blood flowed freely from his head but he was not seriously hurt —Craufurd & Peacocke are both Trinity men & Pupils of Heath; Peacocke is about a foot shorter than Craufurd (— wch he pleaded in excuse for his conduct) —

[29]   The College was then a preserve of lawyers and 7 of the 8 Masters elected between 1689 and 1856 were advocates. Few Masters and comparatively few fellows lived in college before the mid-nineteenth century and 'were apt to regard the few clerical fellows as necessary and useful resident managers' whilst they lived and worked in London (C.W. Crawley, *Trinity Hall*, (1976), p.134). Power had been ordained deacon in 1824.

[30]   In 1837 Isaac Pitman had published *Stenographic Sound Hand* which marked a new era in the development of phonetic systems.

Craufurd brought the matter before the town magistrates[31] who very properly referred it to the College:— we rusticated Craufurd to the end of the term & Peacocke sine die.[32] . . . The Master of Emm & Mrs Archdall were kind enough to take me over to dine at Charles Townleys: met there Mr & Mrs Worsley, Edm. Mortlock & Mr & Mrs Herbert:— I thought Mr Mortlock spoke strangely in the contempt he heaped upon Gibbon; & then most absurdly in despising Guizot & the whole French nation. — Took Dunford in a Fly to the Hospital.

Fri. 17. Dunford is put in the Fever ward (not that he or any body else in the Hosp. has a fever):— drinking is the cause of all his ailment:— he is rather better today. — Another very severe frost. — G.T.R. & many others skated on Cottenham fen — G.T.R. gave a grand leavetaking wine party. . .

Sat. 18. . . . Seniority to report upon the 41st Statute (concerning Hebrew Greek & Divinity Professorships) as by us revised & yesterday exhibited to the Electors into those Professorships:— they wish the said 41st to be referred to the University.[33] (I suppose to a Syndicate):— we therefore apply to the Queen for approval of all the rest, leaving this for the present undetermined. — Dunford a trifle better. . . In the Evening read loud Miss Ferrier's *Destiny*:[34] I like it very much. — Long letter from J. Heywood about the Power of Parliament over University:— answered it. Women not out.

Mon. 20. Dunford much the same. Nasty rainy day: women not out . . . George left Cambridge at 8 this morning to begin his new Artistic career as pupil to Mr. Denning . . . Poor Mr. Langshaw [sic] (Minister of Great St. Andrews) died of consumption in his College rooms[35] . . .

Fri. 24. Dunford better: Lodge passed a good night. — Walk with him & afterwards with M. — Lodge very wisely abstained from dining at the Family,[36] but he looked in upon us after dinner. — We met at Cartmells:

---

31 In 1829 an Act of Parliament gave magistrates a summary power of punishing for common assaults without reserving the privileges of the University. The borough magistrates frequently heard charges of assault against undergraduates. 'Students . . . are naturally anxious to avoid academic punishment and . . . generally make their appearance before the magistrates without their academic dress, and are well content to escape with the payment of a fine which, being paid to the Borough, does not come to the knowledge of the University Authorities'. (*University Commission Report* (1852), Correspondence and Evidence p. 45).
32 I.e. no date was given for Peacocke's return to the University.
33 I.e. the Trinity seniority had approved a revised form of the 41st chapter of the Statutes and submitted it in courtesy to the electors to the three professorships. See Winstanley Chapter XIII for a detailed account of the complicated and protracted sequel.
34 *Destiny,* Susan Ferrier's last novel, appeared in 1831.
35 According to the tablet in St. Andrew's George Longshaw, 'Langshaw', was for more than seven years the faithful, indefatigable and self-denying Incumbent of this parish.
36 A select dining club of which it was, and still is, a great distinction to be a member. On 16 December 1834 Romilly wrote 'Dined for the 1st time at the Family where I have succeeded Thirlwall . . . The Dinner & wines were very good, & the Pineapple — I thought the introduction of pipes & spitting boxes most filthy: but as it is the invariable Custom, one must bear it'. See S.C. Roberts, *The Family: the history of a dining club* (1963).

. . . Cartmell gave us some Game which I never saw before — a Cock of the Woods; — I thought it flavourless & like tough beef. — Stayd till 1 o'clock.

Sun. 26. . . . A very satisfactory letter from George Romilly who finds himself very comfortable at Dennings & has taken a good likeness of Baugh's baby:— sent £10 for buying painting materials. . .

Sun. 5 March. (Last Sunday we began at Trinity to have the Terminal Sacrament on Sunday;[37] — it used to be on the Thursday after Division[38] — We have now imitated the rest of the University in having it on Sunday — We have a compulsory chapel service at the usual hour of 8, without the Communion: then at 11 the service begins with the Communion, is followed by a Sermon & concludes with the Sacrament.) — Lovely bright morning with a hoar frost. — Lord Ellenboro (in consequence of carrying off the Somnauth Gates) is called Sampson Affghanistes[39] . . .

Wed. 8. . . . Today Lucy brought home from the Hospital her protégée Sarah Fordham (with the bad head): she went in 10th Nov. 1841 & has therefore been an inmate of Addenbrooke's 16 months all but 2 days. Her head is still much the same: she has been shaved scores of times:— she is domiciled with us till she goes as a servant to Mrs Shedds, where L is to pay 2/6 a week for her.

Th. 9. Another good letter from Lodge:— found Dunford a trifle better:— he seems sinking into idiocy. — Trial at V.C.'s; 5 men playing billiards at the house of Poulter (who is discommuned)[40] were suspended: 2 of them were Bachelors (Yarranton & Lindsay) & are now reduced to undergraduates till 1844. — Read loud in Evening & copied out the Trial.

Fri. 10. Read prayers at Downing Chapel; 4 or 5 women there, Masters maids & bedmakers . . . Lodge returned from Leamington yesterday Evening. — He is adhering to Jephson's rules; ½ cup of tea in the day; lunch at 1 & dinner at 6:— no beer or wine[41] . . .

[37] Holy Communion was normally administered in Colleges only once a term.

[38] I.e. half-term.

[39] In September 1842 Lord Ellenborough had been overjoyed at the success of Generals Nott and Pollock in rescuing our prisoners and reopening the door to Kabul after the disastrous first Afghan War. The gates of the temple at Somnath (Bombay province) had supposedly been carried off by the great Mahmud to Ghazni in central Afghanistan. Nott returned the gates to Agra where they remained in the lumber-room in the fort and were disappointingly found to be of much later date than the eleventh century and to be made of deal and not deodar.

[40]. I.e. all members of the University, under severe penalties, were prohibited from having any dealings with W. Poulter whose house was in St Andrews Street. Hostility between Town and Gown was naturally greatly increased by discommuning inn-keepers and tradesmen who broke University regulations.

[41] Dr. Jephson was a fashionable physician whom Lord Ashley (later Shaftesbury), amongst other great persons had travelled from London to consult in 1827. Romilly returning from holiday in September 1838 stays in Leamington and writes 'Most places have their Hero: Dr Jephson is the great man of Leamington:— I saw an advertisement 'Cork Models under the Patronage of the Queen and Dr. J'.

Sat. 11. Read prayers again at Downing — Lodge returned this morning to Leamington. — Walk with M. — Evening party at Trinity Lodge to open the newly furnished (Henry VIII) Drawing Room. Mrs Hayles & Henslow & Willis there:— Mathison & Thacker played the piano :— the Chimney piece very beautifully decorated.

Th. 16. M & I left cards at Mrs Graham's — M. had visits from Mrs Ainslie, Miss Apthorps etc. — Last Monday a long visit from Mrs Thompson (an upholsterer in King St who has most humanely taken that poor creature Caroline Fordham (sister of Lucy's protégée Sarah with the bad head)):— she gave us a long account of her illness & Lucy gave an order for her as an In-patient at the Hospital.[42] Letter from Lodge saying that he had had a bad night & was coming back to Cambridge for 2 days. — To Magdalene at 9 to meet Lodge who had just arrived from Leamington:— think Dr Jephson has done him an immensity of good; he has washed out the greater part of the yellow from his complexion.

Sat. 18. Lodge went back to Leamington. His Cousin Edmund is appointed principal of the College at Agra with salary at £45 monthly. My Gyp Dunford's health is so completely broken that I have parted with him: I allow him 4s a week: he went to Ely today.[43] — I have taken in his place Hoppett, as I promised the Bishop of Hereford some years ago . . . Finished Pagets Milford Malvoisin,[44] a story on the subject of Pews . . . The story is entertaining in spite of the ultra detestation of Pews, the praise of the Cavaliers, the admiration of Laud & the ridiculous attack upon Railroads . . . Received from America a very handsome present of 2 large vols of the History of Harvard University: they are sent by the Author Mr Quincy, at the kind suggestion of Mr Savage (who was here in the summer making inquiries about the original founders of his University) . . . Today the Judges (Tindal & Coleridge) came into the Town.

Sun. 19. M, L. Esther & I to Trinity Ch. where Carus preached from Gospel of the day Luk. XI. 2 8 'Yea rather blessed are they etc.': by way of attacking the Romanists he ran down the Virgin Mary somewhat objectionably. — Edw, M & I took a short walk. — I went to St Mary's at 2 to hear Mill who also preached from the Gosp. of the day 'taketh unto him etc.': it was a very excellent sermon showing the existence of fallen angels,

---

[42] People who subscribed two guineas or more annually became governors of the hospital and could recommend patients according to the amount of their subscription.

[43] Perhaps to the large union workhouse which in 1838 had been erected on the Cambridge Road and housed 340 people. (See V.C.H., IV, 46).

[44] *Milford Malvoisin, or Pews and Pewholders* appeared in 1842. Most parish churches in the 1840's contained large, lockable, box pews occupied for a rental by the upper and middle classes. The poor stood or sat on free benches in what space remained. In the towns, where population increased very rapidly, pews took up a quite disportionate space although many churches depended on the money they raised at a time when rates were becoming more difficult to collect. John Mason Neale and the Cambridge Camden Society greatly helped the gradual freeing of seats but feelings ran high on both sides and the issue 'gave rise to one of the legal and pastoral arguments of the age'. See Chadwick, I 520-2 and J.F. White, The *Cambridge Movement*, 1962.

their agency, the reality of demoniacal possession, the power of falling away after regeneration, etc. — In the Evening Edward read loud to us Bp. Thirlwalls Charge.[45]

Mon. 20. The Town Election to fill up the seat vacated by the Resignation of Sir A.C. Grant: Fitzroy Kelly won by 33

F. Kelly	714
R. Foster	681

Up to 2½ Foster was a good deal ahead, so Kelly has probably bribed during the last hour & a half[46] . . .

Tu. 21. Wrote to G.T.R. & Denning (who says that George has made good progress but has been rather distracted this last week by thoughts of his Little-Go).[47] Wrote to R.L. Koe (sending him a Testimonial):— also to Lodge. — This morning a young man (G. Hillman of Magdalene) found dead in his rooms: he had fallen down backwards in an apoplectic fit while pouring out water to wash himself before going to bed:— he was perfectly sober:— he had been very anxious about his Little-Go[48] . . .

Wed. 22. . . . Received a subpoena to produce Subscription Book & Oaths in the case Belaney v Totton for Libel.[49] — The case is this: Belaney (plucked both for Little-Go & Degree) is a red-hot Puseyite: he became curate at Meldreth to the aged Mr. Totton (resident on his other living at Debden):— he banished Pews, introduced week day service, preaching in surplice, etc: & set the Parish in a complete flame:— His Rector (in a private confidential letter to a young man called Sparke, late Churchwarden at Meldreth) calls Belaney 'a Papist in disguise', — meaning neither more nor less than that he was a Puseyite:— Sparke betrays the confidence, communicates the letter to Belaney who (like a firebrand as he is) brings an Action against Mr Totton!!

---

[45] Thirlwall had become Bishop of St David's in 1840. He wrote 11 triennial charges which were a summary of the history of the Church of England during his Episcopate. He was 'by far the ablest academic mind on the bench' and 'brilliant and coherent on paper' though 'hesitant and remote as a pastor'. (See Chadwick, I, 247).

[46] A select committee subsequently found that Fitzroy Kelly (Conservative) was duly elected. One William Smithers had been bribed, but it was not proved that the bribe was given by Fitzroy Kelly or his agents or with their consent.

[47] I.e. the Previous Examination (instituted in 1822) in classics and divinity which all undergraduates were obliged to take in their fifth term of residence. The standard of the examination was 'extremely elementary, owing to the fear of distracting the men from the pursuit of mathematics . . . and deranging the system of college instruction'. (Winstanley p.167).

[48] The verdict after a post-mortem was that he had 'Died by the Visitation of God'.

[49] The book in which subscriptions for degrees were recorded. The University 'required the recipients of all degrees either to declare themselves members of the Established Church or to subscribe to the three articles of the Canons of 1604'. (See Winstanley p. 84). Belaney, whom Venn lists as achieving a B.A. in 1843, became a R.C. in 1852 and lived to be the oldest R.C. priest in Great Britain. Mr Totton was more prescient than he realised. The result of the case was that the Lord Chief Justice instructed the jury to find for the plaintiff with temperate damages (40s).

Th. 23. Seniority (about Leases etc.) — Yesterday was Licensing day:— 154:— 2 old ones were refused (viz. Portland Arms for a Prostitutes Ball & Albion for the publican being in prison for debt to his landlord):— all new applications refused[50] . . .

Fri. 24. In court:— Heard the greater part of the trial of J.F. Mortlock for shooting at his uncle Edmund last November:— Byles was the Prosecutor, & the Prisoner defended himself: he was much overcome at the beginning & sat down for a while; he soon recovered & spoke for near an hour with great earnestness & considerable eloquence about his poverty, his wrongs from his uncles (with regard to his Father's share at the Bank), his persuasion of there being no legal document of resignation of his Father's share (wch document he had demanded over & over again, & should remain quite contented if it could be produced), that he had been accustomed to firearms all his life & that if he had intended to injure his uncle he could have made sure of it, but that he only meant to frighten him. — The Jury found him guilty of shooting with intent to do grievous bodily harm. — Judge Coleridge sentenced him to 21 years transportation[51] . . .

Sun. 26. M, L, Esther & I to Trinity where Edward Allen joined us at Sermon time. Carus preached a very hard sermon from Joh XIII.10 'He that is washed etc' The wind blew so violently that I recommended M. not to take her customary walk with me . . . Amused with the witticism about Ventris the curate of Quy & Chaplain to the Jail: he is called 'Curate of Quy & Chaplain of Quod' — Edw. tea with us.

Tu. 28. . . . Audit of late V.C. (Dr. Archdall)[52] — Our rascally old cat gave birth to 4 kittens. — Dined with V.Ch. to meet the Auditors . . . Found Lodge so melancholy in the Evening that I wrote to Jephson to ask him about allowing him to drink wine . . .

Wed. 29. Letter from George Romilly sending me a pretty original sketch & saying that he is getting on so well that he will decline coming up for the Littlego:[53]— some talk of his being employed to illustrate Vol. of Kenilworth (to receive £2 for each drawing) — Found Lodge so dejected &

---

[50] All Cambridge inns had to obtain the Vice-Chancellor's licence. The publicans of each parish, in alphabetical order by parishes, were called in according to a list prepared beforehand at the Law Schools. The lowest estimated figure of notorious prostitutes in Cambridge was nearly 100.

[51] See also note for 18 November 1842. Mortlock was taken to the Leviathan hulk at Portsmouth after the trial and more than 900 signatures later accompanied a petition to the Home Secretary asking for a commutation of the sentence. Mortlock wrote his own account of his life in Australia, reprinted in 1965 as *Experiences of a Convict* by Sydney University Press. He returned to Cambridge in 1864 and as part of his continued campaign to recover his inheritance published his memoirs in five parts. These he sold on Saturdays in the market place — a stone's throw from his family's bank (now Barclays) in Bene't Street.

[52] The annual University audit usually took place at the end of the Lent term. Dr Archdall had been Vice-Chancellor in 1841.

[53] George had begun his undergraduate career in Trinity on 16 October 1841. He did not take a degree and his uncle, who was so interested in pictures, seems to have been content that he should withdraw from the University and to have been proud of his artistic talent.

miserable that I prescribed a glass of wine & more mutton chops — Walk with him till dinner . . .

Fri. 31. Congregation:— I MD, 2AM, 25 Inceptors:— the Grace for correspondence between Examiners & Professors lost in Black House; 27:19.[54] — Lodge passed a bad night; walk with him. — In the Evening Lodge came up in a towering passion to our house:— he had just received from his cousin John (whom he had sent to Jephson with my Letter) a letter describing his interview with the great man:— he had asked 'Who is this Mr Romilly?' 'How should I know whether wine is good for Mr L. without seeing him' 'He had no business to go away'. 'I wish I had never prescribed for him' — This last speech — (wch John was an ass for communicating) has enraged the Librarian.

Sun. 2 April. Bowtell (the Library Keeper)'s daughter converted to Popery by the Roman Catholic Priest Wolfrey[55] here . . . M, L, Esther & I to Trinity Church where Carus preached from Joh XX.30.31: it was (like all his sermons now) a fling at the Puseyites . . . In the Evening finished Evans 'Bishoprick of Souls' which I like very much[56] . . . Finished also Gresley's Portrait of a Churchman:[57]— certainly his portraits of Herbert the Clergyman & Ridley (his brother-in-law, — a lawyer and afterwards an MP) are those of very good & clever men with ultra high church notions:— but why make them such redhot tories & make them abuse Whigs in such rancorous terms.

Tu. 4. At Dr Mills request wrote to Mrs Lindsay a letter explanatory of the sentence of suspension passed on her son for playing billiards in a discommuned house:— the Gr.Father of young Lindsay (Bp of Kildare) is in high dudgeon & this letter is to soothe him . . .

Wed. 5. Seniority to try Bidgood & Willyams (2 Freshmen) for having been in a Prostitute's house (with other gownsmen & women) making a disturbance last Sunday at 2½ PM! Rusticated them for 3 terms . . .

Sun. 9. (Palm S). The change at St Mary's began today, viz the University Sermon at 10½, & the Parochial service *with a Sermon* at 11½.

---

54 The grace was to carry into effect recommendations made by a Syndicate appointed 'to consider whether it is desirable . . . to secure a correspondence between the Mathematical and Classical Examinations of the University, and the Mathematical and Classical Lectures of the University Professors'. Romilly notes in *UP* 14 no. 967 that almost all of St John's voted against the grace.

55 In 1842 the Rev. H.N. Woolfrey O.C. came to Cambridge to minister primarily to a group of Irish workers settled in the Barnwell area. He presumably ministered for a short time only, as in 1843 Thomas Quinlivan became the first rector of St. Andrews, the small Roman Catholic church built by Richard Huddleston in the slum area of Union Road. The building of this church aroused great indignation in the University and on 5 November 1841 a large group of students attempted to tear up the foundations. A.W. Pugin designed the church which was removed brick by brick to St Ives after the present church was opened in 1890 on a different site.

56 *The Bishoprick of Souls* (1841, 5th edition 1877) was about R.W. Evans's (classical Tutor of Trinity 1814-36) work in his parish of Tarvin, Cheshire.

57 William Gresley was an ardent supporter of the Tractarian movement which he tried to popularise in many writings.

Carus used us shamefully, for without apprising us of his intention (tho' he wrote me a letter last night & sent 2 declamations for me to look over) he deserted us[58] & preached at St Mary's:— we suffered agonies from Hose's preaching, it was his most pompous stile: his text was Matt. 23.34. 'Father, forgive them etc':— the sermon must have been 2 thrown together, for it was much above an hour! Lucy rushed to St Mary's & found Carus had just given the blessing: He had been preaching (as Mayor's Chaplain) Chapman's Obiit Sermon[59] — she gave him a withering look & then went to visit her various paupers. — Lucy had on Friday from the Miss Willimotts an offer of a place for her poor protégée with a bad head (S. Fordham) at Mrs Lutts:[60] she magnanimously refused it & keeps her on at Mrs Shedd's[61] (where she pays 2/6 a week for her) as at a place more free from temptation . . .

Sun. 16. (Easter S.) I preached in Trin Chapel from Luk. XXIV. 34. 'The L. is risen indeed,' — a Sermon of Burders.[62] M & L to Trinity Church where Carus preached an excellent sermon from Matt. XXVIII. 7. 'tell his disciples that he is risen' — The new system at Trinity Chap. (of having prayers at 8, communion sermon & sacrament at 11) makes the service very short:— we were out of Chapel at 12½; M & L did not get out of Church till 2! . . .

Mon. 17. Beautiful day. Sedgwick and I over in a Fly at 1½ to Dungate. — After lunch Sedgwick & I & Phil Frere & Mrs Frere with Mrs Spring Rice & her other 3 daughters[63] & Mrs & Miss Lindsay set forth on a stroll along the Dyke (wch runs about 4 miles):— I enjoyed this ramble; when we got to a little wood (about 1½ mile or 2 miles from the house) all sat down on the ground & after a little rest returned home:— I was however not satisfied with this & went to the end of the Dyke in the outskirts of Fulbourn . . .

Tu. 18. . . . Letter from George Romilly telling me of the death of his pretty friend Isabella Smith. — Also a letter from Baugh telling me of the death of his brother at Cresselly[64] last Saturday:— he had had lately some affection of the chest, but was not thought in a dangerous way:— he died within a quarter of an hour of his seisure. — His loss will be severely felt by

58 I.e. his congregation at Holy Trinity.
59 In 1668 Edward Chapman left the corporation £100 to be bestowed on the poor 'at one time in the year, the first to be about Easter, with a sermon for the benefit of the living'. . . (*Reports of Commissioners . . . into Charities and Education of the poor in England and Wales* Vol VI).
60 The only Lutt listed in Pigot's *Directory* for 1839 and in the 1851 *Gazetteer* was Edward, (Shoe Warehouse) 12 King's Parade.
61 Presumably the wife of James B. Shedd of 6 Pembroke Street, registrar of Marriages.
62 Probably George Burder, (1752-1832) congregationalist minister, secretary of the London Missionary Society, one of the founders of the British and Foreign Bible Society and author of many sermons.
63 Spring Rice had married his second wife, Mrs Whewell's sister, in 1841. His eldest son had married Ellen Mary Frere, daughter of the Master of Downing.
64 John Hensleigh Allen (1769-1843) Baugh's elder brother and the head of the family at Cresselly House, Kilgetty, Pembrokeshire.

his sisters to whom he was a most kind brother & by all his tenants to whom he was a most generous landlord. — Wrote to condole with Baugh. Wrote to the Master of Dulwich to beg his interest for Harry Allen for the Wardenship. — Wrote also to G.A. Browne in answer to a L. of his concerning the D. of Sussex who is suffering from Erysipelas. Declined Mrs Mills Soirée.

Wed. 19. Beginning of Scholarship Examination conducted by me & Martin:— after I had distributed the papers & the young men had been working 5', I was highly amused by Sedgwick stalking in with another bundle of Greek papers:— I told him that he had been strangely misled by his colleague Blakesley, — that the Latin day had been assigned them, & that he must instantly go & set some Latin!! . . . Dined in Hall. Sedgwick, Martin, Heath & Blakesley drank wine with me:— all but Heath looked over papers with me till midnight.

Th. 20. 2d Day of Scholarship:— conducted by Sedgwick & Blakesley. — Dined in Jesus Coll. Hall with the Master & Fellows, being the Rustat dinner:— I never was at a dinner where the waiting was so bad. — I was glad to see my old Clerk Rowe acting as Butler:— his eldest boy followed in his train . . .

Fri. 21. 3d day of Scholarship — Mathematics by the Master[65] & Martin. Sedgwick & I over to Babraham to dine with the Adeanes . . . Before dinner I was much amused with the 3 little Miss Adeanes to whom I read (at their desire) Southeys story of the 3 bears.[66]

Mon. 24. Rather alarmed at hearing Margaret screaming in the middle of the night:— went & knocked at her door to ask if she was ill: she said she was quite well, but had woke suddenly:— I suppose it was some horrid night-mare; — but it left no impression on her memory. She afterwards complained of a little headache & wisely took some physic. — Walk with her: Lucy to the Hospital etc. — Began reading loud Mémoirs of Isaac Milner,[67] & also that amusing new work of Surtees 'the Spa Hunt or Handley Cross'.[68] — To Sedgwick after dinner to look over papers — Went late to the Whist Club at Bateson's: won every rubber!

Tu. 25. The Queen produced a little girl no 2[69] . . . All the morning looking over Scholarship papers . . .

---

[65] These were only College scholarships, but see Winstanley for an account of the duties of a Vice-Chancellor who like Whewell, 'was almost the sole administrative officer of the University'. (pp. 373-4).

[66] Southey's story of *The Three Bears* appeared in Volume 4 of his *The Doctor* which was published in 1837. In Chapter CXXIX of Volume 4 Southey writes '. . . as there are Chapters in it for the closet, for the library, for the breakfast room, for the boudoir . . . for the drawing-room, and for the kitchen . . . so should there be one at least for the nursery'. The story differs from that which includes 'Goldilocks', and Southey did not invent it, as was long supposed.

[67] *The Life of Isaac Milner D.D.* by Mary Milner (1842).

[68] Jorrocks here reappears as a M.F.H. and the possessor of a country seat.

[69] I.e. Princess Alice Maud Mary.

Th. 27. . . . In Chapel at ¼ to 9 to declare the new Scholars. — Then a long College meeting . . . Dined in the Combination room with my brother Examiners — we went to tea at the Lodge where we met Lord Fra. Egerton & son: I should have known Lord F.E. from his likeness to his portrait in that beautiful picture of E. Landseers 'The Return from the Hawking'.

On the 4 May Romilly went to stay in Dulwich with Baugh Allen who from 1805 to 1820 had been Warden and then Master of Dulwich College and still retained a house there in addition to Cilrhiw in South Wales. Romilly breakfasted with the Dennings and 'conveyed to Susan Chune (now maid at the Dennings) a very handsome teacaddy sent by M & L'. He also took a long walk with his nephew George Romilly ('both of us greatly admiring the beauty of the scenery') who was annoyed because Mrs Baugh Allen had framed 'a portrait wch he had made of her son, after having put in beautifying touches of her own'. In London he worked hard on his brother Frank's behalf seeking information about the payment of dividends, but also found time to hear 'his pet preacher', Baptist Noel, preach in St John's Chapel, Bedford Row: 'the place was intensely full, the time 11¼, the 1st Lesson just begun, — no bribery could procure me a seat in the body of the Church, at length with a silver key I got a pew unlocked for Mrs John [Romilly] and I myself stood till the Communion Service:— Baptist Noel preached a learned sermon on Baptism, but not very practical . . . moreover it lasted 70 minutes' . . . Romilly also went to 'Westminster Abbey wch I found hung with black in honor of the D. of Sussex & his arms on the Pulpit pannel'. The Duke, who was the sixth son of George III, had died of erysipelas on 21 April.[70]

On 8 May Romilly began the journey to Dublin where he was to christen the year-old son of his first cousin Sophie and her husband, the Rt. Hon. Thomas Francis Kennedy, P.C. of Dunure, Co. Ayr, and Paymaster of the civil service in Ireland. The 10 o'clock mail train from Euston reached Liverpool at seven in the evening and Romilly 'lost no time getting aboard the mail packet for Dublin . . . we had a favoring Easterly breeze so that we hoisted 2 sails'. Once arrived he went sightseeing, heard a debate 'in the Assembly House (in William St:) walked to the end of the Pier, about 1 mile' and was present at a large dinner-party after the christening. He strongly disapproved of a fellow-guest 'Lord Cosmo Russell (whose levity and indecorous conversation I thought very offensive tho I have no doubt he is much admired in his mess room) . . . After all the company were gone we drank the young Lairds health & I was highly delighted by Sophie's dancing Parisot's hornpipe — of course she was dressed in white for the christening'.

On 13 May our diarist noted that his return passage to Liverpool took the remarkably short time of only 10½ hours. Once there he stayed with his cousin Henry Romilly at 21 Oxford Street and was shown the sights. In London again he went to 'Drury Lane & heard K. John & Fortunio:— I thought Macready & Miss Helen Faucitt very bad successors of John Kemble & Mrs Siddons'.[71] He had put up at 'Mr Woods hotel' and the following morning, Tuesday May 16, records that family prayers were 'at 9½ . . . the congregation consisted of his wife & family & several of the waiters & (I presume) all the chambermaids. Mr Wood set the

---

[70] A correspondent of the *Morning Chronicle* wrote that 'His periodical visits to Trinity were always a source to him of long anticipated and heartily enjoyed pleasure . . . There was no pomp or parade expected by His Royal Highness on such occasions'.

[71] English licensing regulations confined the serious theatre to three licensed houses in London — Covent Garden, Drury Lane and the Haymarket.

opening Psalm . . . & he & the congregation sang very well indeed.' Romilly returned home on the same day leaving the Railway station at 11½ and reaching Cambridge at 3.

Tu. 16. . . . found the women pretty well; — M. had a slight headache & L. a little cold. — M. & I walked for an hour in the Evening during an interval of fine weather. — Dr Chafy (Master of Sidney) died today aged 64: so little did he expect his death that he dined at the Audit last Thursday, & at the moment of his death a pipe of port was bottling off in his cellar,[72] & the butler was going to bring him a glass to taste!

Th. 18. Seniority, about the final revision of our Statutes. — Today there was a great noise in resetting the Kitchen grate, so Margaret accompanied me to College to escape the din. As we were going along we met the 2 Miss Hardings whom Margaret has most amiably undertaken to teach a French Accent (in order to oblige Miss Watson of the Petty Cury). They know French tolerably well but pronounce detestably:— their names are Emma & Agnes:— they are very merry & the youngest very pretty — I know their Father who was wooden spoon:[73] — their brother was not so successful, having been plucked:— They live in Widnalls Cottage at Grantchester. — Margaret gives them a lesson twice a week (viz. Mond. & Th:) — They accompanied M. & me to my rooms, & there did their lessons. — M. & I paid a visit to Mr Roe's shop, & he exhibited to us a pretty picture of mother & child by Gainsboro . . .

Mon. 22. . . . Poor Browne (the V. Master) has been suffering for the last week with erysipelas[74] in the head: he was at one time considered in danger, but is happily now much better tho' dreadfully weak & exhausted . . . The Steward of Trinity College (Humphrey) has kindly made my ex-Gyp Dunford a weekly allowance of 1s 6d a week from the Sacrament money. — Dr Chafy buried this Afternoon[75] . . .

---

[72] The wine offered for sale after Dr Chafy's death amounted to about 600 dozen bottles! For an account of Dr Chafy's hospitality see H. Gunning, *Reminiscences,* Vol. II, p. 369.

[73] I.e. he was the last junior optime, the last name on the honours list. The last wooden spoon was presented in 1909.

[74] Before the advent of anti-bacterial chemotherapy erysipelas was both frequent and dangerous.

[75] The following people preceded Dr. Chafy's coffin in the procession to the College chapel:—

Mutes
two and two
The Undertaker   The furnishing undertaker
The Porter,   carrying staff
The Butler   The Cook
The Mason   Plumber   Bricklayer
Dr Haviland   Dr Thackeray
T.J. Ficklin, Esq.

(*UP* 14 no. 1011).

Tu. 23. At 6 o'clock this morning 10 out of the 12 F. of Sydney met in the Chapel[76] (there is one vacancy & the Senior Fellow Luke who is out of his mind was absent). It was understood that there would be 4 candidates, viz. Temple, B.A. 1817, Garnons, B.A. 1814, Saunders 1824, & Phelps, 1833: I believe Temple retired: Garnons had 3 votes, Saunders 1 (his own) & Phelps 6: Phelps was of course elected, having (as required) a majority of the whole votes:— Phelps was 5th Wrangler & wrote a good book on Optics. — Good letter from G.T.R. giving a favourable account of himself & his studies. — Wrote to him & sent him £5 . . .

Th. 25. Holy Thursday. Got into a great scrape with Lucy by telling her that I had told Carus he had never called to collect her Parker Society Guinea:[77] — she was affronted at his neglect & was very glad to give up the Society, — the publications of wch are most dull:— so I had to write to tell Carus it was all a mistake & that he was not to write to the Society to pay the Guinea in arrears. — Wrote to Master of Caius, Dr Woodhouse, Holditch & Thurtell to solicit their votes for the child of our Butcher (Tom Carpenter) for the Perse School[78] . . . Augustus Lewis of Trinity (underg) asked me to play Whist with him this Evening:— he is a capital player:— but I declined, having been out a great deal this week . . . Lucy went to Trinity Church this Evening & heard Carus read prayers: she might have heard an old man (of the name of Fry) preach, but she bolted . . . Miss Spilling wrote to me 4 days ago to decline the Poplin Gown I brought her from Dublin, as too magnificent for the Matron of a Hospital:[79] — after an interview however with M. & L. she at last accepted it & wrote a grateful letter of thanks.

Fri. 26. . . . We this day sealed our Petition to the Queen for the Revised Statutes of Trinity College.[80] — Election of Hebrew Scholars, Bright (Magdalene) 1st; Lovell (John's) 2d.[81] — With M & L to select a

[76] They met to elect Dr Chafy's successor as Master. 'They & the College Servants (according to Statute) met in the College Chapel, where there was full service & the Sacrament: they met very early, before 6'. (Note by Romilly in *UP 14* no. 1012).

[77] A society established in 1840 under the leadership of the Earl of Shaftesbury and some other prominent Evangelicals to issue 'the works of the Fathers and early writers of the Reformed Church'. It took its name from Matthew Parker, Archbishop of Canterbury from 1559-75.

[78] 'The free scholars are to be elected quarterly by the supervisors after public advertisement of the number of vacancies . . . The supervisors of the trust and the patrons of the school are the master and four senior fellows of Caius college'. (Cooper *Memorials of Cambridge.* Vol. III, p.160). Hamnet Holditch, John Thomas Woodhouse and Alexander Thurtell were all senior fellows of Caius.

[79] On 10 May Romilly had gone shopping with his cousin Sophie Kennedy 'who kindly selected 6 Poplins for me . . . she saved me a good deal of money for she would not allow me to buy any double or figured'. Miss Spilling's responsibility as Matron of Addenbrookes would have been 'merely that of a housekeeper and cook, with some disciplinary duties added'. (V.C.H., III, 108).

[80] I.e. to petition the Crown for Royal Letters confirming the revised statutes. See Winstanley, Appendix B.

[81] I.e. they were the best candidates in the examination for Tyrwhitt's Hebrew Scholarships which took place on the second Wednesday in May.

paper for papering a room of Mrs Shedds. — Dined at Anstey Hall (Trumpington) with Mr & Mrs Eb. Foster to meet Ingle . . . On returning to Cambridge met a torchlight procession with a band of music:— it was a tory rejoicing at the decision of H. of C. that Kelly was duly returned, & that tho there was bribery it was without his knowledge . . .

Sun. 28. . . . Today received Denning's portrait of G.T.R. wch is a charming picture & a most agreeable likeness.[82] M. & I wrote to George: M. also to Miss Wilcox. Edward to tea with us.

Mon. 29. Wrote to F £10 — M. & I caught in another grand storm: asked in by the Hustlers to their lodgings at the University Arms. — Tolerably good letter from Lodge — Mr Brocklebank (Rector of Willingham) dead: Mr Addison of Landbeach dead: much delighted at the B. of Ely having given Willingham to Dr Graham:— it's worth about £800 a year. Tinkler will succeed to Landbeach. It is said that many a Belle longs to become a Tinkler.

Th. 1 June. . . . Heard a good story about the late Incumbent of Willingham & Teversham (Mr. Brocklebank):— He is said on his deathbed to have made the following lament: 'Sad times for the Church! Poor Teversham! When I am dead you will be severed from Willingham, never more to be held by the same Clergyman'!

Fri. 2. Matriculation at 8 in the morning: only 4 Pensioners. — Tolerably good letter from Lodge: wrote to him (as I do every day):— told him that Haviland recommended Carlsbad . . .

Sat. 3. Letter from Lodge saying that he leaves London for Antwerp tomorrow in company with his cousin John Lodge. — Visit to G.A. Browne whom I found very ill from the effect of a sleepless night: he is suffering from *tic douloureux* in the jaw & eyes . . . Dined at Trinity Lodge: a huge party of 16 . . . I attempted to escape from the Coffee room by going thro a side door:— defeated by a maid lurking behind it to wash cups & saucers. — Declined visit to Henslows.

Sun. 4. Whit Sunday. M, L. & I to Trin. Church. Edward came in to the Sermon. — Carus preached a very good Sermon from Joh. XV. 26. — M. & I staid: but Lucy not. — Before she got away from the Chancel door a shower began, which was soon followed by a thunderstorm ending in one of the heaviest falls of rain I ever heard: — Lucy stood up in the doorway all the time, writing in her notebook . . .

Mon. 5. . . . Margaret & I paid visits to Mrs Barker & Mrs Clark. — She had the 3 Miss Hardings (for the [youngest] came today) to read French; & after dinner she most valiantly had out 3 teeth, 2 loosish but the other as firm as a rock. — Whist Club at Eyres: only 5 of us viz. Eyres, Haviland, Birkett, Marquis & I.

---

[82] Mrs Mary Bain, the owner of the portrait, is G.T. Romilly's great-granddaughter.

Wed. 7. . . . Edward in the 4th Class, with which both I & he must be content. Wrote to him & his Father. — Read loud 'The Neighbours'.[83] —Mr Browne rather better.

Th. 8. Walk with M. up the Hills Road; our [first?] walk since Monday, & till her teeth are set to rights . . . Began reading loud Borrows 'Bible in Spain': it is extremely interesting: I cannot however help thinking that the love of adventure (particularly among The Gypsies) is a stronger passion with him than his zeal for distributing the Scriptures. —

Fri. 9. A day of torrents of rain: M. however kept her appointment with Mr Jones the dentist:[84] she went in perfect confidence of suffering no pain, but merely having the false teeth fastened in:— to her surprise & disgust Mr Jones said that he had broken one of the teeth on Monday & he must now draw it: he did with a vengeance, & hurt her so that she screamed with anguish. — Found Browne extremely languid, tho' mending.

Sat. 10. Browne a trifle better: I am now his Private Secretary, & write letters for him daily. Wrote (as Deputy Librarian)[85] to Lord Eliot,[86] to beg the Irish Statutes:— also to Hon. W. Leslie Melville to thank for a Bannatyne Book (viz. Family Papers relating to Scottish History). Declined lunching with Dr Fisher — A cigar & some coffee with Sedgwick who caught me going into my rooms (for wine for one of L's paupers) in the Evening. . .

Tu. 13. M paid a visit to Jones the Dentist (— to have wax model taken of her gums). — To Magdalene in the Evening to receive Lodge (who came by the Times):— most happy in finding him much better than his own report of himself:— he complains of physical weakness, resulting from his disturbed rest:— he has however a bright eye, a clean tongue, a good pulse (tho feeble) & no yellowness mixt up with the natural red of his complexion. — Sat with him till 10 & then went to a Card party at Mr Wilsons (of the Bank):— Sir G. Harnage, Arlett, Mills & that wild man Overton were the other players.

Wed. 14. G.A. Browne had another of his fits while I was with him:— he is however certainly getting better, tho slowly. — Poor H. Hudson (our Cook) is gone out of his mind:— he insisted on seeing G.A.B. the other day, saying that he (G.A.B.) was going to die & he must thank him for all his

[83] Presumably Fredrika Bremer's novel of domestic life in Sweden which was published in 1837 and translated in 1842 by Mary Howitt. There were 2nd and 3rd editions in 1843.
[84] Mr Jones of 63 Trumpington Street advertised in the *Cambridge Chronicle* as follows: 'Mr. Jones, Surgeon and Mechanical Dentist to H.R.H. the Duke of Sussex, Earl of Ivverness [sic] etc. etc. Every description of Artificial Teeth . . . guaranteed to answer all purposes of mastication and articulation, combined with durability and economy'.
[85] Romilly was acting as Deputy Librarian in Lodge's frequent absences and was not officially appointed Deputy Librarian until November 1844. Lodge, genuinely ill in addition to his long-standing hypochondria, tendered his resignation in March 1845. He died in August 1850 aged 57.
[86] Lord Eliot had been appointed chief secretary for Ireland in 1841.

kindness.[87] — Lodge very comfortable this morning: paid him 2 visits, & took a long walk with him, he declaring that he was too weak to walk, wch I laughed at very properly. Our maid Betsy Edwards started this morning for a months visit to her Parents in Wales:— her place supplied by Harriet Gillson.

Fri. 16. Another bright sunny day — Lodge passed an excellent night, & seems to me as well as I ever saw him. — Mr. Browne mending very slowly. — M had her new set of teeth today — Jones charges outrageously, 25 Gns:— this being the 2d set . . .

Sun. 18. Carus still absent. — M. & I to Trinity where Colenso preached (from 131 Ps) on Humility: he gave his Text partly from Bible, partly from P. Book & partly from his own head. I did not much like the Sermon & the manner was far too dull & dismal for my taste — Lucy kept house in the morning but went out with me at 2 to St Mary's to hear Dr Mill, who positively enraged me: he stammered worse than ever & spoke in that rapid bellowing stile at the beginning of a sentence with a sinking of the voice at the close, wch is so irritating:— then if the Sermon had been decently delivered it was insufferably dull . . . It was Lucy's 1st hearing of Mill, & doubtless will be her last . . .

Fri. 23. Wrote to Mr Savory & Mr I'anson, etc. about Mr Browne whose condition is (I think) hopeless . . . Last night or rather 2 A.M. a thief got into the Observatory & was courageously laid hold of by Mrs Challis:[88] he however made his escape. — Today proclaimed Pot Fair.[89]

Th. 29. . . . Jane this Evening left the room in the middle of prayers with hysteric sobs:— after prayers M. had an interview with her. A grand scene it was:— Jane is jealous of the favor shown to Betsy, & it has now come to a head from this 2d visit of Betsy to Wales. — M. behaved vastly well & with much gentleness. — A few days ago Jane gave warning, professing to intend setting up as a dressmaker:— we have taken her this time at her word (she twice before offered to go).

Fri. 30. . . . In the Evening received fees till 9 o'cl. when I went to Trinity Lodge to teach the Master & Mistress Ombre;[90] — I plaid a Vole & won it.

87 G.A. Browne did indeed die on 4 July.
88 The *Independent* reports that 'Mrs Challis was awoke by a noise in the bedroom and immediately alarmed her husband who said it was something on the roof, and went to sleep again'. Mrs Challis got out of bed and 'a man suddenly sprang from the corner of the room towards her; she caught hold of his sleeve, but was unable to hold him, and he made his escape'.
89 The Midsummer fair on Midsummer Common sold earthenware particularly — hence the popular name of 'Pot Fair' — and, being near the river, goods for sale were easily brought to it by water. The fair was proclaimed by the Vice-Chancellor and principal University officers, and by the Mayor and Corporation successively. The proclamation was read by the Registrary, and repeated after him by the Yeoman Bedell.
90 A card-game played by three people which was especially popular in the 17th and 18th centuries. Not surprisingly Romilly won every trick.

Tu. 4 July. Poor Browne died this morning at 7¼:— wrote before breakfast to Savory, I'anson[91] & Searle. — About 12½ Savory arrived by Coach, too late to witness the last moments of his friend. — Lodge now in vigorous health: left Camb. today for Anderby. — M. L. & I went over the 2 dilapidated houses, gardens & 6 cottages belonging to 2 unfortunate maiden Ladies of the name of Bones who have just been removed to Bedford Asylum.[92] Their relation (Mr Michael Headly) kindly showed us over the place: it was a melancholy exhibition: the 6 cottages were all dismantled, the gardens become a wilderness: the house in St Andrews St had never been finished, they having quarrelled with their Architect:— the house facing the Pig market was where they lived. They fancied everything was poisoned: they used therefore to throw aside their bread after smelling to it: we saw at least 60 loaves of bread in different closets, many wrapt up in paper & dated, the greater part mouldy & hard: they had fastened down the register to their stove, tying it to the top bar, because they thought there were spies in the Chimney: they did not venture to speak to each other lest they should be overheard by the spies, but wrote down their thoughts on slates: they slept in the same bed; they spoke to persons from a pannel in the bedroom window: they had no servant but an occasional charwoman; they had not changed their linen for weeks, nor seen the said charwoman: the elder of the 2 sisters had more than £1000 about her when taken away:— they resisted very much (as might be expected) when taken away, & fled from room to room: their little dog defended them stoutly & bit the Policeman. — The house & cottages that were unoccupied would let for more than £150 p.a.:— in one of the gardens was the old decayed chaise of their Father (an Attorney)[93] . . .

Wed. 5. G.[94] & M & I walked together:— G. made today several very clever pen & ink drawings from Shakspere:— Mr Smith of Dulwich has promised him 2/6 for each. — George read loud in the Evening the new no. of Chuzzlewit (— Martin's 1st conversations in America): we thought it

91 William Janson, or 'Ianson' according to the *Clergy List* for 1843, was Mr Browne's Curate at Rettenden, Essex. Mr Browne had been Rector there since 1838.
92 The story of these two sisters who lived at No. 7 St. Andrew's Hill was retold by Miss Enid Porter, in the *Cambridge News* of 31 January and 7 February 1964.
93 John Bones died in 1813 and is commemorated in a memorial tablet on the north wall of Great St. Andrew's Church.
94 George Romilly had arrived by Star on 3 July and was sleeping in his uncle's rooms in college.

insufferable.[95] Today an American of the name of Cutler came to my office to see the writing of an ancestor of his who in 1723 took a D.D. at Oxf. & was then admitted ad eundem:[96] — I copied out for him a very complimentary Grace upon granting him a certificate of this degree sealed with the Common seal:[97] — I showed Mr Cutler the presents I had received from his countrymen Mr Savage & Mr President Quincy. Mr Cutler was in the quiet American manner pleased with his visit, & particularly with the copy of the Grace.

Sat. 8. Poor Mr Browne's Funeral at Chesterton: the Master accompanied the body from the rooms to the Gate. The 4 mourners were Almack (the Executor) Ja. Searle, Skrine & myself. I took the place of Ch. Beales who was to have been the other mourner, but feeling unwell resigned his place to me, knowing that I meant to walk over to Chesterton. — There was only one Coach as Mr Browne had particularly wished his funeral to be quite private:[98] — the Deightons walked over:— Mr Smedley[99] read the service very well:— George Romilly returned to Dulwich today . . . Over to Ely by the Lynn Coach (at ¼ to 2) I was outside:— it rained the whole way. — We did not dine till ½ past 7 as we had to wait for Lord Northampton, Prof. Willis & Hartshorne who were out on an Architectural tour. . . . The whole conversation was upon Architecture & was very amusing: The V.C & Mrs Whewell & Willis went early, & then Hartshorne exhibited rubbings from brasses, & lectured very entertainingly upon them.

Sun. 9. An awful sermon from Mr Minor Canon Clay: his Text was Jerem. IX. 23[1] — for aught that appeared the Preacher might have been a Jew . . .

---

95 Dickens' descriptions of Martin Chuzzlewit's and Mark Tapley's adventures in America are savagely critical of almost everything American. Dickens had sailed to Boston in 1842 and had made speeches advocating international copyright which met with little success. He had been appalled by the sight of slavery and the suppression of free discussion of it and he returned home thoroughly disillusioned and heartily disliking the country despite the immense enthusiasm of his initial reception. On his return to America 25 years later he promised that *American Notes* (1842) and *Martin Chuzzlewit* should not be reissued without mention of the improvements he found. 'Also, to declare how astounded I have been by the amazing changes I have seen around me on every side . . . Nor am I, believe me, so arrogant as to suppose that in five and twenty years there have been no changes in me, and that I had nothing to learn and no extreme impressions to correct when I was here first'. (From the Postscript to *Martin Chuzzlewit*. See also 19 September 1842).

96 I.e. as a graduate of another university he was admitted to a Cambridge degree by incorporation.

97 I.e. the seal of the University.

98 If Browne had not asked that his funeral should be private there would presumably have been many coaches filled with mourners. In addition to being a Senior of Trinity and Rector of Rettenden, Essex, he was a prominent Freemason — Provincial Grand Master for the county of Cambridge and Provincial Grand Superintendent of Royal Arch Masons for the same province.

99 The Rev. E.A. Smedley had succeeded Mr Browne as Vicar of Chesterton in 1836.

1 I.e. 'Thus saith the Lord, Let not the wise man glory in his wisdom, neither let the mighty man glory in his might, let not the rich man glory in his riches:'.

Mon. 10. Master & 7 Seniors (J. Brown, self, Moody, Sheepshanks, Thorp, Rothman & Martin) met in Chapel at ¼ to 9 to elect a Senior. — To my great surprise, Moody & Sheepshanks declared that they could not conscientiously take the oath as they could not discharge the duties & therefore begged to be passed over:— whereupon Archdeacon Thorp was chosen. — Walk with M. — Whist Club at Marquis's . . .

Tu. 11. At 7½ to Chapel to swear in Thorp:— to my great joy & Sedgwicks he consented to become Vicemaster, wch post would otherwise have fallen to Sedgwick or me . . .

Wed. 12. M. & I called on the Archdalls: also on Prof. Cumming to recover George's Pistols:— it turns out that James Cumming & the footboy[2] have broken the stocks of them!! . . .

Th. 13. M. & I called on Mrs Cumming — The Trinity Coll: farm[3] (on the Hills Road) set fire to, & a large quantity of wheat consumed: no doubt it was the act of an incendiary. — M. & I went to see a Picture of Mr Carus by Dawe[4] (at Mason's the printseller): — it is tolerably well painted, but bears very little resemblance: it is 10 years too young & far too serious. — Read loud 'Fair Maid of Perth'.

Sat. 15. Betsy returned today from her month's visit to Swansea. —Set Thompson (Upholsterer) about nailing crimson cloth to protect my books. — M. & I walk in the Evening. — Began that dull work, 'Memoirs of Fr. Horner'.[5]

Th. 20. Dined at Impington Hall. Fly was ordered at ¼ to 6: at ¼ past 6 no fly had arrived, so (tho' it rained) I set off post haste to Hodgson & blew up him & his wife for his misdemeanour:— this was the 2d time, — on the former (a dinner at the Prests) I staid at home. — Kept all the company waiting ½ an hour . . . Swinny has just discovered a fresco painting of St Christopher at Impington:[6]— he told us the beautiful legend of St Christopher sinking under the weight of the child bearing the sins of the world.

---

2   The young domestic servant.
3   The farm was under lease to Col. Pemberton. In 1836 Mr. William Thurnall of Duxford when giving evidence to the commissioners appointed to investigate disturbances in Cambridgeshire was asked 'Have you had any fires?' — 'Yes in the village near me we had 13 fires in one year and a half and we had one lately at the north side of Cambridge'. . . 'To what do you attribute those?' — 'To the desperate state of the labouring class'. Although by 1844 draining and claying the land had led to an improvement in conditions, incendiarism remained a long-term and frightening problem. See also E.J. Hobsbawn and George Rudé, *Captain Swing,* (1969), pp.241-248.
4   Henry Edward Dawe (1790-1848) was a well-known painter and mezzotint engraver.
5   Francis Horner (1778-1817) exercised considerable influence as a political economist and managed to hold the attention of the House of Commons for hours on such dry topics as coinage and currency. *Memoirs and Correspondence of Francis Horner M.P.* was published by his brother in 1843.
6   Mr Swinney was the then owner of Impington Hall. 'Some highly interesting fresco paintings, one of a gigantic S. Christopher, have recently been laid bare' (Paley, *Ecclesiologist's Guide,* (1844), p.8). The fresco dates from the fifteenth century and is on the north wall of the church.

Mon. 24. Lucy's pet cat came home this morning (from her customary nocturnal rambles) with a brass wire round her neck: she had apparently got into a snare meant for a weaker animal & had had strength to break thro' it. — Lucy filed off the wire, & the beast swore & attempted to scratch her . . .

Tu. 25. . . . Visit from the Archdalls who (M & I being out) did our garden the honour of visiting it under the guidance of the gardener. — To Pampisford Hall to dinner.— The Master of Catharine was kind enough to take me in his carriage. We dined at 4 (to suit Dr Procter). The party consisted of 7; viz. our Host & Hostess (Mr & Mrs Parker Hammond) Mrs Nicholson (born Malin & sister of Mrs P.H), a very pretty Miss Malin about 18 (niece I presume of the other 2 ladies), & Edmund Mortlock. —We walked about the beautiful parterres, etc for ½ an hour before dinner:—the house was built by Hardwicke (the Architect of Goldsmith's Hall, of Mr Adeane's at Babraham, etc) — I enjoyed their little party very much: every body was in high good humour. Fire at tea, & then a rubber.

Wed. 26. Looked over a parcel of books in the Library. — Letter from Heywood begging me to review Hubers 'English Universities' for the Eclectic:[7]— wrote in answer, declining . . . Lucy went to the School feast of the Barnwell & New Town Sunday Sch. in Downing Gardens:[8]— she took with her 4 of her protégées Sarah Foulkes, Sarah Fordham, Caroline Howes & Betsy Howes. She was rather frightened about poor Foulkes who was pushed down by the crowd at the gate. — Of course Lucy & her flock did not arrive till 4½, the last bit of cake having been consumed at 4 & the last drop of tea about the same time! — She was very civilly addressed by the handsome wife of a Trinity Undergrad. (a Mrs Faulkner), & also by a Mrs Walters: they both were most communicative & were most eloquent in praise of Mr Perry, Mrs Owen & all the principal he-&-she-saints: the latter is suspected to be a Trinity Bedmaker! . . .

Sat. 29. . . . Jane Smith (our Cook) today left our service, to the great satisfaction of Margaret, who never could endure her uncomfortable manners: she is a woman of religious feeling, perfectly honest & quite steady:— she has naturally weak nerves, & is of a jealous temper:— her jealousy of the great favor shown to Betsy Edwards made her give warning:— she has had much domestic affliction, from the death of her father, & the suicide of her profligate brother (who was suspected, falsely I believe, of having poisoned his father) — She is now intending to set up as

---

[7] *The English Universities.* From the German of V.A.H. [Victor Aimé Huber]. An abridged translation, by F.W. Newman, 2 vols, (London 1843).

[8] On August 20 1840 Romilly had also accompanied Lucy to 'Downing to the Feast given to the Barnwell Sunday School:— 500 of them: boys arranged on one side, girls on the other: after tea & singing (wch they did very indifferently) an allegorical grace about Manna the children went to their sports in wch the teachers &c joined, the boys to Football, the girls to thread-the-needle, &c. — Lucy & I & our protégée attached ourselves to Mrs Owen: we were joined by Lady Harnage, Mrs Scholefield & the Prof. &c: we drank tea under a tent.'

a mantua maker.[9] — Our new Cook arrived by the Beehive:— she came inside & paid inside fare, there having been no outside place. — She is very ugly, talks broad Scotch, is past 30 & is called Sarah Ironsides: she is happily of a very cheerful temper:— she makes most ridiculous curtseys. — Read loud A. of Geierstein.[10]

Wed. 2 August. Great robbery of Plate at Jesus Butteries. All the morning arranging my books: gave Hoppett 10/— & Mrs Carpenter 20/— for the trouble they have had in the grand bustle[11] . . .

Sat. 5. Had an interview with Bowtell to talk with him about seeing his daughter who is now so irrevocably a Papist that she is going into a Convent.[12] — Wrote to Miss Cotton an account of my conference (wch was at her suggestion):— Miss Bowtell says she is prepared to sacrifice every thing for religion, *the very hair of her head,* wch I presume therefore is fine. — Wrote to Lodge to ask leave for Bowtell to go abroad with Deighton,[13] the body of Bowtell being to be supported by Deighton & the mind of D. by B. Cards at Pagets.

Sun. 6. . . . M. & I walked in the Evening half way to Cherry Hinton. — Lucy went to St Mary's in the Evening & heard the whole service (except the 1st ½ of the prayers for wch she was too late) by Carus. The maids were also at Church, so I clambered in at the Kitchen window, never dreaming of Lucy having left the garden door open when there are so many thieves about. — Wrote to G.T.R.

Wed. 9. M. & I voted against walking in the morning as the air was very sultry. — About 4½ in the afternoon came on a storm of thunder & lightning which was accompanied by the most awful hail that I ever witnessed, or perhaps was ever witnessed in this country:[14] it came driving along with irresistible violence from the N.N.E & made havoc of all the windows that were exposed to it. We had not presence of mind enough to

9   I.e. a dress-maker
10   Sir Walter Scott's *Anne of Geierstein* (1829).
11   On 17 July Romilly had set 'Painters, Paperers & Plasterers to work in my rooms'.
12   Father Wolfrey had done his work well. Many fathers at this time feared the priest not only for the moral dangers to which popular belief thought he might expose a daughter, but also because of his role as a rival authority.
13   Lodge, as University Librarian, would have to give permission for the Library Keeper, Bowtell, to have unexpected leave of absence. Bowtell, the nephew of the great bookbinder, was a member of the Library staff for 35 years and it was not the first time that he and Deighton the bookseller, had been abroad together. (See McKitterick p. 498).
14   John Glaisher, Senior Assistant at the Observatory and younger brother of James the distinguished meteorologist, recorded that many of the hailstones 'measured an inch in diameter: some were even larger . . . They fell as closely as the drops from a water-spout and this . . . caused them to do immense destruction . . . Midsummer common was one sheet of water, in the midst of which a burst drain boiled up like a miniature Icelandic geyser . . . birds, even rooks and pigeons, were killed in large numbers, and picked up in the country in all directions . . . The effect on the crops where the storm was most violent was very remarkable. In some instances the straw was actually beaten down and broken up into little pieces almost as if it had been *chopped,* and the ears were as bare as if they had been regularly thrashed'. See the article headed 'Terrific Tempest' in *The Cambridge Chronicle* 12 August 1843.

think of shutting[15] the windows of the dining room & study, which we might have saved. We found afterwards that scarcely any body had more thoughtfulness than ourselves. — Our breakage was as follows: 6 panes in dining room, 3 in the study, 8 on the staircase, 4 in the Kitchen, 4 in my bedroom, 3 in the Attics, & the skylight entirely smashed. — The flowers in the garden & the fruit on the trees were ruined by the Hail. — A flash of lightning set Bowtells chimney on fire, but it was soon extinguished. Happily King's Chapel did not suffer: very little damage was done in the Public Library & Senate H. — about 20 panes in each. — Dr Clark had 170 panes broken. The Churches suffered but little: St Pauls (close to us) seemed most damaged. — Had to sleep in the spare room.

Th. 10. M. & I called on Mrs Clark & heard the account of their sufferings from the storm. The Town presents a very curious & distressing spectacle from the shattered windows & desolated gardens . . .

Fri. 11. . . . With much exertion I induced our Glazier to put in the panes in my bedroom yesterday, but I know not when I shall get the others repaired as there is not ¼ glass enough in Cambridge to mend what is broken . . .

On 15 August Romilly went by coach to Wisbech, among his travelling companions being W. Mortlock, 'who made himself the laughing stock of all the passengers by his mode of talking (constant repetition of 'you know', enquiring every body's business & telling his own'). The Registrary dined with the vicar, Mr Fardell, in a large party of forty, so large in fact that they had to sit down in two halves, he being in the 'grand half' and seated on Mrs Fardell's left. The following morning he walked over to Leverington where he found the fine church 'dreadfully neglected'. 'In a side chapel here', he noted, 'is a credence table, the only one I ever saw.'[16] 'The clerk was a man of profound ignorance:— I asked him what sort of dissenters there were in the parish & I could get no answer from him but 'that they chose to be buried in a different Churchyard'. After his visit to Leverington he went to make some purchases at the bazaar which was being held in Mr Fardell's grounds for the erection of a chapel in the new cemetery; '1s. was paid for entrance & £66 was taken at the gate.' As there had been a sharp shower of rain, the grass was covered with puddles, and the women, Romilly noticed, were 'very draggletailed'. Among the stallholders were Lady Hardwicke, Mrs Fardell, and Mrs Greaves Townley; the diarist himself bought 'a very clever coloured print of Mr Gale Townley's churchwindow for 10/— and a pair of carpet shoes for 20/-'. He noticed too that a model and an engraving of the new chapel, simply and elegantly designed by Willis, were on sale. In the evening he dined again at the vicarage in a huge party of 60, though the numbers must have been larger than was expected since '14 of us had to have a table improvised for us in the library.' Afterwards there was a grand evening party, at which the numbers rose to 150, and a ball: 'Lady Hardwicke sang 2 songs & the pretty Mrs. Jones also sung [sic]; but her singing was very flat after the brilliancy of Lady Hardwickes.' The culmination of the ceremonies, on 17 August, can only be described in Romilly's words.

15 Romilly writes 'shutting' but 'shuttering' would make more sense.
16 A small side table, sometimes placed near the altar by high churchmen to hold the bread, wine and water to be used at the Eucharist. The credence table installed by the Camden Society in the Round Church in Cambridge in 1845 was one of the causes of the undoing of the Society. (See also 25 July 1844).

Th. 17. A grand summer day with a bright sun & a boiling heat. — Mr
Fielding, Mr J.G. Fardell (nephew of the Vicar & Incumbent of Sprotbury)
& I breakfasted together at the Inn. — Then to Church where there was full
service: one of the Curates Mr King, read prayers, & the Vicar preached
from Is. XXVI. 19: a worthless sermon: there must have been 2500 people in
the Church & he raised only £53. The singing & playing were charming: the
Ely Organist & Choir being the performers: they sang the Dettingen Te
Deum, Plead thou my Cause, & the Hallelujah Chorus. I should have said
that at breakfast time we were most agreeably surprised by hearing a band
playing 'the roast beef of O.E.' & on looking out of windows saw 4 Cooks
carrying a Baron of Beef decorated with flowers, wch was to be part of the
Vicarage dinner today. — After the Church Service we went to see the 1st
stone laid of the Cemetery Chapel: the ceremony began by one of the
Curates (Mr Jackson, engaged to Miss Elinor Fardell) reading Joh XX; Ld.
Hardwicke then made a speech concerning the honor paid to his Lady who
was about to lay the 1st stone:— the 100th Ps. was then sung by the Ely
choir, etc., Lady H performed her part of the ceremonial, & the whole
concluded with a prayer from the Vicar (wch I did not hear):— it was
awfully hot during the whole of this proceeding:— I should have said that
there was a long procession headed by the Vicar etc followed by singing
men & boys chanting the Sicil. Mariners hymn,[17] all the sunday school
children & a long train of carriages. After this all the children came into the
Vicarage grounds & were fed with penny buns. — All these doings
consumed the time till past 3 when it was too late to keep my engagement of
going over with Mr Fielding to see the Upwell window.[18] — At 5 we dined
under Canvas, a very large party, about 100: the Baron made a grand
appearance at a separate table of his own:— he was presided over (O!
horrible!) by the Butcher who killed him & the Cook who roasted him. —
This was a dinner to people of all persuasions; a great no. present were
dissenters from the Church, but they all agreed in their esteem for the Vicar
& their appreciation of his good cheer. The Host gave the healths of the
Queen, etc very well indeed: in proposing Ld & Lady Hardwicke he made
rather too warm a eulogy of their virtues (as they were present); however Ld
Hardwicke paid him in coin & made him not only the beau ideal of a Vicar
but the composer of the best sermon ever writ by mortal pen:— it could not
have been that one wch we heard this morning, but Mr F. imagined it to be
so intended & acceded to the request of Ld H that he would publish it:— if

---

[17] The Sicilian Mariners Hymn was introduced into this country about 1800 and became
very popular. It is printed as follows in a contemporary hymn book. 'O Sanctissima O
Puiissima dulcis Virgo Maria. Mater a mater intemerata ora ora pro nobis'.

[18] The only window mentioned by Pevsner in St Peter's Upwell is the ninetheenth-century
East window in the Chancel.

Mr F. had any reputation as an author of sermons this will not add to it.[19] — I was amused with the 9 cheers for Lord & Lady H. being followed by a 10th for their pretty little girl, Lady Agneta. Ld Hardwicke is a finished speaker, & was happy in his efforts this Evening both serious & jocose:— it would perhaps have been better if he had omitted politics in so mixt & large an assembly:— there was much good feeling in his speech & the Vicar's towards the Dissenters of whom many were present. An unhappy lady (Mrs Maul) near me (in the midd. of Ld. H's speech) broke out into hysteric sobs & behaved with all the wildness of a madwoman:— to my surprise it created no sensation, so intent was everybody upon the Oratory of the Ld Lieutenant. — We then went to a Concert arranged by Mr James [Janes] the Ely Organist & performed by the Ely Quire: it consisted principally of Catches, Glees & Madrigals by Stevenson, Bishop etc & the music in Macbeth. — It was very well performed. — Then came fireworks (of Mr Decks)[20] in the Market place wch went off very well, the Night being perfectly dry. — So far so good: now comes the mishap. — In returning to the Vicarage alone I tried to make my way thro the Offices as I had seen done by young Mr Fardell in the day time: & in so doing fell down into the Beer Cellar, the mouth of wch had been left uncovered; the fall was 7 or 8 feet & I hurt myself a good deal: I fortunately after wandering about a short time met a Servant come to draw beer, who escorted me to the upper regions, where I had a basin of water & some tea: I was a good deal stunned & felt much strain'd. However I laughed it off, & told them to go & look whether any body else was caught in the trap: to be sure it is rather curious having an uncovered mouth of a Cellar like the pitfalls of Louis XI at Plessis Les Tours:[21]— I now designate myself a Monk of La Trappe. — I heard Ld and Lady H sing a Spanish song & then hobbled off to my hotel; there I met Mr Fielding who had contrived to walk into the Duckpond close to the back entrance of the Vicarage & was in a pretty state!

Fri. 18. On attempting to get up (after a feverish bad night) at 6½ to return to Camb. I found myself utterly unable to walk, & therefore went to bed again & sent for a Surgeon: he found that I had violently strained the muscles of the knee & clapped me on 8 leeches: I never saw such obstinate leeches, it was at least ½ hr before one would bite so unfleshly a part . . . I had exhausted my books (Mackintosh's England, Plautus's Rudens &

---

[19] The *Cambridge Chronicle* reprinted Mr Fardell's fulsome dedication of his sermon to Lord Hardwicke. It contained the following sentence: 'The pious devotion which marked her (Lady Hardwicke's) whole conduct could not be otherwise than what it was, the theme of universal admiration, and must have left the foot-print of satisfaction indelibly impressed on the minds of all present'.

[20] The fame of Isaiah Deck, Guy Fawkes to his friends, as a pyrotechnist was obviously not confined to Cambridge. For many years he organised firework displays for special occasions and his artistry was commented on many times in R.C.D. The Decks' chemist's business was established on Market Hill before 1800. See Sara Payne's *Down your Street* Vol.I, (1983), pp.120-1.

[21] During the last years of his life Louis XI lived, and in 1483 died, in the cavernous château of Plessis-les Tours just west of Tours.

Erasmus's Colloquies) & was obliged to send to the circulating Library . . .
A ball at my hotel at wch the Vicar danced: a great hubbub up to 5 o'cl. in
the morning, when some of the ball folks . . . sang God save the Q. 3 times
& paraded round the Market with a band of music one of them wearing a
washhand basin for a hat: they must have been mad drunk'.[22]

Next day the vicar's nephew discovered that Romilly was still in Wisbech and he
was removed to the vicarage. That night he dined in a party of 15, largely members
of the family. One of the vicar's daughters, 'the pretty Miss Elinor', was engaged to
another member of the party, the curate of Wisbech St Mary 'greatly to the
annoyance of the Vicar who says he will never perform the ceremony for them:—
his unpardonable crime is poverty, but he is also redhaired and vulgar'. On
Sunday, 20 August, Romilly went to church twice; in the morning the Vicar
preached quite well, but in the evening one of the curates preached 'so dull a
sermon that I had the greatest difficulty in keeping my eyes open.' On Monday he
rose very early and was back in Cambridge by one o'clock. His knee still gave him
trouble and he had to buy himself a stick 'as I hobble awfully'.

Romilly remained in Cambridge slightly over a week before leaving on 30
August for London. He again stayed at Wood's Hotel and as usual spent his
evenings at the theatre. He saw Charles Matthews, Madame Vestris, and Farren at
the Haymarket though 'I thought Farren's acting so indelicate that I would not stay
for the last piece, a farce of Buckstone's called 'Shocking Events' in wch he was also
to play.' On the last day of August he visited an exhibition of cartoons in
Westminster Hall, the best of which were eventually to decorate the walls in the
Houses of Parliament. The subjects were generally historical or illustrative of
Milton and Shakespeare. The scriptural pieces were few; 'one was oddly
catalogued, *Satin,* Sin & Death:— the painting was as bad as the spelling'. Later the
same day he went by water to see Brunel's Thames tunnel between Rotherhithe and
Wapping which had been opened on March 25 1843 '. . . The Toll is 1d in the
Tunnel:— at the foot of the flight of steps on each side of the river there is music: at
one side a man playing the harp: on the other 2 German women playing the Fr.
horn and Clarionet:— I thought the effect delightful'.

On 1 September Romilly left London for Brighton. The train journey was
enjoyable and the scenery lovely; among the places he noticed were 'the
disfranchised Gatton' and the viaduct near Cuckfield 'adorned with a most elegant
balustrade'. At Brighton station 'the distribution of the luggage was novel to me: all
ones luggage is marked with the same number: mine was 24: one stands . . . round
a table under ones own individual number, & upon producing one's ticket receives
every package marked with that number'. At pretty Mrs Wells's boarding house,
dinner was 'at 5½: party 23: a majority of women; only 2 young & none good
looking'. The party did, however, include a Trinity man, John Guthrie, and on the
first evening Talbot (also of Trinity) 'joined us & we had a very agreeable walk &
talk'. All through his stay the weather was very fine and hot. He went bathing and
walked on the pier, which was decked with flags in honour of the royal children
who were staying at the Pavilion. He lay for long hours on the beach, reading
Erasmus' *Colloquies* and Rousseau's *Emile.* In the evenings he played whist and
chess, defeating at the latter game another visitor who had beaten everyone else, but

22 On 21 September an angry letter to the editor of *The English Churchman* contained the
following sentence 'To dance and to let off fire-works at the hour of midnight in the
presence of a large concourse of people, shouting and yelling, and that for the professed
object of obtaining funds for the building of an edifice *where the service for the dead is to be
performed* — are performances more suited to a heathen than to a christian community.'

whom he found 'a whale among the minnows'. On Sunday, 3 September he went to church three times. In the morning he heard the celebrated and much loved Evangelical preacher H.V. Elliott, who discoursed on the profanation of the Sabbath, and made a 'violent & just tirade against Railway Excursions on Sunday'.[23] The afternoon sermon at another church was rather disappointing, but in the evening he heard Joseph Sortain preach one of the most striking sermons he had ever listened to. Though he preached in Lady Huntingdon's chapel, the first to be built for Lady Huntingdon's Methodist-linked Connexion, Sortain wore vestments and used the liturgy. His address, which was extempore, displayed 'eloquence of the highest order', and Romilly found nothing in it which displayed bad taste or which he wished omitted, though it was given with great speed and impetuosity. The chapel was crammed, and the heat was appalling; 'the moisture was streaming down the walls and no quantity of mopping checked the perspiration in my head'.

Romilly saw more of Elliott than merely hearing him preach. They had a long talk about Sunday railway trips at half-price 'to a place called Hassocks 9 miles off:— all the worst part of the population flow thither'. They also visited a school for poor clergymen's daughters, called St Mary's Hall, which Elliott had founded. This had been opened seven years earlier; the designs had been made gratuitously by Basevi and the buildings and grounds had cost £10,000. The pupils numbered 100 and the basic fees were £20 per annum; the whole place, Romilly considered, was very clean and comfortable as well as having 'an extraordinary air of propriety and decorum'. Each girl had a separate bed divided off from the others in the dormitory by curtains; their uniform was a grey print dress, 'very neat: high gowns, perfectly decorous'. Part of the curriculum consisted of 'Callisthenics' gymnastic exercises with hoops and bars, which Romilly thought in general pretty and elegant. He was less certain about one exercise in which 'each girl had a wooden machine (like a racket with the centre part taken away) stuck into her bosom & making a frame for her face: those that were handsome of course looked so much the more piquantes from the bizarrerie of this mask, but the plain ones looked frightful; wearing this machine to throw out their chest & keep their head back they were regularly drilled like soldiers.' Ordinary dancing was not permitted, as the callisthenics teacher was a former dancing mistress who had joined the Plymouth brethren, and now looked on dancing as a great sin; 'she does not think Callisthenics so near akin to dancing as I do.' 'Very similar to this institution,' Romilly noted, 'is the Boy School for sons of the clergy at Marlboro wch is just come into operation: it is for 200 & the charge is £30!'[24]

On 6 September Romilly spent 'almost all the morning lying in the broiling sun on the beach reading Erasmus'. September 7 and 8 were the last days of his holiday and the entries for them deserve to be quoted at length.

[23] Romilly's views on Elliott's sermons had greatly changed. On 5 February 1832 Elliott preached in Cambridge and Romilly's diary was very critical of his sermon in general . . . 'A great deal of bad taste, talking about 'Parades & Bands playing Opera Tunes and Waggons plying on a Sunday etc: An indecent attack upon Paley & Whately: allusion to Cholera & an undue allusion to Politics'. Elliott was in the forefront of the battle for the strict observance of Sunday.

[24] 'The main aim of the founders was to provide education at a low cost for clergymen's sons. They were to form two-thirds of the total number of pupils and to pay thirty guineas a year. The 'lay' boys paid more'. (John Roach, *A History of Secondary Education in England 1800-1870* (1986) p.165).

Th. 7.   Bathed in the sea before breakfast. Brighton is in great excitation this morning as the Q. is expected to land on her return from France[25] . . . accordingly the Pier was closed to the Public: the Royal Children & suite went down at 10, being their 1st walk on the pier: I looked at them thro the Telescope in our Drawing Room: the P. of W. was dressed in a light frock & red sash & with a red rosette in his hat: the Princess Royal was in a green frock & straw bonnet:— I did not observe the little Princess Alicia, tho very likely she was in the arms of one of the attendants:— the other 2 children seemed to enjoy themselves very much & trotted about with all the eager curiosity of childhood. — Wrote to the women. — A very idle day: could not sit for ½ hr together for fear the Queen should arrive just at that time. — The Queen's beautiful steam-yacht (Victoria & Albert) reached B. about 3: it being nearly low water the steamer could not come alongside the pier but the Queen was rowed to the Pier stairs in a 10 oared boat: the stairs & staircase were covered with red cloth: the Mayor & all the B. clergy were on the Pier to welcome the Queen:— the Public were excluded today till after the Queen had quitted the Pier: I got a good telescopic view of the Queen as she was walking down the Pier with P. Albert & the P. de Joinville[26], & was quite close to the Royal carriage as it drove along the Steyne & saw the Q. perfectly. — The sight of today was a very interesting one; the weather was lovely & the place was swarming with people: the seaview also was most striking, there were 12 steamers, 4 line of battle ships & countless boats, — such a display as B. probably never before witnessed. — The manning of the yards, firing salutes, decoration of vessels, houses & even bathing machines with flags, produced a most striking effect. — The Q. was looking in perfect health & seemed a little browned by her voyage. — After the Royal party had quitted the Pier the public were admitted as usual: I followed the multitude there to get a near view of the Q's Yacht & the little fleet that accompanied it:— there were 2 French steamers; one (the P. de Joinville's) fired a royal salute. — In the Evening there was a very slight attempt at an illumination viz, I saw one Star, one Crown, one V.A, & perhaps had I walked all over the Town might have seen a few more. — At night one man of war was beautifully illuminated, giving the outline of the ship & rigging:— it lasted about 10 minutes:— 2 others also but not very successfully:— from other vessels rockets were thrown up & blue lights burned. — Played whist unsuccessfully. lost 8/-.

Fri. 8.   Bathed in the Sea before breakfast. — While at breakfast it was announced that the Q. the P.A. & P. de Joinville were on the Pier: I immediately took a view of them thro the Telescope & then planted myself

[25]   Louis Philippe's daughter Louise was married to Queen Victoria's uncle Leopold I King of the Belgians, and the royal couples' visits to Château d'Eu in 1843 and 1845 helped to cement the Entente Cordiale with France. The meeting at Eu, to the north of Dieppe, was the first visit of a reigning monarch to France since the time of Henry VIII.
[26]   The Prince de Joinville was the third son of Louis Philippe and in 1840 had brought the remains of Napoleon from St. Helena to France.

at the Pier gate to see them drive thro. Nothing could be more simple & in better taste: The 3 royal people were in an open carriage & pair: the servants were in undress liveries (dusky with a red cord over the shoulder & back): the Queen quite simply dressed (yellow gown & white bonnet without feather) with a very small green parasol:— P. de Joinville sat by the Queen: the only approach to state was a couple of outriders . . . Met the Miss Ouvrys & walked home with them. — Then lay under the Pier for 2 hours reading the *Emile* . . .

On Saturday, 9 September, having taken 'a farewell bathe in the sea' and paid his bill (£3.19.0 for 8 days), Romilly left Brighton reflecting that he could never in his life recollect more glorious weather. The train took him to Swindon where the station refreshment room was 'the most magnificent I have seen on any railway' and thence to Cirencester. The last stage of the journey was by coach 'thro 15 miles of beautiful scenery' to Cheltenham where he recorded that he had 'travelled about 170 miles today'. He stayed there over the week-end at the 'Queen' hotel, 'the most magnificent I ever was in'. On Sunday, 10 September he sat down to dinner at 5.30 in 'a superb saloon: 34 of us: I was Vicepresident: a very agreeable party of well mannered men & women'. The same day he went twice to hear the prominent Evangelical preacher, Close, whom he described as 'a prodigious favourite and when he married the Ladies furnished his house. He is a pudding faced unintellectual looking man with large coarse features: he is very fair & has a fine head of brown hair wch is (I am told) curled daily.' Romilly was disappointed with Close's lack of dignity and his preaching which he found dull and repetitive; moreover the sermons were long, 70 minutes in the morning and 50 minutes in the evening. The church, he noted, was large with a striking tower and spire and 'one good round window', though it had an 'awful quantity of galleries'[27]. The singing he found very good.

Part only of Monday, 11 September, was spent in Cheltenham. He took a walk in the Montpelier Gardens and bought himself a cotton umbrella, 'my silk one having got broken in the railway carriage'; later in the day he travelled by coach to Hereford to stay with his old friend the Bishop, riding outside and reading Horace on the way. He found a happy friendly party at the Palace, and he very much enjoyed his five day's stay there. One evening 'Ingle kept us in a continued roar of laughter with his stories . . . He told us an infinitude of ghost stories — we did not get to bed till past 12'. He found his hostess, Mrs Musgrave, and her sister, Mrs Taylor 'two very pretty fairskinned affable ladies'. He paid a number of visits to neighbouring country houses, admired the pictures which they contained and commented on the beauty of their grounds and of the scenery generally. He attended a great missionary meeting at the Town Hall, presided over by the bishop, which was addressed by Archdeacon Robinson (formerly of Madras) 'in the highest style of impassioned eloquence: every word seemed to come from his heart. He spoke of the 4 great fields for exertion, viz. N. America, the W. Indies, Australia & India'. He was shown over the cathedral, which was then under repair, by the dean; the architect, Mr Cottingham, 'explained to us everything with regard to the giving way of the tower, all his own devices for its reparation & for removing all the patchwork upon the original design of the Cathedral. The skreen before the

---

[27] The population of Cheltenham more than doubled during Close's incumbency and he was responsible for the erection of five district churches, with schools, in the town. The Cambridge Camden Society also disliked galleries because they 'were never admitted into ancient churches', but they were of course needed by growing congregations. See J.F. White *The Cambridge Movement*, 1962.

beautiful EE [Early English] Lady Chapel is now removed & the works are to be finished by the end of 1844'.[28]

He returned to Cirencester outside on the Mazeppa coach on Saturday, 16 September; it was a lovely day in which 'the beautiful scenery appeared to the greatest advantage' . . . 'especially the view from the top of Cotswold down on Cheltenham'. He got to London that night, and on the Sunday he again went to hear Baptist Noel in the morning and to the Abbey in the afternoon. The singing there he again thought fine, but noted that 'the Vergers hurry one out . . . very uncivilly.' On Monday 18 Romilly 'Sallied out before breakfast to buy a Birthday present for M. for next Monday' and then returned to Cambridge 'by Telegraph at ¼ to 11'.

Mon. 18. . . . Wrote to Frank £10 . . . also to the Vicechancellor to apologise for having forgotten the Proclamation of Sturbridge Fair:— it took place this morning after a prodigious hue and cry after me and the Proclamation. Kingdon acted for me; the Proclamation was found in my office.

Tu. 19. Consulted Sudbury about the strain in my knee: thought the very little the matter with it was rheumatic & gave me a liniment. — Wrote to Miss Butcher (about her poor friend Miss Pearce who is at this moment without a home). Wrote in a great stew to Gosset about our Examination on Saturday:[29]— the Evening Post brought Gosset's instructions, so I wrote to him again. — Walk with M. after dinner to post my 2d letter. — At night read loud the new no. of Martin Chuzzlewit:— it is a coarse exaggeration of the faults of the Americans:— such publications from a popular writer are very wicked.

Sat. 23. Latin day of Fellowship Examination conducted by Gosset (& me nominally): Gosset made the selections & kindly presided in hall morning and evening. — 8 Fellowships to give away: 21 Candidates. — Court at Sturbridge Fair where Earnshaw enacted Commissary:[30] received fees from only 11:— Court adjourned till Tuesday. — The University Grace abolished the eating part of the Ceremony 18 months ago. The Taxors however (Woodham & Edleston) treated us with oysters at their own expense. — Gosset came to my rooms at 7 & over our coffee & wine we

<hr/>

[28] 'The condition of the central tower, the East wall of the Lady Chapel and other parts of the structure was so insecure that a general restoration was undertaken in 1842-49 under Cottingham'. (Royal Commission on Historical Monuments, *Herefordshire,* I (South-West), p. 91.)

[29] I.e. the Fellowship examination. The examination consisted of Classics, Mathematics, and under the title Metaphysics, of papers in the History of Metaphysics, Moral Philosophy, Political Economy, International Law and General Philology.

[30] It was 'one of the duties of the High Steward or his deputy to hold a Court Leet, at which those found guilty of using weights and measures not sealed by the Taxors were fined'. (Winstanley p.128). The 2 Taxors were nominated by 2 colleges in a fixed cycle every year and had to examine and seal all weights and measures used within Cambridge and its suburbs. Each of the stamps for sealing was cut with the initial letters of the surnames of the Taxors of the day. John Cowling, the deputy High Steward in 1842, wrote that the whole machinery of the Court Leet was 'quite inadequate for the purpose at the present day' and the Borough Council contended that the Taxors' duties could be carried out far better by the ordinary police.

examined all the Verse compositions: finished them in time to go up to the Hills Road to sleep.

Sun. 24. Margaret very nearly recovered from her nervous excitement (occasioned partly by the heat of the weather but principally by overworking with Miss Corfield) . . . Lucy took Miss Corfield & Esther to Trinity where she had a long sermon from Hose (Text: 'Let not your good be evil spoken of') wch made her nearly mad; she suspected some treachery of Carus & rushed to St Mary's only just in time to hear the 'lastly' & the blessing. — Carus (as Chaplain to the Mayor) preached before the Corporation: but the papers did not announce it & he had never told us of this official duty.

Mon. 25. M's birthday:— she is happily now restored to her usual health by the departure of the sultry weather. — Gave her as a birthday Present a little or moulu canopy for holding a smelling bottle:— bought it at Harding's Pall Mall, from wch place Mrs Musgrave (the Bishopess) bought a similar one. — 3d day of Fellowship, Mathematics & Metaphysics by the Master. — The Master & Mrs Whewell took me in their carriage to dine at Fulbourn: besides host & hostess & their son (Tom Townley) & our 3 selves there were Miss Cotton & her sister Lady King, Miss King, Rev. Yorke & an unknown lady. — We had fires. — As we were driving into Cambridge at 11½ a man in a gig drove against us (we being on the right side) & upset himself:— he did not seem hurt. — Amused by driving thro the King's Court[31] etc up to the back of the Lodge: it seemed so magnificent having the great portals unbarred.

Wed. 27. . . . M & I called on the Mills where Dr Mill read to us (from the Christian Observer I think) a furious attack upon Fardell's Bazaar, sermon, ball etc. etc.[32] . . . Received from Frances Wilderspin an inlaid box for holding Letter Stamps . . .

Fri. 29. M. passed so bad a night that I called in Haviland: he prescribed 4 leeches to the temples & drafts *quantum sufficit:* he said he was not surprised that she was unwell, but the wonder was (after such sultry weather followed by very chill) that any body was well. — Visit from Miss Cotton, but she was not admitted as M was just going to have the leeches

[31] The court, now known as New Court, was so called because King George IV had contributed £1000 towards its building. It was begun in 1823 and designed by Wilkins. Additional undergraduate rooms were needed in Trinity because 'of the serious evils arising from the Lodging of great numbers of Young Men in the Town; which evils briefly are: increased expense; scanty accommodations, and consequent unhealthiness in some of the Lodging-Houses; and the impossibility of preserving the same degree of salutary superintendance and discipline' (from a circular soliciting subscriptions).

[32] It was not in the *Christian Observer* but in the high-church *The English Churchman* for August 31 1843. The anonymous author of the letter to the editor criticises in detail the impropriety and secular nature of the fund-raising events on each of the four days and concludes that 'every Christian is bound to protest against such unhallowed abominations as seem to have been practised at this Wisbech Carnival, under the pretence of Charity'. *The English Churchman* for September 14 supported the letter, and added criticisms of its own. If the paper received any letters defending the Carnival it did not print them.

applied. — Today was delicious, sunshine & west wind:— M. L. & I walked together . . .

Sat. 30. Margaret a little better today, tho nervous & headachy. — I was so busy about the Fellowship Examination all day that I could not walk with M . . . At 6 to the Lodge to elect the Fellows: at tea we had (besides Mrs Whewell) Mrs Carpenter who is painting a portrait of the Master: Mrs Carpenter is a plump goodlooking ladylike person of middle age.[33] — The 8 Vacancies were, 2 by death viz. G.A. Browne & H. Goulburn, 1 lawyer Bunbury, Conybeare, Forsyth & Vaughan by marriage, Evans & Field (College Incumbents). — We filled them up with Martineau, Richardson & W. Smith of the 3d year, Munro, Shaw, Denman & Mansfield of the 2d year, & Gray (3d Wrangler) of the 1st year.[34] — Poor Tom Robinson, in spite of all his exertions & his answering every paper, was found too feeble for Election.— this was his last time.

Sun. 1 October. . . . Poor Charlotte Elizabeth Mill (or Lotta as they called her) died today. This dispensation of Providence must be most heartbreaking to her Parents:— she was in her usual health on Monday last, but caught cold at Church that day, without however exciting any alarm. We paid a visit on Wednesday & there was not then the slightest uneasiness about her. — An awful instance of the uncertainty of life! —She was a sprightly, amiable girl of 12 & 25 days whom I much admired: she was fair & blue eyed like her Father:— she had grown much beyond her strength & was in appearance 15 or 16. — M. & I took a walk up the Hills Road.

Mon 2. Abbot the Surgeon died today — Dr Haviland paid 3rd & last visit to M. At ¼ to 9 to Chapel to elect the new Fellows. — Walk with M up the Hills Road to avoid meeting any body as her face is disfigured by the leeches:— of course met shoals who talked to us. — Dined at the Fellowship Dinner in the Combination Room with my brother Examiners. — Consulted Sudbury about the Lumbago with which I have been troubled. He sent a man tonight to rub some liniment into my back. — I slept in College.

Wed. 4. Betsy was today pronounced by Dr Paget to be suffering from Brow Ague. — Lucy this morning wrote to Mr Bernard of Custom House begging his aid in getting John Gilmour (who has just lost his father & with whom L. had been acquainted about 3 weeks) into the London Orphan

[33] Mrs Margaret Sarah Carpenter (1793-1872) was a portrait painter of considerable distinction. She constantly showed pictures at the Royal Academy and the portrait of Whewell was one of four exhibited by her in 1844. In 1866 'The late Rev. W. Whewell, D.D., Master of Trinity College; study from life for the picture exhibited in 1844' was the last picture which she showed there.

[34] A candidate had 3 chances of gaining a Fellowship during the 3 years between taking his first degree and his M.A. and success at the first attempt was rare. Only Scholars and Fellow-Commoners were allowed to retain their rooms in college and the majority of them took pupils. However, the candidates themselves were expected to work on their own and rarely continued to read with their private tutors.

Asylum. Lucy also this Evening went very spiritedly to the Hospital & got 6 Leeches for her poor suffering protégée Sarah Foulkes. Read loud Walpole's Letters & Cast. of Otranto.[35]

Th. 5. To the V. Chancellor to license Rowe (who has just ceased to be our Chapel Clerk) for keeping a spirit shop. — Good account from Lodge. — Wrote to him — sent a packet of books to Lady Cotton[36] — Abbot the Surgeon buried today: all the Physicians & Surgeons of the Town attended. — The Archdalls sent us a leash of birds . . . The following very clever rebus is ascribed to Macaulay

"cut off my head, the singular I act:
"cut off my tail, & plural I appear:
"cut off both head & tail, O wondrous fact!
"Altho the middle's left there's nothing there.

"What is my head cut off? a sounding sea:
"What is my tail cut off? a flowing river:
"And thro their mingling depths I fearless play,
"Parent of sweetest sounds, tho mute for ever.

— Cod —

Fri. 6. At 9 o'clock went to attend poor Charlotte Elisabeth Mill's Funeral. I found in the drawing room Dr & Mrs Frederick Thackeray, Francis & his sisters, & Mrs Wallich. — I was summoned into the Library where I found Dr & Mrs & Miss Mill, the Miss Gouldsbys & Master Gouldsby, etc.:— poor Dr Mill behaved with wonderful fortitude, & spoke to me in a tolerably firm tone of voice. — As the funeral was to be in St

---

[35] Horace Walpole, *Castle of Otranto* (1764).

[36] By the 1840's the University Library's Novel Room offered an infinitely greater variety of novels than the circulating libraries. J.E.B. Mayor (the University Librarian) noted crossly in 1865 that 'for years the principal work of the Library had been to compete with the circulating libraries to the waste of assistants' time and of money spent on rebinding'. The Cottons of Madingley Hall were voracious readers and as Romilly could borrow virtually any number of books he patiently and frequently sent off 'parcels of anything from half a dozen to eighteen volumes to them'. (See McKitterick, 22-3). Romilly's entry for 24 December 1853, the first day of the new Library quarter, reads as follows: 'I followed Lucy's advice & planted myself at the Library door 5' before 10: there were congregated about 20 persons waiting for the opening of the door . . . I placed myself quite close to the door & Rusby told me that I must run upstairs as hard as I could, for that everybody would try to pass me:— I made up my mind that nobody should do that:— so away we went helter-skelter I keeping ahead: I rushed into compartment Y & seized on Lewis Arundel & then turned to catch 'Heir of Redclyffe', but it was snapt up & so was 'My Novel':— I rather hope that Rusby carried off 'Heir of R.' as he said he was come to get a novel beginning with R. for a lady'. The Cambridge Free Library in the old Meeting House in Jesus Lane was not opened until June 1855 under William Ewart's Public Libraries Act. It began with 1,200 books which had to be read in the reading room, but three years later, no doubt to the relief of the University Librarian, the lending library was established. In 1862 this was moved to Wheeler Street.

Andrew's Ch. Yd & St And. Church is not yet consecrated,[37] an additional length was unhappily given to the ceremony:— Dr & Mrs Mill were chief mourners, then followed Miss Mill, the Miss Gouldsbys, the Governess, Master Gouldsby & myself: after these 10 came Dr & Mrs Thackeray &c. — It was a walking funeral. — We first went to Trinity Church where Archdeacon Thorp read the service extremely well, solemnly & with simplicity. — We then went to Gt St Andrews Ch. Yd where the service was completed. — It was the most afflicting funeral I was ever present at: the moans of Mrs Mill were heartrending:— it was most distressing to see how she & Miss Mill lingered over the grave & could scarcely be drawn away by Mill:— he behaved with the resignation of a true Christian. — At the door of her own house poor Mrs Mill was so much overcome that she was obliged to be lifted in. We none accompanied the family into the house except Mrs Wallich. — Walk with M. — Lucy passed the après-midi till tea-time painting a chaise wch she has bought for her Scotch-widow-protégée Mrs Gillmour's children . . .

Sun. 8. Our household rather sickly:— I very stiff with my knee, wch feels all in a flame:— M. poorly still from nervousness (tho Haviland paid a friendly visit yesterday & declares there is nothing the matter with her); Betsy still suffering from headache & brow-ague:— so that we 3 could not go to Church:— Lucy staid at home, because Mr Carus is gone to the North & the day was wet:— Sarah alone of the household to morning Church. . . Lucy went to St Mary's at 2 escorted by M. to the door (the day having cleared up): Lucy heard the new Hulsean, Mr Marsden preach:[38] she thought him too much of a jolly friar Tuck, — too much flesh & too little spirit. . . M read loud a sermon of Barrow: I read one of Massillon. Hare & partridges from Mrs T. Mortlock.

Sat. 14. Betsy recovered: — we ascribe her recovery very much to a mixture of Camphor & Laudanum wch Deck recommended. M. & I paid a visit to Mrs Archdall who has been very unwell. Poor Dr Bowstead (Bp of Litchfield) is dead: recovery having been apparently long hopeless one cannot regret his death. — Mr Perry ill with a bowel complaint which he caught in Ely Cathedral . . .

Sun. 15. M. & I to Trinity Church where Hose did all the duty: he preached insufferably from 1 Pet. 2.9 — M. & I then went thro the walks at the back of the Colleges & left Cards at Perry's, — who is better. — I should have said yesterday that Lucy sent home to her new protégée Mrs Gilmour

---

[37] The new church of St Andrew the Great, designed by Ambrose Poynter and built on the site of the mediaeval church, was consecrated only 13 days after Charlotte's funeral. An etching in Cooper's *Memorials* Vol.3 shows an extensive graveyard round the new church. (See the plate facing p.208).

[38] The duty of the Lecturer as set out in Hulse's will of 1789, was 'to preach and *print* 20 sermons in each year'. The salary was 'nearly £300 per annum' and the subject of the discourses was to 'shew the evidence for revealed religion, or to explain some of the most difficult texts or obscure parts of Holy Scripture — or both.' (*Cambridge University Calendar* 1843, p.136).

(a Scotch widow) a child's chaise, for which she made a most elegant little cushion at the cost of 3 days hard work. . . . Lucy went to Perry's Church at 3 where she heard Mr Ragland catechise the children: there is no sermon at this service. — All the Evening I read my Uncles Memoirs.[39]

Tu. 17. College Seniority to announce the intended visit of the Q. & Prince Albert on Wednesday the 25th inst.[40] — This is very glorious. — I was so busy that I could not come & walk with M, who in consequence never stirred out . . .

Sun. 22. M, L, Esther & I to Trinity Church where Carus preached from the Gospel (Ephes. 4.30): Edward came in for the Sermon, wch was very good, & accompanied with a great deal of graceful & varied action. — Exhibited my rooms to M. L. & Esther; Lucy had not seen my new carpet & curtains before. — Then took them into the Senate House, where Lucy had never been before!!!!: showed them all the preparations there. . .

Mon. 23. Began issuing Tickets at 10 for the Senate house: I was assisted by Bunch, Lodge & Cartmell: left off at 2½. Issued about 220 for Doctors & MAs & the same no. for Ladies:[41] the V.Ch. would not allow me to issue any tickets for Gentlemen today. The V.C to my great delight took the B.A's & Undergraduates off my hands & threw them on the College Tutors . . .

Tu. 24. Tickets from 10 to 2½ with the same kind aid as yesterday. — I previously called on the V.C. & assured him that there would be quite room for Gentlemen in the Pit of the S.H: he accordingly furnished me with a supply, & almost all the applicants of yesterday profited by it. Dined in Emmanuel Hall as Mr Foley's Guest: this was a dinner given by him as Rector of Cadbury to the College:[42]— I went away very early, as it seemed to be a long sitting with hard drinking . . . Read loud Mrs Brunton's Discipline.[43]

Wed. 25. Tickets from 10 to 12, aided by Lodge & Bunch. I gave my Lady's Ticket to Lucy (wch with Miss Vincents she gave to Carus) . . . At 1

[39] The *Memoirs of the Life of Sir Samuel Romilly* written by himself and edited by his sons were published posthumously in 1840. Sir Samuel committed suicide by cutting his throat with a razor four days after the death of his beloved wife. (See also Patrick Mead, *Romilly* (1968) pp.294-301.)

[40] The purpose of the visit was to confer the degree of LL.D. on the Prince, not as an honorary degree but under the old provisions for the admission of noblemen to degrees without examination. But the time for preparation was indeed short. The Vice-Chancellor in his address to the Queen on October 25th 'esteemed it a peculiar instance of your Majesty's royal favourable disposition, that your Majesty has been pleased to make this visit at a time when the occupations and business of the University are proceeding in their ordinary course, and so soon after the announcement of your Majesty's gracious intention that the University necessarily wears its usual aspect'.

[41] 'The raised seats on either side of the Senate-House and the west end of the gallery will be appropriated to Ladies'. (From the notice issued by the Vice-Chancellor on 21 October).

[42] North Cadbury, Somerset, was an Emmanuel College living and the Rev. Richard Foley had been a Fellow of Emmanuel from 1825 to 1842.

[43] Mary Brunton's novel *Discipline* was published in 1814 and reprinted three times.

the Bishop of Ely, Master of Christs, Lord Wriothesley Russell etc. came to my rooms to be ready for the Procession of the Address. — At 2¼ the Queen & P. Albert reached Trinity Gate: the V.Ch. Heads & Bedells were in attendance: the V.C. had the Maces laid down on a table,[44] & the Q. graciously not in words but by gesture ordered them to be taken up: the great Gate was thrown open & the Royal Standard hoisted on the top of the Tower: the Royal carriage then drove as far as the Sundial, & upon its stopping the V.C. &8 Seniors surrendered the College keys to the Q:— she took them in her hand & then graciously returned them:— by the way they were in their usual state & hung on a dirty leather strap.[45] — The Bursar carried them. The Royal carriage then drove to the Clock Tower & so to the door of the Lodge.— The Queen almost immediately showed herself at the window & was welcomed (as when she entered the College & when she stopped at the Dial) with rapturous applause.[46] — The Queen & Prince then went to Luncheon; & we arranged ourselves in a Procession, headed by the High Steward[47] (Lord Lyndhurst) & concluding with the under-graduates:— the head was at the Lodge door (looking S); the procession reached the N & E sides, & ended at the Queens Gate on the S.[48] — It was a most admirably conducted procession & tho we had to wait for a full hour (with no amusement excepting seeing the 3 travelling carriages retire & 3 State Coaches with State Liveries range themselves by King Edw's Gate) perfect silence was kept:— it was a very striking sight. — At ¼ past 3 the V.C. sallied forth from the Lodge[49] & put himself at the head of the procession wch now moved on to the Hall wch was used for a Presence Chamber. A canopy had been erected & a throne (viz. Bentley's Chair)[50]

44 No doubt to avoid handing all three at once to the Queen as had been done when Queen Elizabeth I visited Cambridge in 1564. These maces were presented to the University by George Villiers, Duke of Buckingham when he was Chancellor in 1626. The third Bedellship was abolished in 1863 after the death of Leapingwell.

45 'You never saw such an ample bunch of keys — large, ponderous and rusty — and strapped together by an old greasy bit of leather — thick enough to have bound the limbs of unshaven Samson, and looking as if it had been cut from the flank of a rhinocerus'. . . (Sedgwick in a letter of 30 October in Clark and Hughes, *II*, 58-9).

46 On Tuesday an order had been issued by the Vice-Chancellor 'that the *whole University* should assemble in Trinity Great Court at 1 on Wednesday . . . By 1 o'clock I think every man in the University of every grade was in the court all in full dress, the noblemen in their purple and gold, the doctors in scarlet and every man in a white tie and bands'. (From a lively letter from a Trinity undergraduate to his mother dated 28.10.43 and reproduced in *The Cambridge Review* of February 13, 1908).

47 The High Steward was expected to take a benevolent interest in the University, occasionally to visit it and if necessary act as its spokesman in Parliament. (Winstanley p. 98).

48 The Queen's Gate opens on to Trinity Lane and a statue of Elizabeth I sits in a niche above it.

49 'preceded by the Esquire Bedells & accompanied by the Registrary (carrying the Addresses)'. (See *Victoria and Albert at Cambridge. The Royal Visits of 1843 and 1847 as they were recorded by Joseph Romilly Registrary of the University*, edited by Prof. R.S. Walker and Dr. E.S. Leedham-Green).

50 'usually in the Henry VIIIth's drawing room'. See Romilly's *Account of the Visit of Queen Victoria* 1843. (*Misc. Collect.* 29).

prepared for the Queen: Her Majesty & the Prince had entered the Hall by the door from the Dais into the Lodge, & were standing under the Canopy. — The Gallery over the Skreens was filled with Ladies (among whom were L. M. R[51] & Miss Vincent) — The effect of this magnificent presence Chamber was incomparably more imposing than that at St James or Buckingham Palace. The Vicechancellor read the Addresses[52] with a loud clear voice; the Queens voice tho sweet & harmonious was scarcely loud enough: the Prince read his answer distinctly & well. — The young men behaved admirably:— tho the latter part of the procession must have known that the Addresses would be over before they reached the Hall they kept their places like well-disciplined soldiers:— the undergraduates were 6 or 7 abreast or there would not have been room for them to be ranged round the Court. Directly after the presentation of the Deputation[53] the Q. & P. returned to the Lodge thro the Master's door to the dais:— consequently the backing out was but for a short time.[54] — The Deputation consisted of V.Ch., High Steward, [and Heads except] the Provost who was waiting to receive the Q. at King's College Chapel, & the President of Queens, who wisely nursed himself at home) the Caput, Orator, Proctors, Bedells & Registrary. — Lucy & Miss Vincent were indebted to the kindness of Dr Peacock for getting into College today, & similarly to that of Mr. E. Foster Jun. tomorrow. — Immediately after the Addresses every body rushed to King's Chapel. I had only a ticket for antechapel. The Q. & P. sat with their backs to the Communion Table to the great scandal of the Puseyites:[55] — they had a faldstool before each of the Chairs, & the anthem was printed on white satin & had gold fringe & tassels. — After the Service was over I got into the Quire[56] & examined these accommodations for royal devotion:— there were stools placed for the Royal Attendants. — The Anthem was one of Mozarts 'Have mercy etc.': Pergolesi's Gloria in E. & Handels Coronation Anthem were also played. — I afterwards dined in

[51] I.e. Lucy Mary Romilly.
[52] For the texts of the Addresses see Cooper, 662-4.
[53] I.e. by the Registrary who was himself presented by the Vice-Chancellor.
[54] . . .'the members of the University (not wearing their eyes in that part of their persons where Argus is said to have carried a portion of his eye-establishment) are singularly clumsy in all retrograde movements . . . The odds were that [in backing out] we should come to a dead-lock, and be converted into one melancholy unwholesome mass of Academic jam' (Sedgwick in a letter of 30 October in Clark and Hughes, II, 59).
[55] . . . 'The authorities of King's College are proceeding to erect a throne for Her Majesty on the top of the altar steps of their beautiful chapel, and in such a position as absolutely to obscure the holy table itself . . . Nothing, I am convinced, would insure for our beloved Monarch greater popularity here than a refusal to accept a homage tendered to her in contempt, or at least in utter disregard, of His honour by whom Kings reign.' (Letter to the *Times* of 24 October from Vindex of Christ's College, Cambridge).
[56] Whilst Romilly was examining the choir the Queen and Prince visited Trinity Chapel which was hastily lighted for them. Four undergraduate noblemen held flambeaux so that the royal visitors could examine the statue of Newton. 'This group with the light reflected from their superb dresses, stiff with purple and gold, presented one of the most picturesque exhibitions which greeted her Majesty this day' (*The Cambridge Chronicle.* Saturday, 28 October).

Pembroke Hall with Arlett at 5½. — I went away (without going into the Combination) to distribute Tickets. — At 9½ I went to the Levee at Trinity Lodge:[57] I was too blind & too ignorant of the MA's to help the V.C in presenting them to the Q., but recommended Phelps (the Master of Sidney) as an assistant:— a great many were not provided with cards & occasioned some little embarrassment. I then went with Lodge, Lord Jermyn, &c, to see the Round Church which was lighted up. I thought the Illuminations (especially of Trinity & St Johns Gates) very pretty but I did not go to see the Triumphal Arch[58] & kept sedulously away from the fireworks on Parkers Piece. — Today M staid at home feeling rather poorly:— the maids were let go out, & M's companion was a little girl, a protégée of L's (Gilmour):— M. exerted herself so much to entertain the child that she brought on a nervous attack & sent for Haviland: next day Haviland pronounced her quite well & took his leave.

Th. 26. Declined dining with Eyres. To Chapel this morning: it was at 8 o'clock by way of accommodating the Queen if she should feel disposed to come: she however did not come. Her Maid of Honor Miss Stanley came & was by many of the youngsters taken for the Queen.[59] — Very busy afterwards distributing tickets: I have had that employment also every Evening. At 9¼ went to Trinity Lodge to take the Subscriptions of the Prince

57 This was held in King Henry VIII's drawing-room. The Vice-Chancellor did not know of the Queen's intention to hold a levee until the evening itself 'when hasty notice was sent to the Colleges:— in consequence many persons (Dr Mill etc) never heard of the Levee until it was over'. (See Romilly *Misc. Collect.* 29).

58 On the drive to Cambridge the royal cortege had passed under arches at Tottenham Cross, Waltham Cross, Ware and Royston 'where the High Street presented literally a canopy of flags and triumphal arches' and at what is now Brooklands Avenue before stopping at the arch at the entrance to Trumpington Street. This extended right across the street, was about 18 feet in depth and covered with laurel leaves and evergreens. 'On each side of the arch were splendid stars . . . and in large letters the words, 'Welcome Victoria' and here the corporation stood ready to receive her Majesty'. The mayor presented the corporation mace to the Queen and, preceded by the corporation, then walked by the side of her carriage as far as Trinity College. (*The Progresses of Her Majesty Queen Victoria and His Royal Highness Prince Albert in France, Belgium and England.* Published by William Frederick Wakeman 1844). On 30 October 1843 Prince Albert wrote to his mentor and dear friend Baron Stockmar, 'The enthusiasm of the students was tremendous and I cannot remember that we were ever received anywhere so well as upon the road to Cambridge (to which 2000 horsemen accompanied us) and in Cambridge itself'. And in *UP* 16 75 (10) Romilly records that the Queen's coachman is reported to have said that 'he had never been in such a well conducted mob and that he liked a mob of gentlemen'.

59 In 1843 Miss Stanley, who was Maid of Honour from 1842-62, was 22, the Queen 24.

for Matriculation & Degree:[60] — Archdeacon Thorp also was there to receive the P.'s signature as his Pupil: he desired the Prince to put the date: the P. looked up & said 'I think we have the 26th' — The Cong. in the S.H. was at 10. The company all stood: indeed there were no seats except for the Q. & P.:— the P. however stood all the time till he had taken his degree. — The V.Ch. ought to have asked the Q.'s permission to wear his cap & be seated in her presence: the M. of Magdalene suggested it to him, & (upon his agreement) the M. of Magd. desired the Ld Chamberlain (Ld De la Warr) to ask the Q's permission, wch was instantly granted:— similar leave ought to have been asked for the 2 Proctors Dr. Ollivant & Phelps (who was to have a Mandate DD)[61] but was not. — The Prince ought properly to have been brought from the end of the S.H. by a Bedell, but he stood all the time on the Platform:— he did not put his arms thro his Doctor's Gown but put it on like a Cloke:[62] — by the way he gave £5 to the person who put it on (who was the Masters servant, Taylor the School keeper being too infirm to undertake the office), & £10 to Johnson the University Marshall. The Orators speech had too much about 'Marcellus' & dwelt perhaps too strongly on the Prince's merit as The Father of the future king.[63] — The young men behaved extremely well: they gave rapturous applause to the Q. & P. on their entrance & exit:— they also gave 3 cheers for the P. of W, but upon the V.C. holding up his hand they became instantly silent. The P. is reported to have said afterwards, that the young men did not show such obedience at a place where he had recently received honors:— I cant

[60] 'At nine o'clock the Registrary and the Proctors attended at Trinity Lodge. They found the Prince and the Vice-Chancellor in the first drawing room. Archdeacon Thorp (Senior Tutor) was also in attendance to admit His Royal Highness a member of the College. The Registrary then put into the Prince's hands a copy of the Matriculation Declaration. The Prince signed his name. The Junior Proctor . . . then read the declaration to His Royal Highness, who (at its conclusion) read aloud the words 'Haec omnia in me [recipio et polliceor me fideliter esse praestiturum]'. The Registrary then opened the Subscription book and explained to the Prince . . . what he was about to subscribe. The Prince . . . after having looked at a few pages of the University Statutes . . . wrote his name in the Book of Subscriptions for Degrees'. The Prince could then proceed to his degree without further formalities. (See *Victoria and Albert at Cambridge*, cited in note 49 above.)

[61] On the initiative of the University a Mandate Degree could be granted by the Crown to a person not strictly admissible to it.

[62] 'The Prince was invested with the scarlet robe of a Doctor of Civil Law on the *steps* of the Platform and was presented by the Orator to the Vicechancellor . . . The boards containing the oaths were not forthcoming and the Vicechancellor had to improvise them. Neither was there a Bible to kiss so after some demur, Lord Arthur Hervey, who was there as a spectator, recollected that he had a little church service in his pocket, and produced it, and it was accordingly kissed twice by His Royal Highness and afterwards by the Rev. Mr Phelps.' (Stanley, *Twenty Years at Court*. ed. Mrs Erskine). Romilly in *Misc. Collect. 29* writes of Whewell's improvisation 'The oath of Supremacy was not completely accurate; but not one man in a thousand in such a presence could have done it comparably so well'.

[63] . . . 'Here our attention was diverted from the Orator to her Majesty, who having thus far patiently (for a lady) submitted to the irksomeness of hearing a speech in Latin, addressed herself to Earl De La Warr . . . and during the remainder of the speech her Majesty's attention seemed to be occupied in viewing the crowded galleries and the architecture of the building.' (*The Cambridge Chronicle* Saturday 28 October).

substantiate this on the authority of any person who heard him. — Vivat Regina Vivat Princeps was shouted by the youngsters in the Gallery on the Exit of the royal persons. — I then went to Sedgwick's Museum where very few persons but myself got in in the Royal Suite:— the Queen was much struck with the fossil elk: the Prince paid a good deal of attention to the specimens; upon S. pointing [out] to him the [Solenhofen] stone (wch is used for lithography, & saying that it came from the P's country the P. disclaimed any knowledge of [illegible; ms. worn] but pointed out to the Queen the Libellula[64] in it. — Sedgwick made a very animated exhibiter:— on showing certain bones he said 'we don't know where they came from; I think they are come on purpose to do homage to your Majesty.' The Q. then went to the Public Library (the gownsmen strewing their gowns as they had done last night at the entrance to Trinity Chapel, — Edward Allen being then one of them):— I escorted Mrs Challis & Miss Copsey, into the Library, to wch very few were admitted. — Lodge did the Honors: by the way the Queen walks a great pace & had got to the last room of the old library before Lodge overtook the Royal party & making his bow offered to escort them into the New Library.[65] The Lord Chamberlain (Ld. De La Warr) said 'Mr Lodge, the Librarian, I think?' — Lodge exhibited the Codex Bezae[66] Gospels in Anglo-Saxon &c.: the Q. said 'I think the Paléographie is not finished'.[67] Lodge ventured to set her right & told her it had been completed a 12 month. After this the Royal party went to King's Chapel & then to St John's; — but I gave up any more Queen-hunting & went home to take out Margaret.[68] I took her thro the main streets & showed her all the triumphal arches, decorations, lamps for illuminations &c: we stood quite close to the Prince as he drove thro the Court & saw him capitally, but she never saw the Queen at all. In Trinity Coll. hall we met Lucy & Miss Vincent: the Canopy (under wch the Q. & P. stood to receive the Addresses) was still there. I then took M. into the S.H to see the Canopy

---

[64] . . . 'neither of them seemed in a hurry, and I think the Queen was quite happy to hear her husband talk about a novel subject with so much knowledge and spirit. He called her back once to look at a fine impression of a dragon-fly which I have in the Solenhofen slate'. (Sedgwick in a letter of 30 October, in Clark and Hughes, II, 63).

[65] Only the north side of the new University (Public) Library had been completed by 1843.

[66] This fifth century version of the Gospels was presented to the University by Theodore Beza in 1581.

[67] The Queen's remark is puzzling. The Gospels are not illustrated and for this reason the Queen may have thought them unfinished. Lodge, unused to such simple assumptions, may have misunderstood the Queen and thought she referred to a work issued in parts which Professor R.I. Page suggests may be de Wailly's Eléments de paléographie (Paris, 1838).

[68] After the visit to St. John's the Queen returned to Trinity. Prince Albert, however, went to Christ's, Sidney, Jesus and Magdalene. They then together visited Corpus and the Round Church where 'they were received by the President of the Camden Society . . . the Incumbent . . . & the Churchwardens'. (Romilly, Misc. Collect. 29).

there — The Q. & P. left Camb. for Wimpole about 5.[69] — Lucy spent all today in company with Miss Vincent as she did yesterday:— yesterday she began the day at Mrs Simpson's (having declined Mrs Haviland) & seeing the Queen most imperfectly as she drove by she posted away to Trinity with Miss Vincent & (thro the influence of the Dean of Ely) got into the Hall & saw the Addresses presented. Today she started at 10 with Miss Vincent & went with her & Mrs Simpson to the Fosters Bank, saw the Town Address (beautifully got up),[70] & by Mr E. Foster Jun.'s aid got into Trin. Coll: she afterwards drove with Mrs Simpson &c in her carriage as far as Barton[71] & got a capital view of the Queen. — She didn't get home till past 6.

Fri. 27. George returned to Dulwich this afternoon. — Took M. & L. into the Senate House to see the Fittings up. Today the Magna Congregatio.[72] Tonight was the grand ball at Wimpole:— I was not asked. — The Dorias were there & Harty danced with Lord Fielding in the same Quadrille with the Queen:— the Queen danced 3 out of the 5 Quadrilles: her Partners were Lords Hardwicke, Calidon, & Canning:— in one of them her partner made her laugh by getting on the wrong side & figuring as a Lady: going to supper Ld Hardwicke offered the Q. his left arm:— she said 'No, my Ld, the other arm.' The Q's bedroom was over the ball room; dancing therefore ceased soon after 11.

Tu. 31. Another wet day:— women not out. — This Evening a grand scene. Betsy found her Cow-Box (Subscriptions for buying a cow for her Mother) much lighter than she expected, & broke it open: 16/6 had been stolen out!! there could be little doubt that the thief was Ch. Spink (a young man who had been employed in mending the blind): this is very shocking & annoying:— the Mother is a most respectable, painstaking woman, & M. puts one of the other children to school. — Edw. read Chuzzlewit to us. — Whist club at Birketts . . .

Wed. 1 Nov. . . . Great batch of Graces for the different Examiners. — It was thought indecorous to bring in a Grace for paying the expenses of the Prince's degree out of the Chest,[73] as it would not look well to see the

---

[69] . . . 'Wimpole House, the seat of the Earl of Hardwicke [Lord Lieutenant of the County], which was honoured with their presence till the morning of the 28th of October, when they left for Windsor'. (Cooper *IV* 665).

[70] Fosters' Bank was in Trinity Street; see A.B. Gray *Cambridge Revisited* (1921), p.94. The Mayor, Thomas Stevenson, and a deputation had also attended the Levee in the Master's Lodge and had presented addresses from the Council.

[71] The route to Wimpole lay through Barton.

[72] The Black Leet or Magna Congregatio was held annually in Great St. Mary's and was a ceremony during which the Mayor and Bailiffs of Cambridge were required, on election, to take an oath to observe the liberties and customs of the University. See Winstanley for the intermittent friction between Town and Gown caused by the University's insistence on maintaining a ceremony which since 1317 had stood for the subordination of the town to the University.

[73] I.e. University funds. Dr. Leedham-Green tells us that the University Audit book (U.Ac.2(5), (155)) shows that in addition to Prince Albert's fee for matriculation as a nobleman (£16), also paid by the University, the expenses of his degree amounted to £41.0.6, to include fees of £21 to the Orator and £9.13.6 to the proctor.

announcement of such a Grace in the Papers:— the payment is to be made quietly by the University. . .

Th. 2. Lucy having taken strong measures, & written to Mrs Spink letters threatening a summons against her son, the poor unhappy woman contrived to borrow the money & today restored the 16/6 stolen by her son. — Weather fine again:— good walk with M. — L. had caught a cold & did not stir out. . . Dined with Sedgwick. . . The 2 Miss Smiths sang a great deal, excellently. I outstaid all the company, handed the ladies into their carriages & then sat an hour with Sedgwick & smoked a cigar. G.T.R. went to Belgium this Thursday with W. Smith.

Fri. 3. Lovely day. Long College Meeting: Hudson (Vic. of Kendall) just dead. — Took M. & L. & 3 little protégées of the latter (viz. Esther Bailey, Eliza Gilmour, & Eliza Clark, — all 3 accidently in mourning so they looked like one family) to Trinity Lodge. Mrs Whewell was very kind to us & showed us the State Rooms, the Queen's Bed etc, etc & also the Bracelet given her by the Queen[74] . . .

Mon. 6. . . . Carus called on Lucy to go with her to see the child (John Gilmour) whom she is endeavouring to get into the British Orphan:[75] — the child passed a very bad examination being much frightened: he could not even say the Lords prayer:— Carus gave good admonition . . .

Fri. 10. Began reading Greek Testament (St Mark) with Edward. Walk with M. — Lucy not out. Dined at the Family at Mortlocks & met Drs Tatham, Graham & Paget, Packe, Shaw, Lodge, Power, Smith & Mr Walker: bad dinner, ill-cooked, & the wines said by those who tasted them to be detestable.

Sun. 12. Poor M. so unwell with pain in her side: called in Haviland who said that it was a slight pleurisy, but he thought the inflammation might easily be subdued:— he ordered a blister. — L. & Esther & I to Trinity Ch. where Carus gave us an excellent sermon on spiritual worship . . . Found Lodge in bed, he having had one of his nights of horrors: he was very stiff also from riding: he had not rode for 10 years & a few days ago he bought a horse, & the exercise has perhaps been too much for him. — M. kept her bed all day: so L. & I dined together without her:— unnatural & uncomfortable it felt . . .

Mon. 13. Matriculation.[76] M. had a good night tho (as usual) the blister would not rise. Today Haviland prescribed some stinging vinegar for the side, but neither would that affect the skin. — She kept her bed, but

---

[74] The bed with 'V. and A.' on the headboard is still in the possession of Trinity, though altered. Surprisingly, during her stay in Trinity Lodge 'The Queen furnished all provisions for herself . . . viz. Meat, Fruit, Milk, Coffee, Wax Candles, etc. The College supplied Oil & Ale'. See *Victoria and Albert at Cambridge,* cited in note 49 above.

[75] The British Orphan Asylum in London was founded in 1827 'for destitute children . . . of middle-class parents'. Childrens' Homes in the earlier decades of the century were undenominational.

[76] In 1843 noblemen paid the Registrary as Matriculation Fees £16.0.0., fellow-commoners £11.0.0., pensioners £5.10.0. and sizars £1.5.0.

seemed very cheerful and certainly better. I dined in hall, & then read loud to the women in M's bedroom The Life of Wilkie[77] till teatime . . . The matriculation a very good one.[78]

Tu. 14. Received from Mrs Potts 2 copies of her verses on the Queens Visit[79] — one in gold letters the other in blue. — Dr Haviland considered M. to be recovered:— at length the vinegar etc produced a rising:— M. (after having kept her bed for 2½ days) got up for dinner today: weak indeed & stiff, but thank God without cough or pain in her side . . . Poor Charles Ingle destroyed himself yesterday: He had married his housekeeper last Saturday at Liverpool: she was to have come to his house yesterday — (He had returned home on Sunday for his Clerical duty[80] and had preached on the sin of man withstanding his Maker). He could not stand the world's censure, & shot himself thro the heart with a pistol wch he had grasped with his left hand: he was covered up with the bedclothes & seems to have died instantaneously as the clothes were not disarranged: his face after death is said to have exhibited an awful fierceness of resolution. This housekeeper was a very interesting person & his enemies about the tithe-commutation[81] had insinuated base calumnies about his intriguing with her: he had ventured doubtless upon one of the most dangerous actions, that of directing her reading & cultivating her understanding: the inevitable result was that the affections of both became irremediably entangled; & when he wished to quench the growing scandal by dismissing her from his service he found that her peace of mind & probably her life was at stake. The ill-fated marriage took place as a desperate measure, from wch there seemed no escape. — The unhappy young woman (for she was under 30) is an object of the deepest pity. She was sister of an inn keeper at York: she was interesting in personal appearance, & accomplished far above her position in life, for she played & sang with taste. A sister of hers was C.I.'s housemaid. I have always considered poor Ingle as a most unfortunate & most ill-used man. With talents of the highest order, with a mind stored with all the treasures of literature, with a most retentive memory, & wit only 2d to Sidney Smith's, he was the delight of society: the Archbishop of York & all the nobility of the neighbourhood vied with each

77 Presumably Cunningham's life of Sir David Wilkie, the painter, just published.
78 'The numbers of undergraduates admitted' to Trinity, 'taking every tenth year from 1781 to 1851 are as follows: 41, 42, 46, 64, 107, 152, 135, 148'. (See Robert Robson, ed. *Ideas and Institutions of Victorian Britain*, 1967, pp.322-3). For figures for the whole University see *Historical Register* p. 990.
79 Robert Potts was a distinguished private Mathematical coach. He had sent a copy of his wife's verses to Henry Goulburn M.P. asking him to present them to the Queen. One of the blue copies is in *Cambridge Pamphlets* Folio Series Vol.I 6a in the University Library.
80 Ingle was vicar of Osbaldwick, Haxby, Murton and Strensall — all villages near York.
81 The struggle over the Tithe Commutation Acts (1836-1860) which substituted a monetary tithe rent charge for all tithes paid hitherto was prolonged. On 12 July 1837 Whewell, hoping to persuade Richard Jones to join him on the Continent, wrote You would be much better 'for forgetting during a fortnight that there are such people as country parsons and farmers fighting about tithes'. See I. Todhunter, *Dr. William Whewell. Writings and Letters*, II, 257.

other in making their houses attractive by having Ingle for their guest,[82] — but they suffered him to languish in poverty upon a miserable living of about £150 a year — wch paltry pittance became his lot as the son of a Cambr. Attorney who supported the Rutland Interest.[83] — A melancholy tale! — Ingle had brought up a nephew with him to Coll. at the time of the Queens visit: he had been observed by Sedgwick to be unusually gloomy & upon his unbosoming himself S. (& afterwards Peacock) strongly urged his marriage, & tho the end has been so fatal I think it was the wisest advice.

Th. 16. The day not bad: but I was so taken up with reading with Edward, with visiting Lodge, & Registrarial work that I could not walk with M. who accordingly staid at home. — Letter from Denning saying that G. was returned from Belgium & had brought some sketches as good as could be done by any body of the present day:— that is capital . . .

Fri. 17. Declined dining at Babraham. — Took M. out walking, the 1st time since her illness. — Dined in hall: gave wine to Thompson, Hemery, Roby (private tutor of Mr Russell) Ld Nelson & his freshman brother, Ld Fielding, Mr Russell (Lady de Clifford's son) 2 Spring Rices, Gifford & Edw. Allen. I had asked a Mr James Boone Rowe (of St John's) a friend of Peter Ouvry's, & was rather surprised at his answer: he had scruples of conscience about Friday & must decline. My party went off very well. — The dreadful intelligence of Ingle's suicide reached Cambridge today. — Sedgwick was so much affected by it that he could not come to my party.

Th. 23. . . . Began reading Odyssey B.VI. with Edward. Went with Lucy & Mrs Smith (born Osborne) & a good humoured spinster friend of hers over the Servants-Training Establishment: thought the furniture very shabby, & the 7 maids awkward & hideous (obviously Mrs Scholefields selection):[84] — I am not surprised at the rooms being unoccupied:— there is no garden. Walk with M.

Tu. 28. Wrote to Lodge. Lovely day: M. & I went to see Mr Browne's

[82] 'He was a man of great reading and extraordinary conversational powers . . . at times he was liable to fits of terrific melancholy . . . And then, all at once his soul would emerge from the dark and dismal vapour that surrounded it, and he would blaze out in such a way that it required all one's nerves to endure his vivacity.' (Sedgwick in a letter of 6 January 1844, in Clark and Hughes, II, 65.)

[83] From 1787 or 8 until 1832 Cambridge had been a Manners (Rutland) pocket borough and Ingle's father had died only a few years after the return of Spring Rice (Liberal) in 1832 with his financial affairs in disorder.

[84] Presumably the wife of the Regius Professor of Greek. Mrs Scholefield was lady patroness of the Institution for Training Young Females to fill situations as domestic servants and it would be surprising if she was not aware of the reluctance of many wives and mothers of sons to employ attractive maids. The Institution was on the west side of Parker's Piece and normally trained girls of 15 and over for two years. Sampson Low in his list of *Charities in London in 1861* includes institutions for training and aiding servants amongst the organisations 'for aiding the industrious'. These appealed particularly to Victorian philanthropists.

curiosities,[85] wch are to be sold tomorrow, & more especially a certain hideous green little jug upon wch Mrs Money Kyrle has set her affections & wch I am to buy for her. . . Wine to Thompson (our Fellow) Walton, Harrison, Sykes, Meggison, Sarel, Selwyn, Tooke, Rowe[86] (who don't go out on Fridays, — & who is so shy & dull & stupid that it would be a comfort to one if he went out on nodays), Edw. Allen & Plater. — To Miss Humfrey's ball. — All the world there.

Th. 30.   Dined with the V.Ch. & met the ugliest man in the University Mr Mason (master of the Free School)[87] bearing away the palm for hideousness:— very bad dinner miserably cooked. I had the good luck to take in Mrs Hodgson so I found my position at table very agreeable. I did not go up stairs to coffee, but went to Dr Procters to play a rubber . . .

Romilly spent the first week of December in London. The main events of his visit were connected with his family. He stayed with the Edward Romillys at 14 Stratton Street and saw John Romilly called within the bar at Lincoln's Inn as a Q.C. He began December 6th 'by reading over with Mrs Marcet her new little book of conversations on English History'.[88] But the high light of the day was a grand dinner party at which Miss Edgeworth, the famous novelist, and her sister were present. Miss Edgeworth 'is about 76 . . . and has all the animation of youth. She told several stories (most of them indeed well known) about Madame de Stael & Talleyrand . . . Madame de St. said 'Nous sommes tous les deux représentés en Delphine'.[89] 'Oui,' said he, déguisés en femmes' . . . This in turn led Sir Edward Codrington, the victor of Navarino, to say that 'he had heard Mad. de St. say to Sydney Smith that the French had some words wch are not translatable into a single English word such as 'sentiment'. We express the idea, said S.S., by five words 'My eye & Betty Martin'. Sir Edward talked a good deal about his interviews with the E. of Russia & Louis Philippe:— by way of wonder he did not talk of Navarino:[90] — I hear that on that subject he is called 'Never-end-O''. Romilly also found time for a brief visit to Dulwich where he dined with the Dennings and was 'much pleased with George's 50 sketches in Belgium'. On the 7th December he had the inside of the Telegraph to himself on his journey back to Cambridge.

Fri. 8.   Trial in V.C's Court:— Bates v. Gilby (undergr. of St Joh.) for being in discommuned house:— suspended for 3 terms. — Walk with M. & L. to leave some ink at Carus's. — By the way I had a long interview today with

[85]   G.A. Browne had died on 4 July.
[86]   William Walton of Trinity had taken his B.A. in 1836 and Rowe was in his first year at St John's. The others were all undergraduates at Trinity.
[87]   I.e. the Perse School. Peter Mason, headmaster from 1837 to 1864, was unusual in having been an undergraduate at St. John's and not a Fellow of Caius like almost all the previous headmasters.
[88]   Mrs Marcet lived with her daughter and son-in-law at Stratton Street. She wrote tirelessly for the young on many subjects and Lord Macaulay said that 'Every girl who has read Mrs Marcet's little dialogues on political economy [1816] could teach Montagu or Walpole many lessons in finance'. In 1843 Mrs Marcet was 74, a little younger than Miss Edgeworth.
[89]   Mme de Stael's *Delphine* was published in 1802.
[90]   Admiral Sir Edward Codrington was British commander-in-chief in the Mediterranean when the battle of Navarino was fought in October 1827.

Carus about Thorp's talking of taking St Marys,[91] wch I certainly heard him at a Seniority pass over:— Carus is prodigiously excited & with great reason. — He called on the women 2 days ago to unbosom himself on that all-absorbing grievance . . .

Sat. 9. . . . To the Vicechancellor's about the action against Bates (Proproctor) for an assault: the University is going to claim cognisance[92] & I shall have to go up to London tomorrow night about it.

Sun 10. . . . Again (altho Sunday) to the V.C. about this tiresome Cognisance business, which has prevented our dining till past 5 both yesterday & today. — Wrote to Frank £10. — Wrote also to Lodge. — Left Cambridge in the middle of the night viz 35 past 1 by the Rapid.

Mon. 11. My companions were two farmers: got to London at 7: went to the Belle Sauvage:— did not go to bed. Went at 10 to the London Attorneys, (Jones, Trinder & Tudway) . . . accompanied Mr Tudway at 11½ to the Judge's Chambers: we were detained for 1½ hr amidst a great hubbub. The Judge in Chambers was Pattison: he endorsed our claim of connisance on the affidavit & ordered a summons to the other party to show cause etc:[93] — Bought satin shoes (4 pair) for Bessy Doria, . . . a gown for M. etc: Dined at 3 at the Belle Sauvage; wrote to the V.C. an account of my proceedings. Down to Cambridge at ¼ to 4 by the Star:[94] on the railway I had Jones of Hayleybury for my visavis but in the Star I had no companion but a bankers Clerk. — Reached Hills Road at 9.

Wed. 13. Sent £1 to poor Harvey who has been discharged from his Clerkship at the Pitt Press for negligence in his accounts . . . At Trinity we gave away Kendal to J.W. Barnes and Gt St Mary's to Carus, — Thorp having waived his right & saved J. Brown, myself & others the painful necessity of protesting against him at Chapel, as he had in my hearing at a Seniority passed it in favor of Carus. — Walk with M. up the Hills Road: Carus (on horseback) met us and was in high exultation. In the Evening read loud Wilkies life.

91 As Perpetual Curate, which Carus became in 1844.

92 I.e. the right of dealing with the matter judicially. On 8 December Bates was found guilty of striking Charles Greenaway. Greenaway had been posted outside John Brown's Ram Yard Inn with instructions to blow a whistle if a proctor approached and so warn members of the University who might be playing the forbidden game of billiards there. Bates was fined 20s., but the magistrates hoped that the obstruction of Mr Bates in the execution of his duty would not occur again.

93 The sentence of The Vice-Chancellor's Court was that John Brown be admonished. On 14 December the indefatigable John Brown began another action in the Court of Pleas of the Borough of Cambridge against the Senior Proctor for confiscating gowns found in a billiard hall. Counsel (Cowling of the Temple) wrote that 'my own opinion is that a Replevin [the restoration to a person of goods taken from him] is within the Charter and that the University is entitled to claim Conusance'. He advised that the Court of Pleas of the Borough of Cambridge 'can have no right to try such an action without a grant giving it that power, or a prescription.' See *Privileged Persons and Claims of Cognizance* CUR 36.2 (152).

94 The Star left the Belle Sauvage Hotel on Ludgate Hill every day. There is a reproduction of it doing so in *R.C.D.* facing p.43. The railway line from London had reached Bishop's Stortford on 16 May 1842 and Romilly had presumably taken the coach there.

Fri. 15. Commemoration day:[95] — Cooper preached an excellent Sermon (I am told) in wch he touched on the death of G.A. Browne & Goulburn. — The speeches etc: (especially Bristed's)[96] went off well in the Hall. — there was a species of feast at Dinner in Hall:— I was glad to hear of this partial revival of former times . . . Very lumbaginous. — bought a horsehair belt. — Edward Allen left this morning for Cilrhiw. — M. all the morning at Mrs Marlows school.

Sat. 16. Sarah Foulkes came out of hospital today having been there for 6 weeks . . .

Fri. 22. Yesterday took M. to see the Dissenters Cemetery.[97] — Today M. & L. to Mrs Marlows School (for the annual distribution of rewards): they got away by 2: . . . In the Evening read W. Scotts Pirate.

Mon. 25. (Christmas Day). Declined going to the Dean at Ely. M. & I to Trinity Church where Myers preached from John 5.24. — Lucy reserved herself for Perry's 3 o'clock service[98] & lo! there was none! so Lucy was not at church either yesterday or today. — M. & I took a good walk. — Betsy spent the day at Harston.

Th. 28. Lucy, M. & I paid visits:— they were with *interested* motives, viz. to solicit votes for the British Orphan Election . . . We went into the Hospital & saw Susan Chune etc: Finished Dicken's new work 'Xmas Carol': — think it clever.

Fri. 29. . . . Dined at Trin. Hall Hall where Sir Herbert Jenner Fust presided with great hospitality & good humour: met there Serjeant Telford, Mr Thesiger etc.[99] Mr Thesiger is a regular wag: — He & 3 other lawyers played whist with me:— the table was close to the fire so he said it was 'Burns Justice':— Thesiger being Q.C. I said to him 'I suppose you always lead when you play whist with stuff gowns'.[1]

Sun. 31. . . . M, L, Esther & I to Trinity Church where we had an admirable sermon from Carus, delivered with extraordinary animation: . . . Lucy to her protégées — We are all, thank God, pretty well on this last day of the year.

[95] I.e. of benefactors to Trinity College.
[96] Bristed as 'the author of the First Prize Declamation' could choose his own subject. 'I took for mine *The Principle of Liberality* chiefly for the pleasure of having a fling at the Antediluvians in Church and State'. (Bristed p.228).
[97] The Histon Road Cemetery which was opened in 1843. The original buidings included an entrance lodge and a mortuary chapel, the first in the Elizabethan Tudor style, the second in mid fourteenth-century Gothic. 'The Lodge and the Mortuary Chapel were good examples of their kind'. (Royal Commission on Historical Monuments, *City of Cambridge* Part II, plate 309).
[98] At St. Paul's.
[99] The Trinity Hall lawyers were visible only in the Christmas Vacation. (See 14 February 1843).
[1] I.e. Junior Counsels.

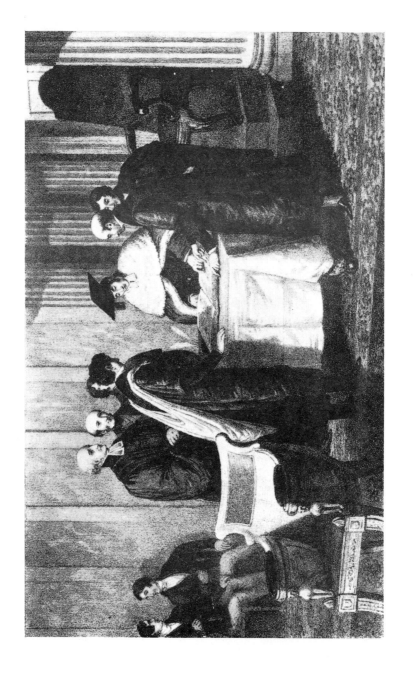

Examination of the Register Book

1844

Mon. 1 January.   Thank God we are all quite well at the opening of the year. — 1st day of receiving fees:— received 130.[1] Dined in Hall & found to my surprise that it was a grand feast day. — Avoided the Combination room & went home & read loud Miss Pickering's Grumbler[2] — Whist Club at Dr Havilands, where I met the Prests &c:— a pretty little g. niece of Mrs Havilands, Miss Scott was there. Lucy sent Carus a lovely pair of carpet shoes.

Sat. 6.   Letter from Lodge, giving a very poor account of himself since his recovery from the Gout. — This Evening received from Admiral Hawtayne a magnificent Turkey fattened at his farm of Catton near Norwich. — Margaret read loud again this Evening & finished 'the Grumbler', the last volume of which is sadly too much. — I was able however to read prayers tonight, M. having acted Chaplain for the last two.[3]

Sun. 7.   Mild day with soft rain, in spite of Murphy's Prediction that it would be the coldest day of the year.[4] M, L, Esther Bailey & I to Trinity Church where Carus preached effectively from the Epistle of the day: his Text was (Rom. XII.1) 'present your bodies a living sacrifice &c'. — Lucy went also at 3 to Mr. Perry's Church (St Pauls) & stood god-mother to Agnes Gilmour (aged 3) the daughter of a Scotch widow who has very recently lost her husband, & whom Lucy has taken under her protection: — she is striving to get one boy (John Gilmour) into the British Orphan Asylum.[5] To Lucy's great sorrow the eldest boy (William Gilmour) age 8! was seduced to join an older boy in robbing Mr Favell's hen-roost: this elder boy was only 15 & had been several times convicted before: he was convicted last Monday at the Quarter Sessions & sentenced to trans-

---

[1]   See 27 June 1842.
[2]   Ellen Pickering's *The Grumbler* was published in 1843, the year of her death from scarlet fever. She had been described as 'at the very head of the Circulating Library School' of novelists and some people thought her books resembled those of Frederica Bremer which Romilly enjoyed .
[3]   Romilly attributed his cold and loss of voice to having stayed at Arlett's until 2 am on January 3rd.
[4]   Presumably a reference to P. Murphy, a popular weather prophet and author of *The Weather Almanac and Barometer of the Seasons for the Year 1844.* (London 1/6d).
[5]   The British Orphan Asylum (1827) admitted 'destitute children . . . of middle-class parents' and was in Clapham Rise, London. 'One of the traditional financial resources of some . . . institutions was the privilege which could be held out to subscribers of selecting the beneficiaries of the charity.' The whole body of subscribers voted in proportion to the amount of their subscription to elect the candidates. (See David Owen, *English Philanthropy 1660-1960.* (Cambridge, Mass. 1965) p.481 and 15 July 1844).

portation.[6] Little Gilmour was acquitted:— but it cost Lucy £1.5.10 in feeing counsel &c. — M. & I took a walk in Trin. & St. Joh. grounds . . .

Mon. 8. Wrote to F: £10. — Also to Madame & her 3 children in answer to very amiable letters upon the New Year.[7] — I was highly amused with a sentence in Sophie's 'Moi j'ai un chat, Fanny un chien: dans le commencement mon chat battoit le chien, & maintenant c'est le chien qui le bat. Je trouve cela bien injuste, car nous devons toujours avoir le dessus.' — Wrote to George Romilly who comes of age tomorrow . . . Poor Mr. Crisford of the Bull (wch Inn he had just resigned) was this morning found drowned in the river:— doubtless his own act.[8] — Mills of the Sun destroyed himself several years ago just after giving up business, & the Landlord of the Lamb at Ely (Beeston or some such name) was very recently saved from intended suicide. — The Whist Club at my rooms: present, Haviland, Skrine, Cartmell, Marquis, Snowball, Prest, Wilson (of the Bank) Arlett & Shaw. — They staid very late & won my money.

Wed. 10. Took M. to see the Figures of Justice, Mercy, Law & Power wch are just erected at the County Courts:[9]— they are very pleasing . . . Declined Mrs Pembertons great Juvenile party . . .

Tu. 16. Refunded (by Letter) to Blacker (Joh) plucked last January. — Carus brought Lucy a present of the new 'Patent Perryian Gravitating Inkstand':— he brought it at our dinner hour, so we did not let him in. — This Evening & yesterday I read loud with interest a new work of Gleig's called 'the Light Dragoon' — it is a well written narrative of the adventures of a private who is made prisoner by the French in a skirmish immediately after his reaching the Peninsula in 1810 . . .[10]

Sat. 20. Meeting of the Master & 16 in Chapel at 9½ to set the College Seal to a Consent to the omission of a Clause (enforcing attendance at the Sacrament under 1s fine) objected to by the Home Secretary (Sir James Graham) in our amended Statutes now awaiting the Queen's signature:[11]— this was the only objection raised:— a very sound one in my opinion, altho our old Statutes had a similar enactment. — at 10 to the Bachelors

6   The governor of the gaol, Mr Edis, said that the boy Creek had been in gaol seven times and that 'he did not know a more dangerous boy in Cambridge'. The Recorder, in sentencing Creek to 14 years transportation, said that 'he would not, however, be sent out of the country, but to a place where every effort would be made to reclaim him'. (*The Cambridge Chronicle* 6 Jan. 1844).

7   I.e. Joséphine Romilly, Francis's (Frank's) wife, and Estéphanie, Sophie and Jacques their children. Estéphanie became Mme Bourlet, Sophie Mme Oger and Jacques Professor of Rhetoric at Nantes.

8   The Bull Inn in Trumpington Street was left to St Catharine's in 1626 by the then Master of Caius. It now houses college offices and undergraduates and is simply known as the Bull.

9   See note for 14 April 1842 and plate 298 in the Royal Commission on Historical Monuments, *City of Cambridge,* Part 2, (1959).

10   George Robert Gleig, chaplain-general of the forces, had served as a very young man in the Peninsular campaigns of 1813 and 1814. *The Light Dragoon* was published in 1844.

11   See 15 April 1842.

Commencement.[12] A beautiful day:— this was the 1st occasion of the new arrangements (about the permanent raised seats &c) being used. — The Vicechancellor had issued a calm notice to the Tutors recommending quietness to the young men: it was an imitation of that of Whewell last year. Everything went off comparatively very quietly & the whole proceedings were over by about 1:— 124 Honors were admitted, & 116 Polloi.[13] Hemming (Joh) was S.W:— he is very young looking but is 24 . . . The Wranglers were 37; the Senior Optimes 44 & the J.O. 36:

> Trinity had 9 Wr; 12 S.O; 6 J.O
> St. Johns — 10 —; 11 S.O; 10 J.O.

The only joke I heard was on Parr & Wren being bracketed together at the tail of the J.O: it was said to be, because the Examiners had determined to admit nobody below par. — Trinity alas had no man higher than 6th Wrangler (Warren): we also had the 7th & 8th . . .

Sun. 21. Read prayers for Hose. M, L. & Esther Bailey were at Church. — Carus preached from 1st Lesson (Isai. 55. 8.9.) a most objectionable sermon at wch Lucy was enraged: he declared that those who had committed a great sin & were truly penitent were sure of acceptance while those who had lived uniformly correct lives & had never learned what penitence was were sure of rejection:— the moral (or rather the immoral) was 'let us go & commit a great sin'. . .

Tu. 23. Looked over a parcel of Books in the Library. — Dined at Jesus Lodge . . . Tonight was the Bachelors Ball[14] so the Ladies were dressed out for conquest: Lady B. in diamonds. I had received a ticket but declined going. — I found the party very pleasant & was very glad to renew my acquaintance with the Miss Giffords whom I had not seen since the days of their childhood. They sang several Jacobite duetts with great spirits:— Lady Braybrooke amused herself & me by desiring me to ask them to sing 'Awa! Whigs! Awa!'.

Th. 25. . . . Page & I dined at Pampisford with Mr & Mrs Parker Hammond where we met his brother Henry & his very pretty, little, spritely wife: she was vastly agreeable & talked away with all the vivacity of a French woman:— she looked about 18, but was old enough to be the

---

[12] See 3 July 1842.

[13] I.e. the Poll or ordinary degree men. These comprised the majority of undergraduates who if their future was secure, saw no reason, even if they were able, to cram for highly specialised honours degrees. They were invariably pensioners and their fees helped to subsidise the more expensive honours courses of sizars and scholars. See Sheldon Rothblatt, *The Revolution of the Dons* (1968), p.184.

[14] The annual Commencement Ball had become one of the great social occasions of the academic year and celebrated the taking of degrees. According to a note by Romilly in UP 11 (no. 313) dated 25 January 1837 'this was the first instance of the new Bachelors giving a Ball'. *The Cambridge Chronicle* (27 January 1844) asserted that the ball this year outshone its predecessors. The Town Hall was decorated with draperies, banners and mirrors; Weippert's band of twelve was engaged, and wines had been sent down from London. Dancing began at 9.30 when Earl Nelson and the Hon. Miss Neville took the floor, and continued until seven in the morning when the last party-goer disappeared.

mother of a fine boy of 10 & a lovely little rosy faced, dimple-cheeked girl of about 5 . . . I was fascinated with mother & child:— the husband is a common-place man, a Clergyman near Ware (B.A. 1829) . . .

Wed. 31. A fall of snow. Over to Ely by Lynn coach: Cross the Coachman gave me a copy of his 'Lament of a Coachman': it is a Parody of Gray's Elegy & has considerable merit.[15] My only companion was Mrs Davy wife of the Lynn Gaoler: her turnkey & maid were outside: after she had satisfied her own hunger & thirst she handed out the remainder of her viands & a green bottle of spirits to the menials, observing to me, that they were faithful, so she fed them well. She gave me a minute account of her journey up to the Millbank Penitentiary with a male convict (her husband being ill, — she had gone beyond her customary duty of escorting the female prisoners): this fellow had been most unruly during the journey & had attempted to commit suicide. — I had offered the Fardells to stay with them,[16] but the Dean with some difficulty persuaded them to let me be his Guest . . .By way of amusing the little boy[17] we played at a new game of chance called 'Running horses' at wch he won a prize to our great pleasure as well as his own. He proposed to me a riddle 'How does it appear that the University Preachers are the greatest gluttons?' — 'Because they pray for all the Commons of the realm'. The party was very lively.

Th. 1.   February A cod fish from Mrs Houghton. Smart Frost. To the Cathedral twice: dull services of Blow & Croft. — Read with much interest Forbys E. Anglian Vocabulary[18] also Alb. Ways admirably edited Promptorium Parvulorum.[19] — Dined at the Palace . . . a party of 12 & a very pleasant one it was . . .

Th. 8.   . . . Dined in Hall:— much pleased with finding the youngsters

---

[15] We have not been able to trace a copy of this parody. Thomas Cross was a local 'character' who after a life at sea had become a stage-coachman. He also wrote poems on historical and religious subjects which attracted the attention of dons and undergraduates. In his *Autobiography* (vol. 3) Cross states that after the advent of trains his only income came from the sale of his literary work, and he records a meeting with Romilly shortly after he had been rudely repulsed when attempting to sell a copy of his *St. Paul's Vision.* Cross did 'not stop to observe his [Romilly's] benevolent aspect, neither was I roused by the kindness of his speech and manner, but moved to pass on. 'Stop', he cried — 'stop — you forget me, I fear'. I looked up and recognised the features of one who had been foremost in the University to praise and patronise my maiden effort. 'What are you doing now?' 'Nothing.' 'Nothing? Have you not written anything lately? You promised me a copy of any future productions long ago.' I immediately handed him one, when he paid me with a coin far above the price set upon his purchase. I was about to give him change. 'No', he said; 'if I like this as well as I did the first, I shall remain your debtor' '.

[16] Presumably in Wisbech, of which Mr Fardell was vicar. The Fardells had evidently come over to Ely for the dinner-party.

[17] Georgy Fardell.

[18] Robert Forby, rector of Fincham, Norfolk, published in 1830 *The Vocabulary of East Anglia; an attempt to record the Vulgar Tongue of the twin sister counties, Norfolk & Suffolk, as it existed in the last twenty years of the Eighteenth Century and still exists: with Proof of its Antiquity from Etymology and Authority.*

[19] I.e. Albert Way's edition of the English-Latin dictionary compiled by Geoffrey the Grammarian in Norfolk in the fifteenth century.

all admitted & standing at their tables to hear Grace said by Vice Master & Dean. This decorous rule began 1st Feb. — Plaid whist at Snowballs very successfully.

Sun. 11. . . . Lucy & I to St. Marys' at 2 to hear Selwyn (whose month it is):[20] . . . it was a sermon of very beautiful language with fine similes, but I thought there was singularly little matter in it: . . . Lucy to her poor protégée Sarah Foulkes. — Today wrote to a quaker lady (Miss Southey) with whom we have established a barter: we give her London Orphan Proxies for British Orphan.[21] — Wrote to Miss Druce on the same matter.

Tu. 13. . . . Lucy in her pauper visitings today was likened by a Mrs Penson to an Angel, — rather an odd one, for it was the Angel wch at the expulsion of Adam & Eve was placed at the gate of Paradise.[22] — Declined Dr. Proctor's [sic] whist & passed the whole Evening sorting Maps for the Bookbinder.

Wed. 14. Yesterday Evening we had a visit from our neighbour Mr Watford who brought us a large Roman funeral urn dug up near Melbourn, just given him in return for his versified Collects:[23]— it was frightful — Dined at Madingley . . . Sir St Vincent developed much hostility against the Queen for keeping Prince Albert in such close attendance on her . . .

Wed. 21. Congregation day . 1 Hon A M, 1 D D — 7 Dunces. — Matriculation 5 F.C, 26 P, 1 S.[24] . . .

Th. 22. . . . Marquis Spineto, Arlett, Power (of Pembroke) & I went over together to Harlton to dine with Fendall . . . Staid till past 12: our driver must have had a cup of the Rectors ale for he whisked us along the hard frozen ground at the rate of 12 miles an hour.

---

[20] I.e. as Select Preacher. In 1802 a grace was passed to appoint 9 Select Preachers, reduced to 8 in 1803, to preach on Sunday afternoons in Great St. Mary's from 10 October to the end of June and also, as from 1803, on the afternoons of Christmas Day and Good Friday.

[21] The voting system had many defects and 'the labour of canvassing subscribers for votes . . . was an absurd expenditure of energy and money for both candidates and sponsors' (David Owen, *English Philanthropy 1660-1960*, p. 481).

[22] Mrs Penson may have lived in Annesley Place (Newtown). The report of the General Board of Health's Inspector in 1849 gives an appalling picture of the filth and overcrowding in the small courts in the central area of Cambridge, particularly between Bridge Street and Trinity Street. Some of these courts were only 2½ feet across and sun and air were excluded from them. Sanitation did not exist. 'The conditions are so wretched as to be a disgrace to civilisation; it is next to impossible for the inhabitants to be healthy, cleanly, moral, decent or modest'.

[23] Dr. Leedham-Green tells us that Alexander Watford, the surveyor, started to versify collects whilst kept waiting for church parade by his sister. He was, happily, advised that he was unlikely to find a publisher for his verses, but his finely written MS is preserved in Lambeth Palace Library to which he sent it.

[24] I.e. 1 Honorary M.A., 1 Doctor of Divinity, and 7 Poll men, who in general had passed their examinations at a second or subsequent attempt, were given degrees. 5 Fellow-Commoners, 26 Pensioners and 1 Sizar were matriculated. The main B.A. congregation was to take place the following day.

On Monday 26 February Romilly went by the Rocket to Audley End where 'I had not been for several years'. He passed the morning of the next day in the saloon 'looking over the beautiful pedigree made by Lady Cornwallis & the Braybrooke illuminated Missal (or rather Psalter)'. On the 28th he returned to Cambridge for a college meeting. 'The New Statutes (with the Royal signature at beginning & end & the great seal) were just arrived.' Saturday 2 March saw him again at Audley End where in 'the Evening we looked over 'Audley Book', & the Bishop of Norwich amused himself & us by exhibiting a Photometer invented by Prof. Wheatston'.[25] The next day Romilly visited Lord Braybrooke's 'picturesque old almshouse with its 2 courts,[26] & then went to the Aviary, where the Bishop delighted the Keeper by promising to send him his book on birds.'

Mon. 4 March. Lady Braybrooke kindly wrote to Alderman Copeland & Lady Manvers in behalf of our Brit. Orph. Candidate; & Miss Stanley also begged a couple of cards. — Left Audley End directly after breakfast. It was a miserable wet day: the Wisbech coach did not run: so I walked on & got all the way to Sawston (8 miles) before I was overtaken by the Lynn Coach[27] . . . Whilst Club at Birketts where I lost my money.

Wed. 13. Breakfast to C.C. Neville, Seymour Neville, Bristed & E.E.A. — Lucy by dint of Tincture of Rhubarb & Brandy quite well this morning: . . . For the last week (while Mrs Clark is at the Hullah class) Miss Corfield has resumed her studies with M.

Th. 21. Exhibited the Library Accounts to Whewell. He, alas! is talking of forming a Syndicate to arrange the new Library, both he and Willis &c, being enraged at the largeness of the new Classes.[28] Dined in hall.

Tu. 26. Seniority about Enfield wch has become vacant by the death of Dr. Cresswell:— the Bp of London recommends dividing it into 2.[29] At 2 to the Woodwardian Lecture room to hear the discussion between Whewell & Sedgwick concerning inviting the British Association to Cambridge in 1845: they both made very animated & clever speeches, Whewell in opposition, & Sedgwick in favor:[30] the Dean of Ely, Peacock, was in the

---

[25] For an explanation of Sir Charles Wheatstone's invention for comparing light intensities see *Photometry* in *The Encyclopaedia Britannica* (11th edition).

[26] Now the College of St Mark.

[27] It seems odd that the Braybrookes did not send someone to check that Romilly was safely in the Wisbech coach when it was raining hard and he was presumably carrying a portmanteau.

[28] See 21 June 1844 and McKitterick p.489.

[29] Trinity was patron of Enfield which according to the *Parliamentary Gazetteer* was divided into three districts each with separate parish officers. In late April and early May Thorp and Carus not suprisingly declined the living which with 3 churches to look after must have been unusually strenuous for the incumbent.

[30] On 22 February 1844 Whewell wrote to Peacock as follows: 'My dear Dean, I am sorry that we should not agree about the desirableness of inviting the British Association here next year. I retain the opinion . . . that it is not desirable that the Association should go on repeating its sittings in its former haunts. I think that such a course would make it an intolerable burthen to the places included in the cycle, & to those of their inhabitants who took a share in its proceedings. And in this way it would lose its most valuable office, which is to stir up the scientific zeal of the places which it visits.' (I. Todhunter *Dr. William Whewell. Writings and Letters.* Vol. II (1876) p. 320).

Chair: Hopkins gave a good statement of what the British Association had already done:[31]— upon the show of hands only one (Blakesley's) was lifted up against altho Heath, Woodham, etc. are notoriously opposed . . .

Th. 28 Little-Go over:— Edward in the 1st class. . . We indulged E.E.A. with whist after tea.

Sat. 30. E.E.A. left for the vacation. — A young man of the name of Fox (undergraduate of St. Johns) died on Thursday last from throwing himself off the box of a 'drag'[32] the reins of wch had broken:— his 3 companions who stuck to the carriage were unhurt, the horses being soon stopped. Looked over a parcel of Foreign Books. This Evening 2 Scotch ladies of the name of Skelton communicated to Lucy their intention of making a present to her protégée Mrs Gilmour:— Lucy highly approved:— they thought a mangle would be a good present:— Lucy thought so too:— they thought they could raise £3 out of the requisite 6, *would L. contribute towards the rest?* This certainly is a charming mode of making presents at the expense of our friends! — Today I was very sorry to hear from Mr & Mrs Gibbs (now in Cambridge) that Frances Wilderspin (who has been going on so well for these 3 years at the Boyers) has a white swelling on her knee. — Wrote to G.T.R. — Whist at Bateson's & met a large party of 14.

Mon. 1 April. . . . M. & I to Trinity Church: Lucy was too much tired to stir out all day. — She had a visit from the Miss Skeltons to whose mangle we all 3 subscribed 2s.6d. Walk with M: in spite of the N.E. wind the day was delightful. At night read the Prairie Bird.[33]

Wed. 10. . . . Looked over foreign books from Bailliere[34] . . . Today the Scholarship Examination began — Greek day by Gosset & Blakesley.

Mon. 15. A hue & cry after the Latin Composition (Translation from Paley's Natural Theology[35]) of the upper year (set by Martin & me & of which I had collected the papers. — Pollock appointed Chief Baron to succeed Lord Abinger, Follett raised from Solicitor General to Attorney

[31] The first meeting of the British Association had been held in York in September 1831 and the first meeting in Cambridge (the third meeting of the Association) in June 1833 with Sedgwick as President. The Dean of Ely was to be President of the Mathematical and Physical Science sectional committee of the 1845 Meeting. (See 20-25 June 1845.)

[32] According to the *Cambridge Chronicle* of 30 March Fox threw himself off the box of a phaeton.

[33] C.A. Murray, *Prairie Bird* (1844).

[34] Hippolyte Bailliere of 219 Regent Street, London also had a branch in New York and was one of the four principal suppliers to the University Library of modern foreign books.

[35] William Paley's *Natural Theology; or Evidence of the Existence and Attributes of the Deity collected from the Appearances of Nature* (1802) of which a twentieth edition appeared in 1820. Paley's Evidences was also a set book for the Previous Examination and in October 1850 a Corpus freshman wrote to his mother 'Paley is the only subject I am at all afraid of — it is however a very serious subject, and requires a very hard grind to get it up. It always sends Trotter to sleep, at whatever hour of the day he is reading it.'

General, & Thesiger Solicitor General:— The partisans of Kelly are much annoyed.[36]

Wed. 17. The papers never found. Donaldson amused me today by saying that he had discovered 2 books wch he thought related to the controversy about the Round Church between Thorpe and Faulkner viz. 'Aedes Althorpianae' & 'Falconer's Shipwreck'.[37] By the way Stokes (Scholar of Trin.) has written some clever Latin Hexameters on the subject. — Chapel at 6. Drank tea with the Master to decide the Scholarships: 17 besides 3 Westminsters:[38]— among the successful candidates was a son of Hallams: among the unsuccessful was a son of the Premier, Fred. Peel.

Th. 18. At chapel at ¼ to 9, to elect the new Scholars: upon this occasion we made the 1st formal use of our Revised Statutes by the Masters reading from the official copy with the Queen's signature . . . Poor Miss Agnes Ainslie (9 years old) died yesterday of water in the brain, & my handsome friend Mrs White (wife of the Surgeon) died on Monday of ossification of the heart. Dined with Master & other Examiners for the Scholarships. I was today asked to dinner by Adeane, C. Townley, Prest, & Dr. Fr. Thackeray! I have told all my friends that Mondays & Fridays are tabooed days: they thought themselves safe in asking me for a Thursday.

Mon. 22. Wrote 3 letters to Lodge today. The last in answer to one from him giving a very poor account of himself. — Carus paid us a visit. — Whist Club at Birketts:— Dr. Haviland sent for in the midst of our playing to my poor goddaughter Bessy Doria whom he found in a considerable state of fever:— she has had the influenza hanging about her some time.

On 25 April Romilly left Cambridge for London outside on the Telegraph. He stayed with his first cousin John at 32 Gordon Square and as usual went to the Opera where 'Grisi was admirable as Norma, in fine clear voice' and 'La Blache was superb', and to several theatres, including 'the French play'. By day he enjoyed seeing friends and relations and on Saturday 27 'not finding the Koes at home I went to Hampstead: just at the outskirts of Camden Town there are some very ornamental red brick almshouses for decayed tailors . . . Enjoyed greatly my walk on the high ground by Jack Straw's Castle'.[39] At the National Gallery he found that

[36] Fitzroy Kelly (Conservative) represented Cambridge from 1843-7. Sir William Follett died in June 1845, having held office for little more than a year, and Sir Frederick Thesiger succeeded him as attorney-general. Fitzroy Kelly's friends then had the deferred pleasure of seeing him appointed to the vacant office of solicitor-general.

[37] *Aedes Althorpianae; or an account of the Mansion, Books, and Pictures of Althorp,* was published in 1822. William Falconer's poem *The Shipwreck* was published in 1762 and reprinted innumerable times. However, it was the Camden Society and not Faulkner which in the end was shipwrecked (see 25 July 1845). Thorpe was President of the high-church Camden Society and Faulkner the low-church incumbent of Holy Sepulchre.

[38] The Elizabethan statutes of 1560 stated that boys from Westminster School should be preferred to other candidates for scholarships, and from about 1589 the College normally elected three Westminster boys annually. See Winstanley, pp. 341-3.

[39] Presumably the well-known Hampstead Heath inn. The site of the manor house which was destroyed by Jack Straw's followers in 1381 is at Highbury in Islington.

the 'only novelties are a small hideous picture of a man and woman by Van Eyck[40] & a marble Statue of Wilkie by Joseph (not bad)'. In Dulwich Romilly saw George and Mr Denning, who was very pleased with George's progress, and went to the christening of Baugh Allen's baby to whom he was godfather.[41] Lady Clementina Villiers was godmother and 'gave the names Clement Francis Romilly'. He returned to Cambridge on 3 May with Dr. Mill as 'my companion outside'.

Sat. 4 May. Had to pay £18.8 to the Stamp Office for the Accumulation of George's Dividends since his Fathers death up to his coming of age.[42] —I think this an iniquitous tax, because I was most desirous of paying the Legacy Duty when I paid the Probate Duty: but I was refused in consequence of the contingent Legacies. — Looked over Books for Lodge. — Walk with M. — In the Evening Edward read the new no. of Chuzzlewit.

Sat. 11. This Evening began reading a new novel of that coarse minded Mrs Trollope:— it is called the 'Laurringtons or a very Superior Family'. I did not like what I read:— I thought it completely out of nature:— it is not (as yet) improper.

Sun. 19. . . . At 2 to St. Mary's to hear H.V. Elliott: his Text was 'Saul, Saul, why persecutest thou me?': he dwelt almost rancorously on the enormity of his character before conversion: I greatly objected to the Preachers exclaiming 'write Satan for Saul:— it would read well'. Parts however of the sermon were very effective, & it created a considerable sensation. — Wrote to Miss Lodge.

Fri. 24. . . . To Ely by Lynn Coach: my companions were Mrs Barnes (wife of Barnes, the Gloveless Fellow of Queens) Miss Chapman (introduced to me by Francis of Trinity Hall) & a conversible Norfolk Esquire . . . Mrs Barnes I thought singularly agreeable: she is about 50, very animated & cheerful & must have been very good looking. The talk went on so well that I never thought of reading my book. — Passing thro Streatham saw the devastation occasioned by the recent fire:— 25 houses & barns! — happily purely accidental:— a spark from a black-smiths forge lighted on a thatch.[43] — 'The Family' dined with our Honorary Member the Dean of Ely. . . The Dinner party was of 14: 9 'Familiars'. . . & other 5 (viz Prebendary J.H. Sparke, Mr. Newcome of Sutton (s. of Irish Arch Bishop & father of Mrs Edw. Sparke), Basevi, Miller, (the historian of the Cathedral) & Hubbe a German Prof. of 'wasserbaukunst' or drainage). I, as

40 The 'Marriage of Giovanni(?) Arnolfini and Giovanna Cenani(?)' had been bought by the Gallery in 1842.
41 I.e. by Baugh Allen's second wife whom he had married in 1841 after the death of the diarist's oldest sister ten years earlier. It is curious that Romilly does not comment on Lady Clementina's looks. For her fame as a beauty see 4 July 1842.
42 George's father, Colonel Samuel Romilly, had died in 1834, leaving him an estate of almost £8000 upon his coming of age in January 1844. Romilly had paid probate duty as an executor and there was now a further payment due in respect of the interest that had accumulated on the capital. The contingent legacies to Margaret and Lucy would only have become effective had George died before his twenty-first birthday.
43 The fire broke out on May Day 1844 and damage was assessed at £20,000.

usual, was Croupier: the usual smoking did not take place, out of tenderness to one of the guests so Shaw, Power & I went into the garden after tea & there smoked a cigar . . . Basevi, Mortlock, Shaw, Power, & I slept at the Deanery.

Sun. 26. . . . Heard 2 good episcopal stories: 'a Clergyman said to the B. of London, 'My Lord, one of my parishioners asked me what present Hiram K. of Tyre made to Solomon & I could not tell him.' 'O said the Bishop, you should have said you were not Solomon & it did not concern you.' — The Bp of Worcester (Pepys) was pompously declaiming at a religious meeting & said 'I have always most firmly opposed the Catholic Faith', — a voice from the other end of the room said 'which Faith unless a man hold stedfastly he shall perish everlastingly'. At Dinner we were a partie quarrée, viz the Dean, Shaw, Power, & I. At 9½ we left the Deanery in a postchaise.

Wed. 29. College meeting:— presented Heath to Enfield. Dined at Master's of Sidney (Dr. Phelps) . . . There was a good deal of excellent conversation between Whewell, Phelps & Mr. Crayke till unluckily they got on the Long Parliament & Ol. Cromwell, when Whewell and Mr. Crayke were of opposite opinions, & the harmony of the Evening would have been marred but for the mildness of Mr. C. — Mrs Phelps sung a duet with the giantess, who afterwards sang 'O thou that tellest' very well indeed. — Mathison & other musical men came in the Evening.

Fri. 31. Lionised W. Smith & my nephews to the Fitzwilliam, Pub. Lib, Trin. Lib., Senate H. & Round Church.[44] — Committed W. Smith & George to the care of Archdeacon Thorp at dinner in hall at 2. They went to town by the Rocket at 3. — Agreed with G.T.R. to make up his income to £260 . . . Total eclipse of the moon tonight.

Sat. 1 June. Found that Lucy had made her cold very bad indeed by gazing at the Eclipse. Lucy's blind protégée Anne Frost died today: she had been brought home from the Liverpool Blind Asylum where she had been for more than a year. Letter from Lodge giving a very sad account of himself. Edw. Allen drank tea with us & read loud the new no. of Martin Chuzzlewit.

Tu. 4. Dunford's leg swelled:— think him in a bad way:— sent him to hospital in a fly:— my bedmaker Mrs Carpenter kindly accompanied him. — Went to see him in the hospital & found him calm. — Yesterday wrote a long Latin Letter to a German Professor Dr. Jan (of Schweinfurth in Bavaria) (about our MS of Macrobius)[45] — Wrote Letters of thanks to various benefactors to the Library . . .

Fri. 7. Lucy's Pauper Sarah Foulkes brought home this Evening by Mr Clark of Haslingfields — who (having his chaise full) kindly tied little

---

[44] George and his friend William Smith had come from London on 29 May.
[45] The most important of Macrobius's works are the many books of the *Saturnalia* (c. 325-385). Ludwig von Jan had published a book on them in 1843 *Symbolae ad Macrobii libros saturn aliorum emendandos.*

Okey (a girl of 11 with whose parents she had been staying) on his horse, & so brought her like a monkey on a dog at a fair. E.E. Allen in 5th Class:[46]— wrote to him. — M. & I walked before & after dinner.

Sun. 9.   Heard from Mrs Clark yesterday that Loraine Skrine who was engaged for 9 days to marry Mr. Blackett of the Navy, on the 10th declined when he said he proposed taking her for 9 months to Van Diemens land to wind up his affairs. The joke is to say that she is willing to go to Sidney. (Dr. Phelps seems unwilling).[47] He had £2500 p.a! Lucy kept house in the morning & upon seeing 2 boys fighting in our garden rushed out & found the younger was William Gilmour (brother to the boy John whom she is trying to get into the Brit. Orphan): they were fighting about a bird wch W.G. had in his pocket & wch the other declared he had stolen. Certain it is that W.G. had staid away from the Sunday School; so L. seized upon the culprit & kept him till the afternoon schooling & then handed him over to Mr. Ragland:— this W.G. is a bad boy & was (not long ago) one of a party who stole fowls. — Lucy went to Perry's Church at 3 & heard him give one of his Confirmation Lectures from Ps. 17.5: it was very sensible.

Mon. 10.   . . . Sarah Foulkes & Betsy Oky [sic] came to tea with the maids.

Fri. 14.   Dined in hall: symptoms of vacation: only 5 of us Thorp (Vicemaster), Cooper, Kingdon, Atkinson & I. Lucy had little Betsy Oaky to dine with her. In the Evening M. L. & I took the little girl to the Philos. Society to see the stuffed birds. — Began reading loud Miss Austin's 'Persuasion'.

Wed. 19.   A little rain today. Dined at Sir Ch. Wale's . . .to meet Mr & Mrs Vignolles (born Pemberton): the rest of the company consisted of Mr & Mrs Prest, Bessy & Harty Doria, Miss Augusta Wale & 3 brothers & Fentall. Lady Wale told a good story of the present Pope: a man said to him 'it is 50 years since I have seen you, & I hope at the end of another 50 years you will be as vigorous.':— 'you mistake, said the Pope, I am stiled 'Your holiness' & not 'your eternity'. Plaid 4 Rubbers at loss of 2s per rubber.

Th. 20.   . . . To a small Evening party at Trinity Lodge to meet the distinguished guests who dine there, viz. the K. of Saxony & his suite, (viz. his minister at our Court the Baron Gersdorff, Dr Carus his physician, & a moustached Major Reichart, Dr & Mrs Hodgson, Worsley, Thorp (Vicemaster) & Paget: . . . The King wished to be here incog; & the invitations were to meet Count Hohenstein; every body however addressed him as your Majesty, altho (to my surprise) Mrs Whewell &c sat down in his presence even when he was standing. — He speaks but very little English & seems a man of few words & would excite but little interest if he were not a King. — He is apparently friendly & laughs heartily: he is said to

---

[46]   I.e. in the Trinity College examination.
[47]   Dr Phelps was Master of Sidney. He could not have remained unwilling for long as he and Loraine were married in All Saints on 4 September.

be well acquainted with Geology & Botany. — He is a man of very active habits & keeps early hours: he was yesterday morning at the top of St Pauls Cathedral before 5 o'clock: tonight he set a very good example by making his bow at 10 & going off to bed.[48] We were all presented to him . . . It was comical enough for Carus to meet a namesake, a cousin German (as he called him):— Carus told me that the K. called him 'carissimus' when presented to him. Dr. Carus is a very eminent physiologist: he has a good recommand of English & talks with much animation:— Paget & Clark thought very highly of him. We all staid till 11 & then took our leave . . .

Fri. 21. 2nd day of Bishop's confirmation. As Deputy Librarian exhibited the Public Library to the K. of Saxony: I had a carpet spread & a table set upon it in the New Library[49] & a chair of state set for his German Majesty: I had placed with the aid of Bowtell the principal book-treasures on the table, viz. Codex Bezae & its facsimile, Caxton's Chess 1474, the Anglosaxon versions of the Gospels & Gregory's Pastoral (this last by King Alfred), a Nuremberg Bible 1483, a beautiful M.S. of Wycliffe's Bible, Coverdales Bible, that printed for William 4, Tippoo Saib's copy of the Coran, the pretty framed copy of Hafiz poems, Edw. VI book of devotions, &c.[50] — I also set out for the King the finest works on Botany. — It seemed to me that the K. took very little interest in any of the books: the sight of the Nuremb. bible indeed elicited a few words in German from the K. to Baron Gersdorff. — My part was now over & the distinguished visitors went under the guidance of Whewell to see sights & finally to lunch with the V.C.[51] (previous to quitting Cambr. for Woburn) . . .

[48] For a very interesting description of the visit see the extract from Dr C.G. Carus's *The King of Saxony's Journey through England and Scotland, in the year 1844* (London 1846) which is reproduced in Cooper IV, 668-72. Carus writes 'After our numerous state dinners in London, our comparatively quiet repast in the society of men of learning and a few highly educated ladies was a true refreshment' . . . In addition to the usual dessert 'a portion of bride cake was particularly pointed out. This cake was a part of that which had been made after the wedding of the master with his very polite and agreeable lady. . .'

[49] C.R. Cockerell's design was intended to occupy the whole site of the then Library and Schools. However, only the north range, nearest to Caius College, was completed. This is in 1993 the Squire Law Library. See Vol. III of Willis and Clark for a chapter on the history of the extension to the Library.

[50] I.e. William Caxton's *Game and playe of the chesse*. Gregory's *Pastoral Care* is the Anglo-Saxon MS. in the translation once attributed to King Alfred. The printing on vellum of William IV's *Bible* was begun by the University Press in 1835 but as William died before he could receive it it was presented to the new Queen on 14 July 1837. (See entry for 14 July 1837 in *R.C.D. 1832–42*). When Tippoo Sahib was finally defeated in 1799 his library was removed to the East India Company in Calcutta. 'Like the Bodleian, Cambridge received a *Koran* of unusual quality' (McKitterick p.377). Mrs Butterworth of the University Library's Near Eastern section identifies Hafiz' poems as *The Divan of Hafiz* No. CCLVI (Add. 267) in Edward G. Browne's *Catalogue of the Persian Manuscripts in the Library of the University of Cambridge* (1896). No. CCLVI is described as written 'between margins ruled in red, blue and gold' which could be seen as frames.

[51] William Hodgson of Peterhouse. Dr C.G. Carus wrote 'We lingered till after midday in Cambridge, and I have there learned and seen much, which seems to me indicative of the commencement of a new and fresh impulse in this otherwise antiquated university . . . May the free spirit of knowledge more and more throw off those chains, in which Puritanic theology has so strictly bound almost everything in England!'

Mon. 24   Lucy's friend Mr Simpson (who had been in a desperate state these 2 yrs, & had gone up to town to be galvanised)[52] is dead . . .

Sat. 29.   Congregation — 1 DD, 1 LLD, 5 MD, 1 LLB,[53] 49 AM, 3 AB, 2 eundem. — Dined in hall. — Read loud Rasselas. — Sat up in state from 8 till 10 to receive fees:— caught very few. Plaid a rubber at Arletts with Mills & Burcham: I think Burcham, poor fellow, in a very bad way:— he has a constant cough . . .

Sun. 30.   . . . There was a fire this Evening in the Black Lion Yard. Bunch (Em.) kindly came to fetch me as the premises were so near my office. — the fire was soon subdued. There was also one in the Brazen George Yard.

Th. 4 July.   Congregation to catch the clumsy people who have come up too late. — 5 AM and 2 eundems . . . Thorp, Paget, J.J. Smith & I over to Ickleton to dine with Mr & Mrs Herbert . . . The day being wet we had fires in the drawing room & dining room. — The 2 little girls, their Governess, Mrs Wick, Miss Lempriere, Thorp, Paget & Mr Wick danced a Quadrille on the carpet . . . Sent off the M.S. of Macrobius to Dr Jan's London friend Mr. Hulle (of 26 Lower Pountney Hill) from whom I heard today . . .

Sat. 6   Lucy & I called upon Mrs Clark ostensibly to see her new greenhouse, but really to get (if possible) some geraniums & handsome flowers:— we got a nosegay, but not such a one as satisfied Lucy who is making up one for Carus:— full-blown roses did not content her. — In the Evening M & I went to Trinity to take the Dean[54] a nosegay, & also a volume (Christian Retirement) lent by him in an unbound state & restored in an elegant dress:— Read loud a short & pathetic tale of Frederica Bremers called the Twins:— a story of a brother & sister of angelic beauty & goodness, who are called 'the Angels', & die of consumption at the age of 16 at the same moment.

Tu. 9.   Received from Lord Jermyn his sextuple proxy for the British Orphan, & His Lady's. — Wrote to Lodge. — At Mrs Worsley's request I selected for her a quantity of music from the Public Library. — Received from Mrs Whewell the bill of fare when the Queen dined at Trin. Lodge on the 25th October, & also a list of the servants[55] . . .

Mon. 15.   Election of British Orphan Asylum. — We sent from Cambridge 36 Proxies containing 333 Votes: John Gilmour was this day elected thro the very active exertions of Lucy backed by the invaluable

---

[52]   I.e. for the fashionable and supposedly therapeutic use of direct current electricity.
[53]   I.e. Doctor of Divinity, 1 Doctor of Law, 5 Doctors of Medicine, 1 Bachelor of Law.
[54]   I.e. Carus, who was Dean of Trinity College. Why the Romillys, who had their own garden and gardener and were so generous as a family, should have been so determined to plunder other people's gardens remains a mystery. Perhaps the seven florists and seedsmen listed in Pigot's 1839 *Directory* did not sell cut flowers.
[55]   See 3 November 1843.

assistance of Mr. Bernard, who has borrowed 48 proxies wch we must repay in January:— John Gilmour had 1519 votes[56] . . .

Th. 18. Dined in hall. M. got well again. — Lucy had an interview (at Addenbrooke's) with the Curator of the Bury Botanical Garden, a Mr. Hodgson who had engaged to take Susan Chune as his servant next week:— he says he makes his servants very comfortable — Miss Susan Apthorp presented M. with a little French China basket. — Mrs Worsley brought to bed of a still born child.[57]

Fri. 19. As I was walking with M. in Trin. this Evening about 6 I was to my great surprise told by the College Porter that I was to dine with the Judges (Alderson & Williams) today:[58] I thought it was to be tomorrow & had already dined at 3 o'clock at home. — However I hastened back to the Hills Road, dressed & was in abundant time, for we did not dine until past 7. The Judges threw their 2 parties into one; the V.C, Heads, Fellows of Trin. & the bar all dined together. It was a good dinner with Turtle & venison:— & I found it very agreeable. — The Masters civility in giving me, & a select few coffee, saved me the customary 2s to the Judges servants — for to my surprise they were not at the door when I went out. — Judge Alderson was very ill-tempered at 1st because it rained when he got to Trinity gate, & he & Judge Williams sat in their carriage for several minutes waiting in vain for the rain to cease, & peste'ing at not being allowed to drive to the back entrance.[59] A double dinner day!

Sun. 21. M. & I to Trinity Ch. where Colenso preached from Rom. XIII.11. His matter was good (tho the sermon had the fault of being without divisions) & some parts contained really fine writing, but his manner is so insufferably dismal that I cannot endure him:— his reading prayers is

56 The winner headed the list of seven successful candidates with 1994 votes. 'To pick a winner to bring one's candidate through at the head of the poll was akin . . . to any triumph on the track, the playing field or the stock market'. (David Owen, *English Philanthropy 1660-1960* p. 482). Proxies were bought as well as borrowed. In May 1833 Romilly had been indefatigable in securing a place for Maria Blencowe in the London Orphan Asylum. One of his many calls was on the Secretary of the Asylum who 'will write to me on the subject of finding un homme a 120 Proxies pour 40 Guineas'. On 23 May he records calling 'on Mr. Kingsley to give him a draft of 40 Gnas for the Blencowe cause'.

57 This was the Worsleys' second great disappointment and after it the marriage remained childless.

58 See 18 July 1842.

59 This was not the first time that the Judges were indignant because they were not allowed to use the back entrance to the Lodge. Trinity regarded the Judges as distinguished guests who, although they were given the exclusive use of certain rooms and offices in the Lodge during their stay, were not allowed to use other parts of it or the approach to them. See Winstanley's *Later Victorian Cambridge* pp.20-3. There is an amusing 'Delectable Ballad of the Judge and the Master' by Tom Taylor, (1817-1880), dramatist, editor of Punch and, briefly, fellow of Trinity, which was published in *Bentley's Miscellany* for 1843. It begins as follows:

    'The stout Master of Trinitie
    A vow to God did make
    Ne Judge, ne Sheriff through his back-door
    Their way from court should take'.

more offensive than his preaching. — Lucy went to St. Mary's at 2 & heard Franks: his Text was Rom. XIV. 22. She found him insufferable: M & I during her absence had a long visit from Mrs Clark & Johny. — Dined in Hall to meet the Judges, the High Sheriff, etc; a party of about 30: the Master was there. Sir. E. Alderson told 2 legal ancedotes wch amused me. Sir Art. Piggott called the word lien (always called lion by Lord Chancellor Eldon, & indeed all the bar) as if it had been written lean. — Upon wch the following epitaph was made,

> Sir Arthur, Sir Arthur, pray what do you mean
> By calling the Chancellors lion lean?
> Indeed & indeed, is it come to that,
> That nought from his kitchen can ever be fat?

The other anecdote was concerning Sir Griffin Williams (Master in Chancery) who in his old age & in spite of nature took to oil painting: he showed one of his daubs to Sir Geo. Rose, & said 'Now, tell me candidly your opinion of it.' 'O! said Sir G., every body would declare that it was by an old Master'. . . Avoided the combination room:— walk with M. in the Evening. Tried to read loud Stephens Article in the Edinburgh on the 'Clapham Sect':— found it intolerable from its verbosity.[60]

Th. 25 . . . Attended as Notary Public at the trial before the Chancellor of the diocese (Sparke) & his assessor Dr Daubeny, concerning the Stone Altar & the Credence Table in St. Sepulchre's Church.[61] — The Court 1st met in the N.W. corner of St. Mary's Church: we then made a procession to St. Sepulchre's to view the state of things, & then went to Trin. Hall Hall, which was kindly lent for the occasion. — Dr. Bayford (of T.H.) spoke for 3 hours against the Stone Altar & quoted a great quantity of Latin, but the Court (i.e. Dr. Daubeny for Mr. Sparke took no part) was manifestly against him from the beginning. He told us that the shape of the Altar originated from the primitive Xns having in times of persecution celebrated the Lords Supper in the crypts upon the tombs of the martyrs. He said that what constituted a Roman Cath. Altar was, 'the upper slab being of stone, or having at least a stone let into it, & Chrism[62] having been used for consecration'. Dr. Phillimore Junior spoke for 1 hour in defence of the altar, etc: he told us the well-known anecdote of communion rails being introduced by Laud because a dog had got to the consecrated elements on one occasion. — Dr. Daubeny pronounced in favor of retaining the Altar:— Mr. Faulkner (The Perpetual Curate) immediately appealed to the Court of Arches. — Dined in Hall:— our hour now during Vacation time

---

[60] James Stephen's article was in *The Edinburgh Review* for July 1844, pp. 251-307. The group of Christian philanthropists and politicians were known as the Clapham Sect because they often met in Henry Thornton's house on Clapham Common. Their most distinguished member was William Wilberforce.

[61] In 1842 and '43 the church had been restored by the Camden Society (see 29 October 1842). A stone altar and credence table were introduced into the church and their legality questioned. Hence the trial. (See link passage for August 15-21 1843).

[62] I.e. oil mingled with balm for sacramental anointing.

being 5; court broke up at 4½.

Fri. 26. . . . Sent 5 dozen of table beer to old Gunning for the use of his son Francis who has been dangerously ill . . .

Wed. 31. Mrs Thompson (Upholsterer) (in gratitude for my employing her husband & recommending his lodgings) brought us a Cushion of her own embroidering as a present:— it is very handsome indeed. — Finished Peter Priggins:— it is a most exaggerated picture of the vices of an Oxford life[63] . . .

Sat. 3 August. Very melancholy letter from Annette Lodge at Strasbourg giving me an account of a very dangerous bilious attack wch Lodge has just had:— at one time she was in the greatest alarm for his life: he is somewhat better poor fellow . . . M. & I caught in a great thunderstorm at Miss Suttons: we took refuge from the rain in her house. She showed us in to her schoolroom, where I mystified a little girl by asking her how many pence there were in 6 pence:— she could not tell, but I gave her the 6d:— Miss Sutton introduced us to her assistant Miss Orvis, whose cheerful manners we much liked & greatly admired her drawings. — Poor Charles Ingle's widow is just brought to bed.[64] — Began reading loud Bulwers Ernest Maltravers:— highly pleased with it. Lucy today paid £3.10. — for a new gold border to the Communion Cloth in Trinity Church:— she packed up a large bag full of presents for Carry Hudson.

Sun. 4. . . . Ludicrous letter from Ibotson (Magdalene) begging Lodge to praise him up to the skies to Archdeacon Sinclair:— the Letter was put in my hands, & I blew the trumpet instead of poor Lodge:— Archdeacon Sinclair has an appointment in his gift which Mr. Ibotson covets.[65]

On 5 August Romilly travelled by Telegraph to London and remained there and in Brighton until the 17th. He went to the Lyceum to see Martin Chuzzlewit and Aladdin (both part of the same bill) and to the Haymarket where, as 'The Queen this morning gave birth to her 2d son . . . God save the Q. was plaid, & of course the whole house stood'. He saw to his and George Romilly's financial affairs and delivered a box of new clothes to Lucy's protégée Carry Hudson. 'She is now in her 15th year: is short & thin: does not walk lame: but is not strong for household work . . . She knew me immediately'. From Carry's mistress's house he went by boat to Westminster and, as last year, to 'the gratuitous exhibition in Westminster Hall of Cartoons, Frescoes & Sculpture. — Of the Frescoes I liked best, 'Peace crowned with Flowers' by Bendixen, 'Cath. Douglas barring the door with her arm' by Redgrave, 'Milton dictating to his daughters' by Bridges, & 'Pucks Mission' by Townsend' . . . In the National Gallery he greatly admired 'the two new Pictures

---

63 T.E. Hook's *Peter Priggins, the college scout* was published in 1841. Many years before Hook had left Oxford under a cloud after two terms. He had volunteered 'to sign forty articles should such be the desire of the authorities' (D.N.B.) Hook was required by the University to subscribe only to the 39 articles of the Church of England.

64 See 14 November 1843.

65 The trumpet blast seems to have achieved its object as in 1845 Ibotson became Perpetual Curate of St James Norlands, Kensington of which the Vicar of Kensington, Archdeacon Sinclair, was patron.

. . . The Judgement of Paris by Rubens as a piece of colouring is quite wonderful:— the Guido is very beautiful:— the subject is 'Lot going from Sodom with his 2 daughters' '.

On 7 August Romilly travelled to Brighton in a second class carriage: 'for ¾ hour there was fierce driving rain wh. made me regret not having come in the 1st Cl.'[66] He again stayed at Mrs Well's boarding house where the bow window of his room looked over the sea and where he took 6 hot baths. The weather was wild and often wet and he was able to bathe in the sea only on his last day. He and John Guthrie, an old Trinity man, walked and went to H.V. Elliott's Church and Lady Huntingdon's chapel and in the evenings he played whist. He found Arthur Stanley's life of Dr. Arnold[67] 'peculiarly interesting as showing how completely he made all his teaching religious'.

After a particularly stormy day Guthrie and Romilly dined with Elliott where the talk was largely about Tractarianism. At tea-time the topic was 'more amusing' — that of mesmerism. 'I was very much surprised at finding 2 clever highly-educated men like Cavendish and Kennaway believers in this mummery. Cavendish told a story of clairvoyance wch we received with shouts of laughter:— he said, a young woman had a letter handed to her wch she forthwith sat upon & repeated its contents. — Guthrie goes the extraordinary length of believing a man to have had his leg cut off while he was in mesmeric sleep & quite unconscious of anything painful'.[68]

Romilly's last day in Brighton was 'lovely & sunshiny'. In London he 'called on Frances Wilderspin & gave her 10s and a keepsake from Brighton', before going to Cambridge by the Star. Once there he bought 'Henslow's remarks on Suffolk Labourers' distress:— read it till dark'.

Tu. 20 Wrote to Miss Lodge & the Librarian. G.T. Romilly came down today: he brought with him a little picture wch he had painted in oils from an indifferent engraving of my Uncle Sir S. in one of the periodicals.[69] Took George and his friend Jos. Smith to dine in hall:— they went to drink wine with Tooke:— I went into the Combination room to chat with Sedgwick who arrived today with his niece Isabel & her brother Dick. Sedgwick told us an interesting story of a young girl who went over to Ostend with him, & who he delivered over to the porter of a nunnery at Bruges: Sedgwick dissuaded her very strongly against taking the vows & told her that she would certainly regret it & be very unhappy:— she answered that she

---

[66] Romilly had saved 4 shillings by travelling second class. In 1844 the fare between London and Brighton at an average speed of 20 m.p.h. was 1st: 11 6, 2nd: 7.6, 3rd: 5.0. According to a letter from C.J. Gale to the President of the Board of Trade printed in *Tracts Railways*, London, (John Murray 1844) 'the improved second-class carriages are much more comfortable than was the outside of a coach'. However the second-class carriages had no cushions on their seats and on 21 July 1840 Romilly recorded 'a good deal of rain which beat in as there are no curtains (much less sashes) to these 2d class carriages'.

[67] I.e. A.P. Stanley s *The Life and Correspondence* of Thomas Arnold, (2 vols. 1844).

[68] English doctors, unlike their European colleagues, were exceptional in not using 'magnetism' as a therapeutic agency. However, in 1841 James Braid, a Manchester surgeon, made a careful study of 'hypnotism' as he was the first to call it, and John Elliotson of University College, London used it as an anaesthetic in surgical operations until the discovery of chloroform in 1848 made it obsolete.

[69] Engravings of the portraits of Sir Samuel Romilly by Sir Thomas Lawrence, Martin Cregan, and others are in print room 21 in the British Museum. The portraits are in the National Portrait Gallery.

thought herself made for a nun, because she was of such a cheerful temper:— poor girl! she was only 16 . . . To an Evening party at the Marchesa's: good Hullah singing. Lucy took Susan Chune to Carus's Lecture in White Hart Yard.[70] It was on the Lords Supper.

Wed. 21. . . . Dinner to Marquis & Marchesa Spineto & 4 Miss Dorias, Prof. Miss & Dick Sedgwick, Ansted, Thurtell, Carus & George. — This was Meggy Doria's 1st dining out: & it was comical enough that my goddaughter Bessy's 1st dining out was also at my rooms. . . . Our principal conversation was about 'Dr. Arnold's Life'. — The night was fine & we walked home with the 6 ladies.

Th. 22. . . . G.T. Romilly gave a wine party & had supper in my rooms. — I did not go to his party . . . Letter from a Mr Horington with whom I had travelled to town on the 5th & praised his philosophical bearing of the loss of his Luggage:— he is an Oxford man:— he sent me the Prospectus of a book of his on 'Consecration of Churchs' [sic]:— — I sent him back a money order for 7s, the price of his book:— I must not be civil to strangers again . . .

Sat. 24. . . . Today Miss Corfield came to take leave of M. on her quitting Mrs Clarks. M. very characteristically prevented an hours sentimentality by reading French with her. Miss Corfield brought her a present of some pretty worsted-work (in a frame) to support a teapot . . .

Sun. 25. M. L. Esther Baily & I to Trinity where Carus preached an excellent sermon from 1 Cor. XI 23.29 on the Lords Supper. — M. & I took a good walk the day being nice & cool. — Wrote to Edw. Allen:— a grateful letter from G.B.A. in answer to mine about his attachment to Miss Dora Eaton![71] — In the Evening read loud the Pilgrims Progress with great delight.

Sat. 31. Scena down stairs (in consequence of W. Barker (the gardeners son) having borrowed £2 of Sarah (at the suggestion of Betsy who declined for herself) the day before his marriage & not having kept his promise of paying.) — : Betsy came up & gave warning, — wch we laughed at . . . Double walk with M. Began reading loud Alice (the continuation of Ernest Maltravers).[72]

Sun. 1 Sept. We met Professor Smyth with his stick & gouty shoe, & were glad to find him much better than he was a year ago: he was very cheerful & conversible in spite of his deafness.

---

[70] The White Hart was in King Street and there was a room in its yard. The only school in King Street at this time was the National School for girls and the infant school in a room attached to it. See 27 April 1842.

[71] George had written to his uncle to say that he was in love 'but that his father objects'.

[72] *Ernest Maltravers* by E.G.E. Bulwer Lytton was published in 1837, *Alice* in 1838.

Mon. 2. Letter from Baugh about George's love affair with Miss Dora Eaton:[73] wrote to him & to George, dissuading marriage till there is 500 a year certain & a foundation of an increasing income from the bar. — Wrote to G.T. Romilly sending him £5. . . .

Wed. 4. Dr. Phelps married to Loraine Skrine. I went to the breakfast where I met the bride's 3 sisters & their husbands, the 3 bridesmaids (Miss Wilkins & 2 Miss Dorias) etc, etc. Little or no crying — Carus called upon Lucy to announce the Feast to his Sunday school today. From Carus's account we expected that he would address the children upon their entering the Trinity roundabout at ¼ to 3 or certainly before 4, so we ordered our dinner at 4½. We (i.e. Lucy & I, for M prudently staid at home) arrived as the children entered the grounds, & witnessed their walk round & their sports (relieved by munching apples & pears handed about by the Teachers in reversed parasols, handkerchiefs etc).:— by the way the girls dances & songs were all about 'kissing', 'sweethearts', 'nice young men all to themselves', & such matrimonial speculations. — A few minutes before 4 Carus retreated: we jealousied[74] that the carnal appetites were conquering the pastoral solicitude:— & so it proved:— for on passing thro the skreens we saw him at his dinner in the hall:— we learned (from Miss Watson) that he would return to the grounds at 5 & make an address to the children; upon the conclusion of the address the children were to sing G. save the Queen & then go immediately to the rooms (in White Ht Yard) to have tea. So from Carus's want of explicitness we missed all that we wanted to hear, for we had no desire to be present at their singing a hymn in the schoolroom before they started. — However our labour was not quite thrown away, for Lucy saved the life of a frog from the inhuman boys. I gathered a beautiful nosegay for M:— & besides the day was lovely & it was delightful to see the sports of the children . . .

Fri. 6. Lucy had a letter from her pretty, unhealthy protégée Susan Chune, — saying that her strength had broke down in her hard place, & that she must quit it. The Lords have reversed the Sentence of O'Connell; so he has had 4 months of false imprisonment![75] — Good letter from

---

73 The Eatons of Parcglas, whom George and Edward had known from childhood, were near neighbours of Baugh's in Wales, so near that on 14 August 1838 Romilly wrote that in 'coming home it was pitch dark and we had the greatest difficulty in finding our way thro Mrs Eaton's trees and over the brook'. During this and many subsequent holidays there were frequent visits to or from the Eatons and although theirs was not an 'old' family like the Allens it is surprising that Baugh was so vehemently opposed to George's engagement. George nevertheless married Dora (Dorothea) in 1847, the year after his father's death and two years later Edward Allen married her sister Bertha.

74 Romilly is using a verb now found only in Scottish and northern dialects. To jealouse means to have a suspicion or to suspect a thing or person.

75 On 30 May Daniel O'Connell, the Irish leader, and his chief colleagues had been sentenced to 12 months' imprisonment and a fine of £2000 for creating discontent and disaffection among the Queens' subjects and for contriving 'by means of intimidation and the demonstration of great physical force, to procure and effect changes to be made in the government, laws and constitution of this realm'.

Lodge giving me an account of a nunnery not far from Leamington which he has just visited, & where he met with marked respect. — which he ascribes to his known Puseyism. — He went to this nunnery (at Princethorp) with a Colonel Morgan & had a letter to the Father Confessor Dr. Thurer: he however was absent & the letter was given to the Lady Abbess, who in ¼ hr came with the Vice Abbess in the Benedictine dress & did the Honors.

Mon. 9.   Letter from Baugh:— rather absurd, says 'he would rather see G. hanged than living at Mrs Eatons' . . .

Wed. 11.   Letter from Miss Butcher about her friend Louisa Pearce who is desirous of setting up a school: the foolish girl has refused to marry Mr. Williams (the clergyman of Hauxton) because he is very ugly & lame & wears a red wig:— sent her £10. Her brother J.B. was acquitted of bigamy, tho both wives are alive . . .

Th. 12.   . . . Lucy walked with M & me to Decks to smell 'Prussic Acid': we found very little smell in it. — Her curiosity had been excited by the trial of Belaney for poisoning his wife with Prussic Acid:— he was acquitted indeed, but the evidence of the Medical men made so frightfully against him that many persons think him guilty.[76] — In the Evening read loud some of Miss Martineau's 'Life in a Sick Room'.

Sat. 14.   A.T. Russell asked me to do duty for him at Caxton (11 miles off) next 2 Sundays:— I declined his somewhat unreasonable request, but gave him a Guinea to get a substitute . . .

Mon. 16.   . . . M. & I picked up a maidservant who fell over the stones lying at Miss Bones's door:— she was carrying a tray to the baker — she fell with her face on the edge of a stone & was much bruised: she was insensible when I took her up & fainted in my arms. Happily Mr. Hammond the Surgeon was passing by & I handed her over to him . . .

Sat. 21.   . . . In the Evening read loud the conclusion of Miss Martineau's 'Life in a Sick room'. A great deal of it is too refined & philosophical for the great mass of mankind, who have not such mental resources. — Religion is scarcely introduced in the whole vol. The love of truth is admirable.

Sun. 22.   Began fires . . . M. & L. called upon the Paupers. Lucy found her protégée Eliza Gilmour had staid away from Sunday Sch. & Church because (forsooth) the new bonnet (making for her by L.) is not yet finished. — Lucy made her put on her old one & took her to Church at 3:— the child had lyingly pretended she was not well. — Finished a List of the Texts preached on by Carus, & presented it to L. In the Evening read loud Pilgrims' Prog.

---

[76] Belaney had ceased to practice as a surgeon in Sunderland and at the time of the trial managed the lime works there which had recently been inherited by his wife. On a visit to London from Sunderland Belany bought prussic acid for, he said, his own medicinal use. The jury had to decide whether Belany had administered the prussic acid draught which he had prepared or whether his wife had drunk it by mistake.

Mon. 23. Visit from Mrs Hayles. — Took M. to see the elegant new Storey Alms houses,[77] & the Dissenters Burial ground. — In the Evening read loud Boswell's Johnson, also Johnson's London, Boileaus 1st Sat. etc.[78]

Wed. 25. M's birthday. — Thank God she is quite well:— gave her a shawl (from Bakers)[79] & Lucy also. — Letter from Denning about G's proposed residence in London: of course highly objecting — wrote to him.[80] At night read loud Miss Edgworth's Birthday Present & Simple Susan:— our Cook (Sarah Ironsides) made M. a present of a pair of soles for dinner in honor of her birthday.

Sat. 28. L. took home to Carus 'Arnolds Life' wch he had lent her, — & gave him a grand nosegay wch she had got out of Mrs Clark's garden by bribing the gardener . . .

Mon. 30. . . . A letter from Mr Bernard saying that votes of unsuccessful candidates at the B. Orphan are to be registered for future occasions: we think this is a death blow to the borrowing system, & that Lucy will have to pay for her borrowed proxies.[81]

Wed. 2 October. Latin day:— conducted by me:— Carus was my sleeping partner. — Dined in Hall. — By our new arrangements we have the Examination over before dinner & dine at 5. — This Evening my portrait came down on the Piano & frightened the women by the din it made.[82] — Lodge returned to Cambridge this night & happily was to all appearance (bating a little cold) in excellent health.

Fri. 4. 4th day Fellowship Ex. — Metaphysics in the morning, Mathematics in Aft. . . . A venison feast in hall: The Master & a large party there. — By the way the Master has given offence by writing (on the 1st day of Examination) to the Examiner (who happened to be Gosset) directing him to desire the candidates 'to write good English'.

Sat. 5. 5th & last d. of Examination — Miscellaneous Paper & Greek composition . . . I found poor Lodge in bed & awfully out of spirits — (his cousin Annette has unfortunately set her affections upon him: he will have nothing to say to marrying her:— an eclaircissement has taken place in

77 The almshouses were founded under the will of Edward Storey who died in 1692. In 1843 the houses for widows of clergymen and others, which had been in Northampton Street, were rebuilt on Mount Pleasant. These were mock-Tudor buildings erected at a cost of about £6000 by order of the Court of Chancery. The inmates each received about £45 a year.
78 I.e. the celebrated poems on London (1738) and Paris (1660), both in imitation of Juvenal's third Satire.
79 In Pigot's *Directory* for 1839 William Baker is listed as having a shop on Market Hill.
80 George moved to 34 Percy Street, Tottenham Court Road on 31 September.
81 See 11 February.
82 Presumably the small water-colour by Miss Hervé which was painted in 1836 and has hung for many years in the University Registry. We know of no other. On 17 March 1836 Romilly wrote 'Called on the Marchesa . . . took her advice & went to Miss Hervé to sit for a miniature: found the artist very gay & agreeable & enjoyed my sitting. — She came over at the revocation of the E. of Nantes . . .' Romilly had six sittings and on 25 March 'Got my miniature from Miss Hervé.'

wch the Father and stepmother etc say Lodge has behaved most honorably:— but of course he can never go to Hawkshead till the young lady or himself is married).[83] — All this has preyed upon his mind.

Mon. 7. M, L. & I went over the house of a Mrs Barker (just dead): we found it a bijou of neatness. — Lodge passed a good night, but still keeps his bed. — All day working at Fellowship papers.

Tu. 8. M, L. & I went over the house of a Mrs Maxey (just dead)[84] & fell in love with a piece of Dresden china (a sleeping boy & a girl blowing a horn in his ear) — Maltreated by my Flyman who never sent a fly for me, & after waiting ½ hr I went to the Blue Boar & found the horse in the stable:— I arrived very late at Madingley . . . Played 4 rubbers: the players were Lady Cotton, Sir St. Vincent, Mrs Charles Townley & I.

Wed. 9. I have this day completed my 53rd year & am, thank God, quite well. Dined at home:— it would have been most unnatural to do otherwise on my birthday. — We had Packe's partridges . . .

Th. 10. To chapel at ¼ to 9 to pronounce the Election. — Got my Clerk to bid for the China: got it a bargain, viz. for £1.7. — & duty 1s.2. . . .

Sat. 12. Election of Caput. — To Ely by the Lynn Coach. — Dr. Lamb & I were outside & the Bishops 2 sons (George & William) inside:— the Bps youngest son is banished by his Father to the Isle of Jersey. — Went to the Palace:— Ld. Spencer pays his annual visit at this time: Ld. Sp's companion in his carriage was a favorite pointer, — as a sort of compensation for missing his favorite sport of shooting . . .

Tu. 15. . . . Consecration of St. Paul's Church: we did not go, but sent the maids. — gave dinner to the Bride (Mrs Phelps) & bridegroom, V. Chr. (Dr. Hodgson) Dr & Mrs Graham, Dr & Mrs Whewell, Mrs Archdall, Mr & Mrs Skrine & Mrs Dav. Stewart. — I had a little bouquet for each guest, & everything was most successful in the cooking, lighting, & attendance:— went off capitally. The Skrines didn't come till ½ hr after the time thro Flymans villainy. — After all the rest of the company was gone the Skrines fly had not arrived, so Mr & Mrs Skrine played whist against me & dumby:— they won both rubbers. — By the way the Bride was dressed in a superb dark coloured dress, which was thrown away upon me, for I took it for mourning . . .

Wed. 16. Today (under the superintendance of Mr Ling)[85] Margaret sent off George Romilly's Piano Forte: it was put in a case sent down by Broadwood. — she sent also his Music Waggon, sword, Chimney

[83] See 3 August 1844. On 17 October Miss Lodge wrote to Romilly 'expressing her hope that her cousin . . . would come to her Fathers as she could remain with her G. Father or her great friend Miss Bliss'.

[84] Mrs Barker and Mrs Maxey lived near the Romillys, Mrs Barker at Osborne Terrace, Hills Road, and Mrs Maxey at Bene't Place. Advertisements for the viewing and sale by auction of their furnishings were placed in *The Cambridge Chronicle* of 28 September and catalogues could be had. The long list of Mrs Maxey's 'Genteel' furniture etc. is a good guide to the contents of a comfortable middle-class home of the day.

[85] Mr Ling's music shop was in King's Parade.

MARGARET
ROMILLY

G.T. ROMILLY

L. BAUGH ALLEN

ornaments &c.[86] — Lodge left Cambridge to-day with his man John Smith for St. Leonards:— they went in a Fly as far as Trumpington to avoid salutations on departure. — Lucy has induced Edw. Romilly (without actual asking) to subscribe a Guinea to the Governesses Institution in behalf of Mrs Mann.[87] — Breakfast to P.T. Ouvry & his brother John North (a freshman of 28, late in the army)[88] . . .

Fri. 18.   Breakfast to the 2 Ouvrys & Wm. Vizard junior (the Father having left Cambridge) & his brother Henry Brougham (a freshman) . . . Baugh's aversion the Baron de Rutzen[89] called on me yesterday to claim for his son the privilege of wearing a hat:— I told him that I believed he had no such right, but would refer him to the V. Ch. & Heads who were the interpreters of our Statutes.[90] — The V.C. indeed forgot at the meeting of the Heads to-day to consult them, but quite agreed with me that he had no right — I communicated the decision to the Baron, who takes it in high dudgeon that a privilege should be granted to the son of an English Baron of yesterday's creation wch is refused to him whose nobility is of 200 years standing. — The Baron de Rothschild's son did not wear a hat:— The Count Charles d'Aglie indeed did wear a hat, but his Father (whose only son he was) had been embassador at our Court from that of the K. of Sardinia, & was therefore Rt. Honorable in England . . .

Sat. 19.   Poor John North Ouvry has been found deficient in classics at our Admission Examination: he has 24 companions but he is extremely dejected & talks of renouncing a College career. — Proclaimed the Markets. — Looked over parcel of books in the Library . . .

Sun. 20.   A letter from George Romilly saying that he had been for 2 years in love with Fanny Smith!!![91] — he has reached 21 years of age & the intended has attained the mature age of 16!!!!! I wrote him a long letter, disapproving of his engaging himself now, & of his ever marrying till he

---

[86]   George was presumably able to house his treasures now that he no longer lived at Mr Denning's. On 3 December 1844 his uncle reported that his lodgings were 'large and sweet'.

[87]   The Governesses' Benevolent Institution helped with pensions rather than residential accommodation.

[88]   On 6 February 1838 Romilly recorded that John Ouvry had come of age '& is therefore going to qualify himself for succeeding to his Aunt's property by assuming the name of North — he & his brother Henry are both with their regiments in Ireland'.

[89]   The Baron's family was Russian. He lived however in Pembrokeshire as did Baugh Allen. This son was the eldest of three who came to the University from Eton and was admitted Fellow-Commoner at Magdalene on 20 October 1844. The other two sons were at Trinity.

[90]   The relevant statute was no. 46 of the 1570 statutes *De vestitu scholarium* whereby scholars were forbidden to wear hats but sons of Lords and the eldest sons of Knights were entitled to wear them instead of caps whilst they were undergraduates. The Baron's son was not so entitled because he was a foreigner. These 1570 statutes remained in force until the 1850's.

[91]   Fanny's father was a stationer and George had known him and his family since childhood. In August 1855 Romilly wrote that he 'was shocked to hear that Mr. Smith (of Dulwich and Long Acre) . . . is ruined:— I thought he had been a wealthy prosperous man'.

has £700 a year: spoke of his own feeble constitution, & of the danger of consumption in the lady:[92] deprecated long engagements, especially for a person of so restless & fickle a temper, & alluded to the possibility of his wishing himself un-married when too late . . .

Tu. 22. Yesterday Lucy sent off to Mr. Bernard 8 Proxies (containing 30 votes) for the Governesses' Institution in behalf of Miss Mann. — Foggy sort of damp November day:— took out M. in spite of some reluctance of hers. — Lucy & I met in the Townhall at a Bazaar for the London Mission's Jubilee (the Society was founded Sept 1795): the great room was fitted up with tea things (& nosegays) for several hundreds, & looked very pretty:— the supper-room was used for the Bazaar: Miss Thoday & other dissenters were the sellers: Lucy bought baby linen:— I bought some trumpery: one paid 6d for entrance. — Today received from Dr. Jan of Schweinfurt (in Bavaria) the Macrobius M.S. wch I had sent him out of the Public Library; he wrote a very civil Latin Letter:— I answered him in the same language
. . .

Th. 24. . . . Miss Corfield wrote to M. to lament her having got into a situation where she fears the mistress is so in more senses than one & fears that she will by cruel treatment beat the child to death. — I wrote to Miss Corfield in M's name recommending her leaving instantly . . .

Sat. 26. Letter from Miss Corfield telling us that she had rushed away from the den of iniquity (with the loss of her linen at the washerwoman's) & is now safe with her mother . . . Dined at Lady Cottons . . . Little Augusta Fisher (5 years old) repeated (very prettily) to me a little French story, but declined singing a French song *before so many people*:— so I am to have that pleasure at some tête à tête. — 5 Rubbers. — Made Dunford an out-patient of the Hospital.

Sun. 27. M. & I to Trin. Ch. Mr. Pym preached for the Jews for 70 minutes (unmerciful man!).[93]

Wed. 30. Congregation day — Hildyard (Christs)'s Grace (for reappointment as Classical Tripos Examiner) thrown out by 17 to 5 in the Black House . . . Thompson (Trinity) gave the 1st Non Placet — Hildyard had made himself most obnoxious to his Brother Examiners last year & had added to his unpopularity by his recent attack on Private Tuition.

Th. 31. . . . Dinner at Magdalene Lodge. — The Master amused me by apologising to me for having survived all our contemporaries & having asked none but youngsters to meet me. There was only one Lady beside the members of the Family, a certain Miss Williams. — I found the party very pleasant. — A rubber at Lewis's (an undergraduate of Caius): the party

[92] In October 1828 George, 'our little man' was 'dangerously ill' and for many years from then on the diaries report his uncle's intermittment anxiety about his health.

[93] On 28 February 1841 Romilly likened him to 'a Republican Puritan come back into the world. He preached with great fluency, entirely extempore, but it was very hard & insufferably long'. See also 30 October 1842.

consisted of a Mr. Croxton (a Fellow Commoner of Caius), Skrine, Mills & Eyres.

Fri. 1 November.   Lodge kept his bed today till near 2 when he got up:— he & Bowtell went off by the Rocket & are to reach Hawkshead tomorrow morning at 11. — Dined at the Family at Shaws: a very small party: 8; viz. Shaw, Tatham, Haviland, Paget, Packe, Power, Cartmell & I . . . Dr. Graham could not come, as Mrs. G. has miscarried:— Mortlock's resignation was announced. — Shaw mentioned the epigram on Ld. Elgin.

> Noseless himself he brings home noseless blocks,
> To show what time can do & what the p —

— Packe convulsed us with laughter by a coachman's account of real gentility: he said 'Sir Henry sat by me all day on the Box: he is a real gentleman: he can drive through a keyhole, — but that ain't it — he didn't break wind once, — as I know of'. — Dr. Haviland communicated a conundrum 'what flower is a nursery full of children like?' — answer 'Everlasting pea.' — A magnificent dinner:— enough for 20 people. —

Sat. 2.   — Wet day: the women not out. — M. & I yesterday visited the Railway works on the Hills Road: 70 men at work:[94]— one asked me to lend him 1s:— I was not rash enough to do so. — Today received a picture from George Romilly: it is a copy of Denning's of his youngest daughter lying on a sofa:— sent him £5 for it. — At night read loud Richard Parkinsons 'Old Church Clock': it is of the ultra tory and high church order:— too little incident in it.[95]

Sun. 3.   Nasty wet morning: we went in a fly!:— Carus preached from 1st Lesson Prov. 2.1-6: it was an excellent address on 'true wisdom' to the freshmen — we had a visit from John Ouvry:— he staid about 10 times too long.— In the Evening read loud with much pleasure 'Some passages in the Life of a Radical by Bamford'. — He was one of the Manchester weavers![96] — The Freshmen of Trinity (150!) were today directed to dine at 5 after the 1st dinner: they did not in fact get their dinner till 5½. — They are to dine at 5 every feastday this term.

Mon. 4.   . . . We ought to have met at Eyres rooms for the Whist Club tonight, but he very uncivilly put us all off till tomorrow, *that he might go out shooting:*— guess he will have a small party. — Heard a rich story about the said Eyres:— viz. that he went over with 3 other fellows of Caius to hold a court at Shelford, & while they were playing bowls he would not wait till

---

[94]   So many labourers were working on the railway lines in 1844 that a Chaplain was appointed to them and services held in St Mary's Chapel, Barnwell. (See UP 16, 399).

[95]   On November 4 Romilly reported after further reading that the 'account of Robert Walker . . . who united great pastoral zeal with rustic labour is very interesting'. Richard Parkinson was a canon of Manchester collegiate church and twice Hulsean lecturer. The *Old Church Clock* was published in 1843.

[96]   *Passages in the Life of a Radical* were published from 1840-44. See *D.N.B.* for an account of Samuel Bamford's life.

they had done, but went back to Cambr. in the Fly by himself, leaving his friends to walk.

Sun. 10. . . . Bright sunshiny morning: about ¼ to 1 it began to reign [sic]:— M. Esther & I went home instantly, but it took Lucy to ¼ past 4 to get home, she stopping at different places in the vain hope of the rain ceasing:— to her great annoyance several people insisted on her coming into their houses: one of these (Mrs Rickard) amused her by the account of her husbands last illness: she described his childishness, his greediness, &c & her own great joy when he was fairly dead . . .

Tu. 12. Lucy caught a bad cold by her long standing up for the rain on Sunday. — Bought of Styles (the chapel marker)[97] another of the China groups which we had admired at Mrs. Maxeys sale . . . Learned that the boy in 'Old Church Clock' who saves the hero from being beaten by his Father . . . was the present President of Queens (Dr. King).

Th. 14. Matriculation — Total 432 — 145 of Trinity viz. 2 N, 6 F.C, 132 P, 5 S; St. Johnns [sic] had 91, viz. 1 F.C, 68 P, 22 S. — Not over till near 3. . . .

Fri. 15. Trial in V.C's Court of our neighbour Mr. Crowe (the builder), Haylock (the Chemist) & Dan. Pate (of the Mechanics Institute) for lending money to an undergraduate of St Johns named Haberden . . .

Tu. 19. Good walk with M, & then one with Peacock to discuss arrangements about Library:— there is to be a Grace to appoint me Deputy Librarian, etc. . . .

Th. 21. . . . Dined in hall:— our nos are now so great that 'the Deans Table'[98] is used for the Freshmen: I not having dined in hall this term

[97] Whewell told the Royal University Commissioners in 1851 that the 'students are required to attend at the [chapel] service once at least every day, and twice on the Sunday. Default of attendance is noticed by remonstrance from the Deans, and by constraints and 'impositions', or tasks imposed by them'. (See Winstanley chapter 16.) William Glover left Cambridge in 1842, having been a chorister, but not a member of the University. In his *The Memoirs of a Cambridge Chorister* vol 2 (1885), 216–17 he describes the duties of the Trinity chapel markers. 'Two 'markers' stand in the centre of the chapel, with something like slate-frames, covered with tightly-stretched canvas, in their hands. On these frames they place very long rolls of paper, made after the fashion of those used in ancient times. The feat of pricking their names is truly astonishing. Five or six hundred men rush forward . . . in utter confusion and take their places, frequently at a great distance from the registrars, who, however, rarely move from their position to ask a question . . . The important pin is pressed into this roll of fame or shame, and rarely can an error be detected in the accounts of these sleepless sentinels.' After the psalms for the day were 'chanted fully, the sacred roll is quickly deposited under the dean's equally sacred cushion, and the markers rush off to another parish'. See also *V.C.H.* Vol. III facing p. 240 for an illustration entitled 'Chapel Service in Trinity College 1842' by R.W. Buss which shows a marker in action. College servants such as John Fynn, head porter of Corpus from 1804-48 sometimes marked in addition to their other duties. Fynn was allowed £4 per annum for marking. See Patrick Bury, *Corpus Christi College* (1952), p.25.

[98] Dr Robson tells us that the two high tables are still referred to as the Vice-Master's and the Dean's tables and that before the dais was extended in the late nineteenth century the Dean's table must have been below the dais and parallel with the other tables there. The Bursar's table, which no longer exists, was presumably one of these.

JOHN LODGE

ADAM SEDGWICK

WILLIAM WHEWELL

WILLIAM CARUS

before was quietly going to seat myself among the freshmen! — The Dean now sits at the Bursars Table . . .

Sat. 23. 3rd & last Court in the usurious transaction:— the 3 Culprits (Crowe, Haylock & Pate) were discommuned. — M. L. & I gave ourselves up to civility: we called on Mrs Whewell, Mrs Barker, Mrs Hayles, Mrs Simpson & Mr Barry:— we got in at only 2 . . . Dined at Cummings . . . Asked also to Magdalene Lodge . . .

Sun. 24. M, L, Esther & I to Trin. Ch. where Carus preached an excellent 3 yr old sermon . . . Mrs Houghton, Lucy & I to St. Mary's where we heard Theyre Smith preach on 'the leaven of the Pharisees wch is hypocrisy':— I was greatly pleased, but Lucy was disgusted with the matter & the manner:— but she was prejudiced . . . & the conclusion (about praying to God in secret) was very fine. Lucy, Mrs Houghton & I then went to Kings: it was very full, L. sat in a stall, Mrs. H. in one of the lower seats & I on the steps: we were very fortunate, for we had Haydn's Pastoral Symphone as a prelude, 'The Marvellous Works' for an Anthem, & were played out with 'The Heavens are telling'. — We then visited Kings Hall, Trin. Coll. Hall (where dinner was going on:— I took them into the Gallery (where the Freshmen were dining) that they might have a good view: I apologised to the freshmen for the intrusion). — I also exhibited the 2 Combination Rooms to them. — E. Allen dined with us:— he came as usual to the Sermon at Trinity.

Tu. 26. Dined in Hall: met there Mr. Peter Cator who is come down to offer 'the Peregrine Maitland' Prize for a triennial missionary Essay' . . .

Wed. 27. Congregation Day — the Missionary-Essay Prize accepted: it was made a high-church & low-church question: in the Black House the nos. were 14 to 4, the dissentients being Blakesley, Dr. Mill, Archd. Thorp & Thompson (of Trinity): in the White House the nos were 19 to 3: the 3 Malcontents being F.A. Paley, Freeman (Pet.) & Goodwin (Caius) — Shirked Mrs Havilands Ball. — Yesterday Evening went to a grand Hullah[99] singing at Trin. Lodge: Hullah himself directed: Mrs Hullah was there:— everything went off capitally: 'Crabbed Age', 'Let us all amaying go' &c were performed:— there was a large party & the room was well lighted, & the company well drest.

On 2 December Romilly went to London and stayed with the Edward Romillys in Stratton Street. He saw to his financial affairs, gave both his London nephews dinner at a Chop-house and then took them to a 5-act comedy at the Haymarket by Boucicault which was followed by one dull and one amusing farce. He inspected

---

[99] On 22 February 1844 Whewell in a letter to Archdeacon Hare, wrote 'I think you would laugh . . . if you were here to witness what we are going to set about tomorrow — a set of singing lessons under the direction of Mr. Hullah — we being forty Masters of Arts, who meet at my Lodge. Many of them want to learn, that they may be able to direct the teaching of singing in their parishes, which they have or hope to have'. In Manchester in July 1842 the number of people attending Hullah's classes was reckoned to be fifty thousand.

the young men's lodgings, visited 'all the principal architectural improvements in London' and was delighted by the recent acquisitions at the National Gallery 'viz. Rubens Judgement of Paris & a Guido (our Lord & John the Baptist as Children)'. On 5 December he and George went 'down to Camb. by the Star'.

Fri. 6. To the meeting of the subsyndicate in the Library:— Lodge had made up his mind to tender his resignation:— but nobody came except the Master of Trinity, — & nothing was done. — Walk afterwards with Lodge to see the Railway works. — George dined in hall with me:— he then had a wine party &c in my rooms . . .

Sun. 8. Sharp frost with bitter N.E. wind. — M, L, & I in Trinity Church where Carus gave us a 3 yr old Sermon . . . Edward (who came to the sermon) walked with me to see the railway works at the Paper-mills turnpike[1] & the osier-bed near Chesterton. — Edward drank tea with us. — Read 'Claims of Labour' by A. Helps.[2]

Sat. 14. . . . Called congregation for Maitland-Prize Examiners. — Declined the Hullah-Sacred-singing at Trinity Lodge . . . today being Commemoration day[3] went to Chapel:— Birks preached a high flown but clever sermon from Colossians 2.2.3 in wch he lashed the Puseyites. — Then to Hall to hear the Prize Eng. & Lat. speeches. — I enacted Senior Dean & gave away the Prizes for Eng. Declamation & for Reading . . .

Mon. 16. Dismissal of Term . . .

Tu. 17. Very cold indeed from a sharp N.E. wind. — My poor late Gyp Dunford went to the Union today:[4] my bedmaker Mrs Carpenter kindly accompanied him:— Dunford is so offensive in his person that no person will lodge him. — I ought to have dined at Madingley today, but I received a letter, to my great amusement, from Lady Cotton, putting me off because she was out of coals! The frost at the Locks has stopped the coal barges[5] . . .

Th. 19. Sent Miss Burdett £6.5. — also a copy of Burders Sermons. — Letter from her, recommending her friend Miss Pearce as a worker of

---

[1] See 27 April 1842.

[2] Arthur Helps's *The Claims of Labour, an essay* was published in 1844. He was a Trinity graduate (B.A. 1835) who had been secretary to Spring Rice and Lord Morpeth.

[3] Commemoration Day was held on or near 19 December until the twentieth century when it was moved to the end of Lent Full Term so as to get out of the way of the entrance scholarship examining which used to happen in December. There is no longer a prize-giving, but the benefactors of Trinity are still remembered annually in chapel.

[4] I.e. to the Central Union Poor House in Mill Road, built in 1838 with room for 250 inmates.

[5] J.W. Clark in his 'Memories and Customs (1820-1860)' reprinted from *The Cambridge Review,* Lent Term 1909, writes that although the undergraduate could light a fire in his rooms 'he was to a certain extent at the mercy of the weather — and in severe winters, when the Cam was frozen over, and barges could not get up from Lynn to Cambridge, the supply of fuel has been known to run out, and chairs, gun-cases, and other articles of furniture to be used until they also came to an end . . . In those days . . . the older members of the University seemed to be quite insensible to cold. I can recollect that so late as 1859 the library of Trinity College was not warmed'.

Collars etc . . . & wishing hereafter for Newton on the prophecies.[6] — Visit from Mrs Heaviside. — Read loud Hallingdon Hall [sic]:[7]— much ridicule of novelties in manuring:— Jorrocks talks indeed of Guano, of nitrate of *sober,* etc, but his cidevant huntsman Pigg always exclaims 'Mucks the Man' . . .

Sat. 21. A letter from a mad Mrs Stone (who cannot be persuaded to leave the town):— the wildest letter I ever had: she began 'heavenly Joseph Romilly' and spoke of herself as 'pretty Nancy'. — Today 2 brothers of W. Newby (the coalmerchant) called on me, saying *that he certainly would die in a few days* & bespeaking my favor for the continuance of his places to his widow. — Dined in hall.

Sun. 22. . . . From the dead letter office a letter of mine to Lodge at Berne:— I had signed it J.R. so it was directed back to J.R. & found me:— monstrous clever fellows those post office agents[8] . . .

Mon. 23. Received British Orphan Asylum proxy from Ld A. Hervey. — Began copying out a sermon of Mr Boyers for Xmas. — Read loud Dicken's new work 'the Chimes':— it is a dreamy sentimental production, not at all to my taste: bought it as a present to E.E.A.

Tu. 24. Finished copying the Sermon. — Sent off 'the Chimes':— had to pay 1/6 postage, wch I thought more than the book was worth. — Read loud Close's sermon 'Restitution of Churches Restitution of Popery':— it is a violent attack on the Camden Society & the Ecclesiologist.[9] — The title is offensive: but there is much foundation for a great part of the attack on the Camdenians.

Wed. Christmas Day. Our gatepost attacked in the night & the copingstone thrown down. — Preached in College Chapel (instead of Sedgwick) a sermon of Mr Boyers from Luk. 2.14. — a very small congregation:— out of Chapel at 12:— the women not out of Trin. Church till past 2. Carus preached from Isai. 9.6 'For unto us etc.' Walked to the railway works at the Paper Mills. — M. & L. called on Miss Apthorps. — I went to St. Marys at 2 where Colenso preached from Luk. 2.13.14:— the anthem was 'O thou that tellest etc', capitally performed. — Miss Vincent dined with us. — A very clever letter from E.E. Allen.

Th. 26. Library reopened. Sent off a parcel of books to Miss Cotton. In the Evening read loud Boswell's Life of Johnson. — Mrs Archdall paid us a visit today.

---

[6] Presumably B.W. Newton's *Thoughts on the Apocalypse* (1844).
[7] Surtees's *Hillingdon Hall or the Cockney Square* (1845) appeared first in serial form and had an ironical dedication to the Royal Agricultural Society.
[8] On 18 December Romilly was amused to note that the Duke of Donkeyton in *Hillingdon Hall* 'calls everything 'monstrous' '.
[9] *The Ecclesiologist* founded in November 1841 was the journal of the Camden Society. Close's sermon was preached on 5 November 1844 not many weeks before the committee of the Camden Society recommended its dissolution. For the influence exerted by *The Ecclesiologist* see J.F. White, *The Cambridge Movement* (1962).

Fri. 27. Looked over a parcel of books. — Willis is extremely angry about the confusion in the New Library.[10] I ordered no fresh ones to be introduced till all the new Class marks are put to the former. — Dined at Trin. Hall Hall: a very large party (39) but no distinguished people. I sat next Sir Herbert & found him very agreeable: he told me that I was the only man who had not in talking with him tried to sift him about the Round Church[11] . . .

Tu. 31. 2nd day of B.A. fees; received 124. Dined in Hall & then went home immediately:— at 8 came to Trin. Comb. Room where we had 2 or 3 card tables: I was Vicemaster, the only other Fellows were Thompson & Thacker. — We had a capital supper . . . At midnight Kemp entered the room & gave the customary toast of 'Prosperity to Trinity College':— I then made a little speech on the New Year & gave the Queen, proposing that 'G.s.t. Queen' should be sung:— Walmesley set it up & we all joined in. — I then gave various toasts, such as 'the Bishop of Ely', 'the Medical Profession', 'the discipline officers', etc. wch were responded to by the Master of Dulwich (the Bishops Son), Dr. Fisher, the Junior Proctor (Goodwin), etc. We did not break up till near 3. — Everything went off well. Declined Mrs Havilands juvenile ball.

[10] See 21 March 1844.
[11] See 25 July 1844.

Railway Bridge at Cambridge.

William Carus preaching

The Great Court of Trinity College

The Reception for the British Association

1845

Th. 2 January. . . . Letter from Lodge talking of resigning as his Cousin Richard thinks the thoughts of the Library prey upon his mind.— Looked over & signed Library bills today:— also read over the copy of the Hulse Accounts &c.[1] Read 'Amber Witch' at night.[2]

Fri. 3. On Lucy's strong recommendation wrote to Lodge in recommendation of his resignation. . .

Tu. 7. Letter from Lodge saying that he will come up to resign in person.— Lucy gave ½ Doz. Audit[3] to that impudent Mr Finch at the Hospital who asked for it:— today Lucy sought out in the Hospital a certain Gypsy Widow Smith, who has been visited by Carus & Mrs. Whewell. . . Dined at Kingsleys of Sidney:— it was a Lady party . . . Poor Mrs. Phelps was overcome by the heat of the room & fainted at dessert time:— after she had recovered she said to me 'do your sisters often treat you with scenes of this sort?' . . .

Wed. 8. — Coward (the successful crammer of polloi men, commonly called Polly Hopkins) married to a rich young widow:— a very grand affair.— Dined in Hall because I had to attend a Seniority in the Combination room at ¼ to 5 to pass the Trinity supplicats.— Read loud 'Ferdinand' a French tale written by the author of 'Oeufs de Paques':[4] it was lent me by Isabel Cumming:— an unfit story for young people, being an account of an uncle trying to murder his nephew . . .

Fri. 10. Skrine lent me 'Scenes de la vie privée et publique des animaux':— the stories are by different authors, such as Balzac, &c: the engravings are by Grandville & some of them very clever.[5]— I read the history of the English Cat Beauty, & also that of the French Cat Minette: the 'Chatte Anglaise' is by Balzac; it is coarse and indelicate it is also a ridicule of 'the Saints', & an ill-natured satire on English manners, sneering at our cleanliness, our humanity & the chastity of our married women. . . M, L. & I called on Miss Vincent. Our neighbour, Ebenezer

---

[1] I.e. the accounts of funds bequeathed to the University by the Rev. John Hulse of St John's who died in 1790. They were for religious purposes including a prize and the salaries of the Christian Advocate and Hulsean Lecturer (or Christian Preacher). The electors and trustees were the Vice-Chancellor and the Masters of Trinity and St John's. In 1845 the prize of about £100 was for a dissertation on 'The influence of the Christian Religion in promoting the abolition of Slavery in Europe'.

[2] The English title of a novel by J. W. Meinhold translated in 1844. It is a vivid account of the Thirty Years' War, fabricated to deceive and so ridicule historians and biblical scholars who claimed to be able to assess the validity of texts on internal evidence. The plot is summarised in the *Oxford Companion to English Literature*.

[3] A special, strong and much sought after ale originally brewed for the College audit day. C.V. Le Grice's 'Sonnet on Receiving a Present of Trinity Audit Ale' (December 1847) is reprinted in E.E. Kellett, *A Book of Cambridge Verse* (1911), p. 223.

[4] Children's tales by Christoph Von Schmid.

[5] P.J. Stahl (ed.), Scènes . . . (Paris 1842).

Foster Junior has just married:— he told me that he had never thought of marriage till that fatal end of poor Charles Ingle.— Read loud 'Krummachers Parables'.[6]

Wed. 15. Day of Caput sitting for the Supplicats &c &c: finished our work very early at 1.— The Master of Trinity strenuous in his complaints against aegrotats[7] in wch the Medical man does not give a full account of himself, his degree, place of abode, &c.— Large Evening party at Marchesa's.

Sat. 18. Declined breakfasting with the Father of Trin: (Atkinson)[8] & his numerous flock— Bachelors Commencement.[9]— went off very well: a little barking like dogs, & a good deal of noise when any person appeared with their cap on:[10]— no personality.— Over at 1½.— M & I called on Miss Apthorps.— Wrote to E.E.A. sending him the Tripos list . . . Dined in Hall.— In the Evening with Lucy's aid corrected for the Press the names of the new B.A.s.

Sat. 25. Visit from Mrs. Challis: we sent word that we were dressing to go out, but she insisted on coming in as she was tired with walking from the observatory:— she made herself very agreeable, & abundantly compensated for our ¼ hours loss of walk.— Poor Lodge still in bed:— very sick:— his man came to me last night, but I could not leave my guests & directed him to fetch Sudbury, wch he did.— In the Evening I went on with the Amber Witch:— it is occasionally unfit for a lady to read, particularly 'the trial' & 'torture Chamber'.— Dined in Hall.— Today Lucy deposited in Carus's Letter-box a fabrication purporting to be an Extract from the Advertiser, offering £50 reward for information about a Gentleman in black who left his college rooms on the 30th ultimo:— the joke succeeded very well & brought a reply from him this evening directly after his return:— he has been absent 3 Sundays & all the days possible short of 4 Sundays.

Sun. 26. Read prayers for Hose who has a bad cold . . . Went to Jones the Dentist, & had one tooth filed & one stopped with cement:— I found one side of my mouth not in eating order.— No walk with M. except to & from Church.— Sat a long while with poor Lodge who is still in bed, tormented with retching:— poor fellow, he suffers a great deal.

Fri. 31. Wrote to Mr Smith of Dulwich (Georges future father in law) to ask him to breakfast tomorrow morning as I hear from G. that he comes to C. tonight[11] . . .

---

6   F.A. Krummacher, German Protestant (d. 1845), *Parables* (1805). There were several English translations, one as recent as 1844.

7   'Aegrotat' literally 'he is ill'; hence a certificate to say that a student is too unwell to attend lectures or sit examinations. An aegrotat degree was awarded if the examiners were satisfied that he could have passed under normal circumstances. Comprehensive medical directories which would have answered Whewell's questions were not readily available.

8   I.e. Praelector of the College who presented members for their degrees.

9   See 7 January 1843.

10   The reference is obscure. But cf. 26 February 1847.

11   George had known the Smith family of Dulwich from his boyhood when he was friends with Fanny's brothers.

Sat. 1. February . . . Mr Smith came into my bedroom at 8 . . . I had some talk with him about George, & learned his failure at the Academy:— Mr S. has lectured him for his want of steady perseverance . . .

Tu. 4. Meeting of Master & Seniors:— received a legacy from the Princess Sophia of Gloster, a beautiful picture (by Sir Joshua) of the late Chancellor of the University her brother when a boy of 4: he is in Vandyke dress: the colours are well preserved:[12] she left us also packets of Letters relative to his campaign under the Duke of York (1795 to 1799) . . .

Fri. 7. Today had a final visit from 'pretty Nancy' as Widow Stone (the poor crazed woman) calls herself:— she brought with her her land-lady at Harston (to whom she owes £2.13.): gave her £5 to pay her debts & take her into Wales, on condition that I was never to hear any more of her.— Met our neighbour Mr. Hurlock (the clergyman) carried on along by 4 men— he having fallen down in an Epileptic fit . . . G.T.R. came on a visit— in spite of the severe cold he came outside (of necessity indeed & not by choice): he caught no cold:— he came by the Telegraph & dined with his Aunts. . .

Tu. 11. G.T.R. & I dined in hall.— He gave a wine party to 12.— I came home & read to myself Mrs. Inchbalds Nature & Art.[13]— Neither of the young men with us in the Evening. Today a College meeting, in wch we were told that the Executors of Princess Sophia of Gloster objected to the Picture of the D. of G. (as a boy in a Vandyke dress) by Sir Josh. being hung anywhere but where she directed viz, the Hall.— At this meeting we discussed the disappearance of more than a dozen MSS from our Trin. Library: several of them have been bought by the British Museum.— Our suspicions strongly attach to Halliwell of Jesus[14] . . .

Wed. 12. G.T.R. & I dined in hall.— Last night the Thermometer down at 14! The river is fast freezing— M. & I walked to see the skating.— The young men drank with us: Edward read loud the Antiquary[15] while George drew a foot from a cast.

Th. 13. Letter from Baugh complaining of Edwards communication that Walton & myself dissuade him from reading for Honors:— Wrote in defence of the advice:[16]— sent him a draft (£8.15.-), the last before I transfer

---

[12] At the age of twelve William Frederick, Duke of Gloucester, had been the first member of the royal family to be admitted at Cambridge, as a member of Trinity College. He had been Chancellor from 1811 until his death in 1834. The painting is reproduced in the Fitzwilliam Museum's *Cambridge Portraits* (1978) where are further details.

[13] Elizabeth Inchbald's *Nature and Art: a Romance,* (1796), a novel replete with villainy and pathos. The plot is summarised in the *Oxford Companion to English Literature.*

[14] On J. O. Halliwell (later Halliwell-Phillipps) the precocious antiquary, see Winstanley's article in *The Library* 5th series, 2 (1948), 250-82, where the thefts are fully described, W.H. Bond in *The Library* 5th series, 18 (1963), 133-40, and A.N.L. Munby, *Phillipps Studies* II (1952), 39-40, 50-3. Halliwell matriculated from Trinity, soon migrated to Jesus and left the University without a degree.

[15] Sir Walter Scott, *The Antiquary* (1816).

[16] Since Grim had only managed to appear in the fifth class in the examinations of the previous June, no doubt his uncle considered the study required for honours was beyond his powers, and that proved to be so (see 5 June 1845).

the money to G.B.A. & E.E.A.— Matriculation in Prof. Corrie's Lecture-Room, because Bell's Scholarship[17] & Classical Tripos are both going on in Senate House:— it was amazingly inconvenient , the table being very low. . . The Bishop of Ely has had a paralytic stroke.

Fri. 14. — M (having corns) did not walk out of the garden: Lucy & I called upon Miss Page (who gave me a penwiper of Miss Phipps making), upon the Miss Chapmans (we saw nobody but their uncle), & Mrs. Whewell (who did the Honors of her house very kindly:— Lucy greatly admired the Picture of Prince William Henry (afterwards D. of Gl.) by Sir Joshua.— George dined with his aunts & then gave a wine party at my rooms.— The Skrines kindly took me over to dinner at Madingley . . . Yesterday the President of the Camden Society (Archdeacon Thorp) announced the withdrawal of the Chancellor of the University, the V.C. & the Bishops of Exeter & Lincoln, & said that it was therefore the unanimous advice of the Committee that the society do dissolve in May:— 'the Christian Kalendar' (written by one of the Secretaries) is probably the deathblow to the Camden Society[18] . . .

Tu. 18. Trial in the V.C.'s court: the Rev. Edward Ventris v W. H. Walker (undergraduate of Queens) for writing a scandalous anonymous letter: Hedger (Cashier at Mortlocks) declared his belief of the anonymous letter being written by Walker from comparison with his acknowledged writing:— Griffin however (his private tutor) saw no reason for pronouncing the identity:— so the case was dismissed as 'not proved:'— there could however be no doubt of W's guilt[19] . . .

Wed. 19. — Congregation day: 3 AM, 2AB.— Lodge unfortunately fallen into one of his fits of low spirits.— Meeting of Master & Seniors at 3 o'cl:— we accepted the Thorwaldsen statue of Lord Byron offered to our Library by Sir J. C. Hobhouse & the other subscribers to the Byron

[17] These scholarships has been founded in 1810 by the Rev. William Bell of Magdalene for the sons of poor clergymen. Elections were made on the Friday after mid-Lent Sunday by a small ex-officio board who were rewarded with a dinner for their trouble. As members of King's College and Trinity Hall were not allowed to compete it is not surprising that Trinity men had made up almost half of the successful candidates. The two men elected in 1845, J.L. Davies and D.J. Vaughan, became Fellows of Trinity.

[18] The Society had over 800 members and at this meeting elected a further 26, including two colonial bishops. Thorp made the issue one of 'obedience' to the University authorities, but many members refused to dissolve the Camden and campaigned for its continuation. S.N. Stokes, author of *A Christian Kalendar* (1845), was a young Trinity graduate and one of the honorary secretaries. It was he who had given the stone altar to the Round Church (see 25 July 1844), and he made a profession of faith in the Roman Catholic church at Birmingham in December 1845. Thorp, as President of the Camden Society, felt obliged to emphasize publicly that anonymous works by members had neither the approval nor sanction of the body. See 8 May 1845.

[19] Ventris, Perpetual Curate of Quy, had received on 4 February a letter signed by 'a hater of humbugs' which described him as 'a whoremaster, a cruel persecutor both to his last wife & a wicked rascal as it respects is[sic] present, for he got all her money & now treats her like a brute. did you ever solicit any girl in the fields. . .' Romilly had to read this and a long exchange of letters between Ventris and Walker before the nine members of the court, and write it up later in V.C. Ct I 20 Acta Curiae, pp. 255-66 (University Archives).

Testimonial:[20] we also discussed the subject of Halliwell & the disappearance of the MSS from the Trinity Library.— Dined in hall.— In the Evening copied out the trial of yesterday.— This Evening received a magnificent Severn Salmon from W. Baxter (an Irishman incorporated 2 months ago as a B.A. at Cambridge, & to whom I had shown some civility) an undermaster at Cheltenham:— very kind & very like a warm-hearted Irishman: I have shown equal attention to hundreds of others without any expression of gratitude.— E.E.A. tea with us.

Th. 20. — Wrote to Denning about my remaining payments for George— Lodge takes his announced resignation very much to heart:— found him in bed.— Walk with M.— In the Evening Edward read loud a very amusing vol. of Poole's 'Christmas Festivities'.[21]— Dined off the Salmon.

Sat. 1 March. Trial at V.C.'s Court. Taxor v a Butcher for light weights & heavy words:— the Butcher was very penitent & ∴ came off with making an apology & paying the expenses of Court 3/6 . . .

Fri. 7. Congregation day— Petition concerning Welsh Bishoprics[22] opposed in the W. H. by Dr. Ainslie: he had only 2 supporters, Dr Lamb & Leapingwell:— the numbers were 50 to 3.— Found Lodge in bed, but very little the matter with him: he complains of want of appetite.— Walk with M. between Congregations. Letter from Rev. G. Williams (of Newton) asking for instructions how to apply for the Librarianship: he said that he was acquainted with all the standard works in English, French, Italian, Spanish, Portuguese, & German, & that his present acquaintance with Oriental languages extends to Hebrew, Chaldee, Syriac, Arabic & Sanskrit!!!— Pretty well![23] Dined with 'the Family' at Cartmells . . . Packe's drollery of the day was 'When a woman has a little behind she puts herself in a great bustle.'. . .

Th. 13. Thermometer last night at 10! Uh!— Grim left this morning at 6 for the holidays: of course he went outside *by preference* !. . . A meeting of

[20] Byron had quit Trinity in 1808, making few short visits thereafter until he went abroad. It appears, however, that stories of him were current in the College: 'there is still an old bedmaker here full of anecdotes of Byron, his pet bear (which he kept in College) his badger and other locomotives (for these famous pets of his were always found where they should not have been)' (Letter of February 1845 from F. H. Bowring (John Rylands Library, Manchester, MS 1231).) The notoriety of Byron's not very private life had caused the authorities of Westminster Abbey, for which Thorwaldsen's statue was intended, to refuse it. After some years in a packing case it was offered to Trinity.

[21] John Poole, *Christmas Festivities: Tales, Sketches and Characters* 4 vols (1845-8).

[22] By an Act of 6 & 7 William IV there was provision to unite the Welsh sees of St Asaph and Bangor when one of them became vacant. The issue took on a significance quite beyond its real importance, and there developed a strong lobby in favour of repealing the act. Its members, who included many of the English clergy and the dons of both the older universities, thought of themselves as friends of the established church in Wales. See 11 March 1846.

[23] Williams was not on the short-list for the Librarianship, and remained in his parish until he died. Three of the seven candidates, including Lodge's choice, Mynors Bright of his own college, withdrew before the election. See McKitterick, pp. 510-13.

the Library Subsyndicate at V.C 's:— Lodge (much against my wishes) attended it:— he was so weak and exhausted when he got to Sidney Lodge that he had to be supported upstairs by Drs. Graham & Archdall:— everything went off smoothly: Lodge agreed to the suggestion of appointing a Syndicate to deliberate about an *underlibrarian* after the Election of L's successor.— Called on Lodge & took him a bottle of E.I. Madeira,— he having expressed a wish to try some:— his stomach revolts at sherry at present . . . I should have said yesterday that Lucy & I paid a visit to the Matron of the Hospital Miss Spilling who is just returned to the Hospital after her visit to Leamington:— she is still very far from looking recovered from her late illness: we also visited 2 of the Patients, Susan Chune & a little boy of the name of Raby (who has very recently had his leg off):— L. took presents to both of them:— In the Evening I went on with the Vicar of Wakefield.[24]

Fri. 14. End of term— Bishop of Ceylon & Master of Harrow admitted DD by Mandate:[25] Ollivant made a good speech with unfailing memory:— he made no pretence of 'the kiss of brotherly love' . . . Visit from Mrs. James Walter & daughter:— she is wife of the Architect, but is so poor that she bakes biscuits for the Combination rooms &c:— she & her daughter were dressed as if they had a 100 a year pin money:— she came begging for a poor old candidate for the Spittle House almshouses[26] (a Mrs. Matthison): gave her 10s:— she staid an insufferably long time & almost talked Lucy & me into a nervous fever . . . At the Congregation today the V.C announced Lodge's intended resignation on the 25th & fixt 3d Apr. at 9 for the day of Election.— I drew up the form & spoke of Lodge as 'Bibliothecarius praestantissimus' & his illness as 'deflenda':[27]— I took an English version of it to the Newspapers . . .

Mon. 17. A thaw.— No walk with M.— Found Lodge in bed, complaining of forgetfulness.— I took him another bottle of Madeira.— His bedmaker is a great croker & is frightened about him:— I am not myself at all: I have seen him so much worse— Finished V. of Wakefield.

Fri. 28. 3d day of Scholarship (Mathematics by Master & Martin).— Looking over papers with Sedgwick all day:— at night drew up for the H. of Commons a return of Degrees & Matriculations & the Fees upon them for

[24] Oliver Goldsmith, *The Vicar of Wakefield* (1766).
[25] See 26 October 1843 .
[26] The old leper hospital of St Anthony and St Eligius in Trumpington Street, used as an almshouse for six poor and aged women. Its meagre endowments had recently been increased by a bequest of £400 and William Mortlock was active in collecting private subscriptions, according to the *Cambridge Guide* (1845).
[27] I.e. 'most distinguished Librarian' and 'to be deplored'.

the last 11 years.— Tawell (the Quaker) today hanged for the murder of Sarah Hart.[28]

Tu. 1 April.   Master of Corpus took me & Dr. Haviland & Carus over to Bishop of Ely's funeral. We were all but Haviland pall-bearers: the other 5 were Baines (Examining Chaplain), James (Rector of Ditton & formerly the Bishop's Curate), Perry, J. H. Fisher (who came from Kirby Lonsdale), & Dr. Graham.— The procession began at 20′ past 1:— We arrived before 12. We were received by Baines & Burder: none of the family appeared. The 3 sons & Miss Allen (to my grief) walked as mourners.— The sight was a very striking one & very touching: the eldest son (the Master of Dulwich)[29] behaved with the greatest tenderness to his sister:— she bore up with more firmness than I expected & uttered no cries that were audible.— The Cathedral was filled (even the triphorium):— everything was conducted with the greatest decorum. The Music & the chanting were excellent: the Dean read the service impressively . . .

Sun. 6.   Sedgwick rode over to breakfast . . . Sedgwick discussed 'Vestiges of Creation', against wch work he and all scientific men are indignant. The authorship is still uncertain: Sir Richard Vivian, Lady Lovelace & some Scotch-man or other are talked of:— Sedgwick thinks the internal evidence in favor of an authoress (in spite of the indelicacy of details about gestation) from the hasty jumping to conclusions. The book is rank materialism . . . Sedgwick has unfortunately declined the invitations of the Editors of the Edinburgh & Quarterly to answer this book wch has run thro 3 editions in a few months[30] . . .

Wed. 9.   Sent G.T.R. £15 to pay his landlord. Congregation: 2 Hon MA, 4 MA, 15 BA, 2 eund.— A grace passed for consolidating the offices of Librarian & Protolibrarian:[31] it was unopposed. I then presented to the

28   John Tawell, a married man and well-to-do chemist (who had returned from transportation to Australia) was found guilty of poisoning his mistress Sarah Hart, and tried and executed at Aylesbury. Both F. Gunning and Sir Fitzroy Kelly had been retained for his defence. The trial attracted large crowds, doubtless increased by Tawell's appearance in the Quaker garb which had led to his speedy apprehension when a description preceded him to London by the new telegraph.

29   G. J. Allen, the Bishop's son, was no relation of Baugh Allen who had also been Warden of Dulwich College. The Wardens and Masters bore the same surname for over two hundred years as required by the school's founder Edward Alleyn. There is a cut of the procession in the cathedral in the *Illustrated London News* (1845), I, 236

30   *The Vestiges of Creation* (1844) by the Scottish publisher Robert Chambers was published anonymously and in great secrecy, leading to much speculation as to its authorship. Both Sir Charles Lyell and Prince Albert were said to have written it. Chambers intended it to be scientific and non-theological, but the book was widely attacked for its central heterodox theory of biological development, which prefigured the work of Huxley and Spencer rather than Darwin. Sedgwick loathed the book and attacked it both in the *Edinburgh Review* (July 1845) and again in 1850 in an inflated edition of his *Discourse on the Studies at the University.* See M. Millhauser, *Just Before Darwin: Robert Chambers and 'Vestiges'* (Middletown, Conn., 1959).

31   The office of Protolibrarian and its salary which Lodge had held concurrently with that of Librarian had been created in 1720, a child of politics rather than scholarship. It had long been anachronistic. See McKitterick, pp.168-71.

V.C. poor Lodges resignation (wch I received last night) which I dated for today (it having been designedly left undated):— the V.C. then appointed Thursday week for the Election of a new Librarian . . .

Fri. 11. Birkett & Mills came to me to mark off the not-created MA's— To a Seniority where we tried a W. Babington for getting out of his lodgings at night:— Gated him & admonished 1st time previous to expulsion.— Wet day : no walk for the women . . .

Th. 17. The Election of Librarian began at 9: Drs. Webb & Graham sat one on each side of the V.C; Birkett & Mills were umpires for Power, Eyres & Prowett for Smith:— Mr Hunt & I attended officially.— At 3½ there was an adjournment for 4 hours: the numbers then were 259 for P, 179 for S.— Dined in hall.— Polling resumed at 7½ :— at ¼ to 10 (with the consent of both parties) the polling closed; Sharpe (of Queens) tendered a vote for S after this,— he having been in the S.H. all day!— Final numbers P 312, S 240.— Went to the grand supper in Clare Hall:— probably no such assemblage there since the time of acting Ignoramus before James 1.[32]— Lord Bayning declined giving Power's health, so it fell to my lot to make a little speech on doing so.— I came away at midnight just at the introduction of the Punch. — Smith bore his defeat very well.

Fri. 18. Wrote to poor Lodge an account of the Election.— Walk with M. on the railway & saw all the plans of the Station &c.— Dined at the Family at Pagets & met Drs Graham, Tatham & Haviland, Packe, Shaw & Cartmell: Guest (the Founder of the London Philological Society), Mr Gwilt (an amusing clergyman, fond of shooting & riding), a stammering Mr Johnson (whom I once met in a bearskin dress), & a Mr [illegible] just come from Egypt. . . There was a horrid Cock-of-the-woods in the 2d course: I ate a mouthful & thought it detestable.[33]— A placard was printed & sent to Smith's Committee Room, 'Vote for Smith & 9 small children', upon wch one of his friends said 'Hang that fat boy Joe, he's always asleep':[34]— this hit upon the corpulence & somnolence of Power is rather smart.—

Sun. 20. I had a letter from a Mrs. Salisbury sending us her double-proxy for Miss Mann & *offering us £5 if she fails:*— I wrote to thank her most warmly.— Carus preached from the Gospel of the day (John XVI.14): the sermon was not bad but it was an hour long:— there were tirades in it

---

[32] A long Latin satire on lawyers by George Ruggle performed before James I during his visits of March and May 1615.

[33] I.e. the capercailzie, largest of the grouse family. The bird, formerly extinct, had been reintroduced successfully into Scotland as recently as 1837 and was no doubt still something of a curiosity. Cf. 24 February 1843.

[34] An allusion to the boy in *Pickwick Papers* who, when not eating, is asleep.

obviously meant against the people who voted for the Maynooth grant yesterday.[35]— M. & E. & I walked, the day being lovely . . .

Tu. 22. Lovely weather:— we are unluckily having the outside of our house painted, so we are not in good odour:— the cat came in thro the balcony today *green* instead of tortoiseshell:— Lucy turpentined her, & then thought she was mad because upon licking herself she foamed at the mouth . . . G.T.R. & G.B.A. came this evening by * [36]. . .

Fri. 25. G.T.R. dined in Hall with me: he gave a wine party with ice to a dozen of his friends.— I went into the Combination room to talk to Mr Sidney who came up with Carus, Henslow, &c.— This morning a Seniority:— we gave away the little living of Masworth to J.I.Smith our Librarian.— I should have mentioned that Lucy honored George Allen on Wednesday by being present in the S. H. when he took his degree: M. gave him £5.— Took Lucy into the Public Library (her 1st visit!!!) & showed her the Codex Bezae:[37]— took her also into the Round Church (also her 1st visit!): the stone altar & credence have recently been removed & were lying (not very decorously) in the church-yard.— At night finished 'the Improvisatore'.[38]—

Sat. 26. G. T. R. left by the Telegraph.— Walk with M. to look at the Skew[39] Bridge on the Hills Road . . .

Mon. 28. Mrs Hopkins this morning called with a letter from a Mrs Crokat asking us to give up all our votes in favour of McGermas *as Miss Mann had no chance*!!! I received the proposal with unbounded indignation:— The Railway Labourers on the Hills Road struck today:—they fought by way of filling up their time.— Whist Club at Cartmells:—Dr. Haviland joined us to our great pleasure.

Tu. 29. Election of a Physician at Addenbrooke's in place of Dr. Thackeray resigned: the Candidates were Fisher, Drosier & Webster.—

---

[35] The College of St Patrick at Maynooth had been founded by the Irish Parliament in 1795 to educate the Catholic priesthood. Government proposals to pay for extra buildings and to increase its annual grant united Anglicans and dissenters throughout the country in violent protest and vituperation. Much was made of the sinful endowment of a rebellious popish seminary; the majesty of Heaven must be offended, and judgment must surely be visited on the nation. An appeal to the University M.P.s in favour of the grant was signed by nearly eighty Whigs in the University (Romilly, Gunning, Sedgwick, Pryme, Power, Leapingwell, and others) but by none of the Heads. There was a separate appeal by some 300 non-residents such as Henslow, Peacock, and Spring-Rice, but the Tory *Cambridge Chronicle* of 12 April was glad to report that a local petition against had some 1,100 signatures. On 11 April in the Commons Macaulay scorned the objections of Oxford and Cambridge, whose wealth, endowments, and comforts he compared at length with 'the miserable Dotheboys Hall' given in exchange to Roman Catholics. Introduced by Peel and backed by Russell, the bill in fact received large support in both houses.

[36] I.e the Star coach.

[37] See 26 October 1843.

[38] Hans Andersen, *The Improvisatore, or Life in Italy* (1834) translated 1845. Romilly thought him 'of melancholy temperament with a prodigious disposition to fall in love.' (22 April).

[39] I.e. the bridge had arches set obliquely to the piers.

The final numbers F. 130, D 118, W 52.[40]— Wrote to an Irishman named *Patrick Knox McKenna* living at Parsonstown Ireland in reply to his query of what I knew *not advantageous* to his character:— I reminded him of having lived 6 months at Ansells in Fitzwilliam St in 1840 & having gone away without paying & that he owes said Ansell at this day about £18.— Also to an enquiring Clergyman McCausland on same subject.

On the thirtieth, accompanied by the two Georges and Grim, Romilly went to his London bank to receive dividends of January and April, and then, more pleasurably, to the Royal Exchange where he was 'delighted' with the frescoes being painted there. On May Day morning he found himself among a large crowd watching the opening of Brunel's 'very beautiful' Hungerford suspension bridge. 'I was pleased with the gallantry of one of the Committee who gave every Lady a coloured engraving of the bridge.' After buying books worth £1-13-0 at the S.P.C.K. for a lending library at Porthkerry where he had once been rector, he had a frustrating afternoon. He failed to see his cousin John from whom he hoped to learn the address of Henry Whittaker who was needed to sign a power of attorney, and George Romilly did not meet him as arranged at the British Gallery. 'The gem of the collection' in Romilly's view was Goodall's *The Widow's Benefit Night,* and he thought other pictures at the 'Water Colour' by Prout, Copley Fielding, and Hunt 'very good'. He returned to the Edward Romillys with whom he was staying, and met at dinner Edward's brother Charles, Lady Georgiana Spedding, and Lady Harriet Russell 'gay & rattling but not pretty—age 18'. Edward presented him with a copy of his translation of Cavour's pamphlet on Ireland, and Mrs Marcet with one of her children's books with 'good cuts' for Margaret. Dr Roget joined him for breakfast on Friday and talked about the British Association which was to meet shortly in Cambridge. Romilly, as so often, dined at the Belle Sauvage before leaving outside on The Star coach which brought him home in time for tea at 9.15 with the women.

Th. 8. May. . . . Election at Governesses' Institution today: we are sure of being beaten.— a grand hubbub at the Camden Society tonight:—the Society declined dying (as they had been requested to do by the vote of Feb. last): furious attack of Stokes (author of Christian Calendar) by Sedgwick.[41]— Visit from Mrs. & Miss French.— Read loud Susan Hopley.[42]

[40]   The election began at the hospital at 10 a.m. and continued until 7 p.m. Besides Romilly other governors present included Sedgwick, Peacock, Carus, Archdall, Hodgson and Paget. Peacock proposed Fisher, Chapman of Caius proposed Drosier, and Archdall proposed Webster.

[41]   The meeting which was held in the Town Hall lasted almost four hours. Only 109 members voted in favour of dissolution, more than 270 against. According to the Society's own report (taken from the newspapers) Sedgwick, who as lately as 1843 had been an auditor for the Society, described the *Christian Kalendar* as 'an insult to the Church and University. (Cheers and uproar)'. In vain he challenged Thorp to confirm Stokes's authorship amid 'great confusion', declaring its author 'unfit to be a member of the Society at all'. The Society removed to London, changed its name to the Ecclesiological Society and became a national rather than a University body, although Thorp remained President. There is a brief *Memorial* of the Society by one its leading members E.J. Boyce (1888).

[42]   Catherine Crowe, *Susan Hopley or the Adventures of a Maid-Servant* (1841). A dramatised version was performed at the Barnwell Theatre on 11 October 1845.

Fri. 9. Miss Mann came off only 5th best! Miss Davies & Miss D-y were elected . . .

Sun. 11. Lucy a good deal better but not well enough to go out.— I read prayers for Hose.— Carus preached from 1 Cor. XII. 4:— M. staid the Sacrament:— we did not get out till past 2.— M. & I walked to the Railway bridge on the Hills Road:— crowds of people, quite like a fair . . .

Tu. 13. All the morning looking over proof sheets of Sedgwicks article in the next Edinburgh against 'the Vestiges of Creation'. . . Lucy sent Mr. Laing (Secretary of Govern: Inst.) a draft for £164.7.9 (to purchase an annuity of £15 for Miss Mann):— this is the wildest of her quixotisms, as she not only never saw Miss Mann nor even ever wrote to her, but only heard of her accidentally from the Bernards asking her support:— all the votes almost wch Miss Mann obtained were got by the incessant exertions of Lucy for many months.— Dined at Pet. H. Lodge: party of 14 . . . No fire in the dining room: obliged to button my coat . . .

Tu. 20. M. & I caught in the rain while looking at the railway works.— Our cook (Sarah Ironsides) has got engaged to a Clerk on the Railway.— Evening party at Sidney Lodge: some very good Hullah singing[43] from Miss Wilkins, Mrs Phelps &c &c.

Th. 29. Breakfast to Mr Alexander Prévost & his brother George: the former is one of the most intelligent agreeable people I ever met with:— Peter Thomas Ouvry was of the party. I showed them the Library of the University & Trinity with some difficulty (today being a holiday in honor of the Restoration),[44] our Chapel &c . . .

Mon. 2. June. A horrid report that Sir St Vincent Cotton had destroyed himself after heavy losses at the Derby:— Trust there is no foundation for any part of the report: most certainly he has not committed suicide[45] . . .

Wed. 4. Carus paid the women a visit;— he has been offered some dignified position (I suspect an Archdeaconry), but has declined it.[46]— His curate Hose (to his C's great joy) is going to leave, having had the small living of Dunstable given him. Seniority: we appointed Brimley our Librarian (in room of J. I. Smith . . .

---

43 See 27 November 1844.
44 The restoration of Charles II was commemorated in the liturgy, and the University kept it as a Scarlet Day. The morning was ushered in by a peel of bells at Great St Mary's where there was a sermon by William Griffin of St John's on the text: 'Submit yourselves to every ordinance of man for the Lord's sake, whether it be to the King as supreme . . .' (1 Peter 2. V. 13). This service was removed from the Book of Common Prayer in 1859.
45 Vinny Cotton, alias Sir Vincent Twist, led a wild life devoted to sport and gambling. Crockford said he had never known his equal in fondness for hazard, but although he ran through a fortune he never lost the Madingley estate. To the sketch of his life in *D.N.B.* one may add that he married his mistress the day before he died. His family papers are in the Cambridgeshire Record Office.
46 The *Cambridge Chronicle* of 21 June denied a rumour that Carus was to be tutor to the Prince of Wales.

Th. 5. The new bonnets arrived from town (from Mesdames Marshall & Co). — All the morning in the office: I am going thro every drawer.— Dined in Hall.— Looked over proof for Sedgwick.— Wrote to E. E. Allen: in 5th Class.

Fri. 6. Looked over more proof for Sedgwick: he is most indignant at a Letter from the Master forbidding his walking with Shindy in College.[47]— Wrote to Bishop of Gloucester to congratulate him on his son Charles James Monk's getting the Greek ode.[48]

Sat. 7. Much astonished at a letter from B. of G. saying his son did not write for the G.O:— more is his luck for he has got the prize with little trouble— Finished Whewell's 'Indications of a Creator' which I think a very instructive & valuable work. Also finished Smyth's 'Evidences' which is a work very characteristic of its author & may be of service to dispassionate sceptics[49] . . .

Wed. 11. Barnaby Lecturers.[50]— The smallest number of BDs ever known on this day, viz. 1: 1AM, 1AB.— There was a Grace for £400 worth of hot water-pipes for warming the Library; & also a Grace for allowing Morgan the assistant observer to keep his residence in the observatory:— Morgan is about to become an undergraduate:— Crick (Orator) non-placeted it, & was supported by Ollivant, Edleston & Frere among the Trin. men & by 4 Johnians: the numbers were 11 to 8 in favor of the Grace.— Looked over more revise for Sedgwick.— It turns out that the V.C. had mismatched the Prizes; Monk got the Epigrams, & it was De Winton who got the Greek Ode.

Sat. 14. In my office all the morning.— Looked over proof sheets with Sedgwick— Dined in Hall— Lucy took Carus a present of a nosegay & a copy of Toller's sermons (with Robert Hall's memoir).[51] We had great difficulty in getting this book as it is out of print. It appears that other congregations tried to seduce away Toller but he clung to his own tho' the

47 Shindy was Sedgwick's white Pomeranian bitch, brought back from a visit to Germany in 1839. The statutes of Trinity forbad the keeping of dogs, a measure originally intended to prevent undergraduates from having hunting dogs, and were hardly appropriate to a domestic pet. See Clark & Hughes, II, 66
48 Sir William Browne (d.1774) founded an annual competition for Greek and Latin verse. The Greek ode, in imitation of Sappho, was in 1845 on Napoleon at St Helena. The prizes were gold medals bearing a likeness of the benefactor and another of Apollo crowning with laurels 'a Scholar with a gown and band, kneeling on the Steps, and praesenting a Scroll in his right hand, and holding his Square Cap with his left hand.'
49 Whewell's *Indications of the Creator* (1845) and Smyth's *Evidences of Christianity* (1845) were intended to counteract the influence and arguments of Chambers's *Vestiges*. Smyth, who had been Regius Professor of History since 1807, had ceased to lecture about four years earlier 'not only because I had become deaf and old, but because I found that I had lost my audience', but he continued to publish.
50 So called as they were elected on St Barnabas' Day. The endowment of Sir Robert Rede in 1524 required that there should be lecturers in humanity, logic, and philosophy. In 1857, however, the University admitted that 'for many years past no duties whatever have been discharged'.
51 Thomas Northcote Toller, *Sermons* (1824). He was a Congregational minister of Kettering. For Hall see 29 December 1846.

salary was much smaller:— his own Congregation upon this raised a subscription of nearly £1000.— vide 4th June for explanation of this present.— M. & I accompanied Lucy in carrying the book & the nosegay in the cool of the Evening:— we went into the Fellows walks & gathered ourselves 3 large nosegays.— We did not get home to our tea till nine o'clock.

Sun. 15. Read prayers for Hose (who today is reading in at his Living of Dunstable).— Carus preached on Mark 10. 13. 14. on the baptism & education of children: it was a pilot balloon: he told us that Mr Myers (who is to preach a charity sermon for the school next Sunday) would probably not speak so much on this point as he thought desirable: he (W.C.) should therefore give them 2 sermons on the subject, one this morning & the other in the Evening at St. Mary's:— Lucy went to both:— M & I were quite satisfied with one.— A boiling hot day:— I fatigued myself by going to the railway bridge (wch is now open) on the Hills Road . . .

Th. 19. First day of the British Association[52] — An old Scotch beggar calling himself Dr Charles Romilly Scott (aged 78) who told me that his mother was a Miss Romilly called on me: he is going to lecture on Temperance & gave me 3000 blessings for a 3s ticket. Went to the Hoop a little before 4 to receive Dr Roget whom I lodge in my rooms:— he was not arrived:— went into Hall without him: we had there Sedgwick in the Chair, the B. of Norwich & a very agreeable party:— Dr Roget made his appearance with the cheese, & afterwards went to the Ordinary (at which the Dean of Ely presided): Dr Roget is my guest, living in my rooms:— we went a little before 8 to the Senate House to hear Peacock's speech on resigning the Presidency & Herschel's on assuming it: Herschel had a bad cold & was nearly inaudible:— he read a very long address, which it was very wearisome to hear as one caught only a word here & there.

Fri. 20. Queen's Accession.[53]— Breakfast to Dr. Roget, E. E. Allen, Huntley & Heywood— A grand dinner in hall at wch the Master presided: Lord Northampton Herschel &c were there as well as Mr Everett (the American Minister), Wilberforce (the new Dean of Westminster)— I happened to sit opposite the Master (as Croupier)[54] with Dr. Roget on one side & an unknown person on the other: presently the Master's servant came to me & asked the stranger's name: I answered I did not know: he was

[52] See the large *Report of the Fifteenth Meeting of the British Association* (1846), and well illustrated, topical accounts in the *Illustrated London News* of 21 and 28 June 1845. One of the more speculative addresses in the zoology and botany section must have been Spineto's *On the Egyptians and Americans.* Besides the lectures, an exhibition, largely of zoological specimens 'in Goadby's fluid', was set out in the Perse school. It also included models of churches, daguerreotypes and talbotypes, encaustic tiles, a machine for beating and brushing carpets, and a 'patent removeable window sash without taking off the bead'.

[53] It was marked by a sermon in Great St Mary's by Dr Sharpe of Sidney on Matthew XXII. 21, 'Render unto Caesar. . .'.

[54] I.e. vice-chairman at the lower end of a table.

not my guest:— the servant soon returned & said to the stranger 'Your name Jerdan?',— 'Yes';— 'Whose guest are you?' 'Professor Sedgwick's.'— It appears that 2 years ago Jerdan in his editorial capacity wrote something wch grievously offended the Master. An angry correspondence between the Master & Sedgwick followed this business.[55]— Poor S. was also lately desired by the Master to part with Shindy.— In the combination room the Master gave the health of Mr. Everett, who replied in a speech of singular beauty.— At 8 we went to the Senate House when Airy gave a lecture on Magnetism in his clear distinct manner. I was separated from Dr. Roget (he being a committee-man & ∴ furnished with a red ticket wch gives the entrée to the platform).— Ladies were very ungallantly excluded without they subscribed;— 173 were found who wheedled their husbands or brothers into paying £1 for them.— Poor Spineto had to pay £5 for Marchesa & 4 daughters!— I sleep at the house during Dr. R's occupancy of my College-bed.— Baugh Allen came to C. this Evening & has a bed in College.

Sat. 21. The Master has given unpardonable offence to St. John's by having Herschel as his guest:— surely nothing can be more unreasonable: the Master of Trinity invited Herschel a year ago: Herschel declined accepting the invitation for a fortnight, waiting to see if an invitation would be sent by his own college:— none coming he then accepted Whewell's.— Clearly no fault either with W or H.

Sun. 22. . . . At 2 I went to St. Mary's & heard a very clever sermon from H. Goodwin (of Caius): I was very glad that Mr. Everett should hear so well-reasoned & so eloquent a sermon.— Took Baugh & Dr. Roget into Hall where was a very grand assemblage . . . No speaking: everything went off very well.— Took Baugh & Roget to Chapel & then we went to St. Mary's, which we found crammed as Wilberforce (Dean of Westminster) was to preach. I was charmed with his manner & his matter: some of his sentences were very vigorous: one was 'the chamber of voluptuousness is the antechamber of hell'. it was a charity Sermon for the District Visiting Society[56] . . . I omitted to state that on Friday there was a very good Horticultural Exhibition in Downing:— an imitation of the Round

---

[55] For Jerdan's account see his *Autobiography,* IV (1853), 292-5. He relates that it was Romilly who insisted on taking him up to the Combination Room and sitting by him when 'the Master's passion was but too obvious'. The offence given by Whewell led to his invitations being disregarded the following night. Murchison finally 'wrung an ungracious apology' from him. Sedgwick is said to have considered this affair 'as only the last of a series of contumelies he had endured from the same quarter', and expressed his satisfaction that it had come to a climax.

[56] It has been reckoned that in the first half of the century new philanthropic bodies were created at the rate of six a year. The General Society for the Promotion of District Visiting had been established in 1828, and was widely supported, for example by Simeon in Cambridge. Many lay middle-class members, especially women, were involved in visiting the poor and sick to whom they gave tickets for relief in kind from local tradesmen. Wilberforce attracted a large congregation who gave £46.

Church, a Lilliputian garden & fountain, were among its attractions:—
there was a collection of electro-typed flowers[57] . . .

Mon. 23. Roget breakfasted with the Marquis Spineto. Took Baugh to
dine in hall (Dr. Roget dining in Peterhouse with a Mr Fuller, who asked
me also): I was in the chair; Airy was on one side of me & made himself
very agreeable, the discontented Colonel Everest (who is remarkable for
having measured an arc of the Meridian) was on the other & made himself
singularly disagreeable by his complaints of the neglect of government of
his great claims.— Dr. Roget & I went to tea at the Observatory, thereby
missing the Evening Lecture in the Sen. H. where Murchison gave an
account of Russia: I was glad enough to escape that, but regret losing a
brilliant speech from Dean Wilberforce in vindication of science from the
charge of irreligion.— The party at the Observatory was very agreeable.
Mrs. Airy & her sister Elizabeth were there & sang:— we drank tea on the
lawn, but were ultimately driven in by the rain.— The Heavens were
clouded & not a star to be seen through the telescope.

Tu. 24. Gave a very gay breakfast with nosegays for each person,
ending with fruit & ice & champagne. It was a large party 19 viz. Sir H. &
Lady Bunbury, Mr & Mrs Bunbury (born Horner) [*note above the line:* as a
child (about 20 years ago) she peculiarly excited my admiration] Mr & Mrs
Lyell (born Horner), Mr & Mrs Leonard Horner & Miss Horner, E. H.
Bunbury (our late Fellow) Prof. Pillans, Henslow & his daughters Fanny &
Louisa, Dr. Roget, Carus, Baugh, Grim & self.— Baugh & Edward went
away at 11½ to Town.— Dr. Roget dined at Caius College.— I avoided the
Promenade in the Senate House where by way of agreeable excitement
electric shocks were repeatedly given to the Company.— I was highly
delighted today by going to the chemical section & hearing a Lecture in
French from Mr Boutigny accompanied by the most brilliant experiments,
particularly the making ice in a crucible at white heat.— Declined
drinking tea with Mrs. Selwyn. I might there have heard Mrs. Airy & her
sister sing & have seen Professor Bogulowski who wears a profusion of
shaggy hair hanging over his shoulders, & by that mark of his proves
himself to be the real lion of the meeting.— Present at a meeting of Master
& Seniors today from 3 to 4:— Sedgwick presided at dinner in Hall where
an Italian professor Foggi had his health drunk, & after returning thanks
for 2 or 3 sentences in English he burst into an Italian sonnet of exultation

---

[57] The show was postponed at the request of the British Association and the organisers seem
not to have made the arrangements to meet in Downing College until a fortnight before
the opening. With its profusion of flowers and plants, Litchfield's tent for ices and
refreshments, and the presence of a band, the show was a great success . Three glass cases
sent in by a Captain Ibbetson attracted much attention with their copper flowers 'formed
by an improved electrotype process whereby their form and growth are most curiously
preserved', and a Mr Catling was awarded a special prize of thirty shillings for his model
of the Round Church decorated with flowers. Members of the British Association were
admitted on their tickets; ordinary admission from 2 to 5 p.m. was half a crown and a
shilling in the evening.

wch he had written on finding himself in the place where Newton had lived.—At one of the dinners (at the Ordinary, I believe) a Frenchman wished to recite an appropriate French poem of 200 lines or more:[58]— the Chairman stopped him, but allowed his 2d request of giving a toast.— he gave 'les dames anglaises'.— I dined at home & took a walk with M. in the evening.— M. had her ear syringed today.

Mon. 30. Slept in Coll. last night to be ready for this morning's busy work: began receiving fees at 8 . . . a great rush of MAs.— 2 BD, 95 AM, 3 LLB, 1 AB, 3 eundem.[59]— A prodigious number of MAs this year 240: In the year 1842 there were 257; in 1818 238:— no other year nearly so large. . .

Wed. 9. July. Yesterday Betsy took a disgust against her cat 'Tom', who had bitten the gardeners & who she thought was going mad:— she had him drowned.— Christened William Anthony Coppin at Trin. Church: Margaret was present & not only gave a sovereign to the Baby's mother (whom she had taught French, Italian, & Music when Kitty Marlow) but generously tipped the nurse:— the husband (Mr Coppin, a baker) was present:— he is a genteelly made man of about 40, with a red face.— Lucy talked of going to the christening but did no more . . .

Th. 10. Our Cook Sarah Ironside married today to John Weavings a Railway Inspector: I performed the ceremony at Barnwell, & Margaret honored the bride & bridegroom with her presence, never having been at a marriage before: Lucy's protégée Susan Chune was of the party, & looked vastly pretty & like a languid fine lady:— she came with M. & me in our fly: in the other were bride & bridegroom, bridesmaid (Betsy Edwards, dressed in white for the occasion), & the giver away of the Bride (a young man of the name of Wootton about the age of the bridegroom, viz. 22 or so— the bride being 36 by her own confession): they were all as smart as hands could make them, particularly Betsy Edwards (who is properly in deep mourning.— There was no crying & no tittering:—everything most decorous. To our great amusement we found Eliza Gillmour in the church.— M. & I afterwards exhibited the Fitzwilliam Museum, the Mesman & my office to Susan Chune & then deposited her at the Hospital. Dined in Hall where I was glad to meet Sherwood of Downing who was passing thro Cambridge.— Letters from Mrs. Kennedy & Miss Lodge: the former was a charming letter, written with all her delightful stile:— Miss Lodge's gave me but a melancholy account of poor Lodge. . .

---

[58] This rhapsodic catalogue, where men of letters appear more often than those of science and we find the bold rhyme Brunel/tunnel, was by M.A. Jullien. It was published in London and dated 18 June as *A l'Angleterre savante et littéraire.*

[59] I.e. *ad eundem [gradum]* admitted 'to the same [degree]' as one held from Oxford or Dublin without examination. The distinction between ad eundem and incorporation was that the former did not require a man to be admitted to a College (H. Gunning, *Ceremonies* (1828), pp. 217–18).

Sat. 12. . . . Went on with Walter Scotts 'Old Mortality':[60] it is very delightful to return to him after every other writer.

Tu. 15. Town Elections— Voted before breakfast Kelly 746, Adair 729.[61]— I took M. a new walk for her, namely along the Hobson Stream into the Via Lambertina,[62] to see the handsome swing gates of the railway there.— Wrote to Edward Allen.— Went on with 'Old Mortality'.

Wed. 16. Dined in Hall: a large party for vacation time: Dr Clark, Prof Cumming, Dr Fisher & John Hutton Fisher, &c were there: I being V.M. went into the Combination room & staid till 8 o'clock.— Kelly not chaired: that was wise on his part:— the Election was turned in Kelly's favor by about 50 dissenters going in after 3½ to vote for him.— A very old man Ingle (past 90) died today in the street while being dragged along in a Bathchair.

Wed. 23. Began reading 'The Sibyl' by D'Israeli.[63]— Very dull I find it.— Letter from G.T.R. to say that his drawing[64] has been accepted at the Academy:— wrote to congratulate him:— sent him a small present of £2— Went on with 'the Sibyl'. It mends:— but it is a book calculated to make the Manufacturers rise upon their employers. Susan Chune left the Hospital today.

Th. 24. . . . At night I went on with 'the Sibyl': mischievous book with painful details about the Tommy shop or truck system; it is certainly clever but very exaggerated.

Tu. 29. Opening of the Railway.[65]— M & I happened by good luck to be at the Station just when the train came in from Ely: the carriages were decorated with flags & produced a very gay effect: it was a very long train: forth from it came the B. of Norwich, Lord Braybrooke & sons, Adeane, the

60 Sir Walter Scott, *Old Mortality* (1816).
61 A sketch of 'the Nomination' is shown in the *Illustrated London News* for 19 July 1845. Kelly left for London by coach, being escorted as far as the Trumpington Road by a crowd with band and banners. It was, according to the *Cambridge Chronicle* (19 July), as Tory party members were proceeding quietly home that 'they were attacked in a cowardly manner by the horrid ruffians of the Whigs, (the leader of whom was a fellow known as 'Tambourine Sam') and a desperate fight ensued in the neighbourhood of Emmanuel College'. A different story appeared in the *Cambridge Advertiser*, alleging menaces and even 'savage violence' against liberal voters in Barnwell by gangs of railway navvies supplied with Tory beer and tobacco. A restrospective commission of 1853 showed that Kelly's agent had bought votes at £10 apiece.
62 Now Long Road, named after James Lambert, Bursar of Trinity, 1789—99.
63 Benjamin Disraeli, *Sybil or the Two Nations* (1845).
64 We have not been able to identify this.
65 The Act allowing the Eastern Counties Railway to construct a line to Cambridge had been passed in July 1844, after the University authorities had inserted draconian clauses which allowed it to supervise student passengers (see Cooper, IV, 672-4). The town was en fête for the grand opening before hundreds of guests and thousands of spectators. There were dinners, a band, flowers, flags, cannon, and inevitable speeches, including those from the Mayor and the Vice-Chancellor. In October the Barnwell Theatre staged a piece called 'Cambridge Railroad Station', and complaints began to appear in the press of the continual changes to 'time bills' and the debonair indifference of the clerks who 'want looking after'. See Enid Porter, *Victorian Cambridge* (1975), pp. 21-4, summarising newspaper accounts, and R.B. Fellowes, *London to Cambridge by Train* (1939).

Dean of Ely, &c &c: the arrival of the train was hailed by firing off little cannon. The Station & the Bridge on the Hills Road were adorned with flags.— The Directors &c dined in a Tent at the Station.— I dined in hall.— Went on with Sibyl.

Fri. 1. August. Dull showery weather.— The vaulting of Trinity Great Gate is beginning.— Work as usual all the morning at my office.— 'Monastery' after dinner.[66]

Mon. 4. A dreadful accident on the Railway (near Littlebury): the Stoker killed, & the Engineer broke his leg.— Went on with the Monastery in the Evening.

On 6 August Romilly left on the 4 o'clock train to Audley End. He had become quite accustomed to rail travel and recorded 'very cautious at starting: we were 5 min. doing the 1st mile'. After looking at the 'miserable' church at Wenden he took a very shaky omnibus to Walden to inspect the church and almshouses before arriving wet at the mansion. It was a family party of Braybrookes who after dinner sat talking almost till midnight. Lord Braybrooke himself 'was full of anecdote & kept up the conversation with little or no help from anybody.' The next day his host entertained him in the gardens and retailed several uncomplimentary anecdotes about Prince Albert: 'a grand present of choice fruit was sent to the Queen one day when she was known to have a large dinner party:— the Prince proposed keeping it till the next day when they might eat it all by themselves:— The Prince took his younger brother out shooting, but kept all the good shots for himself, whereupon his brother said in German,'You always were the most selfish fellow in the world & you are not improved by becoming a great man.' After dinner he displayed various curiosities from the library such as the so-called Vinegar Bible of 1717. Romilly joined in two rubbers 'and won 9 points, but no stake had been mentioned, so received nothing'.

Friday brought a grand cricket match, lasting the whole day between Audley End and the University, whose team arrived in a drag. All the neighbourhood were present and ninety guests were served lunch. F.J. Gruggen was the University hero scoring 67, and his side won despite Mr Morgan's being 'severely hurt by 2 balls striking his knee'. Lady Braybrooke sent Romilly to Wenden station in her carriage on Saturday, a nasty rainy day not improved by Romilly's having mislaid his umbrella. 'It was a quick train; got to the Skew Bridge in 25': had however to wait there 5' because the up-train was under the shed'.

Sat. 16. At the office all the morning as usual . . . Read also some more of Eothen rather dull.[67]— Read loud the 1st dialogue in Defoes 'Religious Courtship':— I bought Defoe's works (20 vols) this day for the

---

[66] Sir Walter Scott, *The Monastery* (1820).
[67] Romilly puts the title in Greek: A.W. Kinglake, *Eothen or Traces of Travel brought Home from the East* (1844).

sake of this work wch I had never read.[68]— I think it very clever indeed:— the arguments are very clearly & vividly put.— A great charge brought against a protégée of Lucy's the other day (Sarah Fordham) by her Master (Mr Palmer) was that she had been reading an improper book:— it turned out to be 'Religious Courtship'!!! the man proved abundantly that he had never read the work, for it is one of the most pious books I ever read.

Mon. 18. Agreeable day, no rain:— M. & I saw a train come in today, the 1st we have seen since the opening.

Tu. 19. Dreadful day for the harvest: rain all day: saw a sickle carried about on a pole, with the inscription 'pity the poor harvestmen'.— Dined in hall.— Found 'the diary of a Physician' too horrible to read loud[69] . . .

Wed. 20. Asked to dine today both by Lady Cotton & the Charles Townleys:— declined both.— Yesterday a slight accident on the Railroad: the engine got off the line at Waterbeach: nobody hurt.— Went on with Eothen: also with 'Religious Courtship', & W. Scotts Abbot.[70]— Also read loud a sermon of our new Trin. Church curate (J. Coombe):— it was a college Commemoration Sermon at St. Johns:— it is rather ultra pious: it is very like a flaming discourse in a Methodist Chapel.— Went on with 'Diary of a Physician' to myself:— read 'the Magdalene': very revolting.

Fri. 22. Charming day: much corn carried: went to look at the Gleaners.— Read loud 'R.C.'

Sat. 23. Another dry day: the thermometer not above 60.— Being Market day M & I walked up the Hills Road.— Finished De Foe's 'Religious Courtship' which we thought very tedious & latterly very twaddling . . . Went on with Eothen: the account of crossing the desert & of the Plague at Cairo is very amusing. The author is pert & flippant in talking about religion, & is an idoliser of Tennyson & all that school of poets,— but he is vastly entertaining . . .

68   Their father left Joseph his Spanish books and a cyclopedia, and Cuthbert all his classical books and translations which in turn passed to Romilly on Cuthbert's death. With his own steady purchases over many years and his sisters' personal collections, these must have formed a varied and well-stocked library. Soon after Lucy's death in 1854 he noted that he had presented a 'considerable' number of volumes to the University, preferring that to 'leaving them all in a lump in my will', in which he made several specific bequests of books, such as all of Lucy's to a great niece. We may presume that George Romilly, as his heir, took what he fancied, and G.B.Allen certainly took the manuscript diary as Romilly had asked him to do. Yet the bulk of the books was evidently sold at the Hoop on 4 November 1864 when many were bought by Robert Potts and presented to the University Library. The sale-catalogue included many omnibus entries;the Defoe volumes, however, are identifiable as lot 129, and other major sets are specified e.g. Goethe, Voltaire, Italian poets, Scott's edition of Swift and Malone's of Shakespeare. There were besides many reference books and 20 volumes of Trinity examination papers.

69   Samuel Warren, *Passages from the Diary of a Late Physician* (1832–38). Warren had been a medical student at Edinburgh, and he was much criticised for divulging professional secrets in these melodramatic pieces.

70   Sir Walter Scott, *The Abbot* (1820).

Wed. 27. Unpacked a box of books in the Library.— Margarets new Piano arrived: cost 55 guineas carriage 2 guineas . . .

On 28 August Romilly played host to Lady King, Miss Cotton, Lord Forbes, Paget, and Pakenham to whom he gave a champagne lunch with bouquets for each person before escorting them to the Fitzwilliam Museum and the University Press. There he was obliged to leave them to catch the train to Wenden where, after waiting an hour for an omnibus, he finally took a fly to Audley End. During this visit the last cricket match of the season took place on a 'glorious fine day' and the visitors from Linton were soundly thrashed, the hero of the day being Charles Neville whose twenty-second birthday it was. Romilly met the young tutor of the Adeane family Russell Day, an Etonian (about to enter King's College), and the Miss Townshends one of whom 'has the blackest moustache & the longest & thickest that I ever saw on a woman's lip'. In company with Lord Braybrooke he called on Ralph Clutton, vicar of Saffron Walden, with the object of sighting his guest the novelist Fanny Trollope, but 'our curiosity was defeated,— we were not let in'.

Mon. 1. Sept. . . . Took my departure at 12: There was no omnibus for the day-mail train, so I had to carry my portmanteau 1½ mile to the Wenden Station.— M. & George met me at the Station.— G.T.R. arrived last Saturday. Today an Excursion train from London to Cambridge & back for 5s enlivened the Town by an importation of about 400 cockneys.[71]— £5 to G.T.R.—

Fri. 5. M. & L. have heard of a cook at last. Her names are Theodosia Russell !!! My olfactory nerves distressed yesterday & today: my new drawers (in my office) are being painted under my nose.— M. & I called on Havilands & Apthorps. G.T.R. gave wine to a couple of friends.— In the Evening we had our first fire & I went on with 'Lady Hester Stanhope'.[72]

Th. 11. All the morning engaged in Lodge's affairs: got his 2 Bonds (£300 each) with £10.19 interest on them from Mr Mortlock . . . Wrote to Lodge to tell him what I had done:— I received from him yesterday a note (authorising me to demand his bonds):[73]— this is the 1st time I have seen his handwriting since he left Cambridge . . .

Sat. 13. M. & I walked up the Cherry Hinton Lane & penetrated further into the fields than we had ever gone before.— In the Evening went on with Lady Hester Stanhope.

Sun. 14. Margaret felt poorly with indigestion:— she & I went to Trinity Church where Coombe did all the duty & preached a ranting

[71] This was the first cheap excursion train from London. Estimates of the size of the 'invasion' varied and the *Cambridge Chronicle* (6 September) which settled on a precise figure of 286, reported icily that 'an immense concourse of persons assembled at the station to watch the arrival of the curiosities, who, by the way, conducted themselves very well during their stay here'. Some disapproved of railways for the new mobility they gave to the lower classes.

[72] The eccentric spinster (d.1839) who had settled in the Levant and adopted eastern ways. Her lengthy *Memoirs* (1845) and *Travels* (1846) were published by her physician.

[73] I.e. the monies held as security during Lodge's tenure of the Librarianship and now returned to him. They were more than his annual salary.

sermon of 55′ on 1 John 2. 10 in behalf of the sufferers at Quebec by the fire:— there were sermons in all the Churches on the same charity:[74]. . .

Wed. 17. Our new Cook 'Theodosia Russell' came today: she has a fine complexion & is very good-looking: she is short & very plump:— seems dull & slow . . .

Mon. 22. Caught cold from having been overheated yesterday in Church & the wind blowing on me:— I had got ½ way to church with a black neckcloth on when I met Coombe's messenger with a note asking me to read: so I had to run home for a white cravat.— Mrs Elizabeth Apthorp died this morning . . .

On 25 September Romilly, who had stayed overnight at the Green Dragon hotel in Bishopsgate Street, had a busy day in London. It was the height of the speculative railway mania and Romilly took his profits. He collected two extra shares in the Cambridge and Lincoln railway, and then sold them with an original four shares for £28-10-0, and 'cleared nearly £20'. Money was much on his mind for he also called on his solicitor Mr Tatham to confer with him about T.P. Romilly's estate. His father had left three-sevenths of the residue of his estate invested for the benefit of his three daughters, with Romilly and Cuthbert as executors. On Cuthbert's death in 1837 his responsibility was transferred to Edward Romilly and Henry Whittaker and it was necessary to obtain a power of attorney from Whittaker, living abroad, to transfer the consols (£1750) into the names of Margaret, Lucy, and Baugh. 'N.B.— I took a legal opinion whether Baugh or his sons were entitled: the decision was for Baugh's right. . .' After a visit to Mrs Boyer and Frances Wilderspin he was obliged (since the Athenaeum was under repair) to dine at the British Coffee House whose accommodation seemed to him 'very mediocre'. He went on to a cigar divan for coffee and a smoke before attending Mrs Keely's Lyceum theatre where he saw some good acting from her and her husband in *Fibbing for a Friend, The Governor's Wife,* and *Open Sesame.*

Romilly spent a couple of hours at the Tower of London on Friday morning, but reached home in time to accompany Packe to Madingley for whist with Lady Cotton, Sir St Vincent, and others of a 'very agreeable & conversible' party. He played four rubbers and won four shillings.

Tu. 30. Last night thieves got into Peterhouse & stole the College Plate to the amount of 4 or £500.[75] Wrote to George Romilly sending him a draft for £25‥16‥9.— Dined in Hall with most of my brother-examiners.— Went on with Kenilworth.[76]

Fri. 10.Oct. At ¼ to 9 to Chapel to elect the new Fellows— Opening of term; 3 AB, 4 AM, 1 eundem.— Dined with my brother Examiners: Archdeacon Thorp was just come into Cambridge;— so we had the pleasure of his company. The Master told us of 2 friends of his going to France & ordering 'des oeufs, chacun deux', wch they pronounced so ill

[74] Fires in May and June had destroyed much of Quebec leaving many thousands homeless.

[75] The thieves who broke into the Buttery took plate to the value of £400, although there was ten times as much within easy reach. Messengers were posted in several directions as soon as the theft was discovered, and by the end of October one William Smith alias 'Billy Go-fast' was held in London for examination though he had to be discharged owing to the unreliability of the man who had informed against him.

[76] Sir Walter Scott, *Kenilworth* (1821).

that the garçon called to the cook 'cinquante deux oeufs pour Messieurs les Anglais'— On my return home read 'Margaret Catchpole'.[77]

Tu. 14.   Sent £25 to George Romilly.— Wrote to Mrs White (born Isabel Kate Lilley) whose scoundrelly husband refuses to surrender the property (of the late farmer Lilley) wch he holds in spite of a decree of Chancery, & is secreting himself from an attachment:— Mrs White wishes to take lodgers at Granchester Cottage, a Gent & Lady:[78]— Wrote a recommendation to the Directors of the Cambridge Railway in behalf of William Clark (commonly called William Wilkins) driver for 10 years of the Beehive, wch coach (the last on the road) is about to be put down[79]
. . .

Wed. 15.   Lucy from her bedroom this morning before breakfast saw a boy (James Swan) ill – using a horse drawing an overloaded cart; out she bolted, got a policeman to take him to the Station & was directed to appear at 11 at the Townhall to substantiate the charge:— she accordingly made good her charge before the Mayor (Bishop) & Mr Fawcett & agreed to let off the young ruffian with a reprimand, wch she took in her own hands (for the Mayor said little except to the lads father) & gave a good round reproof to him, as I heard afterwards from Mr Fawcett.[80]— Poor Basevi today fell from a scaffold at Ely Cathedral & was killed.[81] . . .

Fri. 17.   . . . Finished Cobbold's 'Margaret Catchpole':— the most interesting book I have read a long time.

Sat. 18.   Thorwaldsen's statue of Lord Byron hoisted into Trinity Library thro the south window—Proclamation of Markets.— Seniority:— we rusticated a son of Lord Cottenham for general inattention to lectures & for getting posted at last Examination[82] . . .

Tu. 21.   M. & I called on the Miss Chapmans & also on Mrs Hodgson (where we found the gigantic Miss Tarlton).— M. & I went to Trinity Library to see the beautiful statue of Lord Byron by Thorwaldsen:— we also went to Trinity Chapel where was standing a waggon containing the statue of Lord Bacon[83] (a copy of that at St Albans) generously given us by

[77] Richard Cobbold, *History of Margaret Catchpole* (1845), an instant best-seller based on the true story of a Suffolk woman transported to Australia ; see *D.N.B.*

[78] Romilly had known the disputatious Lilley family of Grantchester for many years, and there are several references to them in *R.C.D. 1832–42.*

[79] The *Cambridge Chronicle*, bidding 'Adieu' to the Stage Coach' on 1 November 1845, marked the passing of the Beehive when 'the contest against all-potent steam was found to be useless', and noted that its driver Wilkins 'has been provided for by a berth upon the rail by Mr G. Fisher, Resident Director.' Advertising himself as 'late coachman of the 'Rocket' ', a James Pryor had opened a fish and poultry shop in Petty Cury a few weeks before.

[80] The lad had used 'most insulting language' to Lucy *(Cambridge Chronicle).*

[81] He was inspecting the western bell-tower, and, having his hands in his pockets, was unable to save himself. He is buried in the cathedral.

[82] Cottenham (Christopher Pepys) an old member of Trinity, sent four of his sons there; the reference is either to Charles (admitted 1843) or William (admitted 1844).

[83] He had been largely 'rediscovered' after Macaulay's essay of 1837. On the Fellows' behalf Sedgwick wrote Whewell a formal acknowledgement quoted by Clark & Hughes, II, 99-101.

the Master: we saw however nothing but the plaster cast (wch is to be placed in the Library), the marble statue was still in its case.— At night read loud that rubbishy 'Royal Favorite'.[84]

Tu. 28. Edward heard from George that his father was rather better.— Breakfast to Latimer Neville, J. Lodge (Junior), Edlin, & Edward.— Wrote to Richard Lodge about an annuity to Mrs Jarvis:[85] wrote also to poor Lodge.— Declined dining with Warter in Magdalene Hall to meet the Master.—Went to a great christening party in the Evening at Sidney Lodge:— It was nearly 9 when I went: the whole party (35!) were in the dining room when I was shown in: the christening had taken place in the College Chapel after the 2d Lesson in the Evening Service:— the Dean of Ely officiated (& took the baby on his wrong arm), the Master of St Johns was proxy for the Godfather the Duke of Northumberland; the Godmothers were Miss Phelps (aunt of Dr. P.), & Miss Frederica Frere:— the baby was to be named Edith Percy, but Miss Frere when applied to for the name professed her ignorance.— A foolish fellow of the College (La Motte) astonished us by asking leave to give a toast:— he gave 'Church & King':— he is a wild high-churchman.— There was a large Evening party;— a mad clergyman of the name of Morgan (a butt of Lord Aug. Fitzclarence & Lord Norreys, when they were in college), but I received him very coolly, having utterly forgotten him.— Chafy (the Foxhunter) was there: he played whist at the same table with Mrs Prest, Skrine & myself:— he made himself very disagreeable; he talked loudly & incessantly to everybody in the room, got up between deals to go into the next room, never played the right card, & once revoked.— Some good Hullah singing; also solos from Miss Wilkins, & Miss Frere.

Wed. 29. Edward heard that his Father was much the same. Wrote to Hankinson (Secretary to the Subscription for Testimonial to memory of Fowell Buxton), who had written me a very civil letter speaking of the manner in wch F. B. had cooperated with my uncle in the amendment of the penal laws: I declined subscribing.— M. & I paid a visit to Trinity Chapel to see the marble statue of Lord Bacon just given by the Master:— it is sculptured by Weekes & is an improvement from the original at St. Albans,— it has taken off his hat & changed for the better the angular position of the right hand: we thought it however very ugly, tho less so than the original, a plaster cast of which has just been stuck up upon a table in one of the Classes of our Library. — The more I see of Thorwaldsen's Lord Byron the more I admire it.

Th. 30. Wrote to G.T.R. at Paris £10:— Trial in V.C's Court; Bates (Christs) & Brock & Mandale (Trinity) for hissing him in the street:— Bates was walking with his friend Hildyard & had just plucked Mandale at the

---

[84] *The Story of a Royal Favorite* (1845) by Catherine Gore, a facile novelist of the silver-fork school parodied by Thackeray.
[85] Lodge's servant.

Little-Go:— it appeared that Mandale was hissing a lying story told by his friend Brock:— they were acquitted but charged not to hiss in the street.[86]— The afternoon's post brought me letters from Meares & George telling me that poor Baugh died on Tuesday:[87] I instantly communicated this mournful & unexpected intelligence to poor Edward who was otherwise coming to my wineparty:— I also wrote to George & Meares . . . Letter from poor Miss Butcher telling me of her having undergone a 4th operation for her dreadful complaint (Cancer):— she sent me a volume of poems by a young cousin of hers (I think his name is Haynes):[88] the subject was the 'Flight of the Spirits'; it is an account of what is seen by 2 female spirits in their flight thro the world:— The author has some power of versification, a good deal of imagination & much knowledge of geography . . .

Fri. 31. Congregation; 1 BD, 5 AM, 1 eundem.— Walk with M. from 1 to 2.— Walk with Lucy from 3 to 4: escorted her to Post Office with her letter containing 50 Governess votes for Mrs. Blamire in return for 22 she had borrowed.— Took L. into Trinity Chapel to see the statue of Lord Bacon:— she thought it frightful.— Poor Grim went off for his Father's funeral by the 4 o'clock train . . .

Sat. 1. November. All Saints:— declined going to the Trinity Dinner . . . M. & I called on Miss Humfrey:[89]— it is quite mournful to see the grounds cut up by a brick wall & all appearance of many tenements springing up on the spot:— a very sad reverse of life for my poor friends . . .

[86] See V.C. Ct I. 20, Acta Curiae, 267–9. Mandale, who had earlier called on Bates to complain of his failure in the Previous Examination, offered at the trial to produce witnesses to swear that he did not hiss, and Brock was prepared to bring others to prove he was in the habit of hissing a story in which he disbelieved 'whether in a room or the open air'. Their tale seems at best implausible, and the formal verdict was ambivalent.
[87] The funeral was in Wales where Baugh had died, and that may be why Romilly did not attend. 'Being of sound and disposing mind but from my advanced age and from approaching symptoms of decay uncertain how long God may permit me to remain in this world', Baugh had made his will on 20 January 1845. He divided his many properties in Wales among George and Edward and their step-mother, who also received an insurance of £2,500, ten shares in the Llanelly Railway Company, and the contents of their Dulwich home. George and Edward also had £200 apiece and a share of books. The furniture, wines, etc. at Cilhriw went to George who proved the will as sole executor. It should be remembered that wills at this time may give a false notion of the size of an estate since they dealt only with what was considered to be personal estate and not with certain real estate.
[88] Henry W. Haynes, author of *Job, a Lyrical Drama, and Other Poems* (1845) and *Pleasures of Poesy* (1846).
[89] Her father Charles Humfrey's financial affairs were becoming increasingly embarrassed, and he had lately been obliged to allow terraced housing on the land round his mansion near Emmanuel College. He had been involved, sometimes with partners like Julian Skrine, in local banking for thirty years. On the same day, 13 August, that he met the officers of the London and County bank who were to buy the bank, he issued a public handbill, explaining that since 'I do not feel that I should be justified in paying or receiving any money on account of my bank at present, business will be suspended for three or four days'.

Mon. 3.   Resignation of V.C.— Wrote to F.R. £10.— Declined dining with Dr. & Mrs Archdall.— Wrote to Mrs. John Romilly about poor Baugh's death, also to Lady Georgy (about London orphan), also to poor Lodge (deprecating the idea of his coming to Cambridge & offering to meet him at Keene Ground or London), also to Miss Lodge (about an annuity to Mrs Jarvis) also to Cruttwell (about Lucy's rent).— Read loud Horace Smith's 'Mesmerism'.[90]— M. & I paid a visit to the Dissenters' Cemetery & went into the chapel wch has very elegant stained windows & is paved with encaustic tiles.— The cemetery was full of flowers: some of the monuments very good.[91]

Tu. 4.   Declined breakfasting with the Senior Proctor Mills.— Election of Tatham as V.C.— Margaret & I went to the Townhall to see a Picture of the children of Israel passing thro the Red Sea: it was by a Flemish Painter of the name of Francaer & painted about 1610;[92] it was in the Quentin Matsys school: there must have been 200 figures, elaborately painted.— I did not go to the V.C's wine or to Birkett's Whist Club.

Mon. 10.   M & L. paid a visit to Miss Apthorp who wished to read to them selections of poetry copied out by her sisters and herself into various copybooks. She also lent them a sermon by her Father on the death of his sister Mrs Wheelwright: I read this loud in the Evening & thought it excellent:— Mrs Wheelwright seems to have been as near perfection as a dismal person can be. — M. & I went to Peters to see the plate (value £84) wch we & others have subscribed for Carus,— very unnecessary in my opinion:— a project of Miss Watsons:— I thought the inscription too long & too canting about 'Christian benefit derived from his ministry'.[93]— Swore in new Mayor Jos. Deighton.[94]

Sat. 15.   Lucy very Quixotic today: she bought some faggots of a drunken fellow, & gave the man's donkey 3 bits of Parliament[95] a penn'orth of bread & a penn'orth of beer! (at the suggestion of his master wch he drank out of a basin.— Lucy succeeded in gaining from the Linton Union 10s for clothing of a poor girl just taken by Mrs Curson as her little maid:— Lucy wrote the letter to the Board of Guardians, & Charles Townley rode over today & paid the 10s to Mrs Curson. — Meeting of Seniors. — Yesterday morning at 6 o'clock the Electors of Catharine Hall viz. the 4 Fellows, Corrie, Philpott, Goodwin & Procter met in the Chapel & elected Philpott: Corrie ∴ could have had only his own vote.

[90]   Horace Smith. *Love and Mesmerism* (1845). a novel.
[91]   See 22 Dec 1843.
[92]   This was exhibited by George Brune, carver and gilder, of Sidney Street. 'It is very finely executed, each figure being delineated with a minuteness of detail truly wonderful'. Francaer seems to be an error for Frans Francken II (1581-1642).
[93]   The coffee pot, part of a breakfast service, was inscribed in part 'from numerous attached friends, as a token of affectionate gratitude for spiritual benfits derived through his ministry, and other labours of Christian love' (*Cambridge Chronicle* 15 November).
[94]   See 9 November 1842.
[95]   With a pun on 'faggot' votes, that is those manufactured by the transfer of sufficient property to persons not otherwise qualified to be electors.

Mon. 17. Went to the Funeral of Dr. Procter: it was very well attended: 11 heads of houses &c: we were summoned at 10½ & did not get away till 1 o'clock: Maddison read the service.— the weather was very beautiful. Heard the history of Philpott's election from Maddison: there must be a meeting *not later than the 3d day from the Vacancy* to fix the time of Election, wch must *begin* not later than the 4th day in the Chapel at 6 AM. Accordingly the latest times were chosen; Dr Procter died on Monday & the Election began on Friday morning.— The Junior (F. Procter) voted for Philpott, Goodwin did the same, & Philpott voted for himself; whereupon Corrie gave no vote, but said 'I agree (or I acquiesce)'.— Corrie behaved as well as possible under his disappointment: he accompanied Philpott to the V.C. & on the Sunday morning (wch was Sacrament Sunday in College) preached on brotherly love. Absurd stories had got around that there were 2 scrutinies & that in the 2d Corrie voted for Philpott[96] . . .

Wed. 19. A great railway-meeting in the Townhall: Hudson, the King of Railways, was there: I went to hear him speak:— he is a coarse vulgar-looking fellow.[97] Dined with the Archdalls . . . Lucy's protégée Sarah Fordham was sent away by her mistress (Mrs Penson) on account of swelling of her face: she was sent back to Mrs Gilmour to Lucy's indignation.

Mon. 24. Warter, Cartmell, Drosier & I went together to dine with the Charles Townleys: we met Gale Townley & his bride (born Pratt), Mr Acland, Mrs Curtis Smith & her brother Mr Green (the sheriff in 1843): He was with Lord Denman when he was refused admittance to the Back entrance of Trinity Lodge: the violence of Mr G. highly amused me : he proposed to Lord D. ordering the javelin men to batter down the Gate & greatly regretted that it was not done.[98]— Mrs Frere & daughter came in the Evening & sung,— most lamentably:— I played 4 rubbers with Drosier against Cartmell & G. Townley.

Wed. 26. Congregation day.— 4 AM, 3 AB, 2 MB, 1 AB incorp, 1 eundem; J. J. Smith's Graces (for change in the Polloi Examination, particularly an alphabetical publication of the polloi in a few classes), deferred till a future congregation in this term[99] . . .

Sat. 29. Wet day: women not out.— Sent £5 to Miss Butcher who has been ill & wants coals.— Recovered £1-10- out of the surplus of the Brit. Assoc: Local Fund,— to wch I had contributed 5 guineas).— Got from

[96] W.H.S. Jones in his *History* of the college (1936), p. 190, described Philpott as 'perhaps the greatest man St Catharine's has produced'.

[97] This meeting, attended by more than 500 locals and representatives of the railway companies, had been convened to discuss railway projects affecting the town. Hudson's speech was businesslike not oratorical.

[98] See 19 July 1844.

[99] To assign a strict order of merit to the polloi served little purpose beyond perhaps embarrassing some of those at the very bottom. They had indeed an ironical celebrity and were given numerous ingenious nicknames which are recorded in C. Wordsworth, *Scholae Academicae* (1877), p. 57.

Coombe a list of the Subscribers to Mr. Carus's plate:— an anonymous Wisbech lady sent £10, wch was the only large contribution: many under 10s . . . Dined in Hall: had an interview with Carus concerning an application from several young men to present a 'Carus Missionary Testimonial' to the Bishop of Calcutta for founding a Scholarship or any other Missionary purpose in India: I dissuaded his allowing it to be called 'Carus Testimonial', but recommended his being the means of conveying their contributions to the Bishop. Sedgwick had asked me to come & talk to some youngsters at wine:— I found him lying on his sofa preparing to go out to dinner, having utterly forgotten that he had asked me!— He gave me a copy of his article in the Edinburgh on 'the Vestiges of the Creation'.

Sun. 30. Very pretty note from Carus who has acted on my advice.— The Pew-opener warned us that Mrs. Twiss desired 2 seats to be retained for her:— however we were not troubled with her presence:— M. L. E. & I at church: Carus gave us an excellent sermon from the Gospel (Matt. XXI. 4).— M. E. & I then walked to the Skew-Bridge at the Paper Mills Turnpike.— M's 1st sight of it.— Went to St Mary's at 2 & heard an admirable sermon from Prof. Blunt on 'Time'.

Romilly spent 3-8 December in London with the Edward Romillys at Stratton St. There was business to do at the Stamp Office where he paid £2731 for degrees and £487 for matriculations (these being government taxes levied on individual members of the University) and left his books to be stamped. As usual he made many visits of duty and pleasure. His sisters had entrusted him with the delivery of a gown to Frances Wilderspin at Mrs Boyers, and he also saw his nephews, Roget and his daughter, and other members of the family. At dinner he met Charles Kemble, the actor 'dreadfully deaf', Sir Thomas Phillips, 'the hero of Newport', famous for having repelled a Chartist attack, and a Mr Brackedon who had crossed the Alps 120 times. There was much much talk of the repeal of the corn laws : 'All London is wild about the announcement in the Times that Ministers are going to repeal the Corn Laws:— we talked about nothing else'.

Romilly, as usual, visited the National Gallery, and had a novel experience on the train to Blackwall; 'this journey amused me highly: the whole of the line is on a level with the garrets of the houses: the propelling power is an endless rope: the beginning of the journey is like being in a room; one crosses several streets in this gigantic sort of box'. From the Society for the Promotion of Christian Knowledge he 'made a great many purchases for Lucy', and yet another 'prodigous quantity of piety' from the Tract Society. On Saturday he sought out old curiosity shops, for Lucy had asked him to buy a teapot — 'so I bought 4 lovely ones'. That evening he had the satisfaction of beating Lady Davy at cards; she said she had once been reckoned a first-rate player who could play over all the cards again after a game. Sunday was less pleasing. He accompanied Mrs Edward Romilly and her mother to Wilton Crescent church but the service was ultrapopish with 'singing men & boys in surplices' and the preacher, whose subject was 'signs in the heavens' went 'uncommonly near to Purgatory'. It was a 'most Puseyitical affair'. Moreover, at the afternoon sermon in Westminster Abbey Wordsworth mouthed an offensive tirade against the government for voting through the Maynooth grant. Before dinner he examined Dr Roget's son, John Lewis Roget, the future undergraduate of Trinity and found he made only 'a very poor display' in classics.

Th. 11. December.   Went to Jones the dentist about a swelling in my cheek wch I have had about 3 weeks, occasioned (I believe) by clumsily biting my cheek:— he said it had nothing to do with my teeth:— he thought it however a good opportunity to gain a guinea by stopping a tooth wch had been stopped before.— Then called on Sudbury who said he would tomorrow apply leeches . . .

Fri. 12.   Mr Sudbury's Pupil (son of our Fellow, Wiles) applied a couple of Leeches to the inside of my mouth; they were marvellously tiresome about biting, but when they had once taken hold they sucked away famously for near 2 hours, & Mr Sudbury (who came at that time) took them off with salt. Uncomfortable having leeches in one's mouth as it is very difficult to swallow one's spittle without giving them a bite:— their bodies hung dangling out of my mouth.— Gave dinner to the Family: everybody present except Cartmell . . . There was one bottle of Champagne corked:— I never heard of such a thing before.— Difficulty in getting up a rubber: the players were Haviland, Paget, Shaw & I.— Asked to wine today by Sedgwick *to keep my nephew (E.E.A) in order!*

Sat. 13.   E. E. A. left Cambridge.— M. broke one of her false teeth: so she & Lucy had to pay a visit to Mr Jones, who substituted another tooth for M. & stopped with mortar a tooth for L wch he had unsuccessfully stopped with gold a year ago.— Lucy had a wonderful letter from Susan Chune, who is going to be married to a very young man (of the name of Thomas Grounds) a mason by trade, a sober steady man with Father, Mother, 8 sisters! (5 of them married) & 2 brothers.— Sarah Fordham admitted to the Hospital today.

Mon. 15.   Dined at Trinity Lodge, a grand party to meet Mr Hallam & son & daughter . . . Mr Hallam was very amusing with his account of the squabbles about the distinguished men to be commemorated in the new houses of Parliament:—there was considerable opposition to *Cowper the poet* & to *Addison:* Lord Brougham remonstrated against the omission of Littleton (on whom Ch. Just. Coke commented) & the Marquis Wellesley:— he said 'Warren Hastings was allowed, who had been tried & acquitted, whereas Wellesley had not even been tried.[1]— The Master made us laugh heartily by a story of a woman whose lips were seen moving after she got into a railway carriage & who upon being spoken to said 'don't put me out, I have a very bad memory & am repeating the list of my packages, — 'large box, little box, band box, bag' 'large box, &c'. — Today there was an extra Congregation: at this Cockerell was appointed successor to poor Basevi as Architect of the Fitzwilliam Museum; that wrongheaded James Hildyard non-placeted the grace; he was supported by Collison of St Johns: the grace however was carried (in a very thin S.H.) by 6 to 2.— This business

---

[1]   Hastings and Wellesley had been Governors General of India at the end of the previous century. Hastings had been impeached for corruption but was finally acquitted; Wellesley, though often attacked in the Commons for his policies, was never charged with any offence.

prevented my being in chapel where Frere preached the Commemoration Sermon:I was however able to go into the Hall to the distribution of Prizes: I there heard an excellent oration from Hallam 'on the development of the Forms of Poetry as dependent on the social progress of a nation':— he pronounced that the Epic & Tragic period were passed, & that this was the age of the Novel, wch had not yet reached perfection.— he quoted Lord Bacon in vindication of Novels being a form of Poetry.— Lushington pronounced (very lowly & indistinctly) a eulogy on Göthe; he punned upon his name as the worker of goeteia.[2]

Th. 18. . . . The Browne Scholar of last year (Stallard) is just dead . . . The University Marshall (Ellwood) today married to Mrs Phelps maid. . . Today Sudbury pronounced the swelling in my cheek to be in a fit state to be lanced,—wch he accordingly did.— Went to a Committee (of the Subscribers to rebuilding St Peters) at Mr Dodds: St Giles Vic. & St Peter's Perpetual Curacy appear to be two separate benefices, tho they are uniformly held by the same person:— no resolutions come to . . .

Sun. 21. . . . M & I went to Trinity Church where we had 2 nasty young Twisses thrust in upon us . . .

Tu. 23. The snow gone: mild weather.— Dined with Dr. & Mrs Whewell to meet Baron & Lady Rolfe (born Carr) . . . Lady Rolfe sung a series of Jacobite airs with the most heart-stirring enthusiasm:— she also sung some German songs: her singing is quite delightful from the expression she throws into it.— She was a musical genius at 4 years old.— The conversation of course was principally about the political crisis.— On Thursday last (a week after Peel's resignation) Lord John Russell agreed to form a ministry: but 2 days after he tendered his resignation (Earl Grey refusing to act if Lord Palmerston were Foreign Secretary): The Queen then sent for Sir Robert Peel who has consented to resume Office.— There is a very good print on the subject in Punch; Lord John coming to the Queen (like a man applying for a situation as footman), who says 'John, you are not strong enough for my place.'— Sir Robert Peel is of course prepared greatly to modify the Corn Laws.[3]

Th. 25. (Christmas)— Nasty wet day.— Lucy but poorly; obliged to take brandy & Tinture of rhubarb:— we all 3 went to Trinity: Mr. Twiss was in the Pew: he was very civil & hoped he had not inconvenienced us.— Carus preached a very good sermon from Luke. 1. 68. 75.—We stayed the Sacrament.— I then went to St Mary's, & heard Goodwin preach a hard

---

2 I.e. 'spells' or 'enchantment'.
3 Peel had resigned on 5 December when Lord Stanley, Secretary of State for War, and the Duke of Buccleuch, Lord Privy Seal, refused to support his proposed repeal of the Corn Laws. In the end Buccleuch relented and Stanley was replaced by Gladstone in the restored Peel cabinet. 'Peel is now forced to undertake the settlement of the question. It is certain he can settle it. It is very doubtful whether we could have settled it. Every man who would have voted with us will vote with him. But many a man will vote with him who would never have voted with us'. (Macaulay, *Letters* 22 December ed. T. Pinney, vol. IV (1977), 280).

sermon from John 1.1:— the anthem was 'There were shepherds &c': very well sung.— Miss Vincent dined with us: she told us that Philpott (the new Master of Catharines) is going to marry Mary Doria,— a capital match for her.— Gave Lucy as a Christmas Box a lovely edition of Goldsmith's poems with engravings, & Margaret a copy of Gellert's works.[4]

On the 26th Romilly began a visit to the Lakes where Lodge's family lived. Despite a journey of twelve hours by coach to Thrapston and then by rail to the Imperial Hotel, Liverpool, he was prepared to turn out in the pouring rain to visit the theatre. He saw only parts of a dull new comedy and of a pantomime with a troupe of thirty-six Vienna dancers: 'I never saw such ungraceful spinning, so inelegant a costume, or so ugly a set of young people'. It took him another day to reach Windermere where the weather was so foul 'blowing a gale & raining torrents' that no one would put out across the lake for him. On Sunday 28 Bowness appeared to him 'like an Italian town at the foot of the Alps', the hills were sprinkled with snow and he had no trouble reaching Keene Ground, half a mile beyond Hawkshead where Viper the dog received him. Lodge (known we learn now to the family as 'York') was still in bed 'looking very rosy and fat & with no apparent bodily ailment'. He was also introduced to Miss Lodge, John's cousin, 'very near-sighted indeed & not at all attractive'. At 2 o'clock they dined and Romilly saw on the table 'a silver cup awarded as a prize in 1810 to John Lodge's Father for 'the best Tup':— Lodge when a freshman communicated to his friends the existence of this cup: of course he got well quizzed, upon wch he exclaimed 'What a pity I ever had any sheep!'.

Romilly had brought various gifts : books for Lodge, including Dickens's *Cricket on the Hearth*, 'far too sentimental for my taste', and a new edition of Goldsmith's poems for Miss Lodge.

Next day the two friends, in the course of 'a very picturesque & beautiful walk', passed James Marshall's place at Coniston. Marshall, the wealthy Yorkshire industrialist, was Mrs Whewell's brother. The day, however, was spoilt by rain, and they returned to whist and to reading aloud from Barham's *Ingoldsby Legends* whose versification and humour Romilly admitted, although he thought it 'not a decorous publication for a Clergyman'. They also returned to a succession of meals— 'Hot supper at 9 as usual:— the hours for meals here are 8 Breakfast, Lunch 11, dinner 2 tea 6 supper 9 — so they are always eating'. The visit continued with further long walks despite the rain. Mrs Lodge was ready with mulled ale and hot wine, and saw that there was a fire in Romilly's bedroom. He met Dr Hickie, master of Hawkshead School, where (as the diarist must have known despite a telling silence) the poet Wordsworth had been educated, and a Mr Park the local and unpopular clergyman at Ambleside whose mother had no reputation and was indeed on parish relief. 'And so endeth this year with me far from home, an event which never befel me before.'

---

[4]   C. F. Gellert, German poet and miscellaneous writer (d. 1769).

Interior of Holy Trinity

Rogers,	Edv.	Em.	LL.B. 1804.
—	Hug.	Jes.	A.B. 1804.
—	Tho. Ellis........	Trin.	A.B. 1805. A.M. 1808.
—	Tho.	Cla.	A.B. 1808.
—	Tho.	*Sid.	A.B. 1811. A.M. 1814.
—	Joh.	Joh.	A.B. 1812. A.M. 1815.
—	Edv.	*Cai.	A.B. 1814. A.M. 1817. M.L. 1819.
—	Tho. Oliv.	Trin.	A.B. 1821. A.M. 1824.
—	Ja. Tho...........	Trin.	A.B. 1831.
—	Gul.	Cath.	A.B. 1833. A.M. 1838.
—	Geo.	Joh.	A.B. 1835. A.M. 1838.
—	Alex. Joh........	Jes.	A.B. 1839. A.M. 1842.
—	Joh. Gurney......	Jes.	A.B. 1839.
—	Geo. Albert	Trin.	A.B. 1840. A.M. 1843.
—	Hen.	Trin.	A.B. 1840. A.M. 1843.
—	Joh.	Trin.	A.B. 1840. A.M. 1843.
—	Joh.	Joh.	A.B. 1840. A.M. 1844.
—	Alf. Edv..........	Regin.	A.B. 1841.
—	Ri..............	Trin.	A.B. 1842. A.M. 1846.
—	Tho.	Trin.	A.B. 1844.
Röhrs,	Joh. Hen........	Jes.	A.B. 1843. A.M. 1846.
Rokeby,	Hen. Rad.......	Down.	A.B. 1830.
Rolfe,	Edm............	*Cai.	A.B. 1785.
—	Rob.	Cai.	A.B. 1788.
—	Rob. Monsey....	Trin.	A.B. 1812. *Down. A.M. 1815.
—	Edm. Nelson.....	Cai.	A.B. 1833. A.M. 1841.
—	Geo. Crabb.	Joh.	A.B. 1834.
—	Rob. Rose........	A. Tr.	A.B. 1838.
—	Edv. Fawcett Neville	Trin.	A.B. 1842.
Rolleston,	Gul. Lancelot.....	Joh.	A.B. 1840.
Rolls,	Hen.	Chr.	A.B. 1816.
—	Edv.	Chr.	A.B. 1819. A.M. 1822.
—	Phil. Mills.	Trin.	A.B. 1826.
—	Glanville Hen. ...	Sid.	A.B. 1846.
Rolph,	Tho.	Joh.	A.B. 1829.
Romaine,	Gul. Govett......	Trin.	A.B. 1837.
Romanis,	Gul.	Em.	A.B. 1846.
Romilly, (a)	Jos.	*Trin.	A.B. 1813. A.M. 1816.
—	Joh.	Trin.	A.B. 1823. A.M. 1826.
—	Edv.	A. Tr.	LL.B. 1828.
—	Hen.	Chr.	A.B. 1828. A.M. 1831.
Romney,	Joh.	*Joh.	A.B. 1782. A.M. 1785. S.T.B. 1792.
—	Joh.	Joh.	A.B. 1841. A.M. 1844.
Rooke,	Joh.	*Pet.	A.B. 1762.
—	Hen.	*Trin.	A.B. 1769. A.M. 1772.
—	Geo.	Joh.	A.B. 1799. A.M. 1803.
Rookes,	Gul.............	Jes.	A.B. 1783.
—	Car.	Jes.	LL.B. 1824.
Rooper,	Joh. Bonfoy......	Joh.	A.B. 1801.
—	Tho. Ri.	Joh.	A.B. 1804.
Roots,	Hen. Shuckburgh.	Jes.	M.B. 1824. M.D. 1829.
—	Aug.	Jes.	A.B. 1833. A.M. 1836.

(a) Registrarius 1832.

A page of the *Graduati*

1846

Romilly left Hawkshead on New Year's Day laden with gowns that Lodge meant as presents for Margaret and Lucy, and a heap of papers for the University Librarian and the Steward of Magdalene. Lodge and his mother said their goodbyes at Kendal and Romilly and Miss Lodge went on by coach to the King's Arms at Lancaster where they had tea and mutton chops. He then read Defoe's *Apparition of Mrs Veal* till bedtime. The next morning a waiter who found him admiring a print of Landseer's *A Distinguished Member of the Humane Society* invited him to see the original, a dog called Lawrence, in the yard. Miss Lodge left him at Preston where Romilly transferred to a second class railway coach : 'I gained 10/6 by this piece of economy, paying £1-11-6 instead of 2 guineas:—it was a very foolish economy for the accommodation was detestable & the company very bad (noisy drunken soldier & sailor &c)'. In compensation he dined very agreeably in the first class refreshment room at Birmingham, and reached London at 9 o'clock and put up at the 'magnificent Euston Hotel.' After tea he read till eleven.

Sat. 3   January. To Cambridge by 11½ train: agreeably surprised to find M & L at the Station. Walk with M till dinner time. Read loud in the Evening 'Black Dwarf' (W Scotts).[1]

Sun. 4.   M. thought the morning damp & uncomfortable & did not go to Church.— L. & I to Trinity Church where we heard a good *old* New-years sermon from Numbers X. 29: we heard the same in 1841.—We had one son of Dr Lamb in our pew & one of those nasty young men sent by the Twisses: Lucy turned away *one,* & complained to the pew-opener, & went herself into the next pew.[2] The weather mended, & M, E & I took a good walk.— Wrote out hymns in the Evening for Lucy.

Mon. 5.   . . . Received from Prof Pillans[3] a very civil letter & a present of his preface to a selection from Ciceros Orations &c: also from Worsley a copy of his publication as Christian Advocate[4] ('Province of the Intellect in Religion'); this book contains a map (in a pocket) of the Beatitudes &c arranged in concentric circles.— Wrote to thank both.—

Tu.6.   Second day of Questionists Fees 123.— Declined keeping Twelfth Night at Trinity (as requested by Sedgwick).— Lucy wrote to Lodge to thank him for the gowns:— she gave him good advice about going to Church (which he unhappily feels a disinclination to):— I also wrote.

---

[1]   *The Black Dwarf* (1816).
[2]   Difficulty with the Twisses, who had lent Romilly the pew several years earlier, had been growing and were soon to come to a head. See *R.C.D. 1832–42* pp. 232-3, and 25 March 1842 and 18 March 1843.
[3]   James Pillans, professor of humanity and laws at Edinburgh and a well-known Whig, had at one time been tutor to T.F. Kennedy who married Romilly's cousin Sophie.
[4]   By the will of John Hulse (d.1790) the Christian Advocate, 'a learned and ingenious' scholar, was elected for several years to publish answers to all 'new and popular or other cavils against the Christian or Revealed Religion, or against the Religion of Nature.' Besides atheists and infidels, he was to controvert 'new and dangerous error either of superstition or enthusiasm' among Christian sects. There is a list of such writings in R. Bowes, *Catalogue of Cambridge Books* (1894), p. 275.

Th. 8. — Looked over box of books for Power.— Had to appear at Townhall against a rascal who had gone about with a lying begging-case with many false signatures: he pretended to be a Farmer suffering from a fire:— I gave him 2/6 which he transformed into 12/6: he tore out this page of his book & tried to swallow it:— it was taken out of his mouth:— condemned to 14 days hard labour: Betsy had to appear to swear to the man (for I did not see him)[5]— To Audley End by 2½ train. . .

Fri. 9. Worsley acted Chaplain.— Walked to Ashdon & had luncheon with Dr Chapman & his nieces (Mrs Barnwell & 3 younger sisters); Mr Barnwell (an Oxford Clergyman, brother-in-law to the Bridegroom, a very merry young man) & Stokes of Caius were of the party:— plenty of eating & drinking & no end of laughing.— They took me over the place & showed me the good points of view: the house is most comfortable & the scenery very pleasing. They took me to a capital farm-house & introduced me to Farmer Hustler & his well-mannered pretty young wife & 3 young boys (the youngest lying in a cot with a bad knee). I here got the keys of the Bartlow Barrows & took with me the Farmers man armed with a spade.[6] Stokes accompanied me & we went into all 4 barrows with some little difficulty from rusty locks & dirt at the door:— of course no reliques left. . . Walk of more than 14 miles; for Bartlow is 2 miles from Ashdon, Ashdon 4 from Walden, & Walden more than a mile from Audley End . . .

Sat. 10. I acted chaplain (for the 1st time in my life).— Miss Neville, Miss Louisa N., Miss Wynne, Miss Dornier (I think) (the amiable sensible governess at A.E.), Mr Wix & I left A.E. a little before 11: we arrived at Wenden at 10' past 11, intending to go to Cambridge by the 11½ train: we staid half hour after hour, fearful of some accident to the missing train, & a pilot engine was despatched in search of it; a little after 1 it came in with the mail train. there had been no accident, but they could not get along for want of steam.— We put ourselves in the Mail-train but could not have a carriage to ourselves: Mr Wix took 2 ladies in one carriage, & I escorted the other 2 (Miss Louisa & Miss Wynne) in another;— the only carriage in which I could find accommodation was 'the Ladies' carriage': an old lady looked very much distressed, & I offered to retire, but she submitted to my remaining.— On arriving in Cambridge we all 6 (2 daughters of a Lord & one of an Embassador!) got into an Omnibus which deposited us at the Fitzwilliam; I exhibited that, & the Mesman, & the Fitzwilliam Pictures, & the Bust of Pitt,[7] & Trinity Library, Chapel & Hall, & Kings College Chapel in a very rapid way & deposited them all again in the Omnibus a little before 4.— At night read loud 'Black Dwarf'.

[5] According to a report in the *Cambridge Chronicle,* he was a seaman called Mackenzie purporting to be one Thomas Roberts of Steeple Morden.

[6] Two of the barrows better known as the Bartlow Hills had been opened in 1835 and 1838 in the presence of Sedgwick, Whewell, and others, who found various artefacts and bones. See *R.C.D. 1832-42* p. 147. On the second occasion Whewell wrote a set of humorous verses for private circulation reproduced by C. Whibley, *In Cap and Gown* (1889), pp. 149-53.

[7] I.e. that by George Gerrard (1808) in the Museum.

Wed. 14. Ball at Mrs Clarks for young folks: a very pretty sight as almost all the young girls were in white: Kate & Louisa Hughes were the belles of the Evening, & Hopkins' son was the most attractive among the beaus. — John Graham (Master of Christ's son) was among the principal polka dancers.— The whole concluded with Sir Roger de Coverley danced with much spirit. — There was a magic lantern exhibited. — A whist table upstairs: the players Dr French, Dr Paget, Skrine, Mrs Prest & I.

Sat. 17. . . . I had a Letter from Mrs Kennedy yesterday telling me that Frank (tho 3½) is of so gay and so selfwilled a temper that she has not begun teaching him a prayer!

Sun. 18. — (2d Sunday after Epiphany).— M, L & I to Trinity Church: we found the 2 hateful young men (friends of the Twisses) in possession: Lucy took the matter into her own hands, told them that Mr Carus had offered them his pew, & fairly turned them out.— Carus preached an excellent sermon from Matt. XVI. 25, 26 — M, E & I took a good walk: Lucy to her paupers.— Wrote to Lady Braybrooke in behalf of Miss Thornton for Governess Association.

Fri. 23. Caput at VC's at 10 to mark off the Honors: hurrah for Trinity, we have the Senior Wrangler (Hensley): he is the 2d from King's College,— Cayley having been the 1st[8]. . . Today a Queensman (named Jolly) paid me his fees: he was very drunk (reeling & stammering) & offered me 6d! he thought (incorrectly) that he was plucked.[9]

Sat. 24. Bachelors Commencement— 127 Honors & 140 Polloi admitted: a small no of Plucked men, viz. 1 for Honors & 16 for Polloi: Senate house immensely full in spite of the wetness of the day.—Edward dined with us, a farewell dinner to him.— By the way he gave a grand dinner to 14 (Hensley the Senior Wrangler being one) in my rooms last Thursday, — I supplying Champagne & other wines.— Today a note from Mr J.P. Twiss saying that 'he regretted being obliged to take entire possession of his Pew to prevent the recurrence of such a scene as last Sunday's'. — Wrote him a polite note thanking him for the indulgence of several years & saying that I should send him the key of the book-closet on Monday.— It is (doubtless) all his wife's doing: extremely rude to give us such short notice. . .

Sun. 25. . . . M & I went & sat in Carus's most uncomfortable pew near the Vestry: there we found a Mrs Roscow (wife of a Fellow Commoner who has just taken his degree) & her little boy who behaved admirably.— A most villainous Sermon on death from Coombe. Paid a visit to Mrs Worsley who has been very poorly; — took a good walk with Edward.— L. to her paupers.

---

8 I.e. both had been educated at King's College, London.
9 'Plucked. Rejected in a University Examination' (Bristed in his account of 'The Cantab Language', I, 30-5). Compare the later term 'ploughed' which superseded it.

Mon. 26. Wrote to F.R. £20 also to Madame Bourlet, Sophie & Jaques. M & Lucy walked with me to Burleigh House Barnwell (Mr Twiss's house); Mrs Twiss sent out the maid to ask me to come in:— Lucy insisted upon accompanying me:— M. staid outside.— Mrs Twiss is a tall high-coloured dark-eyed handsome dashing woman of about 30 (she is a 2d wife): she wished to throw dust in my eyes but Lucy brusqued her in the most pointed manner, & the breach is clearly irreparable: Mrs Twiss has certainly behaved extremely ill. — Dined with Dr & Mrs Clark & met Miss Fanny Okes, Prof & Miss Sedgwick, Prof & Mrs Willis, Dr Fisher & Williamson:— Miss Sedgwick played the piano in a very forte stile.

Tu. 27. Present from Professor Pillans of 2 printed copies of the Latin compliment to Lord J. Russell on making him LLD of Edinburgh & of 2 English Letters between Sir Rob. Peel & himself (concerning Prof. Pillans' recent publication of Cicero's Orations etc.). . . Dined at Trinity Lodge:— A. Spring Rice, Lawrence (the Artist who made the ferocious drawing of Sedgwick),[10] Sedgwick & myself.—The Master made a violent tirade against free-trade principles. . .

Wed. 28. Congregation: 3 Hon MA, 1 LLB, 4 BA, 1 eundem. — It was a nasty rainy morning, but M & L bravely came to the Senate house to see Edward take his Bachelors degree.— Received a cheese from Lancashire: 'by the kindness of Mr Clarke' was on the address, which looked like Lodge's handwriting.— Began reading loud 'the chainbearer' (ie carrier of Surveyor's chain) by J.F. Cooper: thought it dull.[11]

Tu. 3 February. — College Seniority (about Bursarial business only).— Hear that Edleston & Walmisley & some Fellow Commoners dismissed Christmas last night in rather an objectionable stile, viz. by sitting up card playing & smoking in the Combination Room till 7 in the morning! — Very satisfactory letter from G.T.R. at Paris.

Th. 5. Caroline Howe went off this morning:— Lucy took some carpet work of our French nieces to be made up into ottomans as a present for W.C. on 2d March (his birthday). — College meeting to warn Monk & Scarlett (the 2 Fellow Commoners who sat up in the Combination Room all night) against repeating such unstatutable conduct under any sanction of MAs or Fellows of the College: a 3rd Fellow Commoner (Fussell, a married man) was of the party: he was summoned today but had left College.

Consulted today by a newly admitted BA: he wants to go to Oxford as an undergraduate & be examined there for his degree in Michaelmas: told him it was impossible:— his idea was that he might do so any time before the Tripos day. . .

---

[10] Samuel Laurence (sic) did a crayon drawing of Sedgwick in 1844: 'it makes me look a little like a savage; to be perfect it should represent me with a tomahawk in the right hand, and a bloody scalp in the left' (Clark and Hughes, II, 486).

[11] J.F. Cooper, *The Chain-Bearer* (1845), part of an unsuccessful historical trilogy about American life, which Romilly found 'dull & prosy' (5 February).

Sat. 7. Suffering from Lumbago.— I am now preparing a transcript of the Graduati from 1760.[12]— In the Evening read loud Moore's Zelucco: the remarks on the Slave Trade are excellent[13]. . .

Sat. 14. Wrote to Lodge.—Filia famulae meae apud Collegium (famula in Scholâ prope Londinum) a nauta stuprata atque derelicta in summam incidit miseriam & querit Asylum in hospitio faeminarum impudicarum:[14] Dictated a letter to her Mother in answer to one from T.L. Jackson a missionary (as he calls himself) to whom she had applied & sent a money order for £1.2.6. to redeem her clothes. . .

Wed. 18. Over to Audley End. In the railway carriage I met a friend of Dr Rogets a Mr Taylor: he of course recognised me & not I him:— he presented me to his wife & his brother-in-law Mr Snell & Mrs Snell & another Lady, for they were travelling as a grand family party:— 3 fine women they were: they had come from London with a day-ticket to lionise Cambridge & Mr Taylor had called at my rooms.— The party at A.E. consisted of Lord & Lady B, Miss Louisa, Mr Charles, Mr Stanhope & his wife Lady Elisabeth & 2 daughters, Lady Mary Ross (sister of Lady B), Mr Nelson (brother of Lord N) & Mr Baillie (undergraduate of Trinity)— Mr Stanhope is a queer thin uncomfortable-looking dull man, Lady Elisabeth a handsome plump comfortable-looking moderately lively lady, the eldest daughter rather shy, but the youngest very gay & agreeable. — Miss Neville was confined to her room with a bad swelled face. Whist with Lady B against Mr Charles & Lady Elis: won 3s. Lady B told me that her maid said to her the other day when she was going to Magdalene Lodge 'An't you going, my Lady, to the Magdalene'.

Th. 19. Left A.E. by the 11 o'clock omnibus. . . Mr Stanhope & the 4 ladies & I took one railway-carriage, & the 2 young men were left to themselves in another. Mr Nelson kept up a communication with us by constantly putting his head out of the windows and by waving his handkerchief which he had tied to the end of his cane. . . Bateson was to have sent a fly for me at 5½ to dine at Madingley: at ¼ to 6 no fly having arrived I saw there was some mistake & went to 'the Prince Regent' & got a fly for myself: Arrived at Madingley just before Bateson whose blundering Gyp had ordered the fly at 6½! . . .

Sun. 22. (Quinquagesima) — Term Sacrament:— Carus therefore in College Chapel[15]—Lucy nursed her cold & the cat & never stirred out.— I read prayers & Coombe preached on the Queen's letter for Church-building from Revelations 21. 22 'No temple in the city'. —: he alluded very

---

[12] See 9 November 1842.
[13] John Moore's *Zelucco: Various Views of Human Nature taken from Life and Manners* (1786), 'clever but rather coarse & indelicate' (24 January).
[14] I.e. The daughter of my College servant (a servant in a school near London), seduced and abandoned by a sailor, has fallen into total misery and is seeking refuge in an asylum for Fallen Women.
[15] See 5 March 1843.

well to the danger from which Trinity Church escaped last night when Headly (the Ironfounders) premises were on fire[16]. . .

Tu. 24. . . . A curious proof of ignorance was made today: all the candidates (7) for BA on Dunces Day[17] who went into the extra Examination were this day plucked!. . .

Sat. 28. The house divided at last this morning at 3 o'clock: Sir Robert Peel & the ministers had a majority of 97 in the grand free-trade movement. . . This morning Payne (an Upholsterer) sent to my rooms 2 Ottomans made as a birthday-gift for Carus (whose Birthday is 2d March): the worsted part of one is green & the other blue, they are the work of our French nieces:— the frame part is Rosewood;— very handsome.— M. & L. came to my rooms to see them & to superintend the packing them up. They are to be given anonymously: the note which accompanies this handsome present is of Lucy's composition but in the handwriting of M. wch is supposed to be unknown to Carus.— At night went on with Moore's 'Edward'.[18]

Sun. 1. March. (1st Sunday in Lent) — M, L & I went into the Ministers Pew: Carus preached admirably on fasting from Matt. vi. 17-18: he insinuated that people might fast a great deal without the world knowing anything about it: Carus certainly don't look as if he fasted.

Mon. 2. The 2 Ottomans sent to Carus's: Lucy has sent them so carefully anonymously that I believe Carus will avail himself of the opportunity of returning no thanks:— if so, L. will have mystified him a little more than she wished.— Whist club at our new Members, Francis. . .

Tu. 3. M & L sent the maids to see General Tom Thumb: we were amused by seeing his lilliputian coach & 4 driving about the town: the coachman & footman were 2 very little boys wearing wigs like the Ld Mayor's coachmen, the horses were very pretty ponies[19] — Packe & I dined at Lady Cotton's: party of 9; Lady & Miss Cotton, Mrs Gibbon, Dr & Mrs Whewell, Mr & Mrs Adeane, Packe & I: violent tirade from Dr Whewell against Peel.— No cards.

[16] The fire broke out before midnight and raged for three hours as efforts were turned from saving the foundry to neighbouring premises and their contents. During the confusion 'thieves in abundance were on the look-out for opportunities'. The engines included one from Trinity, sent by Whewell, and 'wherever downright *work* was needed, there was to be seen cap and gown, or rather the remnant thereof, and nothing could exceed the vigour and the hearty good-will displayed by their possessors'. Thus The *Cambridge Chronicle* (28 February) whose office abutted the foundry and which led a campaign against rebuilding it in the town centre: 'public safety is not to be sacrificed to private convenience'.

[17] See 21 February 1844.

[18] John Moore, *Edward or Various Views of Human Nature* (1796), a novel.

[19] The American dwarf Charles Stratton, alias General Tom Thumb, was repeating the success of his English debut two years earlier when he had been fêted and presented to the queen.

Fri. 6. . . . Dined at the Family at Shaws. . . A most magnificent dinner with real turtle & *buffalo hump*; this last is worthless being like very coarse stringy oversalted beef:— I had never seen buffalo hump before, & was therefore much pleased at tasting it.— Phelps, Paget, Cartmell & I made the whist table:— at wch I was unsuccessful.

Sat. 7. Election of University Scholars; both Trinity men, viz. C. Evans & Westcott[20]. . . Worked all the Evening at 'the Graduati' instead of reading loud.— Great town & gown row.[21]

Sun. 8. M. L. & I to Trinity Church (where we had one Lady in our villainous pew: we however were there 1st.— Carus preached from 1 Thess. IV 6. M & L then called on Miss Baldrey & gave her 10s & 2 bottles of Sherry: Miss B is suffering from Asthma. Lucy went to Kings College Chapel (because the Porter had been civil to her in the morning & said that he would admit her without an order if she came at 3 o'clock): L. was not quite au fait in the chapel for she did not turn down the seat, till recommended to do so by a neighbour.— She heard 'Comfort ye'.— M & I took a good walk.

Mon. 9. College Meeting to petition against Oxford & Cambridge Railway passing thro Barrington Vicarage.— Trial at V.C.: J.T. Smith & W.M.Williams of Trinity for refusing his name:— to be reprimanded in S.H. & to repeat 100 lines of 6th Iliad to Junior Proctor.[22]— M & I paid a long visit to Miss Apthorp & Miss Cory.— A prodigious row tonight: windows broken at Christs, Emmanuel, Pembroke, &c.— Whist at Mills, who was out till supper time quelling the row. . .

Tu. 10. Lucy's protégé David Gilmour dismissed from hospital after 10 days stay there.— Mr Cotton of Girton dead aged 82:— sent over to Madingley for Sir St Vincent, 3 vols of Defoe, viz. 'Plague', 'Cavalier', 'Capt. Singleton'. Today Lucy went to Hebblewhite's to buy some of the bargains wch they advertised in consequence of damage which their goods suffered from Headly (the ironmonger's) fire:— of course Lucy was too late: the advertisement was still in the windows, but they said they had sold all the

[20] C. Evans was awarded a Craven scholarship (founded in 1649 and worth £75) and B.F. Westcott a Battie scholarship (founded in 1747 and worth about £35). See J.W. Clark, *Endowments of the University* (1904), pp. 283-300. 1846 was a bumper year for Trinity whose members took all the prestigious university honours and prizes.

[21] Tom Thumb's visit provided an excuse for a protracted town and gown row after disturbances broke out in the Town Hall on the sixth. It was more vicious than usual and the hard-pressed police resorted to measures so firm that one of them was dismissed and gaoled. Tom Taylor published a commemorative pastiche in imitation of Macaulay's 'Horatius' in *Punch* X, 163, but the reality was much nastier and on 10 March the authorities issued a notice threatening expulsion or rustication to any student convicted of taking part in riotous assemblage.

[22] Williams had been involved in a town and gown brawl in Rose Crescent, and claimed he had been struck down several times (twice by the police), hit in the face, and kicked in the chest until rescued. He had no wish to be disrespectful to an M.A. His tutor described him as 'of rather excitable temperament and of forward manners like a schoolboy' (Acta Curiae I 21.). Romilly was not always in court for such trials, e.g. Power deputised on 24 March 1846 and Edleston on 28 July 1847.

bargains.[23]— Lord Abinger & son called on us at our dinner time: he is indignant at the conduct of the police in the late row: he is going to prosecute.— At 7 in the Evening to the V.C.'s to swear in special constables: swore in 18 (of the most respectable tradesmen Gent, Bradwell, Dimmock, &c &c). The Mayor also swore in several.— Today the Heads issued an order against riotous conduct of gownsmen.— The town happily quite quiet tonight.— Amusing letter from EEA at Cilrhiw.

Wed. 11. Congregation — no degree except 1 ad eundem:— Graces for Petitions against union (of N. Welsh Bishoprics), for insertions of clauses against Sunday Travelling in all Cambridge Railway bills, for Syndicate for taxing the University for the new Botanic Garden; &c.[24]— The Botanic Syndicate was thrown out in B.H, by 22 to 17; Hildyard (Christs) gave the non placet, & all the Johnians voted with him.— The V.C. reprimanded Williams: he did it very well.— Meeting of Master & Seniors to try 2 of our men, Nicholson for striking Pleasance (rusticated till Feb 47), & Girling for threatening to knock Mathison down if he touched him (rusticated till October).— Dinner in Hall. — At night read loud 'Edward'.

Th. 12. Sent off Petitions to Lords & Commons for keeping the 2 N. Welsh Bishoprics — Dined at Magd: Lodge: besides Master's brother-in-law & wife, Mr & Mrs Swinny there were Latimer Neville, Mr Herbert (Ld Clive's brother), Mr. Barrington grandson of the Bishop & of Earl Grey, & self.— It was extremely agreeable. The Master told me that the Princess Sophia of Gloster might 3 times have been Queen Consort; George IV offered to her before he married Queen Caroline & also after her death, & the Duke of Clarence also made her an offer.— The young ladies played & sang.

Sat. 14. Wrote to Lodge & Edward to give them accounts of our riots. The Assizes began today under Judges Maule & Parke.— Wrote to my stockbroker Witherby.— M & I paid a visit to the Fitzwilliam Museum & greatly admired the genii with expanded wings that are just put up.— Finished Dr Moore's 'Edward' & began 'the Black Falcon' by Fraser (Author of Kuzzlebash).[25]

Sun. 15. Carus sent for me into the vestry & said that we were to have undisturbed possession of his Pew & that he would [give] us the key of the Closet tomorrow. He gave us an old Sermon from Luk. XI. 27.28 (Gasp)[26]: a fierce attack on Popery. . .

---

[23] Frederick Hebblewhite of 5 Market Hill announced the re-opening of his shop for the sale of linen damaged by fire and water 'which will be offered at an immense Sacrifice. One portion of the Stock, consisting of STRAW BONNETS will be nearly given away.' (*Cambridge Chronicle* 28 February).

[24] On the union of the Welsh sees see 7 March 1845. The need to move the Botanic Garden (cf. 15 December 1842) from Free School Lane, now a built-up area 'too confined for the health of the various plants', to the large site on Trumpington Road had been recognised by an act of Parliament in 1831. Money was the chief impediment.

[25] J.B. Fraser, *Dark Falcon or the Tale of the Attruck* (1844), a Persian romance .

[26] 'Blessed is the womb that bare thee, and the paps which thou hast sucked'.

On 18 March Romilly went for a brief visit to the Edward Romillys. Besides performing 'numerous commissions' he called at an exhibition of tableaux vivants in Windmill Street, to see representations such as *Venus Rising from the Sea, Diana and Nymphs,* and *The Graces* with musical accompaniment. 'Very beautiful' it was 'but almost as indecorous as the ballet of the Opera: the exhibiters wear tight drapery fitting close to the figure & stand (under a very strong lamp-light in a darkened theatre) on a platform which revolves'. Two days later he was in Norwich as Sedgwick's guest, conversing in French with Miss Sedgwick's German teacher and talking at Professor Smyth whose deafness incapacitated him. But 'he hears my shrill voice better than anybody's.' From there he made a day-trip to Yarmouth 'much improved by hotels & houses', and passed a great *broad*, 'as they technically call such an expansion of water'.

Tu. 24.   Prof & Mrs Airy & Miss Smith accompanied Clark & me to the railway station: where Airy gave us an interesting lecture on the Electric Telegraph. At Ely we picked up Peacock who got into our Coupée tho he protests against that Carriage as being very dangerous: reached Cambridge at 2½ .— Walk with M.— over to Babraham with Packe to dine with the Adeanes. Met there Lord & Lady Braybrooke, Mr, Mrs & Miss Gambier & 2 Trinity undergraduates. Before dinner I had a good deal of amusement with the young children: at teatime Miss Lucy Neville & the elder Miss Adeanes made their appearance: they played duetts (very thumpy) on the Piano: I addicted myself the whole Evening to talking to the Governess (an elderly well-mannered lady).

Mon. 30.   Passed the whole morning looking over 6 declamations for Carus.— Dined with Carus to meet some *great* friends of his. . . Not long after 10 (before any of the party was dispersed) in came the servants & Carus read 3d chapter of Phil.:— I thought it not a very happy selection for young men,— 'beware of dogs'. He read the lesson extremely well & made no comment on it: he then made an extempore prayer which I thought excellent: it had variety of matter and was not long. . .

Th. 2. April.   Left A.E. by 11½ train: got to Cambridge in 29 minutes!.— M & I called on Mrs Hopkins, Mrs Phelps & Mrs Stuart.— In the Evening read loud 'Falcon Family' or 'Young Ireland':[27] it is rather coarse, but a very amusing caricature.— A rubber at Dr Haviland's: 5 players, viz. Drs French & Haviland, Marquis, Mills & I.

Fri. 3.   End of Term. . . Trassall (Joh) elected Travelling Bachelor.[28]— Dined in Hall.— Went on with 'Falcon Family', — a clever attack on Puseyism, Young England, Young France, & Young Ireland (with *saffron* shirts, shaggy hair, etc): ridicule of Milnes' Poetry & Wordsworth's in which I quite agree. . .

[27] By M.W. Savage, (1845).
[28] William Worts (d.1709) left a hundred pounds a year to two recent graduates, chosen in rotation from the Colleges, for three years. They were to travel abroad by different roads and write every month in Latin to the Vice-Chancellor on what seemed 'worth observing' about foreign manners and customs. He was to preserve the letters in the University Library.

Wed. 8.   M. & L to St. Paul's Church: I was summoned to a trial at the V.C.'s at 11: the culprit was a tailor Nightingale who had employed that rascally attorney Justinian Adcock to serve legal letters on undergraduates without apprising the Tutor:— Court adjourned.[29]— At night read loud 'Dark Falcon'.

Th. 9.   M & L to St. Paul's Church:— I had to attend the adjourned court: Nightingale was discommuned:— a great pity that we had not the power of punishing Adcock also.— Walk with M. after dinner.— All the evening copying out the trial. . .

Fri. 10.   Good Friday — M, L & I to Trinity where we found (on drawing back our red curtain) Mrs Ernshaw & 3 children: I apologised to her & told her that Mr Carus &c &c; I was very civil & she & her progeny turned out. . .

Sat. 11.   As I was going into my rooms I was laid hold of by a Gentleman who was disappointed at finding both Dr Archdall & Mr Brown out of Cambridge; he said he had known my Uncle Sir S.R: his name was Stedman of Horsham: he introduced his 3 daughters (all good looking young women, & (like their Father) very merry.— I lionised them for 2 hours much to my amusement: for the Father continually broke out with such expressions as, 'Girls were you ever so happy in your lives? —Ah, you'll write an account of this (won't you?) to your Mother'. At night a man knocked on the door asking to see me:— he was very unwilling to take a denial:— he came back again & then said 'a person was dying': I didn't believe his tale & sent him away.— Went on with 'Dark Falcon'.—

Sun. 12.   Easter Sunday — Read Prayers for Coombe:— (today was the thanksgiving for our Indian victories under Sir H. Harding, Sir — [sic]Gough, & Sir H. Smith):[30] Carus preached an excellent sermon from 1 Cor. 5. 7.8. — 241 staid the Sacrament: only once before was there so great a no: about the time of Mr Simeon's funeral there were 245 . . .

Mon. 13.   Cheap excursion train:— Great offence given by the passengers being put in the beast vans.[31]— 3 ladies and a girl came to my office on their hunt for the Pitt Press: unhappy wights; they had come 25 miles on a pleasure excursion, & found libraries &c all shut.— M & I called on Mrs Perry & also on the Searles (who are just returned from the Isle of

[29] Nightingale, though summoned, appeared on neither occasion nor sent in a defence. He had instituted legal proceedings against four undergraduates of Sidney in flat defiance of a decree (18 May 1844) of the Vice-Chancellor and Heads which required tradesmen first to approach a man's tutor. Such cases were not uncommon. As so often, *Punch* made Cambridge affairs the subject of humour with a 'Choral Ode to the Cambridge Nightingale', X (1846), 203.

[30] War between British forces and the Sikhs of the Punjab had broken out in the previous December. A couple of local lads were killed early; of the fate of ten others in the Sixteenth Lancers J. Eaton wrote home (2 February) in a letter published by the *Cambridge Chronicle* on 4 April. The war was speedily if temporarily ended after victories at Aliwal and Sobraon and the occupation of Lahore.

[31] The discomforts of the beast vans are well described in the *Cambridge Advertiser* of 15 April 1846.

Jersey & have taken a house in Bene't Place; Eliza has a very sad cough & they are frightened about her; Georgina has had her head shaved. . .

Th. 16. 2d day of Scholarship: Latin set by Martin & Rothman. . . Dined at Jesus Lodge at the Rustat dinner:[32] The party consisted of Dr, Mrs & 2 Miss Frenches, the V.C., Gunning & all the Fellows of the College. It was very agreeable: there was a young man there who described the habits of a chilly animal of the monkey kind, called a honey-bear, which he keeps in his rooms.— To Sedgwick at 9 & looked over papers till midnight.

Fr. 17. 3d day Scholarship:— Mathematics by Master & Martin.— All the morning looking over papers:—

Mon. 20. Wrote to G.T.R. *(£10 for 1st of May);* also to F. (£20): — Declined dining with the Pembertons.— M. went to Mr Jones the Dentist having broken one of her (false) teeth, & paid £2″1″— (having only 1s). — Walked over to Histon Church to meet a Church-exploring party of Swinny's, (viz. Mr & Mrs Swinny, Lady Charlotte Neville, Miss Neville, Lady Mary Legge, the Dean of Ely, Frere of Cottenham & his wife (who came on horseback & Mr Smith the Curate of Histon).— We visited Histon Church (wch has some beautiful Early English parts), Impington Ch. (wch has a fresco painting of St Christopher; — it is grotesque, representing various fish &c in the water), & Girton Church. At Girton we also visited Miss Cotton's school which groupes very picturesquely with the Church & the new cottages which she has built.— Lunched (rather dined) at Impington at 4½ & walked back to Cambridge with the Dean of Ely.— Whist club at Skrine's, the 4 daughters & their 4 husbands dined there.

Wed. 22. Our cook (Theodosia Russell's) Mother, sister & cousin came from town to spend the day with her. — Dined in Hall: Combination room.— Tea at the Lodge to decide Scholarships: a great fight whether we should elect Edlin (a Sizar) on the score of respectable Mathematics, good conduct, & poverty, & very bad scholarship, & throw out Wolstenholme a very respectable scholar, a less good Mathematician than Edlin, & who had been spoken to by the Dean for conduct in chapel:— we decided (including myself) in favour of Wolstenholme.— Wrote to Calthrop (late Tutor of Corpus) to tell him we had elected his nephew, & how well he had done, particularly in a translation of B.4. Paradise Regained into Latin Hexameters: 'and either tropic now gan thunder';— I copied out this translation.— We also elected Barry (son of the architect), Westcott (University Scholar), & the 2 Bell Scholars Davies & Vaughan.

Th. 23. Report that Col. Campbell (Col. of the 9th Lancers)[33] brother of the Marchesa is to be brought to a Court Martial by his brother-officers for cowardice in the late battles on the Sutluj:— how very sad for his relations! — Dined with the Master & Examiners at the Scholarship dinner. . .

[32] Named after Tobias Rustat (d.1694), benefactor of Jesus College and the University Library. See also 20 April 1843.
[33] Alexander Campbell of Craigie.

Fr. 24. Dined at Pagets: this was the dinner that he lost in a bet with Packe about Raphael & A. Durer,— concerning priority of birth. (N.B.— A. Durer was born 12 years before R. & survived him many years).— The party consisted of Drs Paget, Graham & Phelps, Smith, Shaw, Power, Cartmell & myself & (a former member) Turnbull: Dr Haviland had the gout, the V.C. (Dr Tatham) & Peacock colds, & Packe was absent on account of the death of his brothers wife— Power lost an hour in the day and came at 6.25 instead of 5 exact: he declared that he had not been napping!— The old custom of healths was revived at this dinner:— Dr Phelps, Cartmell, Paget & I played whist: 3 dummies after Phelps' departure.

Sat. 25. Seniority today: we struck off the college boards the name of J. Russell (a subsizar B.A. 1846) for profligacy & for disregarding all communications from his Tutor.— M, L. & I to the Railway Station to receive Edward Allen who arrived at 2. M & I exhibited the interior of the Fitzwilliam to him as it was a sunshiny day.— All the Evening I worked at 'Graduati'.

Wed. 29. . . . Today wrote to Charles Romilly to congratulate him on his 3d son, also to Dr Roget to thank him for a present of his Economic Chess Board:[34]— also to Mrs John[35] to wish her joy of John's being seated for Bridport & Cochrane ousted for bribery:— so his majority on the hustings of 1 has served him in little stead.— Philpott married to Mary Doria. Today Lucy received from Miss Critchett a guinea for Miss Thornton (the Governess candidate).— I slept in College on my sofa, George occupying the regular bed.

Fri. 1 May. . . . No chimney-sweep dancing today:— 1st cessation.[36]

Sat. 2. Lucy and I called on Mrs Thomas (about 'cruelty to Animals' society)[37]. . .

Sun. 3. (3d S. after Trinity).— College Sacrament.— Carus gave us no notice of his intended absence:— M., L. G. & E. occupied our slip of a pew & I was received into another: I had (as usual) a black neckcloth on & therefore could not read for Combe (as the verger asked me while coming into church). L. & G. bolted just before the Sermon:—

Fr. 8. G & I called on Dr Badham: he is an admirer of Miss Fanny Smith, but of course gave way on finding her engaged: I thought him a

---

[34] Intended for travellers, 'this was made of cardboard with small pasteboard pieces lying flat on the board and kept in place by the insertion of their bases into folds or pockets' (D.L. Emblen, *Peter Mark Roget* (1970), p. 287). Roget's great grandson played with one early in this century but Emblen failed to find a surviving example.

[35] I.e. the wife of Romilly's cousin John Romilly.

[36] In England May Day was the sweeps' traditional holiday when they dressed up, paraded in public and performed something akin to morris dances. See A.R. Wright, *British Calendar Customs* (1938), II, 238-40, and *R.C.D. 1832-42* p. 215. Romilly had been active some years before in campaigns against using boys as sweeps.

[37] There was no local society of the kind in Lucy's lifetime, and this presumably refers to the London-based R.S.P.C.A.

clever conversible man: he asked me to dine with him today to meet George &c:— I was also asked to dine by Mrs Frere at Dungate. — Edward gave a grand wine party in my rooms to 15, I furnishing wine, fruit &c:— I dined at the Family at the V.C.'s — the party consisted of Dr Tatham (the host) Drs Graham & Paget, Packe, Power, Cartmell, Shaw, Smith, Col. Pemberton & myself. A letter of Dr Haviland's was read, in which he begged to resign: we unanimously refused our consent.— Another bet of a rump & dozen was made between Paget & Packe concerning the mills at Newnham & the end of Mill Lane 'which is the Paramount Mill, that has the right to blow a horn to warn the other mill not to work till itself has got into work':— the Newnham Mill belongs to Caius & the other (the *'King's'*) to the Corporation[38]: Packe bets that the Newnham Mill is Paramount.— The Whist party consisted of Cartmell, Paget, Smith & myself.— When I came home at 11 found 4 of Edward's party playing whist *in my study:* (Edward was gone up to the house) — they staid till 12½, and behaved themselves most soberly & discretely.— I should have said that poor Bowtell has had a great disgrace befall him: his grandson (a boy of 15 named Dearle) is put in prison for having stolen 5 folios out of the Public Library to sell for waste paper.[39]

Sat. 16. Gave an Examination by written questions to Revd Dixon (Fellow of Jesus) candidate for Priest's Orders: I did this at the request of the B. of Hereford.

Wed. 20. G.B. Allen (aged 25) yesterday married to Miss Dora Eaton.

Fr. 22. Adjourned meeting of friends of Bot. Garden:— agreed to send a Deputation tomorrow to the V.C., recommending a Syndicate for the proposal of a Tax to produce funds for scientific purposes. . .

Sat. 23. Attended the Deputation (wch was headed by Dr Clark): well received by the V.C. — Poor Francis Hildyard (Fellow of Clare) was on Thursday thrown from his horse in St. James Park & died last night.— Forgot to mention last Wednesday that I christened Mrs Coppins 2d child (by the names of Catherine *Marie*): the 2d name I presume is to show some of the French wch M. taught her. . . Dined with the V. Provost in King's Hall. . . Went afterwards to the Boat Procession: but (the day being fine)

[38] These were two medieval watermills on the Cam at the end of Mill Lane. The King's miller had had first claim in time of drought and if at other times he had no corn to grind the Bishop's miller could use the supply on payment of a portion.

[39] John Dearle, grandson of the venerable Library Keeper Bowtell, had worked in the Library for a few months when he removed several folios worth over £20 and sold them as waste to George Muncey, a shoeseller in nearby Rose Crescent for twopence a pound. From Muncey they passed through a dealer to Wallis, the bookseller, who took them to the Library Keeper, Page. Dearle pleaded guilty. The Recorder, sentencing him to seven years, called him 'most hardened and profligate', and described the Library as 'a place which ought to be held sacred, and must be guarded against such depredations'. As a result of this scandal a formal borrowing register was opened and kept until interest waned and it was discontinued in November 1847. It shows Romilly's borrowings, novels for the most part. See McKitterick, pp. 516-17.

the crowd was so great that I could see very little. . . At night read 'the Citizen of Prague'.[40]

Mon. 25. . . .Letter from Edw. Allen describing his brother's marriage.— Received today G.B.A.'s wedding cake in the customary Δr box.

Fr. 29. George left:— he is to dine at the Andersons' today.— Asked to Downing Lodge to meet Hope & Lady Mildred H:— unable to go.— By the 4½ Train to Ely to dine with the Dean who today entertains the Family: 6 of us were together in the same carriage, viz. Shaw, Cartmell, Power, Paget, Smith & I: Phelps & Packe were in other carriages.— Went to the Cathedral: the Dean has now restored ½ of the Purbeck columns, has renewed the floors &c in the Norman Tower, &c:[41]— the effect of this Norman Tower is magnificent:— Packe, Paget & I went to the top of it.— Sparke has put up another painted window:— the new one is in the N. Transept, it is very beautiful; — it contains the History of St Paul; viz. his Conversion, Ananias opening his eyes, his working as a Tentmaker, his being let down from the window, his preaching at Athens, & the stoning of Stephen. . . All the Camb. party came back to C by the 11 o'clock Train.

Sat. 30. Dined with the Provost. . .a table had been set out which was large enough for 16: it was laid for 10: we being only 8 were separated from each other as if we had quarrelled. . . the dinner was very ill-drest. . .

Wed. 3 June. . . . The Trinity Examination began on Monday & is to last thro the week:— oppressively hot weather for Examiners & Examinees.— Read loud an amusing little book called 'the Physiology of Evening Parties':[42] it is by Albert Smith (who introduces his former character of Mr Ledbury) & has illustrations by Leach.

Mon. 8. Wrote to Blakesley to wish him joy of the birth of his son & heir.— Letter from Sedgwick at Harrogate declining the Fellowship Examination of course. M & I went to see Mrs Leathley who had been very ill but is rallying. She told a story of Carus saying to her 10 years ago when she told him she was dying 'he was glad to hear it':— she took it as a high compliment.— Walk (as usual) after dinner.— 'Stepmother':[43]

Wed. 10. Letter from S.O. Meares to announce the birth of his child — (a daughter): he also tells of the vacancy of Swansea Living, in which matter I tried to serve him when it was vacant last year: — sent him 3 guineas.— sent Edward his Beveridge on the 39 Art.[44] by Hensley (the Senior Wrangler) who is going down to Llangollen where E. is.— The Revd. T. Dixon (whom I examined for orders at the request of the B. of

---

[40] A translation by Mary Howitt of the German novel *Thomas Thyrnau* by Henriette von Paalzow.
[41] See 8 February 1843.
[42] This reference confirms the year of first publication, hitherto in doubt.
[43] G.P.R. James, *Stepmother or Evil Doings* (1846).
[44] I.e. One of numerous theological works by William Beveridge (d. 1708), Bishop of St Asaph. It was the standard exposition and often reprinted.

Hereford) was ordained last Sunday, and today married to the eldest daughter of Mr Baker the Linen Draper — he is to be Mathematics Master at the Liverpool College.— Dined in Hall to meet Blakesley: he told us an amusing story:— Mr & Lady Mildred Hope called on him the other day & were introduced as Mr & Lady Heliotrope, — the housemaid having consulted the Gardener who told her that there was no such family as the Heliotropes in the immediate neighbourhood tho he knew *there was in Cornwall!* — Quaere— 'What state is a man in between his BD & DD degree? Answer C.D. — At night went on with James' 'Stepmother'.

Th. 11.　Letter from P.T. Ouvry asking me to tie the knot for him & Miss (daughter of Poor Law Commissioner) Nicholl next month:— wrote to express my great willingness.— Congregation — 6 BD, 2 MA, 2 MB, 1 eundem.— The 'Porson Scholarship' deferred, the Kingsmen & others objecting to the restriction to Freshmen.[45]— M & I called on Mr Baker to wish him joy of his daughter's marriage.— Our Betsy Edwards got herself daguerreotyped: she chose an odd time, for she was suffering from toothache; — she looks like an old woman.[46]—

Fr. 12.　Beware of cheap Tea! About 3 months ago Lucy bought some of Kimbells' *mixt* tea for her paupers; but fearing it might have green in it she stowed it away in one of the cannisters of the caddy:— today it was found mouldy & not fit to throw to the hogs.— Dined in Hall: a very small party this holiday time:— John Brown, 2 Chaplains, a stranger, & myself: — 5 only.— Lucy paid Miss Vincent a visit: she continues in the same state.—

Th. 18.　Intensely hot weather; so I get on famously with the Graduati, as I work up to dinner-time & Lucy helps in the Evening by calling out the names. . . Letter from G.T.R. at Boulogne. his companion (Miss Rosa Smith) suffered from sea sickness. . .

Mon. 22.　Wrote to Madame F.R. (£40).— The 1st attempt I made on Downing Garden Gate I broke the key in the lock: it was so stiff that I had to make a lever with another key.— Yesterday Perry stopped in his sermon & scolded some children roundly for their talking. Today got the new key from the locksmith. . .

Wed. 24.　Lucy before breakfast to Brunswick Place to see the Mistress of one of her protégées (Mary Latimer): among some reasonable complaints (for the pretty girl is idle and sulky) Mrs Norton brings the absurd charge of her being a housebreaker! — she went into some

45 The founding of a classical scholarship named after Richard Porson, Regius Professor of Greek who had died in 1808, was long delayed. Acceptance of the offer was again rejected in October, and not confirmed until October 1847. The scholarship was established in May 1848, though not awarded until 1855. For the complicated background see J.W. Clark, *Endowments of the University of Cambridge* (1904), pp. 121-30.

46 Commercial photography came to Cambridge in August 1844 when an establishment offering 'Beard's Patent Daguerrotype or photographic portraits' opened in St Mary's Passage, and was given an editorial puff in the *Cambridge Chronicle* of 24 August.

outhouse that was fastened up:— Latimer however seems to have no mind to give satisfaction:— she will (I fear) come to no good.

Th. 25. There was to have been a grand tea-party this afternoon (tickets 1s/): at these tea parties Carus makes a speech, says Grace, sings a hymn, hands round tea & cake, & makes himself generally agreeable:— He being gone home (to see his sister who is not well) appointed his curate Mr Rowlands to preside:— the flock however did not like 'the deputy shepherd' & refused to buy tickets:— the tea drinking is deferred. — Letter from Lady Cotton sending a list of books she wishes for. Finished 'Deafness'.[47]— Visit from Dr & Mrs Archdall.

Sat. 27. The abolition of the Corn-Laws has passed the Lords & is to receive the Royal Assent today.— Peel however has been in a great minority on the Irish Coercion Bill & is expected to resign.[48]— Poor Miss Butcher has had a severe illness from an affliction of the spine & has had something like an apopleptic fit. Wrote to her.— Lucy (by way of humanity) bought of W. Gilmour a jackdaw, which was this evening made free of our garden.

Sat. 4 July. Congregation — 1 LLD, 1 LLB, 1 BD, 53 AM, 2 AB, 2 eundem.— There was a great fuss concerning the BD: he signed himself Stewart Cranmer Gordon: he has at different times passed by every combination of these names: he appears to have been an illegitimate son: he has passed by aliases enough to hang him.[49]— The Bishop of Gloster's son today recited his Latin Essay:— the Bishop, Mrs & the Miss Monks were present.— Dined with Ollivant: no lady present at dinner except Mrs Ollivant. . . Champagne & Ice:— very agreeable conversible party.— I left at 8½ to sit at the receipt of Custom:— caught only 15 fees.— At 11 at night in came a young man with a most beautiful small dog under his arm: he proved to be a son of Mr Lennard (a friend of Dr Badham, George's former rival in the affections of Miss Fanny Smith):— he brought an invitation for me to dine with his Father & Dr Badham at the Bull tomorrow.— I declined.

Sun. 5. Poor Mr Prest died last night.— Today tremendously hot.— M, L & I staid the Sacrament. We declined the honor of Coombe's presence in our Pew during the service on account of the heat.— We staid the Sacrament.— Carus preached above an hour: now that is very objectionable on a Sacrament Sunday and is indeed blamable on any Sunday.— His text was 1 Joh.2.20.— We had a thunderstorm with some smartish rain just

---

[47] I.e *The Lost Senses* (1845) by the biblical commentator John Kitto (d.1854) who had been deaf from boyhood.

[48] Sir James Graham had introduced the bill in April to check by severe measures the many crimes against persons and property in Ireland which had been exacerbated by the famine. It was opposed by the Liberals (and by others for reasons of their own), and lost on the motion for a second reading on 25 June. Peel was succeeded by Russell who then held office until 1852.

[49] *Al. Cant.* gives him ordinary if obscure parents, Joseph and Mary, of Essex. He was master of Haworth school and soon to become curate to Rev. Patrick Bronte.

before dinner:— the jackdaw had been put in the tree: Lucy was afraid he would get wet to the skin & struck blind by the Lightning: she tried calling & coaxing, & ended by pelting him:— all in vain. Jack would not stir till the storm was over:— then (when nobody asked him) down he came.— The air was nicely cleared by the storm & M & I took a delightful walk on Clare Hall piece:— not a single scarlet-clad Doctor:—All the brilliancy of Commencement Sunday is utterly gone.[50]— About 9 o'clock. Mrs Clark & her son payed us a visit & kept us unconscionably late for our tea.

Mon. 6. Congregation— 1 Hon MA, 101 MA, 1 DD, 2 ad eundem.— The Bachelor's Essay was recited today.[51]— A curious & unfortunate mistake occurred in awarding the Prizes: Byers (Christ's) and Perowne (Corpus) had both chosen the same motto:— a wrong envelope was opened & Byers was printed as the prizeman & actually came down to recite before the error was detected.— M. made me a very pretty cover for an Ottoman which I have had made out of some carpetwork of Madame Bourlet's. . .

Tu. 7. Got up at 6¼ to be ready for distributing tickets to MAs of former years: Creation of MAs began at 7. . .

Fri. 10. Dismissal of Term:— a poor misguided Queensman undergraduate (who had come all the way from the North to get his BA degree, — for which he had been hitherto unfitted from not having paid his College Bills) called on me at breakfast time:— I told him that it was scarcely possible for him to get together 25 MA in an hour, & that I rather doubted there being so many in the University:— he of course had to go back to the North as an undergraduate.— Dined in Hall where I was V.M.— went on with Kitto.[52]

Sat. 11. M, L & I walked in the Garden of the Master of Downing:— Lucy's 1st visit:— saw in the meadow there the white goat & her 2 kids, but we were kept from them by an iron fence.— M & L. then paid a visit to Miss Baldrey in the Hospital.— They yesterday paid a visit to old Mrs Leathley & heard a long story of her distress of mind when there was a report that Carus was lost at sea.— More of Kitto.

Tu. 14. Wrote a great heap of canvassing letters for Lucy's protégé a poor silly simple-minded old Cobbler (Rob. Scarr) who is a Candidate for

---

[50] See 3 July 1842.

[51] Also known as 'Members' Prizes' since they were awarded annually by the University M.P.s for exercises in Latin prose. By this time they were not restricted to bachelors. Envelopes containing the identities of unsuccessful candidates should, of course, have been destroyed unopened.

[52] I.e. the part of *The Lost Senses* dealing with blindness.

the Victoria Benefit Asylum:[53] He is 68 & has had 16 children; the juvenility of his present wife (his 2d) is thrown in his teeth — she is however past 50 on her own confession.

Wed. 15. Letter from Mrs Edward to say they cannot receive me as their house is painting & they are going on a visit to the Strutts.— M. L. & I used our key of Downing private magisterial grounds this Evening to see Perry's school treat.— He sent up 4 balloons; the largest succeeded capitally but the 3 smaller ones soon caught fire:— we met there James Searle & his 3 youngest sisters:— Lucy patronised an unknown little girl who had hurt herself by tumbling while clambering over the iron fence (where of course she had no business): Lucy took her to see the goat & kids & kindly devoted herself entirely to her.— L's protégée S. Foulkes returned today from a 3 weeks visit to Haslingfield:— had she waited till Saturday she might have come home in Mr Clarks carriage, but with the restlessness so natural to an invalid she chose to come back today in the carrier's van.—

On 18 July the notoriously slow Parliamentary train 'in wch 3d class pay a penny a mile' conveyed Romilly to London, a journey of more than four hours. Having secured his accommodation as usual at Woods he went to an exhibition. The paintings of Stanfield and Landseer pleased him, but 'Turner's pictures were as absurd as ever: 'Undine' was a white mist, the 'Angel in the Sun' a yellow mist'. He also noted the marble bust of Sedgwick by Henry Weekes which was later placed at the Geological Society. After dining at the Athenaeum, Romilly went to see Verdi's new opera *I Lombardi;* the music seemed to him 'pleasing without any very striking airs', and though Maria Taglioni danced, he by this time preferred Fanny Cerito 'who is much younger & prettier'.

On Sunday there was a full round of sermons. There were family prayers at the hotel, and afterwards he was pursuaded to attend St Bride's where Thomas Dale was to preach a farewell sermon on leaving after twenty years:

'His address was very straitforward: he praised himself for the sincerity with wch he had at all times preached to the best of his ability the whole truth without any reservation, but lamented that he must have often missed saying 'the word in season' & doing all the good to the souls of his flock that he wished & ought to have done.— The sermon was one to my hearts delight.' This was in contrast with the afternoon sermon at the Abbey — 'essence of poppies' from which 'the only profit seemed to be in procuring deep sleep'. Thereafter Romily refreshed himself with a walk through St James Park 'a beautiful sight from numbers of people' to the Athenaeum where he dined with a late Fellow of Trinity, T. J. Phillips. 'I read & wrote journal till it was time to return to Woods Hotel & go to bed.'

On Thursday Romilly called on Mrs Boyer where he found Frances Wilderspin in great distress over her brother who had tried to kill himself. They had a long conversation and the diarist thought she was much soothed when he left. He

---

[53] The Victoria Friendly Societies' Asylum, established in 1837 and built for twelve families in Chesterton Road, was a retreat for infirm men and women who had been members of local societies for at least ten years, and who therefore were deemed respectable and provident. Elections were in the hands of subscribers. See *The Cambridge Guide* (1845), pp. 227-8, and *The Cambridge Victoria Friendly Societies' Asylum: its Formation, Rise, and Progress* (Cambridge, 1851), which prints the rules and lists benefactors and subscribers including Romilly and Lucy.

collected a half-year's dividends, some £295, before visiting Windmill Street and an exhibition of Tableaux Vivants with which he was very pleased. The evening saw him at Oxford Terrace where the Ouvrys had gathered, and at 9 the whole party went to take tea at Mr Nicholls' house in Hyde Park Street and to witness the signing of the marriage settlements. Romilly seems to have been untypically ill at ease: 'a house on the eve of a marriage is an uncomfortable place for a visitor:— a constant worry & bustle.' The marriage between Peter Ouvry and Jane Nicholls with the diarist officiating took place next day, 21 July, at St John's church with 'no crying, no giggling.' The bride's father proposed Romilly's health, remarking that he had performed the service effectively: 'I said, 'the proof would be if all the bridesmaids & the other unmarried people present immediately got engaged'.'

Tu. 28. Lucy's birthday:— gave her Stanley's life of Dr Arnold.[54]— Went to the wedding of John Haviland with Harriet Doria. The church was quite full. The service was read by Philpott (Master of Cath.) who to my great indignation left out the prayer for children! — I wonder what young people marry for except to have children. There were 6 bridesmaids, viz Bessy & Meggy Doria, 2 Miss Freres, Miss Wilkins & a pretty Miss Scott (a niece of the Havilands).— The bridesmaids were all in white, but were distinguished by having green wreaths in their hair whereas the bride wore silver bodkins & a veil.— No speechifying.— The wedding cake has 3 true-love knots of paste:— within there were a thimble, a crooked 6penny, & a ring, prophetic of spinsterhood, wealth & a speedy marriage:— they fell to the lot of Meggy Doria, Frederica Frere & Miss Scott.— I suppose the distribution was not purely accidental.— Archdeacon Harper (who took his BA in my year) was today by me presented to the Deputy V.C. (Dr Archdall):— he came up to College at the mature age of 25: he obviously has a very high opinion of himself: he did nothing at College (migrated from John's to Queens' & took an aegrotat degree) he has been in India for 30 years:— he wears flowing white hair but seems in infirm health & is very conversible. He criticised the monuments of Heber & Corrie as violating Eastern habits.[55]

Wed. 5. August. — The poor young woman (Emma Stearn) whom Lucy has been visiting for the last 3 weeks sank under her complaint (consumption) and was buried at Grantchester on Monday.— Susan Grounds (born Chune) has been very ill: sent her £2. M had a delightful letter from Mrs Kennedy containing a high eulogy of Mrs P.T. Ouvry (born Nicholls) & also an account of Frank having knocked out a front tooth.— M. a great deal better.— Poor Gunning has just lost his youngest daughter:— & his 2d son (the Counsellor) is now out of his mind (and they

---

[54] A.P. Stanley, *The Life and Correspondence of Thomas Arnold* (1844).
[55] Reginald Heber (d.1826) and Daniel Corrie (d.1837), a disciple of Simeon and brother of Professor Corrie had been active in missionary work in India. There are monuments in St Peter's, Colombo, by Theakston (Heber), and Weekes (Corrie).

say hopelessly): his son Frank has for some years been so: how very sad[56]. . .

Fri. 7. M. still poorly:— we only walked in the Garden. . .Lucy's pet jackdaw was scared away this Evening by a strange cat pouncing upon it in the area.— A case of real spasmodic cholera in the Town: a postboy of the Lion died of it in a few hours.

Sat. 8. M. better today:— The Jackdaw brought back this morning:— the Baker's boy recognised it in the hands of our neighbour Mrs Cornell (whose sons took it out of a tree where it was resting): Mrs C. cut the wing very close.— Lucy was highly indignant & scolded her well.—

Sat. 15. Lucy paid for the coffin of Emma Stearn:— they charged her £3,— which seems very dear. . .

Th. 20. Another wet day.— Over (by the railway) with Ficklin to Audley End Luncheon.— No ladies out of doors: some of us men huddled together in tents there was only ½ hours play, & then a steady unceasing rain made all play impossible. . .

Sun. 23. M. (thank God) well enough to go with us to Church.— Behind us was a bellowing boy who had probably been a chorister till his voice broke:— he sang so loud that Lucy was obliged to ask him to sing more piano. . . M. L, Carus & I then went to my rooms where we had a glass of wine & Carus talked very agreeably for an hour about Mr Simeon & the forthcoming life. . .

Mon. 24. The first page of my 'Graduati' is printed at the University Press. . .

Th. 27. . . . L. & I after dinner paid a visit to Trinity Lodge (I having an errand from the Master for some books):— we went over the house & garden & saw the Golden Pheasant & his wife:— Lucy was indignant at the confined space in wch they lived. . . We then went on a wild-goose chase to Gibbs building (ground rooms in the left corner) to see the vestiges of Mr Simeon's name on the door thro the lairs of superadded paint: we could not make out anything at all. . .

On 31 August Romilly accompanied Paget on a visit to the Whewells' cottage near Lowestoft, a pretty thatched house 'in spite of the bad carpenter's Gothic of the windows',with well-stocked gardens that at night were illuminated by the nearby lighthouse. Whewell took them to see the training of the coastguards: 'a sort of sham fight was got up, but we were a long way off & I could see little but the smoke of the firing', and also to examine the sculls collected by the local surgeon, a Mr Worthington; Paget of course was greatly interested, but 'all his abominations in pickle' made the diarist almost sick. There was sea bathing to enjoy, and good company for dinner including the Hon. Captain Jerningham 'the life of the party'

---

[56] There is no good account of Henry Gunning and his family who were closely allied to several other Cambridge families such as Thackeray, Brooke, and Whish. Ellen, the daughter, died at Newnham on 31 July, and Frank (Francis John) died on 5 October in the same year. There are some details of him in C. Jackson, *A Cambridge Bicentenary* (1990), chapters 7 and 9. According to a deed quoted there Gunning had been incapable 'for a period of two years and upwards' before his death.

who had command of the local coast guard and was 'indignant at the way in which his men were jeered by the natives (who of course take part with the smugglers against the preventive-service)'. He returned home to find a letter from his friend Miss Butcher telling how she had been robbed by night; he sent her five pounds and went to Inspector Thresher of the police 'who will write her a series of questions by tonights post'.

Fri. 4 September. A very good letter from Frank giving a satisfactory account of the end of Jaques' college career: he has taken his Bachelors degree: he was 26th out of 36 successful ; 124 were rejected or as we should say 'plucked'. . .

Sat. 5. Letter from Miss B. saying alas! that there is every reason to suspect her little handmaiden, a very pretty, quiet, kindhearted girl of 12 . . . She humanely declines prosecuting. . .

Mon. 7. . . . A stupid gownsman (2 doors from Mrs Vincents) at Mr Dennys left his candle burning & at 2 o'clock in the morning found the place on fire & began bawling 'police' 'fire' & running about in the garden in his shirt. . . the damage done was not great,—about £30. . .

Sun. 13. To the sorrow of M. our excellent old washerwoman (Mrs Bangles) sailed today with her husband for America, hoping that trade would be brisker and better paid across the Atlantic.

Tu. 15 Grand cricket match on Parkers Piece between Cambridge & all England: Cambridge won. . . Dined in hall & heard from Atkinson (who is just returned from Italy) an account of the earthquake near Pisa. . .

Th. 17. Judge Williams & Bishop Carey dead.— Williams is said to have behaved most generously to a poor Curate of the name of Howes: they were competitors for a Trinity Fellowship & Williams considered Howes to be cleverer than himself; Howes however was not elected & Williams was:— W. sent Howes a £100 a year as long as he lived. . .

Fri. 18. The Kitten lost a joint of her tail by the door slamming on her — Proclamation of Sturb. Fair : the V.C. introduced a novelty; he & the Commissary (Sykes of Pem), the Esq. Bedell & I stood up in the carriage while I made proclamation:— No Proctor, no Deputy Proctor, & only one Taxor, who had a carriage all to himself. — All the morning I was rummaging the Baker M.S.S.[57] — Declined dining with Charles Townley. — M. & I walk in the Evening. — Wrote to Lodge.

Sat. 19. Lucy (having obtained certificates of cure from the Linton Surgeon, Lestourgeon & Brewster) took her Linton protégée (Betsy Fitch) to a place (viz. Mrs Burrell's):— the little one being very unwilling as she was pining to go to a College bedmaker. — Lucy gave dinner to the said protégée: so I dined in hall. — Read loud Guy Mannering.[58]

---

[57] Thomas Baker (d.1740), the nonjuror and antiquary, divided his large collections for the history of Cambridge between the University Library and the Harleian Library. See the account of him in F. Korsten, *A Catalogue of the Library of Thomas Baker* (1990).

[58] Sir Walter Scott, *Guy Mannering* (1815).

Tu. 22. Lucy went to see the furniture &c of my poor friend Humfrey at St. Andrew's Close: I would not go as I think it most melancholy to go under such circumstances into a house where I have for so many years been a visitor & where I have always experienced the greatest kindness.[59] — Took the selections of Greek Verse to the Press. — Went on with Guy Mannering.

Wed. 23. Captain Bailey solicited me to write to Lord Fitzwilliam for him!! Very civilly declined. — Every body is looking out for a place & some most absurdly think that I have interest with Ministers:— if I had I should use it for my own friends & relations & not for strangers.—Handsome present of Grapes from Mr Gunning.— Brace of birds from Lady Cotton.

Th. 24. Lucy had set her heart on buying a mahogany mangle at poor Mr Humfrey's Sale (to give to one of her paupers named Melburn): it went beyond her commission, viz. for £10 — Dined in Hall.— Yesterday finished 'Guy Mannering':— today began 'Castle Rackrent'[60]. . . First fire this Evening.

Fri. 25. M's birthday:— she is, thank God, in her usual health.— Wrote to Mrs. F.R. £20:— to Miss Butcher £5 (stopping £1:5:— as 2d instalment).— Gave M. as birthday gift a new book called 'Wisdom & Genius of Shakspeare'.[61]— Called upon J. Brooks (a portrait painter who keeps a chandlers shop on the Chesterton Road near the Ferry, & who was recently robbed in the middle of the night by housebreakers): gave him 10s, & also 10s from Margaret — Margaret sent £1 to Mrs Wakefield.— This portrait painter has painted the little Grahams at Christ's Lodge, Johnson (the Schoolkeeper), &c:— his merit is small. Poor wretch:— the housebreakers attacked his house again last night. Finished 'Castle Rackrent'.—

Tu. 29. Yesterday we had a visit from Mrs Ebenezer Foster Junior:— she was beautifully dressed: her stile of paying visits is to my thorough satisfaction:— she is obviously intent upon escaping the 1st moment she can. . .

Sat. 3 October 3rd day of Fellowship:— Mathematics by Master & Latin prose by Martin.— Edward, M & I walked together.— In the Evening Edward read loud the 1st part of Dickens' new Novel 'Dealings of Dombie

---

59   The contents of Humfrey's home from silver and paintings to coals and garden tools were sold by auction on 23 and 24 September. Baker's patent mangle seems to be what Lucy wanted. The house and grounds attracted thousands of sightseers and it was reported that good prices were reached and purchases made by locals as well as London dealers. Three paintings of the house by John Ince in 1845 are reproduced (illustrations 10-12) in D.E. Chaffin, 'Charles Humfrey and Early Nineteenth Century Building in Cambridge' (1963), a dissertation in the Cambridge Faculty of Architecture.

60   Maria Edgeworth, *Castle Rackrent, an Hibernian Tale* (1800). She had been a friend of Joseph's aunt, Lady Romilly; see S.H. Romilly, *Romilly-Edgeworth Letters 1813-1818* (1936).

61   First published in 1838 by Rev. Thomas Price, this was a volume of selections with notes and scriptural references.

& Co.'[62]— we were pleased with it.— L. & I as usual looked over a half sheet[63]. . .

Sun. 4. That great philanthropist slave-trade Clarkson is dead:— aged 86. — M. L. E. & I to Trinity Church where we all staid the Sacrament. Carus gave us an excellent sermon from 1st Lesson Ezek. 14.12.13:— his subject was 'national sin the cause of God's heavy judgments:— the Archb. of Canterbury has issued a prayer in consequence of the failure of the Potato Crop.— Lucy went afterwards to Barnwell & (besides a sermon) heard 5 babies christened & 5 mothers churched.— Yesterday M. E. & I went over Jesus College Chapel where great additions are being made, as well as extensive restorations.[64]

Sat. 10. In Chapel at ¼ to 9 to complete the Election.— Edward communicated by the Electric Telegraph his Election to his friend Hensley who was in London.— Holden is very much mortified at not being elected:— he & Rendell were equal as 1st Classics in Classical Tripos.— Lucy better today & got out.— The news travelled from Cambridge to Hensleys House in Town (3 miles from the Shoreditch Station) in 50 minutes: the expense was 6s & 6 pence; viz 3s-6d for the rail & 3s for a Cab.— Hensley was here in Cambridge by 12½.— Dined at the usual Fellowship dinner in the Combination Room. . .the party consisted of the Master, Sedgwick, Self, Rothman, Martin, Jeremie, Carus, Thompson & Grote.— Thompson, Rothman & I migrated to Sedgwick's & smoked Cigars.

Tu. 13. Voluntary Theol. Examination began today.— Edward Allen is an Examinee:— he seems to me most indifferently prepared: 134 go in. Dined with the Master & Mrs Whewell to meet the Bishop of London . . . (18): a very agreeable party:— Mrs Hayles came in the Evening:— The Bishop was very civil to her: she asked him if he had seen the Byron Statue etc., he said 'I've seen nothing but teakettles & coalskuttles':— he has brought up a son. . .

Fri. 16. 4th & last day of Theological Examination. — Edward went off by an afternoon train to his brothers house in the Regents Park.— The Syndics of the Press met today: they agreed to my petition of having the 'Graduati' printed 'typis ac sumptibus Academicis'.

[62] *Dombey and Son* was issued in monthly parts from October 1846 to April 1848. Romilly was not always accurate in recording titles, cf. *The Sybil.*

[63] I.e. of the *Graduati.* Romilly had finished correcting 'the star-bearing' Fellows from the Vice-Chancellor's subscription books on 17 July. At the end of this volume of his diary (MS. Add. 6824), Romilly lists some 63 recipients of the book from the Chancellor, Heads, and eight bishops and ten professors to the Athenaeum Club and the Oxford Registrar, Philip Bliss. A presentation copy to George Phillips of Queens' College in which Romilly describes it as this little book *(opusculum)* is in the University Library.

[64] The College had lately begun an extensive restoration of the chapel, at first under Salvin then Pugin, which was not finished until 1850. See R. Willis and J.W. Clark, *The Architectural History of the University* (1886), II, 145-51, where is reproduced a view of the interior before work began.

Mon. 19. Lucy's protégée Sarah Foulkes desperately ill.— Our late fellow W. Sidney Walker (who has long been out of his mind) is just dead.— College meeting. — Declined the venison feast in hall.— Whist club at Birketts. Edward returned last night: he performed the journey from Regents Park to our house for 5s 2d, viz. 6d for an Omnibus & 4s 8d for a 3d Class carriage!

Wed. 21. Congregation.— 3 AM, 3 AB.— A fight in the Senate House about the Grace for founding 'a Porson Scholarship' for freshmen:— it was unopposed by the Black Hoods, but was thrown out in the White Hood House by an equality of 15:— Rowlands of Kings was the original agitator against it: W. G. Humphrey wrote a series of objections:— Kingsley (the Junior Proctor) voted last, & says that he voted against it *because he thought it absurd for the Grace to be carried by a majority of 1:* any reason more fatuitous can scarcely be imagined.— I should think neither Archdeacon Burney (who offered to found this scholarship) nor any one else will offer us anything for a long while[65]. . .

Sun. 1 November M. L. E. & I to Trin:— Carus preached from the 2d Lesson (Heb. XI 39, 40), — an old Sermon of 1 Nov/46. We all staid Sacrament.— We fell in with Ouvry North on our return & he came to lunch with us. He announced that his Mother &c were coming down to Cambridge tomorrow.— I told him I could not possibly entertain them as I was going to Audley End.— He accordingly sent a message by the Elect. Telegraph to say they must not come.— It was amusing enough: the proceeding was as follows; 'Paid message: call at 49 Oxford Terrace: tell Mr Ouvry he is not to come tomorrow':— they telegraphed back 'have you paid 5s for the Cab?': upon our answering 'yes', the business was complete: the whole thing passed in about half the time that stuttering Phil. Frere could have delivered the message.

Mon. 2. Wrote to F.R. £10: also to poor Thorpe (the bookseller) at Malines & sent him £5.— To Audley End by the 3 o'clock train, having lost my walk with M. from an unreasonable visit which Mrs. Owen paid us.— I was asked to meet the Duke and Duchess of Bedford, but they were commanded to Windsor. Nobody there but the Family & the Family Surgeon (Mr. Wright). . . It was the first day of dining in the dining room since its painting & gilding & new furnishing —: it looked very magnificent, & the carpet & curtains are remarkably handsome.— Played Whist with Mr. Charles against Lady B. & Mr. Henry & won 15 shillings — Showed some Chess Problems to Miss Lucy.— Lady B. communicated several Conundrums (— Vide end of Volume).[66]— Lady B. gave an amusing account of her visit to Hatfield (the M. of Salisbury's) to meet the

---

[65] See 11 June 1846 above.
[66] Three examples: Why is an old sailor likely to know what o'clock it is? Because he is always going to sea. What is the Latin for a Lady's Bustle? Superbum . How did Sir Harry Smith bribe the Sikhs to submission ? By giving them a check on the banks of the Sutlej.

Queen. (Queen Elizabeth was at Hatfield sitting under an oak when she received the news of her sister Mary's death).— The Queen was very gracious: she patted the ponies of a Mrs. Gaussen, — who was (on the Q's departure) offered 100 guineas for them: she said 'nothing on earth should induce her to part with them as the Queen had caressed them' — The Queen was highly amused at Lord Talbot (a large heavy man) sitting down on a sofa, breaking thro' and coming down to the ground with his legs kicking up in the air:— she laughed like a school-girl. — The Queen planted an oak.

Tu. 3. Left Audley End by the 11 o'clock omnibus:— the new Lodge is almost finished & looks very well.— Gave a grand dinner today: the party was 15, viz. 2 Brides Mrs. Philpott (who will be Mrs. Vicechancellor tomorrow), & Mrs. John Haviland (Mary & Harty Doria), & their husbands, Mrs. Haviland, Dr. & Mrs. Ainslie, Dr & Mrs Graham, Dr & Mrs Archdall, Sedgwick, Carus, Edward Allen & self. — Carus acted vice president.— Sedgwick was rather headachy in the Evening and went into a room by himself for ¼ an hour:— but when all the rest of my guests were gone he came to life & sat with me till 12 o'clock smoking cigars.— Exhibited to my Guests some of the new Guncotton which I had got from Decks.[67]— In spite of the Telegraphing the Ouvrys came down on Monday (having thoroughly made up their minds to do so). . .

Wed. 4. V. Chancellor's Election at 10 : Philpott is V.C.:— he made an uninteresting speech talking of his indifference of health, of his acquaintance with the University &c. . . A great hubbub in the University in consequence of Morris (of Trinity) going over to Popery: this weakminded undergraduate had been 3 years at Alford's (our late Fellow) & came to College with a great leaning to Popery, which was well developed by F.A. Paley of St. Johns who is a Papist at heart tho' not yet professed:— Paley introduced him to the Popish Bishop Wareing.— See the whole published correspondence of Alford, Paley &c in 'University Papers': The 'Times' has a grand tirade against Paley.[68]

Fri. 6. Edward to Town & back with a day-ticket.— I avoided Mrs. Phelps soirée, being knocked up with the dissipation of the week.

Sat. 7. M. & I paid a visit to Mrs Clark & heard an account of her summer proceedings — My Volume of Graduati is printed to the end of Z: the Appendix is to be begun on Monday.— Dined with Dr & Mrs Lamb & 2nd son (of Caius) to meet Harford & very pretty daughter & Pulling . . . the daughter is about 17 or 18 & is a most charming sort of a Hebe.— The youngest girl of Mrs Lamb greatly amused me by saying to me when I came

[67] A new high explosive made by steeping cotton in nitric and sulphuric acid. Deck, the master pyrotechnician, was plainly au fait with modern researches.
[68] The local and national press regularly reported conversions (or 'perversions') to Rome among members of the University, often noting, if they were young and obscure, their family connexions with better known public figures.

179

into the room, 'Mr Romilly has come without a Lady' 'poor Mr R.— he has got no Lady':— this little advocate for Matrimony is 3 years old!

Mon. 9. C.E. Brown (Editor of Cambridge Chronicle) elected Mayor.— Went with the V.Ch. & Proctors to swear him.— Edward & I dined with Sedgwick. . . magnificent dinner.— Professor Miller came to tea & gave us an account of Challis's talk this Evening at the Philosophical about his own observations in search of the newly discovered planet:— it is very hard that Adams & Challis should seem likely to lose the éclat attached to this triumph of science: Adams made calculations of the orbit earlier than Le Verrier, & Challis actually saw the planet before Galle (tho he did not know it was the Planet)[69]. . .

Th. 12. F.A. Paley was *recommended* by the Master [of St John's] (Dr. Tatham) to quit College: he accordingly did so : but there was no formal expulsion from the College:— he was not a Fellow:— he has recently published the Orestea of Aeschylus: he is a good scholar, but is a weak man, whose head was turned by the Camden Society & seems to be a Papist if he has any fixt religous opinions at all — It is a good thing for the University that he is dismissed.

Fri. 13. Matriculation from ¼ to 9 to ¼ to 3.— I appointed the times very cleverly & there was scarcely any delay.— a very good Matriculation 437 : the same no once before; never a larger.— 1 N (Lord Durham), 14 F.C. (including 2 horrid tenyearmen), 389 P & 33 S. . . .Some of the names amused me: Parson & Perfect for surnames; Erastus, Charitie, Justice & Angel for Xian names. One man was so nervous that he could not write at first, so I left him till the last of his College, & then he wrote as if he had the palsy or delirium tremens, tho I did all I could to prevent his being flurried. One man could not read 'Haec omnia in me recipio &c'[70] to the Proctors, who came to me in a great dilemma:— I went over & read the words to the young man in the 2nd person & directed him to bow if he acquiesced:— so it passed over:—what his physical infirmity was I know not, — whether stuttering or dreadful timidity or doubt of reading the Latin —Dined at the Family at Smith's. . . One of the best dinners I ever saw on a table: everything superbly drest:— I never before tasted Cavear [sic] without loathing.— Paget, Phelps, Cartmell, Packe & I plaid whist.— I was successful:— I ought to have gone this week to Audley End to meet the D. & Duchess of Bedford (who really came this time).

Mon. 16. M's spasms much the same.— Sent off 3 Dozen Audit to Edward Romilly. M. wrote to Mrs. Edw. for Bonnet & Mantle.— Dined

---

[69] Adams and Le Verrier, who published first, had made independent theoretical calculations about the existence of Neptune in 1845, and a debate arose, warmed by national jealousies, as to who was the 'real' discoverer. English laggardness continued when Challis saw the planet in August 1846 but was unaware of what it was, unlike J.G. Galle of Berlin six weeks later. See W.M. Smart, *Occasional Notes of the Royal Astronomical Society* 2 (1947), 33-88, which includes a photograph of Adams *c.* 1846.

[70] The matriculation oath confirming that a member accepted and would uphold the University's requirements.

with Warter in Magdalene Hall to meet the Master who is paying one of his fly-away visits. The Master was very amusing with the account which he gave of dining at Windsor Castle. . . The Q sits a long time after dinner; the Prince stays ¼ hour after her & then stalks out by himself:— the other men stay 5 minutes after him. The Queen always has cards: she often plays a round game: the stake is a penny & the Q. keeps a large bag of silver pennies to give people change. To a grand ball at Mrs Wilkins. . .

Tu. 17.   Declined dining with the Fendalls:— sent for Dr Haviland who thinks there is very little the matter with her, & that the spasms merely come from the stomach being out of order:— still however they are very uncomfortable. Whist Club at Skrine's: there was a small party & we broke up before 11.— Some impudent gownsmen at night called out 'How d'ye do Mr Registrary?' I answered 'Your humble servant' & came across to speak to my supposed friends:— whereupon they hurried off & burst out a laughing.

Sun. 22.   'Stir up' Sunday.[71]— Carus gave us a very good sermon from the Gospel viz. John VI.14: he preached the same within the twelvemonth, viz. last 23 Nov. 1845. . . M at night fell over the drugget & came down with great violence bruising her forehead:— the drugget is to be banished for ever.

Mon. 23.   Letter from Lodge; very short but it gave me much pleasure as I have not had an autograph from him for a very long time: wrote to him again, altho I wrote yesterday. . . By the way I had a letter 3 days ago from G.T.R. in which he speaks very properly & indignantly about Fanny's conduct to him & threatens to give her up: I wish he would. . .

Tu. 24.   College meeting at which we agreed to commemorate our 300th anniversary next Dec. (22d) by a grand dinner in hall; Carus, the 3 Tutors, the Steward (Humphry) & I were appointed a committee to arrange invitations. . .

Sat. 28.   To the V.C.s about University Scholarship: so missed being present at a Seniority where a man was rusticated for a term por neas heneka.[72]— Had a grand party to drink wine: one of my guests (a Peterhouse Fellow Commoner of the name of Lennard) dined in hall with me: my other guests were Hensley, Edward Allen, Roget, Latimer Neville, Crawfurd, Cumming, Harnage & Mirehouse & Hustler. . .

Sun. 29.   M. E. & I in Trinity Church where an admirable Sermon for the Moravian Mission was preached by John Harding, from 1 Thess. 5.13: I had meant to give half a Crown but ended by giving 8 times as much. . .

Mon. 30.   The Syndics have fixt 9s on my book in sheets & 9/6 in boards, but I may bind it in cloth & charge 10/— They pay for the cost of

---

[71]   I.e. the last Sunday in Trinity, so called from the opening of the collect, 'Stir up, we beseech thee, O Lord, the wills of thy faithful people. . .'.

[72]   I.e. on account of fornication.

printing 500 & I am to pay for the 250 remaining.— M. & I called on Mrs. Worsley & saw all the drawings of the Master during the Summer . . . Edward went geologising with O. North & Roget & dined with the former.— Whist Club at Eyres where I got victimised: small party, viz. Eyres (drest (or rather undrest) most absurdly in a dressing gown), Cartmell, Francis, Skrine, Mills, Bateson & I.

At the beginning of December Romilly visited his London friends and relations. Mrs George Allen put him out of temper for 'she talks so countrified that I thought it quite ludicrous', and was hopeless at whist without 'any notion of the Game'.

Fri. 4 December. Came down by the 11.30 train.— Found Edward & M. at the station ready to receive me.— Dined at the Family at Packe's: this was an Extra meeting, being a bet dinner lost by Packe in a bet with Paget: the bet was wch of the 2 Mills (the one at the end of Mill Lane (commonly called King's Mill or Bishops Mill), or that by the 3 Jolly Millers on Sheep Green) is the Paramount Mill with the right of blowing a horn:— the King's Mill is the paramount. . . It was the noisiest party & the most drinking I have seen for some time.— Played whist till past 12.— The streets like glass when I went home.

Sun. 6. Ouvry North paid us a farewell visit before the Vacation.— We gave a Turkey for dinner to Grim as a regale before his final departure on Tuesday: he has now attended a Course of Corrie's Lectures & has done with the University:— M. has sent by him a pair of Pearl Earrings that were my mothers as a present to Mrs. G.B.A.

Mon. 7. To my great delight Jeremie has at last undertaken the Commemoration Sermon: wrote to thank him.— Seniority to declare the Fellowship: it is a capitally good one, viz. 20 original dividends: last year it was 19.

The material of a Dividend was

£.	s.	d.	
75			Master
200			8 Seniors at 25
40			2 Labourers at 20
102			6 Sixteeners at 17
428.	2.	6.	34 ¼ Majors at 12.10
70			14 Minors at 5
915.	2.	6.	

This is the best Fellowship since 1821 when there were 24 Dividends: the Monster F. of 32 Dividends was in 1817 — Edward ate his last dinner with us.— Read loud M.A. Wellington.[73]— Whist Club at Birketts, where I staid late & lost my money.

[73] R. Cobbold, *Mary Ann Wellington, the Soldier's Daughter, Wife, and Widow* (1846).

Tu. 8. Breakfast to Grylls, North, Edward Allen, H.B. Vizard & S.T. Clarke. . . Gave 'Reform Club Cutlets'[74] to oblige Edward who has bought Soyer (the R.C. cook)s book.— M. L. and I went up to the Station at 2 to see Edward off:— it was very much a touch and go business with Edward: he arrived at the last moment with no end of baggage of his own, & 2 great plaster casts of Tookes: he was assisted by Roget & attended by 2 porters: he was streaming with perspiration & all but too late.— Met at the Station Lord & Lady Jermyn & children. Her brother Lord John Manners is in Cambridge (at Trin. Lodge) escorting the claimant of the Spanish Crown (the Prince of Asturias, or as his travelling title is, Count of Montemolino) & the Duke of Medina Sidonia.[75] Lord John treats the prince as King Louis & always addresses him by the title 'Sir'.— The party dined with the Master in Hall: but I was tired & declined going:— there was afterwards an Evening Party at the Lodge. The Prince & his friend the Duke are short, particularly so when compared with Lord John:— the Prince has no sight with one eye, squints with the other & is rather knock-kneed: he is rather fat & looks more like a Dutchman than a Spaniard:— he wears a moustache:— he speaks a little English.— He conversed willingly & seemed to take an interest in every thing: he spoke about the University of Salamanca & its 3000 students, & said its Colleges were like ours. Carus expressed to him his horror of war:— a topic which the Prince could not be expected to agree in as he is levying troops against the Q. of Spain! — He has been in captivity for 7 years:— he is son of Don Carlos, who resigned his pretensions in his Favor:— he seems about 30.

Fri. 11. A fall of snow during the night: thermometer at 26 at 8½ in the morning.— Dined with the Family at Cartmell's. . . a very good dinner with grouse soup, — a novelty to me. . .

Sun. 13. Very cold & bleak.— M. L & I to Trinity where Carus preached extremely well from the Epist. of the day 1 Cor. 4.1.2. it was an old sermon of the year 1841. — M. then walked with me as far as St. Mary's, where I heard Dr Mill preach a very hard and able Apostolical-Church sermon in opposition to the Evangelical party.— Wrote to G.T.R. in answer to a very right-minded letter of his in which he expresses religious resignation to his grievous matrimonial disappointment.

Th. 17. M. felt but poorly & did not go out.— George arrived about 8 in the Evening: he was a good deal out of spirits, naturally, as his engagement with F.S. is broken up: all presents are returned:— she seems to have behaved in a most heartless manner & to have been (from her coquetishness & capriciousness) quite unworthy of the warm attachment which George has felt for her these three years of their engagement: she is a

---

74 Mutton chops, coated in egg, breadcrumbs and finely chopped ham, fried and served with a thick, spicy Reform sauce. See Alexis Soyer, *The Gastronomic Regenerator* (1846), pp. 294-5.

75 There had been civil war in Spain since Queen Isabella's accession in 1833. Her cousin the Pretender was in Cambridge for two days and was shown the usual sights.

mere child accustomed to be petted & spoiled:— she will not be 19 till 21st Dec.— George is to sleep in College all the time he likes to stay here.

Sun. 20. M. still at home.— L. G. & I to Trinity where Carus preached from the Epist. Phil. 4.4:— an old sermon of 1841:— it was very good, but it lasted an hour.— Had an interview at my rooms with Campbell (Lord C's son) who is coming forward for the Town: he wished for my advice about his address:— I thought his views moderate & sound.[76]— His Colleague as a Candidate will be Shafto Adair (whose Father Sir Rob's mansion Flixton Hall is just burnt down accidentally).— To St. Mary's where Mill preached an excellent sermon on the character of St. Thomas, whom he described as affectionate & faithful but naturally desponding.— Took a long walk with G. & talked over his unfortunate love affairs & all his shameful treatment. He meets with the sympathy & approbation of every body, more particularly of his great Parisian friend Miss Scott (sister of Mrs Anderson of Dulwich). In the Evening read loud 2 of Blunts Lectures.[77]

Mon. 21. G. & I dined in Hall: gave wine to him & Latham & Mr. Taddy (his uncle) & 2 young friends of G's, Leecroft & Holden.—George had a pull in an 8 oar in the middle of the day. . .

Tu. 22. Gave G.T.R. £5 for Chr. box.— G. breakfasted with Clark (one of our Scholars) with whom he leaves tomorrow for Paris.— George left us today by the 3 o'clock train:— he took away (without asking my leave) the oil picture given me by Miss Fanny, — a landscape of her own painting:— I presume he is going to send it back to her.— A very glorious day of bright sunshine & sharp frost.— This is the day fixt upon for our 300th Commemoration of our Foundation.— Took M. & L. & Miss Apthorp to see the preparations in our Hall & Kitchen, with which they were much amused:— in the Kitchen there was a piece of beef roasting which weighed above a hundred weight.— The distribution of the Prizes was at 10 o'clock:— the B. of London &c & 2 Ladies (viz. Mrs Whewell & Mrs Hare (Julius's wife) were present. Vansittart made the 2 prize orations: the English one was 'a comparison of Carthage, Athens & England as naval powers', the Latin an Eulogy of Luther. This last must have been peculiarly interesting to Hare who has recently had a gold Medal given him by the K. of Prussia for his defence of Luther.— At this distribution of prizes there were handed round copies of verses in Greek & Latin on our 300th Anniversary by Evans (University Scholar) Westcott (University Scholar) & Calthrop.— Bickersteth (who has gained the English Ode for 3 successive years) had written some English Verses for the occasion: but they were thought too diffusive & were not printed by the College.— The Commemoration service was at 4; Jeremie preached a most beautiful

[76] Hon. W.F. Campbell of Trinity, son of a Whig peer, was only 22 as his opponents did not allow him to forget. The 'address' was merely a brief paragraph declaring his intention to stand for the Liberal interest. See 30 July 1847.

[77] Perhaps J.J. Blunt's old Hulsean lectures on *The Veracity of the Historical Scriptures of the Old Testament* (1832).

Sermon: he was my deputy & I read the list of Benefactors. The dinner was nominally at 5:— about 350 I think sat down — The upper table A was thus arranged.[78] We had the Band of the Artillery in the Gallery, & they began (as in the days of old) with the Overture to the Occasional.[79] The Anthem after dinner ('Kings shall be &c')[80] with military accompaniments of Walmisley's was performed from the Gallery.— The 1st Toast was the Queen: the band played God s. the Q. & then retired:— their places were filled up by the Questionists &c who had not dined in hall:— all the Scholars, Sizars & Prizemen dined in hall:— the rest in the Lecturerooms.— The Master spoke very well & not too long: his health was given by Lord Fitzwilliam in good stile: B. of London made a good speech for the Church, T. Coltman a poor one for the Law, Lord Hardwicke a noisy one for the Navy, Macaulay a very finished oratorical harangue (his health had been given as a Privy Councillor & member of the Government), the V. Ch. delivered 2 or 3 sensible sentences, Lord Monteagle made a warmhearted address (about old recollections) in proposing the V.M. & Seniors & Sedgwick made an incomparably better in returning thanks. I should have said that the American Minister made a very complimentary harangue which he bellowed out as if he had been in the back-woods halloing:— it was very odd to see him twice in his speech turn round to the Master for confirmation or correction;— for example, 'the students of this College, — *should I say Fellows?*'; 'the magnetic influence is felt at the same instant from pole to pole, — *'am I right?'*. After Sedgwick's speech the Master dissolved the meeting having given Goulburn no opportunity of speaking.— I ought to have mentioned that after dinner with the dessert were put Copies of verses on the table: 3 epigrams on the 3 Towers (one Greek & 2 Latin) by Humphry the Steward, & some Latin drinking verses the joint production of C.B. Scott & A.A. Vansittart.— Shortly after 10 we left the hall:— tea was provided in the Comb. room (which had been our place of assembling before dinner) but the great mass of us went to a Soirée at Mrs Whewells:— there was supper downstairs.— This great day went off to one's hearts content.— Several persons who would greatly have wished to have been present were not able to come: of our 10 Judges only 3 were present, of our 6 Bishops only 1. But of all absentees none felt his compulsory absence so

[78] Here follows a seating plan. There are ephemera in UP 16 and a full account of the day's events in the *Cambridge Chronicle* (26 December 1846) which includes the plan, menu, speeches, etc. Jeremie's sermon on Psalm 143 v. 5, which fortunately was printed afterwards, was so faint that the reporter could hardly hear it, and he had difficulty in following Bancroft, the American Minister, partly from his 'national peculiarity of intonation'. Romilly's own reading of College benefactors was to an outsider 'most tedious and somewhat uninteresting'. In contrast with such grand celebrations was a meeting convened in the Town Hall on 16 December to help the poor with bread and coals. Romilly subscribed £5.

[79] I.e. Handel's.

[80] Cf. Isaiah 49. 23, an apt text for a College which counted Edward III, Henry VIII, and Queen Mary as its founders.

much as Hustler.[81] John Romilly could not come because V.C. Wigram's court sat.— We had down (at Wrays recommendation) 2 of the London Police & we refused admission to the London Press, we also excluded ladies from our Chapel & Hall.— The young men behaved very well during the speechifying: there was only one uncomfortable & suspicious set of sounds (as if of drunken phrensy), & they proceeded from poor A. Gordon our Chaplain who said he would go if he died:— he has very recently had a severe attack of paralysis & is not in his right mind:— he was obliged to be carried home to his rooms, poor fellow!—[82]

Wed. 23. Nasty thaw.— Grand dinner to the College Gyps & Bedmakers (140) at 6 o'clock in hall: Carter presided at one table, & Cranwell (the Library Keeper) at another.— They adjourned to the Lecture rooms where they had tea & coffee & then dancing to 2 fiddles & a piano till 2 o'clock. My hagged old bedmaker (Mrs Carpenter) said she never passed so happy a day: her wedding day was not to compare:— she had had enough of every thing, that all was so good & she had been treated with *so much respect.*— I should have said that yesterday we gave a massy silver tankard to Claydon, & a grand bible to Cranwell in gratitude for their services.— Dined in Trinity Hall Hall. . . in the Evening we had whist & I (unluckily) plaid with Crick (Orator) against Paget & a very good player of Tr. Hall (Humphrey). Not home till near 2!

Fri. 25. M. L. & I to Trinity Church where Carus preached from ('Thou Bethleh. Ephr.').[83] We staid Sacrament & did not get out of Church till past 2. We were all much chilled as the day was very cold:— We had a very small party at our Christmas dinner, namely our 3 selves:— our poor Guest of former years Miss Vincent will never dine out again after her paralytic seisure, & none of our nephews were with us.— We should have acted kindly in asking Miss Apthorp, but we were very snug & comfortable by ourselves.

Tu. 29. Gave breakfast to John, Blunt & Sedgwick:— after breakfast we had cigars & liqueur:— Sedgwick was brilliant: I never heard him more entertaining.— Today I received very agreeable letters of thanks for my Book from the B. of London, Master of Temple (T. Robinson) & Prof. Blunt.— M. & I went to Castle-end to take a present of stockings &c to Caroline How (living at Mr Bells):— Lucy went on numberless benevolent excursions among the poor.— After dinner read loud Rob. Halls magnificent sermon on the death of Ryland[84]. . . Went to a Juvenile Ball at

---

[81] J.D. Hustler's absence is not explained. He was a former fellow and tutor who had married the daughter of W. L. Mansel (d.1820), Master of Trinity.

[82] Whatever his condition Anthony Gordon remained one of the chaplains until 1858.

[83] See Micah V 2, a prophecy of the Messiah.

[84] Hall (1764-1831) spent fifteen years as a Baptist minister in Cambridge and won golden opinions for his oratory. Bohn had published a volume of his miscellaneous works in 1846. John Ryland had been his schoolmaster at Northampton. An additional interest for Romilly may have been that Hall's closest friend and would-be biographer had been Sir James Mackintosh, who had married Baugh Allen's sister.

Mrs Havilands: a very pretty sight. A most unpleasant fracas took place at the Whist table in Dr. H's study. I was playing with the Marquis against Skrine & Heaviside. Skrine accused the Marquis of having revoked, which both he & I stoutly denied:— the Marquis (erroneously thinking the game gone) had pushed the cards together: Skrine accused him of having done so in a tone & manner (but not in actual words) which implied that he had done so fraudulently:— great rage (in spite of all I could do to bring them to reason) was exhibited by both, & the M. left the house telling Skrine he should hear from him.

Wed. 30. Today 3 snipe from Marchesa.— Got up very early & wrote a most urgent letter to the Marq. recommending peace & forgiveness: I had afterwards an interview with Captain Doria & in consequence wrote to Skrine advising him to say that he did not intend the meaning put on his words. Skrine accordingly wrote me a letter to that effect which I forwarded to the Marquis & recommended him to apologise for the anger he had shown. He did so & thus this painful quarrel which was on the eve of a duel has happily ended in peace.

On 30 December Romilly was at Audley End to celebrate the New Year. He must by this time have been on very easy terms with the Braybrookes for on his arrival, finding no one in the saloon, he went 'to my own room & wrote journal till dinner time' at seven. He escorted Lady Longford, 'a handsome most Aristocratic widow who has had about a dozen children, & looks as if she would have a dozen more if she had a husband'. On New Year's Eve' there was snapdragon in the hall and an excellent magic lantern which, however, Charles Neville exhibited 'very flatly & never opened his lips:— One of the slides I thought coarse; it was called 'love in a Coal-hole'.' The older generation were abed by the time the sons of the house shouted in the New Year & sat up drinking and laughing.

Cambs Collection

Christ Church

ELECTING A CHANCELLOR AT CAMBRIDGE.

(A LITTLE ALTERED FROM GEORGE CRUIKSHANK'S "ELECTING A BEADLE.")

1847

On New Year's Day Romilly acted as chaplain before a long morning game of battledore and shuttlecock with the young people; it was amusing and noisy and left him 'sopped thro with perspiration'. Later he walked as far as Ashdon to visit Dr Chapman whose tithe day it was and who intended to give a grand dinner to the payers. A dance began in the evening and Romilly, who no doubt knew he would have to act as chaplain again, retired after the first supper while the young folk went on 'hugging' (as the scandalised Lady Cornwallis described waltzing) till three. When he left on the next day for home Lord Braybrooke presented him with a brace of pheasant for his 'ladies'.

Sat. 2 January. . . . Found Margaret very poorly with spasms in her left side & much out of spirits about herself. The severe weather & the alterations of damp & cold have much disagreed with her . . .

Sun. 3. . . . I had caught a cold from overheating myself at battledore & shuttlecock on Friday. I therefore staid at home & so did M.— L. went by herself & heard Carus preach from Isai. 41.17.18.— In the Evening read loud 'Philosophy of the Plan of Salvation' by an anonymous American;[1]— also a Lecture of Dr Cheever.[2]

Mon. 4. . . . Sent for Dr Haviland: he recommended leaches to the left side.— 1st day of Subscriptions 142, an unusually large number. M. had on leaches in the Evening.

Sat. 9. . . . A long visit from David Melville who is Principal of the new Coll. at Durham, Hatfield Hall. Sent copies of my book to Bps of Hereford, Ely & Edinburgh, Drs Haviland, Ollivant & Lee, &c &c: wrote also to them all.— Wrote a long letter to Miss Lodge — a gossiping affair about Audley End.— Begged Dr Haviland to come & see Margaret, whose side smarts very much (from the leach-bites, I suppose): he ordered her a poultice & wrote a prescription, but does not seem to think anything is seriously the matter with her.— Today letters from F.R. & family: also a letter from George enclosing a copy of a very long & (I think) brusque letter beginning & ending 'Sir' he has sent to Mr Smith: George wishes me to go to Town to see his friend Miss Scott (Mrs Anderson's sister) & also to write to Mr Smith asking him to return all the drawings. I shall write tomorrow declining both one & the other.— George has done 2 things without asking my leave wch I disapprove of: he has sent back the painting wch Miss Fanny gave me, & he has sent to Mr Smith confidential letters of mine in wch I spoke severely of Miss Fanny.— At night read loud Dr Cheever & Madame D'Arblay![3] George's Birthday:— we had a bottle of Champagne to drink his health.— He is 24.

---

[1] 'An American Citizen' (i.e. James Barr Walker), *Philosophy of the Plan of Salvation: a Book for the Times* [1841 ?]. It was often reprinted in Britain and America, and also translated into German, French, and Welsh.

[2] George B. Cheever, an American author of lectures on *Pilgrim's Progess.*

[3] Romilly was reading her *Diary and Letters* (1842-6). See 3 February 1843.

Mon. 11. . . . (Plough M.)[4]— M. decidedly better. I forgot to mention a short time ago a visit I received from Dr Ficke:[5]— I had not seen him for above 20 years & did not in the least recollect him:— 'You don't recollect me?'. 'No I'm sorry to say I do not recollect your name tho I recall your features'. 'Why! it is not much more than 20 years since I saw you, & you really do not know me?'. He was as vivacious as if he had grown 20 years younger instead of older. I received him very warmly when I knew who he was & regularly victimised myself by listening to his translations into English Verse from Schiller &c for *1½* hour:— they were very spirited & clever, but I of course was tired much sooner than he was.— I entirely dissuaded his wild scheme of giving up his London pupils to come to Cambridge as a German Teacher in the Place of Mr Weil who is going away.— A general report that Charles Perry is to be the Bishop of Australia Felix.[6]— Dr Haviland prescribed a belladonna plaster today.— M. did not go out (having taken physic) tho the day was dry & sunshiny, the 1st good one we have had for some time.— Dined in hall.— Read loud Madame D'Arblay's account of her flight from Paris with the Princesse d'Henin at the beginning of the 100 days:— very vivid.

Th. 14. . . . The pain in M's side returned so violently that I called in Dr Haviland who prescribed a blister. . .

Fri. 15. . . . Dr Haviland applied the Stethoscope & pronounces there to be no affection of the heart: he thinks it entirely a case of overloaded bowels: no fever, & the pains fly about. God grant that he may set her up again.— M. kept her bed all day.— Lucy & I dined by ourselves & I did not see M. all day. Lucy sat with her all the Evening.

Sat. 16. . . . Note from Dr Haviland saying he had got an attack of Gout & could not go out but begged me to bring report of M. I called accordingly & made a report of castor oil having been necessary before the aperient would operate: he says this shows great torpor in the bowels & must decidedly be overcome & then he fears nothing.— I declined the Marchesa's soirée this Evening.— Day for receiving Supplicats: very busy.— Letter from G.T.R. asking me to send £12 to Mrs Anderson (wch I did), to get him an introduction to the Embassy at Paris (I wrote to Edw. Romilly to crave his assistance) & to get M. to copy out several airs.—Wrote to G.T.R. saying I would try & procure the airs from the Musicsellers. M.

---

4   On the first Monday after Epiphany by ancient custom farm workers would take a plough from door to door asking for beer money before the labours of the new year began. In 1848 Lucy 'staid at home to escape from the plough-boys —by the way they did not drag about a plough this year'. See E. Porter, *Victorian Cambridge* (1975), p. 42, and her *Cambridgeshire Customs and Folklore* (1969), pp. 96-100.

5   I.e. Whewell's 'very able German friend' Heinrich Fick (sic), 'a person of great literary ability, well acquainted with English, as well as with German poetry' (I. Todhunter, *William Whewell* (1876), I, 168-9). Several of his letters are among the Whewell papers at Trinity.

6   Perry was made first Bishop of Melbourne in 1847. Its western hinterland had been dubbed 'happy' in contrast with the deserts of the interior.

came down for 2 hours in the Evening, but was suffering pain from the blister & was chilly & dejected:— she went to bed again after tea: she is however decidedly better.—

Th. 21. . . . M. very languid.—Dined in hall.—Today the 5 Airs ('Sound the loud Timbrel', 'the Spacious Firmament', 'Come if you dare', 'From Greenland's &c', & Pergolesi's 'Gloria in Exc') arrived from Town, procured for us by Mrs Joseph. They are the Airs wch George wanted M. to copy out for his great friend Miss Scott.—Letter from Edward to say that Frederick would in about 3 weeks introduce George to Lord Normanby[7]
. . .

Fri. 22. . . . M. a little better.—Sent the Music to Miss Scott (at her sisters Mrs Anderson's at Dulwich): wrote to Miss Scott & also to George
. . .

Sat. 23. . . . Bachelors Commencement from 10 to 1¼ : 129 Hon. & 129 Polloi: went off very well & quietly.—*I. Hill* (of Joh) was plucked:— the joke was that the *'igh 'ill* was laid low.— Received from Mr Warwick a copy of his gay 'Camb. O. &c Calendar':[8] sent him in return my sixtieth & last presentation Copy of my 'Graduati.'— Read loud to M. up stairs. . .

Sun. 24. . . . M. kept her bed all day.—Very bad day:— Lucy not out— (Carus at Somersham): Hopkins preached very ably for the starving Irish: Miss Baldry (in the Hospital) sent 6d by me, M. sent £2, I gave £5 (having intended to give only 1): £161 collected at the door! The next largest *Church* Collection was at St Andrews £55.— At the Baptist Chapel I think £400 was collected:— the Dissenters altogether raised £600! Hopkins' Text was 'Think ye those men on whom the tower &c &c.'[9]— Read loud to M. & L. all the Evening . . .

Mon. 25. M. better today.— She got up directly after breakfast & remained up all day:— she kept her room however as she cannot bear her stays on or any tightness on her side where the blister was:— she replaced the belladonna plaster today.—Lovely mild day.—Wrote to F.R. £10.— Meeting of Master & Seniors:— we made a subscription for the poor Irish: the Master & Brown gave £50 each, I gave £30, the rest £25. . .

Tu. 26. Declined dining again at Downing Lodge today.—M. felt much irritation in her side from the plaster during the night & tore it off.— She however got up directly after breakfast.— Another mild lovely day.— Called on Dr Haviland (still laid up with Gout) to talk about M: he thinks there is nothing seriously wrong about her:— prescribed some nervous

[7] The diarist's cousins, Edward and Frederick Romilly. Normanby, an old member of Trinity, was ambassador to France.
[8] I.e. the *Oxford, Cambridge, Durham, London and Dublin University and Ecclesiastical Almanack*. Warwick, having given up the *Cambridge Advertiser* in 1846, returned to compiling specialised reference books of this kind, such as *The Clergyman's Diary* and *Clergyman's Companion*. None of them took hold any more than his *Cambridge University Register* of 1843 and 1844 had done.
[9] 'Think ye those men on whom the tower in Siloam fell' (Luke 13. 4.). The text was a popular one for disasters and invited general repentance; cf. 17 July 1842.

Medicine, viz. stinking Valerian:[10] he says Patients think more of nasty physic.—called on Sir John & Lady Walsham & daughter at the Eagle: they are come for the Bachelors Ball:[11]— I learned from them that Frederic is now a Colonel:— wrote to compliment him.—Lady Walsham is an agreeable person with too many teeth in her mouth, wch is somewhat rabbit-shaped: her nose is too small: but she is pleasing in manners & appearance. Her daughter is a bouncing fresh-look Bowzelinda.— M. came down to Tea & staid over prayers.— Tonight began reading loud 'Jack Brag';[12] I find it as amusing as when I first read it.— Kept away from the Bachelors Ball.

Th. 28. . . . M. much better, thank God . . . Poor Miss Baldrey died in the Hospital this Evening . . .

Fri. 29. M. seems better this morning—Wrote to George £10. Mrs Cleaver has turned off Lucy's protégée Mary Beales; Lucy called on Mrs Cl. to receive the 10 days wages 2s. 2d—Mrs Cl. went into Hysterics when talking about her treatment by M.B: Lucy & she excellent friends & parted with mutual courtesy.—I wrote to old Beales (g. f. of Mary) who is going to receive her tomorrow in Town:— Sent him £1. Lucy lodged M.B. at Mrs Gilmours for this one day.—Dined at the family at Dr Tathams . . .

Sat. 30. M. better.—Mary Beales packed off by Parliamentary Train[13] at 11.20: she was not arrived when the Omnibus stopped, & her bag had to be packed while it was staying! What a dawdling hussey!—Lucy had a long interview with Miss Spilling, & was told all the particulars of her [Miss Baldrey's] death:—she has died worth £65 besides a little plate!—Lucy's protégée Eliza Gilmour is come from town to stay a few days with her mother: the poor Girl seems in a decline. M. down at dinner & staid till bedtime.— Read loud the new number of Dombey with the description of little Paul's death. Also read some of Jack Brag.

Sun. 31. M. decidedly better: she received from Mrs B. Allen a very agreeable letter of thanks for her present of pearl earrings wch had been my mothers.—I staid at home to keep company with M in the morning.— L. went by Herself & heard him preach a Sermon from 1 Cor. 9. 24;—a very old one, the 4th time! . . . M. came down directly after breakfast.— M. played the Piano a little in the Evening, being the 1st time for a long while; she did not venture to sing.

---

[10] A common medicine made from the root of the plant, and also known as 'Allheal'. Haviland seems to have fallen back on it as a tonic; it was given as a stimulant for the treatment of spasms, hysteria, epilepsy, corea, and hypochondriasis.

[11] Walsham, a nephew by marriage of Sir Samuel Romilly, was not a member of the University; his son and heir came up in 1850.

[12] Theodore Hook, *Jack Brag* (1837). When reading the novel on its publication Romilly had enjoyed it despite Hook's 'irresistible tendency to indecency' (*R.C.D. 1832-42,* p.119), and had re-read it in 1844.

[13] So called because by an act of 1844 every company had to run passenger trains daily over its system at no more than a penny a mile.

Th. 4 February. M. going on well.—Mrs Barker very unwell.— We had a ludicrous scene today in trying to get a Chest of drawers up into the Attics: we got into a regular fix & had to send for the Carpenter:— we had been trying an impossibility.—All the furniture (brought from Miss Baldrey's) given to Mrs How & Mrs Gilmour.—By the way Eliza Gilmour is come home with a very bad cough:— Caroline Hudson[14] writes to say she is ill & out of place; & Betsy Fitch has just lost a brother, & her Mother is gone into the Union:— So Lucy's paupers are not prospering.—Declined the Ball at Mrs Thackerays. . .

Fri. 5. Called on Miss Apthorp to give her an account of M.— Ouvry-North returned: brings a very bad account of his uncle John Ouvry & his Aunt Campbell: they are both dying.—Forgot to mention last Tuesday swearing in 11 Special Constables in consequence of the continued attacks on the Proctors[15] . . .

Sun. 7. The organ at Trin. taken down & a seraphine[16] substituted by Carus.—I staid at home to keep M. company:— read her the Lessons &c & 2 Sermons, 1 of Arnold & 1 of Chalmers.—Lucy to church by herself & was nearly poisoned by the paint on our newly-boarded-up pew:— She staid Sacrament wch lasted till nearly 2½! . . . In the Evening Margaret sang as well as plaid;— a great improvement . . .

Mon. 8. Margaret certainly much better.—In proof of it, she cut out a set of nightshirts for me . . .

Th. 11. M. down to Breakfast: hurrah!—Went to see at Roe's a beautiful picture of Landseer's called 'Shoeing': it is the portrait of a horse lent by Bell the Chemist (when horse exercise was prescribed to him): this Picture is Bell's:— the Canvass is well filled with a donkey, & dog, the blacksmith &c.— M. out walking! Her last day of walking was Tuesday the 12 Jan., *30 days since*!. . .

Fri. 12. M. out walking again altho the day was cold & harsh. . . The D. of Northumberland, (aged 62) found dead in his bed yesterday morning: he had been suffering from Influenza.

14 She had been a protégée of the women's Dulwich days when they had sent her to stay at the seaside, paid for her to visit an infirmary, and taken her to Margaret's own doctor about her leg. Lucy left her £25 in her will.

15 Eleven specials were sworn in on 2 February and 10 more on the twelfth. The disturbances arose after the death of Elizabeth Howe, a prostitute from Fulbourn, who in the previous November had been put in the Spinning House for one night by Kingsley, the Junior Proctor. It was supposed that there she had contracted the fever from which she died. The jury at the inquest expressed its abhorrence at a system which allowed the University to apprehend women 'when not offending against the general law of the land, and confining them in a gaol unfit for the worst of felons'. The national press entered the fray but proctorial powers were not diminished.

16 A kind of harmonium invented in 1833 by John Green.

Sat. 13. The Johnians sent up an Address to Lord Powis this morning by the Electric Telegraph[17]—M & I out walking: we went to see Landseer's Picture, with wch she was greatly pleased: met all the world at the Exhibition, viz. the Archdalls, Hopkinses, Paget &c . . .

Sun. 14. Nasty wet day:— Thermometer above 40: more than 10 deg. higher than the last several days.—Lucy went alone to Trin. Ch. & (to avoid the smell of the recently painted boarding in our Pew) sat with Miss Page. . . The organ has been moved from the N. Transept window, has been tinkered up for £20!, & placed on the ground where the Seraphine was last Sunday:— it made a great noise.—I staid at home with M. who did not get out all day . . . I read to her the Psalms, Lessons, Collect &c. &c. & an admirable Sermon of Barrows on our latter End[18]. . .

Mon. 15. Sent Miss Butcher an Octavo Bible of the largest print as she writes me word that her eye sight is failing :— she says the engagement between Mr Williams & Miss Louisa Pearce is broken off because she will not renounce all intercourse with her worthless Father.—Meeting of Master & Seniors: we were unanimous in offering the Chancellorship to Prince Albert . . . Walk with M. in the Garden after dinner:— She complains again of tenderness in her side, & does not fasten her Gown behind.— The Johnians sent off an express to E. Powis (brother-in-law of the D. of Northumberland) as soon as they heard of the D's death, to invite him to stand for the Chancellorship:— His acceptance appeared in this Evening's London Papers.—Communication has been made by Master of Trinity (thro' Anson) to Prince Albert to sound his willingness to accept the Chancellorship: His R. H.'s answer is favourable *if he is unopposed.* . .

Tu. 16. Walk with M. in the Town: she had a visit today from Miss Spilling who came to offer her & Lucy the choice of poor Miss Baldrey's trinkets (according to the directions of her will): she chose the prettiest (viz. a Brooch) for Lucy, & the ugliest for herself (viz. a ring with a Coffin on it).—Congregation to declare the Vacancy of the Chancellorship:—Th. the 25th fixt for the Election. Finished the Danish Tales:[19]— very imaginative.

Th. 18. M.'s 1st day of shopping: she did it handsomely, giving the house 6 Table Cloths.—Letter from Pet. Ouvry to say his uncle John was

[17] Having served as High Steward of the University, Lord Northumberland had been elected its Chancellor in 1840. Powis had not held any office at Cambridge: he was, however, Northumberland's brother-in-law, and well-known for his steady and ultimately successful opposition to the union of the Welsh sees (see 7 March 1845). Powis had been M.P. for Ludlow for many years although it was held briefly by Edward Romilly from 1832 to 1835. On the manoeuvering of the candidates for the Chancellorship and their supporters see Winstanley, pp. 106-21. The election led to much ephemera some of which is reprinted in C. Whibley, *In Cap and Gown* (1889), pp. 207-27.

[18] I.e. *Practical Discourses upon . . . our Latter End, and the Danger and Mischief of Delaying Repentence* (1694). Isaac Barrow, Master of Trinity who died in 1677, was still highly regarded by fellows of the College, three of whom had lately published independent selections or editions of his works. A statue of him was erected in the College Chapel in 1857 (see Winstanley, pp. 436-9).

[19] By Hans Andersen. There were three translations in 1846 alone.

dead.— Wrote to him, & also to his wife. Wrote to E. E. Allen: also to G.T.R. inclosing a letter of introduction to Ld W. Hervey[20] the Embassador's Secretary.—College meeting about the Chancellorship:—there is a strong party in London against Prince Albert as not having been educated at the University & not having a seat in the H. of Lords:— Ld Nelson is the Chairman of Powis's London Committee.—There was today a meeting of the Heads on the matter of Chancellorship:— also a meeting at St Johns.— We announced a meeting of the supporters of P.A. in Trin. Comb. room tomorrow at 11; & sent Atkinson off to the Railway to set the Electric Telegraph to work to order the announcement to be printed in the London Evening papers:— We also sent up Martin at 2 o'cl. to communicate with Lord Monteagle, &c. &c.— Finished reading loud 'F. of Nigel.'[21] M. wrote to Mrs G.B. Allen.

Fri. 19. Matriculation: The least I ever had in the Lent Term:— 4 F.c., 21 P. & 1 S.—Great meeting of supporters of P. Albert in Trinity Comb. room, the Master in the Chair.— Walk with M. from 1 to 2: then worked at our Committee till dinner time: dined in hall: combination room for an hour:—then worked in Committee Room till bedtime.—The V.C. gone to town.

Sat. 20. . . . Worked at Committee all the morning:—Yesterday we telegraphed our resolutions & also sent up Arlett by 3 o'clock Coach.— Dr French & Graham returned from London yesterday:— Cartmell went up yesterday.—We sent up by the 2 o'cl. train a prodigious number of letters under the care of Barnard Smith.— The Prince was to receive the V.C. at 12 today.—At 2 o'cl. there was a telegraphic communication from Town made to Shaw or Dr Graham: neither was on the spot at the time; Ld. Hardwicke, Dr French, Packe & I were there; the other 2 were sent for & were caught on the road coming: [Note in manuscript: 'The Telegraphic Communication was R (For Refusal): the Telegraph was to bring A, C or R (for acceptance, conditional, refusal)] I believe the communication was simply that the V.C. would bring down the Prince's Answer, wch by Ld H. & Dr Fr. is expected to be retirement from the contest.— At 8 in the Evening there was a full meeting in the Committee room & Dr Graham communicated the Prince's Answer in the shape of a Letter to the V.C. & Masters of Senate (written by Col. the Hon. C.B. Phipps (the Prince's Secretary) in the Prince's name: it states the impossibility of the P. entering into a Contest with a subject, but says that he will be both happy & proud to accept the Chancellorship if offered to him.— This we consider as a permission to make the fight & give him the Prize if we win. So we mean to fight valiantly. A copy of the Prince's Letter is to be sent to Ld P's committee in Cambridge & London, & a strong London Committee formed for the Prince.— That wrongheaded Dr Mill has joined Ld P's Committee : Dr Wordsworth, Blakesley, W.

---

[20] One of five brothers who entered Trinity between 1819 and 1833.
[21] Sir Walter Scott, *The Fortunes of Nigel* (1822).

Vizard, &c have given in their adhesion to Ld Powis's party (wch has Ld Nelson for its Chairman, Ld J. Manners,[22] A.J.B. Hope, D. of Buccleuch, &c for members). The Puseyites, the 'Young England' party, the Johnians, the admirers of Punch are all in favor of Lord Powis: Sedgwick says Powis is patronised by 3 P's, Punch, Puseyites & Pigs.[23]—At night read loud Marryatt's 'Settlers'.[24]

Sun. 21. . . . Lucy went at 2 to St Marys to hear Henry John Rose (the preacher of the month) preach on the Q's Letter for The Starving Irish:[25]. . . M. sent £2 by her. . .

Mon. 22. . . . Very good speech of Whewell. Dr French & Dr Graham & many more had been completely depressed on Saturday Evening by the Prince's telegraphed answer: Dr Graham particularly said that he had had private communication & that he conceived his answer to be conclusive, & that we should be behaving disrespectfully to him if we pressed the business. Arlett behaved with great pluck & said the London people thought we were bound to go on vigorously & that the Prince could not but expect it. At 11 at night (Saturday) Cartmell arrived at Trinity Lodge from town & brought a confirmation of Arlett's opinion.— The speaking was all very energetic this morning (Monday) in favor of going on with heart & soul, & from none more than from French & Graham. The Master of Trinity spoke extremely well:— the leading article (from a Correspondent) in the Camb. paper was the echo of his speech & probably sent by him.— Dr Archdall however was croky about possible defeat & the delicate position in wch the Prince was placed by us.— Dr Ainslie proposed 3 resolutions which (after much deliberation & debate & alteration) ultimately passed:— they were only sent to the newspapers & were not circulated in Letters from the Committee Room.

Th. 25. Election — 1 days Polling. Began at 10. At the Table sat the V.C. with the 2 Proctors on his right & Mr Assessor Hunt; the Junior D.D. (viz. Dr S.E. Walker) was opposite the Junior Proctor; on the left of the V.C. sat Birkett & Mills as Scrutineers on the Prince's side, & opposite to them the Scrutineers of E. Powis viz. Snowball & Cookson:— Birkett & Cookson wrote down the names of the voters, & Mills & Snowball checked off the names in the Calendar & challenged the disputable votes. I (as Registrary)

22 Lord John Manners was a leader of 'Young England', a group of largely aristocratic young Tories c. 1840-48 who wished to revive (as they thought) a paternalistic relationship with the working classes. Disraeli put forward their ideas in his novels.
23 *Punch* consistently ridiculed Prince Albert and would doubtless have taken anyone's part against him. Powys was reckoned a Puseyite for his High Churchmanship. For reasons never convincingly explained members of St John's College had been known to others since the seventeenth century as *Johnian hogs* (or *swine* or *pigs*). Cf. *R.C.D. 1832-42*, pp. 86, 211, 227. Elaborations of the joke are in M. Morris, *University Slang* (1950), p. 44.
24 F. Marryat, *The Settlers in Canada, written for Young People* (1844).
25 A circular letter to the clergy asking for charitable collections. Before the years of famine and disease the population of Ireland constituted a third of that of the whole realm. Between 1846 and 1851 it is estimated that almost a million people emigrated and a million and a half died. See C. Woodham-Smith, *The Great Hunger* (1962).

sat at the N. end of the table separating the 2 sets of Scrutineers:— The V.C. the 2 Proctors & Dr Walker (being the 4 Persons who stand in scrutiny officially) gave their votes first; the V.C. & Kingsley for the Prince, Brumell & Walker for the Earl.— There was an immense rush of Voters all day: Dr Bland was knocked down in one crowd which defeated the Constables & broke down the Barrier.— Earl Fitzwilliam (drest in his *scarlet* gown) tendered a vote for E Powis: a wag in the Gallery is said to have exclaimed 'here she is',— to wit the Lady of Babylon. Lord Fitzw. vote was refused, he never having resided 3 terms.— Lord De La Warr's vote (for the Prince) was refused on same ground.[26] The Provost of Eton (for the Prince) was refused, his mandate B.D. giving him no vote.— Sir John Beckett's vote (for the Prince) was much opposed, but the V.C. & both Proctors approved it in opposition to Dr Walker: of course it passed.[27]— Two Trinity MA's (F. S. Williams & Rob. Harris), whose names had been taken off by their Tutor, were of course refused.—One bad vote certainly passed, viz. Clotworthy Gillmor (an incorporate Dublin man, who had never resided):— he voted for the Earl.— An obstinate violent ill-behaved Trinity man (Richard Hodgson, Member for Berwick) tendered a vote for the Earl and was refused as *not created*:[28]— I drew up an affidavit & administered the oath to him before the V.C. with the greatest solemnity:—on his so swearing that he had been created the Grace Book was altered & his vote received. He afterwards backed his cause with Eyres for a sovereign. He disgusted the V.C. (to whom he behaved most impertinently) & everybody else.— Another person made himself obnoxious & ridiculous on our side, viz. Dr Vaughan (LLD) of St Johns: who went about saying that he had brought up 100 voters for the Prince, & paid the expenses of many of them.— It had been intended by Dr Graham that the B. of Norwich should give the first vote today:— there were however 2 or 3 pressed in before him. The Poll closed at 5 o'cl. when the V.C. *continued* the Congregation to 8 in the Evening. The Polling in the early part of the day was in favor of Lord Powis, who was at one time viz. at ¼ to 1 o'cl. 82 ahead: this number was however steadily reduced & at 5 the numbers were 574 for Prince Albert & 582 for E. Powis. The scrutineers (Lund who had taken the place of Birkett) & Birkett) did not agree in their numbers: Lund however ultimately turned out to be right.—but our inaccurate report of the Prince being 10 ahead gained general circulation.—Dined in hall (taking in Lord Wriothesley Russell)[29] at 5½: our youngsters had dined at 4.— There was a large party of MA's, above 240: Sedgwick was in the Chair as V.M., who spoke excellently & in a kind way for both sides: we were too large a party to go up stairs.

[26] Lord Fitzwilliam had taken an honorary LL.D. degree (as had De la Warr) immediately upon entering the University as a middle-aged politician in 1833.
[27] It is not clear why Beckett's vote was opposed. He had been a Wrangler and Fellow of Trinity.
[28] I.e. he had not been formally admitted to a degree.
[29] An elder brother of Mrs Charles Romilly.

Sedgwick gave the non-resident voters & Earl Nelson (London Chairman of E. Powis's Committee) returned thanks:—he proposed Sedgwick's health wch was received with great applause: Sedgwick made an excellent answer.—A little before 8 we went into the Comb. Room for Coffee: At 8 I returned to the S.H:—the Galleries were quite dark: they were crammed: the youngsters howled, & hooted & made themselves hateful. At 9 the V.C. continued the Congregation to 10 tomorrow:— the state of the Poll now was, Prince A. 617, E. Powis 602: making a gross number of 1219, a prodigious one for a single day of 8 hours polling: being at the rate of 5 votes for every 2 minutes.—I slept at the Hills Road.

Fri. 26. Poll recommenced at 10. One of the 1st voters was my dear friend Lodge (who had been solicited by Warter): he was looking very well & had been most anxious for the Prince ever since he heard of the Contest: he came up with his Cousin Richard (who lodged at the Bull, & he himself at Magd):— he wisely did not venture to remain in the hubbub of the S.H:—he was expected by me to return to the North tomorrow:— he however did not go back till Monday,—but I saw no more of him.—John Romilly voted last night, but I never saw him.—The polling was not brisk today: only 372 polled in the 7 hours from 10 to 5—(at the rate of 53 per hour):— The Poll at 5 gave 828 for the Prince & 763 for the Earl.—I dined again in Hall, taking with me A. Malkin who came in obedience to my summons:—A large party, above 200:—Sedgwick in the Chair: he spoke briefly & well:— to the Comb. room a little before 8.—At 8 to S.H.:— the youngsters in the galleries availed themselves of their dark concealment & showered down peas & shot on our heads.—one piece of wood & some halfpence were also thrown: the young men behaved infamously, howling & hooting the whole hour, some blowing horns, others braying like asses (as they were). Their rage had been excited at their defeat in the morning upon the Hat & Cap question:[30] the day was cold & the outvoters wore their hats in spite of a most obstreperous din from the galleries.— The Polling closed at 9: the numbers then were 789 Powis; 875 the Prince; total 1664: only 73 polled in this hour of Babel confusion. The number polled in the hour last night was still less, being only 63.— I went to the Hills Road to read prayers but slept in College.

Sat. 27. Polling began at 9: it was much brisker than could have been expected: it closed at 12 with a majority of 117 for the Prince.—the final numbers were 954 for the Prince, 837 for the Earl; making a total of 1791, an unprecedented Poll. Glost. 468 Rutl. 351:— The Majority for the D. of Gloster in 1811 was also 117.— There was a grand dinner in Trinity Coll: Hall to wch all the Prince's Committee were invited: I however avoided this party & dined quietly at home, having been a good deal knocked up by the insufferable din in the Senate House wch had interfered with my

---

[30] I.e. over the niceties of academical dress, especially as they distinguished the ordinary undergraduate from noblemen and others (see 18 October 1844 and 18 January 1845).

sleeping.— It is said that the Master of St Johns, Prof. Blunt & Dr Hymers were much opposed to the contest & that in Lord Powis's Committee-room at St Johns on Tuesday last there was a division upon going on: 17 were for, & 16 against.— In the Evening read 'Settlers'.

Sun. 28. I staid at home & kept M. company.—Lucy to Church by herself. . . Yesterday besides the bell-ringing, rejoicing was made by hoisting flags at St Mary's & St Michaels:—the flag at St Mary's was hoisted again today.— M. & I had begun last night to sort the 582 Cards of Trinity for Gunning's forthcoming Poll:— we finished them today:—& I left them at his house.[31]—M. not out;—day very cold & harsh.—In the Evening I wrote to Grim & read loud 'Philosophy of Plan of Salvation'.

Mon. 1. March. . . . M. very poorly this morning. She however took a walk with me: we met Warter who told us that Lodge had not gone away till this morning, & that he had been prodigiously excited by that idiot of a Mrs Jarvis telling him that I had said to her 'that he was mad & that nobody ought to mind a word he said'. This annoyed me prodigiously & I wrote him a letter of the most indignant denial, stating 'that when Mrs Jarvis insisted to me on his having promised her a pension for life I said to her that she had no evidence to produce, no paper, no witness: that he had no recollection of it:—that words of kindness (even if he had uttered them) by a person in great suffering showed only the goodness of his own heart, but were in no ways binding:—that besides all this there was no use in applying to Mr L. as he had had the misfortune to lose his memory'.— I hope Mrs Jarvis is only an utter fool: if she has a spark of sense she is extremely wicked in saying such things to a most kind & generous master, as could not but give him the acutest pain & set him at variance with his best friend. I am sure she little deserved the £20 which I persuaded Lodge to give her,—not one farthing of wch would she have received but for me.— Dr Haviland's son Arthur has had the Typhus Fever at Eton, but is now out of danger. . .

Tu. 2. Carus's Birthday: Lucy sent him nothing, but she intends giving him a copy of Gunning's Poll as soon as she receives it:—M. & L. drank his health in a glass of Ale.—Congregation today for reading the Orators letter. It could not be expected that the partisan of Lord Powis would write any thing highly agreeable to the Prince: the letter accordingly is sufficiently cold, it dwells ungraciously on the unanimity of the Election of the D. of Northumberland, & bids the Prince look carefully after the interests of the Church. The 2d Cong. was at 1 that the V.C. & Mr Gunning might start by the 2 o'cl. train: they did so, without the Orator, who would have been a most unwilling & unwelcome actor. I was this morning roused from my

[31] Gunning had printed all the recent polls for important offices such as those for the Registrary (1832), Orator (1836), and Librarian (1845). By now he was almost eighty and failing in health so that help from his friends was indispensable. On 12 March Romilly worked into the early hours with a team making corrections for the press.

bed a little after 7 by the V.C's servant who came for a copy of the Orator's letter: he had injudiciously sent the copy intended for the V.C.to me with the copy which was to be my model for the engrossing for the Prince:— these two copies did not reach my house till late in the Evening & were not put in my hands when I came home. I got up with all speed & posted away to the V.C. who thought it would not be necessary to send (as is usual) a copy by the Post to the Chancellor Elect as the P. had been told by him yesterday that such an official Latin announcement of his Election was to be presented to him today. I then hurried off to my Clerk (whose vellum was all prepared, & who had been prepared by me to receive the Orators Letter yesterday afternoon) & bade him work steadily till it was done. He completed his task by 12. I then sealed it with the University S. on Wafer & deposited it in a box covered with blue morocco leather:— no silver box:— this is according to precedent. My rousing up today was at a more seasonable hour & on a more dignified occasion than that of a short time ago when I was waked up at 5 o'clock by the obstreperousness of a sweep who had come *uninvited* to our house.— I dined in Hall.— At 5½ the Vicechancellor & Gunning came to Buckingham Palace & were received by Lt. Col. the Hon. C.B. Phipps; The Prince not having expected them till 6 was not returned: in about ¼ an hour they were summoned to the Prince (who was attended by nobody but his Secretary Col. Phipps). The V.C. presented the Latin Letter to the Prince saying 'I have the Honor of presenting to your R.H. the Letter of the Senate announcing your R.H. Election as Chancellor':— the Prince took it in his hand, glanced his eye at it & said 'And here is my Answer':— both the V.C. & Mr G. exclaimed 'I hope it is favorable':— 'Oh yes, he exclaimed, I am highly gratified.' He conversed for about 10 minutes on the subject of Professors & their Pupils which he imagined to be on the footing of the German Universities:— he recognised Mr Gunning & spoke to him about his long tenure of office. The Prince did not sit down. The V.C. returned at night.— I today received answers from Col. Phipps & Sir C.G. Young concerning the Prince's Arms & Titles: Col. Phipps Letter was of use as being sealed with the Prince's Arms (without the Crest indeed), & Sir C.G. Young was kind enough to send me a French engraving of the Prince's Arms with all his titles:— this Coat of Arms looked very singular from the multiplicity of crests in a row: Sir C.G. Young however informed me that the central one alone was necessary. I set Roe the Engraver to work as soon as I got these Letters:— the Coat of Arms in Lodges Peerage of 1846 (wch he had begun copying) is altogether wrong, wrong supporters (Lodge makes them 2 Lions, instead of The English Royal Supporters), & wrong quarterings . . . Today wrote to Miss Lodge (concerning that vile Mrs. Jarvis).

Wed. 3. Cong.— No Graces— The Prince's Answer read:— it is not very enthusiastic, but his circumstances (as having refused to be a Candidate) are very peculiar: & I for one am quite satisfied:— not so

Mrs.Gamp[32] (i.e. Dr Archdall) who goes about grumbling & saying 'it is quite a rebuff.'—A few degrees viz lMD, 2MA, 1 LLB, 1 AB. The Orators letter (& an English Translation), & the Prince's answer of acceptance have been all printed.— Vide 'University Papers' — finished 'Siska Rosemael.'[33] At the suggestion of Dr. Graham (& with the V.C's approval) I today began drawing up an account of the last 3 Installations to send to the Prince. I also today left at Wiseman's a copy of my 'Graduati' to be bound in Red Morocco for the Prince's acceptance.

Thu. 4. Yesterday walk with M. between Congregations:—today also walk with M. altho the E. wind is very harsh. V.C's at 2 for Pitt Scholarship;[34] C.B. Scott elected.—All day drawing up account of 'Installations'. Forgot to say that last Monday I went again to Jones & had 2 teeth filed & mortared: I saw the Ether-inhaling apparatus: he has used it a few times, but never without the presence or at least the written consent of the person's Medical Adviser.[35]

Fri. 5. Finished the 'Installations': sent them off to Col. Phipps at Osborne House — Dr Haviland came today to see M: he prescribed for her a mustard plaister & some tonics: Lucy saw him & had a good deal of talk with him about her (M's) feeble dejected state.— Letter from Miss Butcher saying that her horrid complaint of the Cancer is returning & that she is recommended to go to the seaside:— wrote to her & sent her £5.— There is a subscription begun for a testimonial to Ch. Perry (Bp. elect of Melbourne in Australia Felix):— gave £3.3.— to it.— M. did not go out: nasty cold day. Bought a water-bottle for her feet.— Poor Gunning has dreadful afflictions to endure in his family:— his son Francis died mad, his son Frederick is confined in a Lunatic asylum, & now his only surviving daughter Mrs Elger (formerly Mrs Blackman, or some such name) shows very alarming & violent symptoms of insanity! She is much more calm since her Father's return from Town: her violence was during his absence:— she & one of the Miss Frank Gunnings are living with him at Newnham.—Mr Gunning

---

[32] The tipsy, umbrella-carrying, old midwife and nurse in Dickens's *Martin Chuzzlewit* (1843). *Mrs Gamp* was Archdall's nickname in the 'University Sweepstakes', a comic broadsheet by the brothers Andrew and Frederick Long, Fellows of King's. It assigns runners such as Whewell's *Rough Diamond*, Sedgwick's *Robin Goodfellow*, Hildyard's *Cantankerous*, Prince Albert's *The Chancellor*, and Powis's *First Fault*. The list is reprinted from the rare original in C. Whibley, *In Cap and Gown* (1889), pp. 216-17.

[33] I.e. Hendrik Conscience, *Siska van Roosemael* (1844), a novel in Flemish.

[34] A scholarship in honour of Pitt the younger, who at the time of his death was both High Steward and M.P. for the University, had been established in 1813, and awarded to an undergraduate every five or six years by examination in classics. It had to be vacated if he took an M.A. or obtained church preferment. See J.W. Clark, *Endowments of the University* (1904), pp. 307-9.

[35] Ether had been used as an anaesthetic in surgery with excellent results for less than six months. Unlike opium it had no after-effects.There are said to be more than a hundred references to it in *The Lancet* between January and June 1847, and W.S. Daniel, house pupil at Addenbrooke's, was one of many who invented an inhaling apparatus. By November when Margaret Romilly was dying in pain it was used to produce 'the magic effect'.

sent us today a most beautiful Camelia.— Dined at the Family at Shaws
. . . a great Capercailzy in the 2nd course: it did not taste of turpentine, &
that is all can be said in its praise. Phelps, Paget, Cartmell & I played whist
till near 2: lost moderately.

Mon. 15.   M. much the same but sadly languid—The weather has
become charmingly mild; so I took her out for a little walk in spite of the
wind. Called on Mr Gunning & sat some time with him. Today the
invitations arrived for the dinner at Buckingham Palace after the
Installation: the day is to be the 25th; the hour of the Installation 3, that of
the Dinner 7½. The invitations are sent by the Lord Steward: wrote to the
Lord Steward to accept for myself & to decline for Gunning. . .

Tu. 16.   Sent to Buckingham Palace for the Prince a copy of my
'Graduati' beautifully bound in Red Morocco by Wiseman with the
University arms on both covers (cost 14 shillings):— Gunning had his
'Ceremonies' bound to match.[36] I sent them in one parcel to Col. Phipps,
writing him 2 notes begging him to present the 2 Books in Gunning's name
& mine. — Lovely day: Walk with M. she was very lackadaisical &
complained much of fatigue . . .

Sat. 20.   Received yesterday from Buckingham Pal. a letter of Col.
Phipps conveying the Prince's *best thanks* for Gunning's Book & mine.
Short walk with M.—At 3 attended before the Grand Jury to give evidence
(concerning Proctorial powers by virtue of Charter of 3rd Eliz.)[37] in the
case of Brumell (Senior Proctor) & Newman (for rescuing a common
girl).— Dined in Hall.

Mon. 22.   Wrote to F.R. £10; to Madame F.R. £20. . . Today a most
disgusting trial for libel, Chafy & Lindsell: Chafy laid his damages at an
immense sum £20,000: he was defended by Thesiger; Lindsell by Kelly: I
did not go into Court: the evidence was of the most revolting nature:—
Chafy was nonsuited & can never show himself in society: crimen
infandum in propriam uxorem.[38]

Tu. 23.   Yesterday & today short walks with M: we made our first visit:
we called upon Mrs Bayne & Mrs Pryme who are living at the Servants
Training Establishment on Parker's Piece; it is called 'Park House'[39]
. . .

---

[36] Gunning's *The Ceremonies Observed in the Senate-House [etc.]* (1828), a revision of a book by
Adam Wall (1798), containing accounts of examinations, degrees, elections, preachers,
prizes, and scholarships with other miscellaneous material.
[37] I.e. the charter of 1561 allowing the University to seek out and punish lewd women.
[38] I.e. an unspeakable crime against his own wife. W.W. Chafy was son and heir of the late
Master of Sidney, and had married a daughter of a bishop by whom he had at this time
three young children. Neither the *Cambridge Chronicle* nor *The Times* would print the
allegation (based, it was claimed, on what the Chafys' servant and others had said), made
by Lindsell at a hunt meeting in February. See, however, *The Justice of the Peace* XI (1847),
352. Romilly's forecast was mistaken, for Chafy made two respectable marriages after the
death of his first wife.
[39] See 23 November 1843.

Wed. 24. The great National Fast in consequence of the Famine in Ireland.[40]— M. not well enough to venture to Church: she took a little walk with me however. L. & I to Trinity Church where Carus preached a most obnoxious political sermon (against the Maynooth grant[41] in particular & Romanism in general): His Text was Jer. XIV. 7.8.9:—Lucy gave £10.10—; M. £2 & I £1 only. Lucy disliked the sermon so much that she burnt her notes when she came home. . . The sermon was 67 mins! The offertory & the additional prayers made the service very long:—we did not get home till ¼ to 2. I should have said that I passed all the morning yesterday looking over Declamations for Carus.

Th. 25. Breakfasted at the Station at 7½. To Town by the 8.17 Train in company of Dr. Paget, Dr. Tatham, Hopkins, & Dr. Hodgson. Went to the Burlington Hotel in Cork St: I was amused by this unwieldy hotel made out of 4 houses: they were designated by letters A,B,C,D; I slept in the B. House or hive (as I called it)— I wrote out a list of the Deputation & enclosed it in a Letter to Col. Phipps which I took myself to the Palace: Cartmell & Shaw accompanied me in the Cab. At 2 we began to assemble: The Marq. Camden & the Members for the University joined us at the Hotel. We waited a little for Adams (the discoverer of the Planet Neptune) who was deputy of the Senior Proctor (as his Moderator) & who was late from a delay in the Train.— We did not form any procession but went in Carriages hired for the day by the V.C: The V.C. took me & Leapingwell & Hopkins in his carriage & the Patent & the Statutes: Elwood the University Marshall was on the Box.—Crouch & Johnson had been sent forward to the Palace: Johnson was to stand by when the cards were presented by the members of the Senate: Crouch preceded the 2 Esq. Bedells Leapingwell & Hopkins (Gunning was confined to his bed by his accident) in conducting the V.C. to the throneroom. By the way Elwood carried the Patent-Box & the Statutes etc & put them on the table wch was to the right of the Chair of State. The Throneroom was in this Fashion [small plan]: the Throne was railed in, & before it was placed a chair of State: a Folding door led to an adjoining room: the Prince when summoned by the Yeoman & 2 Bedells came thro a door D into this room accompanied by the V.C.— The V.C. & Proctors wore their caps till the V.C. made his speech & remained uncovered after that time. The V.C. sat down for an instant on the Chair of

40 It was fixed by proclamation for 'a grand fast and humiliation before Almighty God, in order to obtain pardon of our sins, and that we may, in the most devout and solemn manner, send up our prayers and supplications to the Divine Majesty for the removal of those heavy judgments which our manifold sins and provocations have most justly deserved, and with which Almighty God is pleased to visit the iniquities of this land, by a grievous scarcity and dearth of divers articles of sustenance and necessaries of life'. 'A Churchman' whose letter appeared in the *Cambridge Chronicle* (20 March) urged abstinence, putting off of jewelry, penitential prayers in the family, and avoidance of work by servants. Shops were closed and the streets quiet, although services were held by all the main denominations who made collections.

41 See 20 April 1845. Carus no doubt found in the famine God's retribution for the error of aiding Catholic education.

State: he made his arrangements very rapidly & the Prince made his appearance the moment he was summoned: he walked with his cap in his hand & had two trainbearers, Col. Bouverie & Capt. Seymour, holding up his train. He did *not* wear bands: he wore the robes of the D. of Wellington:[42] he wore the ribbon of the Garter & The insignia of the Fleece: he had buckles in his shoes. By the way he was on the point of sitting down in the Chair of State as soon as his train was dropped if the V.C. had not stopped him. The Prince stood by the Chair of State: the Proctors stood at P, the V.C. at V.C (with the Registrary on his left holding the Patent): The V.C. took his cap off & spoke an excellent address (for wch see 'Univ. Papers') beginning 'It is my duty to present to your R.H. the Letters Patent of the Office of Chancellor &c'; he spoke it in a calm clear voice without the least hesitation,—having committed it to memory perfectly.[43]— The Registrary then handed the Patent to Mr Kingsley the Junior Proctor who read it aloud having his colleague (Adams deputy of Brumell) standing by his side:— Adams ought properly to have read it: but he has some impediment in his speech.— The V.C. took the Patent when it had been read & handed it over to one of the Equerries:— by the way in the Patent I wrote Dux de Saxe & ought to have written Dux Saxoniae, as Col. Phipps afterwards (at the Prince's command) wrote to the V.C. The V.C. now handed the oathboard to the Prince & he took the Oaths of Allegiance and Supremacy, reading 'I Albert do &c': the oath of office was then administered: the V.C. presented to the Pr. a Copy of the Statutes (wch had been the D. of Glosters) & seated him in the Chair of State: whereupon the Bedells saluted by turning their maces with the broad end uppermost: the Prince put on his cap. The Orator now advanced & made his Latin speech, uncovered.— When this was concluded, the Prince rose took off his Cap & read his speech, which we all thought admirable.— The Prince did not put on his cap or sit down again: he now walked (with his train borne) accompanied by the V.C. but not preceded by the Bedells across the room to the Folding door, where he bowed to the company & retired:— as he walked along the V.C. introduced to the Prince the Members of the Deputation who were standing in the 1st row; I was one of them. The Prince shook hands with very few;— I observed only the Bp of Lincoln & the M. of Christs . . . We now came down to Luncheon in the Library: the Prince did not make his appearance: —a very handsome luncheon with abundance of Champagne. I saw a rich scene: a royal servant was helping a London Clergyman to Chicken & Champagne & said to him: 'I have a Pew in your Church, Sir': 'O' said the Pastor, 'I am sorry that I have not yet had time to call upon you— I will do so—pray how long have you had a Pew?'— 'Six years' said the Page in Scarlet. Poor Clericus was taken aback

---

42 Wellington was Chancellor of Oxford. The Cambridge robe was 'of black damask silk, very richly embroidered with gold. It is worn with a broad, rich lace band, and square velvet cap with a large gold tassel'.

43 Philpott's address and Albert's reply are in Cooper, IV, 685-7.

by the announcement of so long a period & stammered out 'Ah! In so large a parish as mine it takes a very long while to visit every body:— I am very much obliged to you & will take the earliest opportunity of calling!' — He dispatched his luncheon very rapidly & moved to another part of the room. The Yeoman Bedell & the 2 Esq. Bedells then preceded the V.C. to his Carriage: the V.C. took me & Hopkins & Dr Chapman (Leapingwell having preferred walking): The Bedells maces were taken by the Yeom. Bedell who remained behind at the Palace with the U. Marshall & School-Keeper (Elwood & Johnson)[44] & one man of each Proctor: These 5 had an excellent dinner at 4 at the Palace with plenty of wine.— I went to an Exhibition of Modern Artists at the Brit. Institution: it was very bad:—two pleasing pictures of Sant:— I then explored Westminster Bridge &c &c till dressing time. The Dean of Windsor (Master of Magd.) took me & Dr. French in his carriage to Buck. Pal. — We were very punctual to our time 7.30: but we found the D. of Wellington already in the Saloon (the Picture Gallery). The Prince was not there; the company arrived in a few minutes & at ¼ to 8 (or sooner) we were all seated at dinner. Besides the Deputation (consisting of V.C. & 13 other heads (all but the Provost, the President of Queens' & Sir H.J. Fust), the Orator, the Caput (Dr. Banks, Dr. Bond, Maddison (dep. for Prof. Corrie) & Reyner), the Proctors (Kingsley & Adams), the Scrutineers (Astley & Procter), 2 Bedells (Leapingwell & Hopkins), & the Registrary there were present the D. of Wellington, the M. of Exeter, the M. of Northampton, Lord W. Russell, the B. of London, the Members for the U. (Goulburn & Law), the Speaker of the H. of Commons, & part of the P's household (viz, Anson, Bouverie, Phipps, & Seymour). The company sat in the following order [plan of the seating]. The D. of Wellington was looking stouter & better than when he visited Cambridge some 6 years ago. Like most deaf persons he speaks loud: he made an appointment with the Prince for tomorrow to talk about the Field-Marsh's Batons. He told an amusing anecdote about his own Installation: 'You are not all of you expected to know Latin at Cambridge:— we are at Oxford. I had to make a Latin speech when I was installed:— I didn't write it tho':— I got Sir H. Halford to write it for me:— he couldn't keep the Secret however. He dined with me directly after the Installation & before the dinner was over every body knew he was the Author'. There were (I was told) 114 waxlights on the Table: the effect was very brilliant; & there was a profusion of Candles on the sideboard. The display of gilt vases & candelabra (each standing on a separate plateau) was very striking: all these plateaux touched each other & reached from one end of the table to the other: the vases were filled with hothouse flowers: the workmanship of them seemed to me very beautiful:—close to me was a representation of Venus in her Shell. — There was a Band playing during dinner: the musicians were unseen, being in a room above:— the effect was very

---

[44] I.e. custodian of the Old Schools.

pleasing, not loud enough to interfere with Conversation. I found my Neighbour Capt. Seymour very agreeable & conversible.— The waiting was perfect— Every dish is carried round, named & helped by the Servants:— for example; a servant brought me sponge cake with Apricot & said 'Brioche aux abricots': I answered 'if you please', & he helped me to a fitting portion. The great mass of the servants were in Royal Scarlet, some few in plain clothes, one in a jägers uniform, & one (the piper of the Palace) in a highland costume: I learned from Captain Seymour that sometimes he walks round the room piping, as a signal for the servants to retire:— he did not do so on this occasion. The Prince drank wine with no one: of course no person asked another.— I was not struck with the goodness of any thing but the Ice. I asked in a very humble way 'is it possible to have a glass of beer?' — Very soon after he came back with some beer in a short glass with a handle (much like a teacup).— This success of mine excited the envy of the Orator (when told of it afterwards), he having been cautioned against asking for his favorite beverage. — At this dinner Dr. Phelps (who had been out of sorts for some days & who had ventured on a glass of punch after the turtle soup) was taken ill: Dr. Bond (who was near him) beckoned to a Servant & they conducted him out of the room; he fainted away & when he came to himself went home to his hotel. The curious circumstance was, that all was managed so quietly that all of us who sat to the left of the Prince knew nothing of this event. — I believe if he had died every thing would have gone off as noiselessly: it would have been like the death of Ananias, 'the young men arose, wound him up, carried him out & buried him'.[45] After dinner there was a beautiful dessert, but I saw nobody touch it but myself; & I only ate a little cake from the dish opposite me in my fingers, leaving no trace on my plate of what I had done. No wine but Claret & Sherry was handed round after dinner, the Master of Caius (Dr.Chapman) of course could not hear the courtly whisper in wch the servant announced what he offered, & said 'Port if you please': — the servant went to the sideboard & brought him what he had asked.— We did not sit more than 20 minutes at the dessert, & the wine was handed round twice only. There were no toasts, no speeches, no 'God save the Queen' played.—The Prince rose & walked into the beautiful Picture Gallery wch was the Saloon on this occasion (— there are in it choice pictures of the Dutch School, viz. Cuyp, Wooverman, Metzu, Netcher, Teniers, Ostade, De Hooge, & Rembrandt;—also a pleasing Greuze, 2 large pictures of Sir Jos. Reynolds, & a Rubens:— There are also here statues of Canova:— The marble figures supporting the Chimney pieces are very beautiful):— the Prince was allowed a start of a minute and then we all followed: the Prince did not sit down: of course every body stood: Coffee was handed round & then liqueurs: I did not observe any tea. The Prince graciously addressed a few words to every one: he spoke at some length to Mr Adams & showed an

[45] See Acts V, 5-6

intimate acquaintance with the history of the discovery of the new Planet Neptune:— the D. of Wellington also spoke to Mr Adams & said 'I have heard a good deal about you & am glad to see you.— You didn't win in the Contest for the Chancellorship because you hadn't the same confidence in your cause that *we* had in ours.' I think this speech charming.— By the way the Prince spoke very kindly to the Master of St. Johns.—Of the Prince's guests 4 voted for the E. of Powis, viz.the Master of St Johns, the Orator, Adams, Reyner; Mr Law did not vote at all.— At 10 o'clock the Prince bowed to us & we all retired:—he went to the French Play to join the Queen.— The Master of Magd. took the Master of Jesus College & myself back to the Burlington, as he had also brought us. There was some little amusement in the announcement of the carriages:— The B. of London's was called as the *B. of Magdalene's,* & the Master of Trinity's as *Professor Weavell's.* — By the way Punch this week has a fling at Whewell headed 'Extraordinary Modesty', 'The Master of Trinity has said let who will be the next Bishop he shall be content.'[46]

Wed. 31.　　Lucy to the 8 o'cl. prayers.— I went at 11 to All Saints where Maddison read the Service. In the Free Seats was a ragged elderly man with a child of about 2 in his arms: I have seen him about the Streets: he does not beg: I have given him however & he does not refuse: today I gave him a groat on going out of the Church tho I suspect him of being a hypocrite & a humbug:— his little girl (almost as thinly & miserably clad as himself) seemed very happy playing with her doll all church-time:— the doll's body was a short hedge-stick, its head & drapery a filthy coarse cloth with a knot in it . . .

Good Friday 2 April.　　Betsy Edwards Sister Mary today dismissed from the Hospital (where she has been 16 days). Thank God Margaret today ventured to Church again after an interval of more than 3 months:— the last time she was at Church was on Christmas day. She & I went to St. Paul's (where we had the Purchas's pew to ourselves). Perry read prayers: Nicholson preached (stutteringly) a sermon (of some merit) on the Crucifixion. — Lucy went by herself to Trinity Church: a red-haired stranger read prayers, & Hopkins (in preaching attire!) was boxed up in the pew with her:— *her cough was so bad that she came away in the middle of the prayers!* That treacherous Carus had said last Sunday from the Pulpit 'that if his life was spared he would preach to them next Friday & Sunday':— he has left Cambr. & does not return till next Wednesday:—base man! In the Evening I read loud his life of Simeon, a copy of wch he sent (with a note) to

[46]　Whewell was a constant butt of the magazine, now tainted further by his association with Albert's election.

Margaret last Tuesday. Lucy & I had expected copies— but none have come for us yet.[47]

Easter Sunday 4 April. I was required at Trinity Chapel where Cooper preached an excellent sermon from Joh. XIV. 19 "because I live ye shall live": he & Mathison & I assisted the Master in the Sacrament . . . Lucy had today the excitement of well frightening a little boy (named Miller, son of butler of C.C.) for having thrown a stone & hit a little girl of about 3 in the face: she threatened to take him to the Station House.

Sat. 10. Carus wrote to L. to ask her whether the copy of Mr Simeons life (which he had sent *with a note to Miss Romilly*) ought not in her opinion to have been given to me: — I think he had promised Lucy very distinctly & that he ought certainly to have given her a copy whatever he did to me.— It would not have ruined him if he had given each of us a copy:— 'Thrift, good Horatio, thrift'! . . .

Tu. 13. . . .yesterday Lucy had a note from Carus saying she was to have the 1st copy of the 2nd Edition of Mr S's Life. — He paid me a long visit to tell me of the different people who have written to him: he seems most pleased with Sedgwicks & Sir R. Simeon's; the former gives a very favorable & eloquent criticism of the work, & the 2nd states 'that the nice points of family matters have been nicely rounded off.' Carus has written my name in the copy sent up to the house (which indeed was sent back to him for that very purpose).— Dined in Hall. In the Evening began reading loud Peveril of the Peak.[48]

Mon. 19. Last Saturday Lucy took one of her hospital protégés to a slopshop[49] where she rigged him out in a smock-frock & waistcoat:— she was by the mistress of the shop taken for the pauper's mother!!! The boy's name was W. Raby: his leg was taken off in the hospital. . .

Tu. 20. Yesterday wrote to F.R. £10.— To Jones's: had a tooth out:—of course I did not take the Aether:—a woman the other day valued herself upon her courage, & said 'I am come to have my tooth out *with all my feelings.'* Dined in hall: a pious Scholar in the Grace said 'Amen', at wch Thompson behaved very indecorously, for he turned completely round as if to conceal a burst of laughter. In the Evening read loud 'Peveril of the Peak'.—Lady Godolphin dead.[50]

Th. 22. Wedding cards from Mr. & Mrs. Benjamin Webb: she was Maria Mill; he was Dr Mill's Curate at Brasted: he is as high-church as his

---

47 Both editions of Carus's long biography are dated 1847. He had asked for a candid opinion of it 'rather late' when the first edition was at press: 'I think he has mixt up his 'pieces justificatives' with the text. . . all account of ecstatic religious feeling should have been omitted'(4 September 1846). The work was also published in America where it was reprinted several times in an abridged version.

48 Sir Walter Scott, *Peveril of the Peak* (1823) .

49 I.e. a shop selling cheap, ready-made clothes.

50 Elizabeth, wife of Francis, first baron Godolphin, High Steward of Cambridge town and M.P. for the shire in seven parliaments, had died at the family mansion at Gogmagog Hills on the seventeenth.

Rector: he used at College to be called 'Blessed Benjamin': his dress was very peculiar & intended to designate ultra-highchurchism. They now are neighbours of George Allen, living at 3 Park Village East. . . Walk with M:— by the way (in spite of the wind being easterly) the weather has been charming this week. Henslow, Bateson, Atlay (successor of Bateson in Madingley living), & I over together to dine with Lady Cotton. . . Sir St. V. gave a rich account of his pursuit of the Tarrants when they came poaching on his grounds: he was on his pony & Tarrant on foot: — Tarrant crossed the river at the sluice on Jesus Common & turned back to recover his dog wch fell into the water: Sir St. V. was much disposed to forgive him for the gallantry of that action. He had followed Tarrant for hours in heavy rain to run him to his home, having no doubt of his identity tho unable to swear to him.

Sat. 24.   Took a walk with M. to see the pretty houses (with gables) built near the Union (in Mill Lane)[51]for the Railway Porters. In the Evening read loud Mr Simeon's life.

Sun. 25.   . . . Called on Gunning: he is decidedly better: he was lying on a fracture bed.— Lucy received from Mrs Beardmore a letter in praise of the piety & general goodness of Frances Wilderspin:— she wrote to her in reply.—Yesterday my Gardener's son Josua [sic] Barker was pleased to run away from his place (— he was servant to Mr Fendall at Harlton) on account of the sulkiness of the housemaid, & is supposed to have enlisted!— must be mad. . .

Mon. 26.   Hung up in our dining room an Engraving of Mr Simeon wch we have had framed: Carus gave the Print to Lucy . . .

Tu. 27.   . . . Bought 2 sixpenny pincushions of Fanny Henslow: she & her sisters & her Aunts have made 4000!!! for the benefit of the Irish . . .

Th. 29.   A day to be marked with a black stone; Lucy's pet jackdaw disappeared,— stolen beyond all doubt . . .

Wed. 5 May.   Lucy called on a Mr Cooke (Inspector of Schools) concerning putting a young girl of the name of Tyler into the Training School to become a Schoolmistress. the negotiation failed: & she thought Mr Cooke far from polite. — Sedgwick to Town to see P. Albert who has appointed him his Camb. Secretary.[52] Congregation: 1 Hon M.A, 6 M.A, 7 B.A.— Grace for Syndics to increase the Univ. Income so as to make public works for the use & honor of the University:—opposed by Collison & 5 others; carried 15 to 6. . . Letter from Miss Lodge announcing her marriage for the 15th; also one from Edward Allen *acknowledging an*

[51] An error for Mill Road.
[52] The invitation was made by Col. Phipps on 6 April and accepted at once. Sedgwick was to keep Albert informed of local affairs, answer his questions, and occasionally write letters in his name. Winstanley (p. 200) reckoned the duties 'few and unimportant', but another opinion is that they were more than Sedgwick had expected and interfered with his scientific work (see Clark & Hughes, II, 120).

engagement with Miss Bertha. —Wrote to them. Had a visit from Miss Apthorp. Walk with M. between Congregations.— Thunder today.— M. & I called on Mrs Clark & saw her prize plants.— Declined drinking tea with Mrs. Prest to meet Lady Wale & the Skrines. — Read 'Lovell'.[53]

Th. 6. To the 'Cambridge University Musical Society's' Concert in the Town Hall. . . The room was immensely full. Mr. Dykes conducted: he & Mr Martin (Joh) &c sang: the best part of the performance I thought an overture of Kalliwoda & the 12th Symph. of Haydn. The drums & cymbals were to my ears harsh & loud:— the piano parts I thought good:— the singing poor stuff.[54]

Sat. 8. Complete wet day— M. not out.— Lucy (in spite of the rain) went to Mr Brewsters to get physic for the Cat who is apparently dying: she stood up at different places, but got sadly wet . . .

Mon. 10. Walk with M.— Dined with Cartmell to meet Sedgwick, J.G. Blunt, Packe, Peacock & Shaw: the object was to talk about Lefevre as a Candidate for the University. Sedgwick told us a good story of the rude eloquence of a ranter preaching at Liverpool on the Prodigal Son: 'but you will say 'how does this apply to us? we don't feed swine';— What? When your shipmate says 'd— Jack come & drink' & you go & drink till you are beastly drunk—I tell you, you feed swine:— or when a trull asks you to go with her & you do—I tell you, you feed swine.'— Sedgwick rather shocked me by telling this before the bedmaker . . .

Th. 13. Holy Thursday.— Poor Puss died today. Lucy had taken great trouble about her favourite for the last week & had consulted Mr Brewster about her: an old nurse at our neighbours Mrs Helms made herself useful in administering physic to Grimalkin, whom she treated as resolutely & skilfully as if she had been a child:— however neither care nor skill availed: her time was come. . . About 8 o'cl. in the Evening great alarm was excited by the breaking out of a fire in the Kitchen chimney which burnt fiercely for a time & threatened destruction to the Combination room & to Nevilles Court:— most happily there was little or no wind, there was abundant supply of water, & the young men worked admirably (as they always do on such occasions): so that the danger was over at 10 o'cl.— The consternation was very great:— Mr. Smith in a panic terror removed his boxes &c to my rooms where he contrived to break 4 glasses in my study: my bedmaker &c were in such a state of alarm that I gave them wine to keep up their spirits. My young men of course left my rooms & made themselves useful:— Mrs Tooke was very anxious about the safety of her husband, who was very energetic, climbing at top of the roof:— he contrived to tear his breeches, but suffered no other damage.

---

[53] J.S. Knowles, *George Lovell, a novel* (1847).

[54] In March 1845 F.H. Bowring reported to his aunts that this young society 'flourishes extraordinarily'. It 'wholly consists of Univ. men, and is looked on with great favor, as admission is given by Members' Tickets, and no one pays anything' (John Rylands Library, Manchester, MS. 1231). See also F. Knight, *Cambridge Music* (1980), pp. 65-73.

Fri. 14. The V.M. (Sedgwick) called a Seniority in wch we passed a resolution of thanks to the Town & Gown for their services last night.— Sedgwick also printed in the Newspaper a spirited account of the Fire.[55]— Two of our Combination Pictures (D. of Glost. & M. Camden) had holes poked in them in the Confusion of taking them down. . .

Sat. 15. Dan. O'Connell died this day at Genoa.[56] — Felt shaky & ill— Declined Peacock's invitation to Ely for today and tomorrow. Visit from Cannon (Proprietor of Advertiser); he made a wonderful proposition of contributing a large annual percentage (15 p.c.) of his profits (about 3 or £400 p.a.) towards a fund for University Buildings if the University would aid him in obtaining subscribers for his paper (viz. 3000): he wished me to become treasurer!!!! I received him very civilly but most decidedly refused his proposal on my own part & that of the University. [57]— I paid Carus a visit: he has an inflammation in the throat:— he told me a good story of himself & the B. of Winchester going last week to Mrs. Stevens house in town to look at a picture of Mr. Simeon:— they hunted all over the house in vain till at last the house keeper took them into a *Cockloft servants bedroom* where they found pictures of Mr. Simeon & Mrs. Dornford:— 'O. said the old lady, those are pictures of Mistresses *Grandfather* & Grandmother.'[58]— Ate no dinner today.— Having promised Mrs. Prest to play a rubber I went to her house for a short time: left at 9½, slept in College & took physic.— Read loud Arabian Nights to M.

Sun. 16. Wrote Lucy an Elegy of 42 lines upon her poor Cat . . .

Tu. 18. Walk up Hills Road with M.—at the bridge they are making a cattle & sheep pen . . .

[55] The letter appeared in the *Cambridge Chronicle* and referred to 'zealous and effectual assistance in extinguishing the fire. . . which, without such aid and the blessing of Almighty God, would inevitably have caused the destruction of a large portion of the College. I wish to write with no formality: formal language would ill accord with feelings of my brother Fellows in whose behalf I now write. We wish to use the words of heartfelt gratitude. . .'. The damage was estimated at £300.

[56] O'Connell died on his way to Rome aged 71. His life had been spent in a futile attempt to have the Union repealed by legal and consitutional means. He had made a final appearance in the Commons three months before to tell members 'Ireland is in your hands, in your power. If you do not save her she cannot save herself', and to predict that a quarter of her population might perish.

[57] *The Cambridge Advertiser and Free Press,* of broadly liberal sympathies, had been started in 1839, the latter part of its title being changed to *'and University Herald'* when W.J. Cannon became editor in 1846. This bid to increase circulation and others (such as frequent 'free' supplements) failed to attract the entrenched readership of *The Cambridge Independent Press* (Liberal) and *The Cambridge Chronicle* (Conservative). By 1848 it seems that Cannon had entered into an arrangement to put 15 per cent of the profits on subscriptions in the hands of J.J. Smith of Caius for the restoration of Ely Cathedral and the completion of University buildings. But *The Advertiser* never had more than 15 per cent of the market and finally closed in 1850. See M.J. Murphy, *Cambridge Newspapers and Opinion 1780-1850* (1977).

[58] The point of the anecdote seems to be that Charles Simeon was never married. Sumner, Bishop of Winchester, may have become involved in this search with Carus because his son had married one of Simeon's great-nieces.

Wed. 19. Congregation — 2 Mand D.D[59] (Bps Perry & Tyrell), 1 Hon. D D (Bp Eden). . . Such an event as 3 Bishops taking their deg the same day is unparallelled.— A fight about Graces.— Eyres Gr. (for Fitzwilliam Museum for a ballroom)[60] thrown out unanimously in the Caput: the Gr. for Voluntary Contribution to Police was thrown out in B.H. by 35 to 31:[61]— the Grace for hanging up the Pictures &c in the Fitzw. thrown out in W.H. by 13 to 11; this last had also been opposed in B.H., but there passed 12 to 2. The throwing out this Grace was mere childish pique because Fitzw. M. was refused for Ball. — Walk with M. between Congregations— Dined in Hall & went up into Comb. Room.— Sedgwick had today to do his 1st duty as Chanc's Secretary in sending off 2 Petitions & Letters for Mandates (of the V.C. & Professor Maine): I superintended the drawing up the Letters & would not part with him till I had the packet, wch I myself deposited in the Post:— by the way poor Barsham the Postmaster is dead. . .

Th. 20. . . . M, L & I started for shopping (to buy bedroom carpets, gowns &c): the rain caught us & we took refuge at Mrs Brookers, when we met the shy Miss Daguilar.— L. left us & went to her paupers.— M. & I performed our shopping: she bought a beautiful bedroom carpet. I treated her & M. with Scotch Muslin gowns at the small price of 12s each. . .

Tu. 25. Farewell visit from Dr & Mrs Perry . . . Perry gave each of us a little book of devotion wch he has written called 'A parting token:' he also gave the maids each one: they did not see Theodosia (because she thought herself not fit to be seen), but took a very pious leave of Betsy who told them 'that she hoped she should meet them in Heaven.' . . .

Fri. 28. Called on Dr Haviland to talk about M.— he thinks possibly there may be a peritoneal & wishes to see her in bed tomorrow morning at 8: he thinks with me that the seaside might do her good, — but unhappily she is most unwilling to stir, & I almost despair of being able to induce her to go to Brighton (the place wch he recommends).— Phelps, Packe, Cartmell, Shaw, Warter & I went in the same Railway carriage (by the 3.43 train) to dine with The Dean of Ely.— We went to the Cathedral where we heard a good service & were imprisoned by a storm of thunder & lightning & rain. At dinner we were a party of 9 by the addition of Mr. Millers the minor canon (who has just succeeded to a fortune of £5000 a year by the death of his niece) & Stuart. — In the Evening we smoked a Cigar & came into coffee a little after 9 leaving Shaw smoking. We became alarmed by his nonappearance at 10, & he was then brought back by a man who had picked him up: he had gone out of the Deanery grounds, his foot had

---

[59] See 26 Oct 1843.
[60] Cf. *R.C.D. 1832-42* p. 213 and 5 and 6 July 1842.
[61] Although after its creation in 1836 the borough force inevitably came into conflict with the Proctors, who had an ancient authority over members of the University, at times of public disorder each side had to call on the other. The main points of the report behind the rejected Grace are printed by Cooper, pp. 687-8. Whether and how the University should help pay for civilian policing remained a contentious issue for many years.

tripped against a stone & he had had a heavy fall: there was a frightful swelling on his cheek & he seemed very confused. Our fly was at the door to take us to the Station; so we all 6 got into it & returned to C. by the 10.25 Fish-train to wch The Directors kindly attached a carriage for our special use. . .

Sat. 29. Dr. Hav. saw M. this morning in bed:— found no enlargement corresponding to peritoneal inflammation.— I called on him & had a great deal of talk about her:— he confesses that he cannot discover what is the matter with her:— he thinks that the pains are sympathetic pains & that the organ affected is probably the brain.—Found Shaw going on well: leeches applied to his face this morning . . .

Mon. 31. Dr. Haviland called on M. & strongly advised her going to Brighton,— to wch to my delight she has consented.— Meeting at Cartmell's concerning Lefevre's coming forward for the University: nobody there but Sedgwick, Peacock, & I. Whist Club at Mills':— the last of the Term: a small party of 7.

Romilly left on 4 June to conduct his sisters and Betsy to Brighton. He travelled back and forth throughout the month, and was in Cambridge, busily preparing for Prince Albert's installation, when they returned on 2 July.[62]

Mon. 5. July . . .I began Work at 6 & had one continuous tide of people from that hour till 11 without being able to get a moment for my breakfast— I then swallowed a cup of cold coffee & rushed to the S.H.— Degrees 38 MA, 1DD, 9 AM passed in the morning.— A little before 2 arrived the D. of Wellington at the Station (wrapped up in a blowze): Maddison got into a carriage with him & escorted him to Cath. Lodge (where he & Ld J. Russell are to be guests). Shortly after 2 the Queen & Prince arrived in Trin. Court. I was with the V.C. & Heads & the foreign Princes &c &c in the Hall of the Lodge to receive the Queen. She was leaning on The Prince's right arm: she offered her hand to 2 foreign princes who knelt & kissed it. She & the P. went upstairs immediately. In about 20 minutes the Prince came down in his Chancellors robes *with bands on* having his *train borne* by 2 attendants: he asked one of the officers if the Q. were gone & having learned that she was he walked out of the Lodge followed by the V.C. to the College Hall.— He read The Address extremely well from a copy wch he held in his hand, I standing by with the original. The Queen stood the whole time: there was no canopy for her this time. She read her answer in a very clear harmonious voice: but neither Her Majesty nor the P. were heard in the Gallery.[63]— The Prince asked me who should

---

[62] Romilly's account of the royal visit is complemented as in 1843 by his formal record printed in *Victoria and Albert in Cambridge* (1977). The local papers gave minute details and the *Illustrated London News* devoted two issues (10 and 17 July) to woodcuts of the grander events.

[63] Albert's address as Vice-Chancellor to the queen and her reply are in Cooper, IV, 689-90.

kiss hands; I said 'the V.C.'— The Prince of course did not kiss hands: I called the names as usual; the persons called came up very badly, so I had to pass on to others: they came & stationed themselves near me & I called all such over again: the Q. offered her hand not to the V.C. alone, but to all the Deputation, wch was an honor that nobody (not even the V.C.) enjoyed in 1843:— One Head (Qu. Dr. Graham?) had his gloves on: that moon-struck Jun. Proctor Kingsley kept tugging to get his glove off while the Q. was holding out her hand, & Field (the Deputy Esq. Bed. in the room of Gunning) never answered my call.— Last of all I had the honor of kissing the Q's hand.—The Procession in the Court was a complete failure:— no attempt had been made till the last moment at marshalling it: & all was confusion & crowding.— Before the Prince & Deputation came into the Hall the Queen had taken her place upon the dais: she found Lady Hardwicke (with one of her little boys) there & embraced her very cordially: the Countess gave her a great nosegay.— Lucy was in the Gallery & saw every thing capitally:— ices &c were given to the company then. — At 3 o'clock the Prince went to the Senatehouse to confer degrees: a Table was placed for the Chancellor on the Left of the seats for the Q. & himself. —I had the greatest difficulty in forcing my way thro' the dense crowd in the Pit:— I ought to have gone up the Platform entrance. I had no table, but rested my books on the edge of the balustrade by the Proctors, & so took the signatures for Matr. & Deg.—: the Proctors were at their table *below* close under the platform.— The Q. arrived shortly after 3 & the Prince walked down the S.H. to escort her:— it had been thought that she would enter by the platform door, but she bravely encountered the crowd: she was received with rapturous applause, as the Prince had been shortly before. The Orators Speech was insufferably long (an hour!) & the Q. & every body else was sick to death of it: coughing & hissing were resorted to.— The Prince admitted 19 degrees viz: D. of S. Weimar, Prince Waldemar of Prussia, Prince Peter of Oldenburg, Van de Weyer (Belgian Minister), Prince Löwenstein, M. Abercorn, E. Fortescue, E. Spencer, Hon C.E. Law, Hon H. Packenham DD (Dean of St. Patrick's), Sir Geo. Grey, Sir Harry Smith, Sir R.I. Murchison, the Bishops of Oxford, Antigua, Cape Town & Tasmania, Professors Ehrenberg & Von Mohl.— Of these 19, Lords Abercorn & Spencer, Mr Law, D. of St. Pat, Sir H. Smith & Sir R. I. Murchison were real degrees.[64] The Prince held the Colonial Bishops very cheap & said 'they had no rank'. — Immediately after these 19 degrees The Q. & P. left [with] the V.C. — Dr Hodgson then acted as V.C. & admitted the ordinary degrees. At 6½ the Q. &c dined with the V.C. at Cath. Lodge: party

---

[64] I.e. full degrees as distinct from mere titles of degrees, holders of the latter not being members of the University.

of 62: The Q. &c went to the Concert in the S.H. to hear Alboni &c:[65] Jenny Lind was not allowed to sing here.— I dined in Trin. Hall at 6 where Sedgwick presided: he made 2 capital short speeches in giving the Health of the Q. & the P.— A capital party: the Hall quite full; *no Ladies* however, as there were in the halls of many of the Colleges.— I sat by Carus & Lord Wrio. Russell (Carus's Guest in Coll.) who has brought his two boys to the Festivity. Sir Harry Smith, Le Verrier &c were in Hall. [66] Today besides the Honor of kissing the Q's hand I had a long conversation with the D. of Wellington & was introduced to Le Verrier & Sir H. Smith. — The Q. had wished to knight Adams, but he modestly declined. — At 8 I went to my room & distributed tickets till bed time.

Tu. 6. Up at 6 giving tickets & Certificates till 10½ — Dog-tired — Showed my nose in the S.H. for a minute & heard a few notes of the Installation Ode:[67]— the heat insufferable:— the singing at the end of G. save the Q.(in wch the Prince & all the assembly joined Chorus) said to have been very fine:— I should like to have heard it. By the way one of Lord Wrio's boys fainted in the S.H. today.— Took Lucy & Frances to see the Fitzwilliam Museum (the scaffolding &c all removed): it looked beautiful. Then took them to see the cooking &c in our kitchen & larder, & also the superb Gold Plate from Storr & Mortimer for our banquet today. This was a most brilliant sight. — I then showed them the preparations in hall, & afterwards took them into the Great Combination Room where Lunch was going on, & got them to eat something & drink a glass of wine. I here introduced L. to H.V. Elliott who was most kind to her & introduced us to

[65] Among the other performers were Luigi Lablache, the Queen's singing master, and the young Joachim who performed Mendelssohn's violin concerto. The programme included two pieces by the conductor Professor Walmisley, popular arias by Rossini, Mozart, and Donizetti, overtures by Beethoven and Weber, and other favourites. Tickets were priced at 15 shillings and a guinea, and all profits were to go to Addenbrooke's hospital.

[66] An unpublished letter by Mrs Challis dated 23 July tells how Prince Albert invited himself at very short notice to the Observatory. She and Challis left the banquet and drove home where, as the servants had gone off to see the fireworks, they had to make the place ready and light the rooms, and 'just as the carriage drove up everything was ready and Professor with gown on and cap in his hand was upon the steps to receive his Royal visitor and conduct him to the dome where he had the opportunity of seeing all the objects of interest that could be viewed through the large Telescope. The Prince appeared much pleased, made some very sensible remarks and asked some very sensible questions'. She continues with a lively account of Tuesday's events (to which she wore an 'Albert blue' gown), and of a large party who were entertained at the Observatory on Wednesday evening (Observatory Archives:Letters,1847/72).

[67] It is supposed that the ode was largely 'ghosted' for the Poet Laureate, Wordsworth, by his son-in-law. Tennyson had declined when invited by Whewell to compose one. *The Cambridge Chronicle* (10 July) describes how it sounded set to music, and *The Cambridge Advertiser* (Supplement of 14 July) gives a highly technical assessment. Certainly the performance cost enough, almost half (£400) of the total cost to the University chest of the entire installation. Such was the heat and crush that the performance was punctuated by cries of 'air, air', as several gentlemen were got out before they fainted. The largest expenses incurred by the town were £73 for fireworks and £60 for Green's balloon which carried him as far as Bottisham.

one of his St. Mary Hall young ladies.[68] — I then deposited L. & Frances in my rooms: presently up came Mrs. Smyth & her friend Mr. Hewham (who is going to India with B. Perry): I enticed them in & gave them wine & biscuits: I left them there looking out for the Queens departure to the Horticultural Show in Downing.— I went to the Horticultural: thousands of people there: weather most sultry. Lord Hardwicke clumsily tore the Q's dress with his spurs, & a Farmer touched her gown & went about boasting 'I've touched her'. H.V. Elliott said of Ld H's accident 'he should not have expected such an attack of the Town on the Gown'. The Grand Banquet in Trin. Coll. Hall at 6½. I had originally been marked down for a place at the Royal Table, but the Court struck out Sedgwick's name & mine:—It was however stated that S. as V. Master had a fixt place & the Court allowed him to remain: by the way he had most cheerfully acceded to the sentence of exclusion.— I had as good a place as possible for seeing the Queen, being President of the central table [Seating plan]. There was a military band in the Gallery: I thought the noise too great. — The Master (standing between the Q & P) with Sedgwick read the long Grace: 2 Scholars read it after dinner:— no singing— Poor Mrs. Willis was taken ill at the beginning of dinner & was taken home. The Master gave (by the Q's gracious permission) 2 toasts, the Q & the Prince. These toasts were received with reiterated shouts, Ld Hardwicke setting the example of hurraing at the top of his lungs. The Master gave these toasts well & briefly. 'By the gracious permission of Her Majesty who is present I am allowed to propose a Toast— The Queen,— we daily pray for her in this building— God bless her!' — Similarly for the Prince. In one newspaper the toast was spoiled by saying 'we daily *drink her health.'* — Directly after the Prince's health the Q &c left the hall, & every body else went out immediately after.— What was to be done with the ladies who in ½ hour were to be presented at the Queen's *'reception'* (as it is called in the announcement)? Carus kindly threw open his rooms for them.— My excellent friend J.E. Blunt was as near as possible not dining at this Banquet, wch would have been sadly wrong: he was only asked near the last moment.— The programme for presentations this Evening had mentioned Professors & their wives but had omitted *Drs:* the Doctors sent a Petition to the Prince & the Q. commanded their presentation. The presentation lasted above 1½ hour: the Mayor & The Mover & Seconder of the Town Address were presented: Lefevre *not* presented.

Wed. 7. Went to the Prince's Levee at 9 this morning: here I had the great & unexpected honor of shaking hands with the Prince. Took Lucy & Frances to see the Queen go to the Breakf. in the grounds of Trin. & St Johns: at the entrance of the Skreens of Trin. I (having my own ticket in my hand, Lucy holding my arm, & Frances following behind) said 'may these persons with me who have no tickets pass thro just to see the Queen?':— we

---

[68] See September 1-8 1843 (link passage).

were immediately allowed to go through. I placed them at the foot of the flight of steps close to the balustrade: they saw the Queen famously (who came thro the Hall): they afterwards walked with me all over the grounds & saw every thing & every body, but they touched no breakfast;— I afterwards sent £2.12— to Addenbr. Hospital as a compensation for the tickets they ought to have had . . . I introduced Lucy to B. of Norwich, Dr Scoresby, Lady Alderson &c. We had a good deal of conversation with Dr. Scoresby, the Miss Macgregors, Assad Yussuf Kayatt (the Syrian) &c. Lucy was highly pleased with renewing her acquaintance with the Syrian: he introduced us to his 'Lady' as he called her: she is very fair and very fat & he fed her very carefully like a kind husband; he invited Lucy to spend a year with him in Syria; he told us that his son was like his Godfather (Carus) 'always flourishing':— he repeated to us all his long string of names; the 1st of them is Abib, wch he told us was the Syrian for Carus. A few drops of rain made us all crowd into the Cloisters.— The Queen left the Breakfast a little after 2. Lucy & Frances & I came away directly after.— I deposited L. & Fra. at Mrs. Smyth's, & directly after their arrival (10' before 3) the Queen came driving by for her final departure.— With the Queen went the glorious weather, for a sharp rain now began falling. — Bateson very cleverly published a notice 'the navigation of the River will be stopped *by order* on Wednesday' & he moved barges at Clare H. & St. Johns & so prevented an inroad of people without tickets from boats:— the *order* was his own. The Conservators[69] would not venture. . .

Fri. 9. Cong. —dismissal of term. To Senate House fitting Syndicate: voted £50 extra for expenses of singers in the Ode who had to come down on Mond. night because the trains would not bring them in time on Tuesday:— £400! for performance of the Ode!— Worked Degree Lists &c & corrected Newspapers. Sent Le Verrier a list of the passed & plucked for 10 years. Showed the V.C. Whewell's protest against the V.C. having summoned the Heads to meet the Q. at his Lodge:— The V.C. said 'silly man'.— W.W. had also sent a protest to Buckingham Pal. against his Lodge being considered as the Queen's house.[70] By the way the Queen brought with her this time wax candles & gold & silver plate for her breakf. & lunch.— I declined dining at Pampisford today:— also declined going to Bp of Hereford.

Sat. 10. M. not out today.— Wrote to Dr Haviland (who this morning has left for Cromer) concerning a consultation with Ficklin—Lucy & I & Fra. to see the Sen. H: it was ½ pulled to pieces. . . Lucy's bill for Carus's Sunday Sch. children seeing the Q. (on a stand in St. Marys Churchyard) & eating buns &c after her Departure came to £4 7 8 . . .

---

[69] The body empowered to maintain and regulate the river.
[70] See 3 Nov 1843. On 14 July 1847 Romilly had written to Whewell about the visits of Charles I. The Master was firmly on this hobby-horse.

Th. 15. The V.C. has received a Gold inkstand from P. Albert (with the date 6 July), the Prince's name & H. Philpott: no complimentary language engraved, but a very agreeable accompanying letter.— Walk with M. on London road. Received from Mr Brown (the Mayor) a copy of his *Royal* No. of the Camb. Chr. (he printed only 6) & also from Mr Hudson the Bill of Fare at the Royal Table in Cath. Hall (July 5) printed on purple satin.

Fri. 16. This new volume of my life begins, alas, with a continuance of the same feeble state in dear M's health: she does not seem to make any advance whatever in strength & spirits . . .

Mon. 19. Subpoena'd to attend in Court in the Prosecution of Newman for rescuing a Prostitute from the Proctor Brumell:— He pleaded guilty & was bound over in £200 to appear & receive his Sentence when called upon:— if he behaves well he is to hear no more of the business. I was in Court 4 hours before this cause came on!— Dined with the Judge at 7 o'cl: . . . When I came home a little after 10 found that Frances had been much frightened by a man (she says a great fellow) coming into the kitchen not long after 9, & blowing her candle out: on her screaming & Betsy running in the man ran off:— whether an evil-disposed person or some playful frolicsome admirer of Betsy's does not satisfactorily appear:— nothing stolen.

Wed. 21. Miss Apthorp paid a very long visit to M. & tired her exceedingly: she also left money for M. to pay her servants for the next 12 weeks, week by week. — I called on Miss Apthorp & returned her the money, telling her that the commission was too much for her in her present sad state of health.— Poor Miss Apthorp was in a very excited frame of mind about a certain trust that she cannot get Harris (the Attorney) &c to arrange:— I called at Mr. Harris's office & requested his partner (for he was not at home) to call on Miss A. this very Evening.— Walked with M. in the Evening. I dined in Hall.

Mon. 26. . . . The Hon. Rob. Ch. Winthrop (member of Congress for Boston) brought me a letter from my friend James Savage of Boston: he was accompanied by his son (a lad of 12½, very nearsighted). Mr. Winthrop is a tall, somewhat gaunt, man of about 36. He seems to know every body of consequence in England:— he is a well informed conversible man. I lionised him & his son till 1 o'clock: they then had lunch in my rooms & returned to Town by the 2 o'cl. train[71] . . .

On 27 July Romilly arrived at Park Village West, the home of George Allen where there was a small family gathering including Miss Emma Allen, Mrs Hensleigh Wedgwood, and John Allen the son of Mr Allen of Cresselly, who stood as

[71] See 12 July 1842. Savage, the Harvard antiquary, spent many years investigating the genealogy of New England settlers, a project for which knowledge of Cambridge records and rapport with the Registrary were essential. In old age Winthrop published privately *Reminiscences of Foreign Travel* (1894), a dull catalogue of the celebrities he had met on this first visit.

godfather when Romilly christened his first great nephew, John Romilly Allen, the next day. Fond as he was of George, the diarist confided to his journal 'I looked over all his drawing-room chairs & thought them dear & not to my taste'.

Th. 29. 1st day of University Election. Polling is to be from 10 A.M. to 5 P M & from 8 to 9 in the Evening. The Contest is to last 5 days. At 5 o'clock the numbers were Law 522, Feilding 423, Goulburn 296, Lefevre 215. Total 782. Dined in College Hall at 5½: a very large party (altho the Bachelors, Undergr. & Sizars dined at 4). John Brown presided at the V. Masters table & I at the Deans.— My cousin Peter Ouvry was there & I took in for him his friend (Buck of Magd.) who was a brother Curate at Paddington.— At 8 the polling began again: it closed at 9: the numbers then were, Law 583, 466 Feilding, Goulburn 347, Lefevre 248, Total votes 880.— Today Dr. Haviland brought Ficklin to see M. They took a great deal of pains: they found her much emaciated: they prescribed bark. . .

Fri. 30. Gave my vote for Adair & Campbell at the Town Election: H. Manners Sutton is the Conserv. candidate, Humfrey having retired . . . At 5 o'clock our numbers were, Law 935, Feilding 732, Goulburn 610, Lefevre 436, Total 1453. Dined in Hall (where I enacted Dean). At 8 went on with the Polling: brisk polling for the hour. At 9 we closed with Law 988, Feilding 765, Goulburn 679, Lefevre 490, Total 1562. Adair & Campbell were returned triumphantly for the Town.[72] At 10 o'clock to supper at Rothman's to meet Sheepshanks, Moody, Bethune, & Malden.— We played whist afterwards, I furnishing cards & 2 bottles of Steinberg.

Sat. 31. . . . Seniority in Chapel at 9½ to elect a successor to poor Gosset.[73] Remington declined. The Master & V.M. came over from Norwich by an early train for this Election: the other 6 fellows present were Brown, self, Rothman, Martin, Moody & Sheepshanks. Martin took an objection against Jeremie's eligibility on the ground of his holding a living besides his Professorship:— it was overruled.— The Electors took no oath nor did the V.M. read The A. of Parliament.— It was determined to swear in the new Senior today with an understanding that (if anybody scrupled) Jeremie should be sworn again on Monday. The Master administered the oath to Jeremie in the words 'secundum leges & jura &c':— Moody suggested that the right words were 'secundum legem de eo sancitam': it

---

[72] Confident that government policy would call out 'a burst of approbation from the sober and enlightened middle classes', Campbell asked in a speech of 4 June a series of rhetorical questions which he then answered for true Liberals. 'To employ the vantage-ground of civil and religious liberty for the improvement of the largest number; to devote great legislative effforts to the masses of society; to give perfection to the arrangements, parochial, educational, and penal, by which humanity is modified, are ends to which normal [sic moral?] principles engage them, and to which they have been pledged a hundred times by the Rommillies [sic], the Mackintoshes, and the Arnolds' *(Speech addressed to the Electors,* Cambridge, 1847). In the mid-forties the electorate numbered about 1650; see J.C. Mitchell and J. Cornford,' The Political Demography of Cambridge 1832-1868', *Albion* 9 (1977), 242-72. For J.S. Lefevre's awkward part in the University election see F.M.G. Willson, *A Strong Supporting Cast* (1993), pp. 134-8.

[73] Gosset had died on the twenty-fourth.

was accordingly so administered.— One ground for not waiting for 'postero die' was that tomorrow is Sunday. Lefevre's little boy went up to Lady Feilding yesterday & said to her, 'there may be differences in politics, but I am sure that any body who knows my Papa must wish him to win.' Numbers at 5 o'clock were Law 1113, Feilding 855, Goulburn 832, Lefevre 606, Total 1816. Dined in Hall. The Polling from 8 to 9 was dull:— it reduced the majority of Lord Feilding to 12: The final numbers tonight were 1143 for Law, 881 Feilding, 869 Goulburn, 639 Lefevre:—Total 1884.

Mon. 2 August. The polling was not brisk today: but it became immensely interesting from the neck & neck race between Goulburn & Feilding: the 888th vote of Goulburn was given by Ld Milton & made Goulburn for the 1st time 1 ahead. At 5 the numbers were Law 1300, Goulburn 1025, Feilding 1005, Lefevre 763. Total 2176— John & Henry Romilly polled today: John is returned for Devonport. At 8 o'clock the polling was resumed: Goulburn gained 9 upon Feilding & left off with a majority of 29:— the numbers were Law 1349, Goulburn 1074, Feilding 1045, Lefevre 797:— Total 2266.—M. had nothing but a garden-walk today.

Tu. 3. I hear that Carus is going to marry a Miss Selwyn.[74]— 5th & last day of Poll:— Closed at 2. The numbers were Law 1486, Goulburn 1189, Feilding 1147, Lefevre 860:— Total 2491! Exactly 700 more than at the recent contest for the Chancellorship.— It was distressing to see the anxiety of Lady Feilding: she stood up on the highest seat that she might see if it was a carriage of his. I was glad to see her go out at ¼ to 2, before the closing of the poll. The young men in the gallery gave 3 cheers for her husband as he was taking her out:— I thought they acted with good feeling.— The Counting the votes & then reading them was a tedious affair: it was not over till past 5.— I then jumped into a Fly & took all the cards (4682!) to Gunning. . .

Th. 5. Wrote to Lodge.— Went to Mr. Gunnings & fetched away all the Cards & gave them to Maddison, who with Cocker had kindly undertaken to publish the Poll. . .

Sat. 7. Exhibited my office & the Pitt Press to Lucy & Frances:— the latter (very timidly) worked off a sheet of the Bible:— also exhibited to them the Public Library & Fitzwilliam Collection & the Trinity Library & Chapel: also the Anatomical Museum, where Lucy thought justice had not been done to the Cats. . . I dined in Hall. Carus was there: he took me to his rooms to speak about his engagement to Miss Maria Selwyn, wch he says is of 2 years standing altho he had never communicated it to his mother (who, strange to say, disapproves of his marrying). He says that he shall not marry these 8 or 9 years! In the mean time he has been out with his intended at Hemingford Grey rowing her in a boat & walking tête à tête

---

[74] They were not to marry for four years more.

with her in the woods in the Evening. He is said also to have been seen kissing the said lady (who is 27). The consequence was that the poor young lady & himself got talked about in a most unpleasant manner: 2 railway lads seemed to have mistaken another party for them & to have spread evil reports which reached the Magistrates of the place. Carus immediately went from the house of a friend (where he was on a visit) to Hemingford Grey, had an interview with the Magistrates, showed letters of his to Miss M.S., & instantly replaced himself in the good opinion of every body.

Sun. 8. Lucy & Frances to Trinity Church, where Carus preached from Deut. XXXII.10.11.. . . I staid at home with M. & read the Lessons &c to her, & a Sermon of E. Cooper's.[75]— We afterwards went to St. Paul's & heard Nicholson catechise the girls on the birth of our Lord: I thought he was not judicious in calling them 'dear' so often, & in thanking them at the end for their Texts, & in asking a tall young girl of about 15 'when a person feels love for you what do you feel in return?'. . .

Mon. 9. . . .Lucy's protégée Frances Wilderspin returned to Town today after staying more than 5 weeks:— Lucy saw her off . . .

Wed. 1 September. . . . The most interesting event of the last fortnight is the murder of the Duchess of Praslin by her husband who has since destroyed himself:— would that he had been guillotined.[76]— Presents of fruit today from Miss Spilling & Ri.Rowe. Letter from Miss Emma Lilley, announcing her intended marriage with*T. Green (the puseyite bookseller of No. 6 Kings Parade): she has asked me to perform the ceremony: — I have agreed to do so. — Grand feast in hall, but I declined going to it. * It appears (from a trial in the Newspapers) that a Mr. Crisp is the intended: I jumped to the conclusion of T . Green being the intended from her saying in her note that she had embarked all her money in his shop. — Walk with M: we met Dr. Haviland who is just returned from Cromer.

Th. 2. Walk with M (who has now got unhappily to feel faint & sick before breakfast) at 1, because I had to go to the Railroad at 2 to look out for Mrs. Augustus Hare. Sedgwick had written me word that this Lady & her adopted son Augustus (son of Francis Hare) would then arrive from Norwich. I popped my head into every 1st class Carriage, asking 'is Mrs. Hare in this carriage?' till I must have appeared harebrained: — no Mrs. H. was to be found, & my handsome lunch was eaten up by the college cormorants. — I went with the Phelps to dine at Madingley. . . Played 4 rubbers of whist & lost 3 of them: Dr. Paget (who came in the Evening) was opposed to me. — Sir St. V. gave me a brace of birds for M, which I thought most kind & amiable of him.

[75] Presumably Edward Cooper (d.1833), Rector of Yoxall, Staffordshire, author of many sermons.

[76] The duchess, only daughter of a former ambassador to Britain and mother of nine, had been stabbed to death in a Paris hotel on 18 August. Her husband, while refusing to admit his guilt, took poison in custody. The press throughout Europe found copy in this story for weeks, and its combination of mystery, savagery, and sexual passions among the nobility was not to be resisted.

Sat. 4. Walk with M. at 1 that I might go to the rail-road at 2. Dr. Haviland paid M. a visit. Letter from Edward Romilly who is just returned from Schwalbach (where he thinks the waters did his wife good & himself mischief). Mrs. A. Hare & the boy arrived:[77] Mrs. Hare was attended by her maid & man: — I hospitably entertained the servants as well as the mistress. — There was not much time after lunch as Mrs. Hare had ordered a Fly to be at the gate at 4:— We only saw the Library, Hall & Chapel of Trinity, the walks & the interior of Kings. I like Mrs. Hare very much, & think her adopted son a mild intelligent boy: —he sketches nicely: he showed me a book of the drawings which he had just made at Norwich: — he is a Harrovian. — I wrote to Sedgwick an account of Mrs. Hare. Read loud at night.

Mon. 6. Letter from Peacock announcing his intended marriage to Miss F. Selwyn (Sister to B. of N. Zealand): —wrote to congratulate him.— Wrote to Frank £10. Miss Vincent tho so ill herself kindly thought of M. & sent her a brace of partridges. As M. & I were out walking we fell in with Dr. Haviland who was good enough to turn about with us to talk to M. about her illness:— it was one of her most languid days. In the Evening I went on with Coelebs.[78]

Wed. 8. Lionised Miss Neville, Miss Lucy Neville, the Governess, & Lady Augusta Onslow from 11½ to 3. I was greatly pleased with Lady A: she is very quick & intelligent & took great interest in every thing she saw. We went to the Botanic Garden to see the Aloe wch is just beginning to blow:[79]— we went on the top of King's Chapel . . .

Th. 9. Paid a visit to Mrs Henslow at Mrs Hayle's. . . She told me that her eldest daughter (Helen) is engaged to marry a Dr. Hooker (passionately fond of poetry & botany like herself): they are to wait 12 months or more as he is going to the Himmalaya mountains. . .

Fri. 10. . . . I had a very agreeable letter this morning from Lady Braybrooke saying that my lionising had given great satisfaction. Wrote to Lodge & sent him a Poll Book of the University Election . . . Wrote also to Mr. Maitland (at Lambeth Palace) about the words 'Salting' & 'Problem' wch he finds in an old college account which he is about to print:— he thinks 'Salting' was a fee paid by a student on his 1st dining in hall, & 'Problem' his 1st examination on admission (for wch there was also a

---

[77] The boy, A.J.C. Hare, does not record such a meeting in his voluminous autobiography. He was spending the summer with relations at the Bishop's palace in Norwich. As a child he met many Trinity men, friends of his uncle Julius, and 'particularly disliked' Whewell for his 'icily cold' manner. To Sedgwick he was devoted for 'nothing could be more charming than his stories, more attractive and interesting than his conversation, especially with children, with whom he took pains to "be agreeable".' See *The Story of My Life,* I (1896), 164-5 and III, 158 where he repeats a scathing verse about the Whewells.

[78] Hannah More, *Coelebs in Search of a Wife* (1809). This, her most popular fiction, gave rise to the expression 'Coelebs' wife' for a bachelor's ideal.

[79] It was 16 feet high and supposed to have a thousand blooms.

fee):— I think he is right: but I can find nothing corroborative.[80] Today two moustached Americans came to my office to consult about ancestors of theirs of the names of Roger Williams & George Phillips:— I showed their handwriting & communicated all that my office contained about them:[81]— they were agreeable gentlemanlike men, & seemed much surprised at my declining any fee. — Ficklin called today & altered M's Medicine. She was very languid indeed today & crept along most slowly & painfully, so much so that Dr. F. Thackeray (who saw us from the road) drove on to Parker's Piece & offered to take her home. Lucy's Protégée (Eliza Rawlinson:— niece of Mrs. Hatton the hoody went today to the Training School: Lucy has spent 3 Guineas in money in fitting her out, & M & L. have spent a fortnight of time in making her clothes:— I gave her a Bible & P.B.— Lucy went today to the Trinity Roundabout to hear Carus speak to his Sunday-school children. I deposited her at 2½ & left her there that I might go home & walk with M.— We waited dinner for L. till 5 o'clock & then dined without her. That treacherous Carus went away for his own dinner in Hall & did not make his little speech to the children till ½ past 5! The children sang a very pretty Hymn beginning 'There is a Friend we ought to love':[82] it was got up under the instruction of Hopkins (the Curate) who sings well:— it was capitally performed.—L. not home till past 6.

Mon. 13. Wrote to Ficklin begging him to come up early: he did so:— he punched M's side so that she complained all day of the pain. It was a wet day & she did not stir out. She was in a very uncomfortable state all the day & would not play in the Evening. I read loud a story of Theodore Hooks (in the set called the Parish Clerk): this one is named 'the Lieutenants Story': Some Bow St. Runners are cleverly drawn in it.[83]

Fri. 17. . . . In the Evening I received letters from Ch. Romilly & John Lindsay about the living of South Kilworth in Leicestershire:— Lindsay is a Candidate for it: & I had (at Lindsay's request) written to Charles as secretary to the Chancellor in whose gift it is. I don't expect that Lindsay will get it: Charles wrote very kindly about it, & Lindsay very gratefully: Lindsay's Letter was a very interesting one, for it described his gentle modes of dealing with the Independents & how they sent their children to his Sunday school: he also described his mode of training up a Teacher for his school:— he instructs a boy in religion & in common parts of

---

[80] 'Salting' was a crude sixteenth-century initiation rite for freshmen and involved drinking salt-water, or salted beer. By transference it referred also to the associated festivity and its cost (see A.H. Nelson, *Records of Early English Drama: Cambridge 2* (1989), 996-1001); a 'Problem' was an academic exercise in hall whose rules were laid down in the Trinity statutes. Romilly also supplied biographical notes for Maitland's articles on 'Archbishop Whitgift's College Pupils' in *The British Magazine* 32 (1847), 366-7, 370, 651.

[81] For the majority of students this had only ever meant their signatures, and records for matriculation and degree(s).

[82] Perhaps an adaptation of a hymn by Marianne Nunn published in 1817 and much used for children.

[83] Theodore Hook, *The Parish Clerk* (1841).

education, feeds him usually in the kitchen, but on high days & holidays makes a parlour Guest of him.

Sat. 18. Proclamation of Sturbridge Fair:— no Esquire Bedell present, as Gunning (the only one in Camb.) was poorly.—Walk with M. who is a little better:— in the Evening she played a little on the Piano; wch she had not done for the last few days . . . Today I dined in Hall. I was amused by the V.C. telling me that the Queen had sent to Storr & Mortimer for the 2 bouquet vases (at the dinner of the 5th & 6th July) wch stood before her Majesty:— she keeps such things & makes appropriate inscriptions on them:— the taste is rather expensive for her Maj's entertainers. The Bills were sent in to the V.C. & to Trin. College:— the V.C's Vase was silver & cost 8.15.—.; but that used at Trinity was Gold & cost above £40!

Mon. 20. Mrs. Helm (our neighbour) kindly sent a leg-rest for M. A horrid accident happened at our gate today: The son of a coalwaggoner (a boy of 13 or 14) (while his father went behind the waggon to talk to somebody) was knocked down by the horses & a wheel went over his body, wch killed him on the spot![84]— Ficklin called on M. & says he will make her medicine a little stronger. Today the establishment of horses of Hughes entered the Town:—Chariots were drawn by camels & Elephants:— a very pretty sight[85]. . .

On the same day Romilly set out to visit Sedgwick at Norwich, going second class which cost 9s-6d. He was one of many guests including Sedgwick's nieces, Dr William Buckland, the Oxford geologist and Dean of Westminster, with his wife and daughter, and J.C. Adams the discoverer of Neptune. They dined well, on ice and champagne, and a goose 'dressed swan-fashion,viz.with beef in its inside'. Romilly was pleased with Madame Barry de Moncey whom he took in to dinner; she knew 'the unfortunate Duchesse de Praslin who was murdered by her husband the other day:— she was familiar with Madame de Genlis: from reverse of fortune she is now a teacher.'

The centre of all attention was the Swedish soprano Jenny Lind for whom there was a nationwide mania by this time. Romilly had heard her before in opera. She was so tired on arrival that she went to bed and the company had to make do with her spaniel, provoking 'manifest symptoms of jealousy' in Faust the resident dog. Miss Lind herself 'looked very ugly indeed' though Romilly granted she was 'unaffected, well-mannered & well-informed'. On Wednesday 22 September she gave her first guinea concert: 'I have pronounced her right name to be Guinea Lind,wch is adopted in the Close'. She sang nothing in English and it seemed to Romilly that the highlight of the first of her two concerts was her Swedish songs when 'she seemed as much enraptured as her audience'. Romilly of course also went sight-seeing, including the Hudson Gurney and St Helens Hospital (where some two hundred patients were cared for by a dozen nurses), the Jacquard loom works, and a hot and uncomfortable horticultural show.

[84] An inquest at the Prince Regent named the boy as Charles Howsden aged 14. He had caught hold of the forehorse to avoid a load of planks standing in the road, and fallen so that the wheel went over his stomach.

[85] Edwin Hughes who had appeared before the Queen in April was about to retire young and rich from his travelling circus. Among several novel achievements was his harnessing camels and elephants together.

Whewell arrived during breakfast on 24 September to carry the party off to his house near Lowestoft,where Romilly took a solitary bathe and walked until dinner. 'The night being very clear the telescope was set up on the lawn & we peeped at Saturn & Mars & the Moon'. He was not long allowed to forget academic matters, however, for Whewell handed over his 'remarks on Trinity Lodge not being (as it has been called) the Queen's house:— I took them away to copy'. He lost his hat out of the window of the train while changing places with Miss Buckland so she might get a good a view of Ely cathedral. At home he found that Lord Braybrooke and Captain Doria had both kindly sent birds for the table, while there was a petition for a case of distress from Miss Kelty the novelist to whom he sent a pound. This moved him to read aloud her *Wants and Wishes,* 'very clever—but rather hard,& much too long'.

Mon. 27. Commissary's Court at Sturbridge Fair: the deputy Commissary was Mr. Mills (son of the Sun)[86]: made £1.5.4½: gave 6d to the little daughter of one of the publicans: upon which Kingsley said in his indistinct mumbling stile 'what'll you buy?':— 'No Sir, exclaimed the Mother, it's not a boy, it's a girl.'— Present of brace of birds from Lady Cotton & a magnificent nosegay from Gunning:— wrote to thank both.— Wrote to G.T.R. £10: he had written a very amusing letter to M, wch arrived (as he intended) on her birthday (last Saturday,—when I gave her Hallams 'Modern Literature').[87] I wrote also to Madame F.R. £20. Walk round Parker's Piece with M: we met Miss Vincent out in a wheel-chair & found her looking much better. Bought a thick air-cushion & blacksilk cover for M. cost 12/6. At night read loud Belinda[88] & Coelebs.

Th. 30. Ficklin paid M. a visit:— she seemed a little better today: walk with her to the Railway. I had a long visit from Randall (the Attorney): he wished me to interest myself with Government about his brother in the Mauritius (whom I never saw nor wish to see), who has a government appointment there of *£500 a year with house & horse* & is not satisfied, & who has never distinguished himself nor is likely!! I told him that I never meant to ask Favors of Government even for my own relations:— he then consulted me about his only son whom he is going to send to College but wishes to keep back till 19½! I dissuaded such waste of a year.[89]— Dined in Hall: the Master was there. A grand Feast,— Venison given by D. of Rutland & Turtle by Randall. My guests were Shaw & Kingsley: they afterwards came to my rooms (after dessert & tea in Comb. room) & we made up a rubber by the aid of the Marquis Sp., Arlett, Buston & Thacker.

Fri. 1 October. 1st day of Fellowship:— Greek by Thompson & Martin. A very bad day of M:— we however took a little walk:— she was most feeble & complained much of her side.— The Gowns arrived from Norwich: but

[86] His father had been landlord of the Sun Inn in Trinity Street. See 8 January 1844.
[87] Henry Hallam, *Introduction to the Literature of Europe in the Fifteenth, Sixteenth, and Seventeenth Centuries* (1837-9), third edition 1847.
[88] Maria Edgeworth, *Belinda* (1801).
[89] Edward Randall was admitted to Oriel College Oxford in 1849 aged 18.

after all the exertion to get a 2d like my original choice it proved impossible: 2 other patterns were sent for our selection:— the women were well pleased, but I was rather mortified at the failure of my wishes. A new number of Dombey (in wch Mrs. Skewton dies, & Capt. Cuttles landlady makes an invasion on him): it is capital:— Read it loud—Went on also with Belinda.

Wed. 6. Last day of Fell:— Greek Composition, Latin Prose; General Paper; Edward Allen arrived at breakfast (having drunk tea at Birmingham last night): he was looking well & flourishing, & brought with him 2 brace of partridges & 2 hares.— I took him to see the flowering Aloe,— which I think a very shabby affair:— it is now going off. This was a very bad day for poor M: she felt very much pain & didn't get up till 7 in the Evening— Lucy & Grim dined tête à tête: I dined with Paget in Caius Hall at the Caius Commemoration[90] . . .

Fri. 8. Sedgwick called & was received by M. who thought him very agreeable.— I called on Dr. Haviland & begged him to pay M. a visit: he kindly did so; & the sight of him always does her good. She also had a visit from Jones the Dentist to set her false teeth to rights . . . Tea at the Lodge to decide Fellowships: (we elected Grant, Holden & Lushington): Miss Sedgwick & Miss King as well as Mrs Whewell drank tea with us. Lucy sent £10 to The Devonport Female Orphans.[91]

Sat. 9. My birthday: I am this day 56 years complete, & am (thank God) in good health. At ¼ to 9 to Chapel to elect the Officers & new fellows. To my great joy Sedgwick has taken the Vice mastership again. Edward breakfasted with me (as usual). . . I dined with my brother Examiners (The Master, Rothman, Martin, Jeremie, Carus, Thompson, & Grote): Sedgwick went off to Norwich to look after certain Geological papers which he has mislaid, & about wch he is nearly frantic: his place was filled up by Cooper. We had a very agreeable party. By the way Sedgwick found his missing papers in a pigeon-hole at Norwich!

Sun. 10. Wet day. Edward of course breakfasted with me:— I sleep in College all the time Edward stays with us. Edward & I to Trinity Church— (by the way, the rain came into our pew & made quite a pool).— L. came for the sermon . . . I should have said that yesterday there was a grand eclipse (11 digits): this eclipse of the sun was annular in some parts of England, but not at Cambridge:— I got up before 7 to see the eclipse, but the rain made it a failure & I went to bed again.— I of course could not take M. out in the wet: but I took a little turn with Grim & then a good solitary walk to Trumpington.— After dinner I read loud the interesting description of Simeon's death in the Mémoirs. I also wrote a letter to Lodge.

[90] I.e. of its benefactors.
[91] Their cousin John Romilly had just been elected M.P. for the Liberal stronghold of Devonport .

Mon. 11. A 4 horse Coach 'the Defence' began running today.[92]— Opening of term. Baily of Clare is Sen. Proctor:— he amused me by reading Div. Joh. *Divinus* Johannes.— There was a Grace for Gunning to surrender his staff by Deputy. . . E.E. Allen & I dined in Hall, where there was a Polish Prince Leon Sapieha from Galicia, his son Prince Adam Sapieha, the Ct. Ladisl. Zamoyski, & a heap of other foreigners. I was V.M. & of course went up into the Combination room: I found the Prince a very sensible well-informed & well-mannered person: he knew intimately my pupil Ld Wriothesley Russell:— he spoke English well & we conversed entirely in English . . .

Wed. 13. Breakfast to C. Robinson & Edward: Robinson is a lively unhealthy-looking young man — Took a walk with M. in the garden: it was most distressing: she was in constant suffering the whole time & it went to my heart to hear her groans. I went forth in search of Ficklin & Haviland:— to my great annoyance Ficklin is not yet returned from his shooting excursion: he went away 8 days ago, & will not (I fear) return before Sunday. Haviland was out but I saw Mrs. Haviland & wrote a note for H. He kindly came the moment he returned & prescribed anodynes.— The 2 Princes Sapieha & Ct. Ladislaw Zamoyski called on me & left cards, I being out.— Margaret went to bed again at teatime.— Edward & I dined in hall:— I was Vicemaster & went upstairs to talk to the Guests:—amongst others were Dr. Jennings (the Archdeacon of Norfolk) & Alleyne (the Warden of Dulwich): he is a very handsome & very agreeable man: he was educated at Bonn.— Poor Dr. Hodgson (Master of Pet.) had a tumor removed from his head not long ago: he caught cold; has erysipelas in the head, & his life is in imminent danger. — This Evening we saw the bright horrid glare of a fire: it was in the farm of Mr. Webb (a Cowkeeper) at Barnwell:— 3 stacks & a barn destroyed:— happily the cattle uninjured:— the fire was extinguished by 10 o'clock. It is not known whether it was intentional.

Sat. 16. . . . Poor Margaret was in greater pain that ever today: Lucy & I went to Ficklins & brought with us the assistant (Chipperfield): he saw M. & so did Dr. Haviland shortly after: hot lotion was prescribed. M. got up about 12 & went to bed about 5. Thank God she was very much easier after the lotion. I read to her from 6 to 8 & she was cheerful & free from pain. — Dr. Hodgson died today:— poor Mrs. Hodgson has borne up with wonderful fortitude. It was only last Saturday that any alarm began to be felt about The Master of Peterhouse!— So uncertain is human life.— My old protégée Mrs. Okey is dead: her granddaughter called on me for assistance in the Funeral.— Her real name was Okeman: her age 88!

---

[92] Rumours of a new London coach became rife early in August after a steep rise in railway fares for passengers and goods, and it was soon begun after public meetings had raised £1000 of the capital needed in £5 subscriptions. *The Defence* lasted only six months, however, and failed from bad management according to one of the principals (see John Brown, *Sixty Years' Gleanings* (1858), p. 403.)

Edward & I dined in Hall. The day was brilliant like summer. Very agreeable letters to me & M. from G.T.R: he is painting a picture for her:— he has painted a Diana Vernon[93] wch he considers his chef doeuvre. He has now been 2 years at Paris.

Tu. 19. Breakfast to Edward, North, Hensley, & Jeddere-Fisher.— Edward went off to Town by the 10.47 train: I carried his bag, & Hensley & himself the portmanteau.— M. passed an indifferent night:— Ficklin came in the middle of the day & thought M. much the same. I am now returned home again, to my great satisfaction as M. is so dreadfully ill:—It is very curious, but since last Wednesday (when these excruciating pains began) her voice is certainly stronger. I sit with her occasionally & read a little to her: but she does not like my remaining long, as she is most unwilling to pain me by crying out when her agony comes on. Her fits of suffering last ¼ hour & longer & are counteracted by ether. They occur 2 or 3 times in the day, & alas! in the night also now.

Fri. 22. M. (thank God) passed another good night.—Haviland did not come today.— Ficklin called & reported favorably. Poor Dr. Hodgson was buried today: nobody asked but the Heads of Houses, the Medical men, Prof. Blunt & the Fellows of the College: Cookson was one of the Pallbearers:— not an uninterested person![94] . . . Magna Congregatio this morning:— they omitted to furnish me with the List, very careless of the Corporation . . .

Sat. 23. M (thank God) passed another good night. But she took a strong dose of opening medicine at 6 in the morning & was in a state of extreme feebleness all day. I never have seen her looking so ill as today: but during her times of freedom from pain she talks of the skreens she shall paint for Mrs. Blamire intended Bazaar for The Governesses.— Ficklin came as usual. M. was up for about an hour: but she was very uncomfortable; & neither worked nor read all day.— I read a little to her after dinner.— She was so full of pain at 7 o'clock that it was alas! necessary to give her then the soothing draft wch she commonly takes at 10: so that I fear it will be necessary to give her another in the night. — Today the Proclamation of the Markets.— Nasty wet day.— Congregation: 1 eundem, & graces for all the Examiners. — Lucy not able to visit her paupers. Called on Miss Apthorp to thank her for marmalade sent to M.

Mon. 25. I heard M. call out in the middle of the night & went into her room; but found that it was a sort of nightmare, for she was in a deep sleep. She did not wake during the night. In the morning she thought herself better. She was certainly more lively & much less complaining during all the day. Both Haviland & Ficklin came together: they thought her getting weaker:— I think her countenance is altered. She however sat up for near 2

93 The heroine of Scott's *Rob Roy* (1818). George's painting is likely to have been a copy of an existing illustration rather than an orginal. He was unable to earn a living as an artist and in the end found paid employment as a civil servant.
94 He became the Master of Peterhouse.

hours, & two or 3 times in the day made an experiment of lying on her right side for a few minutes, she having hitherto lain entirely on her back.— I did not see Haviland & Ficklin, being at a Court at the V.C's where H. Lyon (Chemist of Petty Cury) was admonished by the V.C. for taking a note of hand & prosecuting A.T. Cooper (a B.A. of Trin.) without communicating with his Tutor.[95]— The Skrines called yesterday & sat some time with me to talk about poor M:— Lady Cotton called today: I went out & spoke with her. I read 2 or 3 times to M. during the day: but after tea she begged me not to come up. Tonight the Whist Club at Birkett's:— I of course didn't go. Mrs. Worsley called to offer M. any thing in her power.

Tu. 26. Another night of uninterrupted sleep (thank God). M. was up for 2 hours today. She seems alas! to gain in nothing but that most invaluable blessing, exemption from severe pain.— Ficklin came late today: it was past 4. I read both in the morning & Evening to M.— I think she grows (if possible) thinner & weaker. Ficklin says the symptoms of these last 2 days are favorable, but I confess myself without hope & think nothing but a miracle can restore her. Lucy much excited by a letter from Upholland today. The writer is an unmarried young woman of the name of Latham: the mother (who is just dead) had shown much kindness to Susan Grounds & her late brother Henry Chune: the writer is indignant at S.G. not paying a debt of above £5 wch H.C. owed her mother, & says every thing that is spiteful about Susan before her marriage,— that she kept very low company & walked out at night &c. I set these charges down to the natural irritation at being swindled out of her money.— Lucy wrote to Susan Grounds.— I wrote to Ja. Bailey.

Wed. 27. Another night of sleep (thank God). M. however was most feeble all day, partly in consequence of some strong medicine taken in the morning. Ficklin did not make his appearance at all. Happily however Dr. Haviland came.— He confesses that he sees no tendency in poor M. to recovery, no advance towards strength.— Carus caught hold of me today to help him in an emergence:— Dr. Achilli had just found his way to C's rooms, & C. wanted somebody as interpreter between them, the languages of Dr. A. being Italian & French, wch C. is not at home in.— I conversed with Dr. A. in French & learned his adventures: he had left London this morning with a Mr. Watt (who seems to act as his interpreter): Dr. A. got out at Wenden to stare about him & the train went off with his friend Watt & left him staring behind:— he came on by the next train. Dr. Achilli was a Romish priest & is now a protestant: he is zealous for establishing protestantism in Malta, & is to attend a meeting for that purpose at

---

[95] The defence was that Cooper was a B.A. and therefore Lyon honestly thought he was no longer *in statu pupillari*. The court took this into account, as it did on 26 November in a similar case when John Hall, a bookseller, was up for resorting to law, having tried for years to get Hamlet Clark of Corpus (B.A. 1846), a future clergyman, to pay the not inconsiderable sum of £14.

Huntingdon tomorrow & one at Cambridge on Friday.[96] Declined dining with Lady Cotton. Bought M. a bouquet of Violets. . .

Th. 28. We have to be thankful for dear M. having again passed a night free from pain:— she however shows no power of rallying:— still she talks of what she shall do when she gets well:— this may be out of tenderness to Lucy & me that we may not think her as dangerously ill as she is. Ficklin (who had been sent for in a hurry to Ely yesterday) came today & found no change. He found on the mat outside the door a Sovereign, wch doubtless had been lying there nearly 24 hours, & was certainly dropped by Dr. Haviland yesterday when I gave him a fee at *the door*:— what an odd circumstance that it should have been unobserved so long!— I read loud to M. morning & Evening: she scarcely said a word.

Fri. 29. . . .She however became very restless early in the day (about 10½) & it was necessary to give her the composing draft.— These ether drafts act like magic: in 10 minutes she forgets all her sufferings & becomes quite cheerful & talks of what she will do when she gets well. . .

Mon. 1. November. M. passed another night of sleep & that without having taken a night-draft. Ficklin thought her a little better this morning.— At 2½ there was a good deal of excitement to poor M. as she was transferred into the next room while her own bed was removed & a water-bed from the Hospital substituted:— gave her a little wine & water after she was placed in the new bed. Wrote to F.R. £10. . . Seniority & then a 16 at wch I received the unusually large sum of 19s/. Today was the 1st day of Christmas in hall, & the whist club at Eyres': I did not go to either. Felt shivery & hotheaded: abstained from meat & ordered myself a dose . . .

Th. 4. Declined breakfasting with the Senior Proctor Baily. M. happily passed a good night. Dr. Haviland was kind enough to pay her a visit: he comes (ever since last Saturday) as a Friend & will not take a fee:— very generous on his part. He thought her a little better. I cannot see it myself: she seems to me still weaker & complains of headache.— Lady Wale & Mrs. Prest called: I was at home & saw them.— Election of V.C. today: Dr. Phelps chosen. — I did not go to his wine-party.— Finished reading D'Israeli's Tancred, which I thought wild dreamy nonsense in spite of much talent[97] . . . M. sat up a little in the Evening (more than ½ hour): the 1st time since being in the water-bed. Ficklin didn't come today. . .

Mon. 8. M. slept well & thought herself better in the morning. Ficklin also thought her better:— I cannot see it myself.— She became restless &

96 Giovanni Achilli, sometime Dominican prior, professor of theology, and prisoner of the Inquisition, arrived in England in May 1847. He was taken up warmly, especially by the anti-Catholics, but later became an embarrassment when scandals about his life were known, went to America, and died in obscurity. See Chadwick, pp. 306-8.

97 Benjamin Disraeli, *Tancred, or the New Crusade* (1847). Romilly gave him his father's spelling, D'Israeli.

excited in the Evening & it was necessary to give her a very little Ether:— she however was up from 6 to 8 at night. She ate with appetite, & altogether it may be considered one of her best days.— I had a visit from Tooke who told me that his wife suffered agonies from tic douloureux: also from Jeddere Fisher who (tho only in his 2nd year) is reading 3d year subjects. Wrote to Lodge.— Didn't go to Whist Club at Francis's.

Tu. 9. M. slept well: but was very restless & excited in the morning till she was soothed by a draft into which Betsy put a small quantity of Ether & so it passed current for a regular Ether draft & produced the magic effect. Neither Haviland nor Ficklin came today.— The people at Devonport have found Lucy out: the other day they applied for an Asylum & she sent £10: today they have applied for a new Church, & she sent £5.5.—. I paid a visit to our most kind neighbour Mrs. Helm: she is an excellent Lady: she sends M. a newlaid egg every day, & had lent her a silver bell & many other comforts for a sick person. I had never seen her before today:— I was very much pleased with her . . . Today made M. a present of an apostle-spoon, also 2 lilliputian spoons for helping ginger or such things.

Th. 11. M. slept well & happily had no decided fit of restlessness all day: she was however heavy & slightly headachy & did no work & very little reading. She was up for more than 2 hours & made no complaint. No medical man today: Ficklin is attending a lady at Ely. I read loud morning & Evening. Today M. had a very agreeable letter from George Romilly: his promised picture of Diana Vernon also came today & we are delighted with it: he reckons it his best work: it is a present to Margaret.— I wrote to George to thank him.

Fri. 12. M. (thank God) again slept well & thought herself better in the morning.— Sent off 3 Doz. Audit to Edw. Romilly:— wrote to him. Wrote also to Mrs. Kennedy, Miss Wilcox, Miss D'Illens, & Miss Corfield.— Ficklin thought M. a little better today: he has ordered her castor-oil pills:— I never saw such curious huge bolusses: she had however no difficulty in swallowing them, the case being gelatine. I read to her a good deal: but she made no observation whatever. Today hung up George's picture between those of my Mother & Margaret:— it looks very well indeed.— After prayers went up to sleep in College. This was the 2nd meeting of 'The Family': Power was the Host: I did not go.

Mon. 15. Went into Margaret's room in the middle of the night being awoke by her cries: Betsy also came: happily it was only a nightmare, for she was without pain when we awoke her. Today was altogether one of her very best.— She got up twice & sat up altogether near 2 hours.— I read a great deal to her: she did some needlework & read with satisfaction to herself.—I had today a visit from Cattlin the artist (who made the American-Savages Exhibition): he brought a letter to me from George Romilly at Paris. He tells me that he wishes to sell his whole collection to The United States: his object in coming to Cambridge seems to be to sell to the Fitzwilliam Museum his Model of the Fall of Niagara: I told him he ran no chance of doing so till the building was complete &c &c. — He is a widower with 3 small children: having lost his wife a year ago & his only boy a fortnight ago.— He is an American.[98] He spoke highly of George's pictorial talent.— It is reported that Musgrave is to be translated from Hereford to York! Hurrah! What a lucky man! Hampden is spoken of as the new Bishop:— a bold step of Ld. J. Russell.[99]

Th. 18. M. passed a good night & got thro'the whole day without ether, tho she was at one time rather fidgetty:— she was heavy & silent: Ficklin didn't come; Haviland kindly paid a visit; he said she was weaker than when he last called. Mrs Skrine sent M. some potted chicken. Mr. Scott (the Clergyman of St. Pauls) called.— Letter from Mrs. Eaton complaining that Edward would not agree to Bertha's fortune being settled on herself & begging my assistance: I think him quite wrong: I wrote to her & to him.[1] Letter from Musgrave acknowledging that he is to be Archbishop of York.

Fri. 19. Weather very cold.— M. passed a good night: she did not sit up more than ½ hour: she was not very restless today, but exhibits no symptom of advancement. Ficklin came today:— he sent M. ½ Doz. Pears. Congregation for a Petition against Jews in Parliament (directed against Rothschild M.P. for London): Sedgwick nonplaceted it in B.H., & Lamb in W.H.: it was carried by 50 to 25 in B.H., & 28 to 14 in W.H.[2] . . . I read a good deal to M. Lucy visited her poor protégée Sarah Foulkes who is returned home very ill & very dissatisfied with a week's visit to Barnwell . . .

Tu. 23. Necessary to give Ether at 4 in the morning.— Letter from T. Robinson to say his stall of Mora is worth nothing: he is endeavouring to

---

98 George Catlin had brought his exhibition of paintings and artefacts illustrative of the vanishing cultures of American Indians to Europe, where, despite some success, he was often in financial straits. The first volume of his *Notes of Eight Years' Travels and Residence in Europe* (1848) contains a catalogue of the collection.

99 R.D. Hampden, Regius Professor of Divinity at Oxford, had been chosen as Musgrave's successor by Russell to strengthen the Protestant character of the church. Yet his orthodoxy was in question among old enemies (many of whom had defected to Rome), and most of the bishops. Graces expressing alarm at Hampden's nomination were thrown out in the Caput on 8 December. After much petitioning, memorialising, and legal wrangling, he was consecrated at Lambeth in March 1848. See Chadwick, 237-49.

1   Since on her marriage a woman's property and income became her husband's (she having no independent legal status), the settlement by deed drawn up before the wedding was a common device in well-off families to protect her or at least her children. Edward relented within days of the marriage in January 1848 after causing great anxiety to Bertha's mother and exasperation to his uncle who described his conduct as 'obstinate, selfish, and unjustifiable'.

2   Jews and freethinkers alike were effectively excluded from Parliament as they could not take the prescribed oaths. Relief bills failed until 1858 when Rothschild was at last able to take his seat (see Chadwick, pp. 485-7). Although the University would admit practising Jews, they could not proceed to a degree since for that they would have to declare themselves members of the Church of England. Even J.J. Sylvester, the second Wrangler of 1837, went down with no degree. See W. Frankel and Harvey Miller (eds.), *Gown and Tallith* (1989).

set up a Society for superannuated Clergymen:— I desired him to put down my name as subscriber. Letter from W.F. Campbell (Member for the Town) asking my opinion about admission of Jews into Parliament: wrote to tell him that I could have wished Rothschild had not been elected for London, but that I saw no danger to Xty from the admission of the Jews, & that I had voted against the University Petition last Friday. Gave 10/ to a widow Mrs. James Barron:— her husband died 4 weeks since: her Father & G. Father (Hall) had been Brewers to the College: She came to me in tears saying The Master had behaved very unkindly to her, telling her she was a beggar, & that her Father ought to have saved money &c &c. . . Ficklin came in the Evening & Haviland in the morning: Haviland thought M. a little less weak: Ficklin could see no progress. She sat up above 2 hours in the Evening.

Th. 25. Good night.— Ficklin came: he has altered the medicine: he now gives bark & recommends milk & soda water mixt in equal quantities.— Letter from E.E.A.: very unsatisfactory: he seems as obstinate as a pig about refusing to settle Bertha's fortune on her.— Present from Richard Neville of engraving of tessellated pavement from the Roman villa discovered by him at Chesterford: wrote to thank him.— Lucy had a grand scene with Mrs. Gilmour about Eliza (who has been dismissed from Railway Station (probably) on account of the attention there paid her by one of the young men employed about the Rail, & who dresses above her station & gads about & seems on the road to ruin): Lucy behaved admirably & did all she could by strong remonstrance to save Eliza:— Mrs. Gilmour behaved obstinately & proudly & like a fool, & will see no danger & will take no precautions.— Wrote to Messrs Christie (Fairfield Factory) & Mr. W. Swindell (Droylsden) Manchester about G. Rawlinson (a boy from the Haverhill Union) whose Sister Lucy has put in the Servants Training School.— By the way Mrs. Scholefield today prevailed on me to become one of the Trustees of the said Training School . . .

Sat. 27. Good night— it was purchased by Ether at 10. To the V.C's about Univ. Schol. — Declined dining at Magd. to meet Dean of Windsor.[3]— Dr. Haviland was kind enough to call (in spite of the wetness of the day): he says *the disease is gone* & that strength only is wanting:— would that I could see the improvement! I can see no advance whatever:— he now prescribes 'Cods Liver Oil' which he says sometimes works wonders.—may it do so now!— Ficklin did not come today.— I read aloud a good deal of the novel called 'Daughters': I think it very clever[4] . . .

Mon. 29. Good night.— Began with the Cod Livers Oil: it is mixt up with milk:— 3 doses a day. Wrote to F.R. £10: wrote to G.T.R. £10.— Wrote to Lord Braybrooke who had written to ask who 'the Tripos' was in days of

---

[3] I.e. George Neville Grenville, Master of Magdalene and brother of Lord Braybrooke.
[4] I.e. *The Daughters,* a new novel by the prolific and popular Elizabeth Caroline Grey.

old.[5] — Received letter from Messrs Christy saying that G. Rawlinson is in their Employ: that he is strong & healthy, clever & industrious, but a most ingenious thief!! he is well fed & clothed, allowed pocket money, works 6½ hrs (being under 13) & goes to school for 3½ hrs. No Doctor today: M. didn't sit up.

Tu. 30. Good night— Mr. Pemberton (at suggestion of Ficklin) sent us some delicious grapes & pears. Seniority about routine business —Went to see a Picture (at Roe's) of Wilkie's: it is Buonap. making the Pope sign the Concordat: did not much like it.[6] Haviland called & pronounced M. better:— Ficklin also made a favorable report:— M. sat up for 2 hours: she was not quite so restless in the Evening. Read loud the new Dombey in wch Mrs. Dombey leaves Dombey, & Florence goes to Capt. Cuttle.

Sun. 5. December. . . . I staid at home & read & talked with M. till 3 when I went out for an hours walk.— A very good day indeed for M: she again sat up for 4 hours, & wore (for the 1st time) her daycap! — a Gown indeed had been talked of, but that was too bold a venture.— No Ficklin. I read all the Evening loud till 9 o'clock when M. became very restless: Betsy however intends omitting the Ether-draft at bed time.— Mrs Willis kindly sent us a brace of birds, & Mrs. How (the drunken Cobbler's wife) a hare.

Mon. 6. I heard M. very restless in the night & got up & woke Betsy who gave her an Ether draft. — M. was very heavy in the day: she sat up for 2 hours, but got very restless & went to bed again. It was a very bad day indeed with her:— she was restless to an unusual extent early in the Evening.— No Ficklin for 3 days running. Miss Spilling again most amiably sent us grapes, blancmange, & beef-tea:— this is the 3rd time. Mr. Gunning also sent us another lovely nosegay & some violets.— Received from Jeremie his 'Thanksgiving Sermon for the Harvest': it is a most eloquent & beautiful sermon: I wrote to thank him: I read the Sermon loud to M. & L. . . . Lucy sent £5 to the Servants Training School Fund: she did this in consequence of the bonus on Bank Stock. . .

Tu. 7. My dearest sister departed this life about 7 o'clock: she has doubtless made a most blessed exchange of earth with all its pain & sorrow for the joys of heaven. But the parting from one so justly loved with whom we had lived on the terms of daily uninterrupted intercourse of affection for so many years is a very severe blow to Lucy & me. God preserve & bless her & comfort her in her sorrow. Nobody was with poor Margaret at the time of her release. We had not the slightest idea that her last moments were so near at hand, altho she certainly had eaten very little dinner & that slowly & reluctantly & had been so restless as to make it necessary to give

[5] For the changes by which the 'Tripos' meant a stool, a man, a speech, a set of verses, a sheet of paper, a list of names, and finally a system of examination see C. Wordsworth, *Scholae Academicae* (1877), pp.16-21.

[6] 'The Emperor Napoleon with Pope Pius the Seventh at Fontainbleau (sic)', exhibited at the R.A. in 1836, and now in Dublin.

her her etherdraft about 8½. She appears to have died calmly: her countenance had no expression of added pain, nor did she utter any cry of suffering, which I should certainly have heard as our bedrooms join.— She will be deeply regretted, for every body loved her.— She showed great resignation during her sad & severe sufferings:— she was always willing to die whenever it should please God to call her, or she was content to live on (altho in pain) if such were his good pleasure. From her naturally quick temper & from the anguish of her malady on the nerves she could not but utter groans & make a moaning during the time of each paroxysm: (She always begged me & Lucy to go out of the room when her pain came on, so anxious was she to spare our feelings at all times): but the moment the intolerable agony was alleviated her native cheerfulness & elasticity of temper broke out. She was habitually impressed with the idea that she should recover, & with her usual generosity spoke about the presents she should make to different people. She was most grateful for every care & attention however trifling, & often quoted the lines 'I've heard of hearts unkind kind deeds with scorn returning. The gratitude of man hath oftner left me mourning':[7] She was fond of speaking of the comforts she had in her sick chamber, & would often admire & praise the neatness & elegance of its furniture & ornaments. She was most affectionately attached to her maid Betsy Edwards, who made indeed an incomparable nurse from her activity & cleverness & readiness & tenderness & firmness: she used always to kiss her before taking leave every night.— (It is a mournful coincidence that my dear Father died on the 7th of December: his death was in the year 1828). Poor Lucy was overwhelmed by this unexpected calamity: she kept her bed till dinner time: when she came down I could see how deeply she had been plunged in grief, but she put on a calm & placid mien, which I thought most amiable as well as characteristic of her great strength of mind.— God bless & comfort her.— Another present of delicious grapes & pears came from Mr. Pemberton[8] . . . Poor Lucy went to bed again at 8 o'clock.— I wrote a prayer which I read at night to the servants.

Th. 9. . . . I received very kind letters from the Marquis Spineto & Mrs. Owen (to neither of whom I had written):— I now wrote to thank them. — I should have said that Sedgwick called on me yesterday & in the kindest manner possible offered to write letters & do any thing that I would entrust to him:— how like his warmheartedness! Miss Jane Page wrote me a very excellent letter & sent 'the Xn mourner' as a present to Lucy:[9]— I wrote to thank her. — Lucy & I each sent to Mr. Morris £5:— his scholars

[7] A slightly mistaken recollection of the last lines of Wordsworth's 'Simon Lee'.

[8] Romilly here records writing more than a score of letters to friends and relations such as his brother, cousins, nephews, Whewell, Sedgwick, Gunning, Carus, Misses D'Illens, Wilcox and Spilling, Mrs Willis and Mrs Skrine.

[9] I.e. a new and anonymous book of verse by a young Scotch minister, John Ross Macduff, entitled *Wells of Baca, or Solaces of the Christian Mourner, and Other Thoughts on Bereavement* (Edinburgh, 1847).

are now very very few. In dearest M's name I sent £10 to the Hospital as a donation from her for the loan of the Water-bed; & 10 guineas as a present from her to Betsy Edwards for her invaluable services as a nurse. — I myself gave £2 to my bedmaker Mrs. Carpenter to put herself in mourning, & sent £2 also to Mrs. Houghton for the same purpose, & gave £1 to Theodosia, £1 to Betsy's sister Margaret (in Wales), £1 to Jane Cook (our former servant), & £1 to Mrs. Helm's nurse. — I today wrote to Henry & Charles Romilly. — A very amiable letter from Mrs. Willis asking for some memorial of dear M. for little Meggy her goddaughter,— a prayerbook on any other thing of hers. Lucy to bed at 8.

Sat. 11. Dear Lucy apparently a little more composed today.— She & I sent to Dr. Haviland as a mark of our gratitude & as a memorial of dearest M. 'Hallams Modern Literature' (the copy wch I had given her in Sept. as a birthday gift.)— He wrote a very amiable letter in reply:— he called on me today, but I declined seeing him: I was convinced that it was to offer to attend the funeral, I therefore wrote to him to decline his doing so. — Neither Roget nor Jeddere Fisher (whom I asked) can attend in consequence of the Examination . . . I heard that the Fellowship was today declared:— 19 original dividends, which is very large indeed considering the expenses of the year from the Election & the Royal Visit. A clever Iceland friend of J.H. Fisher's (named Grimur Thomsen)[10] called on me today with a letter of introduction: I of course would not see him — I wrote a note to him at his hotel.— Lucy's cough a little better: she went to bed a little after 8; but she must have been most painfully excited by hearing the undertaker's men at work.

Mon. 13. A most painful day.— I took Lucy in a fly to College, having ordered fire & breakfast in the study, & charged my Gyp & Bedmaker not to show themselves. She put an extraordinary command on herself; but it was too plain that she must have passed a most wretched night, & she was deeply dejected. I prevailed on her to have a cup of tea & a mouthful of dry toast:— I left her at ¼ to 9.The Funeral was to leave our house at 9½: in the 1st mourning coach were Ouvry-North & myself; in the 2nd were the maids Theodosia Russell, & Betsy Edwards, & her Sister Mary. My bedmaker also attended. I thought the service finely read by Mr. Titcomb's curate. At a little past 11 I went to College to fetch dear Lucy: I found her without any fire & in a most melancholy state of dejection. If she gave way to a torrent of grief I should have better hopes of her recovering her composure. She shut herself up in her own room on returning to the house, & would not allow any one to see the depth of her sorrow. God be praised she has been supported to go thro this trying day better than I had dared to hope. I (at her kind request) took a long walk: I went to Girton — I was rejoiced that she come down to dinner at 4: she went to bed at 8 directly after tea. — I today

[10] A young Icelandic poet and essayist who had written a book on Byron (Copenhagen, 1845) that was influential in Denmark and Scandinavia.

wrote to Frances Wilderspin & sent her a pound to buy black ribbons.— I today had a kind affectionate letter from Geo. Romilly (who also wrote to Lucy): I had also admirable letters from Frank, & from Miss D'Illens (one of the best letters I ever read): also a kind one from Mr. Scott (the successor of Perry in St. Pauls). — After Lucy was gone to bed I wrote to George, Frank, & Mr. Scott. — I tonight sent off to Rd. Neave at Chelsea Hospital a declaration that Frank Romilly was the officer of that name who fought in the Deccan in 1818-9: this declaration was signed by me, & attested by the V.C. (as a County Magistrate) Mr. Scott (as Clergyman of the Parish), Mr. Asby (as a *respectable* acquaintance) & the Postmaster.[11]— A 3rd Dividend began to be paid on 1st Dec.

Tu. 14. Lucy very much dejected.— She is also suffering from cold & cough.— She wrote today a very warm-hearted letter to Frank. The remains of my dearest Sister are laid in the Churchyard of Christ Church Barnwell: the Vault is at the N.E. corner, next to the monument of Earnshaw:— she had spoken of being buried in the Cemetery but it appeared that Dissenters only were buried there.[12]— Today there was a called Congregation (for a Mandate to Gibson B.A. Trin.who is Chaplain to E.I. Company): one B.A. degree. Cartmell kindly officiated. . . The amiable Mrs. Worsley sent us a little nosegay & the Life of Mrs. Fry. — I was summoned away after dinner to draw up a letter to The Chancellor for Gibson's mandate: Sedgwick ought to have done it, but he is on a visit to The Queen at Osborne House! have no doubt he will highly please her Majesty.

Th. 16. Lucy's cold no better. Dismissal of term: Cartmell took my place.—Commemoration of Benefactors at Trinity:— I did not attend:— the sermon must have been poor stuff, for Marsh was the Preacher. Today is Shaw's Birthday: under happier circumstances I should as usual have been present.— Walk to Histon: Lucy not out, alas! Today I opened dearest M's Will: she has left £500 to Geo. Romilly her godson, & every thing else equally between Lucy & me.[13] I wrote to Frank & to George. In the Evening

11 Sir Samuel Romilly had bought Frank a commission as a young man. His army service, though not apparently long, took him as far as India, and after settling in France he only rarely visited England. Presumably he lived on a pension and his private income, including the many small sums that Joseph advanced regularly.
12 The Histon Road Cemetery (see 3 November 1845) being unconsecrated, was popular with but not exclusive to nonconformists. By 1847 the town churchyards like Holy Trinity had no room for new graves, and that may account for the choice of Perry's new Christ Church. The Mill Road cemetery was much needed when it opened in 1848.
13 The will had been written on a half-sheet of notepaper in March 1837, soon after the death of Cuthbert when it had been decided that the sisters would move to Cambridge. On 29 January 1841 Margaret signed it with Betsy Edwards and Jane Smith as witnesses. Romilly proved the will in the Prerogative Court of Canterbury on 6 January 1848. After the legacy to George and duties there was some £5,200 to be shared between Joseph and Lucy.
It may be a sign of the importance Romilly attached to it that he sent Betsy to the registrar to give particulars for Margaret's death certificate. The cause was given as 'atrophy – 6 months', doubtless Haviland's verdict.

I went on with Mrs. Fry: Lucy sat up till 9, which I thought rather an improvement.

Sun. 19. . . . Lucy's cold still bad:— spirits very dejected indeed. I went to Trinity Church & Lucy came in for the Sermon. Carus preached an admirable sermon from the Epistle (Phil. 4.5,6): we heard it from him 5 years ago.— To my great joy Lucy today paid a visit to her poor friend S. Foulkes.— No rain today.— I walked to Granchester to pay a visit to Lucy's protégée Mrs. Cann:— I found her very dirty; & confessedly she had not been to Church: gave her a lecture & some money to make the lecture go down.— I met Sedgwick who told me that at his visit to Osborne House last Wednesday[14] the Prince had asked him if he would like to see the Royal children:—he (S.) told them a story about a person lost in the snow in his vivid manner which delighted them: at dinner the Queen said to him, 'Princess Royal tells me that you told them an interesting story:— will you tell it me?' — So he told it over again at the Royal Table.— Wrote to Fra. Wilderspin desiring her to thank Mrs. Beardmore for a kind letter of hers to Lucy.

Fri. 24. Lucy still keeping house from the badness of her cold. Wrote to Henslow in answer to his letter: also to Mrs. Worsley to thank her for the Life of Mrs. Fry: also to the Rev. Edm. Edw. Allen who was ordained last Sunday by B. of Lichfield. Today E. Smith made the appraisement of dearest M's clothes, &c. Letter from Miss Butcher who fears that her letters are opened at the Post Office & wishes me to send her word of the mark on every letters seal!! she usually seals with letter P. —Lucy & I made this our Christmas day & had our turkey today.

Sun. 26. Another damp, dismal, sunless, miserable day. Lucy not out:— alas! she has never been out since last Sunday:— she has a nasty cold & cough.— I went to Trinity Church. I invited into the pew a modest gownsman who had placed himself in the free seats:— I wish I had left him there, for he groaned awfully & sung villainously. Downton read prayers most dolorously, & Hopkins preached an enraging sermon about wisdom, (in wch I thought he showed none): his Text was Job 28.22: it was a Charity sermon for the Old Schools.[15] I thought there was but one sensible sentence in the sermon, 'it is better to pay schools for teaching than a police for punishing children'. In the plate in which I put my 2/6 I saw nothing but halfpence, & I don't wonder. — Took a good long walk,— to Shelford. After dinner went to Decks about Betsy who has a touch of the Influenza, we fear: he prescribed (of course) dose & pill. Read loud a Sermon of A. Hare (on Grace & Peace).[16] — Wrote to Lodge.

[14] See Clark and Hughes, II, 131-40.
[15] Otherwise known as Whiston's Charity Schools, established in 1703 and supported by voluntary contributions, they comprised the Free School for boys and the King St School for girls. Carus was treasurer. Cf. 27 April 1842.
[16] I.e Rev. Augustus William Hare, brother of Julius, whose *Sermons to a Country Congregation* had been published posthumously in 1836.

Mon. 27. Lucy's cold much the same.— She didn't stir out tho the day was much less disagreeable.— Kind letter from Miss Cotton: wrote to her & sent her some books from the Library . . . Began reading loud the Life of Bishop Burgess (by Harford of Blaize Castle):— the book was recommended to me by Mrs. Henslow for its piety. The early part (about Scholarship) is vastly dull.[17]

Tu. 28. Same damp dismal weather.— Lucy's cold much the same: she didn't go out.— A Mrs. Warren (late of The Roebuck) came to my rooms & cried me out of £1: she is in distress about rent: she said that her late husband was one of 4 natural children of old Hailstone (Vic. of Trumpington) & that he (H.) as long as he lived allowed her £50 a year.[18]— Went to the Victoria Asylum to see old Mrs. Jordan (aged 87) & give her a Christmas box:— she was out: so I paid a visit to her kind fellow-lodgers the Simpsons. He worked for many years at The Pitt Press, but he has now little or no use of his hands & feet: I went into his bedroom & had a long talk with him, which seemed to give him pleasure, & he expressed himself very grateful. I then went into the sitting-room with his wife & 2 daughters & made the youngest read the Testament to me: she did it greatly to my satisfaction.— Today a Mand. M.A. was conferred on J.D. Gibson (Trin.) who is going out Chaplain to Bombay.— Poor Miss Rennie (Mrs. Leapingwell's daughter) died today:— she was 3 times at Roman Catholic Chapel on Christmas day & twice on Sunday: she had been most charitably active in distributing blankets &c to the poor: — yesterday she was taken ill, & today this interesting handsome young girl of 18 who was engaged to be married is cut off in the bloom of life:— an awful instance of the uncertainty of life!— I heard that inflammation of the bowels was the cause of her death: it was internal abscess in the Chest. Today the Dean & Chapter of Hereford are to make their reply to the Congé d'elire.[19] Dean Merewether in a 2nd letter to Lord John Russell has said that no power on earth shall induce him to elect Hampden & that he will encounter the penalties of praemunire. Lord J. Russell wrote in reply 'Sir, I have received your Letter in wch you tell me of your intention to violate the Law!' Today Sedgwick was to appear in town against a thief who (at the railway Station) attempted to steal his portmanteau: a policeman asked the man 'if it was his?' : he said 'yes, yes, get me a Cab':— the policeman put his hand on the

[17] Burgess, bishop of St David's from 1803 to 1825, founded the college at Lampeter on a site given by J.S. Harford of Blaise Castle, Gloucestershire, for the education of the Welsh clergy. Harford, who published the biography in 1840, was said to be the hero of Hannah More's *Coelebs* (see 6 September 1847).

[18] John Hailstone, formerly Woodwardian Professor of Geology, had died at Trumpington vicarage on 9 June aged 87. He had married late in life, his wife predeceased him, and these natural children must have belonged to his younger days.

[19] I.e. permission to elect the crown nominee (Hampden) as Bishop of Hereford. In theory any refusal by the Dean and chapter would have entailed dire penalties under a statute of praemunire dating from the time of Henry VIII. Merewether, long disappointed in his own hopes of preferment, was obdurate.

direction & said 'as it is yours, what is the direction?' :— the vagabond threw it down & attempted to escape:— he was condemned to years imprisonment & hard labour. At night went on with Bp Butler.

Wed. 29. Lucy's cold rather better.— To my great joy she went to several of her paupers today: among others to a Mrs. Murcutt (14 years help to G. Allen's bedmaker Mrs. Radcliff) whom she is anxious to establish as a bedmaker: she got me to write a letter to each of the 3 Tutors in behalf of the poor drudge. — Today received from Mr. Fenton the papers requisite for swearing me in as Executor: it was necessary for me to have Betsy Edwards sworn at the same time as subscribing witness to the will. I was at liberty to appoint as the *commissioners* any of the authorities of Trinity College or any Clergyman of a parish adjoining to Cambridge:— I chose Thacker & paid him the fixt fee of £1.1.—:— I got Betsy to attend at my rooms & Thacker came to administer the oaths. Today I wrote an epitaph (see next page) upon my dear Sister wch I sent to Bradwell the Bricklayer.— I today wrote to George Romilly. — I received a very warmhearted letter from Frank & amiable ones from all his family. Another instance of the uncertainty of life occurred today: Townson (F. of Qu.) died this morning: ill only for a few days! . . .

Th. 30. Lucy's cold a little better.— Today the 1st snow:— snow & rain & sleet fell all day:— I only went to College & back. Letter from Latham to tell me he was made Tutor of T.H. & to thank me for my exertions in his behalf. The Marq. Spineto today sent me an Italian poem written by him in the name of dearest Margaret. It was very amiable of the dear good Marquis to do this[20] . . . Today Lucy wrote to Mr. Christy (Fairfield, Manchester) offering to give money for the good of a Factory boy (G. Rawlinson) in his employ:—the boy may mend & I hope he will, but Mr. Christy wrote me word that he was *ingeniously dishonest.*— Yesterday a letter from the Rev. E.E. Allen saying that he had preached on Sunday: he has also begun visiting his flock & has performed a Funeral: he says 'I preached at the great Church. I made myself heard, wch was one point, & my advice tho given in a rambling unconnected sort of way was good enough if the cong. had taken it.' Characteristic of the writer.

---

[20] On Spineto's life and poetry see Bruce Dickins in C.P.Brand et al., *Italian Studies presented to E.R. Vincent* (1962), pp.18-23.

[21] This inscription on the Romilly tomb, itself one of few remaining in the churchyard by 1987, does not survive. Lucy's was only partly legible by 1990. Joseph's is quite clear.

[22] The College, originally known as the Hall or House of Valence-Mary, was founded by Mary, widow of Aymer, Earl of Pembroke. She bought the site in 1342 and Edward III signed a licence for the foundation of the College on Christmas Eve 1347.

Fri. 31. Lucy's cold a little better. She however would not stir out tho the day was not very bad. — The Epitaph I wrote for my dear Sister was as follows:

Sacred to the Memory of

M.C.R.

Daughter of T.P.R. Esq. of London

& Jane Anne his wife.

born 25 Sept. 1784 — died 7 Dec. 1847.

She was blest with a cheerful temper,

the most unselfish disposition,

& the kindest of hearts.

She was liberal to the poor,

& beloved by all who knew her;

but her virtues & accomplishments

gave a peculiar charm to her home.

Her life was spent in

endeavouring to serve others.

She endured a long & severe sickness

with Christian Resignation.

Her only hope was in the merits

of her Saviour.[21]

I was very sorry to hear today that dear Professor Smyth had had a stroke of apoplexy. — The Marquis Spineto (who was his most intimate friend) is deeply affected by it. He wrote me the intelligence in a very feeling letter.— Today sent up a certificate of the Burial, wch is required at the Bank.—I dined today in Pembroke Hall to commemorate their 500th birthday:— about 70 guests sat down.[22] The dinner was magnificent, & the hall was very tastefully decorated with holly &c. Dr. Ollivant made a dull speech: & Shaw (Chr.) pretending that he was falling asleep threw himself back (forgetting that he was not in a chair) & fell with the back of his head on the stone floor. I was much frightened, but happily he was not seriously hurt. Some of the speeches were good, especially those of French, Graham, Arlett, Turner (a former Fellow & a distinguished lawyer), & Serjeant Talford. I did not hear this last, for I went away at ¼ to 10, being the 1st to go. — By far the best speech I heard was Dr. Graham's, & I think Lord Hardwicke's was one of the worst.—Lucy tonight (for the 1st time) sat up to prayers:— she seemed much affected, tho with her usual great self-command she endeavoured to conceal her feelings. I thank God that her frame of mind appears far more composed than it was, & her bodily health is very much in its usual state.— For myself I have abundant reason to be most thankful for the very good health which I am now enjoying.

21-22   *For notes see opposite on p. 240.*

Appendix
Romilly's Family

The following summary account puts references in the Diary in context. There is extensive material on the family, together with a chart pedigree (c. 1677-1906), by Henry Wagner in *Proceedings of the Huguenot Society* VIII (1905-8). See also the Romilly entries in Burke's *Landed Gentry* (18th ed. I, 1965), and in Burke's *Peerage* (105th ed.1970), which continue various lines into recent times. For the Allen family of Wales see Burke's *Landed Gentry* (18th ed. II, 1969) under 'Evans formerly Harrison-Allen'. There are entries in the *Dictionary of National Biography* for Joseph Romilly, his uncle Sir Samuel, his cousins Sir John Romilly and Peter Mark Roget, Dr and Mrs Marcet, and for his great-nephew John Romilly Allen (1847–1907) whom he christened on 28 July 1847.

Stephen (or Etienne) Romilly of Montpellier, a Protestant, settled in England about 1701 and died in 1733 having married Judith, co-heiress of Francis de Montsallier of Shoreditch. They left with other children a younger son, Peter. Peter Romilly (1712-84) married Margaret (d.1796), daughter of Aimé Garnault, another French refugee, and they had three surviving children, Thomas Peter, Catherine, and Samuel.

* Member of Trinity College, Cambridge.

I. Thomas Peter Romilly of Dulwich (1753-1828) married 1780 his cousin Jane Anne (1756-1803), daughter of Isaac Romilly, F.R.S. They had nine children:

1. Caroline Jane (1781-1831) married 1813 Lancelot Baugh Allen* (1774-1845), Master of Dulwich College, and had two sons:
    i. George Baugh* ['G.B.A'](1821-98) married 1846 Dorothea Hannah, daughter of Roger Eaton. They had five sons and three daughters.
    ii. Edmund Edward* ['E.E.A'] (1824-98), alias 'Grim' married 1848 Bertha, daughter of Roger Eaton. They had five sons and six daughters.
2. Samuel (1783-1834) married 1820 Amelia (d.1824), daughter of James Walker, Judge of the King's Bench in Canada.They had an only son,
    i. George Thomas* ['G.T.R'] (1823-93) married 1848 Margaret (d.1907), only child of John Mirrielees of Aberdeen. They had four sons and five daughters.
3. Margaret Catherine ['M'.] (1784-1847) unmarried.
4. Peter Randolph (1786-1808) unmarried.
5. George Thomas (1787-98).
6. Cuthbert Stephen (1789-1837) unmarried.

7. Joseph* (1791-1864) unmarried.
8. Francis (Frank) (1793-1863) married Josephine — and had three children,
    i. Estéphanie married Adolphe Hippolyte Bourlet.
    ii. (Louise) Sophie married Félix Ogier, Professor of History.
    iii.(François) Jacques (sometime Professor of Rhetoric at Nantes).
9. Lucy Mary ['L'] (1797-1854) unmarried.

II. Catherine (1755-1835) married 1778 John Roget (1751-83), and had a son and a daughter:
    1. Peter Mark Roget (1779-1869) married Mary Hobson (d.1833). They had a son and daughter: Catherine Mary (1825-1905) and John Lewis* (1828-1908).
    2. Anne Suzanne Louise, 'Annette' (1783-1866).
        (See D.L. Emblen, *Peter Mark Roget, the Word and the Man* (1970).

III. Samuel (1757-1818) married 1798 Anne (d.1818), daughter of Francis Garbett of Knill Court, Herefordshire. When she died he committed suicide leaving six sons and a daughter:
    1. William* (1798-1855) unmarried.
    2. Sophie (1800-79) married 1820 Thomas Francis Kennedy (d.1879) of Dunure. They had a son Francis Thomas Romilly (b.1842).
    3. John* (1802-74), barrister, M.P for Bridport, 1832-5 and 1846-7, and for Devonport, 1847-52. Knighted 1848. Master of the Rolls 1851. Created Baron Romilly of Barry, 1866 (title extinct 1983). Married 1833 Caroline Charlotte (d.1856), daughter of William Otter, bishop of Chichester. They had four sons and four daughters: William* (b.1835), Anne (b.1837), Edward of Caius College (b.1838), Mary (b.1841), Henry* (b.1845), Sophie (b.1846), Lucy (b.1848), Arthur* (b.1850).
    4. Edward of Christ's College (1804-70), M.P. for Ludlow, 1832-5. Married 1830 Sophia (d.1877), daughter of Dr Alexander Marcet and his wife Jane.
    5. Henry of Christ's College (1805-84) married 1850 Rosa (d.1892), daughter of J.P. Morris.
    6. Charles (1808-87), barrister, M.P. for Canterbury, 1850-2. Married 1842 Lady Georgiana Elizabeth Russell (1810-67), daughter of the sixth Duke of Bedford. They had six sons: John (b.1843), Francis (b.1845), Charles Edward (b.1846), Cosmo (b.1848), Alfred* (b.1849), George* (b.1852).
    7. Frederick (1810-87), Lt-Col. Scots Guards. Married 1848 Lady Elizabeth Amelia Jane (1820-92), daughter of Gilbert, Earl of Minto.

They had three sons and two daughters : Samuel Henry* (b.1849), Frederick William (b.1854), Hugh Hastings (b.1856), Elizabeth Mary (d.1950 aged 97), and Gertrude Emily (d.1952).

From Francis de Montsallier Joseph Romilly shared a common descent with the Fludyer family which included Sir Samuel Fludyer, baronet (1800-76), Mary, Baroness Dacre (d.1808), Caroline, Countess Brownlow (d.1824), Mary, Countess of Onslow (d.1830), and Elizabeth, Lady Musgrave (d.1861). From Aimé Garnault he shared a common descent with the Ouvry, Gilson, Vautier, and other families; see *Proceedings of the Huguenot Society* XIV (1929-33), and J.J. Howard and F.A. Crisp, *Visitation of England and Wales* III (1895), 167-9, and the accompanying volume of *Notes* V (1903), 51-6.

INDEX OF PERSONS

Abbreviations:
adm. (admitted), pens. (pensioner), C. (Curate), R. (Rector), V. (Vicar).

Abbott, Alexander Scott, of Jesus Lane. Surgeon to Addenbrooke's Hospital 1817-43, and sometime mayor and J.P., died 1843 aged 53, 23, 74-5

Abercorn, James Hamilton, Marquis of (1811-85), Groom of the Stole to Prince Albert 1846-59, brother-in-law of Mrs Charles Romilly, 214

Abinger, Robert Campbell Scarlett, Lord, adm. pens. at Trinity 1811, 162

Achilli, Father Giovanni, 229-30

Acland, Mr, 148

Adair, Robert Alexander Shafto, adm. pens. at Trinity 1828, M.P. for Cambridge 1847-52, 139, 184, 219

Adams, *probably* Dennis, surgeon, 23

Adams, John Couch, adm. sizar at St John's 1839, Fellow 1846-52, Lowndean Professor of Astronomy 1859-92, 41, 180, 203-5, 206-7, 215, 224

Adcock, Justinian, attorney of Market Street, 164

Addison, Edward, Fellow of Corpus Christi 1798-1824, R. of Landbeach Cambs. 1821-43, 57

Adeane, Henry John, of Babraham Hall, adm. pens. at Trinity, 1806, called to the Bar 1814, M.P. for Cambs., 1830-2, died May 1847, 53, 63, 98, 139, 160, 163

Adeane, Mrs, i.e. Hon. Matilda Stanley, wife of H.J., 160

Ainslie, Agnes, *presumably* daughter of the next, 98

Ainslie, Emily, née Marsh, wife of Gilbert, 11, 48, 179

Ainslie, Gilbert, Master of Pembroke 1828-70, Vice-Chancellor 1828-9 and 1836-7, 1, 11, 18, 127, 179, 196

Airy, George Biddell, Plumian Professor of Astronomy and Experimental Philosophy 1828-36, Director of the Cambridge Observatory, Astronomer Royal 1836-81, 33, 136-7, 163

Airy, Richarda, née Smith, wife of George Biddell, 'as agreeable and winning in her manner as ever', 27, 33, 137, 163

Albert, Prince, 1-2, 12, 70-1, 77-83, 95, 129n, 140, 181, 194-200, 203-7, 209, 213-18, 238

Alboni, Marietta (d. 1894), Italian contralto, 215

Alderson, Sir Edward Hall, Fellow of Caius, Baron of the Exchequer 1834-57; cross-examined George Stephenson on the first railway case, 20, 104-5

Alderson, Georgina, Lady, wife of Sir Edward, niece of Baugh Allen, 217

Aldrich, Ira (d.1867), negro actor, 21

Alford, Henry, Fellow of Trinity 1834, V. of Wymeswold, Leics., 1835-53, later dean of Canterbury, 6, 179

Alger, Samuel, dishonest stall-holder, 26

Alicia, Princess (i.e. Alice), 53, 70

Allen, Clement Francis Romilly (b.1844), son of Baugh by his second wife, Romilly's godson, 99

Allen, Edmund Edward ('Grim'), second son of L.B.Allen and Caroline Romilly. Born 1824, adm.

pens. at Trinity 1842, later R. of Porthkerry and Prebendary of Llandaff, 20, 27-9, 31-4, 43, 48-50, 57-8, 77, 82-4, 86-7, 89, 96-7, 99-101, 108, 117-19, 124-7, 131-2, 134-5, 137, 139, 145-6, 149-50, 155, 157-8, 162, 166-8, 176-83, 195, 199, 209, 226-8, 232-3, 238, 240

Allen, Emma, 218

Allen, George Baugh, elder son of L.B.Allen and Caroline Romilly. Born 1821, adm. pens. at Trinity 1838, practised in the Temple 'the last of the great special pleaders', 6, 9-10, 108-9, 117, 126, 131-2, 141n, 145-6, 167-8, 209, 218, 240

Allen, Mrs George Baugh, née Dorothea Eaton, 108-9, 167, 182, 192, 195

Allen, George John, adm. pens. at Trinity 1828, son of Joseph, Bishop of Ely, Master of Dulwich College, 1843-57, 7(?), 53, 112, 120, 129

Allen, Georgiana Sarah, née Bayly, second wife of Baugh, 54

Allen, Henry, (?) Harry, 53

Allen, (Lancelot) Baugh, adm. pens. at Trinity 1794, of the Inner Temple, brother-in-law of Joseph Romilly, Master of Dulwich College 1811-20. One of the six clerks in Chancery 1825-42, 47, 52-4, 58, 99, 109-10, 113, 125, 136-7, 143, 145-7

Allen, John Hensleigh, of Cresselly, Pembrokeshire, adm. pens. at Trinity 1789, elder brother of L.B.Allen. High Sheriff of Pembrokeshire and M.P. for Pembroke 1818-26, 52-3

Allen, John Romilly, eldest child of George Baugh, 219

Allen, Joseph, Fellow of Trinity 1793, Bishop of Ely 1836-45, 44, 57, 78, 94, 102, 112, 126, 129

Allen, Margaret, née Ashley, wife of Joseph, Bishop of Ely, 27

Allen, William, son of Joseph, Bishop of Ely, 112

Alleyne, John Gay Newton, Warden of Dulwich College 1843-51, 227

Almack, Henry, scholar of St John's 1825, Fellow, R. of Fawley, Bucks. 1844-84, R. of Aberdaron, Bangor, 1843-84, 61(?)

Anderson, Mrs, née Scott, 184, 190

Anderson, Charles Cuyler, admitted pens. at Pembroke 1839 and re-admitted 1847, 'the Fair Maid of Pembroke', 34

Anson, Sir George (d. 1849), Groom of the Bedchamber to Prince Albert, 194, 205

Ansted, David Thomas, Fellow of St John's 1840-51, Professor of Geology at King's College, London 1840-53, 29, 108

Antigua, Bishop of, Daniel Gateward Davis, 214

Apthorp, the Misses, of Botolph Lane, 29, 48, 104, 119, 124, 142-3, 147, 161, 184, 186, 193, 210, 218, 228

Archdall, George John, Master of Emmanuel 1835-71, Vice-Chancellor 1835-6 and 1841-2, 1-2, 7-9, 12, 15, 17, 20, 26, 46, 50, 62-3, 76, 128, 132n, 147-8, 164, 170, 173, 179, 196, 201

245

Archdall, Jemima Elizabeth, née Kinterside, wife of George John, 46, 75, 112, 119, 147, 170, 179

Arlett, Henry, Fellow of Pembroke 1826-69, 34, 58, 80, 92, 95, 103, 195-6, 225, 241

Armagh, Archbishop of, *see* Lord John de la Poer Beresford

Asby, Mr, *perhaps* Charles the Cambridge Councillor, 237

Assad Yusuf Kayatt, 'the Syrian', 217

Astley, John Wolvey, Fellow of King's 1828-49, 205

Asturias, Prince of the, 183

Atkinson, Michael Angelo, Fellow of Trinity 1838 and tutor 1838-55, 101, 124, 175, 195

Atlay, James, Fellow of St John's 1842-59, V. of Madingley 1847-52, 209

Babington, William, adm. pens. at Trinity 1844, 130

Badham, Dr, 166-7, 170

Bagot, Richard, Bishop of Oxford 1829-45, 13

Bail(e)y, Esther, protégée of Lucy Romilly, 6, 23, 48, 50-1, 73, 77, 84, 89, 91, 93, 108, 116-17

Bailey, James 'Beast', scholar of Trinity 1813, head-master of the Perse school 1826-36, impecunious classical scholar and author, 229(?)

Bailey, Miss, orphan daughter of a clergyman, 11(?)

Bailey, Capt., 176

Baillie, Evan Montague, adm. pens. at Trinity 1844, 159

Baily, William Percival, Fellow of Clare 1831, Senior Proctor 1847, 227, 230

Baines, Edward, adm. pens. at Christ's 1819, V. of Bluntisham, Hunts. 1841–59, 129

Baker, William, linen-draper of Market Hill, 169

Baldrey, Lt Andrew Doughty, Senior Assistant at the Observatory; retired 1843 from ill-health and died in October of that year, 19

Baldrey (Baldry), Miss Sarah, daughter of Joshua the Cambridge artist, 161, 171, 191-4

Bancroft, George, United States minister to Great Britain 1846-9, 185

Bangles, Mrs, the Romillys' washerwoman, 175

Banks, Samuel Horatio, adm. pens. at Trinity Hall 1815, Vicar of Dullingham 1828-82, 205

Barker, Mr, schoolmaster of Prospect Row, 24

Barker, Mrs, 57, 117, 193

Barker, Joshua, son of the Romillys' gardener, 209

Barker, Mrs Mary (d. 1844), of Osborne Terrace, 112

Barker, W., son of the Romillys' gardener, 108

Barnes, Joseph Watkins, scholar of Trinity 1827, Fellow 1830, V. of Swineshead, Lincs 1840-3, 88,

Barnes, Eliza, née Atkinson, wife of George, 99

Barnes, George, adm. sizar at St John's 1792, Fellow of Queens' 1799; well-known for never wearing gloves, 99

Barnwell, Mrs Mary Ann, niece of Dr Chapman, married September 1845, 156

Barrington, Charles George, adm. pens. at Trinity 1845, 162

Barron, Mrs James John, widow of a livery-stable keeper, 233

Barry, Alfred, adm. pens. at Trinity 1843, 165

Barry, Charles Upham, adm. Fellow-Commoner at Trinity Hall 1836, C. of St Edward's, Cambridge 1841-7, of Benet Place, 117

Barry de Moncey, Madame, 224

Barsham, William, Cambridge postmaster for 16 years, died 16 May 1847 aged 70, 212

Basevi, George, architect of the Fitzwilliam Museum etc., 9n, 99-100, 144, 150

Bates, William, Fellow of Christ's 1838-50, Proproctor 1844, 87-8, 145

Bateson, Willam Henry, Fellow of St John's 1837, Master 1857-81, V. of Madingley 1843-7, 30-1, 36, 53, 97, 159, 182, 209, 217

Baxter, William, of Sidney Sussex, incorporated from Dublin, 127

Bayford, Augustus Frederick, adm. pens. at Trinity Hall 1824, rowing 'blue' 1829, advocate in Doctors' Commons 1839, 105

Bayne, Mrs, 202

Bayning, Henry William-Powlett (born Townshend), Lord, adm. pens. at St John's 1816, R. of Brome with Oakley, Suffolk 1821-47, 130

Beales, 'Old', grandfather of Mary, 192

Beales, Charles, adm. Fellow-Commoner at Peter-house 1814, coal and corn merchant of Newnham, 11, 61

Beales, Mary, protégée of Lucy Romilly, 192

Beard, William, gentleman farmer. A fellow-pupil of Romilly's at Mr Boyer's school, 16, 28

Beardmore, Mrs, 209, 238

Beckett, Sir John, bart., Fellow of Trinity 1797, 197

Bedford, Francis Russell, Duke of (1768-1861), brother of Lord John Russell, half-brother of Wriothesley Russell and Mrs Charles Romilly, 178, 180

Belaney, James Cockburn, surgeon, tried for murder, 110

Belany, Robert, adm. pens. at St Catharine's 1834, C. of Meldreth, Cambs. 1841-3 and of Long Melford 1843, V. of Arlington, Sussex 1843-52 when he converted to Rome, 49

Beresford, Lord John de la Poer, Archbishop of Armagh and Primate of Ireland 1822-62, 15, 17

Bernard, J.F. of Custom House, 74, 104, 111, 114

Bernards, the, *presumably* the family of Hermann Bernard, teacher of Hebrew in Cambridge 1830-57, 133

Bethune, *perhaps* John Elliot, adm. pens. at Trinity 1819 as Drinkwater, Counsel to the Home Office 1833-47, 219

Bickersteth, Edward Henry, adm. pens. at Trinity 1842, 184

Bidgood, Charles Harry, adm. pens. at Trinity 1841, no degree, 51

Birkett, Robert, Fellow of Emmanuel 1832-51, 1, 9, 13, 31, 57, 83, 96, 98, 130, 147, 178, 182, 196-7, 229

Birks, Thomas Rawson, second wrangler, Fellow of Trinity 1834, R. of Kelshall 1844-66, 118

Bishop, William, Mayor of Cambridge 1844-5, 144

Blakesley, Joseph Willam, adm. pens. at Corpus Christi 1827, President of the Union 1829, Fellow of Trinity and member of the 'Apostles', V. of Ware, Herts., 1845-72, 7, 10, 53, 79, 97, 117, 168-9,

195

Blamire, Mrs, 146, 228

Bland, Miles, Fellow of St John's 1808, R. of Lilley, Herts. 1823-67, 197

Blomfield, Charles James, adm. pens. at Trinity 1803, Bishop of London 1829-56. 'Set himself to reorganise the established Church', 14-15, 17, 96, 100, 177, 184-6, 205, 207

Blunt John Elijah adm. Fellow-Commoner at Trinity 1814, barrister, 216

Blunt, John James, Fellow of St John's, Lady Margaret's Professor of Divinity 1839-55, 149, 184, 186, 199, 210, 228

Boguslowsi (Boguslavsky), Prof. P.H.L. von (1789-1851), Director of the Breslau Observatory, 137

Bond, Henry John Hayles, of 56 Trumpington St, adm. pens. at Corpus Christi 1819, trained at St Bartholomew's Hospital, Regius Professor of Physic 1851, 19, 26, 205-6

Bond, Mary, née Carpenter, wife of Henry John, 26-7

Bones, the Misses, Sophia and Mary Ann of 7 St Andrew's Hill, 19, 60, 110

Boodle, Thomas, adm. pens. at Trinity 1826, Perpetual C. of St Andrew-the-Less, Barnwell, 44

Bourlet, Madame, née Estephanie (Fanny) Romilly, 92, 158, 171

Boutigny, Pierre Hippolyte (1798-1884), French chemist, 137

Bouverie, Col. Everard, adm. pens. at St John's 1807, Equerry to Prince Albert, 204-5

Bowstead, James, Fellow of Corpus Christi 1824-38, Bishop of Lichfield 1840-43, 76

Bowtell, Alicia, daughter of the next, 64

Bowtell, John (1777-1855), library-keeper, nephew of the book-binder, 51, 64-5, 102, 115, 167

Boyer, James (Bowyer) (1736-1814), master of Christ's Hospital 1767-99. Later he kept the private school which Romilly attended. Coleridge, Lamb, and Leigh Hunt testified to his brilliance and severity as a teacher, 119 (?)

Boyer, Mrs (daughter-in-law of James ?), 143, 149, 172,

Brackedon, Mr, 149

Bradwell, bricklayer, 240

Bradwell, 16

Bradwell, *perhaps* William, grocer of Sidney St, 162

Brass(e), Miss, daughter of John Brass (d.1833), Fellow of Trinity, and niece of Miss Milner, 5

Braybrooke, Jane, Lady, eldest daughter of Marquis Cornwallis and wife of R.G.N., 93, 96, 140, 157, 159, 163, 178, 222

Braybrooke, Richard Griffin Neville, third baron (d.1858), adm. nobleman at Magdalene 1811. First editor of Pepys's *Diary*, 96, 139-40, 142, 159, 163, 189, 225, 233

Brewster's *i.e* the chemists' shop of William Brewster in Sidney St, 210

Bright, Mynors, Fellow and tutor of Magdalene, editor of Pepys, 56, 127n

Brimley, George, adm. pens. at Trinity 1837, Librarian of the College 1845-57, 133

Bristed, Charles Astor, American adm. at Trinity 1840, scholar 1844, wrote *Five Years at an English*

University, 89, 96

Brock, Henry Frederick, adm. pens. at Trinity 1843, 145-6

Brocklebank, John, adm. sizar at Pembroke 1804, R. of Teversham, 1817-43, and of Willingham 1824-43, 57

Brooker, Mrs, 212

Brooks, J., chandler and painter, 176

Broome, John, prize-fighter, 7

Brown, Charles Edward, printer, editor of the *Cambridge Chronicle* and alderman, 180, 218

Brown, John, Fellow of Trinity, Vice-Master 1830-42, V. of Bottisham 1828- 37, 8, 40, 43, 62, 88, 169, 191(?), 219

Browne, George Adam, Fellow of Trinity 1797-1843, Vice-Master 1842, chaplain to the Duke of Sussex, 11, 17, 25, 40-1, 43, 53, 55, 57-61, 74, 86-7, 89

Brumell, Edward, Fellow of St John's, Proctor 1846, 197, 202, 204, 218

Brune, George, picture-dealer of Sidney St, 147n

Buccleuch, W F.M.D. Scott, Duke of, adm. nobleman at St John's 1825, Hon LL.D. 1842, Lord President of the Council 1846, 196

Buck, John, adm. pens. at Magdalene 1834, adm. Lincoln's Inn 1843, 219(?)

Buckland, William, Professor of Mineralogy at Oxford 1813, Dean of Westminster 1845, 224

Bull, Mrs, 3

Buller, Sir Francis (1746-1800), judge, 8

Bunbury, Charles James Fox, adm. pens. at Trinity 1829, married Frances Horner, 137

Bunbury, Edward Herbert, adm. pens. at Trinity 1829, Senior Classic 1833, called to the Bar 1841, M.P. for Bury St Edmunds 1847-52, 30, 74, 137

Bunbury, Sir Henry and Lady, parents of the two above, 137

Bunch, Robert James, Fellow of Emmanuel 1829, C. of Toft, Cambs. 1841, 13-15, 77, 103

Bungaree, Australian prize-fighter, died of injuries April 1842, 7

Bunsen, C.C.J., Chevalier, Prussian minister in England 1841-54, 15, 17

Burcham, Thomas Borrow, Fellow of Trinity 1832, Recorder of Bedford 1848-56, 103

Burder, Mr, secretary to the Bishop of Ely, 129

Burdett, Miss, 118

Burney, Charles Parr, Archdeacon of Colchester 1845-64, 178

Burney, Richard, adm. Fellow-Commoner at Christ's 1818, served in the Bengal army, 19

Burrell, Mrs, 175

Buston, Roger, Fellow of Emmanuel 1835, 225

Butcher, Miss, impoverished lady helped since 1832 or earlier by the Romillys, 11(?), 72, 110, 146, 148, 170, 175-6, 194, 201, 238

Byers, Timothy, adm. pens. at Emmanuel 1840, migrated to Christ's, Master at Oakham School 1844-64, 171

Byles, *presumably* John Barnard, serjeant-at-law 1843, leader of the Norfolk circuit 1845, 50

Byron, George, Lord, the poet, adm. nobleman at Trinity 1805, 127n,

Caledon, James du Pré, Lord, representative Irish peer, cousin of Lord Hardwicke, 83

Calthrop, Henry, Fellow of Corpus Christi 1826, R.

of Great Braxted, Essex 1841-75, 165

Cambridge, Duke of, Adolphus Frederick, (1774-1850), seventh son of George III, Hon LLD 1842. 'Not a disagreeable man, though he does chatter, and talk very loud', 14-16, 18

Camden, George Charles Pratt, Marquis, adm. nobleman at Trinity 1816, son of a former Chancellor of the University, 203

Campbell, Col. Alexander, K.H., of the Lancers, brother of Marchesa Spineto, 165

Campbell, Francisca, née Ouvry, 193

Campbell, Hon. William Frederick, adm. pens. at Trinity 1842, President of the Union 1847, Liberal M.P. for Cambridge town 1847-52, nephew of Lord Abinger, 184, 219, 233

Cann, Mrs, protégée of Lucy Romilly, 238

Canning, Charles John, Viscount (1812-62), third son of the statesman, 83

Cannon, William Jeary, attorney who succeeded Warwick as editor of the *Cambridge Advertiser*, 211

Canterbury, Archbishop of, *see* William Howley

Cape Town, Bishop of, Robert Gray, 214

Carlisle, Bishop of, *see* Hugh Percy

Carpenter, Mrs Margaret Sarah (1793-1872), portrait-painter, 74

Carpenter, Mrs, Romilly's bedmaker to whom he left £10 and his glass, crockery and coals in College, 64, 100, 118, 186, 236

Carpenter, Tom, son of the Romillys' butcher, George, of St Andrew's St, 56

Cartmell, James, Fellow and later (1849-81) Master of Christ's, 13-16, 33, 46-7, 77, 92, 115, 127, 130-1, 148, 150, 161, 166-8, 180, 182-3, 195-6, 202-3, 210, 212-13, 237

Carus, Dr Carl Gustav, 101-2

Carus, William, Dean of Trinity 1832-50, Perpetual C. and Lecturer of Holy Trinity 1832-51, 5-7, 11-12, 20, 23-6, 28, 30-2, 34-5, 39, 48, 50-2, 56-7, 59, 62, 64, 73, 76-7, 84, 87-9, 91-3, 95, 98, 102-3, 108-11, 115, 117-19, 123-4, 129-35, 137, 147, 149, 151, 157, 160-4, 166, 168, 170-1, 174, 177-9, 181, 183, 186, 189, 191, 193, 199, 203, 207-9, 211, 215-17, 220-1, 223, 226, 229, 235n, 238

Catlin, George (1796-1872), the American artist, 231-2

Cator, Peter, adm. pens. at Trinity 1814, Registrar of Supreme Court of Madras 1826-39, represented subscribers to the Sir Peregrine Maitland Prize in 1844, 117

Caulfield, Miss, *see* Corfield

Cavendish, *probably* William, adm. at Trinity 1825, second Wrangler and F.R.S. Later Duke of Devonshire, Chancellor of the University 1861-91, 107

Chafy, William, Master of Sidney 1813-43, Chaplain-in-Ordinary to the Queen, 55

Cayley, Arthur, Fellow of Trinity 1842-52, the mathematician, 157

Ceylon, Bishop of, James Cameron, 128

Chafy, William Westwood, son of the above, adm. Fellow-Commoner at Sidney 1832, 145, 202

Challis, James, Fellow of Trinity 1826-31, Plumian Professor of Astronomy 1836-82, Director of the Cambridge Observatory 1836-61. 'a spectacular failure as a scientist... has immortalized him', 59n, 180, 215n

Challis, Sarah, wife of James and widow of Daniel Copsey of Braintree, 59, 82, 124, 215n

Chambers, Robert, author of *Vestiges*, 129n

Chapman, Benedict, Fellow of Caius 1792-1820 and Master 1839-52, R. of Ashdon, Essex, 1818-52, 56, 126, 132n, 156, 189, 205-6

Chapman, the Misses, the three 'rattle-brained nieces' of the preceding, 99 (?), 126, 144

Chatturzie, Chunder Mohur, 18

Child(e), James Gay, adm. pens. at Magdalene 1840, 45

Childe, George Edward, adm. pens. at Trinity 1838, 7

Chipperfield, Ficklin's assistant, 227

Christie (Christy), Messrs, 233-4, 240

Chune, Henry, brother of Susan, 229

Chune, Susan (Mrs Grounds), protégée of Lucy Romilly, 54, 89, 104, 108-9, 128, 138-9, 150, 173, 229

Clark, Dr. 139

Clark, Mr, of Haslingfield, 100

Clark, Eliza, protégée of Lucy Romilly, 84

Clark, John Willis (born 1833) son of William, Professor of Anatomy. Later Fellow of Trinity, Registrary, architectural historian, and antiquary of Cambridge, 105, 171(?)

Clark, Mrs Mary, sister of Robert Willis, wife of William, 11, 23, 28, 57, 65, 96, 101, 103, 105, 111, 157-8, 171, 19, 210

Clark, William, Professor of Anatomy 1817-66. Friend of Byron. 'Bone Clark' who 'laid the foundation of the school of biological science at Cambridge', 11, 65, 102, 158, 163, 167

Clark, William, alias Wilkins, coach-driver, 144

Clarke, Samuel Thomas, adm. pens. at St John's 1843, 183

Clay, William Keating, adm. sizar at Jesus 1824, minor canon of Ely, 1838-54, 61

Claydon, Charles, butler of Trinity College, 186

Cleaver, Mrs, 192

Close, Francis, adm. pens. at St John's 1816, evangelical divine and author, Perpetual C. of Cheltenham 1826-56, arch-enemy of the Camden Society, 71, 119

Clutton, Ralph, Fellow of Emmanuel 1828-44, V. of Saffron Walden 1844-70, 142

Cocker, John, Fellow of Peterhouse 1837, 220

Cockerell, Charles Robert, the architect, 102n, 150

Codd, Edward Thornton, adm. pens. at St John's 1835, C. of St Giles with St Peter, Cambridge 1843-5, Perpetual C. of Cotes-Heath, Staffs. 1844-59, 40

Codrington, Admiral Sir Edward (1771-1850), 87

Colenso, William, Fellow of St John's 1837-46, Bishop of Natal 1853-83, made for the Zulus a Zulu grammar and dictionary, 59, 104, 119

Coleridge, Sir John, judge, Fellow of Exeter College, Oxford, nephew of S.T. Coleridge and friend of Wordsworth, Arnold, Pusey and Newman, 48, 50

Collison, Frederick William, Fellow of St John's 1838-55, 150, 209

Coltman, Sir Thomas, adm. pens. at Trinity 1798, judge, 185

Conybeare, William John, elected Fellow of Trinity

INDEX OF PERSONS

1839, Principal of Liverpool Collegiate Institution 1842-8, 74

Cook, Jane, servant of the Romillys, 236

Cooke, Mr, Inspector of Schools, 209

Cookson, Henry Wilkinson, Fellow and Tutor of Peterhouse, Master 1847-76 Proctor 1843. A distinguished geologist, godson of William Wordsworth, 13, 30-1, 196, 228

Coombe, John Adams, Fellow of St John's, C. of Holy Trinity, Cambridge, 141-2, 149, 157, 159, 164, 166, 170

Cooper, Allen Trevelyan, adm. pens. at Trinity 1843, 229

Cooper, John, Fellow of Trinity 1837-59, Pro-proctor 1842, V. of St Andrew the Great 1843-58, 7, 89, 208 (?), 226(?)

Coppin, Catherine Marie, daughter of the next, 167

Coppin, Thomas, baker, married Kitty Marlow, 138

Coppin, William Anthony, son of Thomas and Kitty, 138

Copsey, Miss, later Mrs E.T. Codd, 82

Corfield, Miss, governess, 23, 25, 28, 73, 96, 108, 114, 231

Cornell, Mrs, 'our neighbour', 174

Cornwallis, Lady, Louisa, widow of Charles the last Marquess, and mother of Lady Braybrooke, 96, 189

Corrie, George Elwes, Fellow of St Catharine's 1817, Professor of Divinity 1838-54, 147-8, 182, 205

Cory, Miss, 161

Cottenham, Christopher Charles Pepys, Lord, adm. pens. at Trinity 1797, Lord Chancellor 1836-41 and 1846-50, 144

Cottingham, Lewis (1787-1847), architect active in the Gothic revival, 71-2

Cotton, Ambrose Alexander, adm. pens. at Pembroke 1782, R. of Girton 1807-46, uncle of Sir St Vincent, 161

Cotton, Lady, Philadelphia, daughter of Sir Joshua Rowley and widow of Admiral Sir Charles Cotton, Bt of Madingley Hall, 25, 75, 112, 114, 118, 141, 143, 160, 170, 176, 209, 225, 229-30

Cotton, Philadelphia Letitia, daughter of Lady Cotton, 41, 64, 73, 119, 142, 160, 239

Cotton, Sir St Vincent (1801-63), sixth and last baronet, gambler, pugilist, cricketer, and driver of the Brighton coach, 95, 112, 133, 143, 161, 209, 221

Coward, Thomas, adm. sizar at Queens' 1829, married Mrs Alice Gulston, 123

Cranwell, Edward, Library-keeper of Trinity College, 186

Craufurd, Edward Henry John, adm. Fellow-Commoner at Trinity 1837, president of the Union 1839, called to the Bar 1845, 45-6, 181

Crayke, Mr 'a clever Scotchman', 100

Crick, Frederick Charles, adm. sizar at St John's 1826, brother of Thomas, R. of Little Thurlow, 1848-85, 16

Crick, Thomas, Fellow of St John's and R. of Little Thurlow 1825-48, Public Orator 1836-48, 1, 15-16, 39, 79, 81, 134, 186

Crisford, Stephen, of the Bull Hotel 'family and

posting', Trumpington St, 92

Crisp, Horace, 221

Critchett, Miss, 166

Crokat, Mrs, 131

Cross, Thomas, coachman and poet, 94

Crouch, John, Yeoman Bedell, 203

Crowe, William, builder, of Gonville House, 116-17

Croxton, George, adm. Fellow-Commoner at Caius 1843, called to the Bar 1847, 115

Cruttwell, 147

Cumming, Isabel, *probably* daughter of the next, 123

Cumming, James, adm. sizar at Trinity 1796, Professor of Chemistry 1815-61, 'seems to have made an independent discovery of thermo-electricity', 5, 27, 62, 117, 139

Cumming, James, adm. pens. Caius 1843, son of Professor James, 27, 62, 181(?)

Cumming, Sarah, wife of Professor James, 27, 62

Curson, Mrs, 147

Cutler, Mr, visiting American, 61

D'Aglié, Count Charles, adm. Fellow-Commoner at Magdalene 1838, 113

Daguilar, Miss, 212

Dale, Thomas, adm. pens at Corpus 1817, V. of St Bride's, Fleet St, 172

Dalton, James Edward, Fellow of Queens' 1832-52, C. of St Sepulchre, Cambridge, 1834-52, 9, 41

Daubeny, *probably* John, D.C.L. of Merton College, Oxford, who died in Doctors' Commons 1847, 105

Davies, John Llewelyn, adm. pens. at Trinity 1843, 126n, 165

Davies, Miss, 133

Davy, Mrs, wife of the King's Lynn gaoler, 94

Dawe, Henry Edward (1790-1848), painter and mezzotint engraver, employed by Turner, 62

Day, Russell, adm. scholar at King's 1845, 142

Dearle, John, thief, 167

Deck, Isaiah, chemist of 9 King's Parade, 7, 67, 76, 110, 179, 238

De La Warr, George John Sackville, Earl, adm. nobleman at Trinity 1828, Hon. LL.D. 1828, Lord Chamberlain of the Household 1841-6, 15n, 81-2, 197

Deighton, John, Cambridge bookseller, 26, 61, 64

Deighton, Mrs John, Susanna, died at Margate aged 42, 26

Deighton, Joseph Jonathan, Mayor of Cambridge 1845, 147

Denman, Hon. George, son of Thomas, adm. pens. at Trinity 1838, Fellow 1843, outstanding rowing 'blue', called to the Bar 1846, 26, 30, 74

Denman, Thomas, adm. pens. at St John's 1796, Lord Chief Justice 1832, Baron 1834, 148

Denning, Stephen Poyntz, of Dulwich, miniature and portrait painter, curator of Dulwich art gallery 1821-64, frequent exhibitor at the Royal Academy, 40, 46-7, 49, 54, 57, 86-7, 99, 111, 115, 127

Denny, Mr (Thomas?), of Downing Terrace, 175

Derry, Mrs, a hosier, 15

Devon, William, Earl of, High Steward of the University of Oxford 1838-59, 17

De Winton, Henry, adm. pens. at Trinity 1842, third Classic 1846, 134

D'Illens, Miss, a Swiss governess and old friend of the Romillys, 231, 235n, 237

Dimmock, James, carver, gilder, etc. of Sidney St, 162(?)

Dixon, Thomas, Fellow of Jesus 1845-6, Assistant Master at Liverpool Collegiate School 1846-51, married Mary Ann Baker at Great St Mary's 1846, 167-8

Dobler, Ludwig, famous German conjurer who in 1842 lit 200 candles instantaneously by firing a pistol, 12

Donaldson, John William, elected Fellow of Trinity 1835, Headmaster of King Edward's, Bury, 1841-55, 98

Doria, family name of Niccolo Spineto, the Marquis,

Doria, Captain Alexander, son of Spineto by his second wife, of the East India Company, 31, 187, 225

Doria, Elizabeth ('Bessy'), daughter of Spineto, god-daughter of Joseph Romilly, and later wife of Rev. William Bain, 88, 98, 101, 108, 173

Doria, Harriet ('Harty'), daughter of Spineto, married John, son of Professor Haviland, 83, 101, 108, 173, 179

Doria, Margaret ('Meggy'), fourth and youngest daughter of Spineto, later wife of Dr Thomas Bumpsted, 108, 173

Doria, Mary Jane, daughter of Spineto, married Henry Philpott of St Catharine's, 108, 152, 166, 179,

Dornford, Mrs, 211

Dornier, Miss, governess at Audley End, 156

Downton, Henry, adm. sizar at Trinity 1836, C. of Holy Trinity 1847-9, 238

Drosier, Wlliam Henry, Fellow of Caius 1845-89, 131-2, 148

Druce, George, adm. pens. at Peterhouse 1839, Fellow 1844, 20

Drummond, Edward, private secrerary to Peel, murdered, 42

Ducrow, Andrew (d.1842), equestrian and showman, 24

Dunford, Romilly's gyp, 46-8, 55, 100, 114, 118

Durham, George F.D.Lambton, Earl of, adm. pens. at Trinity 1846, 180

Dykes, John Bacchus, adm. pens. at St Catharine's 1843, the future hymn-writer, 210

Earnshaw, Samuel, adm. pens. at St John's 1827, Senior Wrangler 1831, 'a very successful coach' 1831-47, 72

Eaton, Mrs, neighbour of Baugh Allen, widow of Roger and mother of Dora and Bertha, 110, 232

Eaton, Bertha, married 1848 E. E. Allen, 210, 232-3,

Eaton, Dorothea Hannah ('Dora') of Chrinow, Wales, see Mrs. G.B. Allen,

Eden, Robert John, Fellow of Magdalene, D.D. 1847, Bishop of Sodor and Man 1847-54, 212

Edgeworth, Maria (1767-1849), novelist and writer for children, 87

Edinburgh, Bishop of, see Charles Hughes Terrot

Edleston, Joseph, Fellow of Trinity 1840-63 when he married Harriet, daughter of Professor James Cumming, 20, 72, 134, 158

Edlin, William James, adm. sizar at Trinity 1843, 145, 165

Edwards, Betsy, devoted parlour-maid of the Romillys, later Mrs James Spink, 35, 59, 62-3, 74, 76, 83, 89, 108, 138, 156, 169, 212-13, 218, 231, 234-8, 240

Edwards, Margaret, sister of Betsy, 236

Edwards, Mary, sister of Betsy, 207, 236

Egerton, Lord Francis (1800-57), statesman, poet, and patron of the arts, created Earl of Ellesmere 1846, 54

Ehrenberg, Professor C.G., Hon M.A. 1847, 214

Elger, Mrs, daughter of Henry Gunning, 201

Elgin, Thomas Bruce, Lord (d. 1841), of 'The Marbles', 115

Ellenborough, Edward Law, Earl of, adm. nobleman at St John's 1807, Governor-General of India 1841-4, brother of C.E.Law, and cousin of H.J. Adeane, 47

Elliott, Henry Venn, Fellow of Trinity 1816. First preacher of the proprietary chapel of St Mary's, Brighton; founded a school for daughters of poor clergyman in 1836, brother-in-law of Whewell, 69, 99, 107, 215-16

Elliot, Hon. George Francis, fourth son of the Earl of Minto, admitted pens. at Trinity 1839, called to the Bar 1847, 11

Ellwood, William, University Marshal after T. Johnson, married 1845 Hannah Hammond, 151, 203, 205

Ely, Bishops of, see Joseph Allen and (after May 1845) Thomas Turton; Dean of, see G. Peacock

Ernshaw, Mrs, 164

Eton, Provost of see Francis Hodgson

Evans, Charles, adm. pens. at Trinity 1843, 161, 184

Evans, Robert Wilson, Fellow of Trinity 1813, 74

Everest, Col. George, surveyor general of India 1830-43, 137

Everett, Edward (1794-1865), American minister to the Court of St James 1841-5, Hon LLD 1842, 15-17, 135-6

Exeter, Bishop of, see Henry Phillpotts

Exeter, Brownlow Cecil, Marquis of, adm. nobleman at St John's 1811, Groom of the Stole to Prince Albert 1841-6, 205

Eyres, Charles, Fellow of Caius 1835-51, recommended admitting dissenters, 31, 57, 80, 115, 130, 182, 197, 212, 230

Fardell, Henry, adm. pens. at St John's 1813, V. of Waterbeach, Cambs. 1821-54, V. of Wisbech 1831-54, 65-8, 73, 94

Fardell, Elinor, daughter of Henry, 66, 68

Fardell, Eliza, wife of Henry, daughter of B.E. Sparke former Bishop of Ely, 65

Fardell, John George, adm. pens. at Christ's 1828, R. of Sprotborough, Yorks., 1837-56, 66-8

Farrar, John, distinguished Wesleyan teacher, 29

Farren, William (1786-1861) actor-manager, 68

Faulkner, Mrs, perhaps the wife of Henry M. of Trinity, 63

Faulkner, Richard Rowland, adm. sizar at St John's

1813, re-admitted 1844, a 'ten-year man', V. of Holy Sepulchre 1825-73, 98, 105

Favell, Mr, 91

Fawcett, Mr, magistrate, 144

Feilding, *see* Fielding

Fendall, James, Fellow of Jesus 1831-40, V. of Comberton 1833-67, R. of Harlton 1839-67, 95, 101, 181, 209

Fenton, Mr, 240

Fetch, Joseph, solicitor of Peas Hill, Cambridge, superintendent registrar of marriages, births, deaths, 30

Fick, Heinrich, German man of letters, 190

Ficklin, Thomas John, surgeon of Petty Cury, always 'very amusing and agreeable', 55n, 174, 217, 219, 223-5, 227-34

Field, *presumably* Frederick, Fellow of Trinity 1824-43, R. of Reepham, Norfolk 1842-63, patristic scholar, 74, 214

Fielding, *perhaps* Henry, adm. pens. at Emmanuel 1816, R. and patron of Salmonby, Lincs. 1840-68, 66-7

Fielding (Feilding) Viscount, Rudolf William Basil, son of the Earl of Denbigh, adm. pens. at Trinity 1841, married Louisa June 1846, 1, 2, 83, 86, 219-20

Fielding, Louisa, Lady, née Pennant (d.1853), 220

Finch, 'impudent' Mr, 123

Fisher, Augusta, presumably the young daughter of Mrs Fisher, née Martin, and Thomas the banker, 25, 114

Fisher, John Hutton, Fellow of Trinity 1820-31, V. of Kirby Lonsdale 1831-60, brother of William Webster, 129, 139, 236

Fisher, Thomas, banker of Thomas Fisher and Sons, Petty Cury, sometime mayor, 20-1, 31, 80, 83,

Fisher, Mrs Thomas, 25

Fisher, William Webster, Fellow of Downing 1834-44, Downing Professor of Medicine 1841-74, physician at Addenbrooke's hospital 1845-73, brother of John Hutton, 1, 6, 58, 120, 131-2, 139, 158

Fitch, Betsy, protégée of Lucy Romilly, 175, 193

Fitzpatrick, James, adm. pens. at Peterhouse 1842. Rusticated and name taken off the boards 1844, 42

Fitzwilliam, Charles William Wentworth, Earl, Hon. LL.D. 1833, former M.P., President of the Statistical Society 1830-40 and 1847-9, 176, 185, 197

Foggi, Professor of Mathematics in the University of Pisa, 137

Foley, Richard, Fellow of Emmanuel 1825-42, R. of North Cadbury, Som., 1842-61, 77

Follett, Sir William, adm. pens. at Trinity 1813, Solicitor General 1841-4, 97

Forbes, Lord, 142

Forbes, Henry Erskine, adm. pens. at Queens' 1840, subsequently a regular army officer, 8

Ford, Henry, adm. pens. at Trinity 1839, adm. solicitor 1846, 8

Fordham, Caroline, sister of Sarah, protégée of Lucy Romilly, 48

Fordham, Sarah, protégée of Lucy Romilly, 34, 47-8, 52, 63, 141, 148, 150

Forsyth, William, third Classic and Chancellor's medallist 1834, Fellow of Trinity 1835-42, barrister, 74

Fortescue, Hugh, Earl, LL.D. 1847, former Whig M.P., Lord Steward of the Household 1846-50, 214

Foster, Ebenezer, of Anstey Hall, Trumpington, banker of Foster and Co, Trinity St. Liberal in politics and active in town affairs, 19, 57

Foster, Mrs Ebenezer, 11 (?)

Foster, Ebenezer (Jr.), of E. & E. Foster, solicitors of Green St. In 1847 listed as living at Union Road, 19, 79, 124

Foster, Eliza Jane, née Edwards, wife of Ebenezer (Jr.), 176

Foster, Richard (Jr.), nephew of Ebenezer senior, 49, 83

Fo(u)lkes, Sarah, protégée of Lucy Romilly, 28, 34-5, 63, 75, 89, 95, 100-2, 172, 178, 232, 238

Fox, Edward Jones, adm. pens. at St John's 1838, 97

Francis, John (b.1822), would-be assassin of the Queen, 10–12

Francis, Clement, adm. Fellow-Commoner at Trinity Hall 1838, Solicitor to the University, 75(?), 99, 160, 182, 231

Franks, James Clarke, scholar of Trinity 1814, chaplain 1819, C. of St Mary's Whittlesey 1844-54, 105

Freeman, Philip, Fellow and tutor of Peterhouse, 1842-53, 117

French, William, Master of Jesus 1820-49, 1, 2, 26, 53, 93, 157, 163, 165, 195-6, 205, 207, 241

French, Mrs and Miss, 132

Frere, Ellen Mary, eldest daughter of Mary, married to Lord Monteagle's heir, Stephen Spring-Rice, 52n

Frere, Frederica, 145, 173

Frere, John, adm. pens. at Trinity 1826, R. of Cottenham 1839–51, nephew of William late Master of Downing, 165

Frere, Mary, Mrs, mother of Ellen, Frederica and Philip, widow of William, Master of Downing (1812-36), singer, 52, 148, 167(?)

Frere, Philip Howard, adm. pens. at Trinity 1830, Fellow of Downing 1837. Linguist and agriculturist, managed Downing's estates, 6, 52, 134, 151, 178(?)

Frost, Anne, protégée of Lucy Romilly, 100

Fry, either Thomas R. of Emberton, Bucks since 1804 or John R. of Desford, Leic. since 1800, 56

Fuller, Mr, *perhaps* Frederick, Fellow of Peterhouse 1843, 137

Fussell, John Thomas Richardson (formerly Curry), adm. pens. at Trinity 1844 aged 27, 158 (?)

Galle, Johann Gottfried (1812-1910) astronomer at Berlin, 180

Gambier family, 163

Garnons, William Lewes Pugh, Fellow of Sidney 1817, V. of Ulting, Essex 1848-63, entomologist and botanist, 56

Gaskin, Thomas, apprentice shoe-maker in Penrith, adm. sizar at St John's 1827, Fellow of Jesus 1832-42, Proctor 1841-2, F.R.S. 1839, 1, 16, 18-20

Gaussen, Mrs, 179

Geldart, James William, Fellow of St Catharine's 1809-21, Regius Professor of Civil Law 1814-47, R. and patron of Kirk-Deighton, Yorks, 1840-62, 1

Gent, 'respectable' tradesman, 162

Gersdorff, Baron, Ernst C.A. von (1781-1852), Saxon minister, Hon LLD 1842, 15, 101-2 'Giantess, the', i.e. Miss Tarleton, sister to Mrs Hodgson, 100, 144

Gibbs, Mr and Mrs, 97

Gibbon, Mrs, 160

Gibson, John Dawson, adm. pens.at Trinity 1841, Chaplain of Bombay 1848-65, 237, 239

Gifford, *probably* George, Earl of, adm. pens. (and nobleman) at Trinity 1842, 86

Gifford, the Misses, 93

Gilby, William, adm. pens. at St John's 1841, 87-8

Gillmor, Clotworthy, adm. St John's 1844, M.A.inc. 1845, Vicar of Dartford 1845-56, 197

Gilmour, Agnes, god-daughter of Lucy, 91

Gilmour, David, protégé of Lucy, 161

Gilmour, Eliza, protégé of Lucy, 80, 84, 110, 138, 192-3, 233

Gilmour, John, 74, 84, 91 101, 103-4

Gilmour, Mrs, Scottish widow helped by the Romillys, mother of the above and next, 76, 97, 148, 192-3, 233

Gilmour, William, 'an unmanageable youth', 91-2, 101, 170

Gillson, Harriet, maid to the Romillys, 59

Girling, William, adm. pens. at Trinity 1843, 162

Gloucester, Bishop of, *see* James Henry Monk

Gloucester, William Frederick, Duke of, Chancellor of the University 1811-34, 125-6, 198, 204

Godolphin, Elizabeth Charlotte, Lady, 208

Goodeve, Thomas Minchin, adm. pens. at St John's 1839, adm. Inner Temple 1840, 41

Goodwin, Charles Wycliffe, Fellow of St Catharine's 1840-7, Junior Proctor 1844, called to the Bar 1848. Elder brother of Harvey. 'An enthusiastic Egyptologist from the age of nine', 120, 147-8

Goodwin, Harvey, scholar of Caius 1837, second Wrangler 1840, Fellow 1841-5, C. of St Giles 1845-8, later Dean of Ely. Joint founder of the Camden Society, 117, 136, 151

Gordon, Anthony, adm. pens. at Trinity 1812, Chaplain there 1838-58, 186

Gordon, Stewart Cranmer, adm. at St John's 1833, a 10-year man, Headmaster of Haworth School 1846-54, 170

Gosset, Thomas Stephen, Fellow of Trinity 1813-47. C. of the Chapel Royal, Windsor, 25, 72, 97, 111, 219

Gough, Sir Hugh (1779-1869), Commander in Chief in India 1843-9, 164

Goulburn, Henry, adm. Fellow-Commoner at Trinity 1801. M.P. for the University 1831-56, Chancellor of the Exchequer 1841-6. Friend and executor of Peel, 35-6, 185, 205, 219-20

Goulburn, Henry, son of Henry, adm. pens. at Trinity 1830, second Wrangler, senior Classic, and Fellow 1835, called to the Bar 1840. Died 1843, 74, 89

Gouldsby, the Misses and Master, 75-6

Graham, Sir James, Hon. LLD. from Trinity 1835, M.P. for Dorchester 1841-7, Home Secretary 1841-6, 1, 92. 170n

Graham, John, Master of Christ's 1830-48, R. and Rural Dean of Willingham, Cambs. 1843-8, Bishop of Chester 1848-65, 1, 9, 33, 40, 43,57, 78, 84, 112, 115, 128-30 166-7, 179, 195-7, 201, 204, 214, 241

Graham, John, son and heir of John above, born 1834, 157

Graham, Mary, née Porteous, wife of John, 48, 112, 115, 179

Grant, Sir Alexander Cray, adm. Fellow-Commoner at St John's 1799, West Indian planter. M.P for four constituencies before sitting for Cambridge 1840-3, 49

Grant, Alexander Ronald, adm. pens. at Trinity 1838, Fellow 1847, 226

Gray, Benjamin, adm. pens. at Trinity 1838, third Wrangler and Fellow 1843, called to the Bar 1848, 41, 74

Grays, the, protégés of the Romillys, 24

Green, sheriff in 1843, 148

Green, Charles (d.1870), balloonist, 215n

Green, T., bookseller of King's Parade, 221

Greenaway, Charles, 88n

Grey, Sir George, Secretary of State for the Home Department 1846-52, 214

Griffin, William Nathaniel, Fellow of St John's 1837-48, 126, 133n

Grisi, Giulia (1811-69) Italian opera-singer, 98

Grote, John, Fellow of Trinity 1837-66, 177, 226

Grounds, Susan, *see* Chune

Grounds, Thomas, 150

Gruggen, Frederick James, adm. sizar at St John's 1839, Fellow 1846-51, 140

Grylls, *probably* Thomas Glynn, adm. pens. at Trinity 1844, 183

Guest, Edwin, Fellow (and later Master) of Caius 1824-80, philologist, 130

Guillemard, *probably* William Henry, Fellow of Pembroke 1838, lecturer in classics and successful coach, 27

Gully, John (1783-1863), prize-fighter, horse-racer, M.P., and colliery proprietor, 11

Gunning, Francis John (Frank), solicitor of Gunnning and Francis, son of Henry. Closely involved in the challenge to the 'entrenched power of the Corporation'. Town Clerk 1836-40, 106, 174, 201

Gunning, Frederick, son of Henry, barrister on the Norfolk circuit, 129n, 173, 201

Gunning, Henry, adm. sizar at Christ's 1784. Esquire Bedell 1789-1852 and author of *Reminiscences* 1854, 1, 19-20, 42, 78-9, 106, 131n, 165, 173-4n, 176, 199-203, 209, 214, 220, 224-5, 227, 234

Guthrie, John, adm. pens. at Trinity 1812, V. of Calne and Perpetual C. of Cherhill, Wilts 1835-65, 68, 107

Gwilt, *perhaps* Daniel, Fellow of Caius 1802, R. of Icklingham 1820-56, 130

Haberden, *see* Heberden

Hailstone, John, Fellow of Trinity 1783, Professor of Geology 1788-1818, V. of Trumpington 1817-47, 239

Halford, Sir Henry (d.1844), 205

Hall, former brewer to Trinity College, 233

Hall, Robert (d.1831), 186

Hallam, Henry, the historian, father of the next, 150

Hallam, Henry Fitzmaurice, scholar of Trinity 1844, an 'Apostle', 98, 151

Halliwell, James Orchard, adm. pens. at Trinity 1836, 125, 127

Hammond, Josiah, of Rhadegund Buildings, trained at St Bartholomew's, surgeon to Addenbrooke's hospital, 23, 29, 110

Hampden, Renn Dickson, D.D.inc. 1835, Regius Professor of Divinity at Oxford 1836, 232, 239

Hankinson, Robert, adm. pens. at Trinity 1786, evangelical V. of St Andrew's, Walpole, Norfolk, 1808-63, 5, 145(?)

Harding, Agnes and Emma and their younger sister, daughters of Derisley, 55, 57

Harding, Derisley, adm. sizar at Trinity 1808, Scholar of Pembroke 1811, V. of Barton 1835-71, but living in Grantchester, 55

Harding, Henry John, adm. sizar at Pembroke 1837, B.A. 1842, died 1845, son of Derisley, 55

Harding, John, preacher, 181

Hardinge, Sir Henry (Viscount 1846), Governor-General of India 1844-7, 164

Hardwick, Philip (1792-1870), architect, 63

Hardwicke, Admiral Charles Philip Yorke, Earl of, matriculated from Queens' and Hon. LL.D. 1835, Lord-Lieut. of Cambridgeshire 1834-52, one of the Lords-in-Waiting 1841-6, 65-7, 83, 185, 195, 216, 241

Hardwicke, Susan, Lady, sixth daughter of Lord Ravensworth, wife of Charles Philip, 65-7, 214

Hare, Augustus J.C. (1834-1903), adopted son of Augustus and Maria Hare, 221-2

Hare, Mrs Augustus, née Maria Leycester, 221-2

Hare, Jane Esther, née Maurice, wife of Julius Charles, 184

Hare, Julius Charles, Fellow of Trinity 1818, R. of Hurstmonceaux 1832-55, 184

Harford, John Scandrett, adm. pens. at Christ's 1820, 179

Harnage, Sir George, R.N., second baronet, of Fitzwilliam St, 58, 181(?)

Harper, Henry, adm. sizar at St John's 1809, Archdeacon of Madras 1836-46, 173

Har(r)ington, Edward Charles of Oxford, 108

Harris, presumably Henry Hemington, attorney, of Free School Lane, 218

Harris, Robert, adm. pens. at St John's 1829, migrated to Trinity, V. of Brierley Hill, Staffs. 1833-59, 197

Harrison, John Branfill, adm. pens. at Trinity 1841, 87

Harrod, John, publican of The Three Swans, 33

Hart, Sarah, murdered, 129

Hartshorne, Charles Henry, adm. pens. at St John's 1821, Perpetual C. of Cogenhoe, Northants. 1838-50. Founder member of the British Archaeological Association, 61

Harvey, Mr, clerk at the Pitt Press, 88

Hatton, Mrs, 'the Hoody', 223

Haviland, Arthur Coles, youngest son of John, born 1831, 199

Haviland, John, Fellow of St John's 1810-20, Regius Professor of Physic 1817-51. Lived on Huntingdon Road, 7-8, 23, 30-1, 33, 39, 42, 55n, 57, 73-4, 76, 79-80, 84-5, 91-2, 98, 115, 129-31,142, 150, 163, 166-7, 181, 189-91, 201, 212-13, 217, 219, 221-2, 226-34, 236-7n

Haviland, John (Jr), adm. pens. at St John's 1839, V. of Pampisford 1845-63, married Harriet Doria, 173, 179

Haviland, Mrs Louisa, née Pollen, wife of John, 42, 83, 91, 117, 120, 179, 187, 227

Hawtayne, Admiral Charles S.J., of Catton, Norwich, 91

Hayles, probably Mrs Jane of Melbourne Terrace, 28, 48, 111, 117,177, 222

Haylock, Robert, chemist of Sussex St, 116-17

Head, George, adm. pens. at Trinity 1841, son of Sir Francis the colonial governor and author, C. of Doncaster 1845-6, 11

Headley (Headly), Henry, medical practitioner, in 1839 listed as resident in Jesus Lane, 7

Headly, Michael, relation of the Misses Bones, a long serving town Councillor, 60

Heath, John Moore, Fellow of Trinity 1831-45, 45, 53, 97 100

Heaviside, James William, Fellow of Sidney, Professor of Mathematics at Haileybury 1838-57, married Mira, daughter of Julian Skrine, 187

Heaviside, Mira, née Skrine, 35, 119,

Hebblewhite, Frederick, draper of Market Hill, 161-2

Heberden, William, adm. pens. at St John's 1841, later in the East India Company, 116

Hedger, cashier at Mortlock's bank, 126

Helm, Mrs, perhaps Mrs A.E. of 2 Hills Road, 210, 224, 231

Hemery, James, Fellow of Trinity 1839-44, R. of St Helier, Jersey 1844-9, 86

Hemming, George Wirgman, adm. pens. at St John's 1840, Senior Wrangler 1844, Fellow 1844-53, 93

Hensley, Lewis, Senior Wrangler 1846, Fellow of Trinity 1846-56, 157, 168, 177, 181, 228

Henslow, Frances (Fanny), daughter of John and Harriet, later married J.D. Hooker, 137, 209

Henslow, Harriet, née Jenyns, wife of John S., 3, 222, 239

Henslow, Helen, daughter of John and Harriet, 222

Henslow, John Stevens, adm. pens. at St John's 1813, Professor of Botany 1825-61, R. of Hitcham, Suffolk 1837-61, recommended Darwin as naturalist for The Beagle and planned the new Botanic Garden, 3, 48, 57, 107, 131, 137, 209, 238

Henslow, Louisa, daughter of John and Harriet, 137

Herbert, Mr, lawyer of Ickleton, 46, 103

Herbert, Mr, i.e. a younger son of the Earl of Powis, 162

Hereford, Bishop of, see Thomas Musgrave

Herschel, Sir John Frederick William, Fellow of St John's 1813-29 whose 'position as celestial explorer is unique', 135-6

Hervey, Lord Alfred, son of the Marquis of Bristol, adm. pens. at Trinity 1833, called to the Bar 1843, 119

Hervey, Lord William, adm. pens. at Trinity 1822,

Secretary of the embassy in Paris 1843, 195

Hewham, Mr, 216

Heywood, James, adm. pens. at Trinity 1829, B.A. 1857, M.P. for North Lancs 1847-57. Dissenter instrumental in the abolition of religious tests at matriculation, 46, 63, 135(?)

Hickie, Dr, of Hawkshead, 152

Hildyard, Francis, Fellow of Clare 1834, barrister, brother of James, 167

Hildyard, James, Fellow of Christ's 1833-47, Senior Proctor 1843-4, R. of Ingoldsby, Lincs 1846-87, 17n, 26n, 30, 114, 145, 150, 162

Hill, Isaac, adm. sizar at St John's 1843, B.A. 1847, 191

Hillman, George, adm. pens. at Magdalene 1841, 49

Hind, John, Fellow of Sidney 1823-4, mathematical author, 28

Hind, Miss, *probably* daughter of John above, 11

Hind, Mrs *probably* wife of John, 27

Hodgson, Mr, owner of livery-stable, perhaps John of the *Blue Boar*, Trinity St, 62

Hodgson, Mrs Charlotte, née Tarleton, wife of William, 87, 144, 227-8

Hodgson, Francis, Fellow of King's 1803-15, Provost of Eton 1840-52, 197

Hodgson, Richard, 197

Hodgson, William, Fellow of Peterhouse 1825, Master 1838-47, Vice-Chancellor 1843-4, 75, 77-81, 87-9, 101-2, 104, 112-13, 116, 132n, 203, 214, 227-8

Holden, Hubert Ashton, adm. pens. at Trinity 1841, Senior Classic 1845, Fellow 1847-54, 177, 184, 226

Holditch, Hamnett, Fellow of Caius 1821-67, remarkable for his shyness. Son of a pilot and harbourmaster of King's Lynn, presented with the freedom of that town on becoming Senior Wrangler in 1822, 56

Hook, Walter Farquhar, V. of Leeds 1837-59, Chaplain in ordinary to the Queen, 21

Hooker, Joseph Dalton (1817-1911), the botanist, 222

Hope (*post* Bereford Hope) Alexander James, adm. pens. at Trinity 1837, M.P. for Maidstone 1841-52. Wealthy politician, author, and patron of the arts, married 1842 Mildred, daughter of the Marquis of Salisbury, 18, 26, 168-9, 196

Hopkins, Caroline, née Boys, wife of William, 32, 131, 163

Hopkins, William, adm. pens. at Peterhouse 1823, Esquire Bedell 1827-66. A renowned mathematical coach who had nearly 200 wranglers as pupils, 1, 19, 78-9, 97,194, 203, 205

Hopkins, William Bonner, adm. pens. at Caius 1840, Fellow 1844-7, C. of Holy Trinity 1846-7, 191, 207, 223, 238

Hoppett, Dunford's successor as Romilly's gyp, 48, 64

Horner, Leonard (1785-1864), the geologist, 137

Hose, Frederick, adm. sizar at Queens' 1826, C. of Holy Trinity 1830-45, 23, 52, 76, 93, 124, 133, 135

Houghton, Mrs, old lady staying with the Romillys in Nov. 1844, 94, 117, 236

Housto(u)n, William, adm. pens. at Trinity 1841,

did not graduate, adm. at the Inner Temple 1842, 7

How, Mrs, drunken cobbler's wife, 193(?), 243

Howe, Elizabeth, Fulbourn prostitute, 193n

Howes, Betsy, protégée of Lucy Romilly, 63,

Howes, Caroline, protégée of Lucy Romilly , 63, 158, 186

Howley, William, Archbishop of Canterbury 1828-48, 15, 177

Howsden, Charles, 224n

Hubbe, Professor, 99

Hudson, Carry (Caroline), protégée of the Romillys since she was a child in Dulwich, 106, 193

Hudson, George (1800-71), 'the Railway King', 148

Hudson, H., Trinity College cook who lived at 1 Camden Place, 58, 218(?)

Hudson, John, adm. sizar at Trinity 1793, Senior Wrangler 1797, Fellow 1798, V. of Kendal, Westmorland 1815-43, 84

Hughes, Edwin, circus-owner, 224

Hughes, Kate and Louisa, presumably daughters of Thomas, 157

Hughes, Robert Edgar, adm. pens. at St John's 1841, migrated to Magdalene, 45

Hughes, the, *i.e.* Thomas Smart, former Fellow of St John's, Trinity Hall, and Emmanuel, R. of Fiskerton, Lincs. 1829-46, Canon of Peterborough 1827-47, and his wife Ann Maria, née Foster, and daughter, 11, 34

Hullah, John Pyke (1812-84) composer and teacher of singing, 117-18

Hullah, Mrs, née Foster, first wife of John Pyke, 117

Hulle, Mr, Dr Jan's friend, 103

Humfrey, Charles, banker, architect, and mayor of Cambridge 1837-8, 20-1, 146n, 176, 219

Humfrey, Elizabeth, daughter of Charles, 87, 146

Humphrey, Mr, Steward of Trinity College, 55

Humphrey, *perhaps* J.H. Humphreys (sic) adm. pens. at Trinity Hall 1798, R. of Tenby 1831-52, 186

Humphry, George Murray, adm. Fellow-Commoner at Downing 1847 having trained at St Bartholomew's; surgeon to Addenbrooke's 1842-94, Deputy Professor of Anatomy 1847-66. Brother of William Gilson, 23, 29

Humphry, William Gilson, Fellow of Trinity 1839, Junior Proctor 1845-6, brother of George M., 23, 178, 181

Hunt, William, Fellow of King's 1788-1852, Assessor to the Chancellor since 1805. 'The most notorious drunkard in the University', 130, 196

Huntingdon, Lady, 69

Huntley, *presumably* John Thomas, adm. pens. at Trinity 1808, R. of Binbrooke, Lincs 1845-81, 135

Hurlock, 'our neighbour', 125

Hustler, farmer of Bartlow, 156

Hustler, James Devereux, Fellow of Trinity 1807, R. of Euston with Little Fakenham 1829-49, married Elizabeth, daughter of W.L. Mansel, Master of Trinity, 57, 186

Hustler, James Devereux, adm. pens. at Jesus 1846, son of the above, 181

Hymers, John, Fellow of St John's 1827-53, Lady

Margaret's Preacher 1841-52, 199

Ibotson, William Haywood, adm. Fellow-Commoner at Magdalene 1832, Perpetual C. of Addlestone, Surrey 1841-5, 106
Ingle, Charles, scholar of Trinity 1811, Fellow of Peterhouse 1825, V. of Strensall, Yorks 1827-43, 19, 57, 85-6, 124
Ingle, Susannah, wife of Charles, 85-6, 106
Ingle, William, of Hills Road, 139
Ironsides, Sarah, succeeded Jane Smith in 1843 as cook to the Romillys, 64, 76, 108, 111, 133, 138

Jackson, *probably* Frederick, adm. pens. at St John's 1836, C. of Elm, Cambs 1842-3, V. of Parson Drove, Cambs 1844-1904, 66
Jackson, T.L., missionary, 159
James, Miss, 12 James, William Browne, adm. sizar at Trinity 1820, V. of Harston 1837-43, R. of Fen Ditton 1844-77, 129
Jan, Ludwig von, philologist, 100, 103-4
Janes [James], Robert, organist at Ely cathedral, 'published a psalter pointed for chanting at a time when singers chose their own divisions', 27, 66-7
Janson (or Ianson), William, 59-60
Jarvis, Mrs, Lodge's servant, 145, 147, 199, 200
Jeddere-Fisher, Cyril, adm. pens. at Trinity 1846, 228, 231, 236
Jenner-Fust, Sir Herbert, Fellow of Trinity Hall and Master 1843-52. Never lived in College. Official Principal of the Court of Arches 1834-52, 45, 89, 120, 205
Jennings, 'archdeacon', 227
Jenyns, *probably* George Leonard, adm. pens. at Caius 1781, V. of Swaffham Prior 1787-1848, Prebendary of Ely, 1802-48. Of Bottisham Hall, 44
Jephson, Henry (1798-1878), physician, 47-8, 50-1
Jerdan, William (1782-1869), editor of *The Literary Gazette,* 136
Jeremie, James Amiraux, Fellow of Trinity 1826-50, Professor at Haileybury 1830-50, 177, 182, 184, 185n, 219, 226, 234
Jermyn, Frederick Hervey, Earl, adm. nobleman at Trinity 1819, M.P. Bury St Edmunds 1826-59, Treasurer of the Household 1841-6, 80, 103, 183
Jermyn, Katherine Isabella, Lady, daughter of John, Duke of Rutland, 183
Jerningham, Hon. Capt., 174
Jersey, Sarah Sophia, Lady, wife of the fifth Earl, 15
Joachim, Joseph, the violinist, 215n
Johnson, Thomas, University Marshal and later School-Keeper, 42, 81, 176, 203, 205
Joinville, François, Prince de (1818-90), 70-1
Jolly, Henry Parker, adm. sizar at Queens' 1842, died May 1846 aged 22, 157
Jones, John, the Romillys' dentist who had worked in Cambridge since about 1821, 32, 58-9, 124, 150, 165, 201, 208, 226
Jones, Luke, adm. pens. at Queens' 1829. School-master of Parker's Piece in 1846, 24
Jones, Richard, adm. pens. at Caius 1812, Professor of Political Economy at Haileybury College 1835-55. Perhaps Whewell's closest friend, 88
Jordan, Mrs, in the Victoria Asylum, 239

Joseph, Mrs, 191

Kaye, John, Master of Christ's 1814-30, Bishop of Lincoln 1827-53. Married 1815 Eliza, daughter of John Mortlock of Cambridge, 126, 204
Kelly, Sir Fitzroy, K.C. 1835, Solicitor-General and knight 1845, Tory M.P. for Cambridge 1843-7, 49, 57, 98, 129n, 139, 202
Kelty, Mary Anne, the novelist, 225
Kemble, Charles, the actor, 149
Kemp, *presumably* Trinity's Combination Room butler, of Malcolm Street, 120
Kennaway, Charles Edward, Fellow of St John's 1824-30, Perpetual C. of Christ Church Cheltenham 1843-7, V. of Chipping Campden 1832-73, 107
Kennedy, Sophie, only daughter of Sir Samuel Romilly, wife of the next, 54, 56n, 138, 155n, 157, 173, 231
Kennedy, Thomas Francis, P.C.(1788-1897), Whig politician, Scottish husband of Sophie, 54, 155n
Kent, Duchess of, mother of Queen Victoria, 1-2
Kielmannsegge, Count, Hon. LL.D. 1842, 15
King, Joshua, Senior Wrangler 1819, President of Queens' 1832-57, Lucasian Professor of Mathematics 1839-49, 40-1, 43, 79, 116, 205
King, Miss, niece of Miss Cotton, a daughter of Sir Richard King, bart, 73, 226 (?)
King, Maria Susanna, Lady, née Cotton, wife of Sir Richard, 73, 142
King, Robert Jarrold, adm. pens. at St Catharine's 1810, C. of Wisbech 1818-54, 66
Kingdon, George Thomas, adm. pens. at Trinity 1834, Chaplain 1842-8, brother of Samuel N., 72(?), 101
Kingdon, Samuel Nicholson, adm. pens. at Trinity 1823, cricket 'blue', Fellow of Sidney, assistant C. at Great St Mary's 1841-3, brother of George T., 23, 35
Kingsley, William Towler (d. 1916), Fellow of Sidney, Junior Proctor 1845, 123, 178, 193n, 197, 204-5, 214, 225
Knight-Bruce, Sir James Lewis(1791-1866), judge. In 1835 and 1837 he unsuccessfully contested the borough of Cambridge. Vice-Chancellor of court of Chancery 1841, knighted and Chief Judge in Bankruptcy 1842, 36
Knowles, Edward, surgeon, 23, 29
Koe, John Herbert of Lincoln's Inn and his wife, London friends of the Romillys. Among their thirteen children was Robert Louis, 49
Koe, Robert Louis, adm. pens. at Clare 1838, migrated to Christ's 1841, ordained deacon 1844, 49

Lablache, Luigi (1794-1858), opera singer, 98, 215n
Laing, Mr, 133
Lamb, Mrs Anne, née Hutchinson, wife of John, 179
Lamb, John, Master of Corpus Christi 1822-50, Dean of Bristol 1837-50; a stout Whig, 44, 112, 127, 129, 155, 179
Lamb, John, adm. pens. at Caius 1844, son of the above, 179
La Motte, Matthew Gallye, Fellow of Sidney, C. of Cove, Devon 1841-56, 145
Landseer, Edwin Henry (1802-73) the painter, 12,

54, 155, 172, 193-4

Langshaw, George, Fellow of St John's 1830-43, V. of Great St Andrews 1835-43, 46

Latham, Miss, 229

Latham, Henry, adm. pens. at Trinity 1841, 184 (?), 240

Latimer, Mary, protégée of Lucy Romilly, 169-70

Laurence, Samuel (1812-84), portrait-painter, 158

Law, Miss, poetess, 40

Law, Charles Ewan, adm Fellow-Commoner at St John's 1810, Recorder of London 1833-50, M.P. for the University 1835-50, brother of Lord Ellenborough and cousin of H. J. Adeane, 36, 205, 207, 214, 219-20

Law, Edward, see Ellenborough, Earl of

Leacroft, Charles Holcombe, adm. pens. at Trinity 1843, 184

Leapingwell, George, adm. sizar at Corpus Christi 1818, an Esquire Bedell 1826-63. Called to the Bar 1830, Commissioner of Bankrupts in Cambs. and Hunts. Married 1843 Sarah, née Campbell,' papist' widow of George Reddie, 1, 18-19, 78-9, 127, 131n, 203, 205

Leathley, Mrs, 'canting old protégée of Margaret's', 168, 171

Le Blanc, Thomas, Master of Trinity Hall 1815-43, 42

Lee, Samuel, adm. pens. at Queens' 1814, Regius Professor of Hebrew 1831-48. One of the greatest linguists of the century he had been an apprentice carpenter till brought to Cambridge under the auspices of C.M.S. and Isaac Milner, 41, 189

Leecroft, see Leacroft

Lefevre, Charles Shaw, adm. pens. at Trinity 1810, Speaker of the Commons 1839-57, 205

Lefevre, John George, Fellow of Trinity, Vice-Chancellor of London University 1842-62, brother of Charles, 210, 213, 216, 219-20

Legge, Lady Mary (1796-1886), younger sister of Charlotte wife of George Neville, Master of Magdalene, 165

Lempriere, Miss, sister of Mrs Herbert of Ickleton, 103

Lennard, Mr, 170

Lennard, Thomas Barrett, adm. Fellow-Commoner at Peterhouse 1846, 181

Lestourgeon, Charles (d.1853), surgeon to Addenbrooke's hospital from 1813, having served in the Napoleonic wars. Father of Charles (Jr.), 23

Lestourgeon, Charles (Jr.), adm. pens. at Trinity 1824. Surgeon to Addenbrooke's Hospital and partner of J. Okes at 34 Trinity Street. Married Elizabeth, daughter of Ebenezer Foster of Anstey Hall, Trumpington, 23, 29, 42, 175(?)

Le Verrier, Urbain J.J.(1811-77), the astronomer, 180, 215, 217

Lewis, probably Charles Warner,(not Augustus), adm. pens. at Trinity 1839, called to the Bar 1846, 56

Lewis, Waller Augustus, adm. pens. at Caius 1841, a fine whist-player, 114 114

Lilley family of Grantchester, 144n

Lilley, Emma or Emily, youngest daughter of Edward, married Horace Crisp, Sept. 1847 at Grantchester, 221

Lincoln, Bishop of, see John Kaye

Lind, Jenny (1820-87), Swedish soprano, 215, 224

Lindsay, Charles Philip, adm. pens. at Clare 1838, 47

Lindsay, Henry, adm. pens. at Trinity 1842, President of the Union 1845, 51

Lindsay, John, 223

Lindsay, Maria, née Marryat, wife of Henry, V. of Croydon, mother of Henry and Charles Philip who had lived with her in Cambridge since January 1843, 8, 28, 51-2

Lindsell, Mr, 202

Ling, Mr, of the music shop. presumably Joseph, a teacher of music in Pembroke St in 1847, 112

Locke, Thomas Bentley, adm. pens. at Trinity 1838, adm. at Inner Temple 1843, 8

Lodge, Annette, cousin of John the Librarian, 99, 106-7, 111-12, 138, 147, 152, 155, 189, 200, 209

Lodge, Edmund, adm. pens. at Magdalene 1836, son of Richard, physician, of Hawkshead, and nephew of John, the Librarian, 39, 48

Lodge, John, Fellow of Magdalene 1818, University Librarian 1822-45, R. of Anderby, Lincs 1835-50 when he died, 6, 11-15, 21-3, 29, 33-4, 39-41, 46-51, 57-60, 64, 75, 77, 80, 82, 84, 86-8, 91, 98-100, 103, 106-7, 111-13, 115, 118-19, 123-4, 126-8, 130, 138, 142, 145, 147, 152, 155, 158-9,162, 175, 181, 198-9, 220, 222, 226, 231, 238

Lodge, John, adm. sizar at Magdalene 1842, brother of Annette and nephew of the Librarian whose 'very negligent if not dishonest' executor he became, 51, 57

Lodge, Richard, cousin of John the Librarian, 123, 145, 198

London, Bishop of, see Charles James Blomfield

Longford, Georgiana, dowager Countess of, 187

Lovell, Henry, adm. sizar at St John's 1837, Crosse scholar 1841, C. of All saints, Northampton 1845-6 when he died, 56

Löwenstein, Prince Wilhelm of, student friend of Prince Albert, 214

Luke, Robert, Senior Fellow of Sidney when he died in 1844, 56

Lund, presumably Henry adm. pens. at Trinity 1833, barrister, 197

Lushington, Franklin, adm. pens. at Trinity 1840, Senior Classic 1846, Fellow 1847, 151, 226

Lutt, Mrs, 52

Lyndhurst, John Singleton Copley, Lord, adm. pens. at Trinity 1790, raised to the peerage and made Lord Chancellor 1827, elected High Steward of the University 1840, 1-2, 15, 78-9

Lyell, Charles, inc. M.A. 1831, the geologist, 129n, 137

Lyon, Henry, chemist of Petty Cury, 229

Macaulay, Thomas Babington, Fellow of Trinity 1824-52, 131n, 144n, 151n, 161n, 185

McCausland, Irish clergyman, 132

Macfarlan, probably George, Fellow of Trinity 1804, V. of Gainford, Co. Durham 1824-62, 13

McGermas, charity candidate, 131

Macgregors, the Miss, 217

McKenna, Patrick Knox, 132

Macleod, Henry Dunning, adm. pens. at Trinity 1838, called to the Bar 1849. Writer on political economy considered unorthodox by contemil1poraries, 11

Maddison, George, Fellow of St Catharine's 1832-9, V. of All Saints, Cambridge 1838-56, 26, 148, 205, 207, 213, 220

Maine, Henry James Sumner, Fellow and Tutor of Trinity Hall, Regius Professor of Civil Law 1847, 212

Maitland, Samuel Roffey, adm. pens. at St John's 1808, Librarian at Lambeth Palace 1838, 222-3

Malden, *presumably* Henry, Fellow of Trinity 1824, Prof. of Greek at London 1831-76, 219

Malin, Miss, 63

Malkin, Arthur Thomas, adm. pens. at Trinity 1820, 198

Mandale, Blain, adm. pens. at Trinity 1843, 145-6

Mann, Miss, 113-14, 130-1, 133

Manners, Lord John James Robert, adm. pens. at Trinity 1836, M.P. for Newark 1841-7, son of the Duke of Rutland, 183, 196

Manners-Sutton, (John) Henry Thomas, adm. pens. at Trinity 1831, M.P. for the borough of Cambridge 1841-7, 219

Mansfield, Horatio, adm. pens. at Trinity 1838, Fellow 1843, called to the Bar 1853, 74

Marcet, Mrs Jane (1769-1858), mother of Mrs Edward Romilly, 87, 132, 149

Marlow, Catherine, pupil of Margaret Romilly, witness to Lucy's will. Later

Mrs W. Coppin, 23, 138, 167

Marlow, Mrs, Mistress of the King St school until 1855, and presumably mother of Catherine, 7, 9, 89

Marsden, John Howard, Fellow of St John's 1827-41, R. of Gt Oakley, Essex 1840-89, 76

Marsh, Henry Augustus, Fellow of Trinity 1841-9, 237

Martin, Francis, Fellow of Trinity 1825-68, Senior Bursar 1837-61, 25, 53, 62, 78, 97, 128, 165, 176-7, 195, 219, 225-6

Martin, *probably* William George, adm. pens. at St John's 1844, founder of the Licensed Victuallers' Choral Association, 210

Martineau, Alfred, adm. pens. at Trinity 1836, Fellow 1843, called to the Bar 1846, 74

Mason, Peter, adm. sizar at St John's 1819, third Wrangler 1823, headmaster of the Perse School, Cambridge 1837-64, 87

Mason, William, print-seller of St Mary's Passage, 62

Mathison, William Collings, Fellow of Trinity 1840-68, a considerable pianist, 48, 100, 162, 208

Matthews, Charles (1803-78) comic actor married to Madame Vestris, 68

Matthison, Mrs, pauper, 128

Maturin, Charles Henry, Fellow of King's 1822-46, Senior Proctor 1840, 9

Maul, Mrs, an unfortunate lady, 67

Maxey, Mrs Sophia, of Bene't Place, 112, 116

Meares, Samuel Owen, adm. sizar at Trinity 1828, Perpetual Curate of Uzmaston, Pembrokeshire 1840-68, 146, 168

Medina Sidonia, Duke of, 183

Meggison, Augustine, adm. pens. at Trinity 1841, 87

Melburn, protégée of Lucy Romilly, 176

Melville, David (1813-1904) of Oxford, first principal of Bishop Hatfield's Hall, Durham, 189

Melville, Hon. William Leslie (1788-1856), son of the Earl of Leven, 58

Merewether, John, M.A.(inc.) 1827, Dean of Hereford 1832-50, 239

Mill, Charlotte Elizabeth, youngest daughter of William Hodge, 74-6

Mill, Maria, natural daughter of Hon. James R. Elphinstone of Bengal, and wife of William Hodge, 8, 53, 73-6,

Mill, Maria Elphinstone, daughter of W.H., later Mrs Benjamin Webb, 75-6, 208

Mill, William Hodge, former Fellow of Trinity, Hulsean Advocate 1839-44, V. of Brasted,Kent 1843-53, Regius Professor of Hebrew 1848-53, 18, 33, 35, 41-3, 48, 51, 59, 73-6, 99, 117 183-4, 195, 208

Miller, Mr, 99

Miller, son of the butler of Corpus Christi, 208

Miller, William Hallowes, Fellow of St John's 1829-44, Professor of Mineralogy 1832-80, 180

Millers, *presumably* George, adm. sizar at St John's 1793, R. of Hardwicke, Cambs 1825-52, kept a school at Ely for many years, 212

Mills, Mr, former publican of the *Sun Inn*, Trinity St, 92

Mills, Mr, son of the above, 225

Mills, John, Fellow of Pembroke 1831-60, 13, 58, 103, 115, 130, 147, 161, 163, 182, 196, 213

Milton, W.T.S. Wentworth-Fitzwilliam, Lord, adm. pens. at Trinity 1833, 220

Mirehouse, *perhaps* John Campbell, adm. pens. at Trinity 1806, Serjeant-at-Law 1833-50, 181

Money Kyrle, *perhaps* Rosa Elizabeth, née Pridham, wife of Rev. James of Emmanuel College, R. of Yatesbury, Wilts. 1843, 87

Monk, Charles James, adm. Fellow-Commoner at Trinity 1843, B.A. 1847, only son of James Henry, 134, 158

Monk, James Henry, Fellow of Trinity 1805, Professor of Greek 1808-23, Bishop of Gloucester 1830-56, 134, 170

Monteagle, Lord, *see* Spring-Rice

Moody, William, elected Fellow of Trinity 1817, called to the Bar 1820, Standing Counsel to Trinity College, 62, 219

Moore, Mr, a clergyman, 32

Morgan, mad clergyman, 145

Morgan, cricketer, 140

Morgan, John Holdsworth, of the Observatory, adm. pens. at Jesus 1845, 134

Morris, Mr, *perhaps* Edward who kept a day school in Union Street in 1839, 235

Morris, John, adm. pens. at Trinity 1844, 179

Mortlock, Edmund Davy, son of John, the Cambridge banker, Fellow of Christ's 1811-46, V. of Great Abington Cambs 1835-45, R. of Moulton, Suffolk 1845-73, 32, 46, 50, 63

Mortlock, John F., the convict, grandson of John the banker, and nephew of Edmund, 32, 50

Mortlock, Thomas, senior partner in Mortlock & Co., the Cambridge bankers, 33, 84, 100, 115, 142(?)

Mortlock, Mrs Thomas, wife of the above, 76

Mortlock, William, *probably* son of John Mortlock and with him commemorated in St Edward's

Church. 'Distributor' of stamps in Benet St. 65

Munro, Hugh Andrew Johnstone, adm. pens. at Trinity 1838, second Classic 1842, Fellow 1843-85, 26, 74

Murchison, Sir Roderick Impey, matriculated from Trinity 1847, President of the Geographical Society 1843-58, 136n, 137, 214

Murcutt, Mrs, 'a poor dirty miserable old drudge', 240

Murcutt, Mrs, 35

Musgrave, Catherine, daughter of Richard Cavendish, Lord Waterpark, wife of Thomas, 71, 73

Musgrave, Thomas, Fellow of Trinity 1812-37, Bishop of Hereford 1837-47, Archbishop of York 1847-60, 48, 71, 85, 167, 169, 189, 217, 232

Myers, *presumably* Charles John, Fellow of Trinity 1825-9, V. of Flintham, Notts. 1829-70, 89(?), 135

Neale, John Mason, scholar of Trinity 1836. Unable to qualify in mathematics he took an ordinary degree. A founder of the Camden Society. Liturgical scholar and hymnwriter, married July 1842, Sarah Webster, 44

Neave, Richard, of the Chelsea Hospital, 237

Nelson, George, adm. pensioner at Corpus Christi 1839, 31-2

Nelson, Horatio, Earl, adm. pens. at Trinity 1841, 1-2, 86, 93n, 195-7

Nelson, Mr, *presumably* Hon. John Horatio, adm. pens. at Trinity 1843, younger brother of Horatio, 86, 159

Neville, Charles Cornwallis, adm. pens. at Magdalene 1842, second son of Lord Braybrooke, 96, 142, 159, 178, 187

Neville, Lady Charlotte, née Legge, wife of George, Master of Magdalene, 165

Neville (or Neville-Grenville), Hon. George, Master of Magdalene 1813-53, brother of Lord Braybrooke. Dean of Windsor 1846 and Chaplain to the Queen. Co-discoverer of Pepys' *Diaries*, 1-2, 15, 81, 114, 181, 205, 207, 233

Neville, Henry, third son of Lord Braybrooke, 178

Neville, Latimer, adm. pens. at Magdalene 1845, later Fellow and Master, fourth son of Lord Braybrooke, 145, 162, 181

Neville, Louisa Anne, second daughter of Lord Braybrooke, 156, 159

Neville, Lucy Georgina, youngest daughter of Lord Braybrooke, 163, 178, 222

Neville, Miss, *i.e.* Mirabel Jane (1821-1900) eldest daughter of Lord Braybrooke, 93n(?), 156, 159, 165, 222

Neville, Richard Cornwallis, heir of Lord Braybrooke, 233

Neville, Seymour, adm. pens. at Magdalene 1841, Fellow 1845-8, third son of Hon. George, Master of the College, 96

Newby, William, coal merchant of St Andrew's St, 119

Newcome, Mr, 99

Newman, Frederick, 202, 218

Nicholls, George, Poor Law Commissioner 1834-47, father of Jane, 169, 173

Nicholls, Jane, Mrs P.T. Ouvry, 169, 173, 195

Nicholson, Mrs, née Malin, 63

Nicholson, John Young, Fellow of Emmanuel, clergyman of St Paul's, 207, 221

Nightingale, Luke, 164

Noel, Baptist Wriotesley, adm. pens. at Trinity 1817, sixteenth child of Sir Gerard Noel. A leading evangelical and Chaplain to the Queen, resigned from the Church of England in 1849 and was publicly re-baptised by immersion, 54, 72

Normanby, Constantine Henry Phipps, Marquis of, adm. nobleman at Trinity 1814, Home Secretary 1839-41, Ambassador in Paris 1846-52, 191

North, John North Ouvry, adm. pens. at Trinity 1844, brother of Peter Ouvry, and Romilly's distant cousin, 113, 115, 178, 182-3, 193, 228, 236

Northampton, Spencer J.A. Compton, Marquis of, adm. nobleman at Trinity 1808, President of the Royal Society 1838-48, 61, 135, 205

Northumberland, Charlotte Florentia, Duchess of, daughter of the Earl of Powis, wife of Hugh Percy. Governess to the Queen when princess, 17

Northumberland, Hugh Percy, Duke of, adm. nobleman at St John's 1802, High Steward of the University 1834-40, Chancellor 1840-7, 1, 12-13, 15, 17-18, 126, 145, 193-4, 199

Norton, Mrs, 169

Norwich, Bishop of, *see* Edward Stanley

O'Connell, Daniel, Irish politician, 109, 211

O'Connor, Denis Prittie, Lodge's curate at Anderby 1841-8, 23

Ogier, John Creuze, adm. pens. at Trinity 1841, President of the Union 1844, 7

Okes, Fanny, *presumably* a sister or child of John, 158

Okes, John, adm. Fellow-Commoner at Sidney 1826, whilst in practice apprenticed to his father Thomas Verney Okes of Cambridge. Surgeon to Addenbrooke's hospital 1817-42, lived at Cherry-hinton Hall, 23

Okey (Oaky), Betsy, a child, 101

Okey, Betsy, Elizabeth, widow of Edward Oakman of Crutch Alley, an old protégée of Romilly, 227

Oldenburg, Prince Peter of, Hon. LL.D. 1847, 214

Ollivant, Alfred, Fellow of Trinity 1823, Vice-Principal of St David's College, Lampeter 1827-43, Regius Professor of Divinity 1843-9, R. of Somersham, Hunts. 1843-9, 41-3, 128, 134, 170, 189, 241

Ollivant, Alicia, née Spencer, wife of Alfred, 170

Onslow, Lady Augusta (1819-91), 222

Orator, Public, *see* Thomas Crick

Orvis, Miss, school-mistress, 106

Ouvry, the Misses, no doubt Francisca and Sarah Mary, younger sisters of P.T.Ouvry, 71, 173

Ouvry, John, uncle of Peter Thomas, died at Worth, Sussex, 16 Feb.1847 aged 78, 193-4

Ouvry, Peter Thomas, adm. pens. at Trinity 1829, Romilly's distant cousin. C. of St John's Paddington 1838-47, 18, 86, 113, 133, 169, 173, 194, 219

Ouvry North, John, *see* North

Overton, *probably* Thomas, Fellow of St John's 1831-56, 58

Owen, Mrs, 63, 178, 235

Oxford, Bishops of, *see* Richard Bagot (1829-Nov.45) and Samuel Wilberforce (1845-69)

Packe, James, Fellow of King's 1824-48, 84, 112, 115, 127, 130, 143, 160, 163, 166-8, 180, 182, 195, 210, 212
Packenham, Hon. Henry, Dean of St Patrick's 1843 and of Christ Church, Dublin, 1846, 214
Page, Miss, 126, 194, 235
Paget, George Edward, Fellow of Caius 18332-51, Physician to Addenbrrooke's Hospital 1839-84, reformed the medical curriculum and examination sysstem, 12, 23, 33, 64, 74, 84, 101-3, 115, 130, 1322n, 142, 150, 157, 161, 166-8, 174, 180, 182, 186, 194, 202-3, 221
Pakenham, 142
Paley, Frederick Apthorp, Scholar of St John's 1836, a nephew of the Misses Apthorp, became a Roman Catholic in 1846 and was then asked to give up his College rooms, 117, 179-80
Palmer, Mr, 141
Parker Hamond, Henry, adm. pens. at St John's 1825, R. of Widford, Herts. 1831-77, and his wife Sophia 93,
Parker Hamonds, i.e. William, adm. pens. at St John's 1812, and his wife Margaret, of Pampisford Hall, 63, 93
Parr, John Robert, adm. sizar at St John's 1840, ordained priest 1845, 93
Pate, Daniel, 116-17
Payne, *probably* Elliot, cabinet-maker of Bridge Street, 160
Peacock, George, elected Fellow of Trinity 1814, Lowndean Professor of Astronomy & Geometry 1837-58, Dean of Ely 1839-58, 13, 27, 44, 79, 83, 86, 89, 94, 96, 99-100, 116, 131n, 132n, 135, 140, 145, 163, 165-6, 168, 210-13, 222
Peacocke, George Montague Warren, adm. pens. at Trinity 1839, called to the Bar 1846, 45-6
Pearce, Miss, 72, 118
Pearce, J.B., 110
Pearce, Louisa, sister of J.B., 110, 194
Peel, Frederick, adm. pens. at Trinity 1841, son of Sir Robert, 98
Peel, Sir Robert, Prime Minister 1841-6, 2, 42, 151, 158, 160, 170
Pemberton, Francis Charles James, adm. pens. at Emmanuel 1796. Of Trumpington Hall, Col. of the Cambs militia, 26, 33, 165(?), 167, 234-5
Pemberton, Frances, née Keene, wife of F.C.J., 92
Pennethorne, John (1808-88) architect and favourite pupil of Nash, 10
Penrose, Charles, adm. pens. at Trinity 1834, schoolmaster, son of 'Mrs Markham', the writer for children, 43-4
Penson, Mrs, 95, 148
Pepys, Henry, Fellow of St John's 1806-23, Bishop of Worcester 1841-60, 100
Percy, Hon. Hugh, adm. Fellow-Commoner at St John's 1802, nephew of the Chancellor, Bishop of Carlisle 1827-56, 15
Perowne, John James Stewart, adm. at Corpus Christi 1841, 171
Perry, Charles, Fellow of Trinity 1829-41, V. of St Paul's Cambridge 1842-7, first Bishop of Melbourne, Australia 1847-76, 9, 20, 29, 63, 76-7, 89, 91, 129,

169, 172, 190, 201, 207, 212, 216
Perry, Mrs Charles, née Frances Cooper, 164, 212
Perry, Mrs Jane, hosier of King's Parade, 35
Peters, silversmiths of St Mary's St, 147
Phelps, Edith Percy, child of Robert, 145
Phelps, Loraine, née Skrine, wife of Robert, 100-1, 109, 112, 123, 133, 163, 179
Phelps, Robert, Fellow of Sidney 1838-43, Master 1843-90, notorious for his conservatism, 56, 80, 81n, 100-1, 109, 112, 126, 128, 130, 134, 139n, 161, 166, 168, 180, 202, 206, 212, 221, 230, 233, 237
Phillimore, Robert Joseph, advocate, son of Joseph, Regius Professor of Civil Law at Oxford, 105
Phillips, Sir Thomas, 149
Phillips, Thomas Jodrell, Fellow of Trinity 1830, barrister, 172
Phillpotts, Henry, Bishop of Exeter 1830-69, 126
Philpott, Henry, Fellow, and Master 1845-60 of St Catharine's, Vice- Chancellor 1846-7. Married Mary Jane Doria, 147-8, 152, 166, 173, 179-81, 185, 195-201, 203-5, 213-14, 217-18, 224, 229
Phipps, Miss, 126
Phipps, Col. the Hon. Charles Beaumont (1801-66), Secretary to Prince Albert, brother of Lord Normanby, 195, 200-5
Pillans, James, Professor of Humanity and Laws at Edinburgh 1820-63, 137, 155, 158
Plater, *probably* Charles Eaton, adm. pens. at Christ's 1843, scholar 1844, 87
Pleasance, 162
Pollock, Sir Jonathan Frederick, Fellow of Trinity 1807, Attorney-General 1841-4, 97
Potchett, William, Fellow of St John's 1798-1807, V. of Grantham, Lincs 1817-56, 'a red-hot Tory', 16
Potts, Anna Horlick, née Hulbert, first wife of Robert, 85
Potts, Robert, adm. pens. at Trinity 1827, private coach, 141n
Poulter, W., publican, 47
Power, John, scholar of Pembroke 1837, Fellow 1841, Master 1870-80, 95
Power, Joseph, Fellow of Trinity Hall 1829-44, of Clare 1844-68, University Librarian 1845-64, 33, 45, 84, 100, 115, 130, 131n, 156, 166-8, 231
Powis, Edward Herbert, Earl of, adm. nobleman at St John's 1803, Tory politican and bibliophile, accidentally shot dead January 1848, 194-9, 207
Praslin, Duke and Duchess de, 221, 224
Prest, Mrs Mary Ann, wife of Samuel, 145, 157, 210-11, 230
Prest, Samuel, of Stapleford Lodge, Cambs, 33, 91-2, 98, 101, 170
Prévost, Alexander and George, 133
Princess Royal, *i.e.* Princess Victoria (b. 1840), 70
Procter, Francis, Fellow of St Catharine's 1842, nephew of the next, 147-8, 205
Procter, Joseph, Master of St Catharine's 1799-1845, 36, 63, 87, 95, 148
Prowett, Charles Gipps, Fellow of Caius 1841-74, 130
Prussia, Prince Waldemar of, Hon. LL.D. 1847, 214
Pryme, George, adm. pens. at Trinity 1798, Fellow 1805. First Professor of Political Economy 1828-63, M.P. for Cambridge town 1832-41, 18, 131n

259

Pryme, Jane Townley, daughter of Thomas Thackeray, surgeon, wife of George, lived at Barnwell Abbey, 14, 18, 23

Pulling, impoverished clergyman, 35, 179

Pym, William Wollaston, adm. pens. at St John's 1809, V. of Willian, Herts 1816-52, 29, 114

Quincy, Josiah (1772-1864) American politican, President of Harvard, 48, 61

Raby, W., protégé of Lucy, 128, 208

Rachel, Elisa (1821-58), the great French actress in London 1841 and 1842, 12

Radcliff, Mrs, bedmaker, 240

Ragland, Thomas Gajetan, adm. pens. at Corpus 1837, Fellow 1841, C. of St Paul's, Cambridge 1842-5, secretary of the C.M.S. 1845-54, 77, 101

Randall, Edward, only son of Frederick, 225

Randall, Frederick, solicitor of Trumpington St, 225

Rawlinson, Eliza, protégé of Lucy Romilly, 223

Rawlinson, G., from the Haverhill Union, brother of Eliza, 233-4, 240

Reichart, Major, 101-2

Remington, Thomas, Fellow of Trinity 1826, Perpetual Curate of Cartmel, Lancs 1834-55, 219

Rendall, Frederick, adm. pens. at Trinity 1841, Fellow 1846-8, 177

Rennie, Henrietta, step-daughter of Leapingwell, died 1847, 239

Reyner, George Fearns, Fellow of St John's 1840-76, 205, 207

Richardson, *presumably* the butcher, 26

Richardson, Thomas Pierson, adm. pens. at Trinity 1837, Fellow 1843-7, 74

Rickard, Mrs, *perhaps* the wife of James, builder of St Andrew's St, 116

Roberts, Mr, Oxonian friend of George Romilly, 16-18

Robinson, C., friend of E.E.Allen, 227

Robinson, Thomas, scholar of Trinity 1810, Archdeacon of Madras 1828-35, Lord Almoner's Professor of Arabic 1837-54, Master of the Temple 1845-69. Father of Thomas, 71, 186, 232

Robinson, Thomas, adm. pens. at Trinity 1836, scholar 1840, 74

Roby, William, adm. pens. at Emmanuel 1824, private tutor, Domestic Chaplain to Baroness de Clifford, 86

Roe, Robert, print-seller and engraver of 10 King's Parade, 55, 193, 200, 234

Roget, John Lewis, adm. pens. at Trinity 1845, only son of Peter, 149, 181-3, 236

Roget, Kate, only daughter of Peter, 29, 149

Roget, Peter Mark, cousin of the Diarist, physician and scientist, secretary of the Royal Society 1827-49, founder of the Society for the Diffusion of Useful Knowledge, author of the *Thesaurus* (1852), 29, 132, 135-7, 149, 166

Rolfe, Laura, Lady née Carr (1807-68), married 1845 Sir Robert Rolfe, Baron of the Exchequer, 151

Romilly, Charles, the Diarist's cousin, son of Sir Samuel, barrister, married 1842 Georgiana, half-sister of the Duke of Bedford and Lord John Russell, 132, 166, 223, 236

Romilly, Cuthbert, the Diarist's brother, 141n, 143, 237n

Romilly, Edward, adm. pens. at Christ's 1822, first cousin of the Diarist, M.P. for Ludlow 1832-5, 33, 87, 113, 117, 132, 142, 149, 163, 180, 190-1, 194n, 222, 231

Romilly, Mrs Edward, née Sophia Marcet, 33, 87, 117, 149, 180 172

Romilly, Fanny, daughter of Frank, *see* Bourlet

Romilly, Frank, the Diarist's younger brother, a former army officer who lived in Paris, 13, 54, 72, 88, 92, 147, 158, 165, 175, 178, 189, 191, 202, 208, 222, 230, 233, 237, 240

Romilly, Mrs Frank, Catharine Joseph Cinte, the French wife of Frank and mother of Sophie, Fanny, and Jacques, 92, 169, 176, 202, 225

Romilly, Frederick, the Diarist's cousin, soldier, 191

Romilly, George Thomas, the Diarist's nephew, son of his elder brother Samuel, 9-11, 13, 16, 18, 20, 23-9, 31-6, 40, 43, 46-7, 49-50, 52, 54, 56-7, 60-2, 64, 83-4, 86-7, 92, 97, 99-100, 106-9, 111-15, 117-18, 124-5, 127, 129, 131-2, 139, 141n-5, 158, 165-9, 181, 183-4, 189, 190-2, 195, 225, 228, 231-3, 237, 240

Romilly, Henry, adm. pens. at Christ's 1824, the Diarist's cousin, merchant of Liverpool and Manchester, writer on the death penalty and on secret ballots, 54, 220, 236

Romilly, Jacques, Frank's son, 92, 158, 175

Romilly, John, adm. pens. at Trinity 1818, called to the Bar 1827, M.P for Bridport 1846-7 and for Devonport 1847-52, the Diarist's first cousin, Master of the Rolls 1851, and Baron Romilly 1865, 87, 98, 132, 166, 186, 198, 220, 226n

Romilly, Mrs John, née Caroline Charlotte Otter, second daughter of the Bishop of Chichester, wife of John, 54, 147, 166

Romilly, Lucy, 3, 6-7, 10, 12, 14-16, 18, 20, 23, 28, 31, 34-5, 39, 47-8, 50-3, 55-6, 59-60, 63-4, 74-7, 79, 82-4, 86, 88-9, 91-3, 96-7, 100-1, 103-6, 108-119, 123-4, 126, 128, 131, 133-5, 138, 142-4, 146-50, 152, 155, 157-61, 164, 166, 169-78, 183-4, 186, 189-94, 196, 199, 201, 203, 207-12, 214-17, 220-1, 223, 226-9, 231-41

Romilly, Margaret, 4-11, 14-16, 20, 23-31, 34-5, 39, 42, 46, 48, 50-2, 55-60, 63-5, 72-4, 76-7, 80, 82, 84-9, 91-3, 97, 101, 103-6, 108-12, 114-19, 123-7, 130-3, 135, 138-9, 141-7, 149-51, 155, 157-8, 160-1, 163, 164, 166, 168-72, 174-9, 181-4, 186, 189-94, 196, 199, 201-3, 207-13, 217-18, 221-38, 240-1

Romilly, Sophie, daughter of Frank, 92, 158, 171

Romilly, Thomas Peter (d. 1828) the Diarist's father, 141n, 143, 235

Roscow, Mrs., wife of Thomas Tattersall Roscow, adm. Fellow-Commoner at Downing 1842, 157

Rose, Henry John, Fellow of St John's 1824-38, R. of Houghton Conquest, Beds 1837-73, 196

Ross, Lady Mary, younger sister of Lady Braybrooke, 159

Rothman, Richard Wellesley, Fellow of Trinity 1825-56, Registrar of London University 1838-56, 62, 165, 177, 219, 226

Rothschild, Lionel Nathan, Baron (1808-79) 113, 232-3

Rowe, Chapel clerk of Trinity until 1843, then spirit-shop keeper, 75

Rowe, James Boone, adm. pens. at St John's 1843, 86-7

Rowe, Richard, Romilly's clerk until 1840, 53, 221

Rowlands, John, Fellow of Queens' 1834-50, C. of Great St Mary's, Cambridge 1844-9, 170, 178(?)

Russell, Arthur Tozer, adm. sizar at St John's 1824, V. of Caxton 1830-52. He 'acquired the name of Cuckoo from his invasion of other peoples' houses', 110

Russell, Lord Cosmo, ninth son of the Duke of Bedford, brother of Wriothesley, 54

Russell, Hon. Edward Southwell, adm. nobleman at Trinity 1843, a cousin of the Duke of Bedford, 86

Russell, Lady Harriet, 132

Russell, James, adm. sizar at Trinity 1842, 166

Russell, Lord John, Prime minister 1846-52, 158, 213, 232, 239

Russell, Theodosia, the Romilly's cook, 142-3, 165, 212, 236

Russell, Lord Wriothesley, adm. pens. at Trinity 1823, son of the Duke of Bedford, brother of Mrs Charles Romilly, R. of Chenies, Bucks, 1829-86, Chaplain to Prince Albert, 78, 197, 205, 215, 227

Rutland, John Henry Manners, Duke of, adm. nobleman at Trinity 1794, High Steward of Cambridge town 1800-35, father of Lady Jermyn, 225

Rutzen, Charles Frederic, Baron de, adm. Fellow-Commoner at Emmanuel 1813, 113

Salisbury, Mrs, 130

Salvin, Anthony (1799-1881), architect and church-restorer, 5, 36

Sapieha, Prince Leon and his son Adam, 227

Sarel, Henry Andrew, adm. pens. at Trinity 1842, later a distinguished career soldier, 87

Saunders, James, adm. pens. at Sidney 1820, Fellow, 56 Savage, James (1784-1873) Harvard antiquary and genealogist, 19, 40, 48, 61, 218

Savile or Savill, Charles Stuart, adm. Fellow-Commoner at Queens' 1833, son of the Earl of Mexborough, novelist, 10

Savory, perhaps 'Lucullus', 59-60

Saxe-Weimar, Karl Friedrich, Duke of (1783-1853), LL.D. 1847, 214

Saxony, Frederick Augustus, King of, 1836-54, 101

Scarlett, William Frederick, adm. Fellow-Commoner at Trinity 1845, son of Lord Abinger, 158

Scarr, Robert, cobbler, 171

Scholefield, Harriet, née Chase, wife of James, 233

Scholefield, James, Fellow of Trinity 1815-27, Regius Professor of Greek 1825-53, Perpetual C. of St Michael's 1823-52, a leader of the Cambridge evangelicals, 26

Scoresby, William, adm. sizar at Queens' 1824, the arctic explorer, V. of Bradford 1839-47, 217

Scott, Charles Brodrick, adm. pens. at Trinity 1842, Pitt Scholar 1847, 185, 201

Scott, 'Dr' Charles Romilly, quack, 135

Scott, Miss, sister of Mrs Anderson of Dulwich, 184, 189, 191

Scott, Henrietta, great-niece of Mrs Haviland, 91, 173

Scott, John, adm. Fellow-Commoner at Caius 1842, Perpetual Curate of St Paul's, Cambridge 1847-62, 232, 237

Searle, Eliza and Georgina, daughters of William, 165

Searle, James, friend of G.A. Browne 60-1, 172

Searle, probably William, treasurer of the Horti-cultural Society, and partner in a Cambridge brewing firm, and his family, 164-5

Sedgwick, Adam, Fellow of Trinity 1810-73, Wood-wardian Professor of Geology 1818-73, Canon of Norwich 1834-73. One of the brilliant group of northcountrymen known as 'the Northern Lights', and 'probably the most popular man in the college and his rooms the chief centre of attraction', 4-5, 8, 13, 17, 44, 52-3, 58, 62, 82, 84, 86, 96, 107-8, 128-9, 131n-7, 144n, 149-50, 155-6n, 158-9, 163, 165, 168, 172, 177, 179-80, 185-6, 196-8, 208-13, 215-16, 219, 221-22n, 224, 226, 232, 235, 237-9

Sedgwick, Dick (Richard), adm. pens. at Trinity 1846, brother of Isabel and nephew of Adam, 107-8

Sedgwick, Isabel, niece of Adam, 107-8, 158, 163, 226(?)

Selwyn, Edward John, scholar of Trinity 1843, son of Edward, R. of Hemingford Abbots, Hunts; future brother-in-law- of W. Carus, 87

Selwyn, Frances Elizabeth, married 1847 George Peacock, 222

Selwyn, Maria Elizabeth, daughter of Edward, Carus's intended, 220-1

Selwyn, Mrs, 137

Selwyn, William, Fellow of St John's 1829-32, Canon Residentiary of Ely 1833-75, V. of Melbourne 1846-53, brother of Mrs Peacock, 95

Seymour, Capt. Francis (1813-90), Groom in Waiting to Prince Albert, 204-6

Shak(e)spear(e), John Joseph Arthur, adm. pens. at Trinity 1839, called to the Bar 1848, 8

Sharpe, John, adm pens. at Sidney 1816, V. of Doncaster 1817-60, 135n

Sharpe, probably William adm. sizar at Queens' 1806, V. of Cromer 1831-52, 130

Shaw, Benjamin, adm. pens. at Trinity 1838, Fellow 1843, 74

Shaw, Joseph, Fellow of Christ's 1807-59, Master January-February 1849, 34, 84, 92, 115, 130, 150, 161, 166-8, 195, 202-3, 210, 212-13, 225, 237, 241

Shedd, Mrs, presumably the wife of James Blackman, registrar of marriages, 24, 47, 52, 57

Shedd, Emma, 24

Sheepshanks, Richard, Fellow of Trinity 1817-55. One of the brilliant group known as 'the Northern Lights', promoted the building of the University Observatory, 62, 219

Shelford, perhaps Henry James Sheldon adm. pens. at Trinity 1841, 7

Sherwood, Thomas Moulden, adm. Fellow-Commoner at Downing 1835, clergyman, 138

Sidney, Mr, 131

Simeon, Charles, Fellow of King's and evangelical V. of Holy Trinity 1783-1836, 164, 174, 207-9, 211, 226

Simeon, Sir Richard (d.1854), nephew of Charles, 208

Simpson, Mr, doubtless W. who died 22 June 1844 aged 56 'after a lingering illness', 103

Simpson, Mrs, 83, 117

Simpson, Thomas, V. of Pannal, Yorks., 21-2

Simpsons, the, in the Victoria Asylum, 239

Sinclair, *presumably* John, V. of Kensington 1842-75, Archdeacon of Middlesex 1843-75, 106

Sinclair, William James, adm. pens. at Trinity 1840, did not graduate, 7

Sismondi, J.C.L., the Swiss historian and economist, brother-in-law of Baugh Allen, 20

Skelton, the Misses, two Scotch ladies, 97

Skinner, Mrs, née Chassereau, 27

Skrine, Almeira, née Weightman, wife of Julian, mother of Myra, Julia, Louisa, and Mary Loraine, 112, 126, 210, 229, 232, 235n

Skrine, Julian, retired Cambridge banker formerly in India, ruined in 1848 and fled to France where he died, 5, 31, 34, 61, 92, 112, 115, 123, 126, 145-6n, 157, 165, 181-2, 187, 210, 229

Smedley, Edward Arthur, adm. pens. at Trinity 1822, Chaplain 1830-6, V. of Chesterton 1836-73, 61

Smith, curate of Histon, 165

Smith, Misses Agnes and Elisabeth, 84

Smith, Mrs, née Osborne, 86

Smith, 'Gypsy Widow', 123

Smith, Barnard, Fellow of Peterhouse 1840-61, 84(?), 195

Smith, Mrs Curtis, 148

Smith, Elliot Macro, of Trinity St, appraiser, 238

Smith, Elizabeth, sister of Mrs Airy, 137, 163(?)

Smith, Fanny, daughter of Joseph of Dulwich, fiancee of G.T. Romilly, 40, 113, 166, 170, 181, 183-4, 189

Smith, General Sir Harry (1787-1860) hero of the Sikh war, 164, 214-15

Smith, Isabella, presumably a daughter of Joseph, 52

Smith, James Ind, adm. sizar at Trinity 1831, Librarian of Trinity 1840-5, V. of Marsworth, Bucks. 1845-7, 131, 133

Smith, Jane, the Romillys' cook until July 1843, 23, 59, 63, 237n

Smith, John, manservant to John Lodge, 40, 113

Smith, John James, Fellow of Caius 1828-49, Senior Proctor 1839-40 and very unpopular 'for his diligence and severity'. One of the founders of the Cambridge Antiquarian Society, 1, 7, 9, 33, 103, 130, 148, 161(?), 166-8, 180, 211n

Smith, Joseph, of Dulwich and Long Acre, wealthy printer and publisher, father of Fanny, William and *probably* Joseph, 60, 124-5, 189

Smith, Joseph, friend of George Romilly,

Smith, Rosa, 169

Smith, Sydney (1771-1845), wit and author, Canon of St Paul's, 33, 85, 87

Smith, Theyre Townshend, adm. pens. at Queens' 1823, Assistant Preacher at the Temple 1835-45, 117

Smith, William, adm. sizar at Trinity 1837, Fellow 1843-64, 74

Smith, William, of Dulwich, son of Joseph and friend since childhood of G.T. Romilly, 84, 100, 107

Smyth, Mrs, 216-17

Smyth, William, Fellow of Peterhouse 1788-1825, Regius Professor of Modern History 1807-49, 19, 108, 134, 163, 241

Snell, Mr and Mrs, 159

Snowball, John Charles, Fellow of St John's 1830-55, Inspector-General of births, marriages and deaths until 1855, 92, 95, 196

Sophia Matilda, Princess (1773-1844) elder sister of the Duke of Gloucester, former Chancellor of the University, 125, 162

Sortain, Joseph (1809-60), author and pastor of North St Chapel, Brighton, 1832-60, 69

Soyer, Alexis Benoit (1809-58), chef, 183

Sparke, John Henry, Fellow of Jesus 1815, Canon of Ely 1818, Chancellor of the Diocese of Ely. Married Agnes, youngest daughter of Sir Jacob Astley, 99, 105

Sparke, Mr, late churchwarden at Meldreth, Cambs, 49

Spedding, Lady Georgina, 132

Spencer, Frederick, fourth Earl, Lord Chamberlain of the Household 1846-6, 214

Spencer, John Charles, third Earl, adm. nobleman at Trinity 1800 where Allen, later Bishop of Ely was his tutor. Lover of country life and reluctant politician, 112

Spilling, Miss Charlotte, matron of Addenbrooke's Hospital 1834 to 1848 when she resigned after complaints of mismanagement, 18, 56, 128, 192, 194, 221, 234-5n

Spineto, Elizabeth, née Campbell, Marchesa di Spineto, second wife of 'the Marquis', 28, 108, 124, 136, 187, 190

Spineto, Niccolo Maria Doria, Marchese di, 'the Marquis', father of the Dorias(qq.v.). Teacher of Italian in the University; published verse. Lived at 41 Rhadegund Buildings opposite Jesus College, 28, 39, 57, 62, 92, 95, 108, 135-7, 163, 187, 225, 235, 240-1

Spink, Charles, 83-4

Spink, Mrs, mother of Charles, 83-4

Spring-Rice, Aubrey, son of Thomas, 158

Spring-Rice, Marianne (Lady Monteagle), née Marshall, second wife of Thomas, sister of Cordelia Whewell, 52

Spring-Rices, the, *presumably* sons of Thomas, *i.e.* Aubrey and William, adm. pensioners at Trinity 1841 and 1842, 86

Spring-Rice, Thomas, adm. Fellow-Commoner at Trinity 1809, M.P. for Cambridge town 1832-9, Chancellor of the Exchequer 1835-9, Comptroller of the Exchequer 1839-65. Created Baron Monteagle 1839, 118n, 131n, 185, 195

Stael, Madame de, 87

Stallard, John Stockdale, adm. pens. at Peterhouse 1843, died at Leicester November 1845, 151

Stanhope, Mr and Lady Elizabeth, *i.e.* John Spencer Stanhope and his wife, a daughter of the Earl of Leicester, 159

Stanley, Edward, adm. pens. at St John's 1798, Bishop of Norwich 1837-49, a vigorous reformer, 5, 96, 135, 139, 197, 217

Stanley, Eleanor, Maid of Honour to Queen Victoria 1842-62, 80

Stanley, Miss, *either* Kate *or* Mary, daughters of the Bishop of Norwich, 96

Stearn, Emma, protégée of Lucy Romilly, 173-4

Stedman, Mr, of Horsham, Sussex, 164

Stevenson, Thomas (d. August 1845), Mayor of Cambridge 1842-3, 31, 83n

Stewart, Mrs David, née Louisa Skrine, wife of David James, adm. pens. at Trinity 1833, C. of Adderbury, Oxon 1843-8, 112

Stokes, Scott Nasmyth, adm. pens. at Trinity 1840, author of controversial *Christian Kalendar*, barred from entering the church, 98, 126n, 132

Stokes, William Haughton, Fellow of Caius 1828-53, 156

Stone, Mrs, the madwoman 'pretty Nancy', 119, 125

Storr & Mortimer, 215, 224

Stuart, 212

Stuart, Mrs, 163

Styles, chapel-marker, 116

Sudbury, John Linley, of 36 Sidney St, surgeon. Son of a Nottinghamshire farmer, married Frances, née Hippisley Jackson, and died 1848 aged 39, 23, 29, 72, 74, 124, 150-1

Sumner, Charles Richard, adm. at Trinity 1810, Bishop of Winchester 1827-69, 14-15, 44n, 211

Surtees, Robert Smith (1803-64), sporting novelist, 119

Sussex, Augustus Frederick, Duke of, sixth son of George III. LL.D. 1819. 'A strong and consistent Liberal'. 53-4

Sutton, Miss Mary, mistress of the 'ladies boarding' school at Llandaff House, Regent St, 106

Swan, James, 144

Swindell, W. of Manchester, 233

Swinny, Edith Anne, née Newton, wife of the next, 162, 165

Swinny, Henry Hutchinson, Fellow of Magdalene 1836-40, V. of St Giles and St Peter, Cambridge 1840-4, 7, 36, 62, 162, 165

Sykes, Godfrey Milnes, adm. pens. at Trinity 1832, Fellow of Downing 1842, 6

Sykes, John, Fellow of Pembroke 1841-65, 175

Sykes, John Henry, adm. pens. at Trinity 1842, R. of Foxholes, Yorks 1848-50 when he died, 87

Taddy, John, Fellow of Trinity 1807-18, Perpetual Curate of Northill, Beds. 1811-58, married Catharina Latham, 184

Tagore, Dwarkanauth, 18

Talfourd, Thomas Noon, called to the Bar 1821, serjeant-at-law, M.P. and author of *Ion* etc., 89, 241

Talleyrand-Perigord, Charles Maurice de, 87

Tarleton, 'the gigantic' Miss, 100, 144

Tarrant, publican of The William & Mary, 33, 209(?)

Tasker, Henry, Fellow of Pembroke 1817, V. of Soham, Cambs 1832-72, 45

Tasmania, Bishop of, Francis Russell Nixon, 214

Tatham, Mr, Romilly's solicitor, 143

Tatham, Ralph, Public Orator 1809-36, Master of St John's 1838-57, Vice-Chancellor 1845-6, 1, 40-1, 43, 84, 115, 130, 145, 147-8,157, 162, 165-7 175, 177-7, 180,192, 199, 203, 207

Tawell, John, murderer, 129

Taylor, Mr and Mrs, friends of Roget, 159

Taylor, surgeon, 23

Taylor, John, School-Keeper for 26 years, died 3 August 1845 aged 85, 81

Taylor, Mrs Juliana, daughter of Lord Waterpark, sister to Mrs Thomas Musgrave, 71

Taylor, Tom, Fellow of Trinity 1842, wit, 104n, 161n

Temple, Nicholas John, Fellow of Sidney, C. of Chirk, Denbigh 1825-53, 56

Tennyson, Alfred, the poet, adm. pens. at Trinity 1827, 141, 215n

Terrot, Charles Hughes, Fellow of Trinity 1813, Bishop of Edinburgh 1841-72, 189

Thacker, Arthur, Fellow of Trinity 1839-57 when he died, 48, 120, 225, 240

Thackeray, Frederick, adm. Fellow-Commoner at Emmanuel 1800, surgeon to Addenbrooke's Hospital 1796-1845, physician 1827. Brother of Mrs Pryme and brother-in-law of Thomas Crick, 55n, 75-6, 98, 131, 223

Thackeray, George, Provost of King's 1814-50, Chaplain-in-Ordinary to George III and his successors, 40, 43, 79, 168, 205

Thackeray, Mrs, *probably* Mary, née Crick, wife of Frederick, 193

Thesiger, Frederick (1794-1878), called to the Bar 1818, Solicitor-General 1844-5, Attorney-General 1845-6. M.P. Knighted May 1844, 89, 98, 202

Thodey, Miss, probably daughter of Rev. Samuel of Meetinghouse Lane, 114

Thomas, Mrs, 166

Thompson, Mr and Mrs, upholsterers of King St, 48, 62, 106

Thompson, William Hepworth, Fellow since 1834 and later (1866) Master of Trinity, Regius Professor of Greek 1853-67, 1, 18-20, 86-7, 114, 117, 120, 177, 208, 225-6

Thomsen, Grimur (1820-96), Danish poet, 236

Thornton, Miss, 157, 166

Thorp, Thomas, Fellow of Trinity 1820, tutor 1833-44, Vice-Master 1843-4, Archdeacon and Chancellor of Bristol 1836-73. First President of the Cambridge Camden Society, and 'the senior member generally invited to lend official respectability to University societies in the thirties and forties', 7, 11, 17, 25, 45, 62, 76, 81, 88, 95, 98, 100-1, 103, 117, 126, 132n, 143

Thorpe, bookseller, 178

Thresher, Charles, police inspector, 175

Thurnall, A.W., surgeon, apothecary's apprentice to Addenbrooke's 1825-30, 23, 29

Thurtell, Alexander, Fellow of Caius 1830-49, H.M. Inspector of Schools 1847, R. of Oxburgh 1848-84, 7, 56, 108

Tindal, Sir Nicholas Conyngham, adm. pens. at Trinity 1795. M.P. for the University 1827-9, Lord Chief Justice 1829-46, 48

Tinkler, John, Fellow of Corpus Christi 1829-43, C. of Grantchester until 1843, R. of Landbeach 1843-71. Married 1844 Rebecca Hutchinson of Watermillock, Cumberland, 57

Tom Thumb *i.e.* Charles Stratton, 160

Tooke, Mrs, 210, 231(?)

Tooke, Thomas Hammond, adm. pens. at Trinity 1841, Fellow-Commoner 1847, 87, 107, 183, 231

Townley, Cecil, née Watson, wife of Richard Greaves, 65, 73

Townley, Charles, adm. pens. at Trinity 1812, R. of Hadstock 1838-70, 46, 98, 141, 147-8, 175
Townley, Mrs Charles, wife of the above, 112
Townley, Gale and his wife (nee Pratt), 148
Townley, Richard Greaves, adm. pens. at Trinity 1802. Of Fulbourn Manor, Cambs. M.P. for Cambs 1831-41 and 1847-52,
Townley, Tom (Thomas Manners), adm. pens. at Trinity 1844, son of Richard Greaves, 73
Townley, William Gale, adm. pens. at Trinity 1805. R. of Upwell, Norfolk 1812-62, and for many years chairman of Isle of Ely sessions. Brother of Richard Greaves, 4, 65
Townshends, the Miss, 142
Townson, Joseph, Fellow of Queens' 1839-47, C. of Grantchester 1846-7, 240
Travis, William John, adm. pens. at Trinity 1826, chaplain there 1833-44, 2
Tudway, Mr, London attorney, 88
Turnbull, 166
Turner, George James, Fellow of Pembroke 1821, Q.C., 241
Turner, Joseph Mallord (1775-1851), the painter, 12, 172
Turton, Thomas, Fellow of St Catharine's 1806, sometime professor of mathematics and of divinity, Bishop of Ely 1845-64, 189
Twisses, the, i.e. James P. Twiss of Barnwell and his wife, 3, 149, 151, 155, 157-8,
Tyler, M.A., protégée of Lucy Romilly, 209
Tyng [Ting], Stephen Higginson (1800-85), American episcopalian, author of Recollections of England (1847), 10
Tyrell, William, adm. pens. at St John's 1827, Bishop of Newcastle, N.S.W., 1847-79, 212

Van de Wyer, Sylvain, Belgian minister in London 1831-67, 214
Vansittart, Augustus Arthur, adm. pens. at Trinity 1842, Second Classic and President of the Union 1847, 184-5
Vassall, William, adm. pens. at St John's 1842, 163
Vaughan, Charles John, second Classic 1838, Fellow of Trinity 1839-42. Headmaster of Harrow 1844-59, 74, 128, 197
Vaughan, David James, adm. pens. at Trinity 1844, 126n, 165
Vaughan, John, adm. pens. at St John's 1820, Perpetual Curate of St Matthew's, Brixton 1841-56, 197
Ventris, Edward, adm. pens. at Peterhouse 1821, Perpetual C. of Stow-cum-Quy 1825-86, 50, 126
Vestris, Madame Lucia Elizabeth, singer and actress, wife of C. Matthews, 68
Victoria, Queen, 1, 2, 11-12, 46, 53, 56, 70-1, 77-84, 86, 92, 95, 98, 103, 106, 120, 140, 179, 181, 213-17, 224, 237-8
Vignolles, Mr and Mrs, née Pemberton, 101
Villiers, Lady Clementina, daughter of Lady Jersey, died unmarried aged 34 in 1858, 15, 99
Vincent, Miss, friend of the Romillys and governess at one time to the Spineto children, 35, 77-8, 82-3, 119, 123, 152, 169, 186, 222, 225
Vizard, Henry Brougham, adm. pens. at Trinity 1843, brother of William, 113, 183

Vizard, William, adm. pens. at Trinity 1831, brother of Henry Brougham, Deputy Registrar in the Court of Bankruptcy 1839-60, 113, 196
Von Mohl, Prof., 214

Wakefield, Mrs, 176
Wale, General Sir Charles (1763-1845), squire of Little Shelford, Governor of Martinique 1812-15, 12, 31, 33, 101, 210, 230
Wale, Henrietta, Lady, third wife of Sir Charles, 12, 29, 101, 210, 230
Wale, Miss, daughter of Sir Charles, 32, 101
Wales, Albert Edward, Prince of (b. 1841) 70
Walker, Mr, 84
Walker, Samuel Edward, adm. pens. at Trinity 1827, R. of St Columb Major, Cornwall 1841-69, 196-7
Walker, [William] Sidney, Fellow of Trinity 1820-9, eccentric, died 1846 aged 50, 178
Walker, William Henry, adm. pens. at Queens' 1843, 126
Wallich, Mrs, perhaps the wife of Nathaniel, the botanist, 75-6
Walmisley, Thomas Attwood, Mus.B. from Trinity 1833, Professor of Music 1836-56, composer and organist of Trinity and St John's, 16n, 120, 158, 215n
Walsham, Sir John James (1805-74), nephew of Anne, Lady Romilly, 192
Walsham, Sarah Frances, Lady, 192
Walter, Mrs James, 128
Walton, probably William, adm. pens. at Trinity 1831, George Romilly's private tutor. Later known as 'Old Father Time', 13, 25, 36, 87, 125
Wareing, William, Roman Catholic Bishop, 179
Warren, Mrs, of 'the Roebuck', 239
Warren, William Newton, scholar of Trinity 1843, called to the Bar 1847, 93
Warter, Edward, adm. pens. at Magdalene 1830, fourth Classic 1834, Fellow 1835, 30, 145, 148, 181, 198-9, 212
Warwick, William Atkinson, editor of the Cambridge Advertiser, Cambridge University Calendar, Warwick's University Register, etc. Printer and publisher, 16, 40, 191
Watford, Alexander, neighbour of the Romillys, 95
Watson, Master, 25
Watson, Miss, of Petty Cury, Sunday School teacher; in 1838 at Holy Trinity Sunday school, 35, 55, 109, 147
Watson, Mrs Elizabeth, widow of Thomas, died 1842 aged 65, 26
Watt, Mr, Achilli's chaperone, 229
Waud, Samuel Wilkes, Fellow of Magdalene 1825-44, V. of Madingley 1837-43, R. of Rettendon, Essex 1844-87, 11
Weavings, John, railway inspector, married S. Ironside, 138
Webb, Anne, née Gould, wife of William, 36
Webb, Benjamin, adm pens. at Trinity 1838, a founder of the Cambridge Camden Society, C. of Christ Church, Regent's Park, 1847-9. Married 1847 Maria Elphinstone Mill, daughter of W.H. Mill, 208-9
Webb, cowkeeper of Barnwell, perhaps Henry of

Newmarket Road listed in 1847 *Post Office Directory*, 227

Webb, William, Master of Clare 1815-56, Vice-Chancellor 1817-18 and 1832-3, 1, 130

Webster, Miss, later Mrs Neale, daughter of Thomas, Fellow of Queens' and Rector of St Botolph's until his death in 1840, sister of J.H. Webster the surgeon, 4, 44

Webster, the surgeon, 132n

Weil, Gottlieb, teacher of languages of 58 Trumpington Street, 190

Wellington, Arthur, Duke of, 15, 204-5, 207, 213, 215

Wells, Mrs, keeper of Brighton boarding house, 68, 107

West, George John Sackville, Earl *see* De La Warr

Westcott, Brooke Foss, adm. pens. at Trinity 1844, 161, 165, 184

Whately, Miss, daughter of the next, 8

Whately, Richard (1787-1863), Archbishop of Dublin, worked indefatigably to administer an educational system which might be acceptable to catholics and protestants alike, 8, 12

Wheelwright, Mrs, née Apthorp, 147

Whewell, Cordelia, wealthy daughter of John Marshall of the Leeds flax-spinning family. She married Whewell in October 1841, a month before he was installed Master of Trinity. Sister of Marianne Spring-Rice, 4, 11, 14, 26, 31, 35, 59, 61, 73-4, 84, 101-2, 112, 117, 123, 126, 151-2, 160, 177, 184-5, 226

Whewell, William, Fellow of Trinity 1817-41, Tutor 1823-39, and Master 1841-66. Professor of Mineralogy 1828-32 and Knightbridge Professor of Moral Philosophy 1838-55. A man of great versatility and influence and an important figure in nineteenth-century English science and philsophy, 1, 2, 4, 6, 10-11i, 13, 25-6, 28, 30-4, 36, 39, 40-3, 47, 50, 53, 59, 61-2, 72-5, 78-81, 92-3, 96, 98, 100-2, 104, 111-12, 117-18, 124-6, 128, 134-7, 143-5, 150-1, 156, 158, 160, 162, 165, 174, 176-7, 185, 190n-91, 194-6, 207-8, 215n-17, 219, 225-6, 233, 235n

White, Mrs (née Isabel Lilley), 144

Whittaker, Henry, 132, 143

Wick, Mr, curate in the neighbourhood of Ickleton. He does not appear in the *Clergy List* 1844, 103

Widnall, Samuel, florist and nurseryman of Grantchester who exported dahlias to America and Russia. Lived in what is now 'Lyndwode' until his death in 1848, 16, 18, 55

Wilberforce, Samuel, Dean of Westminster 1844-5, Bishop of Oxford 1845-69, 135-7, 214

Wilcox, Miss, 57, 231, 235n

Wilderspin, Frances, protégée of the Romillys since 1838, at one time servant of the Boyers in London, 73, 97, 107, 143, 149, 172, 209, 215-18, 220-1, 237-8

Wiles, Mr, son of Henry, Fellow of Trinity 1805, 150

Wilkie, Sir David (1785-1841), the painter, 12, 99, 234

Wilkins, Miss, 109, 133, 145, 173

Wilkins, Mrs, 181

Wilkinson, Mrs Caroline, née Watson, died 1842 aged 26, 26

Williams, Miss, guest at Magdalene Lodge, 114

Williams, Mr, fiancé of Louisa Pearce, 110, 194

Williams, Frederick Sims, adm. pens. at Trinity 1830, equity draftsman and conveyancer, 197

Williams, George, adm. sizar at Trinity 1828, V. of Hauxton with Newton, Cambs 1837-90, 127

Williams, J., C. of Meldreth or of Barrington with Hauxton, Cambs., 110

Williams, Sir John, Fellow of Trinity 1800, Solicitor-General and Attorney-General to Queen Adelaide 1830, Baron of the Exchequer 1834, 20, 104-5, 175

Williams, William Masterman, adm. pens. at Trinity 1845, cadet with Madras infantry in 1846, 161-2

Williamson, William, second Wrangler 1825, Fellow of Clare 1827-50, ordained priest 1842, 9, 158(?)

Willimotts, the Misses, of whom one was probably one 'of the chief saints' at Addenbrooke's hospital, 52

Willis, Mary Anne, daughter of Charles Humfrey, and wife of Robert. She 'is a peculiar favorite of mine', 158, 216, 234, 235n-6

Willis, Meggie, daughter of Robert and Mary Anne, 236

Willis, Robert, Fellow of Caius 1826, Jacksonian Professor of Natural Philosophy 1837-75. Co-author of *Architectural History of the University*, 10, 44, 48, 61, 65, 96, 120, 158

Willyams, James Neynoe Vivian, adm. pens. at Trinity 1842, Lieut. Royal Miners' Artillery, 51

Wilson, Mr, clerk at Mortlock's bank, 25, 58, 92

Winchester, Bishop of, see Charles Richard Sumner

Winthrop, Robert Charles (1809-94), Boston congressman and historian of Massachussetts, 218

Wiseman's, *i.e.* Henry Richard Wiseman's bookbinding shop in Trinity St, 201-2

Witherby, Romilly's stockbroker, 162

Wix, Joseph, adm. pens. at Peterhouse 1829, V. of Littlebury, Essex 1840-88, Chaplain to Lord Braybrooke, 156

Wolstenholme, Edward Parker, adm. pens. at Trinity 1843, 165

Woodham, Henry Annesley, Fellow of Jesus 1841-8. Married Elizabeth, daughter of Charles Humfrey, 72, 97

Woodhouse, John Thomas, Fellow of Caius 1804-45, physician at Addenbrooke's hospital, amateur painter and devotee of cock-fighting, 56

Woolfrey, Rev. H. N., succeeded Father Shanley in 1842 as R.C. missioner to Cambridge, 51, 64n

Wootton, wedding guest, 138

Wootton, Charles Nathaniel, industrious third Library Keeper, 34

Wordsworth, Christopher (d.1846), Master of Trinity 1820-41, brother of the poet, 21, 44

Wordsworth, Christopher, Fellow of Trinity 1830-8, Headmaster of Harrow 1836-44, son of the former Master. Married Susanna, niece of William Frere Master of Downing, 41-3, 101, 195

Wordsworth, William, adm. sizar at St John's 1787, the poet, 152, 163, 215n

Worlledge, John, adm. pens. at Trinity 1827, Fellow 1831, called to the Bar 1838, on the Norfolk circuit, 20

Worsley, Katharine, née Rawson, daughter of a wealthy industrialist, wife of Thomas, 27, 46, 104, 157, 182, 229, 237-8
Worsley, Thomas, Master of Downing 1836-85, 'the finest skater in Cambridge', 27, 46, 103, 155-7
Worthington, surgeon of Lowestoft, 174
Wray, 'Receiver of the London Police', 18, 186
Wren, Thomas, adm. pens. at St John's 1840, C. of Gt Chesterford, Essex, 1845-9, 93
Wright, family surgeon at Audley End, 178
Wynne, Miss (Charlotte?), 156

Yarranton, Thomas Cook, adm. pens. at Sidney Sussex 1839, ordained priest 1845, 47
Yorke, Lady Agneta (b.1838), daughter of Lord Hardwicke, 67
Yorke, Rev., 73
Young, Sir Charles George (1795-1869), Garter King of Arms, 200
Young, Henry Loud, scholar of Trinity 1842, adm. at the Inner Temple 1841, 4

Zamoyski, Count Ladislaw, 227

INDEX OF SUBJECTS AND PLACES

ad eundem degrees, 61, 138
Addenbrookes hospital, 14, 17-19, 23-5, 28-9, 46-7,
  53, 56, 75, 89, 100, 104, 114, 123, 128, 131-2, 138-9,
  150, 161, 171, 191, 201n, 207, 215n, 217, 230, 236
addresses, presentation of, 1-2, 11-12, 79, 82-3, 204,
  213
aegrotat degrees, 124n, 173
All Saints, 207
arson, 62, 227(?)
Ashdon, 156, 189
asylums, 19, 60, 75, 84, 89, 91 95-6, 100-1 103-4, 111,
  159, 172, 201, 231, 239,
audit ale, 123, 180, 231
audits, 8-9, 34, 50, 55
Audley End, 27n, 96, 140, 142, 156, 159, 163, 174, 178-
  80, 187, 189

Babraham, 53, 63
Bachelor's essay prize, 171
balloons, 172, 215
balls, 16-18, 50, 68, 73, 83, 87, 93, 120, 157, 181, 186,
  192-3, 212
baptisms, 54, 138, 145, 167, 177, 219
Barnaby lecturers, 134
Barnwell, 6n, 24, 51, 63, 132n, 138, 139n, 158, 177,
  227, 232, 237
Bartlow Barrows, 156
Barton, 21, 83
Battie Scholarship, 161n
bedmakers, 63-4, 100, 118, 127n-8, 175, 186, 210, 236,
  240
Bell's scholarship, 126
Belle Sauvage, 88, 132
bets, 7, 11, 166-7, 182
billiards, 47, 51, 88
Black House, 9, 30, 51, 114, 117, 162, 178, 212, 232
Black Leet (Magna Congregatio), 83, 228
Blue Boar, 112
boats
  procession of, 9, 167
  races, 9n, 18
Botanic Garden, 34, 162, 167, 222
bribery, 11, 49, 57, 139n
Brighton, 40, 68-71, 106-7, 212-13
British Association, 13, 96-7, 132, 135-8, 148
Browne medals, 134
Buckingham Palace, 1-2, 79, 200, 202-7, 217
Bull Inn, 92, 170, 198

Caius College, 56, 92n, 114-15, 137, 167, 226
Cam, river, 9, 118, 125, 167n, 209, 217
Camden Society, 21n, 29, 48n, 65n, 71n, 82n, 98,
  105n, 119, 126, 132, 180
cancer, 11, 20, 146, 201
Caput, The, 1, 40-1, 79, 112, 124, 157, 205, 212,
  232n
Catharine Hall (St Catharine's College), 26-7, 147,
  214, 218
Caxton, 110
cemeteries, 65-6, 89, 111, 147, 237
Chancellor of Cambridge University, 1, 12-13, 17,
  126; see also elections

Cheltenham, 71-2; College, 127
Cherry Hinton, 64
Chesterton, 6, 61, 118,
chimney sweeps, 166, 200
cholera, 174
Christ Church, Barnwell, 237
Christ's College, 32, 82, 161
Christian Advocate, 123n, 155
Cilrhiw, Pembrokeshire, 54, 89, 162
circus, 224
Clare Hall, 9n, 14, 16-17, 130, 171, 217
Clarence House, 2
coaches
  Beehive, 64, 144
  Defence, 227
  Lynn, 27, 29, 61, 94, 96, 99, 112
  Rapid, 88
  Rocket, 29, 96, 100, 115, 144
  Star, 13, 88, 107, 118, 131-2
  Telegraph, 20, 36, 72, 87, 98, 106, 125, 131
  Times, 58
Commemoration of Benefactors, 89, 118, 151, 184,
  237
Commencement
  Bachelors', 39, 41, 93, 124, 157, 191
  July, 13-14, 18, 103, 171
Communion Service, see Sacrament
compulsory Chapel, 92, 116
concerts, 17, 67, 210, 215, 224
Confirmation, 5, 101-2
Congregatio Magna, see Black Leet
congregations, University, 11, 15-16, 30, 34, 41, 51,
  81, 95, 103, 114, 117-18, 126-9, 146, 148, 150, 158,
  162, 169-71, 178, 194, 197-200, 209-10, 212, 217, 228,
  232, 237
conundrums, 178
Corn laws, 149, 151, 160, 170
Corporation, Cambridge, 28, 31, 73, 80, 83, 167,
  228
Corpus Christi College, 82n, 116n,
Cottenham fen, 46
Courts
  Commissary's, 72, 225
  County, 4n, 5-6, 50, 91-2, 202, 218
  of Discipline, Vice-Chancellor's, 7-8, 26, 32-3, 36,
    42, 47, 51, 87-8, 116-17, 126-7, 145, 161, 164, 229
  ecclesiastical, 105-6
  magistrates, 46
cricket, 24, 140, 142, 174-5
Craven scholarship, 161n

dentists, 32, 57-9, 124, 150, 165, 201, 208, 226
Devonport, 220, 226, 231
discommunion, 47, 87, 117, 164
Dissenters, 22, 29, 65-7, 69, 89, 107, 111, 114, 139, 147,
  191, 223, 237
District Visiting Society, 136
Ditton, 32, 129
Downing College, 6, 10, 27, 47-8, 63, 136, 168-9, 172,
  191, 216
Dublin, 17, 54, 56, 138n, 197, 234n
Dulwich, 1, 20, 40, 53-4, 60-1, 87, 113n, 120, 124,

146n, 184, 191, 193; College, 129, 227

Eagle Hotel, 30, 192
education
National, 7, 77, 108n, 131, 135-8, 203, 209, 219n, 223-4, 233-4, 238
theological, 9, 14, 84, 155, 163, 177, 182, 203, 212, 221
elections
Chancellor, 13, 196-9
Heads of Houses, 45, 56, 148
Librarian, 130
parliamentary, 30, 49, 57, 139, 219-20
physician to Addenbrooke's hospital, 131-2
Professors, 40, 41-4, 46
Trinity Fellowship, 26, 74, 143, 175-6, 225-6
Ely, 27, 29, 44, 48, 61, 76, 78, 89, 94, 99, 112, 129, 139, 144, 163, 168, 211-12, 225, 230-1
Emmanuel College, 15, 19, 77, 139n, 146n, 161
Esquire Bedells, 1, 8, 19, 43, 79, 81, 175, 203, 205, 224
ether, 201, 208, 228, 230, 231-5
Evangelicals, 10, 54, 56, 69, 71-2, 105, 117
examinations
children, 7, 77, 84, 168
Honours, 11, 30, 41, 93, 114, 126, 158, 236
Scholarships, 3-4, 53-4, 97-8, 128, 165
Trinity Fellowship, 25-6, 72-4, 111-12, 143, 168, 175, 225-6
theological, 8-9, 14, 177, 167-8, 177

Family, The, 33, 46-7, 84, 99, 114-15, 127, 130, 150, 161, 167-8, 180, 182-3, 192, 202, 231
Father, College, i.e. Praelector, 124
fees, 13-14, 17n, 25n, 34, 59, 72, 80, 83-4, 91-2, 103, 120, 128, 138, 155, 157, 170
Fellow-Commoners, 7n
fires, 28n, 32, 62, 65, 99, 103, 143, 156, 160, 175, 210-11, 227
fireworks, 16, 67-8n, 80, 215n
Fitzwilliam Museum, 9, 16, 18-19, 24, 100, 138, 142, 150, 156, 162, 166, 212, 215, 220, 232
flower shows, 25, 136-7, 216, 224
Fulbourn, 52, 73,
funerals, 26, 55, 61, 68n, 75-6, 129, 146, 148, 173, 227-8, 236, 240

gambling, 33
gaol, Cambridge, 6, 50, 92n
Girton, 9, 161, 165, 236
Governesses' Institution, 113-14, 132, 146, 157, 166, 228
governesses, 23, 28-9, 96, 103, 108, 114, 156, 163, 222
Graces, 1n, 9, 14, 51, 61, 72, 83-4, 114, 116, 129, 134, 148, 150, 162, 178, 200, 209, 212, 227-8, 232n
Graduati, 31, 159, 161, 166, 169, 174, 177, 179, 181, 186, 189, 191, 201-2
Grantchester, 55, 144n, 173, 238

Harlton, 95, 209
Harrogate, 21-2, 168
Harston, 125
Harvard, 19, 40, 48, 61, 218n
Haslingfield, 100, 172
hats & caps, 31, 113, 124, 198

Hauxton, 110
Haverhill, 233
Hawkshead, 21, 112, 115, 152, 155
Hemingford Grey, 220-1
Hereford, 71, 232, 239
High Church (see also Oxford Movement), 12-13, 21, 34, 40, 44, 48-9, 51, 59, 73n, 79, 110, 115, 117-19, 145, 149, 196, 208-9
High Steward, The, 2, 17, 72n, 78-9, 194n, 201n
Hills Road, 8, 58, 74, 88, 141, 211
Histon, 165, 237
Holy Trinity, see Trinity Church
honorary degrees, 15, 95n
Hoop Hotel, 135, 141n
horse races, 11
Hull, 22
Hulsean benefaction, 6, 76, 123, 155n
Huntingdon, 22, 230

Impington, 62, 165
Installation of Chancellor, 13-18, 201, 213-17

Jesus College, 16, 28, 53, 64, 82n, 93, 165, 177
Jews, 29, 61, 114, 232-3
Johnian pigs, 196
Judges, 20, 48, 50, 88, 104-5, 148, 162, 218

King's College, 9n, 14, 17, 117, 126n 142, 167, 222
King's College Chapel, 65, 79, 82, 117, 156, 161, 222
King's College, London, 157

Landbeach, 57
law, 6, 8, 45-6, 49, 84, 88-9, 94. 97-8, 109-110
Leamington, Warwickshire, 26, 47-8, 110, 128
Leeds, 21
letters, testimonial, 43, 49, 106
Library, Public (i.e. University), 24, 40, 63, 65, 75n, 82, 93, 96-7, 100, 102-3, 113-14, 116, 118-20, 123, 131, 133-4, 141n-2, 163n, 165n, 220
licensing, 7n, 26, 33, 50, 54n, 75
Linton, 147, 175
Little Go, 49-50, 97, 146
Littlebury, 140
Liverpool, 54, 152, 169, 210

Madingley, 75n, 95, 112, 114, 118, 126, 133n, 143, 159, 161, 221
Magdalene College, 11, 15, 30, 36n, 48, 58, 82n, 114, 117, 145, 159, 162, 181, 198, 233
magic lantern, 157, 187
Maitland, Peregrine, prize, 117-18
Manchester, 233, 240
market, cattle, 24
markets, proclamation of, 28, 113, 144, 228
Marlborough College, 69
matriculation, 57, 81, 84-5, 116, 126, 128, 180, 195, 214
Maynooth grant, 131, 149, 203
Mayors of Cambridge, 20-1, 31, 80, 83, 139n, 144, 147, 162, 180, 216, 218,
Mechanics' Institute, 116
medical treatment, 3n, 7-8, 11, 30, 39-40, 42, 46-8, 51-2, 55, 57-9, 67, 72-6, 80, 84-5, 89, 96, 98, 110, 124, 150-1, 189-92, 212-13, 219, 223, 225-34
Mesman pictures, 19, 138, 156

mesmerism, 107
Midsummer Common, 14n, 59
Mildenhall, 7-8
mills, 23, 167, 182
Museum of Geology, 8, 29, 82

National Schools, 6-7, 20, 32, 83(?)
Neptune, 180, 207
Newmarket, 7
Northumberland House, London, 13
Norwich, 219, 221-2, 224-6

oaths, 6, 49, 81n, 83n, 180n, 197, 204, 219, 240
Observatory, The, 59, 124, 134, 137, 215n
omnibus, 140, 142, 156, 159, 178-9, 192
Orator, 1, 79, 81, 199-201, 204, 214
Outwell, 4
Oxford Movement, 5n, 13, 21, 43n, 107, 149, 163; see
 also High Church

Pampisford, 63, 93, 217
Paris, 92n, 145, 158, 184, 190, 221n, 228, 231
Parker's Piece, 80, 202, 223, 225
Pembroke College, 30, 80, 161, 241
Perse School, 56, 87, 135n
Peterhouse, 12, 35, 133, 137, 143
petitions, 56, 127, 161-2, 212, 232-3
Philosophical Society, Cambridge, 101, 180
photography, 135n, 169
Pitt Press, 19, 23, 88, 142, 164, 174, 176-7, 220, 239
Pitt Scholarships, 201
Plough Monday, 190
police, 18, 26, 32-3, 60, 144, 161n, 162, 175, 186, 212,
 238-9
polloi, 93, 123, 148, 157, 191
Porson Scholarship, 169, 178
Porthkerry, 132
Pot Fair, 14, 59
Praelector, see Father, College
prize-fights, 7-8
prizes, 118
proctors, 1, 4, 7, 9, 14, 18, 20, 30, 79, 81, 88, 120, 161,
 175, 180, 193, 196, 202-5, 212n, 214, 218, 227
promenades, 14-15, 17
prostitutes, 50-1, 193n, 202, 218
Protolibrarian, 129
Public Orator, see Orator
Punch, 104n, 151, 161n, 164, 196, 207

Quy, 50, 126n

railways, 20-1, 34, 48, 54-5, 68-9, 71, 88, 107, 115, 118-
 19, 130, 133, 135, 139-44, 148-50, 155-6, 159, 161,
 163-4, 168, 172, 177-8, 182-4, 192, 212-13, 228
religious tests, 49, 106, 232
Roman Catholics, 49, 51, 64, 100, 105, 107, 110, 126n,
 131n, 162, 179-80, 203n, 230n, 239,
Round Church (St Sepulchre's), 6, 65n, 80, 82n, 98,
 100, 105, 120, 126, 131, 136-7
Rustat dinner, 53, 165
rustication, 7-9, 32n, 42-3, 46-7, 51, 87, 144, 161n, 162,
 181

Sacrament, 6, 31, 35, 44, 47, 52, 54-5, 92, 133, 148, 151,
 159, 164, 166, 170, 177-8, 186, 193, 208
Saffron Walden, see Walden

St Andrew's Church, Great, 46, 76, 191
St Catharine's College, see Catharine Hall
St Edward's Church, 6
St Giles's Church, 40, 151
St John's College, 15n, 16, 36, 39, 41n, 80, 82, 92, 136,
 141, 195, 199, 216-17
St Mary's Church, Great, 6, 14, 23, 35, 48, 51-2, 59,
 64, 73, 76, 88, 95, 99, 103, 117, 119, 133n, 136, 151,
 183-4, 196, 199, 217
St Mary Hall, Brighton, 69, 216
St Michael's Church, 199
St Paul's Church, 20, 65, 77, 89, 91, 101, 112, 164, 207,
 221, 232, 237
St Peter's Church, 5, 36, 151
'salting', 222-3
Scarborough, 22
Senate House, 9, 15-16, 18, 28n, 30, 41, 65, 77, 81-3,
 100, 126, 130-1, 135-7, 157-8, 161, 178, 198, 213-15,
 217
Senior Wrangler, 41, 157, 168
Seniority, Trinity College, 5, 7, 11, 20, 25, 30, 32, 43,
 45-6, 50-1, 55, 62, 77-8, 88, 96, 123, 125-6, 130-1, 133,
 137, 144, 147, 158, 162, 166, 181-2, 191, 194, 211, 219,
 230, 234
Servants' Training Establishment, 86, 202, 209, 233-
 4
Shelford, 12, 29, 31-2, 101, 115, 238
Shire Hall, 5n
Sidney Sussex College, 56, 82n, 100-1, 109, 128, 133,
 145, 164n
skating, 46, 125
smoking, 8, 24, 33, 46, 58, 84, 100, 143, 158, 177, 179,
 212
snapdragon, 187
Somerset House, London, 33
Spinning House, 23, 193n
Spittle House, 128
statues, 92, 99, 126-7, 144-6, 177, 194n
statutes, 5-6, 32, 46, 55-6, 81n, 92, 96, 98, 113, 204
Storey's almshouses, 111
Sturbridge Fair, 14, 25, 72, 175, 224-5
Sunday Schools, 24, 63, 66, 101, 109-10
Supplicats, 41, 123-4, 190

tableaux vivants, 163, 173
Taxors, 72, 127, 175
Teversham, 57
Theatre Royal, Barnwell, 24, 27-8, 132, 139
theatricals, amateur, 27
Town Hall, 24n, 114, 132, 144, 147, 156, 161, 185,
 210
Town v. Gown, 7n, 26, 33, 72, 83, 161
Travelling Bachelor, 163
Trinity Church, 3, 5-6, 10, 14, 23, 29, 31-2, 34-5, 48,
 50-2, 56-7, 73, 76-7, 84, 89, 91, 93, 97, 104, 106, 108,
 114, 130, 133, 135, 141-2, 149, 151, 155, 157, 160-2,
 164, 166, 170, 174, 177-8, 181, 183-4, 186, 189, 191-4,
 203, 207, 221, 226, 238
Trinity College
 Chapel, 6, 14, 31, 35, 43, 47, 52, 54, 62, 73-5, 80, 82,
 89, 92, 98, 112, 116, 118-19, 133, 136, 143-6, 151, 156,
 159, 165-6, 177, 184-6, 208, 219-20, 222, 226, 237
 Great Court, 61, 78-9, 82, 140, 213-17
 Hall, 14, 17, 53, 78-9, 82-3, 89, 91, 95, 101, 111, 115-
 20, 135-9, 143, 146, 151, 156, 169, 178, 183-6, 197-8,
 208, 213-17, 219, 221-2, 225, 227, 230

Library, 58, 100, 125-7, 131, 133, 144-5, 156, 220, 222
various, 4-6, 8, 10-11, 16-17, 20, 26, 28, 31-3, 39-41, 48, 54-7, 59, 61-4, 80, 84, 86-9, 92-3, 100-4, 107-9, 115-18, 120, 148, 150, 155-8, 165, 174, 177, 184-6, 195-6, 199, 210-12, 224-5, 227-8, 230, 240
Trinity Hall, 35-6, 42n, 45, 89, 99, 105, 120, 126n, 186, 240
'Tripos', 233-4
Trumpington, 57, 226, 239
tutors, private, 13, 17, 25, 30, 85n, 114,

University Library, *see* Library, Public
University Press, *see* Pitt Press
Upwell, 5, 66

Vestiges of Creation controversy, 129, 133-4n, 149
Via Lambertina, 139
Vice-Chancellor (activities of), 1-2, 7-8, 12-16, 30-4, 36, 41-3, 47, 50-1, 72, 75, 77-82, 87-8, 93, 95, 101-3, 112-18, 123n-4, 126-8, 130, 134, 144-8, 150, 157-8, 160-2, 164, 167, 169-71, 175, 178-81, 191, 194-201, 203-7, 212-17, 224, 228-30, 237
voting for charitable institutions, 74-5, 84, 89, 95-6, 103-4, 111, 113, 119, 130-3, 146

Walden (*i.e.* Saffron Walden), 140, 142, 156
Wales, 59, 109n, 125, 146; *see also* Cilrhiw *and* Welsh bishoprics controversy
Waterbeach, 141
weddings etc., 20, 109, 168-9, 173, 209, 221-2
weights and measures, 72
Welsh bishoprics controversy, 127, 162, 194n
Wenden, 140, 142, 156, 229
Westminster School, 98
whist, 7, 25, 27, 31, 33-4, 39, 41, 53, 56-7, 62, 68-70, 83, 91-2, 95-8, 101, 112, 114-15, 120, 131, 140, 143, 145, 147-8, 152, 157, 160-1, 163, 165-7, 178, 180-2, 186-7, 202, 211, 213, 219, 221, 225, 229, 230-1
White House, 9, 30, 117, 127, 178, 212, 232
Willingham, 57
Wimpole, 83
Wisbech, 4, 65-8, 73
workhouse, union, 118-19 209

Yeoman Bedell, 203, 205
York, 22, 85, 97n
'Young England', 196

CAMBRIDGESHIRE RECORDS SOCIETY
General Editor: P.C. Saunders, B.A., D.Phil.

The Cambridge Antiquarian Records Society was founded in 1972 as the result of a decision by the Cambridge Antiquarian Society to form a separate society for publishing documentary sources relating to the history of Cambridgeshire and neighbouring areas. In 1987 its name was changed to the Cambridgeshire Records Society.

Membership is open to all interested persons, and to libraries, schools and other institutions. Members receive one free copy of each volume when published and can purchase back volumes at a special price. Further details and application forms for membership can be obtained from the Secretary, Cambridgeshire Records Society, County Record Office, Shire Hall, Cambridge, CB3 0AP.

Volumes published so far and still available are:

1. *Letters to William Frend from the Reynolds Family of Little Paxton and John Hammond of Fenstanton 1793–1814* edited by Frida Knight

2. *John Norden's Survey of Barley* edited by J.C. Wilkerson

3. *The West Fields of Cambridge* edited by Catherine P. Hall and J.R. Ravensdale

4. *A Cambridgeshire Gaol Delivery Roll 1332–1334* edited by Elisabeth G. Kimball

5. *The King's School Ely* edited by Dorothy M. Owen and Dorothea Thurley

6. *The Church Book of the Independent Church (now Pound Lane Baptist) Isleham 1693–1805* edited by Kenneth A.C. Parsons

7. *Catalogue of the Portraits in Christ's, Clare and Sidney Sussex Colleges* by J.W. Goodison

8. *Accounts of the Reverend John Crakanthorp of Fowlmere 1682–1705* edited by Paul Brassley, Anthony Lambert and Philip Saunders

9. *A Peasant's Voice to Landowners by John Denson of Waterbeach 1830* reprinted with Masters' history of Waterbeach and an introduction by J.R. Ravensdale.

10. *Romilly's Cambridge Diary 1842–1847* edited by M.E. Bury and J.D. Pickles.

The following volumes are in active preparation:

Court Rolls of the Manor of Downham 1310–1327
edited by Clare Coleman

Edmund Pettis's Survey of St. Ives 1728 edited by Mary Carter

A Cambridgeshire Lieutenancy Letter Book 1595–1605 edited by
Eugene Bourgeois

The Parish Registers of Holy Trinity, Cambridge edited by Mary Siraut

Other projected volumes include:

The Ely Coucher Book 1251 for Cambridgeshire and Huntingdonshire
edited by Edward Miller

Cambridgeshire Population Sources 1086–1801 by Margaret Spufford
and Eric Carlson

The Cartulary of St. John's Hospital Cambridge edited by Miri Rubin

The Tallage of Cambridge 1304 edited by David Gleave

The Sawtry Abbey Cartulary edited by K.J. Stringer

Kirtling Hall Accounts edited by Susan Oosthuizen